The History of Government

VOLUME III

The
History of Government
From the Earliest Times

VOLUME III

EMPIRES, MONARCHIES, AND THE MODERN STATE

S. E. Finer

OXFORD UNIVERSITY PRESS

Oxford University Press, Great Clarendon Street, Oxford OX2 6DP
Oxford New York

Athens Auckland Bangkok Bogota Bombay Buenos Aires
Calcutta Cape Town Dar es Salaam Delhi
Florence Hong Kong Istanbul Karachi
Kuala Lumpur Madras Madrid Melbourne
Mexico City Nairobi Paris Singapore
Taipei Tokyo Toronto Warsaw

and associated companies in
Berlin Ibadan

Oxford is a trade mark of Oxford University Press

Published in the United States
by Oxford University Press Inc. New York

British Library Cataloguing in Publication Data
Data available

Library of Congress Cataloging in Publication Data
Data applied for

ISBN 0–19–820666–6

3 5 7 9 10 8 6 4 2

Printed in Great Britain
on acid-free paper by
Biddles Ltd., Guildford and King's Lynn

CONTENTS

Book IV

Ancient Empires and New Monarchies
1500–1776

Overview

The fate of government throughout the entire world was galvanized, between 1500 and 1776, by two technological advances—firearms, especially artillery, and the ocean-going sailing-ship—and the union of these two in what were effectively 'floating castles enveloped by all-round batteries of quick-firing guns'.[1] These ships enabled the Europeans to take and settle America and to establish fortified trading posts throughout South and South-East Asia. But they could not penetrate the latter beyond the protection afforded by their gunships. Their significance, then, was that for the first time post-Roman Europe had a significant role to play, alongside the three other great state systems—the Islamic, the Indian, and the Chinese. The significance of the siege-gun was more indiscriminate than that of the new type of ship; it strengthened central governments throughout the globe. That artillery could batter down the curtain walls of baronial castles and centralize power in the hands of the monarch is part of the conventional wisdom of European history. The so-called 'New Monarchies' were its direct consequence. But what happened in Europe happened in the Asian polities also and for the identical reason. Its consequence was the emergence of what have been called the 'gun-powder empires'.[2] The centralized power of the Mogul Empire (Babur, 1525), Muscovy (Ivan III, 1480), and the Ottoman Empire (the seizure of Constantinople, 1453) were all founded on the use of artillery. True, this was not so in the founding of the Safevid Empire, but it became so under Shah Abbas (1587–1629). The Manchu conquest of China (from 1642) was supported by artillery that was superior to that of the Ming; and the termination of inter-clan war and establishment of a centralized polity in Japan was due in large part to hand-guns and to the siege-guns that broke down the daimyos' castle walls. The use of these firearms was repugnant to the traditions of both the Chinese and—more especially—of the Japanese military establishment, and once the

---

[1] Quoted by M. Howard, 'The Military Factor in European Expansion', in H. Bull and A. Watson, *Expansion of International Society* (Clarendon Press, Oxford, 1984), 34.

[2] I do not know if McNeill invented this phrase (in which case he is to be congratulated), but he uses it extensively. Cf W. H. McNeill, *The Pursuit of Power: Technology, Armed Force, and Society since AD 1000* (Blackwell, Oxford, 1982), 79, 95.

latter country had sealed itself off from the world in 1638 the samurai abandoned hand-guns and went back to the traditional sword.

There is no question of the world being dominated by Europe or even likely to be so dominated at the beginning of this period. In 1500 the future still must have seemed to belong to the traditional imperial polities of Asia, particularly to the Muslim ones, for Islam had more than compensated for its retreat in Spain and Muscovy by expanding everywhere else—in the Balkans, Africa, India, South-East Asia, and North-West China.

Two-hundred-and-fifty years later however, that outcome was looking rather shaky. While most of those empires still appeared to be in good shape, a new factor had, since 1500, begun to enter into the world equation. In brief, at long last Europe had reinvented the state. This is the so-called 'European state' which, although it was structurally akin to monarchical polities we have already encountered, was possessed of some quite new characteristics and was the direct ancestor of today's world-wide model unit of political affairs. Moreover, this state was ferocious, piratical, intrepid, and, with those guns and ships already mentioned, most formidably armed.

Some historians maintain that the European state system was superior to the Asian polities (potentially at least) as early as 1500.[3] Indeed, there are enthusiasts who would trace its inherent superiority back to perhaps the twelfth or thirteenth centuries.[4] There are even one or two who allege that the roots of the superiority were struck in Europe's Dark Ages which, they assure us, are dark only because we are in the dark about them.[5] But others, more temperate, affirm that Europe started to assert its superiority over the Asian polities only after, say, 1700.[6] Braudel, who must always command attention, puts the date as late as the first quarter of the nineteenth century.[7] My own inclination is to situate the period when the Asian empires were in clear decline *vis-à-vis* the West in the second half of the eighteenth century. The best way to proceed without foreclosing this issue is to compare the polities of the world as they stood in 1500 with what they had become *c.*1750.

We have reached a point at which this *History* begins to acquire a certain fugal quality. At the beginning it described discrete polities: the states of Egypt and Mesopotamia and those, in their interstices, which were largely modelled on them. The Greek, the Hellenistic, and the Roman polities

---

[3] e.g. E. L. Jones, *The European Miracle* (CUP, Cambridge, 1981).

[4] e.g. J. A. Hall, *Powers and Liberties* (Blackwell, Oxford, 1985).

[5] M. Mann, *The Sources of Social Power* (CUP, Cambridge, 1986), i. 377. R. Hodges, *Dark Age Economics* (Duckworth, London, 1982). Just read Gregory of Tours!

[6] W. H. McNeill, *The Rise of the West* (University of Chicago Press, Chicago, 1963).

[7] F. Braudel, *Civilisation and Capitalism: Fifteenth–Eighteenth Centuries*, 3 vols. (Collins, London, 1981–4), iii. 467–533.

followed in increasing interpenetration, but in China a wholly independent development had emerged. More and more distinctive state-systems appeared, often isolated from one another: pre-Columbian America, Western Europe, South and South-East Asia, the Far East. Indeed they could be aptly described as 'worlds unto themselves' whose inhabitants 'were scarcely aware of a world outside their empire'.[8] But from the sixteenth century, with Europe conquering South America and beginning to penetrate the East, the interdependency and imitation proceeds faster and faster. As in a fugue, first one polity comes in, then another, then comes the transposition of certain polities, then their blending together, until, in 1750, the world stands on the brink of becoming one single state-system: an *oikumene*.

Europe, of course, is simply the western promontory of one single land-mass. The conventional dividing line is the Ural mountains, and it is to the east and subsequently to the west of this geographical location that the following political gazetteer of the worlds' states in 1500 proceeds.

East of those mountains, then, stretched that immense flat plain embracing today's Siberia, the former Soviet Central Asia, and Mongolia. Siberia proper then contained perhaps as few as 200,000 inhabitants;[9] the southern, Soviet Turkistan area, where the powerful Khanates of Khiva and Bokhara and Ferghana were situated, contained, however, as many as 3.5 million people at this date. The population of Siberia was largely nomadic and Mongoloid; the southerly Khanates just mentioned were based on oases and their peoples were chiefly of Turkic stock. Here the usual pattern of rule was the traditionally Islamic one of the bisection of authority between *ulema* and Khan, with the leaders of powerful clans disputing rather than sharing power with that ruler. Though somewhat ramshackle, with fluid frontiers and a high turnover of rulers, these states were powerful enough to beat off the horse-nomads of the northern steppes.

Immediately to the south lay Iran: large in area, but with a small population of only some 4 million. This ancient state had been in semi-deliquescence under the Mongolian Ilkhans, then the Timurids, and finally the dynasty of the White Sheep Horde. But at the very point when this gazetteer commences, in 1502, a certain Shah Ismail overran the state to found a renascent and durable Safavid Empire.

East and south-east of it lay teeming India with its 100 million inhabitants, and here, the Afghan Babur ('The Tiger'), with a powerful park of

[8] O. Hintze, *The Historical Essays of Otto Hintze* (OUP, Oxford, 1975), 165.

[9] This estimate of population and the following ones are derived from two sources: C. McEvedy and R. Jones, *Atlas of World Population History* (Allen Lane, London, 1978), and J. R. Hale, *Renaissance Europe, 1480–1520* (Fontana, London, 1971). (The latter deals only with the European states, the former with Asian as well, but the two sets of figures for Europe do not diverge significantly.)

artillery, smashed the army of the ineffectual Sultan of Delhi to found the
mighty Mogul Empire. Tiny Ceylon, with a mere million people, was by
contrast fragmented and feebly governed under an indigenous monarchy.

South-easterly lay the four Burmese kingdoms (4 million people), then
the powerful Thai kingdom (2 million inhabitants), which itself adjoined
the aggressive Vietnamese kingdom of Annam and Tongking and the
Khmer kingdom of Cambodia (altogether some 4 million in population);
whilst the Malay Archipelago was hopelessly fragmented into hundreds of
tiny states.

The Far East, however, was dominated by the apparently unshakeable
colossus of the Ming Empire, now at its height, with a population of 105
million. Japan, with 17 million inhabitants, formed a sorry contrast; for this
strife-torn country was now entering a century of such interminable clan
warfare as to merit the title of 'the Epoch of a Warring Country'.

Asia numbered some 270 million people. Europe, even including the
Ottoman Empire, added up to only 90 to 100 million.

Immediately west of the Urals lay the great open spaces of the Orthodox
Christian Principality of Moscow. Only a few years before 1500 this had
been tributary to the Muslim Tartar Golden Horde, located in the south,
but in 1480 Ivan III, with the support of his heavy artillery, seized Novgorod, and threw off the Tartar yoke. Declaring himself Tsar, he ruled as
autocrat of a land with no city or regional particularisms to contend, but in
their place, over-mighty landowners—the boyars. Except in the frozen
north, Muscovy was land-locked. Between her and the Black Sea stretched
the still formidable Khanate of the Crimean Tartars, and south of them the
Ottoman Empire, while to the west she was cut off from the Baltic by the
Teutonic Knights of Prussia, and by Poland-Lithuania.

The Sunnite Muslim Ottoman Empire was the fourth of the great Asian
empires. 'An anti-Europe, a counter-Christendom', of 'planetary dimen-
sions',[10] its population (even including its European possessions) was yet
no greater than 10 million people. The empire, which had nearly disintegrated in the fifteenth century under the blows of Timur, had since entirely
obliterated the Byzantine Empire by taking Constantinople in 1453 and
annexing Syria and Mamluk Egypt in 1517—in both cases, be it noted, by
the use of heavy artillery. In 1521, when Suleiman the Magnificent acceded, it
reached the very zenith of its power. Already it extended over the Balkans up
to the Danube.

Between its eastern frontier there and the frontier of Muscovy lay the
extensive Roman Catholic state of Lithuania–Poland (population 9 mil-

[10] Braudel, *Civilisation and Capitalism*, iii. 467.

lion). The regime there was antipodal to that of Muscovy. Its monarchy was elective (albeit it still remained in the family of the Jagiellons) but power was shifting dramatically to the *szlachta* (the nobility); a *Sejm*, consisting of a Senate of great nobles and a House of Legates of the lesser nobles had materialized in 1493. In 1501 the state officially called itself a 'republic'. The southern borders of both Poland–Lithuania and Muscovy tailed off in wild steppe-land inhabited by fugitives from both these realms: the Cossacks, who established a primitive form of organized self-rule.

Poland, because it was in the Latin Christian community and also because it had been sheltered from the Mongol invasions and Muscovy's subsequent Tartar captivity, was more 'European' than the barbarous primitivism of the Russian state. This was even more true of Poland's western neighbours, the elective kingdoms of Bohemia (population 3 millions) and Hungary ($1\frac{1}{4}$ millions). Their monarchs, like the Polish, laboured under heavy constraint from their powerful landed nobilities.

Apart from Hungary (whose people were Magyars) all the foregoing independent states of East Europe were inhabited by Slav peoples. In the middle band of Europe immediately to its west, the far north was inhabited by the Scandinavian peoples, central Europe by Germans, and south of the Alps, the Italians. Tucked in between them lay the Swiss Confederation and the Grand Duchy of Austria. The Grand Dukes of Austria were Habsburgs and in the course of their family's history had come to rule over the adjacent territories of Styria and Tyrol. This was the kernel of the nascent Habsburg Empire, whose happy fate it was to expand not by way of arms on the battlefield but by legs in the matrimonial bed. This bunch of disparate territories, whose peoples all owned allegiance to one family, was the very paradigm of what in the European context is called the 'dynastic' state or *haus-staat*. At this stage it was little more than a personal union of several provinces rather than state in its own right. The Swiss Confederation (of only 750,000 inhabitants) was a loose union of warlike peasant-cum-burgher communities: hence that rare thing, a republic.

Northwards as far as the Baltic, the land we should now call Germany was a congeries of many hundred statelets, some very small indeed, with a total population of about 17 to 20 millions. Most of these statelets were purportedly part of the political configuration which possessed virtually none of the characteristics of statehood: the Holy Roman Empire. The Imperial Crown, though elective, had come usually to reside in the Habsburg family; since 1438, continuously so. At this particular juncture the new emperor, Maximilian (1493–1519), was about to try to endow this shadow of statehood with common political institutions.

The Scandinavian kingdoms of Norway, Sweden, and Denmark, united by the Union of Kalmar in 1397 (total populations some 2 millions), was in collapse and in 1523 Sweden was to expel the hated Danes and resume her independence under the founder of a masterful and warlike dynasty, Gustavus Vasa.

Below the Alps, meanwhile, the Italian peoples had evolved a highly sophisticated balance-of-power system of eleven small states: Venice (population 1½ millions), a city republic with a great sea empire; the Duchy of Milan (population 1¼ millions); Florence, a city-republic (¾ million); the Papal States run by nominees of the pope (2 millions); the smaller Republics of Genoa, Lucca, and Siena, and the small duchies of Ferrara, Modena, and Urbino, along with the Marquisate of Mantua; and, in the south of the peninsula, the Kingdom of Naples, known as *il Regno*. The total population of these Italian states was some 10 million.

Finally, we come to the polities variously called the Atlantic Powers, the New Monarchies, the National States. England, as has been snidely observed, is only 'half an island', for the relatively poor and weak Scottish kingdom lay to its north with a population of half-a-million. (Ireland, an English colony, numbered some 800,000 persons, and these spoke the Erse language.) England's population was only 3 million. The country had only just recovered from the Wars of the Roses but was beginning the so-called 'Tudor Revolution in Government' which centralized power in the Crown and Parliament and began the disarming of the nobility. The hereditary enemy, France, was much larger and richer. Over the last fifty years one great apanage or fiefdom after another had fallen to the French Crown so that this was now exercising direct centralized power over (roughly speaking) all territory west of the Meuse–Rhône line. With some 20 million inhabitants, France was by far the most populous unitary polity in Europe. Her most formidable rival was Spain, at this time known as *las Espanas*—a reflection on its very recent unification. The marriage of Ferdinand of Aragon and Isabella of Castile in 1479 united these two ancient kingdoms, and in 1492 these *Reyes Catolicos* went on to conquer the Moorish kingdom of Granada. Navarre was still independent and so was the Atlantic kingdom of Portugal. The latter's population was about 1 million, Spain's, 6½ millions; but what gave these two little states immense military weight was the outcome of the great voyages of exploration, starting with Columbus in 1492. To antedate Canning's famous phrase, 'the New World had come into existence to redress the balance of the Old'.

This gazetteer of the 1500s can be contrasted, now, with that for the 1750s. By then Europe's population, recovered from the ravages of the Black Death, had swelled to 140 million—a 55 per cent increase on the 1500s. Yet

Asia's populations had increased by some 77 per cent and now reached the comparatively staggering total of 496 million. India's population alone was larger than that of all Europe.

One immediate difference from the earlier period, and which was of truly global significance, had occurred in the Siberian–Central Asian 'heartland'. For two millennia this region's invincible armies of horse-nomads had poured out to destroy or conquer East Europe, India, China. Nevermore.

The arrow of the horsed archer who advances, shoots, and then slips away was for Antiquity and the Middle Ages a mode of indirect fire that for its day was almost as effective and demoralizing as that of our artillerymen nowadays.

Why did that superiority end? Why is it that from the beginning of the sixteenth century the nomads could no longer dictate to the sedentary peoples? Precisely because the latter brought artillery against them. Overnight they thereby acquired a factitious superiority which reversed the relationships of thousands of years. The cannonade by which Ivan the Terrible dispersed the last heirs of the Golden Horde, that by which the Chinese K'ang-hi Emperor struck fear into the Kalmuks, marked the end of a period in the history of the world. For the first time but also for ever, military technology had changed sides. Civilization had become stronger than barbarism.[11]

In the southern oasis lands the Muslim Khanates still survived, but Siberia proper was now the Russians'. Their eastward expansion (they reached the Bering Strait in the 1740s) was halted only by the powerful Ch'ing Empire which established the border at the Amur River. South of the Khanates lay Iran (population $5\frac{1}{2}$ million). Only three years before 1750 that empire, under Nadir Shah, had been at the very peak of its military power and political ascendancy only to collapse and become a political cipher from the moment he died in 1747. Still further south, India's population had swelled to 175 millions, but the Mogul Empire had dissolved into numerous warring states, and their deadly rivalries afforded opportunities for the astute activities of the French and English companies trading to India. Almost at the turn of the half-century, in 1751, Clive seized and withstood siege in Arcot, the capital of the Carnatic. The date is historic. It was to usher in two centuries of political subjection to Britain.

Meanwhile, Ceylon ($1\frac{1}{3}$ million inhabitants) had long been under Dutch control, as were, effectively, Malaysia and what we nowadays call Indonesia (17 million inhabitants). The Philippines ($1\frac{3}{4}$ million people) had been discovered by the Spanish and annexed, colonized, and Catholicized from as long ago as 1517. But the Europeans found South-East Asia more resistant. Vietnam had split into two kingdoms but they were still inde-

---

[11] R. Grousset, *L'Asie Orientale des origines au XVe siècle* (Presses Universitaires, Paris, 1941), 11.

pendent. A palace coup in Siam had expelled all Europeans and sealed the country off for the next 150 years, and a reunited Kingdom of Burma (5½ millions), pursuing an aggressive policy of expansion towards all its neighbours, was also left alone by the Europeans. It was not until much later, in the nineteenth century, that its forays into the north brought it up against the British Empire in India.

But China and Japan were not just independent, they were worlds of their own. The Ch'ing Empire of China, with no less than 215 million inhabitants, and which at this very moment (1751) was swallowing up Tibet, Dzungaria, and the Tarim Basin, was at a level of peace, power, and prosperity unequalled in its entire previous history. By a deliberate act of policy its only contact with the Europeans was via the licensed treaty-port island of Macao. And a similar decision had been taken in 1638 by the Tokugawa Shogunate government of prosperous Japan (population 29 million) which—with the power of heavy artillery—had united the country under its rule since 1600.

So, in 1750 the Asian polities were still rich, populous, and powerful. True, the once-mighty empires of Iran and India had now fallen; but the former had a long history of breakdown and subsequent recovery and, as far as India was concerned, any idea in 1750 that the subcontinent was on the brink of losing its independence would have been wholly fanciful. Indian, like Iranian, history had always known periods of disunity succeeded by reunification with greater strength than before. The only location where conspicuous European penetration did take place lay in the multitudinous archipelagos of South-East Asia. This fact provides the explanation of the situation in 1750: the Europeans could and did penetrate the coastal areas as far as the range of gunships and gunship-protected ports permitted (unless expressly expelled as in Japan and China), but they were neither numerous nor strong enough to conquer the interior.

For all that, the wonder is not that the Europeans had failed to conquer all of Asia but that they had penetrated so far. Surely something momentous must have been happening in that continent over the two-and-half-centuries that had passed since 1500. So indeed it had. Europe had now taken the lead in science and technology and with every passing year was increasing its gap over an intellectually stagnant Asia. Nowhere was this technology more advanced than in the matter of 'guns and sails', as we have been at pains to stress; but this superiority reflected a general advance in the intellectual, economic, and political domain, all together. As far as the economy was concerned, the European states, particularly south and west of the Rhine–Danube line, had developed extensive trade among themselves and—as is evident from the last few paragraphs—with the entire world outside the sealed-off areas of China and Japan; and that trade, together with the improved technology in manufacture and agriculture, had resulted in much higher per-capita wealth over that of the 1500s *and* permitted the great jump in population already noticed.

Furthermore, in place of the gangling, decentralized feudal *regnum* of the Middle Ages, the Europeans had re-created the state: a sharply defined, discrete territorial unit, possessing a common political superior, recognizing and being recognized by other similarly constituted units as entirely free to do what it pleased inside its own boundaries: in short, as *sovereign*. Since 1500 or thereabouts virtually all[12] such states, whether they were autocratic like Russia or conciliar like Great Britain, had developed at least five novel and signally non-medieval features: standing armies, professional bureaucracies, fiscal centralization, extensive trading networks, and institutionalized diplomatic dialogue with fellow sovereign states. These features by no means exhaust the singularity of the new European states. As a matter of fact, if one left aside the practice of continuous diplomacy and permanent embassies which (with the beginnings of international law and the evolution of a theory and practice of balance-of-power politics) were specifically European, the Asian polities not only manifested all the other features but had done so since time immemorial, as we have seen. The new European states did, however, have certain superadditional characteristics that made them specifically quite *different* from all Asian polities without exception, of which their *law-boundedness* was the chief. This is not the time to particularize; the matter will be fully treated at the appropriate place. Nevertheless it is so important, it marks such an innovation, it had such world-wide sequels that it must be noted here, right away.

Bearing these remarks in mind, we can proceed as before, that is, from the Urals westward. Russia was now a huge empire of serfs ruled autocratically by a tsar and his service nobility, which stretched from the Baltic to the Pacific and was confined in the south only by the waning Ottoman power. This vast state of 18 million people was now playing an active military and diplomatic role in the European state system, and continually aggrandizing itself.

Russia's chief opponent was the Ottoman Empire (population 24 million). This had reached its fullest advance in Europe when it besieged Vienna in 1683, but by the treaty of Carlowitz (1699) it had surrendered Hungary, Transylvania, and Croatia-Slovenia to the Habsburg Austrian Empire. Yet despite repeated reports of its death, its demise proved always

---

[12] The chief exceptions will be noted below—they were acephalous Poland, the Swiss Confederacy, and the United Provinces of the Netherlands.

to have been much exaggerated. In 1750 it was still wealthy. It exerted a monopoly over the internal Asian caravan trade, excluded foreign ships from the Red Sea, and shut the Black Sea to foreign shipping too until forced to open this up to Russia by the Treaty of Kutchuk Kainardji (1774). Certainly, its political and military institutions were in decline, but it was not until the first quarter of the nineteenth century that the empire began to go into economic collapse, first in the Balkans, then in Egypt and Syria.[13]

To its north lay Poland and this country, whose population had remained stationary at some 7 million, was now in the sorriest of conditions. It had long ago lost its southern steppe-land when the Cossacks there decided to throw in their lot with Russia, and in 1772 Russia (along with Prussia and Austria) was to seize a great slice of its territory. This was the 'First' Partition of Poland; the Third (1795) was to end in Poland's total extinction as a state. For this it had to thank its nerveless political system, a landlord oligarchy carried to its ultimate, self-frustrating excess.

The former elective monarchies of Hungary and Bohemia were now but provinces in the wide-spreading Habsburg Empire which (as we have just seen) was acquiring still more Balkan territory as the Ottoman power waned, as well as its share of Poland. With a population of 24 million, this empire was still a loose conglomeration of provinces, duchies, and the like, but on the point of receiving powerful new centralizing institutions from Maria Theresa and Joseph II. 'Germany' (about 23 million inhabitants) was still made up of numerous statelets, modelled after the now common centralizing and bureaucratic pattern, as indeed were the statelets in Italy (with a total population of 15 millions), with the exception of Venice, which still retained its oligarchical republican form. But one of these German states, quite unremarkable in 1500, was now a most formidable military power despite a diminutive population of only $3\frac{1}{2}$ million people; this was the kingdom of Prussia, another dynastic state, but one where from 1640 onwards a line of able and iron-fisted Hohenzollern rulers had centralized, bureaucratized, and militarized the scattered territories of their house to make it one of the best-regulated and certainly the most regimented state in all Europe. The kingdoms of Denmark–Norway and of Sweden, long past their military peak, were also absolute monarchies.

Two exceptions to the general monarchical tradition of the European states were Switzerland and the United Provinces. (The transient and embarrassed phantom-monarchy of Poland, where each senator enjoyed a

---

[13] Braudel, *Civilisation and Capitalism*, iii. 469–83.

full veto, has already been noticed.) Switzerland maintained its republican institutions but all these had fallen into the hands of oligarchies. The United Provinces of the former Habsburg Netherlands, which had successfully revolted against the Spaniards and established their own sovereign state, adopted a confederal structure with some central leadership residing in its *Stadthouder*. The merchant oligarchs who controlled it had, as we have hinted, come to rule a quite formidable and very rich overseas trading empire in Ceylon and the East Indies. Elsewhere, however—for example, in North America—their colonizing or trading outposts had fallen to the forces of the three westernmost European polities: the so-called 'national' states. The England of 1500 had become the Union of England and Wales in 1536 and then, united with Scotland by the Treaty of Union (1707), Great Britain ($7\frac{1}{4}$ million population). Ireland (3 million inhabitants) was a semi-autonomous province. Meanwhile France was at perhaps its peak of power. It was by far the most populous unitary state in Europe, with 24 million inhabitants, and was correspondingly formidable both militarily and economically. A singular characteristic—for this great power did, after all, have access to the Atlantic and the Mediterranean—is that its overseas extension was so slight. France was above everything else a great land power, perhaps the greatest on the continent at this time. Finally, in the Iberian peninsula Portugal had resumed its existence independent of Spain (population $9\frac{1}{2}$ million). Here, since 1713 when they became the ruling dynasty, the Bourbons had rigorously centralized on the French Bourbon model, but the state's economy and military power were in full decline.

None the less those monarchies fronted the Atlantic but did not stop there. The most dramatic change in their circumstances since 1500 was precisely that, through them, 'Europe'—whatever that may mean—had extended itself into so many 'ghost acres' across the seas, into the vast New World. Portugal controlled a huge empire in Brazil. Spain held the rest of the subcontinent and pressed her claims beyond California up to what is now New Mexico. In North America the French were being excluded by the English. They had settled in the area of Quebec but had to cede this territory to the British in 1757. Southwards, they nominally held the interior of North America west of the Mississippi, whereas the English had planted a string of thirteen populous, prosperous, and vigorous colonies strung along the Atlantic coasts. They had cleared the Dutch away from the Hudson area and renamed New Amsterdam as New York.

Each of these imperial Atlantic powers transplanted its own peculiar brand of political institutions to the New World: the Portuguese and Spaniards, the autocratic model; the British, representative institutions and the common law. All of them, without exception, traded in, imported, and exploited slave labour. As Braudel puts it, there was an identity of action *vis-à-vis* Africa by both Islam and Western Imperialism, both being 'aggressive slave-trading civilizations'.[14]

[14] Braudel, iii. 434.

PART I

Asia

I

Tokugawa Japan, 1600–1745

*J*apan is a late-comer in the history of government. Its history as a state only really begins with the Taika reforms of AD 645. Even so, it is of but limited interest to the historian of government until 1600, the year when the warlord Ieyasu Tokugawa defeated all his baronial rivals in the great Battle of Sekigahara. Up to that point Japan's constitutional history had been a premature attempt at imperial centralization *à la* T'ang, followed by a progressive and cumulative morcelization of authority and power, an interminable Wars of the Roses fought by armoured knights of rival houses: what Milton would have called the wars of the kites and the crows. The constitutional significance of the early Imperial (Nara and Heian) period is that it explains the nature of the subsequent feudal anarchy, which in turn is significant in that the Tokugawa Shogunate was (originally at any rate) little else but anarchy institutionalized.

The outcome is something unlike anything we have so far described in Asia, but not at all unlike what we have already described for medieval Europe; and this in itself is a cause for curiosity. Here we have something like the late medieval regime in England or France at the time of so-called 'bastard feudalism', but frozen in that mould for two-and-a-half centuries. Yet it is out of the ordinary, not like anything we have come across so far. Thus its feudal structure, though it resembles the European, was amalgamated with a set of social values which are characteristically East Asian, indeed, in most particulars, Sinic, for example, institutionalized inequality, no individual rights, no rule of law, and a duty of unquestioning obedience. The resultant regime was a mosaic of despotisms held together and controlled by a super-despot, the shogun, through a huge hereditary caste of knights legally supreme over the rest of the population; stratified by law; socially immobile; thought- and behaviour-controlled; and yet, withal, peaceful, well-ordered, and prospering.

From the standpoint of this *History* the Tokugawa regime is significant in four ways. First, its feudalism, similar though not identical to Europe's, is a true feudalism in a sense that the Muslim *iqua*, for instance, is not; and this in complete isolation from any European contact. Secondly, the regime is interesting not only in itself but by way of comparison with other possibly cognate regimes like the Mamluks or, again, like other composite states of a federal, confederal, or satrapal variety. Thirdly, it provides an almost if not entirely unique instance of the transformation of a hereditary standing army into a civil bureaucracy. Finally—but this is for Book Five—the way the social structure and the economy developed inside the shell of the shogunal political institutions, so as in the end to became antithetical to them, prepared the way, opened by Commodore Perry's ironclads in 1853, for Japan's embracing the model of the modern European nation-state in the Meiji Restoration of 1868.

1. THE LAND AND THE PEOPLE

The shortest distance between Japan and the mainland is 110 miles. This proved short enough for Chinese culture to penetrate but far enough for the Japanese to keep themselves to themselves when they wished; so that periods of self-conscious and self-motivated borrowing from the outside have alternated with periods of self-isolation. Since the only people who spoke Japanese were the Japanese, while the remnants of the aboriginal population had been virtually eliminated by the eighth century, the Japanese were, from a very early age and to a remarkable degree, 'a racially homogenous people unified by a common language and culture'.[1] Consequently, in the course of the long periods of seclusion the original exogenous impulses were modified and Japanized.

Those impulses could come from only one source: from powerful, super-lative, and sophisticated T'ang China. Accordingly, over the sixth to tenth centuries the Japanese took from China Buddhism and Confucianism, the Chinese script and the use of the Chinese tongue, their canons of art and literature, and at one mighty blow, the entire T'ang apparatus of imperial centralized rule: a most extraordinary thing for a primitive, poor, and basically tribal society to attempt.

[1] Reischauer, *Ennin's Diary*, 462.

Each and all of these were, in time, to assume distinctively Japanese forms. Buddhism was conflated with native Shinto animism, for instance; it took on salvationist forms like Pure Land (*Jodo*) or Lotus (*Nichiren*), or contemplative ecstatic ones like Zen which were less well-regarded in China, if at all; and its sectaries, especially the fanatical *Nichiren* monks, organized like the military orders of Latin Christianity in the medieval West, fought between themselves and against the government too. Confucianism—which was omnipresent from the very beginnings of the 'Chinese period' onwards, though its influence waxed and waned before ultimately it came to wield almost monopolistic political influence under the Tokugawa—was indeed highly consistent with many native Japanese attitudes; nevertheless it too suffered significant alterations in the Japanese climate. For instance, though the family was very important and salient in the Japanese scale of values, it did not hold the paramountcy that it did in Chinese Confucianism. To take another example: Chinese Confucianism extolled *wen* (civility) over *wu* (warfare), despised the soldier, and made the literati the leading class in the social scale. But the Japanese élite of the seventeenth century were, by contrast, bloodthirsty and militaristic and made a feature and a virtue out of this, culminating in establishing the samurai caste as the governing class in law! (To accommodate this signal departure from traditional Confucianism, it was later laid down that the samurai must devote himself to learning and the arts as well as to arms.)[2]

On the other hand, Confucianism accorded well and gave philosophical underpinning to many deep-seated native Japanese attitudes. Like the Chinese, the Japanese thought, felt, and acted in terms of groups not individuals, so that it comes as no surprise to find that entire families might be punished or even exterminated for the crime of a single member; nor that villages were collectively responsible for paying tax; nor that their inhabitants were bound together in collective frankpledge groups of five or ten families, just as they were in China. And the conservatism of Confucianism, its exaggerated respect for tradition, and above all its doctrine of the Five Relationships, went to justify and reinforce the indigenously Japanese respect for inequality, hierarchy, and status. The reformers of the 'Chinese period' followed the T'ang in the grading of the court and its officials into so many ranks, all distinguished from one another by uniforms and prescribed precedences and rituals. As in China, too, the relative position of every individual was signalled to himself and by himself via the gradations of bowing and a wide variety of polite forms of address, both of these being found to some degree even in Japan of the present day.

[2] See p. 1100 below.

Status was inherited—the notion of inheritance was very deep-rooted—and such a hereditary status continued to command respect even if in other ways, such as financially, the holder had fallen on evil times. So, for instance, village headmen or elders were chosen, if not exclusively then certainly *inter alia*, for their inherited status and not for their wealth. As for the notion of equality, this was completely absent and with it, *in toto*, the notion of individual rights against one's superiors. All the emphasis fell on obedience and loyalty. Japan was what has been called a 'vertical' society. It is the verticality of the feudal relationship in Japan and the absence of a corresponding 'horizontality' (i.e. the notion of contract) that distinguishes Japanese feudalism from Western Europe's.

But the Japanese held, also, a number of irreducibly native values and sentiments which owed nothing to Chinese philosophies or religions or rationales, and some of these were of political importance. Such in particular was the sentiment of honour and its counterpart, shame, akin to the Chinese 'loss of face' and which impelled the Japanese who was faced with some insoluble moral dilemma to commit *seppuku* (ritual suicide). Japan was a 'shame' society, and the heroic tradition was the other side of this coin. The way of the warrior was to court death and never to surrender. That was as unacceptably shameful to the Japanese samurai as it was to the ancient Spartans. The 'way of the warrior' which we know as *bushido*, a chivalric code similar in many respects to that of medieval Europe's, was a late rationalization which came into existence, paradoxically, just when the samurai's military function had become redundant (i.e. in the seventeenth and eighteenth centuries); but the great military heroes' stirring feats of arms undoubtedly existed long before the 'invention' of *bushido*, and were indeed the inspiration for its code of courage and dauntlessness even to death, if only honour were saved.

2. CHRONOLOGICAL OUTLINE

Japanese constitutional history can be visualized and periodized in a number of ways. In all of them it is clear that an initial period of tribalism was succeeded by one of imperial centralization which, however, by want of a bureaucratic underpinning failed to maintain order, so that it was in part replaced by a government of warriors who could and did (1192). This in turn broke down to give way to a similar type of militaristic regime, but one with much less control over recalcitrant members of the military class (1336); which in turn broke down in a century of incessant provincial wars, until one of the warlords was able to conquer and impose his will on the rest (Hideyoshi, 1590).

Another version, not incongruent with the former, would see the evolution in terms of the changing social origins of the governing class. In the imperial period they were court aristocrats and members of the imperial house, many of whom went out as provincial governors, but later sent deputies in their place to allow themselves the pleasures of the court, though drawing income from their lands. These gilded butterflies constituted the aesthetically gifted but epicene court aristocracy of the Heian period (captured in Lady Murasaki's *Tale of Genji*).

But the emperor had no standing army to speak of and so, as law and order broke down in the capital, could maintain the peace only by calling on the marcher lords of the west (who were still fighting the Ainu aborigines). These lords were the younger scions of the court families and of the imperial line who had sought their fortune in the provinces. Ultimately, these families came to blows with one another until the Minamoto family established its hegemony, which lasted until 1333. This ruling group of minor noblemen was established as military governors (*shugo*) and estate-stewards (*jito*) and as such shared the land revenues with the ancient court aristocracy who still retained proprietorship. This arrangement broke down as a new class of self-made war-lords arose to dispossess both the ancient court aristocrats and this minor aristocracy, cementing their estates into great centralized contiguous domains (*han*), and fighting each other until the all-conquering Tokugawa imposed its peace upon them all, a peace which it sustained for two centuries and a half.

Or again, the history may be conceived in terms of the development of feudalism. The system of direct imperial control via the population's customary deference to the court aristocracy gave way (1192) to the hegemony of the marcher lords who ruled through their vassals, the first and primitive form of Japanese feudalism. This was followed by the secondary and developed form involving, *inter alia*, sub-infeudation and rear-vassalage, and the formalities of swearing allegiance. The final stage, that of the Tokugawa, evinces this second-stage format of feudalism brought under the control of an overwhelming central domain, to which the various fiefs served—as in medieval France—as the *mouvance*.

There are certainly some parallels between what happened in Japan and in some other Asian countries. For instance, Japan's imperial period might be likened to China's Western Chou era, both being followed by the breakdown of central authority and its increasing parcellization among local war-lords until it is almost totally fragmented, whereupon these scattered morsels of authority begin to become concentrated in the hands of fewer and fewer powerful war-lords until in the end one swallows up the rest and so re-creates the imperial system. But this analogy is bad. In the first place the successor states to the Chou were not feudal but centralized and became even more so as time went by. Secondly, in Japan the various fiefs were not absorbed into the victorious Tokugawa domains; they retained their separate identities and autonomy, but inside a Tokugawa framework.

European experience comes nearer the mark. We could compare the Imperial (Nara–Heian) period with the empire of Charlemagne. Both were premature in that the central government's stretch far exceeded its grasp, lacking as it did both the military and administrative means to make and keep its rule effective in the provinces. In both cases the central government's authority fragmented as local war-lords took over in coexistence with, or doubling up for, the still-in-post imperial agents and governors. In both polities this fragmentation became extreme until the day arrived when the greater war-lords succeeded in swallowing up the lesser, so creating a small number of well-organized provinces, which owed only a nominal allegiance to the monarch, and which was expressed in feudal terms. But the monarch too had his domains and he too consolidated them by warring down his own recalcitrant minor baronage, and raced the great provincial barons as to who could consolidate most territory fastest. A point came when the monarch's domain was large enough and his authority extensive enough for him to be able to control the activities of his feudatories and yet leave them in post in their domains.

So far the parallel holds. But whereas in Europe this stage was followed by further provincial consolidation and renewed contest with the Crown, until in the end the latter was able to wear down its rivals and finally absorb them into a centralized system, this stage did not occur in Japan. On the contrary: at that very point where the lord of the victorious domain had established his hegemony over the lesser lords, he progressed no further. He simply froze the situation in that shape. It is this peculiar petrification of the state of affairs that constitutes not just the unlikely outcome but the great idiosyncrasy, and for that reason, interest of the Tokugawa regime.

These alternative ways of presenting Japanese constitutional development, may, it is hoped, assist in interpreting the chronology that now follows.

2.1. *Ancient Period:* AD 250–710

Large group of clans (*uji*) under the head (*mikado*) of the hegemonic hence 'imperial' clan of the Yamato. Hence the YAMATO period. From *c.*230, steady expansion over the indigenous peoples.

Ancient Period

*c.*400–450	Adoption of Chinese script and literary language
538 .	Introduction of Buddhism
593	Prince Shotoku (d. 639), Buddhist and reformer
625	The first of the 'Six Nara Sects' introduced from China
645	Accession of Emperor Kotoku
646	The TAIKA REFORMS: wholesale copying of T'ang imperial institutions

2.2. *The Imperial State (Nara–Heian Period): 710–1192*

Emperor (the *tenno*) the executive head and chief priest: a Council of State headed by *dai jokan* (chief minister). Provincial and local government modelled on the T'ang. Brilliant flowering of culture. Efforts to make Buddhism the official religion.

Imperial State

710	The capital fixed at NARA. The NARA PERIOD
743	Reclaimed lands go to reclaimer in perpetuity, undermining T'ang land-reallocation system
792	Abolition of the local militias. Provincial guards instead
794	Emperor Kammu moves capital to HEIAN (modern Kyoto), severs ties between Buddhism and the state, slows down reallocation of fields. The HEIAN PERIOD

Vast material privileges of the court aristocracy who double as the bureaucracy. Aesthetic civilization at its height. Tax-exempt estates grow at expense of land reallocation. Peasant 'commendation'[3] begins, leading to (tenth century) the end of independent peasantry. The over-elaborate T'ang-model central administration simplified to three ministries for Audit, Archives, and Police.

T'ang

838	Last embassy to the T'ang: symbolic *end of the 'Chinese period'*
858–1160	FUJIWARA period—Fujiwara clan-head controls emperor either as regent (*sesshu*) or counsellor (*kampaku*), marries daughters to emperors, so ensures succession in Fujiwara female line
*c.*900	Introduction of the *kana* syllabary marks the beginnings of the written vernacular literature and the end of Chinese influence

---

[3] Whereby poor peasants surrounded by predatory neighbours were driven to donate or 'commend' their plots to greater landowners in return for protection. G. Sansom, *A History of Japan*, vol. 1, *to 1334* (1958), vol. 2, *1334–1615* (1961), vol. 3, *1615–1867* (Dawson, Folkestone, Kent, 1963), i. 235.

902	Despite efforts to prevent concentration of land, the emergence of the *shoen* (manors) held by scions of the aristocracy and the imperial clan
*c.*1001–5	Putative date of Lady Murasaki's *Tale of Genji* and of Sei Shonagon's *Pillow Book*. Heyday of the effete Heian court culture, the 'World of the Shining Prince'
1073	The inception of the INSEI ('cloistered') emperors: Go-Sanjo abdicates, takes Buddhist vows, rules from his retirement
*c.*1100	Increasing disorders in capital; the Minamoto and Taira clansmen called in to keep order
1156	Contest between reigning emperor and the *insei* emperor starts HOGEN War. Taira victorious, control emperor
1180	The Gempei War, Minamoto versus Taira
1185	Minamoto Yoritomo's forces crush Taira (at Dan-no-Ura)
1192	Yoritomo is made shogun (generalissimo). Court at Kyoto, but the *bakufu* (military tent) at Kamakura

2.3. *The Kamakura Bakufu, 1192–1333*

The *bakufu*, a military feudal government vested in three commissions; military governors (*shugo*) in all the Provinces and stewards (*jito*) on every estate, acting on its behalf. The *shiki-shoen* system.

Kamakura Bakufu

1199	Death of Yoritomo. Power passes to HOJO clan. Unable to assume title of shoguns because their lineage is too humble, hence act as deputies (i.e. *shikken*) for the shogun, who is acting for the emperor, in the presence of the cloistered (*insei*) emperor!
1221	Emperor Toba attempts personal power, rebels, fails; supremacy of the *bakufu* reinforced
1274	First Mongol Invasion
1281	Second Mongol Invasion. Decline of the *bakufu*, unable to reward samurai following defeat of the Mongols; new local families, e.g. the Ashikaga, concentrate ownership and challenge its authority. Enfeebled by inability to control a dynastic dispute. The Hojo family widely unpopular
1318	Accession of Daigo II; he dissolves the *insei* court, seizes personal power, is supported by the Ashikaga
1333–6:	The KEMMU RESTORATION. End of the Kamakura *bakufu*; personal rule of Daigo II
1336	Ashikaga overthrow Daigo II. Set up their own 'Southern' emperor
1338	Death of Daigo II. Ashikaga Takauji appointed shogun

2.4. *The Ashikaga Shogunate, 1338–1573*

Weak control of ever-more mighty provincial lords, fiscal inadequacy, military governors (*shugo*) raise their own taxes, defect from government. Rise of the townsmen and guilds (*za*). Peasant revolts.

Ashikaga Shogunate

1336–92	Dynastic dispute, the Northern Court and the Southern Court, latter supported by the Ashikaga, further enfeebles the *bakufu*
1392	The dynastic dispute resolved
1467–77	Economic distress, dynastic dispute, famines, peasant uprisings
1477	The ONIN War. Marks onset of endemic civil war. Self-protection in countryside, dispossession of aristocratic absentee landlords and *shugo* by new, base-born daimyo (=great name)
1573	The *bakufu* overthrown. End of Shogunate

2.5. *The 'Warring Country' (Sengoku) Period, 1573–1603*

Military governors extinguished. Daimyo take over, concentrate domains, introduce their house-rules as local law, recognize no common superior. In towns, rise of communes and guilds; monasteries playing increasingly temporal role; the rise of the samurai class and the introduction of firearms in 1543; 10,000 harquebusiers at Battle of Nagashino (1575).

Warring Country

1577	Victory for Nobunaga, *kampaku* (regent), imposes unity
1582	Assassination of Nobunaga
1585	Hideyoshi, the 'Japanese Napoleon', as *kampaku*
1587	Hideyoshi becomes master of all Kyushu
1588	The 'sword hunt', disarming of population except the samurai class
1590	Hideyoshi the master of all Japan
1591	Samurai forbidden to enter any other trade or profession
1595	Osaka Castle Bulletin establishes basic rules for public affairs
1598	Death of Hideyoshi: government by the Five Regents
1600	Tokugawa Ieyasu defeats regents at Battle of Sekigahara
1603	Ieyasu appointed shogun. Beginning of TOKUGAWA SHOGUNATE (1603–1868)

3. THE FEUDAL FOUNDATIONS OF THE TOKUGAWA SHOGUNATE

3.1. *Stages of Development*

3.1.1. FROM THE COMING OF THE KAMAKURA *BAKUFU* TO ITS END (1192–1333)

The imperial government ruled the provinces through governors (*kami*) and the commanderies by sub-governors (*suke*). In the eleventh century these officials came under increasing challenge from the local gentry. There was no strong, central standing army so they formed private armies to protect their estates. This was the first appearance of the samurai class.

In 1185 Yoritomo became shogun, that is, the military dictator of the country. He planted his retainers, as *jito* (land stewards) and *shugo* (provincial protectors) alongside the imperial governors. Their authority was limited to military and policing matters. After the emperor's unsuccessful revolt in 1221, *jito* (hitherto appointed in only a limited number of areas) were set up everywhere. The *shugo* gradually turned themselves into military governors, the *jito* expanded their tax-powers.

The imperial court continued to sit at Kyoto, but Yoritomo established his government far away, at Kamakura. This government was called the *bakufu* (the curtain erected around the tent of the general in the field). Initially it was purely concerned with the interests of the new military establishment but, as it was the locus of effective power, it was not long before it became the true government of the country, with the imperial system operating in parallel as a distinctly junior partner. Yoritomo legitimized this usurpation by making the emperor grant him the title of shogun, or generalissimo.

How 'feudal' was this system? Not very. For one thing, the imperial system and the private *shoen* (manors) persisted in large part, completely outside any fiefs (which alone are the mark of a feudal system). For another, the relationship of *shogun* to his followers was 'simple-direct'; there was no sub-infeudation. The situation was one of 'a victorious army exercising its dictatorship through its chief'.[4] 'It needed the civil disorders of the subsequent period', says de Longrais, 'for the warriors to fan out across their lands and there assume a new independence and precipitate the emergence of a decentralized landed feudalism.'[5]

---

[4] F. J. de Longrais, *L'Est et l'ouest*. (Institut de Recherches d'Histoire Française, Paris, 1958), 113.
[5] Ibid.

3.1.2. THE DECAY OF THE KAMAKURA AND THE SWAY OF THE ASHIKAGA *BAKUFU* (1338–1547)

The Emperor Go-Daigo, supported by a coalition of enemies of the then-ruling Hojo family, destroyed the *bakufu* and assumed personal power—the 'Kemmu Restoration'—but was deposed (1336) by his leading supporter, Ashikaga Takauji. The latter, having installed his own puppet emperor in Kyoto, became shogun at the head of the Ashikaga *bakufu*.

The Ashikaga Shogunate was incapable of subduing local war-bands and the epoch was marked by frequent private wars. 'One-level' feudalism now gave way to a stepped hierarchy. In the course of the civil wars the simple warriors commended themselves to the *jito* of their locality, who by now had acquired proprietorial rights from the former owner of the *shoen*. Thus they were now true lords—*seigneurs*—the more so because in the process they had also acquired the right to levy the land tax (*shoto*). However, the *bakufu* was too feeble to guarantee their new rights, so that they in their turn commended themselves to the most powerful war-lords of the area, the daimyo. For their part these had profited from the general confusion and anarchy to become independent. Most of them had previously been *shugo*, and they now extended their *shugo* military role to seize other people's lands, raise their own taxes, and administer justice. Thus they became the *de facto* chiefs of provinces, the *kokushu*. This role, beginning after 1333, swelled to its full in the civil wars of the *Sengoku* period of the sixteenth century. In this way there emerged a pyramidal structure of daimyo, their vassals, and the vassals of these in their turn.

Here we must anticipate what follows to draw attention to two striking and vastly important differences between Japanese and European feudalism. In Japan it was impossible to be, at the same time, a vassal or *gokenin* on one estate, and *kenin* on another; nor could any *kenin* or *gokenin* serve more than one lord.[6]

3.1.3. THE *SENGOKU* AND THE ADVENT OF THE TOKUGAWA SHOGUNATE (1467–1547)

In the fifteenth century an entirely new generation of leaders arose and built contiguous and centralized domains. True feudalism now emerged. Hitherto the lord–vassal link of fidelity had been one thing, the grant of land another. In the civil strife they began to correspond. Moreover, unlike in the Kamakura regime, the *gokenin* were no longer all the direct housemen of the *shogun*.

---

[6] J. W. Hall, *Government and Local Power in Japan, 500–1700: A Study Based on Bizen Province* (Princeton UP, Princeton, 1966), 197.

After the pointless and inconclusive Onin War (1467–77), the country dissolved into chronic civil warfare, waged by the daimyo, the newcomer military strong-men mentioned above. As in the English Wars of the Roses, the older local families killed one another off and were replaced by new ones like the Hojo and the Mori, or sometimes by men with no family background to speak of at all, like Hideyoshi. All these secured and maintained their domination through sheer military power. As in contemporary Europe, the mounted warrior was in full decline. With the ascendancy of infantry a new category of soldier emerged, the *ashigaru* (light-foot)—rather like the ancient Greek *peltasts*—who supported the two-sworded samurai in the field (only samurai might wear the two swords). They were chiefly recruited from among the peasantry. Later they were to come under the strictest military discipline, but during this period they were notorious for robbing and pillaging friend and foe alike, like the *écorcheurs* and other mercenary *bandes* in medieval France. Armies grew vast by contemporary European standards. Japan's population was in the region of 20 million—double the population of France at this period and four times that of the British Isles. Now in 1476–1528 the size of major European field armies was steady at about 25,000–30,000. In 1591 England was keeping 17,000 troops in Ireland, and in 1610 France could count some 51,000 troops in being.[7] But these were the military establishments of entire countries; whereas in Japan, individual daimyo, the equivalent of European dukes and counts, were leading 25,000 men into battle (Okehazama, 1560), and armies of 16,000 and 18,000 men respectively into battle at Kawanakajima, 1561, and Mikata-ha-hara, 1572.[8] At the great Battle of Sekigahara (1600), the Western Army numbered 80,000 with another 13,000 in reserve, while Ieyasu's Eastern Army numbered 74,000![9]

The ancient chivalric norms had gone. Instead, these wars were brutish, full of deceptions, intrigues, and betrayals. Espionage and infiltration had become a major part of military tactics. Sekigahara was won for Ieyasu by the flagrant treachery of one of the enemy's major contingents at the height of the battle.

These daimyo had completely replaced all the former local officials—governors, *shugo*, *jito*, and the like. They had consolidated the scattered estates into huge centralized domains (*han*), which they ruled in independence by their own house rules which laid down the conduct for their subjects in the most minute and oppressive detail and were backed up by

---

[7] J. R. Hale, *War and Society in Renaissance Europe, 1450–1620* (Fontana, 1985), 63.

[8] S. R. Turnbull, *Battles of the Samurai* ('Arms and Armour', London, 1987), 37, 47, 71.

[9] S. R. Turnbull, *The Samurai: A Military History* (Osprey, London, 1977), 240.

ferociously cruel punishments. In the course of their consolidation they absorbed the few remaining private lands still belonging to the imperial house and the ancient court nobility, bringing them to destitution. And with the *shoen* long gone as the unit of local land management, the village community took its place and was to prove the basic unit of government in the next three centuries.

The daimyo now fought great wars among themselves: and in turn first Oda Nobunaga, then Hideyoshi, and finally Tokugawa Ieyasu imposed their rule. In short, one particular 'super-daimyo' imposed himself over all the other daimyo, who were or had to become his obedient vassals, these in turn ruling over and through their rear-vassals. In this way a quite new, pyramidal type of structure, based on levels of vassaldom, was erected. This was to prove the skeletal frame of the new regime of Ieyasu: the Tokugawa Shogunate. This represents fully developed feudalism, whose characteristics will now be described.

3.2. *The Nature of Japanese Feudalism*

3.2.1. THE EXTRA-FEUDAL POSITION OF THE EMPEROR AND HIS COURT

In the West, the king or emperor was both *rex* (extra-feudal) and *dominus*, that is, the head of the feudal hierarchy. The Japanese emperor stood completely outside the latter. That hierarchy culminated in the shogun, the emperor's surrogate. The relationship of the two was in no way feudal: the shogun was not the vassal of the emperor but his appointed 'commander-in-chief'. Furthermore, the shogun strenuously distanced his vassals from the court—his vassals could only communicate with it through his own officials, if at all, and while the imperial court still lay at Kyoto, the shogunal court was in Edo Castle. Unlike the Martels, mayors of the palace who received the pope's permission to depose and replace the ruling Merovingian line, shoguns were content to strip emperors of their imperial functions. They never sought to acquire the imperial title for themselves, for the emperor was a sacral monarch, a *kami* (divinity), descended from the sun-goddess Amaterasu.[10]

3.2.2. THE CARDINALITY OF THE PERSONAL TIE

The lord–vassal tie was personal and so close that it approached that of child to parent. (Compare, in this regard, Roman sentiment about client status.) It took time for this personal relationship to generate a military

---

[10] Cf. M. Bloch, *Feudal Society*, ii. 382.

obligation on the part of the vassal and still longer for this obligation to be conditional on a grant of land. In France the Franks had imposed such a connection from above, just as William the Conqueror was to do in England. In both cases the vassalage link was tied to a specifically military *beneficium*. Whereas the link between Yoritomo and his men was personal, and, moreover, they did not serve him in return for past favours but for spoils to come. It was not till the fourteenth-century civil wars that the personal and the land tie began to coincide, and only when this had happened had a true fief come into existence.

3.2.3. BENEFICE AND *ONKYU*

Onkyu means 'a favour', a 'boon'. The *onkyu* closely paralleled the western 'benefice' in that it was the consequence of a request, usually oral, made by the suitor, in return for his giving certain services (sometimes written down), and which was immediately revocable if the latter were not carried out, the donor having the final word on whether that was the case. Furthermore, the beneficiary only enjoyed the usufruct of the estates; he had no power to alienate them.

The *onkyu* concept went beyond the usufruct of land to apply to any kind of conditional right to do certain things—for example, for a *gokenin* to serve as *jito* (steward) on estates belonging to other persons. Furthermore the condition under which the *onkyu* was granted was not confined to rendering military service; it could be any other kind of service.[11]

3.2.4. SEISIN AND *CHIGYO*

The term *chigyo* was not juridically defined before the Ashikaga. Like seisin in the West, it implied the physical possession founded on legal title of a parcel of land. This possessive right could be pleaded by prescription. In the thirteenth century it took effect after twenty years, later extended to three generations.[12]

3.2.5. NOT CONTRACTUAL

This is perhaps the central, certainly the most important distinction between Japanese and European feudalism, and it is the one that caused Maitland to consider that the Japanese variety was not 'true' feudalism (a conclusion that is today almost universally rejected). The Japanese feudal tie was not a quasi-contract between equal parties. It was a relationship 'of submission',[13] freely entered into by an inferior with his superior, so that

---

[11] de Longrais, *L'Est et l'ouest*, 125–30.   [12] Ibid. 139.
[13] The phrase is that of Bloch, *Feudal Society*, ii. 447.

the respective obligations of the two parties were correspondingly different from those of their European counterparts. The loyalty that the *bushi* owed his lord was vague and general: it is impossible to specify and categorize the feudatories' obligations as one does in the European case; the loyalty consisted of a 'vague ensemble'.[14] Secondly, utterly unlike the European situation, in Japan no lawsuit was ever permitted or even contemplatable between lord and vassal; the latter could not, ever, appeal to a superior lord or suzerain, or even to the shogun. (This peremptoriness and lack of any right of appeal is part and parcel, we may observe, of the general absence of juridical rights of any kind in pre-modern Japan.) The vassal simply had to put up with the situation or quit.

That the vassal could or should revoke his allegiance did not arise in the Kamakura period, when there was only one recognized feudal overlord, the shogun. But between 1336 and 1392 there were two rival imperial courts, and since the feudal lords lined up on one side or the other, not only were the *bushi* forced to make choices, but either choice they made was legitimate. Unsurprisingly, then, it is from this time onwards that the *bushi* recognized nobody as his lord but the man who led him into battle. It followed, too, that if that lord changed his allegiance from one court to the other, his *bushi* followed him.

We may ask, where lay this famed fidelity on which *bushido* so prided itself? The tales of treachery, betrayal, double-dealing, and espionage met with in the *Sengoku* period contradict it. Yet, paradoxically, it did exist in the sense that when a vassal gave himself to his lord he gave his all, even to the death. If, because he was disillusioned with his treatment, he left that lord to join another he brought the same indefinitely deep commitment to his new lord—or so at least we are told.[15] It is worth noticing that this revocability was expressly forbidden once Tokugawa Ieyasu had seized control. From his day on, allegiance was irrevocable.

3.2.6. THE DUTIES AND OBLIGATIONS OF VASSALS

The Japanese equivalent of the European homage was *genzan*. It was less formal than in the West however. The ceremony, if that is what it can be called, amounted to a would-be vassal going to the lord's castle, being interviewed by him, and then as a mark of being accepted receiving such

---

[14] de Longrais's phrase, *L'Est et l'ouest*, 147.

[15] Ibid. 149–53. Even this author seems somewhat embarrassed at the answer he gives, reproduced above. On the basis of the histories, especially of the great battles of the samurai, it seems to me that we ought to distinguish between the loyalty of the *gokenin* to his lord and that of the lord to his suzerain. The latter seems to have been a very tender plant, whereas the loyalty of the 'troops' to their war-leader seems absolute.

gifts as horse and sword; also, it might be, the exchanging of cups of rice wine amidst pledges of fidelity for 'three lives', a characteristc piece of Oriental hyperbole meant to convey deep sincerity.[16] The vassal's oath of fidelity, so given, was a written promise sworn in the name of the gods. In the civil wars such pledges became increasingly formal, but once the Tokugawa had seized power they exacted them and made their vassals honour them.

In the West, the act in which a vassal was invested with his fief was a solemn occasion; in Japan the vassal simply received a charter that explained and confirmed his title.[17] The vassals' duties consisted, inter alia, of guard duty in castles and on highways; military assistance generally, when called for; giving counsel at the lord's request; assisting him financially if need arose. But all this was expressed as favour on the part of the lord and duty on the part of the vassal; not as an act of reciprocity as in the West.

At the risk of being repetitious, it is necessary to return to the two essential differences between Western and Japanese feudalism. The first is this superior–inferior exclusivity about Japanese feudalism—its lack of a horizontal dimension. The Japanese concept of authority was fundamentally different from that of Western Europe. In Europe the symbol of suzerainty was the right to hold a court; lord–vassal relationships were governed by legal procedures; it could prove very awkward for kings and emperors who chose to try to override such procedures. In brief, in Europe authority was based on law, whereas in Japan it was based on a social pattern which simply reproduced the family pattern, that is, extended patriarchy; and of course, Confucianism lent great support to this attitude. The vassal was a type of 'child' and frequently did indeed became the adopted child, bearing the family name, of his feudal superior. In Japan, 'nothing in the religion, mores, political theories, or habits of thought of the people justifies resistance'.[18]

The second great difference, mentioned already, is that a vassal could serve only one lord, and no individual could be feudal lord of one domain but a vassal to another lord in the latter's domain. The fact that this could and did occur in Western Europe was what made it trans-territorial, an eccentric characteristic which as we saw—and shall see later—took time to disappear in favour of the territorial basis of sovereignty-allegiance which was the foundation-stone of the modern European state form.

[16] de Longrais, L'Est et l'ouest, 153–4.   [17] Ibid. 157.
[18] J. R. Strayer, 'The Tokogawa Period and Japanese Feudalism', in J. W. Hall and M. B. Jansen, Studies in the Institutional History of Early Modern Japan (Princeton UP, Princeton, 1968), 8.

3.2.7. THE 'KNIGHTLY CLASS'

The first of the ways in which the samurai class, a noble class, differed from the 'knightly' class in Europe was by reason of its size. In England the maximum number of knights' fees at any time was some 6,000, so that the number of actual knights was much smaller. But the samurai class made up some 5–6 per cent of the total population which, c.1600, would have amounted to no less than 1 million people!

But, secondly, this knightly class differed from those in Europe in its stratification. Not all samurai held fiefs. In Europe household retainers were never a very substantial sector and had almost disappeared by 1100.[19] But in Japan only the upper strata of the samurai class were enfeoffed; the lower were paid stipends in measures of rice. When, under the Tokugawa regime, the daimyo made their samurai quit the villages to reside in their castle-towns, these vassals increasingly became mere parts of a large army-type organization, and in this the number of enfeoffed vassals shrank inexorably while the proportion of stipendiaries increased *pro tanto* so that, by 1700, nine out of every ten samurai was on stipend.[20]

4. THE TOKUGAWA SHOGUNATE

4.1. *The Basic Institutions, 1600–1640*

4.1.1. STRUCTURE

The Tokugawa *bakufu*, more usually styled the Tokugawa Shogunate in the West, was decided by the Battle of Sekigahara in 1600, formally instituted by Ieyasu in 1603, and faced down its last serious revolt, the Shimabara Rebellion, in 1637. It had developed all its structural features by then, and 1639, the year in which the government closed the country to virtually all foreign intercourse, in effect marks the 'end of the beginning'.

Those structural features were imposed by military force and so maintained. It would be no exaggeration to describe them as a government of the samurai by the samurai for the samurai, and they remained in force for the following 250 years. But that long period was one of rising prosperity, complete peace, and virtually no disorders; so, geared up and indeed constructed to be able to give immediate battle, how did these institutions respond to this vastly protracted period of total peace? This is perhaps the most fascinating aspect of the Tokugawa regime.

---

[19] J. R. Strayer, 6.
[20] J. W. Hall, 'Feudalism in Japan: A Reassessment', in Hall and Jansen, *Studies in the Institutional History*, 47.

By common consent, Tokugawa society reached its peak in the *Genroku*, the short period 1688–1703, while politically this period till, say, 1750 is that of the 'mature' *bakufu*. Its structure had not changed but its practice had. What is proposed here is to sketch the institutions as established in the founding period, 1600–40; but thereafter, in the passages that consider the various components of the government in detail, to do so in the light of how they had come to operate *c.*1700. The rest of this section, then, will outline the basic institutions, as they were set up, 1600–40.

The Japanese call this regime *babuhan taisei*, a type of 'decentralized feudalism under overall central control'. We can visualize it as a compound of a lateral dimension which is territorial, and a vertical one which is jurisdictional. The entire land of Japan was deemed to belong to the shogun, who parcelled it out among the domain lords. Among these various domains the shogun's was far larger, richer, and more strategically placed than any of the others alone or even in any feasible combination. Such was the horizontal dimension. The vertical dimension consisted of, first, the unqualified duty of the domain lords to return undelimited services to the shogun in recompense for his grant of land, and secondly, a similar relationship between these domain lords and their own retainers whom they provided with fiefs or (increasingly) paid by rice stipends. We have already drawn attention to the absoluteness of the vassal's obedience to his lord. That absolute obedience to one's superior ran all the way up to the shogun at the peak of the feudal hierarchy, and by the same token his despotic authority reached all the way down to its base. One way of looking at this vertical dimension of the Shogunate would be to describe it as 'stepped despotism'. Its principal distinguishing feature from European feudal states was, precisely, this concentration of power in the hands of the superior at each step in the feudal pyramid. In practice the domain lords enjoyed despotic sway inside their own *han*, as long as they kept within the framework of such general laws or conditions as the shogun laid down.

Effectively the shogun was a despot; that is to say, there was no power or authority, legal or physical, which could check the exercise of his will whenever he chose to exert it. The structure of his government was dual. On the one side lay the domanial administration of the shogun, that is to say, his *bakufu*, his 'house government'. On the other lay the indirect but wholly effective control over the population exercised by his domination of their immediate overlords, his vassals.

Altogether, there were (at various periods) between 295 and 265 *han*, embracing three-quarters of the territory. The shogun's *han*, however, was seven times as large as that of the largest daimyo *han*, covering one-quarter of the land surface and containing one-third of the population of the whole country.[21] Something more than half was under the shogun's direct control, and the remainder was distributed among his 'liege vassals', the *hatamoto* (bannermen) and *gokenin* (honourable housemen). Their rank, wealth, and occupations were all strictly correlated by the rigid rank/office system. The organs through which the shogun governed this domain consisted, basically, of a small council of *Seniors* (the *roju*) and another of *Juniors* (the *wakadoshiyori*), and a handful of highly influential individual posts such as the governor of Osaka Castle, to be described later.

The vassals fell into three classes, the first consisting of the three junior branches of the Tokugawa: the *shimpan*. The Ieyasu line of the family was wary of these families. They were not trusted with governmental posts; their duty was, effectively, to be there to provide the succession to the Shogunate in the event of Ieyasu's line failing. The second class was that of the lords who had been neutral or inimical to Ieyasu at Sekigahara. These were the *tozama* or 'outside' daimyo, some of whom were very powerful, like the Shimazu of Satsuma, or the Maeda, Hosokawa, and the like; their domains all lay far from Edo. It was these that the Tokugawa had most to fear. The third and most numerous class consisted of the *fudai*, that is, the vassals or allies of Ieyasu before Sekigahara, the so-called 'hereditary' vassals. The shoguns took much trouble to place *fudai* domains in strategic locations vis-à-vis the *tozama* ones, and generally to divide up all the *han* so as to minimize the risks of a hostile coalition. This object was also secured by shifting daimyo from one domain to another.

The individual daimyo was an autocrat as long as he did not transgress any of the shogunal laws. Only very wealthy vassals could be daimyo, those whose estates yielded the equivalent of an annual 10,000 *koku*, some 50,000 bushels of rice. Each daimyo had, like the shogun, his own vassals and retainers and could if he wished enfeoff them with sub-fiefs. The daimyo managed his *han* in his own way. His house rules had the force of law and nobody but he alone exercised any fiscal authority whatsoever.

The daimyo's obligation to the shogun was to provide him with any sort of assistance he required at any time. The chief form was, of course, military assistance, but the daimyo were also obliged to contribute to the repairs to shogunal castles, help build palaces, and construct roads and harbours,[22] all of which was expensive. On the other hand, daimyo did not pay taxes to the shogun (though they did give 'presents').

Since no shogunal administrators operated inside his *han*, a daimyo could do what he liked there, subject only—with a certain qualification to be

[21] Sansom, *History of Japan*, iii. 4.   [22] Ibid. 20–1.

mentioned below—to the laws the shogun chose to lay down. The question then is how did a shogun get the daimyo to follow those laws? What happened if they did not? This is the perennial problem of the central–local relationship, arising, as we have seen, between pharaoh and nomarch, Great King and satrap, caliph and governor, for example. And as we have seen, in none of these cases was central control uniformly effective and in most it frequently collapsed into territorial revolts. This did not happen at all in Japan until the third decade of the nineteenth century. On the contrary: shogunal control over the daimyo was absolute and complete. This was partly due to the deep-rooted cultural tradition of absolute loyalty of which we have already spoken, but it was also guaranteed by a whole battery of institutional devices, some of them unique to Japan.

The daimyo had to swear allegiance to Ieyasu,[23] and this oath was repeated at the accession of every new shogun. They were periodically convened to hear the recitation of *Laws Governing the Military Houses*[24] promulgated by Ieyasu in 1615. In some cases, the loyalty was reinforced by marriage into the Tokugawa family. But at the same time the daimyo were not free to intermarry among themselves unless the shogun, assured that no hostile alliance would result, gave his consent. This is in sharp contrast to late-medieval England where the practice, being permitted, led to the creation of vast and hostile domains like those of the dukes of Lancaster.

Nor could the daimyo, without permission, repair or erect fortifications or engage troops. Furthermore, it was for the shogun alone to decide that a vassal had failed in his duties and, as time went on, maladministration of his *han* or what was deemed an improper exercise of his power there came to attract the same treatment as rebellion or breaches of loyalty: reduction in the size of the *han* enforced removal to another *han*, or the dissolution of his house. We saw the daimyo had no recourse or appeal against such decisions and, for reasons already cited plus the two about to be mentioned, no daimyo, not even the most powerful, was ever in a position to make armed resistance.

The strongest of the controls over the daimyo lay in two institutions. In the first place, the daimyo had to keep wife and children, household officials, and numerous retainers at Edo, the shogun's capital, throughout the year, as so many hostages. The second was the unique institution of

---

[23] See p. 1092 above.

[24] For a summary, see Sansom, *History of Japan*, iii. 7–8. This document lays down, importantly, that the study of literature must be practised along with military training. It also charges the daimyo to report all building works on any castle, to expel any soldier in service charged with murder or treason, to expel anybody who has broken the laws, to limit residence to those born in the *han*, and to denounce conspiracies and factions rumoured in their neighbourhood.

sankin kotai, that is to say, the system of 'alternate attendance'. Every daimyo was compelled to come to the capital every year (sometimes alternate years) accompanied by quite enormous trains of servants and retainers,[25] and reside there for some six months, during which time he had to attend monthly audiences so as to keep himself in view of the shogun, who looked on in silence from behind a screen. The cost of the retinues and the extravagance of the daimyo mansions in Edo was enormous and contributed—deliberately, of course—to weakening the daimyo's financial resources. But in addition, the six-month attendances were arranged in a roster in such a way that at any one point in the year one-half of all the vassal daimyo were absent from their domains.

Finally, although the daimyo was master in his domain, this did not mean that he could go unobserved. On the contrary. The shogunal court disposed of a corps of *metsuke*, which is sometimes translated as 'spies' or 'informers', but is more usually translated as Censorate (on the Chinese Ming model). They were in fact intelligence officers and would visit and might even temporarily reside in the daimyo's court and report back to the *bakufu* in Edo. Not a mouse could move throughout the entirety of Japanese territory but that the *bakufu* knew of it.

This minute surveillance along with all the other measures mentioned combined to keep the vassals in a state of total subjection to the shogun, a subjection which they in turn exacted from their own subjects. It was thus that the Japanese feudal polity was contrived to form that 'stepped despotism' of which we have spoken. Unlike in Europe, in Japan feudal authority existed in only a vertical and not a horizontal dimension: Tokugawa feudalism consisted in the subjection of inferior to superior at every level of the feudal pyramid, without right or possibility of appeal, up to the very top.

4.1.2. THE 'VERTICAL' SOCIETY

We have noted how the later Roman Empire, Ming China, and many other governments tried to 'freeze' their societies so that they would endure in that same shape for ever, but the Tokugawa Shogunate is unique both in the completeness and the success of its social engineering.

---

[25] See e.g. E. Kaempfer, *The History of Japan* (J. Maclehose & Sons, Glasgow, 1906), ii. 330–7. 'The train of some of the most eminent among the Princes of the Empire fills up the road for some days . . . The retinue of one of the chief Daimios as they are called, is computed to amount to about 20,000 men more or less, that of a Sjiomo to about 10,000 . . .' (Kaempfer says elsewhere that *sjiomo* means 'lesser name'.) These retinues had to space themselves out along the road, taking three days for the rear to catch up with the head of the column. Since the other daimyos were also going up or coming down from Edo at the same time, inns and the like had to be carefully reserved in advance.

Once he had beaten all his enemies at Sekigahara, Ieyasu sought to maintain his supremacy. The political structure he erected was only one facet of this enterprise. The other was a set of far-reaching enforcements designed to institute and then perpetuate a distinctive social order. All potential centres of disturbances were smashed. Here Ieyasu benefited from the efforts of his predecessors, Oda Nobunaga and Hiyedoshi. The former, for instance, destroyed forever the political power of the Buddhist monk-armies. It took him eleven years of besieging and burning down their great monastery-fortresses, ending with the fall of the Honganji, which was the cathedral of the *Ikko* sect, and thought to be impregnable by reason of its fortifications and the numerous military detachments from the sect's power-ful congregations in all parts of Japan. Its fall in 1580 ended for ever the violence and the political challenge of the Buddhist sectaries.[26]

The *Sengoku* period had seen popular uprisings as well as these sectarian ones.[27] It was Hideyoshi who put a stop to this by the 1588 'sword hunt' which at one stroke totally disarmed all but the samurai.

The cities had thrived. They and their guilds (the *za*) had often come near to achieving something like semi-independence, and for similar reasons to those in Western Europe, that is, the fragmentation of political authority. Ieyasu quashed such aspirations by putting the most populous towns under the direct and iron control of his own commissioners (see below for details), while in the *han* the daimyo achieved the same effect by founding their 'castle towns', which became thriving centres but always under the shadow of their frowning fortress.

The linked policies of eradicating Christianity and isolating Japan from the outside world similarly sprang from this determination to eliminate every possible source of destabilization. Christianity had been introduced after 1543 by Portuguese and then Spanish missionaries and had made great headway among some of the daimyo and tens of thousands of the common folk. The persecutions had been sporadic only, until Ieyasu's son, Hidetada, concluded that the missionaries were an advance guard for European invaders. (This was a plausible notion in the light of recent events in South-East Asia.) After 1617 persecution was unremitting and merciless. The final act of extinction occurred when a desperate Christian peasant revolt at Shimabara in 1637 was crushed (with the military assistance of the Protestant Dutch traders).

Dread of similar uprisings gave a final push to the decision to cut Japan off from the outside world (the policy of *sakoku*). The Spaniards were

---

[26] Sansom, *History of Japan*, ii. 283–4, 289. For further details on the fall of Hiyeizan, see Turnbull, *The Samurai*, 152–3, and for the Honganji, 160–2.   [27] Reischauer, *Ennin's Diary*, 577.

thrown out in 1624, the Portuguese were made to follow them in 1638; then, in 1639, the Japanese were forbidden to leave the country, while any who did so and returned were to be executed. No ocean-going vessels might be built. And the only foreigners permitted to reside in Japan were a few Dutch traders who were pent up on a tiny island off Nagasaki.

Hideyoshi's 'sword hunt' foreshadowed an ever-more complete hierarchicalization of society by Ieyasu and his successors. There was one ruling group, a hereditary warrior caste, the samurai. There followed in rank order the farmers, artisans, and merchants. (The sequence is known, in Japanese, as the *shi-no-ko-sho*.) The rule called *kirisute gomen* means 'permission to cut down and leave'; it referred to the understanding that 'if persons of low degree such as townsmen and farmers be guilty of insulting speech or rude behaviour they may, should it be unavoidable, be cut down'. Admittedly, as time went on this rule was interpreted more and more restrictively, but its very existence is indicative of the position of the samurai in the state. The distinction between them and the commoners applied throughout most of the legal code, too, a matter that will be expounded below. A decisive step in drawing this distinction occurred by command of their daimyo overlords, when they left the villages in order to reside in the castle-town; henceforth, physically removed from the peasantry, they belonged to a quite different sphere. The axiom was that all the rest of society existed for the purpose of maintaining the military class.[28]

Meanwhile, the farmers, who formed at least 80 per cent of the population, were both helped and harmed by Hideyoshi and the Tokugawa. Hideyoshi ended the last vestiges of *shiki* shares in ownership, and by a sort of 'copyhold' gave the farmer secure tenure of his land. But at the same time he became tied to his village. Both results were accomplished by virtue of Hideyoshi's census (1590), and in 1591 his decree commanding the expulsion of 'vagrants' (i.e. anybody who had entered a village after September 1590).[29]

This unequal social order required a justification; but Buddhism neither would give it (since ultimately it was a salvation religion) nor could do so (because its intellectual vigour ceased at the same time as its military prowess). Ieyasu and his successors found that instead the neo-Confucianism of Chu Hsi was a perfect ideology for justifying and supporting it. We have already seen how it originated in Sung China.[30] What appealed to Ieyasu was its emphasis on loyalty, on the hierarchical family, and on the 'five relationships' and, generally, its conservatism. It most

[28] G. Sansom, *Japan: A Short Cultural History* (1st edn., 1931; Cressett Press, 1987), 465.
[29] Sansom, *History of Japan*, ii. 332.　　[30] See pp. 456–7, 810 above.

emphatically contradicted the *Sengoku* period notion of *gekokujo* (the 'over-throw of superiors by inferiors') in favour of the contrary virtue of *kenshin* (dedication) which linked filial piety and *chu* (loyalty) together. The trouble was that Chu Hsi Confucianism set filial piety over all else and the mandarin or *literatus* at the apex of the social hierarchy, with only contempt for the soldier. Ieyasu therefore only espoused this neo-Confucianism with two far-reaching modifications.[31] Loyalty to the ruler completely overrode loyalty to one's family; and the samurai were 'assimilated' to the Chinese literati by the double device of regarding them as like Platonic 'guardians' but also insisting[32] that, for the samurai, learning must go hand-in-hand with the military art. Thus modified, neo-Confucianism proved a fantasti-cally successful ideology of Tokugawa power.[33]

Together with his legal and social privileges, however, the samurai was expected—expected, we repeat—to feel a sense of obligation, like the Roman 'sense of empire' or the concept of *virtus*. In fact the samurai did indeed internalize the sentiment of duty (*giri*) and gratitude for favours (*on*), and a sense of discipline and self-control. Whereas in Europe the Christian notion of original sin was internalized to generate such attitudes (in so far as it ever did, about which one might be justly sceptical), in Japan it was the sense of shame.[34] Moreover, these notions spread down-wards throughout the rest of society. The way this occurred, and its vehicles, will be described later. All that need be said here is that it was highly effective.

4.2. *The Role of the Emperors*

The Japanese emperor, being directly descended from the sun-goddess Amaterasu, was a god-king. He was high priest. His person was too holy for him to be allowed to walk, so that he had to be carried; his hair and nails so sacred they had to be supposedly 'robbed' from him when he was sleeping. He could deify persons whose miraculous deeds or appearances seemed in his opinion to merit this.

---

[31] See the entry 'Japan, History of', *Encyclopaedia Britannica* (1979), x. 73. Sansom, *History of Japan*, 70–4.   [32] See the 'Way of the Warrior, the chivalric code *Bushido*', above, pp. 1080, 1091.
[33] Early shogun had influential neo-Confucian advisers, e.g. Hayashi Razan, Yamazaki Anzai, etc. Yamaga Soko (1622–85), for instance, is quoted as writing: 'Among major matters [of concern to the samurai] there are the maintenance of peace and order in the world; rites and festivals; the control of feudal states and districts . . . and the disposition of suits and appeals among the four classes of people. In addition, there is military command and organization . . .' and elsewhere he writes of the samurais' obligations to discharge loyal service to their masters, to be faithful to friends and to devote themselves to duty above all else. (Quoted in C. D. Totman, *Politics in the Tokugawa Bakufu: 1600–1843* (Harvard UP, Cambridge, Mass., 1967, 249).   [34] See p. 1080 above.

The extreme sacredness of the Japanese emperor was on a quite different plane from the Chinese conception: *there was no Japanese doctrine of the Mandate of Heaven.* That doctrine implied that the emperor was a mandatory of the divine, but the Japanese emperor *was* divine. There was no conditionality about his tenure of the throne. He was *absolutely* absolute. So that when he 'delegated' this authority to a shogun, then this absolute absolutism rubbed off on the latter too.

In antiquity emperors possessed both secular and sacerdotal authority, but from early historical times, with rare, short-lived, and inconsequential interruptions, their secular power was being exercised by somebody else purporting to act in their name. In the ninth century the Fujiwara clan-chief acted as regent (*sesshu*) even for an adult emperor, or else as his counsellor (*kampaku*). The nomenclature changed but not the substance when in 1185 Minamoto Yoritomo, at the head of his triumphant samurai, had the hapless emperor make him generalissimo, *shogun*. So strong was this custom of clandestine rule 'from behind the throne' that when Yoritomo left only an infant to succeed him, the Hojo family permitted the child to succeed as shogun but exercised all effective power themselves, with the title of 'deputy' shogun (*shikken*).

For all this, as long as an emperor owned lands he carried some political weight and the imperial court was always regarded with the utmost suspicion by the shoguns, who kept themselves and their vassals away from it. For, wherever the *de facto* locus of power resided, it was undisputed that the sole source of legitimacy, authority, and honours and the ultimate guarantor of all titles was the god-emperor. It was unthinkable for any regent, *kampaku*, or *shogun* to aspire to the imperial throne. On the contrary, they claimed they were legitimate because the god-emperor had devolved his secular responsibilities on to them.

Not all emperors were prepared to put up with this shadow-rulership, but their attempts to regain absolute power even when temporarily successful had no lasting effect. Their power to resist came to a stop during the *Sengoku* period when the daimyo confiscated their last estates. In 1615 Ieyasu made regulations which, in effect, robbed the court of all but ritual functions, and its compliance was jealously supervised by the shogun's military governor of Kyoto and its castle. This senior official cried out this supervision through two court officials who transmitted the shogun's wishes, and regulated all appointments. Ieyasu granted the emperor a not-inconsiderable salary which sufficed him but left the nobility so indigent that Kaempfer says some of them were reduced to making and selling straw baskets. In his rather good phrase, the court was remarkable for 'a splendid poverty'.[35]

[35] Kaempfer, *The History of Japan*, i. 263.

Thus, emperor reigned and shogun and his *bakufu* governed. When Kaempfer described the Japan of 1702, he portrayed it as having two emperors. The one he calls the *kubo* or *seogun*; but the other he calls the 'Ecclesiastical Hereditary Emperor'—a 'person most holy in himself, and . . . Pope by birth'.[36]

4.3. *The Shogun and the* Bakufu

4.3.1. STRUCTURE

The shogun governed from inside the so-called Central Interior, that is, his private apartments in the vast castle complex of Chiyoda in Edo, in whose 'Exterior' lay the myriad offices for his officials, guards, and commanders.[37] The central administration was built up by degrees, reaching its mature form *c.*1650. Effectively there were three levels of officials: the seniors or *karo*, who were the top policy-making officials, the field officers called *bugyo* at the intermediate level, and the district officers or intendants called *daikan* at the lowest level.[38]

What follows may be better understood in the light of the Organization Chart (Fig. 4.1.1). The key policy-making and administrative body was the council called *roju*, consisting of the *toshiyori*, 'senior elders', with sometimes three or as many as six members. They presided over relations with the throne, court, and great monasteries; supervised the daimyo (vassals with over 10,000 *koku*[39] of rice-land); supervised the management of the shogunal domain; prescribed the form of official documents; and *inter alia* controlled the mint and public works. Conformably to the Tokugawa paranoia at leaving any single individual in sole charge of any important function (on which more shortly), each elder served in rotation for one month at a time. The most influential, as will be seen, was the senior (or 'the great') elder, the *o-doshiyori*.

The *hyojosho* was a kind of administrative tribunal, a *conseil d'état*. It consisted of the *roju* plus various high commissioners (*bugyo*) who headed certain executive departments.

Corresponding to, but under the jurisdiction of, the *roju* (the *toshiyori*) was the *waka-doshiyori*, or junior elders. Their number varied between four and six. Just as the senior elders supervised the activities of the great daimyo, so one of this council's chief duties was supervising the *hatamoto* ('bannermen') and all other vassals owning less than 10,000 *koku* of rice-land. In addition

---

[36] Kaempfer, 259–60.   [37] See p. 1110 below for a further description of the castle complex.
[38] Totman, *Politics in the Tokogawa Bakufu*, 20.
[39] A *koku* consisted of some five bushels of rice, weighing about 300 lbs.

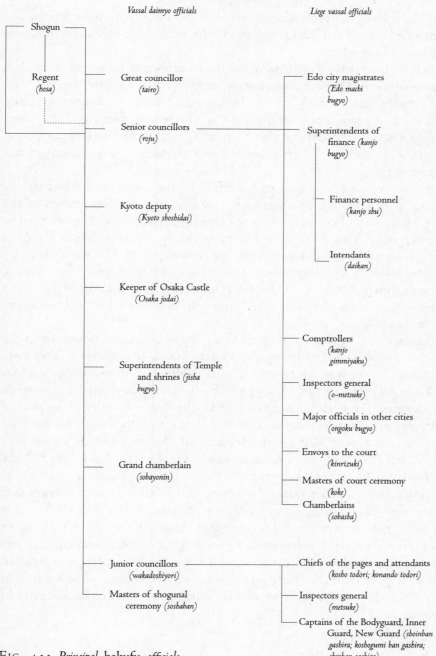

Vassal daimyo officials

Liege vassal officials

Shogun

Regent
(*hosa*)

Great councillor
(*tairo*)

Senior councillors
(*roju*)

Kyoto deputy
(*Kyoto shoshidai*)

Keeper of Osaka Castle
(*Osaka jodai*)

Superintendents of Temple
and shrines (*jisha
bugyo*)

Grand chamberlain
(*sobayonin*)

Junior councillors
(*wakadoshiyori*)

Masters of shogunal
ceremony (*soshaban*)

Edo city magistrates
(*Edo machi
bugyo*)

Superintendents of
finance (*kanjo
bugyo*)

Finance personnel
(*kanjo shu*)

Intendants
(*daikan*)

Comptrollers
(*kanjo
gimmiyaku*)

Inspectors general
(*o-metsuke*)

Major officials in other cities
(*ongoku bugyo*)

Envoys to the court
(*kinrizuki*)

Masters of court ceremony
(*koke*)

Chamberlains
(*sobasha*)

Chiefs of the pages and attendants
(*kosho todori; konando todori*)

Inspectors general
(*metsuke*)

Captains of the Bodyguard, Inner
Guard, New Guard (*shoinban
gashira; koshogumi ban gashira;
shmban gashira*)

FIG. 4.1.1 *Principal* bakufu *officials*
Source: C. D. Totman, *Politics in the Tokugawa Bakufu, 1600–1843* (Harvard UP, Cambridge, Mass., 1967), 41

they supervised the professional corporations, inspected public works, and controlled the officials and personnel in the great shogunal castles in Kyoto, Osaka, and elsewhere.

Below these two councils were ranged a number of boards or individual commissioners. The *o-metsuke*, already mentioned in another context, were the corps of Intelligence Officers who kept close watch on all daimyo. There were four of them, answering directly to the senior elders, and they controlled sixteen subordinates who themselves were supervised by the Junior Elders. Also, there were four commissioners for religious establishments and clergy: the *jisha-bugyo*.

At the intermediate level of government, the great imperial castles of Osaka, Kyoto, and Sumpu were administered by governors known as the *jodai*. Kyoto was administered by a military governor, the *shoshidai*; other cities like Nagasaki, Yamada, and the like by *bugyo*, who, like the French *intendants*, were responsible for administration, justice, and police. The vastly extensive domain-lands of the shogun were governed, under the aegis of four finance commissioners (*kanjo-bugyo*), by field administrators: in certain provinces four *gundai*, but for the most part by forty to fifty officials called the *daikan*, or deputies.

The internal organization of all these departments and boards from the *roju* downwards was grotesquely dysfunctional. It reflected Tokugawa paranoia. Ieyasu was, of course, a most cunning, devious, and suspicious individual, typical of the *Sengoku* period; it is wholly in character that when he organized the departments he had the *Sengoku*'s terrible record of betrayals, treachery, spying, and murder at the front of his mind. Security was his paramount object—the security of the shogun. Only one post might be filled by one sole individual: the one he held himself, the Shogunate. All others were organized so that every official was yoked to, spied on, and constrained by others of his same rank. So, important posts were always held by at least two persons alternating in office, for example, two commissioners to govern a town, or the *roju* where, as we have already seen, the elders took monthly turns in rotation. But there was more: each member of a board assumed, on his spell of active duty, all executive powers of the entire board, *but* whenever he wanted to act he had to collect the co-signatures of all his colleagues before his decision could become valid.[40]

---

[40] And see p. 1113 below.

4.3.2. PERSONNEL

What determined which posts were open and which closed to an individual was his hereditary rank, so this enormously restricted job-mobility. Secondly, there were no formal methods of testing for appropriate qualifications, such as the Chinese examination system. Thirdly, most posts were filled on a hereditary basis. Only warriors held these posts and they did so *qua* vassals of the shogun, their overlord. We thus have the extraordinary spectacle of a military caste transforming itself into a civil bureacracy.

The most senior posts of all—the *roju* and the like—were barred to the *shimpan* daimyo, that is, the collateral branches, and to the *tozama*, the 'outside lords'. Such posts were confined to the *fudai* (Ieyasu's vassals before Sekigahara), mostly to the intermediate ones.

Administration (as opposed to direction), whether it involved policy-making or was simply implementation, devolved instead on the shogun's bannermen and honourable-housemen (the *hatamoto* and the *go-kenin*, sometimes referred to as his 'liege vassals'). There were some 5,000 *hatamoto* and 17,000 *gokenin*. Every one was liable for military service but, as there was no enemy to fight after 1640, it proved impossible to find jobs for all of them and for all the efforts to 'make work' for them, over 5,000 were unemployed.[41] An 'upper' group were potentially involved in policy-making, and formed a reservoir for posts of responsibility. Their posts were hereditary but only in the negative sense that, although hereditary rank determined what posts were open to *hatamoto*, there was eager competition within each such rank, since there was only one worthwhile job for every two candidates.[42] The posts filled by the 'lower' group, the *gokenin*, were much more hereditary in nature. They consisted of the 'host of additional messengers, guards, attendants, serving personnel, cleaners, porters and so on . . .' which were created as the *bakufu* institutionalized itself. Such posts generally had a small office stipend attached to them.[43]

4.4. Government in the Fiefs

An early *bakufu* decree had said that 'laws like that of Edo' were to be observed in 'all matters and in all provinces and places'.[44] At first little more than a velleity, by 1800 it had become the general practice except in the case of two or three of the Great Houses. But this assimilation of local house rules and *bakufu* decrees did not alter the fact that the daimyo were,

---

[41] Totman, *Politics in the Tokogawa Bakufu*, 141–3.   [42] Ibid. 146.   [43] Ibid. 145.
[44] Sansom, *Japan*, 461.

inside that framework, sovereign lords. When, in 1868, a few years before the elimination of the daimyo, an effort was made to specify what had previously been only customary, the daimyo's powers were defined thus: 'Within his *han* to adminster the shrine and population census registers, to promote the welfare of the *samurai* and people, to spread moral principles, to encourage good conduct, to collect taxes, oversee labour service, judge rewards and punishments, administer the registration of Buddhist priests, and command the *han* troops.'[45]

Hall[46] has described the internal administration of Bizen, the *han* of the Ikeda House. The daimyo resided in his fortress in the castle-city of Okayama, his chief retainers and many of the lesser samurai living in concentric circles around it. They consisted of some 5,000 families and were divided into ten ranks with six elders (*karo*) at the top and 1,900–2,600 *ashagaru* at the base. Immediately below the daimyo, the *hyojosho*, or high council, staffed by two of the elders and other top officials, was the supreme decision-making body. The military establishment was a separate organization and consisted of guards regiments whose membership was hereditary in certain families, but the great bulk of the samurai were now a civil bureaucracy. This was headed by two councils of three members apiece, the senior and the junior councillors respectively. They were served by an echelon of staff officials such as chamberlains, inspectors, secretaries, and recorders. The executive functions were performed by magistrates for various sectors of administration, notably the *gundai* for rural affairs and others for finance, towns, temples and shrines, and schools. A record of a shogunal inspection of 1764 shows, *inter alia*, that the Ikeda daimyo counted 1,568 enfeoffed vassals and 4,725 stipended vassals; that his *han* boasted eight districts with 634 villages and thirty-eight branch villages; that the tax-rice, excluding the income of fiefs, was in the order of 103,000–105,000 *koku* (i.e. about 14,000 tons), about half of which was paid out in stipends; and finally, that there were two schools, one for samurai children, the other taking 'even farmers' children'.[47] But the record also shows the *han* as being 'governed tightly under severe security measures and a meticulous control system which regulated the status, residential location and the comings and goings of every resident'.[48]

---

[45] Quoted in J. W. Hall, *Government and Local Power in Japan, 500–1700* (Princeton UP, Princeton, 1973), 411.   [46] Ibid. 411–20.

[47] Ibid. 417–18.   [48] Ibid. 419. And see below, p. 1109.

4.5. *Local Government: Village and Town*

In the countryside, home to 80–85 per cent of the population, the basic unit of government was the village, and the lord's high officials, the *gundai* and the *daikan*.[49]

Villages functioned through what were in effect two different orders of government, one responding to the commands of the government, the other to the village's own internal concerns; but there was some overlap between the functions of the two. In the former, the chief officers were the headman (*shoya* or *nanushi*), three or four elders (*toshiyori*), a number of delegates (*hyakushodai*), and the leaders of the five-man bonded groups we have been calling the frankpledge groups (the *goningumi*). Headmen and elders were paid salaries out of the village's rice crop. The headman was always of an ancient lineage, often inheriting his position; was frequently wealthy as well; and was often the nominee of the lord. He was so important that he had a surname and was allowed to carry a sword—privileges otherwise confined to the samurai. The headman kept all the important records, the census, and a register of changes among the population; he allocated and collected the land tax, oversaw public works, adjudicated disputes, and reported violations of the law to the higher authority. The elders were his assistants. The delegates seem to have been the representatives of the ordinary peasants, keeping an eye on their headman and also giving him the benefit of their advice. The *goningumi*, as already indicated, were law-enforcement devices and will be discussed in that context later.

Alongside this structure there existed the village's agencies for self-regulation. A village was governed by its rule-book. Some of the rules overlapped with those dealt with in the parallel, government-orientated agency, for example, taxation, policing, and so on; but they also covered areas where disputes and conflicts inside the village were likely to arise, such as the management of commons, irrigation, and property boundaries. The major instrument for giving effect to these rules was the village assembly, which met from time to time to draw up new rules, deliberate on violations, and the like. It also laid down the punishment for such violations: usually ostracism, banishment, fines—or having to apologize. While it is not always easy to establish the precise membership of these assemblies, it is clear that the actual control in and through them lay with the élite families. An associated village institution was the shrine association or *miyaza*, for this had acquired the right to choose the village

---

[49] See pp. 1099, 1104 above.

officials. The *miyaza* restricted this choice to its own members and these consisted exclusively of the élite families![50]

Town government appears more complicated and naturally so, because the populations of the biggest towns were huge in both absolute and relative terms. In 1720 the population of Edo is reckoned to have reached 1,200,000, the most populous city in the world; and at around this time Kyoto had about 400,000 inhabitants and Osaka, 350,000. But in fact the general pattern of town government followed that of the village, but on a larger scale: the lord's commissioner, a group of city elders, and below these a set of headmen for the individual streets or quarters of the city.

The most important towns were under direct shogunal control. They were administered by a pair of commissioners who governed in alternate years, since each in turn had to go up and reside in Edo, in the way already described.

Kaempfer, who was stationed in Nagasaki 1700–2, has left a highly detailed description of its government.[51] There were three commissioners at any one time, two on the spot and a third in Edo. Their staff officers consisted of ten *bugyo* (who were minor noblemen) and thirty junior staff. Side by side with his commissioners, the shogun had also appointed a *daikan* to keep an eye on them, another reminder of the mistrust and suspicion which pervaded the entire administrative system.

The city officials were headed by a council of four hereditary elders, with a few deputies to assist them. Kaempfer next describes four officers, annual appointments, who seem to play the sort of role that the 'delegates' did in villages, for they had a room in the commissioner's palace where they waited to deliver the people's petitions and in turn to pass on the commissioner's wishes. These individuals—like the elders' deputies—were chosen from among the ablest of the city's various headmen. Kaempfer then branches off to describe what was in effect the city's police-force: a group of messengers who also served as bailiffs and police constables. These men—'good wrestlers', Kaempfer notes—went around carrying a halter and wore two swords like samurai. They were all members of a group of thirty families who lived side by side on the same street, and their office was passed on from father to son.[52]

Kaempfer then goes on to describe the basic units of town government. In Nagasaki these were the streets. (In Edo, which was huge and continually expanding into suburbia, the basic unit was larger: the *machi* or township, of

[50] This account is derived from Befu, in Hall and Jansen, *Studies in the Institutional History*, 301–14. Cf. also Sansom, *History of Japan*, iii. 97–106; C. J. Dunn, *Everyday Life in Traditional Japan* (Batsford, London, 1969), 71–6.   [51] What follows is a summary, Kaempfer, *The History of Japan*, i. 91–129.
[52] Ibid. 108.

which there were more than 1,000.)[53] Every street (gated at each end and containing between thirty to sixty houses) came under an officer whom he calls the *ottona*, but who clearly corresponds to the village headman. He kept the census, reported on arrivals and departures, conciliated and adjudicated disputes—and in addition was fire-chief, commandant of the watch, and summary magistrate for lesser crimes. He was paid a salary equal to one-tenth of the income of the street (in Nagasaki this was a sum paid out to every street from profits on the foreign trade). This headman was chosen by the inhabitants of the street in a regular election, using ballot papers.[54] He was assisted by three deputies.

These headmen or *ottona* worked down to the five-family frankpledge units, which consisted only of proprietors (*not* tenants). There were some ten or fifteen of these in each street. Each was headed by its own elder who was its leader and answerable for the other members. But the street had other officers too: the public notary, who prepared and promulgated all written instructions, issued passports, kept the census and details of the inhabitants; the treasurer; the messenger—for carrying petitions; and sets of guards, the one (the head guard) for special security duties, the other, a permanency, to look out for fires and thieves and to keep the gates at each end of the street.

5. THE POLITICAL PROCESS

5.1. *Politics in the Palace*

Tokugawa Japan was, in our parlance, a Palace polity. Its great peculiarity in this class of polities, of course, is that political power was most extensively decentralized, not just in practice but *de jure* as well.

This peculiarity may be expressed in another way, if we start by regarding Japan as one kind of 'composite' state, so that it would be akin, albeit in its own highly individual way, to such political systems as the Greek confederations, the Italian confederacy of which Rome was the hegemon, and systems like the Swiss or the Dutch confederations and the like. We may thus visualize Tokugawa Japan as a mosaic of some 250 despotisms held together by the hegemony of a super-despot, the shogun. Japan is best seen, in fact, as a unique amalgamation of Palace-type 'process' and composite 'structure' of government.

In such composite states—and for that matter in satrapal empires of the Achaemenian kind—the political process is, as we have seen, situated in two

---

[53] D. F. Henderson, 'The Evolution of Tokugawa Law', in Hall and Jansen, *Studies in the Institutional History*, 216.   [54] Kaempfer, *The History of Japan*, 110.

planes: the struggle for power inside the palace, and the struggle *for* the palace between it and the local strong-men—a struggle that often ended in the state's disintegration. Only the first took place in Japan. Under the seclusion policy, dissident daimyo could not rely on foreign help, nor could foreigners stir up unrest among the daimyo. Furthermore, there was no organized opposition from Church or the lawcourts or the merchants and bankers as there was in Europe. The shogun was far and away wealthier and more powerful than vassals, alone or combined: nor did he ever need extra money and men to fight foreign wars. Consequently, he was never dependent on vassals or other social elements. Whereas in Europe, as we have already seen, the monarchs' desperation to get financial and military assistance drove them to establish representative assemblies.[55] And, finally, the daimyo's lands were their own and outside the sphere of politics; they were ideologically committed to the Four Estate social order which the shoguns were promoting, and the *status quo* suited them very well.

This is why, in Japan, unlike almost all other polities visited so far, the central–local relationship did not generate a political process. But when we turn to the palace itself, we find the pattern which must surely be over-familiar to us by its constant repetitiousness (Imperial Rome being the huge exception): the subterranean struggle of the ruler and his circle of confidants against the senior ministers at the head of the bureaucracy.

A shogun lived in the so-called Central Interior of the labyrinthine Chiyoda Castle; here were his private apartments, where only he, his guards, and his male servants could move. (Note that eunuchs have absolutely no place in Japanese court life.) The first three shoguns were all highly energetic, and so were one or two of their successors, notably Yoshimune (who served from 1716 to 1745), but in general the shoguns lived an isolated life and for the most part they are anonymous figures in Japanese history. Cut off from affairs, seeing their highest officials for brief consultations only, remote from the imperial court, the shogun made contact with the outside world primarily through his personal atttendants.

The Central Interior led on one side to the Great Interior and on the other to the Exterior. The former was the harem quarter, populated by 1,000 women. There was no way a member of the Exterior could interfere here unless he had a woman friend there who would carry messages. And this was none too easy, for they had to secure exeats to leave the harem. On the other side the Central Exterior led to the great Exterior via the two great council chambers where the shogun held his silent monthly 'audience' with his

---

[55] But cf. Bloch, *Feudal Society*, ii. 452, for another comment on the two different outcomes.

daimyo. The Exterior, a veritable maze of offices for officials, guard detachments, military commanders, and the like, was the administrative quarter.

Up to 1651 highly active shoguns[56] took the helm, with the assistance of
the group of personal attendants each brought with him on his accession.
Then, under the shogun Ietsuna (1651–80), the senior officials, and notably
the senior elders (*roju*), discovered that they themselves could exercise *de facto*
power. But in 1684 a scare that the shogun might be assassinated led to the
relocation of the administrative offices at a considerable distance from the
Central Interior, and this necessitated the use of couriers to pass messages
between them. Of these the most senior was the grand chamberlain and he
soon became the key intermediary. So an ambivalent era set in when now the
shogun, now the senior councillor, but for the most part the chamberlain
came to exercise a personal dominance over policy. The vigorous shogun
Yoshimune (1716–45) resented the dominance of his grand chamberlain
(who himself had effectively supplanted the predominant president of the
senior elders) and reverted to the use of his own *hatamoto* as personal
adjutants. They were the indispensable go-betweens in fixing interviews,
recommending appointments and promotions, handling agreed reports, and
so forth. But Yoshimune's immediate successors were ineffectual. Personal
shogunal rule ceased, and confused and fluctuating struggles for leadership
took place between the senior elders and the grand chamberlain. After the
senior elders got control over the shogun's personal adjutants and resumed
power in this way, the shoguns, to escape them, fell back on the grand
chamberlain, who once more became the essential link-man. This ascendancy reached its peak when the humble but extremely able Tanuma was
raised to the post of chamberlain, from which he secured his elevation to the
post of president of the senior elders itself. Tanuma's extraordinary corruption irretrievably damaged the cause of chamberlain government. From 1787
onwards the president of the senior elders (the *roju*) became the effective
head of the government.[57]

5.2. *Politics and the Administration*

By the eighteenth century, except for the small fraction that constituted the
guards regiments, the shogun's 22,500 *hatamoto* and *gokenin* had become a huge
and intricate civil bureaucracy. If, as described above, leadership in the *bakufu*
passed from the person of the shogun to the 'Exterior', this did not signal

[56] Ieyasu (1603–5), Hidetada (1605–23), Iemitsu (1623–51).

[57] For Tanuma, see Sansom, *History of Japan*, iii. 174–7. Note here how he was helped in
manipulating the shogun Ieharu (who liked him, anyway) through one of the shogun's mistresses,
who was a relative of his wife.

the closure of the political process, for this now became a struggle as to which official should control the Exterior. The form the political process then took was dictated by the structure of the samurai bureaucracy, but it was also necessitated by it; for that structure was so awkward and cranky that without such a political process it would seize up, if indeed it could work at all. So politics in the palace was also politics in the civil administration, and both were the cause and also the outcome of the latter's peculiar format.

The political domination of the *bakufu* fell to the 'medium' daimyo, since they came to monopolize the position of senior elders. Over time these medium daimyo came to follow a sort of *cursus honorum*: master of shogunal ceremonies, then a concurrent superintendent of temples and shrines, then if a clique (see below) favoured him, the keeper of Osaka Castle, and finally a senior elder. A minor daimyo, on the other hand, would be more likely to go from master of shogunal ceremonies to the great guard or to the command of some other guard unit, and then, if fortunate, secure promotion to junior elder (from which some could rise to senior elder). However, advancement was not easy, since there were just not enough posts to go round.[58] To get an active post and, even more, to get promotion, the medium daimyo would be forced to rely on hereditary role, nepotism, or 'contacts'.

These 'contacts' were established by and through membership of a 'vertical clique', as it has been called. The latter, however, was at one and the same time the mode by which one of the high ministers, for example, one senior elder or another, came to dominate the civil service establishment and the lubricant which enabled that ossified structure to move at all. The 'vertical clique', as its name implies, extended from the most highly placed *fudai* officials down through the lower echelons to the liege vassals with basic stipends as low as a mere 100–500 *koku*.[59] Since there was such a rigid association between official post and hereditary rank, it was necessary, in order to keep the chain unbroken, to have a supporter on each descending level. Furthermore, these rank distinctions had resulted in fixing the routine duties of each post and thereby established job-demarcation which was so inelastic that one official could not perform the duties pertaining to another official, to the extent, even, that a senior echelon could not override the fixed routines of a lower echelon. So for this reason too it was necessary to have a supporter at each lower echelon.

But it was unnecessary for the clique to have much 'horizontal' extension at each of these echelons, owing to the 'duty rotation' system, already

---

[58] Totman, *Politics in the Tokugawa Bakufu*, 176.   [59] The following is based on ibid. 181–201.

described.[60] As we saw, the 'inactive' officials were expected to append their signatures to validate the actions of their 'active' colleague but, once given, the signatures could not be retracted. Hence it was only necessary to collar one of the concurrent officials in a given bureau or division and wait for his turn of active office to come round, for then through the 'joint signature system' he could commit all his partners.

Given the close association of hereditary rank and certain types of posts along with the rigid job-demarcation that prevented superior echelons from altering the procedures of the lower ones, one sees that this vertical clique—extending from top to bottom and radiating out at each echelon—was necessary to make the system work. But other devices were used also: one incumbent could be shuffled off for a more reliable supporter, one post could be abolished and a new one created. Another technique was to set up an *ad hoc* committee.

The most important posts to control were: the presidency of the senior elders, and these elders, generally; the junior elders; the Kyoto deputy, and the keeper of Osaka Castle. Then, among the liege vassals, the posts of Edo city magistrate (urban security) and superintendant of finances (litigation, real property law, economic conditions of the domain and the *hans* of the enfeoffed vassals, currency and taxes—the duties ranged very wide). The finance officials worked from the Castle in an office which boasted twelve chiefs of division and 200 junior personnel, so that the patronage was extensive, too. Another important kind of post was that of inspector, because they were required to be able to act in a variety of *ad hoc* roles, in sharp contrast to the general prevalence of pre-established fixed routines. As such they were, as Totman remarks, 'ideally suited for verticial clique politics'.[61]

In all this the most prestigious and potentially most powerful post of all was the president of the senior elders. Why did no such high minister ever come to usurp the shogun's place or govern from behind his authority as in many other Palace systems, and indeed as the 'regents' had done in Fujiwara times and the Hojo *shikken* had in the Kamakura Shogunate?

The obstacles were formidable. Tokugawa legitimacy was immense. No opportunities for usurpation arose, since the Tokugawa line never at any time lacked legitimate candidates for the succession. (The rules as to eligibility were firmly laid down by tradition—first the eldest son, then the cadet sons, then the Lords of the Three Houses, the *shimpan*.) Also, almost the entire ruling caste had its reasons for supporting the Tokugawa. The Three Houses, as Tokugawa, had an obvious interest, the medium

[60] See p. 1104 above.   [61] Totman, *Politics in the Tokogawa Bakufu*, 201.

daimyo knew they had a chance of acquiring political power via the *roju*, and the liege vassals of the shogun would gain absolutely nothing by a change. This left only the *tozama*, and they, cut off from any foreign succour, could do absolutely nothing. Finally, the medium daimyo who contended for this and the other senior posts naturally resisted the efforts of any one of them to acquire a perpetual dominion. By the same token, the formation of a vertical clique provoked the formation of a counter-clique to take its place.

In the last resort the answer is always the same: in Tokugawa conditions the only way a daimyo of the Exterior could come to wield power was by getting control of the bureaucracy via his vertical clique and, in that position of administrative dominance, governing under the shelter of the shogun's name.

6. GOVERNMENT SERVICES

The most striking difference between public provision in Japan as compared with all states so far is the ever-diminishing importance of the military establishment—the bizarre and paradoxical outcome of a regime founded on, and ruled by and in the interests of, its warrior caste.

6.1. *The Army*

The army did not evolve. It devolved. Its numbers shrank, its fighting capacity disappeared, its weaponry actually stepped backward! We should distinguish between the wartime army and the peacetime army. As to the first: in 1603 Ieyasu could in theory have mobilized 400,000 men. In practice he would probably have been able to bring a quarter of a million men into the field. But after the suppression of the Shimabara Revolt in 1637–8 and the adoption of the seclusion policy, the wartime army simply withered on the vine. About one-quarter of the liege vassals were expected to provide personal retainers, but by 1862 only 10,000 such troops were being called for. True, in addition, the vassal daimyo were expected to be able to contribute another 130,000 troops, but they were never called on to do anything like that. And their troops, like the *bakufu's*, were useless: all were engaged on routine duties, they received no campaign training, they were ineffectually organized for tactical deployment, and they never moved on beyond swords and suits of armour.

The peacetime army was, of course, smaller. The Great Guard of 1,020 men constituted, along with their rear vassals, a total force of some 5,000 men in the 1630s, but by the nineteenth century this had shrunk away. These and other guards troops performed garrison duties, for example, in the shogunal castles at Chiyoda, Nijo, and Osaka, and (paranoia again) they were regularly rotated between such locations. The Edo guards units were primarily an anti-riot squad.

Enrolment in a guards unit was prestigious and the first step in a career, but it neither connoted nor demanded any great military skill. There were no training programmes and even when they were introduced, for instance, by Yoshimune, they were ineffectual, and in the long peace the military skills withered away. These guards units were not a force to win a war, but a domestic gendarmerie.[62]

But the most extraordinary feature of the Japanese armed forces was not just the ever-diminishing numbers of effectives nor their progressive loss of military skills, but their abandonment of firearms. The harquebus came in 1543. It had played the critical part in the battles that ended the civil wars. But once the wars ceased the Japanese simply turned their backs on these unworthy, unchivalric weapons—as the great chevalier Bayard and his like had wanted to do, but unavailingly, in Europe a century before. They returned to the traditional and sacramental weapon—the sword. Not that firearms were abolished; there were specialized units such as the Vanguard Harquebusiers. But the prestige order for weaponry was first and foremost the sword, followed by the bow, then the pike; firearms came last.[63] And even then they were never updated. They were primitive matchlocks. When the Dutch traders at Nagasaki gave the Japanese a dozen of the new European flintlocks (1636) the weapons were politely received and then put away in a vault![64] Japanese artillery was even more obsolete, if that was possible. In 1776 their twelve-pounder cannon mounted to protect Tokyo harbour was being test-fired only once every seven years, and then only by means of a match at the end of a long pole.[65]

From the gendarmerie role of the army, it is logical to move to crime-repression and public security. But the way there must first pass through a consideration of the legal system.

6.2. Law and Justice

Did Tokugawa 'law' exist?

The Edo shogunate was a minimal sort of government that had at great risk and effort managed to impose itself upon a largely hostile society, and understandably in the formative years its chief function was the basic task of maintaining peace and

---

[62] Totman, 48.   [63] Ibid. 47.

[64] N. Perrin, *Japan's Revolution with the Sword, 1543–1879* (Godine, Boston, 1979), 68–9.

[65] Ibid. 69.

security by maintaining the shogunate itself—something not to be taken lightly in the light of the preceding century . . . Accordingly . . . [its] use of law was, perhaps necessarily, self-centred i.e. confining itself to defining its structuration (the social hierarchy, the feudal ties etc.) and to protecting itself from its enemies and detractors by harsh criminal penalties . . . This kind of self-serving law . . . was the core of the legal tradition in the courts of both Japan and China on the country-wide level during their respective traditional periods . . . The criminal law (*ritsu*) was little more than a repressive auxiliary to maintain official power and policy (*ryo*). Beyond this there was little 'national' law of any practical consequence . . . So, society existed separately and was largely self-regulated; private relations and private 'law' were local matters to be dealt with by customary accumulations of folk-law without the intervention of the new 'national' law or courts. Thus although the . . . regime was thoroughly authoritarian, it was not totalitarian . . .[66]

Since civil suits were handled by local custom and adjudicated by the elders (and like officials) of the village, the street, or in difficult cases, even the town authorities, it is only with public and criminal law that we are concerned here.

There were neither specialized tribunals nor specialized judges. The administrator—the *daikan* or his equivalent in the *han*—dispensed summary justice from which no appeal was allowed. Nobody had a right to access to a court. As a matter of fact nobody had *any* rights at all against a legal superior. The regulations and the activities of government and its officials were not justiciable in any way whatsover. Even the appeal to the sovereign himself—a right and a practice which we have seen in every polity so far and which seems to correspond to some primordial quality perceived as inherent in the very nature of government, that is, its central duty to dispense justice—was totally precluded in this country until Yoshimune in the middle of the eighteenth century.[67] A social inferior was punishable if he brought suit against a superior. For instance, a 1655 edict decreed prison for a servant who brought his master to court. Domestic suits against family superiors were similarly discouraged. The settlement of such disputes was left to the will of the master, father, teacher, or whoever was superior in the given situation.[68] But even worse befell the inferior who actually appealed over the head of his superior: if his petition was found false, he was crucified.[69]

The criminal law was unequal: samurai and commoners were liable for

---

[66] This admirably succinct summary comes from Henderson, 'The Evolution of Tokugawa Law', 214–15.   [67] Cf. Sansom, *History of Japan*, 156.

[68] Henderson, 'The Evolution of Tokugawa Law', 222. But this must be qualified a little; some suits were accepted—if the interests of the shogun were involved or if the master was seriously at fault, and, also, in some suits concerning property succession.   [69] Ibid. 223.

different crimes and received different punishments. The laws of succession were different for these two categories. One Japanese collection of laws (the entire corpus was never codified) states bluntly that: 'All offences are to be punished in accordance with social status', a rule that was observed in practice.[70]

Trials were summary, but the accused could only be convicted on his own confession. As elsewhere (including Europe) where this rule applied, the corollary was to extract the confession by torture. Punishment was very harsh. Furthermore, as in China, it could be and often was collective and vicarious—family, neighbours, and the like all being punished for the crime of one individual. Kaempfer cites a case where the steward in the household of the *daikan* at Nagasaki was found trying to smuggle out some swords and other weapons to Korea, a trade that was strictly forbidden. For this he and his accomplice were crucified, and his son of seven years beheaded in his sight as he hung upon the cross. The *daikan* himself, as vicariously responsible, was stripped of his post and banished with his two sons.[71] Sansom recites a string of barbarous penalties: drawing and quartering (as in contemporary England for crimes of treason), burying the culprit up to the waist and giving leave for anybody to carve him up with a bamboo saw before he was despatched; in cases of arson, burning alive.[72]

Decrees having the force of law were of two kinds—'notices' (*tatsu*) and proclamations (*ofuregaki*).[73] The first were addressed from a higher to a lower shogunal office, not to the public, since they listed the penalties, the discretion, the mitigating circumstances, and so on. They were, therefore, strictly confidential, yet in the eighteenth century were so widely known as to be as available in the bookshops as any novel. But the substance of the law was contained in the proclamations and the authorities went to considerable pains to disseminate these. In the towns they were sent all the way down until they reached the street or township headmen and the leaders of the five-man frankpledge units. In the villages the families of the frankpledge units had to sign a register to attest that they were made aware of laws. In addition the *bakufu* reached the population of town and countryside alike through great placards.[74] But perhaps the most revealing feature of these placards was what Kaempfer reports:

---

[70] Sansom, *Japan*, 465.   [71] Kaempfer, *The History of Japan*, ii. 128–9.

[72] Sansom, *Japan*, 464–5. He also records that often the samurai were permitted to test their swords on the corpses. This reminds one of the Japanese army bayoneting Chinese prisoners to death at Nanking in 1937. But the author does not tell us how often the punishments were imposed—some historians think, infrequently.   [73] Henderson, 'The Evolution of Tokugawa Law', 215.

[74] For the methods of communicating, see ibid., 216, 218. In some cases the law or decree was read aloud, also.

There is no reason given how it came about, that such a Law was made, no mention of the Law-giver's view and intention, nor is there any determined penalty put upon the transgression thereof. Such a conciseness is thought becoming the Majesty of so powerful a Monarch. It is enough that he should know the reason of his commands, whose judgment 'twere treason to call in question'.[75]

On the one side, *sic volo, sic jubeo*; on the other, 'I hear and I obey'.

6.3. Security and Public Order

Some of the matters we have mentioned, like the *bakufu*'s use of *metsuke* (the intelligence service), the *sankin-kotai* residence requirement and the taking of daimyo family hostages, the rotating commissionerships and headships in the administrative departments, have already suggested the paranoid nature of the regime, and this is amply confirmed by a glance at its security arrangements.

In the first place all movement was strictly controlled. The road barriers, inherited from early times were used to check passports. Women who travelled from Edo had to carry special exeats which carried a full description of their appearance (to prevent daimyo women-hostages from escaping). Commoners desirous of travelling from their homes had to get a certificate of good behaviour from their five-man frankpledge group who pledged to go bail for them, and on the strength of this apply for a passport from the town elders.[76] In the villages the headman, as keeper of the census, had to report any changes in the population, and under the early decrees of Hideyoshi and Ieyasu[77] this necessarily included any migration or immigration, so that the villager too had to get a passport.

One might have thought that townsfolk could have evaded such surveillance by simply changing their address, but just the reverse. Kaempfer has left detailed descriptions of the street-life of Nagasaki. Its inhabitants were shut into their streets by a gate at each end every night and often in the daytime too, at times of high security risk such as when a foreign ship had come in or was about to sail out. On these last occasions the headman would conduct random searches to see if anyone had slipped on board the foreign vessel. Any inhabitant who had urgent reason to leave the street at these junctures had to get a wooden tally, on showing which he was escorted by a member of the street-watch to the headman of the next street, and so on from street to street until he reached his destination. Moving house was almost as difficult as it is to migrate and acquire residence in a foreign country today. The householder had to get permission of the *ottona* (the

---

[75] Kaempfer, *The History of Japan*, iii. 326.   [76] Ibid. ii. 118.   [77] See pp. 1099, 1109 above.

headman), the latter sent a description of the man and his character to each inhabitant of the street he wanted to move to, and any single member of that street unit could blackball him. If nobody opposed, however, he got appropriate documents from his *ottona* and was then free to move, though his troubles were not necessarily over. He had to sell his old house and this he could only do with the common consent of all the inhabitants of his former street-unit.[78]

The five-man frankpledge unit (the *gonin gumi*) was, to repeat, designed to make an entire group responsible for the conduct of any one of its members. In the villages its duties were multiplex: it had to certify marriages, successions, wills, contracts, and so on, take joint liability for tax-arrears, and sign a register which contained a long and highly detailed list (to be described below) of duties of omission and commission. This list was read out loud to the entire village population by the headman several times a year. If these *gonin gumi* groups really had carried out all the duties laid on them, they would indeed have taken the polity a long way towards totalitarianism. But how far they did so is highly controversial. Sansom does not think they did;[79] Befu thinks that they were of limited impact, though 'sometimes useful in controlling the peasants';[80] while the Japanese scholar Nomura thought that 'the organization of the five-man group was almost entirely a mere matter of record-keeping and in practice it scarcely had any meaning'.[81]

Commenting on the condition of the inhabitants of Nagasaki, Kaempfer wrote: 'the Inhabitants of Nagasaki are kept to a very great degree of slavery and submission, which indeed is scarce to be paralleled'.[82] We have already sketched out this traveller's account of policing in Nagasaki.[83] We can conclude this survey of Tokugawa security management with a sketch of the way it was done among the million or so people of Edo.

The city was administered by two commissioners (*machi-bugyo*) who alternated in office every month, though in practice the business had become so heavy that a commissioner had to spend his entire 'free' month in his office to catch up on his paperwork. These commissioners were police prefects, chief executives, and judges in both civil and criminal cases. The post went to fairly humble grade samurai—a 500 *koku* man—but it carried the additional stipend of 3,500 *koku* which brought it into the medium *hatamoto* range.

Administering over a million people as they did, these two commissioners shared the services of twenty-five assistant magistrates, the *yoriki*. These were

---

[78] Kaempfer, *The History of Japan*, ii. 116–19.   [79] Sansom, *History of Japan*, 103.
[80] H. Befu, 'Village Autonomy and Articulation with the State', in Hall and Jansen, *Studies in the Institutional History*, 305. After c.1800 there is no doubt, however, that Sansom and Nomura were correct.
[81] Ibid. 305.   [82] Kaempfer, *The History of Japan*, ii. 114.   [83] See p. 1108 above.

samurai of the 200 *koku* grade, and by the end of the seventeenth century their offices had become hereditary. They all lived in the same quarter of the city.

Since each *yoriki* was responsible for some 40,000 inhabitants, it is unsurprising that each one commanded 120 *doshin* ('companions'). The *doshin* too inherited their posts. They were samurai, but of the lowest grade, entitled to wear only one sword. Just as the Nagasaki policemen went around carrying halters, so these *doshin* went around with a steel crook, to catch the clothes of offenders. Each had two or three assistants of his own—townsfolk, who were often informers. These *doshin* did most of the police work of the city; only rarely was a case so dangerous that the armour-clad, mounted *yoriki* had to make an arrest.

6.4. *Taxation*

In every polity discussed so far—the city-states seemingly the conspicuous exceptions—our account of fiscal matters and taxation has been one of mismanagement, corruption, and illegalities on the part of the administrators, and extortion and even torture were the lot of the subjects. That is not the case in seventeenth-century Tokugawa Japan.

The neo-Confucianism of the early shoguns caused them to reject taxes on anything but land, though by the end of the period a significant proportion of revenue was, by various devices, being derived from the towns and commerce. Hence this account is confined to the administration of the land tax on the shogunal estates (one quarter of the land surface and one-third of the population of the country).

Here the superior officers were the *bugyo* and the *daikans* (see above pp. 1102–4), and it is noteworthy that as in France, where the *intendant* was an *intendant de justice* and *de finance*, so were these officials. What is more, as one of the spin-offs from their fiscal duties they filed back reports on local conditions to the *bakufu*. In the early days these officials were arbitrary and abused their powers: some of them were the local big men who had been running the neighbourhood before Ieyasu, and they did not see why they, themselves, should pay any taxes. Nor were the procedures fixed and laid down. But these conditions had all but passed away by the end of the seventeenth century, and their numbers, at one time 127, were reduced till there were in the period of Tsunayoshi no more than some forty *daikans*. Furthermore, the inheritance of the *daikan* office was ended by the shogun Tsunayoshi in 1681, in a wave of dismissals, while in 1725 Yoshimune abolished the practice whereby the *daikan* deducted his local expenses and sent the *bakufu* only the net balance (a very common practice in all fiscal systems and one that prevailed, under the name of 'drawbacks', in Britain till the middle of the nineteenth century).[84]

A *daikan* was a pretty big fish. After all, there were some 10 million inhabitants in the domain, and only forty to fifty *bugyo* and *daikan*s to administer them all. Their staffs, large by the then-standards of administration, consisted of their own personal retainers, and below these, samurai guards and menial assistants (the *shugen*). These staffs acted as assistants and clerks who kept the records and accounts and inspected the villages. The total complement varied according to the size of the *daikan's* circuit. Permissable floor-space was strictly regulated. In one typical case the *daikan* had, apart from his own vassals, only twenty-nine staff to administer a fief whose daimyo had some 1,000 vassals, and which produced 50,000 *koku* of rice. And the total office space allowed for this was a mere 20 yards by 20 yards![85] One begins to sense that this Japanese field administration was not unlike that of eighteenth-century Prussia, where salaries were so stingy that they gave rise to our still-current phrase— 'travailler pour le Roi de Prusse'.

The *daikan* headquarters kept detailed records of the putative yields of each village, and on this basis it assessed the corvée (for castle-repair, road and irrigation works, and transportation[86]), and the land-tax bills. The headman allocated the global sum among the villagers and was responsible for having it delivered. Apart from this, the *daikan* had nothing more to do with the village as long as it did not disturb the peace. The village headman delivered the tax rice—or currency—to officials who checked the amount and gave him a receipt. Before it went off again to the *daikan* warehouses it was checked a second time. The records of these transactions then went to the Edo Office of Finance for final verification. This Office had a very large staff. In 1635 there were twelve finance officers, but in 1733 there were no less than 186, with a large number of menial assistants making a total of some 2,000.[87]

6.5. *Moulding Society*

We have already recounted how Hideyoshi and Ieyasu determined to enforce the *shi-no-ko-sho* four-estate system and fix it for all time. Their successors maintained it in its entirety. Social differentiation did take place, but inside each estate, not between them.

[84] Totman, *Politics in the Tokugawa Bakufu*, 64–9.   [85] Ibid. 74.
[86] T. C. Smith, 'The Land Tax in the Tokugawa Period', in Hall and Jansen, *Studies in the Institutional History*, 289.   [87] Totman, *Politics in the Tokugawa Bakufu*, 76 ff.

The Tokugawa also had views as to how to fill this rigid fourfold mould. In many of the societies we have encountered religion might be relied on to reinforce social order. The Tokugawa certainly endowed shrines and temples and established a ministry for their upkeep, but religion had lost its savour in their society: Shinto, with the pilgrimage to its great shrine at Ise, had always been a this-worldly religion, and the fire seemed to have gone out of Buddhism, for all the support the state gave to its temples and its *sangha*.

Where the religions did not inculcate moral codes the *bakufu* stepped in. The neo-Confucian tradition was entrenched by the fact that the samurai's literary education was based on reading the Confucian Classics in the original Chinese. In addition the *bakufu* issued strings of decrees and regulations designed to make people conform to Confucian-type morals and behaviour. Where they could not prohibit, they regulated: thus they institutionalized prostitution by confining it to certain areas of the cities, like Yoshiwara in Edo. They realized they could not suppress the new and exciting kabuki theatre, but they could and did put a stop to the employment of women actors, and later, even of young men to substitute for these in the female roles. Nor did the *bakufu* try to suppress the circulation of novels, even of the 'penny dreadful' or the erotic kinds, and it allowed the free circulation of philosophical ideas. But—and this was a very big but— these ideas, we must realize, were the ones available only within the isolated world of Japan. Not until the mid-eighteenth century did a reforming shogun, Yoshimune, make the first break in the seclusion policy by relaxing the ban on certain books from China. (European books had never been banned, as it was thought that few if any people could read them.)[88]

The chief focus of their preoccupations was the peasantry. Earlier we mentioned how various admonitions were put on placards or read aloud in villages. Sansom quotes a relatively short one of only fifteen articles. Dated 1658 it tells the villagers how they must treat visiting officials, clear roads, treat dogs and cats; that they must clear ditches, leave no lands uncultivated, repair all roads and bridges; that there must be no gambling or bribery— and so forth.[89]

The *bakufu* issued detailed sumptuary laws for the townsfolk and samurai. Yoshimune forbade ladies to have expensive hairdos and wear costly fabrics; nobody, not even the daimyo, was to buy expensive lacquer-ware; no more than ten palanquins might be used in a wedding procession. These economy orders were repeated again and again, but to no avail.[90] Towards the close of

[88] Sansom, *History of Japan*, iii. 168–70. For so-called 'Dutch Studies', see J.-P. Lehmann, *The Roots of Modern Japan* (Macmillan, London, 1982), 22–3, 124–5, 128.
[89] Sansom, *History of Japan*, iii. 102–3.   [90] Ibid. 160–1.

the eighteenth century ever-new regulations prohibited the use of barbers and hairdressers, prostitutes were bundled away to Yoshiwara, men and women were segregated in the public baths, and betting and gambling were forbidden. Enforcement relied on an extensive network of spies and common informers.[91]

But the *bakufu*—and for that matter the individual daimyo—did have one great success in the field of morals and good, Confucian-type behaviour, that is, schools. Samurai had their own schools whose curriculum ran to the Chinese Confucian Classics in Chinese, and the martial arts as well. Whereas in Ieyasu's day the samurai were near-illiterates, by the eighteenth century almost all were literate and some were even accomplished verse-writers. The greatest educational success, however, was among the commoners. In the end nearly every moderate-sized village had its school with a professional teacher who taught, for the most part, the three Rs. By the end of the Edo period, 40 per cent of boys and 10 per cent of girls were attending formal schooling, and the literacy rate may have been in the order of 50 per cent.[92] This compares favourably with Europe at that time, and far more so with dozens and dozens of Third World countries today![93]

But the importance of the extensive school network, especially in the rural areas, went far beyond the inculcation of skills. The school is one of the great instruments of socializiation, that is, the process of inculcating a generation with the values of its society. The Tokugawa's prodigious success in this matter will be taken up in the ensuing section.

7. APPRAISAL

That Tokugawa Japan was despotic, harsh, unequal, and bureaucratic hardly needs saying. As one authority writes, it was a 'highly effective police state'; and he quotes the slogan of the time: *kanson minpi*, that is, 'revere officials, despise the people'.[94]

The most intriguing feature of its polity seems to me to be the sequence of mismatches between immediate intentions and their longer-term outcomes.

To begin with, there were certain cases where the *bakufu* failed in its stated intention, *and yet* the unintended outcome proved benign. The most conspicuous instance was the fiscal administration's under-assessment of agri-

[91] Sansom, 206.

[92] Cf. R. Dore, *Education in Tokugawa Japan* (Routledge & Kegan Paul, London, 1965); J.-P. Lehmann, *The Roots of Modern Japan* (Macmillan, London, 1982), 115–21.

[93] Cf. C. Cipolla, *Literacy and Development in the West* (Penguin, Harmondsworth, 1969), chs. 2 and 3.

[94] Lehmann, *Roots of Modern Japan*, 58.

cultural yields. This very elaborate branch of the bureaucracy was supposed, it will be remembered, to make a cadastral survey of fields, allowing for acreage, quality, and nature of crop, as is usual in such surveys. It may be remembered, too, that the Ming dynasty started off with a new nation-wide cadaster of this kind, just as the Tokugawa inherited the detailed country-wide cadaster of Hideyoshi. In both countries—in fact in pretty well all countries attempting this technique (including England)—the outcomes were the same. It was too complicated and time-consuming for pre-modern administrators to make the frequent readjustments required, so that either they used out-of-date registers or they settled for some conventionally fixed sum (like the English Tenths and Fifteenths). The Tokugawa Finance Department used registers that were sometimes a century out of date.[95] But agricultural productivity improved throughout the seventeenth century. In consequence, instead of the peasant paying 50 per cent of his produce in tax he came to pay only 40 per cent, or even less in some cases, so that peasant incomes rose even into the nineteenth century. However, peasants were now producing for a market in certain areas. This made them particularly vulnerable to ruination. This accounts for the increase of peasant revolts in such areas.[96] Thus, in the century under review there was only one peasant uprising per annum, but from 1760 onwards there were six times as many.[97]

To critics who stigmatize the illiberal authoritarianism of the regime, its failure to control the dress, pleasures, and morals of its subjects will also seem a benign outcome. That failure in intention reinforces the earlier comment, that although the polity was utterly authoritarian, it was not totalitarian. Providing the villages paid up and kept the peace, what they did was their affair, and similarly in respect to quarrels and minor crimes in city street-units.[98] The polity's basic concern was self-preservation; it struck deep but not wide. Vast tracts of social life were self-regulating. The folk-ways and the mores had taken over.[99]

But though some failures of intent had benign outcomes, in some cases the long-term outcomes were disastrous, and nowhere more so than in the military sphere. None of the *bakufu*'s efforts to maintain samurai training and battle-readiness, not even Yoshimune's, were effectual. To this one must superadd its contempt for firearms and the semi-religious mystique of the

[95] Smith, 'The Land Tax', 283–99.

[96] Ibid., and T. C. Smith, *The Agrarian Origins of Modern Japan* (Harvard UP, Cambridge, Mass., 1959), 159 ff.

[97] Lehmann, *Roots of Modern Japan*, 63. Also, most of the riots were directed at merchants and usurers, not at landlords.   [98] Kaempfer, *The History of Japan*, ii. 110.

[99] Cf. W. G. Sumner's *'Folkways'* (Mentor edn; New York, 1960), esp. 76–8.

sword. The consequence was that the country lay wide open to the incursion of the West in 1853.

On the other hand, in two highly important areas where the long-term result was just what had been intended, the result was highly felicitous. The first of these was to get a civil service that was both efficient and cheap. The labyrinthine, ex-military civil service was both exceedingly bureaucratic (the Japanese term is *kanryo-shugi*, 'bureaucratism') and arrogant. But up to at least the mid-eighteenth century its standards were relatively high. It is true that gift-giving to superiors was rampant, but although we should call this 'corruption' nowadays, it was an accepted feature of the system in those days, and in any case was usually limited by custom.[100] For the rest the bureaucracy, despite its military origin, and despite, too, its foot-dragging collegiality, obstructive job-demarcation, largely hereditary appointments, and absence of formal proficiency tests, was both competent and economical. 'Most administrators were absolutely loyal to their superiors, scrupulously honest, meticulous in the performance of their duties and efficient, at least by pre-modern standards.' The *daikans* maintained order and levied the taxes on the shogunal domain, 'with a thoroughness and at a cost that would have been the envy of any regime in the world in the eighteenth century'.[101] Unlike Ch'ing China, where mandarins' stipends were pegged so low that corruption was the only way they could maintain their position, let alone make a worthwhile livelihood out of it, in Japan the stipends were high enough to disincline the *daikans* from the extortion and illegalities we have noted in almost every other polity to date. The cost/tax-yield ratio was very low even by today's exacting standards: it cost 1,000 *koku* to raise 17,500 *koku* of tax—a ratio of only 5.7 per cent. Compare this austere ratio with the wholesale plundering built into the fiscal system of the Caliphate![102]

The second area where the *bakufu*'s intentions were successfully implemented was the one we briefly touched on at the end of the last section—the moulding of popular attitudes and perceptions in respect of rank and authority. The school system disseminated to the masses the twin sets of upper-class values: the Four Estate hierarchy, and the rulership of the warriors. The former was transmitted through the (somewhat vulgarized and etiolated) medium of neo-Confucianism: for instance, in Ishida Baigan's *shingaku*, which cult ran eighty-one schools with government encouragement,

---

[100] E. O. Reischauer, *The Japanese* (Harvard UP, Cambridge, Mass., 1977), 238. In any case, the notion that a civil servant and, for the most part, a politician should not use his office to make money is recent and its practical application, even now, is so limited that it is hard to apply it to quite a number of advanced industrial countries—the USA, Japan, Russia, and a dozen others spring to mind. And the notion does not apply at all to the majority of Third World countries.

[101] Ibid. 238.   [102] Above, Bk. III, Pt. I, Ch. 2.

all over Japan).[103] But the latter was made to complement this by the wide circulation of the chronicles and histories, the 'blood-and-thunder' novels, the kabuki plays (with their subversive content), all celebrating the heroic deeds of the great samurai heroes of the past, particularly those of the Minamoto in their wars against the Taira. This is how it came about that, although Japan was entirely civilized by the end of our period, her people were nevertheless imbued with martial attitudes.[104]

Brought up in such a way, the population came to see the Four Estate hierarchy, the etiquettes and niceties of rank and degree, and the primacy of group over oneself as the natural order, all the more so because 'seclusion' prevented even acquaintanceship with any competing ideas from the outer world. Consequently, for no less than eight entire generations the population had no notions of the individual, social order, and polity but their own. In these circumstances a people comes so to internalize such ideas that they produce automatic responses.[105]

But the final word must go to the unintended and, from the bakufu's point of view completely *counter-productive*, consequences of its conspicuous successes in the political field: 'seclusion', the Four Estate and feudal order, and domestic tranquillity—for disturbances were few, and in the event, neither important nor consequential.[106] Herein lies a paradox: the rulers created a political system, this system guaranteed tranquillity and order, the tranquillity and order promoted economic and social changes—but ones that made the shifting contours of society run, increasingly, counter to the fixed ones of the political system. In the political structure the samurai were the ruling caste, with merchants at the bottom of the pile. In the new socio-economic structure, however, these roles were reversed: merchants were on top, and the samurai in debt to them.

Sealed-off and at peace, Japan was now highly monetized, agricultural

---

[103] Cf. Dore, *Education*, and note his comments on how the teaching called *Jitsugo-kyo* 'reduced to stark simplicity' the generalized exhortations of more sophisticated texts and stressed the same reverence for authority and filiality. 'Your father and your mother are like heaven and earth; your teacher and your lord are like the sun and the moon. All other relationships may be likened to useless stones' (p. 279). Cf. also M. B. Jansen and L. Stone 'Education and Modernization in Japan and England', in C. E. Black (ed.), *Comparative Modernization: A Reader* (Macmillan, London, 1976), 214–37, for the role of education in 'modernization' in Tokugawa Japan and Tudor England.

[104] Kaempfer, *The History of Japan*, iii. 307–12, is most revealing on this. But in this context note particularly his remarks: 'Commemorating, as they do, the great exploits, and noble actions of their illustrious ancestors, they keep up in their minds a certain martial ardour, and earnest desire of glory and reputation. In the very first stage of infancy, when they cry, and are out of humour, warlike songs and ballads are made use of to appease them. The boys at school, who learn to read and write, have scarce any other book, or copy, allowed them but the remaining letters and histories of the illustrious heroes . . . etc. etc.' (pp. 311–12).*   [105] Cf. Sumner's reflections on this, 'Folkways', 76–7.

[106] For a list of the most important, see Reischauer and Fairbank, *East Asia*, 620–1.

acreage and yields had improved, the wealthier farmers were producing for the market, and coast-wise shippers, wholesalers, and retailers had sprung up in the ports to subserve it. The despised merchants were getting rich, the towns were expanding, and so was the artisanate, in textiles, metalwork, and the like. The great period of the Tokugawa, the *Genroku* (1675–1725), is famous for the artistic and literary products of a rich urban and *bourgeois* culture.

But while the merchant class waxed fat, the samurai became poor. The shogun's cunning *sankin-kotai* (alternate attendance policy) impoverished the daimyo finances by making them maintain extravagant palaces and retinues in Edo. These absorbed 80 per cent of a daimyo's cash-outlay.[107] Now although, by the mid-eighteenth century, agricultural production and hence the rice tax on it was rising only very slowly, daimyo conspicuous consumption was racing ahead; for instance, the number of daimyo mansions in Edo rose to some 600.[108] In the other societies we have examined the response would have been to increase taxes. But these had become fixed by custom: daimyo altered them only at their peril.[109] Instead they borrowed from the merchants, and reduced (sometimes even, in times of financial stringency, suspended) the rice-stipends of their *gokenin*, nine-tenths of whom were now stipendiaries and not fief-holders.[110] Furthermore, the stipends being a fixed amount of rice, these retainers suffered from any adverse fluctuation in the currency. So, in all these ways the incomes of the lesser samurai fell. But they too had extravagant habits. A few economized, many went into professions, especially teaching and the civil administration, for many were well-educated.[111] But the great majority sank deeper and deeper into debt to the merchants.

The full force of this development did not occur till the point where our present period closes, *c.*1750. From then on the perils of *bakufu* political success became more and more serious as the social pyramid turned into the converse of the political one. They became visible at last when the American warships dropped anchor in Edo harbour in 1853. So was initiated the quarter-century of self-questioning that was to culminate in one of the world's most remarkable political revolutions from above—the Meiji Restoration of 1868.[112]

---

[107] Lehmann, *Roots of Modern Japan*, 85.   [108] Ibid. 85.

[109] The stability of the level of taxes is demonstrated by Smith, 'The Land Tax', 283–99. Cf. also Smith, *Agrarian Origins*, 159 f. For the fear of peasant risings, Lehmann, *Roots of Modern Japan*, 85.

[110] See p. 1105 above.

[111] Dore, *Education*, 150–2. The abler people in the bureaucracy could and did qualify for 'top-up' stipends.

[112] See below, Bk. V. [This intended section of Bk. V was never completed (eds.).]

Obviously, nobody in the Western world of today would fancy living in Tokugawa Japan, and for that matter nor would any Japanese. But it is really no use bemoaning its despotic, unequal, and harsh character. Tokugawa Japan was a world of its own, on its own, with values of its own; and if these values were completely antithetical even to those of the Europe of that time, let alone today, the important thing to realize is that domestic Japanese critics of the things that we find repugnant did not begin to emerge till after 1750.[113] The regime has to be assessed in its own terms. Kaempfer was perhaps indifferent to its ruthlessness; he thought, for instance, that though its justice was rough and ready and might go wrong, it was preferable to the protracted legal convolutions of Europe.[114] For all that, he was a cultivated and well-educated European and, taking the Japanese as he found them, he pronounced this verdict:

Happy and flourishing . . . United and peaceable, taught to give due worship to the Gods, due obedience to the Laws, due submission to their superiors, due love and regard to their neighbours, civil, obliging, virtuous, in art and industry exceeding all other nations . . . abundantly provided with all the necessities of life, and withal enjoying the fruits of peace and tranquillity.[115]

[113] James Clavell's historical novel *Shogun*, which fictionalizes the career of Will Adams with Tokugawa Ieyasu, is at its best, precisely, when the author is conveying the Elizabethan English sailor's stupefying culture-shock. [114] Kaempfer, *The History of Japan*, iii. 319.

[115] Ibid. 336.

2

China: The Golden Century of the Ch'ing,
1680–1780

1. THE MANCHU TAKE-OVER: CONTINUITIES AND QUIRKS

*B*ook Three, Chapter Four of this *History* left China convulsed, the
central government paralysed by the life- and-death struggle between
Mandarinate and eunuchs, and the capital itself under threat from popular
rebellion from the south and from the formidable Jürchen (later 'Manchu')
proto-state which was poised to pierce the Wall at a point only 200 miles to
its north-east. It is not proposed in this chapter to dwell on the subsequent
Manchu, or as it called itself, *Ch'ing* ('pure') regime in the same detail as that
devoted to earlier phases of Chinese government. What is presented here is,
rather, an updating; and this for the simplest of reasons: the early Ch'ing
polity is, basically, the Ming updated and—above all—made to work.

The Manchu (a name of obscure etymology which the Jürchen Prince
Abahai adopted for his people in 1636) were substantially Sinicized and had
already seized imperial territories in the Liaio-tung area when, in 1644, their
armies were invited inside the Wall by its Chinese commander so that they
could jointly march on Peking and save it for the emperor from the rebel
forces. In this they were successful, but with the emperor dead by suicide,
the Manchu regent, Dorgan, seized the throne in the name of the infant
prince, Shih Tsu, known by his era name, the Shun-chih Emperor (1644–61).
Ming pretenders put up the most stubborn resistance in the Yangtse area
and in the south—much the most populous and wealthy part of China and
the one whose literati had long predominated among the Ming élite. The
destruction of the imperial pretenders was largely effected by the forces of
three turncoat Chinese generals in return for the effective rulership over
three huge apanages, but to resist being curtailed they renewed the war on
the Manchus for ten more years (1671–81) before they, too, succumbed.
When the Manchu stormed the island of Taiwan in 1683 the wars were over
for good and the Manchu domination total. At the cost of what some put at
80 *million* deaths, China, under semi-tribal aliens whose ethnic origin and
native language were quite different from the Han Chinese, who initially
pursued a policy of extreme brutality, tyranny, and expropriation, entered an

era which by its own historical standards, or those relative to any con-
tempory states, or in absolute terms, was its Golden Age.

China was internally at peace; politically stable; its peasants' living
standard not inferior to that in Europe; and its economic growth 'sufficient
to support a population, a society, a state and a higher culture that were at
least the equals in size, complexity, sophistication and quality of those of
any European nation prior to the eighteenth century'.[1] Indeed, one authority—himself a Frenchman—claims that 'the Chinese peasant of the Yung-
cheng era and the first half of the Ch'ien-lung era was in general, much
better and much happier than his equivalent in the France of Louis XV. He
was usually better educated.'[2] And with all this China was far and away the
most enormously large and populous state in the entire world—5,247,000
square miles of which 'China Proper' took up only 1,370,000 square miles,
with a population, by 1800, of some 300 million.[3] Peripheral states acknowl-
edged its suzerainty and paid tribute; from Korea in the north to Annam,
Burma, and Siam in the south-east, and Nepal and Bhutan in the south-
west, and far into Central Asia up to the fabled oases of Bukhara and
Khokand.

1.1. *The Rise of the Ch'ing*

CHRONOLOGY

Rise of the Jürchen (Manchu) state (1583–1644)

1583	Nurhaci becomes Chieftain of the Jürchen: a 'marcher lord' subject to the Ming
1601	Organizes his tribes into Four 'Banners'
1607–13	Conquers the other Jürchen tribes
1616	Proclaims his state as the *Chin* and himself as its 'Heaven-designated Emperor'
1618	Attacks and defeats the Chinese
1625	After capture of Mukden (1621), makes this his capital
1626	Nurhaci dies: his eighth son, Abahai, accedes. Defeats Korea and raids Peking
1631	Establishes a civil administration patterned on the Ming (e.g. the 'Six Boards')

---

[1] A. Feuerwerker, *State and Society in Eighteenth-Century China: The Ch'ing Empire in its Glory,* Michigan Papers in Chinese Studies, 29 (Ann Arbor, Mich., 1976), 80.

[2] Gernet, *History of Chinese Civilization,* 481. And see below, sec. 3.1.1.

[3] Feuerwerker, *State and Society in Eighteenth-Century China,* 95. Its area today is 3,691,500 sq. miles, much the same as the USA (3,615,122 sq. miles). Its 300 million population in 1800 compares with Russia—36 million—and France, Japan, and the UK, all 28–30 millions.

1635	Entitles the state and people 'Manchu'
1640	Seizes Chinchow, then conquers Mongols north to the Amur
1640	Death of Abahai. Accession of 6-year-old Fu-lin with uncle, Dorgan, as regent
1644	Chinese rebel Li Tzu-ch'eng advances on Peking. General Wu San-kuei invites Dorgan through Wall for joint advance to defeat Li. Li flees, Dorgan enters Peking, proclaims Fu-lin emperor, his reign-name the *Shun-chih Emperor*

The Conquest of China (1644–1683)

1645	In south, Ming resistance under rival princes
1646	Koxinga, supporter of Prince Kuei, seizes Amoy and Quemoy as bases, sets up civil administration
1646–59	Manchu victories
1659	Koxinga's fleet defeated: retires to Taiwan
1662	Death of Koxinga
1674	Revolt of the 'Three Feudatories' (i.e. turncoat Ming generals in charge of the south). War continues until
1681	Final defeat of all anti-Manchu forces in southern mainland
1683	Conquest of Taiwan

The Ch'ing Emperors (1644–1796)

These are best known by their era names:

1644–61	the Shun-chih Emperor
1661–1722	the K'ang-hsi Emperor
1722–35	the Yung-cheng Emperor
1735–96	the Ch'ien-lung Emperor—abdicates 1796

1.2. Continuities, Quirks, and Changes

The Manchu came in as the new ruling class. They simply took over the Ming apparatus of government in its entirety. The changes their conquest made reduce themselves, effectively, to two. First, the Manchu tribesmen enjoyed a highly privileged political and social position. Secondly, and far more important, up to the abdication of Ch'ien-lung at least, the Manchu emperors energized the governmental system and made it work as it had never worked before. For the rest, eighteenth century Ch'ing China represents the veritable culmination of all that had ever gone into the Chinese political tradition, and the synthesis, as ultimate as humankind could be expected to make it, of the Confucian society, beliefs, and political institutions.

So there will be no need to re-describe the administrative system, the division of its duties, and its system of recruitment; nor the legal and judicial system; nor the *pao-chia* and the *li-chia* at village level. Our concern will be, rather, with the refinements and modifications to the apparatus, for example, the revised law code or the revision of the tax arrangements, but chiefly with the few but critically important changes that the Manchus did indeed effect or preside over. These were, notably, the active role of the emperor *vice* Confucianist passivity, the substitution of the Grand Council for the Secretariat as the dynamo of government, the new bannerman military system, and the ever-growing political influence of the local élites, the so-called 'gentry'.

One set of changes, however, is best described as a quirk. This is what has been styled the Manchu–Chinese 'dyarchy'. In view of the concord between Manchu and Chinese that marked the eighteenth century, it is as well to remember that the initial conquest was carried out with the most extreme brutality. The Manchu intended, originally, to live as lords over an enserfed Han population, not unlike the Arabs in their first century of empire. In this, it is fair to say, they were assisted by their Chinese quislings—Chinese captives or their descendants whom they had captured and enslaved as their 'bondsmen' in their campaigns of 1618–44 and then incorporated into eight Chinese Banners to fight alongside the eight Manchu ones—as well as by defecting Chinese generals like Wu San-kuei. The Manchu rulers forbade their bannermen to marry the Chinese,[4] segregated them into enclaves in the cities, and excluded the Chinese from Manchuria itself so as to retain their pristine tribal identity. They made the Chinese adopt the Manchu robe, to shave their heads, and to wear pig-tails; they massacred those who resisted. They expropriated the peasantry to create great Manchu enclaves worked by Chinese prisoners-of-war and expropriated peasants as so many slaves to be bought and sold like cattle, brutalized, and tied to the soil.[5] Only when they ultimately came to see that this terrorization made the peasants flee and the landlords fight did the Manchu gradually give up such enclave-estates and allow the peasants repossession. From 1685 further confiscations were prohibited and by 1700 the enclaves and the peasant-slaves that worked them had, to all intents and purposes, faded away.

But the Manchu still clung to their exclusivity, prohibiting intermarriage and forbidding the Manchu bannermen to take up any other pursuits; so that they became a hereditary warrior caste, pensioned and stipended by the state. The emperors took none but Manchu as their wives and concubines. More importantly, although they were a trivial minority in China, they

---

[4] They were, however, allowed to marry into the families of Chinese bannermen.

[5] Gernet, *History of Chinese Civilization*, 466.

never took less than one-half of key posts for themselves. For instance, between 1736 and 1793 they constituted 48 per cent of the provincial governors-general or governors, and shared an equal number of posts with the ethnic Chinese in the key institutions such as the Secretariat and Grand Council. All official documents had to appear in Manchu as well as Chinese.

Furthermore, in certain matters there was not even parity but exclusive Manchu control. Thus the 'Colonial Office' (the *Li-fan Yüan*) was staffed exclusively by Manchus. Again, the Manchus kept control of the military command, for although there were Chinese and Mongolian bannermen, the Banner Army was predominantly Manchu, commanded by Manchu generals (the *Chiang-chün*, or 'Tartar generals') with Manchu brigadiers under them.[6] The remnants of the Ming army and additional forces, which were formed into an auxiliary 'Army of the Green Standard', was a gendarmerie, not a fighting force. Here the commands were shared equally between Chinese and Manchu.

2. THE REGENERATION OF THE CENTRAL GOVERNMENT

2.1. *The Central Characteristic of the Regime*

The great innovation of the early Ch'ing monarchs was to regenerate the government of the empire, and they did this by bringing to bear a new, positive political will and a set of appropriate means. They tried and they succeeded in making a nominally emperor-ruled state one where the emperor really did rule personally; that is, they rejected the passive role which the later Ming emperors had been made to accept by the Confucian establishment and Mandarinate,[7] in favour of active and energetic leadership. As we have seen, the constitutional history of China (if this is what it can be called) from Han times to the fall of the Ming had witnessed a swaying battle between wilful emperors on the one side and their court and administrative officials on the other, and that this had frequently taken the shape of a contest between the emperor and the eunuchs of his Inner Court, and the officials, backed up by the literati generally, of the Outer Court: and that furthermore, this contest had been such that it produced paroxysms in the central government of such violence that they precipitated the fall of no less than three great dynasties: the later Han, the later T'ang, and the Ming

---

[6] In 1735 there were (nominally, at any rate) 678 Manchu companies to 207 Mongol and 270 Chinese ones. E.O. Reischauer and J.K. Fairbank, *East Asia: The Great Tradition*, vol. 1 (Modern Asia edn.; Houghton Mifflin, Boston, 1960), 364–5.

[7] See above, Bk. III, Ch. 4, 'Government under the Ming'.

had all collapsed in this way. This did not happen under the early Ch'ing emperors, so the grand question is 'how was it done?'

2.2. *The Active Emperor*

The K'ang-hsi, Yung-cheng, and Ch'ien-lung emperors who ruled the empire for a span of 135 years were richly educated in the Confucian Classics and Chinese literature, and trained for the imperial tasks. They threw themselves into these with an almost obsessive attention, seldom if ever evinced by any earlier rulers. Unlike their Ming predecessors, who were unable or unwilling to leave the palace precincts, these Ch'ing emperors made wide progresses throughout their empire. K'ang-hsi, for instance, made no less than six great visits to the lower Yangtse, and it was common for them to spend the hot summer months in their native Jehol; so they could at least see for themselves how their subjects lived.[8] It will be recalled how the Confucianist literati finally stopped emperors from going on campaign. Compare this with the brave K'ang-hsi Emperor leading his troops in 1696 on an exhausting and perilous march into the heart of the Gobi Desert to crush the Dzungars at Ulan-Bator.

These emperors were, in truth, workaholics. Their attention to administration was unremitting. K'ang-hsi demoted a prefect who had boasted of being able to handle 700–800 items of business in one day because, he explained: 'I've been ruling for forty years, and only during the *Wu San-kuei* [i. e. the Three Feudatories] rebellion did I handle five hundred items of business in one day. Nor did I myself hold the brush and write the documents, and even so I could not get to bed before midnight. You may fool other people but you can't fool me.' He went on: 'In other military campaigns there were sometimes up to four hundred memorials but usually there are about fifty a day and it's not too hard to read them, and even to correct the mistakes in them.'[9] These emperors would commonly start reading the memorials at five o'clock every morning. One official of the Ch'ien-lung Emperor marvelled:

Ten or more of my comrades [in the Council] would take turns every five or six days on early morning duty and even so would feel fatigued. How did the Emperor do it day after day? Yet this was in ordinary times when there was no (important) business. When there was fighting on the western border and military reports arrived even at midnight he must still see them in person and would be inclined to summon the Grand Councillors and give instructions as to the proper strategy,

---

[8] J. D. Spence, *Emperor of China: Self-Portrait of K'ang-shi* (Jonathan Cape, London, 1974), 54–6.
[9] Ibid. 46.

using a hundred to a thousand words. I would draw up the draft at the time; from the first rough draft to the presentation of the formal version it might take one to two hours, and the Emperor having thrown on some clothes, would still be waiting.[10]

Lord McCartney, the British Envoy to the Ch'ien-lung Emperor in 1793, reports that the monarch rose at 3 a.m. to go to the Buddhist temple, then read memorials until breakfast at 7 a.m. After a short break for relaxation he summoned the councillors and others and after running over business with them, went on to give the regular audience, before stopping work at 3 p.m. He went to bed at seven in the evening.[11]

How did the emperors manage to exercise such mastery without reliance on their eunuchs or thraldom to the Mandarinate, or—worst of both worlds—without provoking a disastrous struggle between the two? In two chief ways: by a set of new institutional devices, and by the seduction of the Confucianist establishment. To these we might perhaps add a third—secure frontiers.

2.3. Novel Institutions for Personal Rule

2.3.1. EUNUCHS OUT, BONDSMEN IN

On the suicide of the Ming emperor in 1644, the imperial eunuchs put themselves at the disposal of Dorgan, the Manchu regent and real ruler of the country, but the mandarin officials contested this until, in 1661, they persuaded the four regents who were governing *vice* the infant K'ang-hsi Emperor to dismantle the thirteen eunuch-staffed household offices, and to degrade eunuch status. Thenceforward they were the poorly paid and strictly controlled subordinates of a different class of imperial household servants. These were the *pao-i*—bondsmen—and from this time onward they alone managed the emperor's domestic affairs, in the *nei-wu-fu*, the 'Imperial Household Department'.

Three clear points of difference stand out from the Ming Inner Court: first, the status of the *pao-i*; next, the *non-political* yet, thirdly, the enormously influential financial and administrative role of what was in effect an emperor's own private and secret bureaucracy.

The *pao-i* can be described as bondsmen or, equally, as household slaves. Many if not most of these were Chinese prisoners-of-war from the 1610–20

---

[10] J. K. Fairbank and S.-Y. Têng, *Ch'ing Administration: Three Studies*, Harvard Yenching Institute Studies, 19 (Cambridge, Mass., 1960), 61, n. 51.

[11] Cited, P. C. Hsieh, *The Government of China*, 1644–1911 (Johns Hopkins Press, Baltimore, 1925; repr. Frank Cass &; Co., 1966), 32.

campaigns or their descendants. Thus they were just as dependent on the emperor's personal whim as the eunuchs had ever been and could easily be used as their functional equivalent. They were drawn from the three 'upper' or Imperial Banners, those the emperor commanded personally.

To serve in the *nei-wu-fu* was the ambition of every *pao-i*, just as it had been for eunuchs. To be an imperial *pao-i* was to start what could be a most remunerative career. Organized under the Manchu 'banner' system, these hereditary bond-slaves attended special schools, and if successful, became junior clerks in the household. Thence they were promoted by seniority. But it was very difficult to get into the upper half of the league table and especially into the top posts, where an emperor was always liable to place his own personal favourites.[12]

The *nei-wu-fu* was an elaborate and extensive bureaucracy. It had fifty-six bureaux, many of which were divided into sub-bureaux. In 1662 its personnel numbered 402, but they were 939 in 1722 and no less than 1,623 in 1796.[13] The largest department in that year was the Privy Purse (personnel 183). The *nei-wu-fu's* functions were to feed, clothe, and house the emperor, provide him with the wherewithal of entertainment such as the harem of 'Palace Maids' (a pretty modest establishment under the Ch'ing), libraries, theatrical performances and so forth, and above all, to administer his finances. This activity, handled by the Privy Purse office, branched out far beyond the palace precincts. Necessarily so. For one thing it had to administer the imperial estates throughout the empire, but for another, the Ch'ing emperors were heavily involved in commercial enterprise. They held the monopoly of the very lucrative ginseng trade. They were a major participant in the copper trade. Special, 'excess' customs were raised on their behalf in the ports, especially Canton, the centre of the foreign trade. More traditionally, the emperor had his own armouries and his own manufactories for silk and other textiles in Soochow and Hangchow and he received some fraction—we do not know how large—of the revenue from the salt monopoly.[14] The first importance of all this is that it gave the emperor quite enormous revenues independently of the fiscal system controlled by the mandarin bureaucrats, that is, the Outer Court, and secondly, it both prompted and enabled him to place trusted *pao-i* in key posts in the various government commissions (like the Salt Commission) or departments (like the Customs) that comprised the extensive *public* economic agencies. In short, the emperor controlled a network of personal retainers

---

[12] P. M. Torbert, *The Ch'ing Imperial Household Department: A Study of its Organisation and Principal Functions* (Harvard UP, Cambridge, Mass., 1977), 60–78.   [13] Ibid. 28–2.

[14] Ibid., ch. 4, *passim.*

in key economic positions throughout the empire who provided him not only with money but information, and not just information but critical appraisals of the work of the regular bureacrats.

But this *nei-wu-fu* was quite unlike the Ming eunuch establishment in that, though assuming that group's economic role, it never ever played any part in the policy-making process, nor ever enjoyed any military power at all. It was a parallel bureaucracy to the official one, not a substitute. So the grand question—how did the emperors manage to dominate the bureaucracy where their predecessors had failed?—still remains to be answered.

The first part of the answer is, in brief, that they did so by bypassing it (the bureaucracy). This involved two novel institutions which related, respectively, to information and to action.

2.3.2. THE PALACE MEMORIAL NETWORK

The Ch'ing started off by abolishing the eunuch *wen-shu-fang* as the central organ for receiving and processing information and suggesting action to the emperor, and returned these functions to the Grand Secretariat.[15] Under this arrangement, memorials from the provinces flowed into the Transmission Office which had considerable powers to refer them back to sender; and those from the metropolitan boards and commissions into the Grand Secretariat's sub-bureaux which drafted alternative forms of rescripts and endorsements and sent these to any one of the grand secretaries themselves, for any alterations and thence for onward presentation to the emperor. The point here is that, in either case, officialdom got the information and tinkered with it before the emperor knew anything about it. The struggle between the mandarin establishment and the court eunuchs under the last Ming emperors had been the struggle betweeen the Grand Secretariat and the Transmission Office on the one hand and the eunuch *wen-shu-fang*, for the right to do just this.

In 1970 Professor Silas Wu published a book called *Communication and Imperial Control in China—The Evolution of the Palace Memorial System, 1693–1735,* in which he disclosed for the first time the existence of an entirely separate circuit of information-inflow and decision-making by the emperors personally. This he called the Palace Memorial system and it was developed under the K'ang-hsi and the Yung-cheng emperors. Like many an important insitution, it had curiously trivial origins.

They start with the K'ang-hsi Emperor. This ruler had great troubles over his heir-apparent who seems to have been deranged and had to be deposed, so that the emperor was consequently beset by intrigues from the

---

[15] See Bk. III, Ch. 4, 'Government under the Ming'.

prince and his party. Quite unrelatedly, this emperor was extremely appre-hensive about *weather reports*. As we have noticed before, weather was regarded by all good Confucians as a heaven-sent portent. The K'ang-hsi Emperor nourished the illusion that he could interpret such reports scientifically. Unfortunately, the reports he received were worse than valueless, since provincial officials failed to report bad weather conditions because such were deemed a reflection of Heaven—a judgement—on their handling of affairs. Hence the emperor started asking selected officials—frequently members of his *nei-wu-fu* on secondment to provincial posts—to report back to him in absolute secrecy (no file copies kept), and he returned the report, again in absolute secrecy, to the sender, along with his comments. These letters came to him in a box to which only the sender and the emperor held the keys.

In 1700 the K'ang-hsi Emperor extended this system to the regular field-officials. After deposing the heir-apparent in 1712 he widened the net still further, ordering all court officials of the third grade and above (i.e very senior offfficials indeed) to send him similar letters. They were carried by express messengers and in this emperor's reign they came in at the rate of about ten a day. All the same, at this stage the arrangement amounted to no more than a flow of secret information to the emperor. Its full potential was not realized until 1726, as a by-blow to the Yung-cheng Emperor's war with the Dzungars.

2.3.3. THE SUPPLANTMENT OF THE SECRETARIAT BY THE GRAND COUNCIL

In 1726 the secret messages which the Yung-cheng Emperor was receiving from the front became so numerous that he set up a special Secretariat to handle them. This was not in itself particularly innovatory: the K'ang-hsi Emperor had relied on his Southern Library staff to draft edicts and decrees and the Yung-cheng Emperor had been using what he called an 'Office of Administrative Deliberation' made up of seconded civil servants. In order to handle the military campaign, this emperor was convening a kind of war Cabinet of trusted advisers—the *chün-chi chu*—literally, the 'Military Plans Office'. In 1729 its existence was made official. This body is translated as the 'Grand Council' and the point here is twofold: first that it was a highly confidential 'kitchen Cabinet' but, secondly, that the emperor, through his Palace Memorial network, received non-routine information before this council did. From 1729 it was to this Grand Council that the emperors worked, and the Secretariat was shunted into the sidelines to handle routine formalized business only.

Palace Memorials bypassed the old-established Office of Transmission as well as the Secretariat. Instead, they came to a small Chancery of Memorials (the *tsou-chih ch'u*) which existed simply to pass them on to the emperor and to pass back his replies as directed. This could be in one of four ways. The first was totally private—he wrote his comments on the letter and sent it straight back to the sender. The third was the 'regular' method—he sent that particular memorial on to the Secretariat for routine treatment. The fourth was open publication of his reply. But the second is the method that concerns us here. This was by the 'Court Letter'. The contents of such a memorial were made known to a tiny group only, in effect, the Grand Council and its small staff of senior secretaries. In this way the emperor received his political intelligence independently of the Mandarinate and sent it to a body which bypassed it.

The system worked in the following way. First of all, this Grand Council was informal. The number of councillors was not fixed, and comprised whatever officials the Emperor chose: usually from among the heads and deputy heads of the Six Boards, from the grand secretaries, and sometimes from among the thirty-two senior secretaries of the Council.[16] There were usually six grand councillors but only half were Chinese and the ranking councillor was always a Manchu. The secretaries too were divided equally between the two ethnicities. The councillors held their posts concurrently with their civil service ones, so that there was in effect an overlap between the Grand Secretariat, the Six Boards, and the Grand Council itself.

Next, it was secret, like the British Cabinet. There were no clerical assistants, simply the thirty-two senior secretaries who themselves drew up the edicts and decrees. In fact, not a great many documents came before it—perhaps some fifty to sixty per day.[17] But they were the important ones. The Chancery of Memorials sent the boxes it had received to the emperor, who opened them, each with its own particular key, and read them between 5 and 7 a.m. He then selected those he wished to discuss further and had them sent to the Grand Council. This had begun its work at 3 a.m., so as to be ready for audience with the emperor after he had breakfasted at around 7 a.m. On the completion of business with him the councillors retired to draft 'audience memorials' and at a subsequent session presented these to the Emperor. If approved they went back to the Council who had copies made, and sent these out for promulgation as decrees and edicts. All this was transacted very rapidly, thus:

---

[16] Fairbank and Teng, *Ch'ing Administration*, 57–8.   [17] Ibid. 58.

Day 1: *Dawn*—memorials from the capital handed in at the palace gate, those from the provinces arrive at all hours. Matters go as explained—the emperor reads these and then sees his councillors.

Day 2: *Morning*—to the Council. The matter is resolved and action is taken as above. But where further discussion is required it goes:

Day 3: *Morning*—to the Council. A final decision. Thence as above.

Finally, the Chancery returns the memorials to the sender.

This was the routine process. In matters of urgency it could be shortened to a few hours.[18]

In this way the Grand Secretariat—the stronghold of the Mandarinate—was completely bypassed by the emperor's private council of advisers, and this itself could be and sometimes was bypassed by his one-to-one communications with the memorialists. The emperor scored by virtue of knowing more and knowing it earlier than his councillors, by the non-executive nature of the Council, which was forbidden to issue orders directly to the Six Boards or to communicate with the provincial authorities, and finally, by his secret one-to-one communications with particular memorialists.

Why then did the Confucianist establishment inside and outside the bureacracy not resist the emperor's personal rule—as they had always done before? And the more so now, one would have surmised, considering that the emperors were aliens? The answer is simple: they were seduced.

2.3.4. THE SEDUCTION OF THE INTELLECTUALS

Initially the intelligentsia remained remarkably loyal to the Ming and refused to collaborate with the invaders. The resumption of civil service examinations in 1646 did do something to bring about a rapport but it was not, really, until the reign of the strongly Confucianist and cultivated K'ang-hsi Emperor that the Manchu began to woo and ended by seducing them. In 1679 he invited 188 scholars to participate in an examination. Some Ming loyalists refused but fifty candidates were successful, and were drawn into what was soon to become a great ocean of literary and scientific enterprises, which the Ch'ing emperors financed lavishly and which appealed to the literati, not just because it was congenial work but because it was, in effect, a great, a monumental celebration of *Chinese* culture. The successful scholars mentioned above were set to work on the official history of the Ming. (Earlier, seventy scholars in Chekiang Province had been executed for compiling their private history of that dynasty.)[19] In 1710 the great

---

[18] Fairbank and Teng, 66–7.

[19] Cf. J. Gernet, *A History of Chinese Civilization*, trans. R. Foster (CUP, Cambridge, 1982), 475.

K'ang-hsi Dictionary was commissioned, to be completed in 1716. The year 1713 saw the publication of a great phrase-dictionary (the *P'ei-wen yün-fu*). The great Encyclopaedia, four times the length of the *Britannica*, was begun in 1701 and completed in 1721. One of the greatest of the enterprises was, surely, the famous *Ssu-k'u*. This was a canonical edition of no less than 3,462 major works of literature, many culled from rare manuscripts and books from private libraries all over the empire. It took twelve years to complete this publication (1773–85). Seven manuscript copies were made, each of 36,000 volumes, and deposited at various points in the empire. But in addition to acquiring and editing the texts, the editors wrote critical reviews of the entire 10,230 titles they had started out with, and issued these as the Imperial Catalogue to the Complete Library. This Chien-lung reign saw other majestic literary enterprises, such as the beautiful reprint of the twenty-four standard Dynastic Histories.[20]

The compilation of the Complete Library had its dark side. Between 1772 and 1788 Ch'ien-lung launched what is sometimes called a 'literary inquisition' against what he conceived to be anti-dynastic publications, as a result of which over 2,500 books were totally or partially suppressed. Scholars differ in their assessment. One considers it 'odious tyranny';[21] another comments that the Ch'ing record was 'one of co-optation rather than suppression'.[22] We shall consider the matter later, in our appraisal of the regime. But one thing is certain: even Gernet, the stern critic cited above, accepts that the Manchu emperors' seduction was complete, and that 'the educated classes rallied to the support of the new regime'.[23]

2.3.5. SECURE FRONTIERS

The Manchu were a martial people; one might almost say that they had lived by war, and in the Banner system Nurhaci had invented a highly efficient tactical formation. Each Banner had originally been commanded by a Manchu prince: the early emperors took three of them, henceforth known as the Superior Banners, under their direct imperial control. Yung-cheng brought the remainder under his direct control and in this way the emperor was in direct command and communion with each individual Manchu bannerman, a very far remove indeed from the fastidious reserve with which the later Ming emperors had regarded their troops. Moreover, these earlier Ch'ing emperors were themselves warlike when they were not, indeed, active warriors like the K'ang-hsi and Yung-cheng emperors, in sharp contrast to

---

[20] Feuerwerker, *State and Society in Eighteenth-Century China*, 31–3; Gernet, *History of Chinese Civilization*, 472–5 and 503–15.   [21] Gernet, *History of Chinese Civilization*, 475.
[22] Feuerwerker, *State and Society*, 33.   [23] Gernet, *History of Chinese Civilization*, 503.

every Ming emperor after the unfortunate Ying-tsung in 1449.[24] One has only to look at the pages of K'ang-hsi's reflections to experience the gusto he felt when campaigning against the Dzungars, how intimate and caring was his communion with the rank-and-file, how discriminating and yet masterful his relationship with his generals.[25]

With the Manchu warriors inside the empire and in charge of it, the former external menace to the empire had now become its formidable military asset: the armed poacher had turned armed gamekeeper. The perceived threat came from the western Mongols—the Dzungars mainly—and the more so because they might receive support from the Russians who were pushing up behind and to the north of them. This explains the Dzungar and Tibetan wars. In 1690 the Dzungar chieftain, Dalgan, raided into Jehol before K'ang-hsi defeated him in 1696. In 1717 Dalgan's sucessor occupied Lhasa. Fearing a Dzungar–Tibetan coalition, the Ch'ing sent an expedition into Tibet which expelled the Dzungars and established Tibet as their protectorate (though this did not reach its final form until 1750). Yung-cheng had to face the Dzungars again in 1736–9; but a final reckoning came under the Ch'ien-lung Emperor. By the 1755–9 wars the Dzungar proto-state was totally destroyed and the way into Central Asia laid wide open. China was for the first time in centuries freed from northern pressure (the Russians had been seen off and compelled to accept a recognized frontier by the treaties of Nerchinsk, 1689, and Kiakhta, 1727). A list of northern and western conquests would run something like this:

1697	Outer Mongolia (Khalka)
1720 (finalized, 1750)	Tibet
1755–7	Ili Protectorate
1759–60	The Tarim Basin and Eastern Turkestan (Sinkiang, i.e. 'New Province')

In addition, Chinese military power established a ring of vassal, tributary states. Korea became a vassal in 1637. However, a series of campaigns into South-East Asia from c.1770 failed to do more than to compel states like Burma, Siam, and Tongking to acknowledge a formal tributary status. This was no recompense for the enormous drain on the imperial treasury, a drain which precipitated the Ch'ing decline. But in the meantime, and up to that point, the unexampled security of the northern and western borders greatly contributed to the prosperity and tranquillity of China's Golden Century. It

---

[24] See Bk. II, Ch. 4, 'Government under the Ming'.

[25] By 'K'ang-hsi's reflections' I refer to Spence's *recueil*, Spence, *Emperor of China*, 17–22, 34–9.

provided the framework within which these Ch'ing emperors were enabled to perform the apparent conjuring-trick we have been describing: pursuing vigorous—and enlightened—personal policies without dependency on either eunuchs or Mandarins, or provoking a destructive contest between the two.

3. THE ARTICULATION OF THE TERRITORY

3.1. *The Confucianist Linchpin: The 'Gentry'*

> *I can call spirits from the vasty deep.*
> *Why, so can I, or so can any man:*
> *But will they come when you do call for them?*[26]

It is common to hear the Chinese Empire described as 'centralized', but a genuinely centralized state was an impossibility before the twentieth century. The Ch'ing Empire in particular was much too vast and complex to carry out any policy at a distance, and in practice it was impossible— as indeed it always had been since later T'ang times—for the central government to carry out its policies without the co-operation of the local élite. We have met this situation again and again in dealing with the pre-modern agrarian empires: the interface of officialdom and the local decurions (Rome), notables (Islam), and in the Chinese case, the so-called 'gentry'.

We have already noticed the spreading influence of this group in the later Ming Empire. In the Ch'ing it became the most important single political influence in the empire, which, indeed, some authors describe as the 'gentry state'. They formed the effective central–local linchpin. They were even more than that; they were a kind of cement that unified the entire society: a unified and distinct stratum that overlay and guided the whole political and social structure. It played the same role in Ch'ing China as the decurionate had under the Antonines.

The 'gentry' was not a caste or class, whatever these terms may mean. It was a status group and you entered it by virtue of possessing an academic degree. Being a *literatus* was a necessary condition for entering the 'gentry', but not sufficient; for that, one had to possess an academic degree, and this was obtainable in the vast majority of cases only by passing in competitive examinations. A minority, however, were able to enter by virtue of a rather shabby diploma, which was obtainable by purchase in much the same way as Oxford and Cambridge BAs today purchase their MAs which, elsewhere in

[26] Shakespeare, 1 *Henry IV,* III. i.

the UK, are obtainable only by result of an examination.[27] Since the avenue to gentry status was scholarship, something must first be said about the empire's educational facilities.

3.1.1. THE SPREAD OF EDUCATION

The Ch'ing continued to maintain the State Academy, with an enrolment of some 300 scholars—a research establishment rather than a university. They encouraged official provincial schools, each province having its own educational director, but more important were the numerous private academies funded by wealthy landowners and by the rich merchants. In the rural areas elementary education was provided in public and in private schools that were 'so numerous that comfortably-off peasants could easily pay for the education of their children' and, to make the point at which we ourselves are driving at here, 'Some great *literati* of the eighteenth century were of quite humble origin.'[28] The children of merchants, artisans, shopkeepers, landlords, and the more well-to-do peasants would tend to frequent such schools for a few years. During this period they would follow the standard curriculum, dating from the Sung dynasty, which started off by imparting a reading knowledge of some 2,000 characters and proceeded to the Four Books and the Five Classics. Such students finished knowing and writing several thousand characters. Aware of the importance of education, parents tried as far as their means permitted to send their children to even better schools in the hope that, as scholars, they could acquire the coveted academic degree and enter the 'gentry'. Finally, the village children attending school might do so for shorter periods, perhaps during the slack agricultural season. They mastered a few hundred characters, enough to cope with simple accounts and carry out transactions but offering no basis for advancement.[29] It is impossible to say how many were 'literate' in either of these classes; unquestionably a far smaller proportion than in contemporary Japan which made a feature of promoting mass literacy. But in absolute terms their numbers provided an ample supply of aspirants for the competitive degrees and subsequent acquisition of gentry status.

---

[27] Hsü, *Rise of Modern China*, 72–5, 79. The Oxford/Cambridge mode of awarding MA degrees pre-dated the efforts of other British universities to award the same by examination. The latter would perhaps have been wiser to have adopted a different title for their degrees from the start.

[28] Gernet, *History of Chinese Civilization*, 481.

[29] E. S. Rawski, 'Literacy', in B. Hook (ed.), *Encyclopaedia of China* (CUP, Cambridge, 1982), 131–3.

3.1.2. THE PERFECTION OF THE EXAMINATION SYSTEM

This explained the increased competition for degrees and hence the extremities of complication in the public examination system. Its general features were outlined earlier.[30] Briefly, you could end up with a first degree as a *sheng-yüan* ('government student'); or go on to take a higher degree, the *chü-jen* ('employable man'); or take the advanced degree, the very prestigious *chin-shih* ('advanced scholar').

The examinations for the first degree were taken at *hsien* level, for the higher degree at provincial level, and for the advanced degree at the capital. Each examination consisted, however, of three sub-examinations. The exams for the first degree were held twice every three years. They began with the candidate presenting a guarantee of origin and good character from a member of the gentry. Then followed the examination, conducted by the *hsien* magistrate. The successful candidates were reassessed by a similar examination, held at the *chou* or *fu* level. If they passed, they went on to the final examination at the provincial capital. It was success here that entitled one to the *sheng-yüan* degree: and it will be seen how hard it was to obtain by the fact that the government quota for the total of successful candidates in any completed examination was a mere 1–2 per cent of the total number of competing candidates!

These students were now stipended and encouraged to go on for the higher degree. The examination for this took place every three years. This too consisted of three sub-examinations, sat over a period of nine days, the candidates shut away in tiny individual cells. In Canton the examination area spread over 16 acres and contained 8,653 cells. Into these the candidate took his bedding, food, and writing materials: for two of the three sessions he would be immured there for three days and nights! The quota for successful candidates—*chü-jen*—was only 1,400: roughly 5 per cent of the candidates.

These *chü-jen* were now members of the upper gentry, and received travelling expenses to sit for the advanced degree at the capital. This also occupied three sessions. The results of the first were known in one month; the successful candidates went on to the second session; the next was the palace examination, six weeks later; and then the ten best papers went to the emperor who himself graded them into a top, middle, and lower grade, all entitling the examinees to an imperial banquet, presents, and the highest honours. Only 238 candidates received the *chin-shih* degree at each examination: one in every six of those who sat it. Altogether, it will be seen, a minimum number sitting for the first degree was something like 1,255,446, of

---

[30] See Bk. III, Ch. 4, 'Government under the Ming'.

whom 238 got the *chin-shih*, in short, 0.19 per cent: 1 in every 5,270 of the total competitors!

It has been said that the entire system of competitive entry was bogus in that only the wealthy had access to higher education and the system merely confirmed the privilege of the already privileged classes. That is substantially true, but by no means wholly so. The system did permit a fair degree of upward mobility. Over the entire Ch'ing era, 19.1 per cent of those prestigious *chin-shih* came from families which had contained no degree-holders at all over the last three generations, and another 19.1 per cent of them came from families that had produced one or more first degree (*sheng-yüan*) holders but no better; and only 505 came from the families which had thrown up *chin-shih* holders in the last three generations. So at least one-third of the *chin-shih* came from families that had low or nil educational backgrounds over the last 100 years.[31]

In the 1830s the total number of degree-holders was 1 million. Of these only 47,500 had the advanced degree, and another 25,000 had advanced military degrees. Yet, though the examination system's original rationale had been to provide the best-qualified candidates for the public service, only half of these degree-holders actually held office at that date.[32] Certainly, some were waiting with every expectation of office. But in view of this great superfluity of successful graduates, why was the competition so fierce? Because, though the degree did not automatically bring its bearer an official position, it had one certain consequence: however humble his origin, it entitled him to immediate membership of the gentry.[33] Why was this so desired?

3.1.3. 'GENTRY'

The gentry enjoyed the most prodigious deference. They were privileged at law. They were qualified for public office. Many were or had been public officials. There were rich gentry and poorer gentry, but that was not the point; they formed *the* privileged stratum of Chinese society.

Gentry wore different dress from commoners. Only they might attend the Confucian temple ceremonies. It was usually they who led the ancestral clan rituals.[34] At law, commoners who offended them received harsher

---

[31] Hsü, *Rise of Modern China*, 78.   [32] Feuerwerker, *The Foreign Establishment in China*, 42.

[33] The most splendid—and extremely funny—example of this occurs in Wu Ching-Tzu's (1710–54) novel *The Scholars*, which I have referred to earlier, where the miserable Fan Chin, henpecked by his wife, bullied by his butcher father-in-law because he cannot earn enough for them even to feed themselves, falls into a swoon when he learns that he has passed the *sheng-yüan*, from which he is finally awoken to find himself visited by a local ex-magistrate and accepted, straight away, as a member of the gentry! This is a great book! The relevant excerpt has been reprinted in H. F. Schurmann and O. Schell, *China Readings*, vol. I (1967), 85–98.

[34] Hsü, *Rise of Modern China*, 72.

sentences than if they had committed the offences against fellow-com-
moners; commoners could not call them as witnesses; they did not have
to witness in person—they could send a servant; and they could not be
prosecuted by a magistrate—a fellow-member of the gentry—unless and
until the provincial educational commissioner was persuaded to strip them
of scholar-status. They enjoyed important economic privileges, also. They
were exempt from the corvée. A 'gentry' household paid only about a third
of the tax paid by an equivalent commoner household.[35]

They became the natural leaders of the locality. They took the lead in all
manner of economic, educational, and philanthropic enterprises. And
whereas the *hsien* magistrates, aliens to the area, came and went every three
years, they were a permanency. They became, therefore, the 'eyes and ears' of
the magistrates: were consulted by them, advised them, and intermediated
between them and the population. For there were no other groups of society
that could do this—neither villages *per se*, nor guilds, nor merchants. How
they co-operated will become clearer in the following discussion of the
district (*hsien*) magistrate.

3.2. De Jure *Centralization*, De Facto *Decentralization*

3.2.1. THE TERRITORIAL LEVELS AND THEIR OFFICIALS

Distances

The country was much too large for effective centralization. The methods
of communication had not changed since the days of the Han or earlier.
The Ch'ing took over an imperial network of roads and courier stations
from the Ming, who in turn had taken it over from their predecessors, until
one reaches back even to the days of the Spring and Autumn annals.[36] Five
great routes radiated out from the capital, Peking. Use of the service was
regulated by means of tallies which entitled the bearer to horses and
conveyances. The couriers were strictly regulated; the courier had to 'clock
in' at every station *en route*. The speed of the very expensive 'urgent' courier
was laid down at 200 miles per twenty-four hours (identical with that in the
ancient Persian Empire); that of the ordinary 'express' courier half that.
This, of course, was on horseback. Speeds recorded in the early nineteenth
century are illustrative of the huge stretch of the empire: it could take as
long as forty-one days to get from Peking to Canton; the median was twenty
days. To Nanking the corresponding figures are twenty-five (max.) and ten
(med.) days; to Sinkiang, thirty-seven (max.) and thirty-four days and over

[35] Hsü, 73.   [36] Fairbank and Teng, *Ch'ing Administration*, 3.

(med.).[37] Officials, halting *en route*, were taking from four to six weeks to get from Peking to Canton or Szechuan in 1842.[38]

The Territorial Units

The Ch'ing confirmed the provisional Ming division of the empire into provinces. There were eighteen of these, each ruled by a governor, grouped usually in pairs but sometimes in threes, under governors-general. These were often known in the West as viceroys, with justice, for 'the size of a province nearly matches that of a state in Europe (in fact some provinces' area was bigger than many states in Europe').[39] In view of the slow-rate state of communication, these provinces (it has been remarked) 'worked much more like the states of the American Union under the articles of Confederation than the departments of France'.[40] However, there were also institutional reasons for this autonomy. For instance the viceroys, governors, and finance commissioners were directly responsible to the emperor and exercised their powers without having to obey the central departments, so that in course of time the size and condition of their militias, the fiscal arrangements, and the like escaped rigorous central control.[41]

There is little point in giving anything but the most summary account of the arrangements above the *chou/hsien* level because they were, in Chinese terminology, the officials in charge of officials. The *chou/hsien* magistrates, by contrast, were called 'officials in charge of affairs'.[42] Each governor had three commissioners under him, all appointed by the emperor—for finance, the judiciary, and education. He was served by a staff, which was also appointed by the emperor. The regular army came under the independent command of the provincial commander-in-chief; also independent of the governors were various special commissioners, for example, for the salt tax. Below the province there were the *tao* or circuits and below them the *fu* (prefectures). At the base were the *chou* and *hsien*. All their senior officials were aliens to the locality and were shifted around every three years. They were appointed, promoted, and moved around by the central board of the Civil Office. They were all subject to central government regulations in respect of administration, finance, budget, and the like. Each level was subject to review by the superior echelon.

---

[37] Fairbank and Teng, 30.

[38] J. K. Fairbank, *Chinese Thought and Institutions* (University of Chicago Press, 1987), 34.

[39] Quoted in Hsieh, *Government of China*, 318.   [40] Ibid. 289.

[41] Ibid. 318–19, quoting Wang Tao, *Historical Development of the Provincial System*. Hsieh's fierce critique of the Manchu's provincial administration is postponed to the close of this chapter.

[42] T'ung-Tsu Chü, *Local Government in China under the Ch'ing* (Harvard UP, Cambridge, Mass., 1962), 14.

This is a useful point at which to insert the numbers of officials of each echelon in the provincial administration. The total number of ranking civil officials did not vary much from the norm of some 20,000.[43] Nine out of ten of these were in the capital. The distribution of officials in the provinces was as follows (according to figures in Hsien, *Government of China*, 289–90):

PROVINCIAL LEVEL	8 Viceroys, 15 Governors,
	18 Commissioners of Finance,
	13 Commissioners of Justice,
	Salt Controllers,
	13 Commissioners of Grain
TAO LEVEL	92 Intendants
FU LEVEL	185 *Chih-fu* (Prefects)
	41 *T'ung-chi* (independent sub-prefects)
CHOU/HSIEN LEVEL	72 *chou* magistrates
	1,554 *hsien* magistrates
TOTAL:	2011

District (*Chou* and *Hsien*) Government

The average population of a *hsien* at the end of the eighteenth century was some 200,000. The *hsien* magistrate was responsible for all that passed within it. Hence he was known as the *fu-mu kuan*, the 'father and mother official'.[44] His two principal preoccupations were taxation and justice, and his official assessment-rating was based on how well he handled these two matters.[45] He worked from his *yamen*, what the English would call a town-hall and the Americans a court-house. It opened at dawn. The magistrate would spend the morning on administrative work, and take lawsuits in the afternoon until the *yamen* shut at 7 p.m.

The nature of district administration—it was the same all over the Empire—derived from three characteristics of the *hsien* magistrate—his tasks, his training, and his transience.

The central government provided him with no more than a handful of officials: one or two assistant-magistrates, a gaol-warden, and a few miscellaneous officials such as postmaster, tax-collector, and granary supervisor.[46] Their numbers were trivial: as late as 1899, over the entire empire there were only 925 sub-district (*hsün-chien*) magistrates (effectively police-

---

[43] Feuerwerker, *The Foreign Establishment in China*, 39–40. This author lists 7,000 military officials also.   [44] Ibid. 22.
[45] Chü, *Local Government*, 16.   [46] Ibid. 8–9.

commissioners), only sixty-five postmasters, and forty-five sluice-keepers.[47] Such a staff was irrelevant. So vast—indeed limitless—were the magistrate's responsibilities and so extensive his territory that he needed a whole battery of people to handle the paperwork, and even more numerous 'runners', that is, petty employees, to go and get the villagers to do what was required of them. The magistrate who came to take up his appointment found in his *yamen* and around it a very—in many cases excessively—numerous unofficial civil service already in place.

Among them the clerks' role was unique because, unlike the magistrate who left after three years, they were natives, and though they were supposed to terminate employment after five years they found devices to prolong it or at least pass it around the family so that, in effect, they were permanencies. They were highly influential, and as such, perfect targets for bribery, since they prepared the documents on which the entire administration turned, knew (as the magistrate would not) the details of the rules and regulations, and finally, handled—and hence could mishandle—the files.[48] In the 1618–55 period there could be as many as 1,000 clerks in a large *hsien* and 100 in a small one.

These clerks came mostly from the propertyless class. They had to be of 'good' family, and able to read, write, and calculate. The runners, on the other hand, were the lowest of the low. They belonged to the legally denominated, de-classed 'mean' status—for instance, they could not sit the civil service examinations. 'Runners' is the name for the host of miscellaneous messengers, guards, and policemen who were needed to mobilize the corvée, get the peasants to provide carts and beasts of burden, deliver summonses and warrants, make arrests, keep gaol, even to act as sedan-chair bearers, pipers, drummers, and so forth. They were the magistrates' 'teeth and claws'.[49] The government drew up official quotas of employment but magistrates were permitted to exceed these on proof of need. There were hundreds and hundreds of 'runners'. In the Chekiang province's *hsien* they numbered some 1,500–1,600; the same in Shantung; in Szechuan their numbers ran to 7,000. Interestingly, it was here that a vigorous magistrate dismissed 6,700 of them and worked his district perfectly well with the remaining 300![50]

Where did the pay for these people come from? It came neither from the government nor from the magistrates' own pocket, but from what was called *lou-kuei*: the 'customary fees'. And so, to a large extent, did the pay of the magistrate himself. This mode of payment provides one key to the under-

<hr />

[47] Chü, 9–11.   [48] Ibid. 37.   [49] Ibid. 57.   [50] Ibid. 59.

standing of the quality and nature of government at ground level. The reason is this.

A magistrate's salary was nominal: a mere 80 taels in the *chou* and 40 taels in the *hsien*. This was so absurd that the Yung-cheng Emperor added a supplement to it, known as 'honesty-nourishing money'. But even so it went almost nowhere towards meeting the expenses the magistrate had to find from his own pocket. These included hiring private secretaries, a very highly paid class as will be seen; entertaining and making gifts to superiors; occasional capital levies to make good some shortfall in tax income; and so forth, the total amounting (1753–1809) to some 5,000–6,000 taels excluding the cost of the private secretaries, food, clothing, entertaining, and *per diem* expenses! So the question of pay is a question of how this shortfall was met, and the answer lies in the institution of the *lou-kuei*. The magistrate would levy fees on every possible occasion, for every conceivable function. They were neither legal nor illegal. They were simply unofficial—customary, tolerated, and expected. The nature and quantity of such fees varied from one *hsien* to another—there was a complete lack of uniformity across the country.[51] At one point the central government tried to regulate the fees, but to no avail. On the other hand the magistrate could not arbitrarily increase the fees, for these were set by custom. Nevertheless, at the end of the day the magistrate was usually able, by virtue of these fees, to manage a small surplus.

Now in the same way the *yamen* clerks and runners were also funded by *lou-kuei*. For instance, the clerks received fees for 'pen and paper', for registering documents, for expediting cases, and for other matters which, as a contemporary put it, were 'as numerous as the hairs of an ox'.[52] And in like manner the 'runners' too lived off the 'customary fees'. Country-wide, the aggregate of these customary fees equalled the government's total official regular tax revenue.[53] The scope offered for corruption is too obvious to need elaboration. (A brief survey of the forms it took will be offered later.) The government knew this, but could have addressed it only by paying regular salaries out of public taxation, which of course would have entailed raising taxes; but K'ang-hsi had actually frozen taxes in 1713 (as will be seen), and no subsequent emperor cared to contemplate changing an ancestor's edict.

Albeit they did it with a rapacity and corruption that was proverbial, these swollen trains of *yamen* underlings did, at all events, enable the magistrate to tackle his paperwork and implement his decisions. This, then, is how the problem of his *tasks* was addressed. But another problem

[51] Ibid. 26–30.   [52] Ibid. 49.   [53] Feuerwerker, *The Foreign Establishment in China*, 19.

arose out of his *training*. The magistrates were the products of the civil service examinations, and so were trained in literary skills; yet their chief tasks were the technical ones of assessing and raising taxation and dispensing justice according to the law. Left to themselves they could not have managed these, and the entire administration of the empire would have gone down in a welter of confusion. Furthermore, left to themselves, and getting the country into such a mess, they would all have been dismissed, at the very least. So they hired technical experts to advise them. These were the professional private secretaries, very grand, regarded as equals, styled *mu-yu* or *mu-pin* (house guests) and paid handsomely (from 200 to 250 taels, rising to some 800 by the century's end). They were experts who had specialized in tax matters and in law. They were recruited from ex-clerks, former officials, failed civil service candidates, most of them holders of the first degree. Indeed, when acting as private secretaries it was their practice to take time out to sit the higher examinations. They trained by going to a private tutor or to an existing private secretary. As scholars these private secretaries were also members of the gentry.[54]

There remained a final, a very daunting, hurdle—due to the magistrate's *transience*. He came from another part of the country and in three years' time he would leave this new district to go to a different part of the country. He came to find a well-established social order in place, with its own ways of doing things, its own things that were being done, and families who were either influential or not in such community affairs. The latter were, of course, the local gentry.

Under the Ming this group had become powerful enough to be able, effectively, to decide who the local *hsien* magistrate should be. The Ch'ing put a stop to all that and reined back some of the fiscal privileges which sundry members of the gentry had been abusing, for example, the registration of their houses as 'scholars' residences'. It must be emphasized that the *hsien* magistrate was a very important man, academically as well as politically, since he was much more likely than not to be *chin-shih*, the intellectual *crème de la crème* of a population which, in 1800, numbered 300 million. A magistrate was no push-over. He was independent; so, relationships between him and the gentry were either those of collaboration or of opposition, but never was one party a dependant of the other.

The magistrate went in mostly for the more public works, irrigation and the like; but as he was short-stay, it fell to local consortia of gentry families to construct irrigation works for river tributaries and lakes and so forth. The magistrate would do what he could to fulfil the government regulations

[54] Chü, *Local Government*, 93–115.

respecting schools, poor-houses, and the like, but the gentry supplemented his efforts to the point of overshadowing them: they raised funds to build the canals, dikes, dams, roads, and bridges for the local community; they supported the Confucian temples; they endowed schools and shrines; they funded the publication of local histories and gazetteers; they were called in to arbitrate between litigants; they established charitable trusts and founded poor-houses and hospitals. Importantly, they financed and led local militias.

Sometimes they abused their position. For instance, their houses, as we saw, were taxed more lightly than those of commoners: for a consideration they would register those commoners' hereditaments as their own. The *Dream of the Red Chamber*, that famous eighteenth-century novel, is familiar in the West. Chapter 4 is renowned for the scene where a newly arrived magistrate is about to order the arrest of a known murderer's relatives for interrogation when he is checked by his clerk, who produces for him a confidential list of 'the most powerful, wealthy and high-ranking families in the area'—and then tells him that the family he wants to interrogate is one which the magistrate 'cannot afford to offend'.[55]

And sometimes the interests of the generality of gentry ran counter to public policy. For instance, the magistrates promoted conservation of lakes and reservoirs as protection against droughts, whereas the gentry wanted to reclaim lakes and neglect streams in order to reclaim as much land as possible for cultivation. Again, the magistrates were supposed to update their land cadasters so as to readjust the tax-assessments; this was resisted by the gentry who, of course, wanted those assessments to remain static.

The Village: *Pao-chia* and *Li-chia*

The Ch'ing, as we know, took over the Ming *li-chia* (the bonded taxation group) and *pao-chia* (the police and security bonded group). Effectively it was the magistrate who appointed the heads of these organizations. How they functioned is controversial, but one or two things are clear enough. One main task of the *li-chia* was to update the land-and-population registers but, as will be explained later, in 1713 the K'ang-hsi Emperor froze the corvée and land tax and in 1740 the two were run together into a single payment, set—as it was to remain to the very end of the dynasty—at that 1713 level. In these circumstances, registers kept by the central government would be pointless. They were abandoned, and instead it was the *pao-chia* unit census that was relied on. In 1722 the quinquennial registration for the corvée was abolished and the chief function of the *li-chia* became that of urging its members to pay taxes on time. In some cases the old obligation

---

[55] H.-C. Hsao and N. Kao, *A Dream of Red Mansions* (Foreign Languages Press, Peking, 1978), 54–5.

remained whereby the head of the *li-chia* was held responsible for the full quota of the unit's tax liability. The *pao-chia* continued to function as a bonded group for reporting on births, deaths, and movements in and out of the villages, but its functions as a custodian of its members' activities and morals seem to have progressively weakened.[56] Indeed, an edict of 1726 confesses that it had become nominal.[57]

4. THE ACTIVITIES OF GOVERNMENT

4.1. *Defence, Law, and Order*

In the last quarter of the eighteenth century the empire began to witness great popular disturbances that were to recur with ever-greater intensity up to the present day, and from 1840 the army realized it was living in a time-warp, and lay open to the fleets and fire-power of Western forces. But in respect to this early Ch'ing era, its heyday, all that need be said is that no invaders ever crossed the borders, the revolts of outlying subject-peoples were effectively put down, and the population was quiescent and at peace.

The judicial system continued on the same lines as before, that is, the Ming code. The Ch'ing retained the format of this code but shortened the number of its articles, and published the revised and definitive code, known as *The Statutes and sub-Statutes of the Great Ch'ing*, in 1740.[58]

Like its Ming model, the subject-matter fell under seven great headings. Only one of these is concerned with 'Civil Law', and it covers a mere fraction of what we mean by this term in the western Roman and Common law traditions. As before, the vast bulk of civil cases were handled by customary local law and by conciliation procedures rather than by suits at court. The Ch'ing seem to have been even more fervent in keeping private persons from bringing their private grievances before the imperial courts than previous regimes. An edict of 1692 orders the magistrates to make the courts so dreaded that the people would not take their quarrels there[59] and civil cases should thus be settled by arbitration. It was criminal to give legal advice to a private person, even to help would-be litigants by drawing up petitions for them.[60]

The administrative and penal codes remained as authoritarian and per-emptory as ever, but there seems to have been some softening in the penalties. The code retained the traditional description of the punishment,

---

[56] Hsü, *Rise of Modern China*, 58; Chü, *Local Government*, p. 5.   [57] Chü, *Local Government*, 152.
[58] Bodde and Morris, *Law in Imperial China*, 60–1.
[59] S. van der Sprinkel, *Legal Institutions in Manchu China* (1962), 76–7.
[60] For an example, see Case 203, Bodde and Morris, *Law in Imperial China*, 413–17.

but the actual punishment fell short; for instance, the penalty of '100 blows of the heavy bamboo' had in fact come down to forty.[61] Against this is the undisputed fact that—for reasons which are unexplained (possibly a difference in the mode of calculation)—the number of offences punishable by death had leapt from the Ming's 249 to 813, and also that certain supplementary punishments had been introduced which, by European standards, were 'cruel and unusual': for instance, the wooden cangue (a neck-yoke) which weighed 33 lbs.[62] As usual, the penalties for treason and rebellion were much fiercer than for other crimes, these being among the 'Ten Abominations' that attracted the penalty of 'death by slicing'.[63]

Unlike the equally harsh and authoritarian Tokugawa judicial system, the Ch'ing, building on all their predecessors, developed an elaborate machinery of appeal, notably in respect of the death sentence, which in normal cases had to be approved by the Board of Punishments in Peking. Bodde and Morris remark on the 'great care and seriousness with which the Board . . . performed its work'; it quashed a high proportion of the lower courts' verdicts.[64] Furthermore, for all its harshness, the judicial process was not arbitrary or capricious. It was a 'rule of law' in the sense that due process was stringently observed, and it was an absolute requirement that at every judicial level the pronouncement of sentence must be accompanied by citation of the relevant statute and sub-statute.[65] Ch'ing jurisprudence did indeed permit reasoning by analogy, which can certainly be abused, to bring uncertainty into the law; but it made strenuous efforts to rationalize such reasoning and make it foolproof. In 1739 the government drew up thirty Rules of Analogy.[66] It is also true that there were some 'catch-all' crimes such as 'Doing what ought not to be done' or 'Violating the Imperial Decrees', but all but one of these were for very minor infractions.[67]

4.2. *Fiscality And Taxation*

The first thing that needs saying about the tax system is that the peasants had to pay far more than they should have, and the second thing is that what they should have paid was not all that much. In short, the legal fiscal

---

[61] Ibid. 99.   [62] Ibid. 77–8, 96, 99, 103–4.

[63] Ibid. 93–4, who also note that the extent of the dismemberment incurred under this penalty is highly controversial.   [64] Ibid. 173–4.

[65] Ibid. 173–5. The emperor could indeed intervene but this was very rare and—to judge by the instances in Spence, *Emperor of China*—varied the penalty, not the decision.

[66] Bodde and Morris, *Law in Imperial China*, 177.

[67] Ibid. 177–8. They correspond to such offences as the British army's 'conduct to the prejudice of good order or military discipline', or the Football Association's offence of 'bringing the game into disrepute'.

burden was light but corrupt administration and manipulation increased it. Corruption was in one sense built into the system since, as we saw, only about one half of the public revenue was statutorily authorized, the rest coming from the 'customary fees'. The swarm of runners and their collaborators, the clerks, hung around the *yamen* precisely in order to exploit the system for their own benefit. But their malpractices extended also into the statutory tax system. There is no point at all in recounting the details. We have heard it all before: manipulation of the scale, false receipts, bribes to keep taxpayers off the 'overdue' list, delays in the examination of weighing of the tribute grain, paying the peasant's tax in advance without his consent and then demanding high interest for the unsolicited 'advance'. The important thing to note is that an edict of 1736 maintained that the 'wicked clerks' had pocketed for themselves the equivalent of 20–30 per cent of the land tax. Compare this with the frugal 5 per cent cost of collecting this tax in Tokugawa Japan![68]

But the official tax burden itself was light. Most came from the land tax and the poll tax, along with miscellaneous revenues from the monopolies of salt and tea, and customs duties in Canton. The taxes were levied, originally, on the cadasters of 1646, that is, immediately after the Manchu invasion. But as peace returned so did prosperity. The population was increasing rapidly and the tax-yield increased with it. The dynasty began to make tax remissions. By 1711 these amounted to 100 million taels, more than the central government's revenues; in consequence the K'ang-hsi Emperor decreed in 1712 that the quotas of the land tax and corvée (the *ting*) were to remain fixed at that year's level. And so they were. As a consequence the revenue did not notably increase. In so far as it rose, this was largely due to the increase in land cultivation: in 1644–61, at 28 million taels; in 1736–95, at 43–5 millions.[69] By the end of the century the taxes, it is reckoned, amounted to not more than 5 per cent of the GNP.[70] This is not to say that the taxes were collected without pain—far from it. Magistrates were demoted for failing to meet their quota, promoted for exceeding it.[71] On the basis of a list of tax-defaults, it was common form for them to order the defaulters to be flogged (or, more frequently, the runners, since they were more accessible than scattered peasants).[72]

The undisclosed half of the revenue that came in the 'customary fees' went, as we have seen, to maintain the local government establishments. In

---

[68] Chü, *Local Government*, 49–51, 67–9. For Japan, see Bk. IV, Ch. 1, 'Tokugawa Japan'.

[69] Hsü, *Rise of Modern China*, 59.

[70] S. Naquin and E. Rawski, *Chinese Society in the Eighteenth Century* (Yale UP, New Haven, Conn., 1987), 219.   [71] Chü, *Local Government*, 133.

[72] Ibid. 138–9.

the mid-eighteenth century the disclosed and official income of the government was about 44 million taels, and its expenditure some 35 million taels—some 9.5 million being central expenditure and some 26 million local. About 64 per cent of the two combined budgets went on the military and 16 per cent on the civil establishment. Until the 1780s the central treasury was in surplus by about 9 or 10 million taels a year.

4.3. The Quality of Administration

When the Ch'ing took over the Ming bureaucracy intact it took over all its vices too. There is no need, therefore, to expatiate any further on the defects described above in the chapter on the Ming. Suffice it to say that the cardinal sins of excessive reliance on the document in lieu of observation, the intermittent character of censor surveillance, factionalism, wire-pulling, and corrupt practices continued as before. These vigorous early Ch'ing emperors did what they could by their Palace Memorial intelligence network, by tours of inspection where an emperor would set out to quiz his subjects and encourage them to canvass their grievances,[73] by their household pao-i, who served as informants in sensitive posts throughout the empire, but even they could make little headway. For all the apparent rationality of selection and grading, promotions and propitious postings depended not so much on what the civil servant knew but whom he knew. The network of personal relationships—the kuan-hsi or factions—in short, wire-pulling and the 'old school tie' circuit—prevailed. 'You people with the chin-shih and chü-jen degrees', ran an edict of the K'ang-hsi Emperor of 1729, 'like to form cliques to advance your own personal interests. In order to climb to high office you have given each other undue assistance and protection . . .' But though he warned them, he could not eliminate but only contain this log-rolling, and the more brusque Yung-cheng Emperor's rather more successful efforts did not outlast his reign.[74]

It is conventional wisdom that the regime went into administrative decline after about 1780 and that this accelerated through the nineteenth century until it collapsed. The causes of this were latent in the eighteenth century, some of their evil consequences already, indeed, manifest. The manifestations were excessive slowness, bribery, corruption, and embezzlement, and the steady dripping away of central authority to the extremities. All three became steadily worse throughout the eighteenth century and all stemmed effectively from this: there were not nearly enough civil servants

---

[73] Spence, Emperor of China, passim, for the K'ang-hsi Emperor, for example.
[74] Naquin and Rawski, Chinese Society, 13.

nor sufficiently well-paid civil servants. To take the latter point first, civil servant salaries had been fixed in the early days of the Ming Empire back in the fourteenth century, and the Manchu simply confirmed these salaries. They were, of course, virtually nominal. The only way the officials could continue in office was by making illegal exactions. It was to stop this that the 'honesty-nourishing money' was introduced, which in the higher grades, could multiply the nominal salary by 100 times,[75] though the increase for the *chou* and the *hsien* magistrates was much more modest than this[76] and was, as we have already remarked, completely inadequate to meet their expenses. At the same time the competition for posts had heated up; we have noted that only one in two degree-holders received an appointment.[77] Increased competition lengthened the period between making the first examination attempt and attaining the degree, so it increased the amounts the candidates had to borrow in order to sustain their non-productive studies over all this time. Hence, even if the salaries had been adequate to meet their current expenses, it would not have sufficed to pay off their debts. The consequence was a still more frantic effort to make money on the side. The higher ranks of the civil service were simply riddled with corrupt practices. The relative helplessness of even the most exemplary emperors is demonstrated by their inability to prevent peculation and embezzlement by their *pao-i*. For instance, the salt censor Kao Heng embezzled nearly 11 million taels from the salt-monopoly revenue, a sum which is one-quarter of the entire annual revenue of the empire.[78] The Ch'ien-lung Emperor, we are told, 'was so familiar with the misdeeds of the *pao-i* officials appointed to the salt monopolies and the customs bureaux that he despaired of their ever abandoning their base bondservant habits'.[79]

The bureaucracy's second vice of origin was much more serious; it was to lead to decrepitude and ultimately to virtual dismemberment of the empire. That vice was the insufficient number of established civil servants. It was barely different from the number in Han times. It is suggested that it increased some 13 per cent over the eighteenth century, but the population over the same period increased by 300 per cent! This understaffing had two unfortunate results. It was responsible in the first place for that uncon-

---

[75] Hsü, *Rise of Modern China*, 62.   [76] Chü, *Local Government*, 22–3.
[77] Feuerwerker, *State and Society in Eighteenth-Century China*, 42.
[78] Torbert, *Ch'ing Imperial Household Department*, 139. The case should be bracketed with the earlier estimate (see p. 1156 above) of the clerks pocketing some 20–30% of the land-tax revenue. Clearly if individual frauds of this magnitude be added to the general short-fall in the land-tax revenue, the amount lost by the fisc must have been in the order of half the entire annual revenue, at least!
[79] Ibid. 180. For further instances of corruption in the imperial household, see pp. 117, 131–6, 136–72, 179–80.

trolled expansion of hangers-on and leeches, the clerks and runners, in the *yamens*. Obviously, since the government would not pay for junior clerking and menial staff in the *hsien*, government could only be carried on by freelances, and we have already seen what rogues and vagabonds these turned out to be. In this way, government on the ground drifted further and further away from the control of the centre.

The second unhappy consequence was to bog the administration down in a sea of paperwork and lengthy delays. Four grades of administrative area were too many. Thus

when something was to be done in a place, the approval of the Governor or Viceroy was necessary and the petition might be filed or an order to execute it might follow. But the inadequate means of communication might mean several days to reach a district magistracy and weeks to reach the prefect, the circuit intendant and then the viceroy's office. When it got to the provincial capital, it had to go through the commissioner's office, and thence to the governor. By the time it reaches the governor an immeasurable amount of time and money is already wasted

. . . and so forth.[80]

One cannot fail to be struck by the contrast with the relative efficiency and frugality of Tokugawa Japan. The reason is that China was so extensive and became so very populous that its very limited number of officials grew ever more remote from the people they were administering; whereas in Japan government was typically carried out in the fiefs, and even in sub-fiefs—small areas where the officials of the daimyo or even of his vassals sat right on top of their local population. Even the shogun's own domain lands were only a quarter of the land area of Japan.

The fundamental reason why China's system sufficed in the eighteenth century was because on balance government was so marginal to the life of the common people. Its basic function was to provide peace and public tranquillity without overtaxing its subjects. Seen in its context in the enormous society around it, says Fairbank, the old Ch'ing regime shrinks to a thin stratum of tax-gatherers, magistrates, and military who performed architectonic functions of a centralizing and supervisory sort but were peripheral to the life of the people.[81] Now, interestingly, this same author had also written the following: 'The government . . . was a relatively small, highly centralized body that floated in a sea of isolated peasant communities. The point of contact between the two was the prefectural town, where a governor and perhaps two or three other central government

[80] Hsieh, *Government of China*, 319–20.   [81] Fairbank, *Chinese Thought and Institutions*, 20.

appointees dealt with the village heads, landed magnates and other local leaders.'[82] Yet what this passage is describing is not the Ching at all, but the Han Empire of nearly 2,000 years before !

For all that, China was much happier under the Ch'ing than under the Han or under any previous dynasty, and as happy, if not happier, than any other state in the entire world. The early Ch'ing century was an era of peace and marked prosperity. The revenue was buoyant. The population trebled, because it was able to expand into new lands where New World crops were planted, and new agricultural techniques like double cropping of rice or the alternation of winter wheat and barley with summer millet were introduced. While the central government looked after the dikes and drainage of the great rivers like the Yellow River and the Yangtse, locally the gentry funded and organized the irrigation of the farmlands. It was they, too, who supplied funds for temples, poor-houses, hospitals, and schools. And—as in Toku-gawa Japan—through the schools and the pervasive influence of this very Confucianist-educated gentry, the peasantry internalized the Confucian patterns.

And among these cultivated gentry and the wider literati, the arts, learning, and letters enjoyed lavish patronage and an ever-wider extension. If one were to measure the performance of a polity by comparison with its contemporaries, one would have to say that in respect to external peace, internal tranquillity, the standard of living, and the state of the arts, letters, and crafts, this early Ch'ing era was indeed China's Golden Century, the century in which she became more than a Confucianist empire: rather, a Confucianist society.

Its tragedy was that it was to fall victim to three pressures. Two of these were impossible for it to have foreseen. One was the internal pressure, relentless, of ever-increasing numbers on a fixed quantity of land and the other, the outside pressure of predatory nations with technology so advanced that, from the Chinese standpoint, they might have come from another planet. These two pressures nourished a third, at first tenuous, but which later grew to be overwhelming: an underground of xenophobic Chinese resistance movements to the Manchu overlords.

The oldest was the White Lotus Sect, for it dated back to c.1250, possibly earlier, as a quasi-religious secret organization. It had strongly opposed the Mongol domination and for this reason became a staunch support of Hung-wu. Now it vowed to destroy the Manchus and restore the Ming. Another secret anti-Manchu society was the Ko-lao Brotherhood Association which came into being during the reign of the Ch'ien-lung Emperor.

---

[82] Reischauer and Fairbank, *East Asia, the Great Tradition*, 96.

The one with which Westerners are familiar is the so-called Triads organization. Its full name is the Heaven and Earth Society and it was founded
in the 1670s by five Ming loyalists who had retreated to a monastery in
Fukien and vowed to promote the overthrow of the Ch'ing and the
restoration of the Ming. It was called the Triads because its emphasis on
the harmony of Heaven, Earth, and Man was often symbolized by the
Three Dots. This society set up Five Grand Lodges and Five Minor ones,
and branches and affiliates sprang up throughout the provinces, though
mostly in the coastal areas. Each of these societies perpetuated the anti-
Manchu opposition, but it seems to me that they needed the stimulus of the
previously mentioned two pressures to enable them to make an outright
challenge to the dynasty. The first big revolt—by the White Lotus Sect—
was launched in 1793. Repression and mass arrests further goaded the
members into another revolt in 1796 which spread quickly through several
provinces. Significantly—in view of what we have said about the seduction
of the literati and the key role of the gentry in the Ch'ing Empire—the
gentry organized militias and built fortresses against the rebels. For all that,
the revolt was not crushed till 1804 and during the reign of the Chia-cheng
Emperor (1796–1820) unrest was continual.

As the nineteenth century wore on and the Ch'ing system became more
and more obsolete and the population so pauperized by the pressure of
limited land resources, the influence of such societies strengthened and
became one of the strands which, accompanied by the West's subversion
of China's traditional belief-system and its military weakness, brought about
the degradation and, finally, the death of the dynasty, and indeed of the
entire 2,000-year imperial tradition. But that is a later story.[83]

[83] In general, Hsü, *Rise of Modern China*, 127–30. For specific detail, see F. L. Davis, *Primitive
Revolutionaries of China* (Heinemann, London, 1977); J. Chesneaux (ed.), *Popular Movements and Secret
Societies in China, 1840–1950* (Stanford UP, Stanford, 1972).

3

The Ottoman Empire:
The Classical Age, c.1566

1. THE SIGNIFICANCE OF THE OTTOMAN POLITY

*T*he year 1453, when the Turks took Constantinople, conventionally marks the close of medieval and the beginning of modern European history and, just as that date straddles the medieval and the modern, so did the institutions of the Ottoman Empire. The date is a reminder that this reached its peak a good century or more before Tokugawa Japan and Ch'ing China. As the last two chapters have indicated, the heyday of the Tokugawa regime lay *c.*1710 and that of Ch'ing China around, perhaps, 1750; but by either of these two dates the classical and highly effective institutions of the Ottoman Empire had disappeared, its central government had lost grip over its local officials, and its territorial expansion had not only been halted but turned back.

The Ottoman is the second of the two great historic Muslim empires. Its area was less than half of the Arab Caliphate's[1] (the populations being much the same at some 28–30 million), but it was much more powerful and also more durable. This longevity, together with the uniqueness of its institutions in its prime, are its principal claims to be considered in this *History.*

The state-form with which it invites comparison is its great Islamic forebear, the Abbasid Caliphate. Taking a large view, these two great polities appear similar. They were both very extensive, full of ethnic and religious minorities, and basically agrarian. The scope of their government was limited to war, law and order, and taxation. Both were Palace polities,

---

[1] I calculate the area of the Arab Caliphate at its height in 750, as approximately 4,888,000 sq. mls. In calculating the area of the Ottoman Empire I have omitted the area of the coastal strip that runs between the present Egyptian border through Algiers, and likewise Podolia and the Khanate of the Crimea, so that my figures are on the low side. Anatolia and the Arab territories make up 1, 941,390 sq. miles, the European territories make up 326,170 sq. miles. The grand total is, therefore, 2,267,560 sq. miles. This figure can be compared with my calculations for the Assyrian Empire (580,130 sq. mls.), the Roman Empire (1,454,000 sq. mls.), and the Achaemenian Empire (2,275,400 sq. mls.). The relatively vast expanses of the latter and of the Caliphate are accounted for by the Central Asian territories east of Iran.

nominally centralized. In both, political power resided in a narrow ruling stratum consisting of a standing army and professional bureaucracy headed by an absolute monarch, and sharply distinguished from the subject masses. Both, finally, were Islamic, so that like the Caliphate, the Ottoman Sultanate had to come to terms with an extremely influential religious establishment, to cope with social grievances dressed up as religious dissent, and above all, to exercise that bisected authority expressed as *sharia vis-à-vis mazalim*, or (in the Ottoman case) *sheriat vis-à-vis* the *kanun*.

But within this broad framework the differences between the two polities were very striking indeed. The Ottoman Empire was much more linguistically, religiously, and ethnically heterogeneous; hence one of its most characteristic—and successful—institutions, the *millet* system of communal autonomies. Next, the Ruling Institution's soldiers and bureaucrats were the sultan's slaves and furthermore, till mid-seventeenth century, the élite among them were not ordinary slaves but specially recruited and trained non-Turkish ones! But in contradistinction to this, the military and civil administration of many of the provinces and the supply of the empire's cavalry forces rested on the sultan's granting fiefs (*timars*) in return for military service. This Ruling Institution was the lay power. The Religious Institution at its side consisted, unprecedentedly for Islam, in a religious hierarchy of *ulema*, which one might almost call a quasi-church. This religious hierarchy provided the empire with its local administrators, the *kadis*, who, unlike in the Abbasid Caliphate, indifferently administered both the *sheriat* (Turkish for *sharia*) and the sultan's secular *örf* (his prerogative power) especially as codified in his *kanuns*—the latter being one of the Ottomans' greatest and most beneficial innovations.[2]

In addition, a professional and trained bureaucracy was so firmly entrenched that it kept the empire going despite degenerate sultans, incompetent ministers, harem intrigues, military mutinies, and depositions, all of which increasingly troubled the government after the death of Suleiman in 1566. Alongside this civil establishment, the vast and warlike military forces again and again proved able, despite a decline in their training and discipline after 1600, to see off the empire's increasingly powerful European foes. So, despite the misgovernment, maladministration, corruption, and impoverishment that set in after 1600, the Ottoman Empire repeatedly staged

---

[2] The fact that the *kadi* courts applied both the *sheriat* and the *kanun* (for which see pp. 1197–8 below) did not, however, dispose of the inherent incongruity between political need and religiously inspired jurisprudence: so that although the *kadi* courts did not have to share jurisdiction with *mazalim* courts as under the Abbasids, they were nevertheless encroached on by the summary jurisdiction of governors and other administrators in the provinces—so that the old problem resurfaced in this new form.

astonishing recoveries. This massive and protracted durability stands in marked contrast to the fragility of the Arab Caliphate. And this leads to the final point of contrast between the two polities: warfare.

The Caliphate's phase of active warfare, which began in 632, reached its term under al-Mansur (754–75) and thenceforward settled down to increasingly routine raid and counter raid across the Byzantine frontier. Apart from these formidable but defensively inclined Byzantines, the Caliphate had no great powers to face. It was far otherwise with the Ottoman Empire. To the East it found a ready and equal opponent in the revived Safavid (and Shiite) Empire of Persia. To the West it faced European powers whose technological edge and financial resources were increasing all the time, and a vast new opponent was arising to its north in the shape of Russia. The empire engaged in aggressive warfare on all these fronts. If one divides 1400–1789 into three periods, the Ottoman Empire is in every case one of the four most warlike states. Between 1400 and 1559 it was, like the Holy Roman Empire, engaged in 114 years of warfare—72 per cent of the entire period. From 1559 to 1648 it ranks just behind Spain's eighty-three years of war (or 74 per cent of the total period), with seventy-nine years of war (70 per cent of the entire period). And from 1648 to 1789 it ranks equally with its adversaries Russia and Austria, with seventy-seven years of warfare, 55 per cent of the total period. Out of the 389 years between 1400 and 1789, it was engaged in war for 270: an average of seven years in every ten.[3]

2. CHRONOLOGY

The Turks have already appeared in this history, as the slave troops of the Caliphate who ended up by taking it over, and again, as the Oghuz tribesmen who established the Seljuk Empire in Anatolia after their victory at Manzikert. This empire collapsed after the Mongol victory at Kösedag in 1243, and powerful nomadic Turkish tribes—Turcomans—fled ever-westward through the enfeebled remains of the Seljuk Empire to reform on the mountainous regions of western Anatolia which formed the frontier with the shrunken Byzantine Empire. In search of new lands and booty the leaders of these Turcoman populations incited them to *jihad* against the Christians and built up marcher lordships. In preference to the term *jihad* the Turks used *ghaza*, 'a campaign or raid in the cause of Islam'. One who undertook a *ghaza* was termed a *ghazi*. Osman Ghazi (1299–1326) created a

---

[3] Figures derived from E. Luard, *War in International Society* (Tauris, London, 1986), ch. 2, and app. 1–3. The calculations for the Ottoman Empire are probably underestimates—it is unclear whether they have given due weight to the Asian campaigns. On my own count, derived from Luard's tables (pp. 421–34), the total is 303.

lordship in the lands closest to the city of Byzantium and the Balkans. This Osman is the founder of the Ottoman Empire. 'Osman' is the Turkish pronunciation of the Arabic *Uthman*, whence 'Ottoman'. It is probable that Osman's original name was the purely Turkish 'Toman', which was piously assimilated to the name of the third caliph.

From that point on the story up to 1566 is one of campaigns that swung alternately against the European and Christian north-west and the Turkish and Muslim south-east. Victories over the European armies at Nicopolis (1395) and Varna (1444) guaranteed the annexation of the Balkans. The spectacular capture of Constantinople in 1453 supplied the symbolic as well as the geographical link between the two distinct lobes of the empire—on the one side Christian Europe, on the other Muslim Anatolia. And the third great event is the defeat of the Mamluks in 1517, whereby the empire came to embrace not only the North African coast and the whole of Egypt, but all the Arab lands of the Middle East, including—of the utmost importance— the Holy Places of Mecca and Medina. Thus the Arab, the Turkish, and the south-east European worlds were united under a single diadem. And sub-sequently the empire came to expand even beyond these areas: into Roma-nia, Hungary, Podolia, and the Crimea.

The empire lived by war and off war. So it seems wisest to preface this chronology with a list of the major wars.

THE PRINCIPAL WARS OF THE OTTOMAN EMPIRE*

1399–1401	Byzantium
1400–02	The Mongols
1413–21	Wallachia, Bosnia, Hungary, Venice, Serbia (from 1419)
1422	Byzantium
1429–40	Serbia, Greece, Venice, Hungary
1442–8	The Papacy, Hungary, Poland, Lithuania
1443–61	The Albanians
1452–3	Byzantium
1455–64	Serbia, Hungary, Bosnia, Wallachia, Athens, Morea, Greek Islands
1461	Trebizond
1463–79	Venice, Albania
1463–70	Persia
1470	Karaman (Anatolia)
1475–6	Moldavia, Crimea
1478–9	Albania, Ionian Islands
1480	Naples (Otranto)
1481–3	Hungary
1485–9	Moldavia, the Tartars, Poland
1485–90	Egypt (Cilicia)

1492–5	Bohemia, Hungary
1497–9,	Poland, Moldavia, the Tartars
1499–1503	The Papacy, Hungary, Venice
1509	Egypt, the Knights of Malta
1514–16	Persia
1516–17	Syria, Egypt
1521–3	Hungary, Venice, Rhodes
1525	The Yemen
1528–9	Persia
1537–40	Algiers, Venice, the Emperor
1538	Moldavia
1538	Aden
1541–7	The Emperor, Transylvania
1548–54	Persia
1551–62	The Emperor
1559–64	Spain, Venice
1565	Malta, Spain
1566–8	The Emperor
1569	Russia (Astrakhan)
1570–8	The Papacy, Venice (till 1573), Spain
1576	The Hejaz
1578–90	Persia
1593–1606	The Papacy, the Emperor, the Tartars
1603–12	Persia
1615–18	Persia
1616–17	Poland
1620–1	Poland, the Emperor, Transylvania, the Tartars
1623–31	Persia
1625–7	Poland, Hungary, the Tartars
1631–4	Poland, Hungary, the Tartars
1635	The Yemen
1644–69	Venice
1658–61	Poland, Transylvania, the Tartars
1663–4	Austria
1672–6	Poland, the Tartars, the Cossacks
1677–81	Russia, the Cossacks
1682–99	Austria, German states, Poland, Venice, Russia (from 1685)
1710–13	Russia
1714–18	Venice, Austria (from 1716)
1722–4	Persia
1725–6,	Afghanistan
1729–30	Afghanistan
1729–36	Persia
1734–9	Russia, Austria (from 1737)

1768–74   Russia
1787–92   Russia, Austria
(* Derived from Luard, *War in International Society,* 421–34)

GENERAL CHRONOLOGY

1261–1310   Foundation of the *gazi* principalities in Western Anatolia, including Osmanli (Ottoman)
1326   Capture of Bursa
1326   Death of OSMAN. Accession of ORHAN
1331   Capture of Nicaea
1354   Capture of Gallipoli and of Ankara
1361   Capture of Adrianople (Edirne)
1362   MURAT I
1389   Serbia crushed at Battle of Kossovo
1389   BAYAZIT I (*Yildirim*—'The Thunderbolt')
1389–1402   Alternating seizures of territory in Balkans and Anatolia
1394–1402   Blockade of Constantinople
1396   The European states smashed at Nicopolis. Further conquests in Balkans and central Anatolia
1402   Bayazit defeated and captured by Timur at Battle of Ankara
1402–13   First Civil War: between Bayazit's four sons
1413   MEHMET I
1421   MURAT II
1421–2   Second civil war against his brother Mustafa
1422   Siege of Constantinople
1440   Failure to take Belgrade
1444   Decisive defeat of Europeans at Varna: the definitive conquest of the Balkans
1444   Abdication of Murat: accession then deposition of Mehmet II
1444–51   Second reign of Murat II
1451–81   MEHMET II, 'the Conqueror'. Seizes Constantinople, 1453; adds Trebizond, Karaman (Eastern Anatolia), Morea, Albania, Bosnia, and Wallachia to empire
1481–1512   BAYAZIT II. Third Civil War, against his brother Jem
1495   Death of Jem
1512   Deposition of Bayazit II, accession of SELIM I, 'the Grim'
1517   Defeat of the Mamluks; the conquest of Egypt. Submission of the sheriff of Mecca
1520   Death of Selim I
1520–66   SULEIMAN 'the Magnificent'. The conqueror of, *inter alia,* Hungary and Rhodes; besieges Vienna (1529), takes Tunis (1533), Transylvania. 'The Law Giver'—codifies the *kanun*, reforms judicial system. The empire at its height
1566–74   SELIM, 'The Sot'

1570	Conquest of Cyprus
1571	Major naval defeat at Lepanto, but rapid naval recovery
1574–95	MURAT III
1595–1603	MEHMET III. Shah Abbas of Persia defeats Ottomans at Lake Urmia, takes Iraq and Baghdad
1603–17	AHMET I
1617–18	MUSTAFA I. Deposed
1618–22	OSMAN II. Deposed (strangled, 1622)
1622–3	Mustafa I restored then deposed
1623–40	MURAT IV, 11 years old at accession, faces Janissary mutinies, unrest. Later, ruthless suppression of Janissaries, purge of administration
1625	New uprisings ferociously suppressed
1638	Recapture of Baghdad, Treaty of Kasr-i-Shirin establishes permanent frontier with Persia. Reorganization of the *timars*, efforts to reduce Janissary numbers and reform army. From now on the *devshirme* becomes increasingly sporadic (the last recorded cull took place in 1704)
1640–8	IBRAHIM. Insane. Deposed (executed 1648)
1648–87	MEHMET IV. Aged 6 at accession. Anarchic conditions
1656	Venetians at Dardanelles
1656–61	Mehmet Köprülü, grand vizier, ruthless administrator: curbs Janissaries, purges court, raises taxes, confiscates property, beats off Venetians
1661–78	Ahmet Köprülü (son of Mehmet), grand vizier
1664	Signal defeat by Austrian general, Montecucculi, at St Gotthard
1669	Final conquest of Crete from Venice
1672–6	Conquests in Podolia and Polish Ukraine, hence first contacts with Russia
1678	Kara Mustafa, brother-in-law of Ahmet Köprülü, grand vizier
1683	Vienna besieged. Unsuccessful
1687	Second Battle of Mohacs. Ottomans defeated by Charles of Lorraine. Panic in Istanbul. Deposition of Mehmet IV
1687–91	SULEIMAN III
1689–91	Mustafa Köprülü, grand vizier. Great military and fiscal reforms. The *timar* system revived
1691–5	AHMET II
1691	Mustafa Köprülü defeated and killed at Slankamen
1695–1703	MUSTAFA II
1697	Eugene of Savoy defeats Ottomans at Zenta
1699	Treaty of Karlowitz. Ottomans cede Hungary, Transylvania, Croatia, and Slavonia, the Morea, Podolia. Reforming grand vizier, Huseyin Pasha (of the Köprülü family), opposed by the Sheikh-ul-Islam, dies 1702. Troops mutiny. The Edirne Incident. Mustafa deposed

1703–30	AHMET III. Luxurious court life: the 'Tulip period'
1730	Defeat by Nadir Shah of Persia. Mass riots in Istanbul. Sultan abdicates
1730–54	MAHMUT I. A relatively peaceful period. Cultural progress under Grand Vizier Ragib Pasha (1757–63). Weakening central hold on provinces: the rise of the *derebeys* in Anatolia
1754–7	OSMAN III
1757–74	MUSTAFA III
1774	Treaty of Küqük Kaynarja. The victorious Russians secure right to navigate the Black Sea

3. SUMMARY OVERVIEW OF THE OTTOMAN POLITY, *c*.1600

The empire consisted of the following territories: south-east Europe from the Aegean to the Dniester and the Bug rivers; the Black Sea, which was a Turkish lake, for it was enclosed by the tributary lands of the Crimean Khanate in the north and the Straits of Constantinople in the south; the Anatolian heartland, stretching eastwards as far as Kars and Lake Van; and the Arabic-speaking lands of the ancient Caliphate, stretching from the frontiers of Persia down through Egypt and along the entire North African coast.

Its territorial units were not uniform. On the European marchlands lay various Christian tributary states with their own rulers but under the obligation to obey and to pay tribute. Certain other lands were ruled by governors who paid a fixed sum to Istanbul and kept the remaining revenues for their local administration. These were called *salyane* provinces. Here policing, tax-assessment, and collection were carried out directly by the government, unlike the remaining and by far most numerous group of units, called *beylerbeyliks* at this time, and later, *eyalets*. The governor of such a province was called a *beylerbeyi*, with the rank of pasha. Military, security, and fiscal arrangements of the *beylerbeyliks* were quite otherwise than in the *salyane* provinces. Here the land was parcelled out into so many fiefs, called *timars*, and the fief-holder (or *timariot*) gave military service in return for the product of his fief, wherein he collected the taxes, maintained security, and administered low justice. For judicial purposes, provinces were divided into *kadas*, so called because they were the jurisdictions of a *kadi*; and a kadi was effectively more a local administrator than a judicial magistrate.

In all provinces without exception all officials and *timariots*, and so on, were appointed and dismissed by the central government. This was absolutely in the hands of the sultan, who stood at the head of the so-called Ruling Institution and, in a manner of speaking, at the head of the ecclesiastical hierarchy also. The Ruling Institution consisted of all who served the sultan officially; and in civil law they were his *kul*, his slaves, which meant in effect that they had no personal or property rights against him. The Ruling Institution comprised an administrative group of top officials under the sultan's grand vizier; a numerous secretarial group, the civil service; and the third component consisted of the *askeris*, the soldiers, the 'Men of the Sword' as against the 'Men of the Pen'. These fell into two categories: first, the *timariot* levies who received no pay and were only called out in wartime. The second were dubbed 'slaves of the Palace', and formed a standing force of cavalry and, far more numerous, infantry, known as the Janissaries. These troops, who were paid and quartered in barracks, formed the *corps d'élite.*

This narrow Ruling Institution was sharply distinguished from the commonalty, known as the *re'aya* ('the flock'), and its most remarkable characteristic was that all its senior officials, the upper civil service and the palatine Janissaries and *sipah*, were not merely slaves: they were not, nor could they be, Turks! Ethnically, they were aliens. They were recruited either via the regular slave markets or through the peculiar Ottoman institution of the *devshirme*. This was a levy, or cull, of the infant males of Christian families, who were carried off to the capital to be raised as Muslims and trained as soldiers or civil officials. The Ruling Institution was, in fact, a corps of alien slaves.

Side by side with this Ruling Institution went the so-called Religious Institution. Popular Islam was to be found in the numerous *tarikats* (religious orders) and among holy men who raised a sect, often in opposition to the government; but unlike the Caliphate, the Ottomans created an official Muslim hierarchy, headed by the Sheikh-ul-Islam who, along with all the lesser posts, was appointed—and dismissed—by the sultan. Entrance to and promotion in this hierarchy, which alone gave access to the office of *kadi*, required passing a series of increasingly demanding examinations in government-established *medreses*.

Ottoman government was conspicuously shallow in its penetration of everyday life—more so than most agrarian empires. Its role was to make war, acquire plunder, slaves, and revenues, raise taxes, and keep order. It was, in short, predator, revenue-pump, and policeman. The villagers and towns-folk lived out their lives through all kinds of private religious, commercial, and industrial corporations and it was through their leaders that the public authorities made its limited contacts with them. For the rest, Islam took meticulous care of the domestic life of two-thirds of the empire's popula-tions, while the Orthodox Christians, the Jews, and the Armenians respec-tively composed three autonomous, self-governing communities called *millets*, headed by their own religious leader who was responsible for fiscal and public-order matters. For the rest, the *millets* were free to look after themselves.

4. THE 'RULING INSTITUTION'

4.1. *The Sultan*

4.1.1. THE KEY INSTITUTION

The sultan was the head and source of all authority. The Ruling Institution depended absolutely on him, unless, that is, his duties were discharged by his deputy, the grand vizier. The classic example is the rescue and resuscitation of the empire by the gifted Köprülü dynasty of grand viziers (1656–91). But a sultan was always free to dispense with his vizier's advice—or even have him strangled. It is significant that legend says that Mehmet Köprülü, the restorer of the empire in 1656, exacted a pledge from the sultan that he would have a completely free hand and no interference. Another difficulty was that it required a sultan to be a good picker. That depended on his character and training. These in turn were related to the mode of succession.

4.1.2. TRAINING AND SUCCESSION

Remarkably, the dynasty of Osman ruled for almost 650 years (1281–1924) in unbroken succession in the male line, with never a suggestion that it should be removed or supplanted until Atatürk in 1923. What makes this even more remarkable is that there was no law or custom regulating the succession. The view was that since this lay in the hands of God it would be impious for mortals to establish a fixed rule.[4] In the event, the prince who got to the capital, seized the treasury, and won over the support of the Janissaries and the *ulema* was proclaimed sultan. The result of a civil war was regarded as a divine decree, akin to the rationale of the western 'trial by battle'.[5]

But the way the first ten sultans came to the throne was quite different from that of their successors. They were formidably able characters, active both in war and administration. Their successors, on the other hand, were, with two or three exceptions, grotesque failures and the reason lies in a change in the mode of accession.

At first, following tradition, the sultan's sons were sent to be governors in the old administrative capitals of Anatolia and there learned something of administration. Since the succession was open, they often engaged in civil

---

[4] It may be remembered that the Byzantines believed—or professed to believe—the same thing. See Bk. III, Pt. 1, Ch. I.

[5] Admittedly, largely obsolete in the 13th cent. but last used (successfully) in England in 1818, and not abolished there till the following year!

wars. The one that followed the death of Bayazit I involved four brothers and lasted eleven years. It was to prevent this that Mehmet II, the Conqueror, enacted the notorious 'Law of Fratricide'. 'For the welfare of the state, the one of my sons to whom God grants the Sultanate may lawfully put his brothers to death. A majority of the *ulema* consider this permissible.'[6] Murat III had his five brothers strangled and Mehmet III ordered the execution of nineteen brothers, two sons, and—so it is said—fifteen slave-women made pregnant by his father.[7] But from the early seventeenth century this ceased to be the rule and princes were instead confined to the Fourth Court of the Topkapi Palace, known by an expression as unpleasant as were their dwellings, namely, the *kafes*, 'the cage'.[8] There they languished all their lives as prisoners: forbidden to have children, knowing little or nothing of the outside world, and receiving no instruction in what might turn out to be their royal duties.

The effect of this treatment on the character and competence of the sultans was disastrous. For one thing, it meant that no sultan had children until after his accession, so that many were minors when he died. (In many cases the confinement had sapped their virility and made them incapable of generating children at all.) For another, these princes received no worthwhile instruction during their confinement and, certainly, no training in statecraft or administration. Many, when they acceded, were psychopathological cases.[9] Whatever the faults of their predecessors, they had won the throne through practising to be sultans and then conquering in the field. There were great exceptions like the energetic and ruthless Murat IV, but the generality of the post-1600 sultans were effete and degenerate incompetents, and characteristically no longer led their armies in battle. The more marked their insufficiency, the more the sense of power grew among their entourage of court cliques, Janissaries, and *ulema*.

4.1.3. THE NATURE OF SULTANIC ABSOLUTISM

The sultan was 'absolute'—but in the Islamic sense already encountered in the Caliphate. He could do all things not expressly forbidden by the *sharia*, a convenient formula which effectively gave him free reign in the spheres of

---

[6] Quoted in H. Inalcik, *The Ottoman Empire: The Classical Age, 1300–1600* (Weidenfeld and Nicholson, London, 1973), 59.

[7] D. Alderson, *The Structure of the Ottoman Dynasty* (Clarendon Press, Oxford, 1956), 31. Interestingly, he suggests that the extent of the practice has perhaps been exaggerated in the West. Did Europeans baulk at the practice (for which there were many European precedents), or at its legalization? After all, he pleads, over the 650-year span of the dynasty there were only 80 such executions (p. 27).

[8] Cf. N. M. Penzer, *The Harem: An Account of the Institution as it Existed in the Palace of the Turkish Sultan, with a History of the Grand Seraglio from its Foundations to Modern Times* (Spring Books, London, 1965) for descriptions. Penzer himself calls the *kafes* the 'Princes' Prison'.   [9] Alderson, *Structure*, 33–4.

what we should regard as the 'political' and made even wider in that, just as in the Caliphate, the jurists were not averse from 'bending' the *sharia* to fit the rulers' reasons of state and, as Sunnis, preached total passive obedience to them however mad or bad they were. However, the line between a greater or a lesser latitude was not fixed but jerked to and fro by fits and starts. This was due in general to the relationship of sultanic legislation to the *sharia*, and in particular to the Sultan's relationship to the ecclesiastical hierarchy and particularly to its head, the Sheikh-ul-Islam.

More will be said, later, about the general relationship of sultanic legislation to the *sharia* but let it suffice for now that the Turkish tradition was to act by fixed laws. Hence, in their prerogative sphere sultans issued laws they called *kanun* (derived from the Greek, *canon*) and many of them conflicted with the *sharia* but nevertheless went unchallenged by the *ulema*. This was because a sultan rarely did anything important without first requiring an opinion from the Sheikh ul-Islam, who delivered it in the form of a *fetva*. Usually a Sheikh ul-Islam would anticipate his sovereign's wishes and issue a *fetva* in accordance with them. However, with a weak sultan and an arrogant sheikh the situation could be reversed. Powerful monarchs like Mehmet II and Suleiman the Magnificent had no difficulty in handling their Sheikhs ul-Islam. Thus, in the Edirne Incident of 1703, the sheikh got rid of the grand vizier and established himself as the sultan's supreme counsellor—in which capacity, we might add, he provoked a riot and a military revolt which resulted in him being executed and the sultan being deposed. On the other hand, when a Sheikh ul-Islam contradicted Murat IV, the latter had him strangled. The influence of the Sheikh ul-Islam was episodic, but the supremacy of the *Kanun*, generally speaking, over religious objections was the normal state of affairs.

Within these limits the sultan was supreme. The most extreme expression of this supremacy lay in his absolute power to appoint and dismiss officials. He could make, pick, and choose his Sheikh ul-Islam (just as the Byzantine emperors had been able to select complaisant patriarchs), and he wielded in the most capricious way a literally despotic power over the life, liberty, and property of all his officials since they all were his *kul*—his slaves. And it should be remarked at once that this latter power was no dead letter. On the contrary, sultans exercised it to the full.[10]

[10] This aspect of Ottoman government enormously impressed Rycaut: 'the absoluteness of an Emperour without reason, without virtue, whose speeches may be irrational and yet must be laws; whose actions irregular, and yet examples; whose sentence and judgement, in matters of Imperial concernment, are most commonly corrupt, and yet decrees irreversible . . . When I consider . . . how men are raised at once by adulation, chance and the sole favour of the Prince, without any title of noble blood, or the motives of previous deserts, or former testimonies and experience of parts or

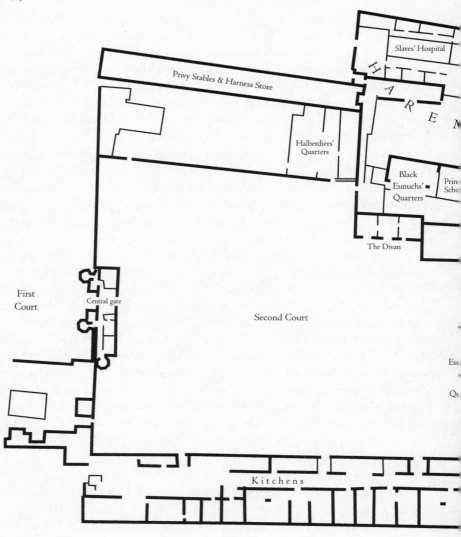

They had to, if they were to translate their political absolutism into practice. To exercise the unfettered sway that was his right, a sultan had to negotiate a difficult passage past several dangerous obstacles. There were the court factions, in which the harem came to play an increasing role from the

abilities, to the weightiest, the richest, and the most honourable charges of the Empire; when I consider how short their continuance is in them, how with one frown of the Prince they are cut off . . .' Sir Paul Rycaut, *An English Consul in Turkey: Paul Rycaut at Smyrna, 1667–1678* (Clarendon Press, Oxford, 1972), 2.

Royal
Saloon

The
Cage

New Library

Royal
Chamber

Third Court

Hall
of the
Treasury

Chamber of the
Chief Physician

Third gate

Fourth Court

0   30   60   90   120 ft

The Topkapi Palace

reign of Suleiman the Magnificent onward; the Janissaries, who had to be placated with victories and booty and 'accession money'; the *ulema*, since they had a great influence on the mob; and this itself, ever ready to riot in the capital. And in the provinces there were frequent disturbances or rebellions where a religious preacher capitalized on the discontent that was rarely far from the surface. The first ten sultans, strong-minded men and successful war-leaders, with full treasuries and an ever-expanding empire, were able to surmount all such obstacles. But with the onset of economic and military decline in the seventeenth century, the obstacles just enumerated became more and more destabilizing at the very time when the institution of the *kafes* had sapped the sultans' mental and physical capabilities.

4.1.4. THE PALACE AND THE ROUTINE POLITICAL PROCESS

The sultan lived secluded in the Inner Palace.[11] Here were situated his Privy Chambers, along with the Privy Purse and Wardrobe offices that pertained to them. The harem was adjacent. Here too lay the chambers where embassies were received, or the Imperial Divan held its meetings. Connecting this Inner Palace to the Outer Palace was the Gate of Felicity, a spacious vestibule where the sultan met with his vizier and dispensed justice. This Outer Palace housed the *agha* (the commandant) of the Janissaries, and the 'Gardener corps' who policed the grounds, along with various groups of messengers and the like. It contained offices for those personnel who served both the administration of the empire and the palace: for instance, the chief architect and his staff, the commissioners of the mint, and the sultan's physician, who was also the head of the medical profession through the empire. All these officials of the Inner and Outer palace formed a single complex and highly regulated hierarchy. This vast corps, which numbered some 30,000 civilian personnel in 1609 as well as 60,000 military or military-related men, accompanied the sultan on campaigns.

Routine decision-taking and administration lay with the sultan, the grand vizier, and the *Divan-i Humayun*, the Imperial Council. The Divan was, essentially, a court of justice: anyone, regardless of his status, could petition it directly and the investigation of complaints and rectification of grievances was considered to be its most important duty. Often subjects sent delegations to the Divan. The Divan also acted as a court of appeal from the sentence of a local *kadi*. When original petitions came to it, it sent the *sharia* issues to the *kadis*, and the others to the appropriate member of the Divan or other relevant minister. After 1475 the sultan merely watched over the proceedings from a listening-window[12] and later, when this practice itself had disappeared, authority to review grievances passed to the grand vizier. Then, after the session, the sultan came down and met the Divan members in the Gate of Felicity in order to review and approve their decisions.[13]

---

[11] See the Plan of the Topkapi Palace, derived from S. J. Shaw, *History of the Ottoman Empire and Modern Turkey*, vol. 1 (CUP, Cambridge, 1976), 116. Penzer, *Harem*, gives a splendid description of the palace, and his plan (reproduced here) shows the very various categories of individuals who lived in it.
[12] Inalcik, *Ottoman Empire*, 91–3.   [13] Ibid. 92.

But the Divan was also the grand vizier's advisory council. The Code (*kanunname*) of Mehmet II ran: 'The Grand Vizier is the head of the viziers and commanders. He is greater than all men; he is in all matters the Sultan's absolute deputy. The *defterdar* is deputy to the Treasury, but under the supervision of the Grand Vizier.'[14] The lesser viziers, the governors (*beylerbeyi*s) and the military commanders all had to put their petitions through the grand vizier, who either handled them himself or put them to the sultan. No appointments were made but were submitted to him first. He was authorized to take independent action on a wide range of important issues. Often the grand vizier led the army on campaign and it was then that his powers were at their height, for he could take decisions without consulting the sultan and make appointments and dismissals at will.

For all that, his authority was not unchecked. Before making important decisions he was under an absolute duty to consult the other Divan members. Again, the heads of the financial and judicial branches made their own appointments. Though he supervised the *defterdar* (treasurer), only the latter could authorize payments.[15] The commander of the Janissaries and the grand admiral were appointed directly by the sultan. Nevertheless his authority was immense: he had the right to supervise and direct all departments, control all appointments and dismissals, and countersign any order of the sultan. It became a convention that the sultan would never reject any decisions made by the Divan which the grand vizier had himself confirmed. Under autocratic and masterful sultans like Selim the Grim or Mehmet II or Suleiman, the grand viziers took a back seat. But under weaker monarchs they could attain virtually dictatorial powers, like the Köprülü dynasty of viziers mentioned above.[16]

The Divan consisted of any officials the vizier cared to convene, but always contained the two *kadiaskers* (representing the judiciary) and the *nishanji* (as head of the Chancery); including the vizier, these men were styled the four 'Pillars of the Realm'. One would usually expect, also, some of the more important *beylerbeyi*s who held the rank of pasha with three horse-tails (the highest number carried on a pasha's standard; the grand vizier's had five, the sultan's seven), the *agha* of the Janissaries, and the grand admiral. The head of the scribal corporation (the *reis ul-kuttab*) and the chief translator also attended the Divan and could participate but not vote.[17]

Of course, the petitions on which the Divan's decisions were founded did not spring straight out of its members' heads by any means; for the most part, they would have emanated from or at least been processed and advised

[14] Ibid. 94.   [15] Ibid. 94–5.   [16] Ibid. 95–7.
[17] Shaw, *History of the Ottoman Empire*, 118.

on by their respective departments, as will be seen in the later section on the structure of the administration.

4.1.5. THE PATHOLOGY OF THE POLITICAL PROCESS

A pathological kind of politics was played out by such as the court cliques of vizier families and their rivals, harem factions, Janissaries and *timariot*, *sipahis*, the *ulema*, the street, and populist religious revivalists and dervishes and their followings in the countryside. Their methods ranged over military mutiny, street riots, religious demagogy and casuistical *fetvas*, court and harem intrigues and conspiracies, and quasi-religious uprisings. They were prompted by the power vacuum at the end of a reign or by some disaster, usually a military one, in the course of a reign. The motivations might be purely personal, like harem rivalries between the various mothers of the sultan's sons, but they relied on—or were used by—wider forces. These were roughly of three kinds: one variety was the popular and quasi-religious rebellion against oppression, another the rivalry between the old Anatolian barons and the new ex-Christian *devshirme* elements, and a third was the Janissaries' determination to preserve and expand their privileges and also improve their donatives and chances of booty. The influence of the principal actors waxed or waned over time; so did motivations and preoccupations; and as they changed, so did political alliances. To disentangle all these elements in the situation and to illustrate them would effectively be to write the political history of the empire.

We are, it must be remembered, describing conditions in the mid-sixteenth century and so we must stress that the confusion did not reach major proportions until the seventeenth century and after. This is because the *kafes*, in so far as it imprisoned all the possible successors inside the Fourth Court, had transferred the choice of sultan from the battlefield to the palace. The influence of harem women may indeed be said to have begun in Suleiman's reign, under the influence of his Russian-born wife Hürrem Sultan (Roxelana). It is widely believed, and very likely true, that it was she who engineered the disgrace and execution of the brilliant and energetic Italian-born Ibrahim, the sultan's second self, and later convinced Suleiman that his heir (by another wife) was a traitor and contrived the latter's execution to open the succession for her own sons. But we have to wait till the career of Kösem Sultan (d. 1651) to savour the fullness of harem intrigue. Widow of Ahmet I and mother of his sons Murat (later Murat IV) and Ibrahim (later Sultan Ibrahim), this extraordinary woman manipulated the succession, helped put Ahmet I's brother Mustafa on the throne, and went on to dominate his reign, then the early part of that of her son, Murat IV, then that of the mad Ibrahim, his brother, and finally, when her 6-year-old grandson Mehmet IV acceded, tried to poison him and bring about the enthronement of his madman cousin, Suleiman. Characteristically for such harem brawls, Kösem's plot was anticipated by her daughter-in-law, the mother of the child sultan. She, equally characteristically, managed to have the old lady strangled.[18]

Similarly, although Selim the Sot allowed himself to be blackmailed into giving 'accession money' to the Janissaries to secure their support and so set the precedent for their direct involvement in the succession struggles, one must wait until 1622 before witnessing the deposition of a sultan, and the riots and sack of the capital; and till 1648–51 for the anarchy to be so bad as to earn the title 'the Sultanate of Aghas'.[19]

The ulema had certainly been influential in politics before Suleiman created the post of Sheikh ul-Islam. Thereafter, though the sheikh's fetva was always sought by sultans in order to legitimize their actions, it was also sought and sometimes received by their enemies for the selfsame reason. For instance, in the case of the execution of Kösem Sultan cited above, the conspirators went to her armed with the sheikh's fetva. It is easy to see that in disordered times the sheikhs' influence would be at a premium, but we repeat what was said earlier: that sultans could dismiss the sheikh and, indeed, go further. 'When Sheikh ul-Islam Ahi zâde Hüseyin Efendi protested, Murat IV had him dismissed and then strangled (1633), doing away with ulema and bureaucrats alike whenever they resisted his orders or were accused of misdeeds.' Murat even ordered the execution of the kadi of Istanbul, one of the greatest scholars of the day, on the grounds that he was responsible for the shortage of butter in the capital!'[20]

These fragmentary examples may serve to indicate the kind of persons involved in high palace-politics under the kafes regime, and how they seem motivated by self-interest alone. But we are interested in the classical period, when the rival princes fought it out between themselves, and here it is indeed possible to detect an underlying rationale: this was the rivalry between the Turcoman notables and the Palatine personnel—first the kapikulu troops, then the Janissaries, and finally the devshirme class as a whole. It was to counteract the power of those notables, which was waxing greatly

---

[18] Her story is told in detail and with great drama by Paul Rycaut, secretary to the British ambassador at the court of Mehmet IV (Rycaut, English Consul in Turkey, ch. 4). The old woman was over 80 and toothless to boot, but she struggled to the end. She drove off her first strangler by biting his thumb. Thereupon four other executioners set on her, and finally left her for dead. But she was not. As they moved off she she began to move her head. They ran back and finished her off by twisting the cord around her neck with the haft of a hatchet.

[19] Shaw, History of the Ottoman Empire, 192–3, 196, 203–4.

[20] Ibid. 198. The kadi was spared only by the intercession of the queen-mother.

as a result of the fiefs and plunder they were receiving from the conquests, that Murat I began creating a personal guard of Christian vassal soldiers and *kapikullari* converts. It is then that he went on to introduce the *devshirme*. As this consisted of Europeans, it came into conflict with the Turcoman notables over the theatre of war—Anatolia (as the *devshirme* wanted) or Europe (as the Turcoman notables wanted); over peace or war (usually the *devshirme* and the frontier lords were the war party and the Anatolian notables the peace party); over the format of the army—infantry armed with firearms and artillery (the *devshirme*), or light cavalry, *sipahis* (mostly Turcoman); and finally, over access to the civil bureaucracy and the vizier-ship itself. Here the notables regarded themselves as the 'natural' counsellors of the sultan and the *devshirme* as 'new men'. When civil war broke out between the princes at each vacancy of the throne, the *devshirme* followed one and the notables would follow the other. In the struggles to succeed Bayazit I, Mehmet I owed his throne to the Anatolian notables and their leading family, the Chandarlis. The Chandarli family, in point of fact, well illustrates the hold these Turcoman oligarchs had on the central administration: the viziership of Kara Halil Chandarli under Murat I passed from father to son for the next four generations, up to 1453.

Under the young Mehmet II the last Chandarli vizier opposed the siege of Constantinople which was being pressed by the sultan's former tutor, the Greek Zaganos. After the city fell Mehmet had Chandarli executed and made Zaganos vizier in his place: and so, for the first time, the *devshirme* was seizing the high ground in the civil bureaucracy. When Suleiman appointed his bosom friend, the Italian-born Ibrahim, as grand vizier it was emblematic of the triumph of the *devshirme* class in both the military and civil spheres.

The course of events as depicted above is reflected in the incidence of depositions. In the period up to 1618, there were only three, and the first does not really count, but from 1622 to 1730 (i.e. 108 years) there were seven, as shown in Table 4.3.1.

These depositions call to mind those of the Byzantine emperors. True, they are less frequent, since they occur at about half the rate of the Byzantine ones; but the reasons for them—military failure—and the court intrigues that preceded them do indeed have a familiar ring. The greatest difference between the two situations is that in Byzantium the depositions frequently marked a change of dynasty, whereas the house of Osman, as we have already pointed out, continued to hold the Sultanate from the beginning to the very end of the empire. Yet the two situations were similar in this: although the throne might totter, the regime never budged an inch. And the principal reason for this in both cases was the existence of a well-

TABLE 4.3.1. *Depositions of Ottoman Sultans, 1402–1730*

Sultan	Date	Details
Bayazit I	1402	By Timur—defeat.
Mehmet II	1446	By (Turcoman) viziers and Janissaries as being too junior to rescue the empire. Re-accession, five years later.
Bayazit II	1512	By son Selim and Janissaries; military failure.
Mustafa I	1618	By viziers: for insanity. Re-accession four years later.
	1623	By viziers; for insanity; survived sixteen years.
Osman II	1622	By Janissaries; for opposition to their corps. Murdered one day afterwards.
Ibrahim	1648	By popular riots and palace intrigues; for debauchery and military failure. Murdered twenty days later.
Mehmet IV	1687	By viziers; for military failure. Survived five years.
Mustafa II	1703	By viziers; for military failures: 'Edirne Incident'.
Ahmet III	1730	By a demagogue, Patrona Halil, and the army; for westernization, idle luxury, and military failure. (The reaction to the 'Tulip Period'.) Survived six years.

Source: Alderson, *Structure of the Ottoman Dynasty,* 76.

trained, professional civil service. It is one of the chief reasons, possibly the most important one, for the longevity of the Ottoman Empire.

4.2. *The Bureaucracy*

4.2.1. THE DEPARTMENTAL STRUCTURE

The layout of the central departments derived from Seljuk times and before. It is of little interest compared with the way in which its personnel were recruited and trained. But since this bureaucracy was essential to the empire's survival, a brief summary of its major dispositions seems called for.

At this time the vizier did not have his own department: the *bab-i-âli* or, as the Europeans put it, 'The Sublime Porte', did not arrive until 1654. He did, however, head the Chancery, whose head was the *nishanji*, an official so important that he had an *ex officio* place in the Imperial Divan.

The major departments which the vizier supervised or directed, known collectively as the *küttab* (scribes), divided into those working to the Imperial Divan on the one side and those working to the Treasury on the other.

The official in charge of these Divan departments—the head of the civil service, as it were—was the *reis ul-küttab*; he was the head of the Scribal Guild, which was already important but was, in the post-1600 period, to become so predominant as to make the *reis* the most consequential of all the officials.

Four departments made up the council side of the administration. The Minutes and Drafting Department (the *Beylikci Kalemi*) took minutes, recorded decisions, and translated them into the appropriate decrees, proclamations, or treaties. The *Tahvil* Department handled the appointment, dismissal, transfer, and promotions of senior government personnel including the *timariots*; while the *Nishan* Department did the same for all junior appointments. The fourth of these Divan departments dealt with foreign affairs.

The Treasury division was headed by the chief *defterdar*, another official important enough to be *ex officio* member of the Imperial Divan. He was the *ex officio* treasurer of Rumelia, and controlled and directed the treasurer of Anatolia and his subordinate offices. The four Treasury departments were, first, the Imperial Treasury Department, which handled all revenues and especially the *jizye* paid by non-Muslims; the Chief Treasurer's Department, responsible for customs duties, mines, and monopolies of all kinds; the Mortmain Department, which looked after estates that for one reason or another had reverted to the sultan; and the fourth department was concerned with fortresses. This is perhaps the best place for showing how this great Treasury Division related to the provincial *defterdars* who will be mentioned later in connection with provincial government. Briefly, each province had its own *defterdar* in charge of four major departments: Registry, Accountancy, Audit, and Mortmain properties. The Registry itself contained three divisions: one to prepare a summary budget for the province, a second to handle its detailed accounts, and the third to check on the second in respect to all payments. The Accountancy Department kept, *inter alia*, a separate record of all receipts.[21]

4.2.2. PERSONNEL: RECRUITMENT AND TRAINING

'The *kul*—slave—system was the foundation-stone of the Ottoman state.'[22] The Ottomans, like the Caliphate and the Mamluks, mainly used slaves for military service until Mehmet II began to appoint men of slave origin as grand viziers. In the fourteenth century most slaves were prisoners-of-war or

[21] Shaw, 118–21. H. Gibb and H. Bowen, *Islamic Society and the West*, vol. 1, pts. 1 and 2 (Royal Institute of International Affairs, London, 1950 and 1957), 107–36. Inalcik, *Ottoman Empire*, 100–3.

[22] Inalcik, *Ottoman Empire*, 77.

had been bought in the flourishing slave markets (in the seventeenth century some 20,000 slaves were sold in the markets of Istanbul).[23] But in the fifteenth and sixteenth centuries, with which we are concerned, most of these slaves were provided by that singular Ottoman institution the *devshirme*.[24] This was a levy or, as I prefer to call it, a cull of the male children of the Christians in the European provinces. In every village the local kadi and *sipahi* summoned all male children between the ages of 8 and 20 along with their fathers, and chose the ones they thought were fit. Apart from Bosnia, where the Moslem inhabitants insisted on being subject to the *devshirme*, only children of Christian cultivators were conscripted and single children and town children were exempt. The district commissioners (a sultan's commissioner and a Janissary officer) enregistered the boys and sent them in drafts of fifty or 100 to Istanbul. The levies took place according to need; on the average, every three to seven years. One authority estimates the intake at 1,000 boys per annum, another at 3,000.[25] Once in the capital they underwent training so as to furnish the *corps d'élite* of the Ottoman army and its top civil servants.

The *devshirme* (in the sense of a conscription) began to fade out in the early seventeenth century and the last cull took place in 1703; but it is clear from Rycaut's description (1668) that the Ottomans were still drawing the candidates for 'the great offices of state' from 'such as are of Christian parents, taken in war, or presented from remote parts' (he instances the Barbary pirates).[26]

The great majority of these children were packed off to farms in Anatolia to learn Turkish ways and become good Muslims. Later—as described— they would become Janissaries. But the most promising were selected as *ich oghlans* (pages) and assigned to the palace schools at Pera, Edirne (Adrianople), or Istanbul. Under the very harsh discipline of eunuchs, they lived in dormitories, with every minute of their day accounted for. Here they were instructed in the Muslim faith and learned Arabic and Persian. The training was literary. (Rycaut remarks with some sarcasm on their ignorance of logic, physics, metaphysics, mathematics, and geography.)[27] Then, once they were strong enough, they were taught to bear arms and, particularly, to bend the bow.

Then a second selection was made. The cleverest went to the Greater and the Lesser Chambers of the sultan's palace, while the rest went to serve in the *kapikulu* (i.e. the personal, palace-based) *sipahi* cavalry. The former

---

[23] Ibid. 78.
[24] Records show it already existed in the fourteenth century, according to ibid. 78.
[25] Ibid. 78.   [26] Rycaut, *English Consul in Turkey*, 25.   [27] Ibid. 32.

category were still subject to the severest discipline, every hour of training accounted for, and compelled to remain celibate till the age of 25 or 30. Finally, after a third selection, the most able of these went to the Chambers for personal service to the sultan and the remainder joined the *sipah* cavalry.[28] This was a nursery for future provincial *beylerbeyis*, headships of departments in the Outer Palace, and senior commanderships in the *kapikulu* regiments. Their Muslim devotion bordered on the fanatical, and above all they were the slaves to the sultan, utterly dependent on him.

Such was the training for the superior posts in the civil bureaucracy. Yet the main body—'scribes' or 'clerks' (*küttab*)—were recruited and trained quite differently. Certainly, many of the clerks to the Imperial Divan were palace graduates, and the head of the *Nishan Kalemi* (Chancery) often came from among the *ulema*. But basically the *küttab* was a self-recruiting, self-training, and self-perpetuating corporation. It was a guild, headed by the *reis ul-küttab*. Apprentice clerks were usually relatives or dependents of the clerks in post. They were admitted as probationers and taught on the job by the senior secretary, a *haje* (plural *hajegân*) or an overseer (*kalfa*). This internship lasted a long time. The *hajegân*—that is, the Heads of Department—corrected the work of these apprentices, who then had to to pass an examination and receive the *hajegân's* approval to qualify merely as a candidate for the scribal guild. He had to wait for a vacancy. A secretary who died would be succeeded by his son if qualified; otherwise the post was allotted to the most able of the qualified candidates.

By any of the standards we have encountered so far, this is a rigorous system of recruitment and training, and it was so effective that in the end, when the old institutions of the empire were crumbling in the eighteenth century, it is unsurprising that the *reis ul-küttab* became more consequential than his master, the grand vizier.[29]

4.3. *The Army*

The army consisted of two types of force: the *kapikulu* and the provincial.

4.3.1. THE KAPIKULLARI

These were the standing army. There seems to be general agreement that the Janissaries (the *yeni cheri* or 'new troops') were founded by Murat I in the mid-fourteenth century from prisoners-of-war and purchased slaves and that recruitment via the *devshirme* came about half-a-century later.[30] The

[28] Inalcik, *Ottoman Empire*, 79–80.   [29] Shaw, *History of the Ottoman Empire*, 280–2.
[30] Rycaut, *English Consul in Turkey*, 190–6.

devshirme children who had been sent off to peasant families were subsequently called up and enrolled, as the occasion arose. They were then entitled to pay, food, clothing, and lodging. Discipline was extremely severe; they were not permitted to marry, they had to live in barracks and to train regularly. They were not permitted to take up any trade. These troops were on a permanent basis. They were, by far, the earliest standing army on the continent of Europe.[31]

The Janissaries began as archers, but by the sixteenth century they were harquebusiers and later musketeers. Unlike all Turkish cavalry forces the Janissaries took to hand-guns, and as warfare shifted away from cavalry to infantry elsewhere in sixteenth-century Europe, so in the Turkish case too the Janissaries became the centre-piece of the army. Under Suleiman they numbered some 30,000, divided into 101 battalions. Over and above these units there were *segban* battalions who acted as the sultan's personal guards and on this account tended to provide officers for the other units. There was also another force called the *agha bölüks*, which is to say 'commander-units'; originally these were the bodyguard of the Janissary commander (the *agha*), but now they undertook a range of duties including guarding the sultan, keeping order in Istanbul, and forming the *corps d'élite* of the Janissaries who were themselves the *corps d'elite* of the entire army. One other point about the Janissaries is noteworthy, something that strengthened their *esprit de corps* and also gave them a distinctive ideology that could put them in opposition to the palace: they were intimately associated with one of the Muslim sects, the *bektashi*. So close was the relationship that in the late sixteenth century the *bektashis* were formally attached to their corps and the sect's grand master was posted commander of the corps' 99th Battalion.

In peacetime the Janissaries served as police in the capital and rotated as garrison troops through the main cities of the empire. They might also serve as the city police-force.

The Janissary corps was not the sole component of the *kapikulu* infantry. Far fewer in numbers, of course, but of enormous military significance were the gunners and the engineers. For the formidable Ottoman prowess in war owed much to the use of super-heavy artillery: Mehmet II's huge guns were what enabled him to breach the walls of Constantinople. The Ottomans were quicker than the Europeans to adopt the cannon and for a long time theirs were superior to the European ones.[32] The cannon corps (*Topju Ojaghi*) was formed by Murat II. It consisted of 1,100 men in 1574, but increased to 5,000 in the seventeenth century. It is important to note,

---

[31] The next earliest would be the French *compagnies d'ordonnance* of 1445.

[32] See esp. C. Cipolla, *European Culture and Overseas Expansion* (Penguin, Harmondsworth, 1970), 73–8.

however, that these guns were principally used in sieges. They were far too heavy for the battlefield (though they did play a decisive role at Mohacs). The Ottomans failed to develop field-guns, an omission which was to cost them their defeats at Austrian hands in the late seventeenth century.

Side by side with the *kapikulu* infantry there was a *kapikulu* cavalry, the *sipah* (not *sipahis*, which were the provincial cavalry still to be described). There were six squadrons of them. They were better paid and more prestigious than the Janissary infantrymen, and the two forces hated one another. We have already said that *ich oghlan* cadets who were deemed unsuited to high civil administration were posted to this corps. Other recruits came from families of existing members of the corps, from non-Turkish Muslims such as Arabs, Kurds, and Persians, and from Janissaries who had distinguished themselves in battle. Two of the squadrons had the special responsibility of guarding the person of the sultan during campaigns. They were salaried. Like the provincial *sipahis*, they disliked hand-guns and continued to use bows, sword and lance, and battle-axe. Late in the sixteenth century they numbered some 6,000. In the late seventeenth and early eighteenth centuries the number had risen to about 21,000.[33]

4.3.2. THE TIMARIOT *SIPAHIS*

By far the great bulk of the Ottoman army consisted of provincial forces. Some were frontier units. Fortresses, when not manned by Janissaries on secondment, were garrisoned by *azab* troops, originally salaried but, by the sixteenth century, young men conscripted from among all the Muslim population of the border areas, as well as by units of enlisted men who were maintained by their villages. There was also a small number of troops who manned fortified villages or guard-posts along the roads; they were recompensed either by receiving a fief or by tax-exemptions and were known variously as *derbent*, *martolos*, or (in Bulgaria) *voinic*. The *akinjis*, who were light-cavalry raiders, were disbanded at the end of the sixteenth century, however, after having suffered a disastrous defeat in Wallachia.[34]

The great majority of the provincial troops were the field-army cavalry: the *sipahis*. Unlike the *kapikulu* troops they were not a salaried standing force at all. On the contrary, they were a feudalistically organized levy whose basis, the equivalent of the occidental fief, was the *timar*.

The *timar* system was simply a a variant on the Arabic *iqta*, and for that matter, the Byzantine *pronoia*. Like them it was, basically, a benefice of the tax receipts from a village or number of villages, inalienable, revocable, and granted in return for service—in this case, military service. It formed the

[33] The account is based on Shaw, *History of the Ottoman Empire*, 122–5.   [34] Ibid. 127–9.

foundation of the Mamluk polity in Egypt. The Ottomans found it in place in Anatolia, and something not unlike it in the remnants of the Byzantine Empire and the primitive Balkan kingdoms. It was natural and logical for them to utilize this same system as their *ghazi* armies pushed forward into Europe. Where the *timar* system somewhat differed from the usual form of the *iqta* was that the *timariot* had police powers on his lands. It was not just a military device but—like Occidental feudalism—was an integral part of the civil administration of the provinces. It should be noted too, that the *timariot* could not sub-infeudate.

The wealthiest *timars*, that is, those bringing in more than 100,000 akches, were called *has*. Those that yielded between 20,000 and 99,999 akches were called *ziamet*, and their holders were the *subashis*. The standard *timar* was one that brought in below 20,000 akches. Every *timar*-holder, great and small, had to maintain horses and provide arms, food, and other materials for himself and the retainers (*jebeli*) he was obligated to bring on campaign, whose number was determined by the wealth of his fief. A revenue of 6,000 akches (in Rumelia—it was 1,500–3,000 elsewhere) obliged the *timariot* to present himself and his equipment whenever required. Every extra 3,000 akches revenue of the *timar* (but 5,000 to the *ziamet*-holder) entailed bringing in one additional retainer and horse.

When a *timariot* died his holding (less any increments added for various reasons as a bonus, or *terakki*) went to his eldest son if of age and qualified to perform the service required; if underage, the heir was allowed to send a retainer instead. An invalided *timariot* was allowed to retire on a portion of the *timar*, with the balance going to his son and other *sipahis*. Bonuses earned during the lifetime of a *timariot* and reverting to the local *bey* on his decease were pooled into a reserve which funded similar bonuses to other *timariots*. If a *timariot* died with no male issue the entire *timar* went back for redistribution to another capable cavalry soldier. Sipahis who failed to perform their service for seven years lost their holdings and status, and became *re'aya*.

At first it was the local *beylerbeyis*—governors—who had distributed the *timars*, but under Suleiman this was taken over by the palace. Thenceforward, the persons who held the rich *has* and *ziamet* fiefs were usually palace officials. A provincial governor's fief would be worth 1,000,000–600,000 akches per annum; a *sanjak beyi's* would be 600,000–200,000; the *subashi beyi's* was worth anything between 200,000 and 20,000. The average income of the *sipahi*—and of Janissaries too—was only about one-hundredth of the *sanjak beyi's*.[35] *Beys* and *ziamet*-holders were immensely rich—that is why the line engravings

[35] Inalcik, *Ottoman Empire*, 115.

made by western travellers always show these pashas with vast retinues and in magnificent luxury.

The *sipahis* lived in the village where his *timar* lands were situated. He did not cultivate the land himself but saw that the peasants complied with the land and fiscal laws—for it was on these that his own income depended—and then collected in kind. When fines were levied he kept half for himself. It was in these ways that he became an integral part of the fiscal and public-order machinery. When called out on campaign the *sipahis* would arrange for a number of their fellows to stay behind to keep order and collect the taxes.

The *sipahis* used lance, axe, scimitar, and the bow, and wore shield, helmet, and armour. Like the Egyptian Mamluks they disdained hand-guns. On the summons to a campaign they rallied, under the command of the *subashis*, to the standard of the *sanjak*[36] *bey*, and from there to join the *beylerbeyi* of the province. These provincial forces then joined up with the sultan or his vizier. However, like all feudalistically supported armies, they could not remain in the field during the entire year since the harvests had to be gathered in and their share of it collected. Consequently the campaigning season tended to open in March and close by October, with only about two months for actual fighting.

In 1527 the empire contained 37,521 *timar*-holders, of whom 27,868 were regular *sipahis*. With their retainers they formed a force of some 70,000–80,000 men, as against the *kapikulu* who did not number more than 27,900. Another 9,653 *timar*-holders performed garrison duties in the fortresses. Together, these *timar*-holders absorbed 46 per cent of the total land revenues of Rumelia, 56 per cent in Anatolia, and 38 per cent in the Arab provinces.

It was calculated in 1607 that the *timars* produced a cavalry army of 105,339 men. Shaw concludes from this that 'Ottoman military supremacy was not achieved by superiority in numbers as often was claimed by their defeated European enemies' but instead by superior quality, training, and so forth.[37] But one must add to these *sipahi* numbers the standing forces, at some 30,000–40,000, and also a host of irregulars who brought their own arms and equipment along to join the army on the march, so that the total concentrations surely go way beyond what the Europeans were fielding in the sixteenth century. Suleiman commanded an army of 100,000 on his second Hungarian campaign and 250,000 men and 300 cannon on his third in 1566. In 1532 the Holy Roman Empire mustered some 100,000 men against the Turks; in 1552 Charles V had as many as 150,000 men under arms, but these were scattered throughout the Empire. The next largest concentration

---

[36] *Sanjak* means 'banner' in Turkish and then 'subdivision of a province'.
[37] Shaw, *History of the Ottoman Empire*, 127.

of forces to the Ottomans' was the Spanish army in the Netherlands, which was estimated at 86,000 men in 1574.[38]

4.4. *The Navy*

It is from Mehmet II's creation of a flotilla to blockade Constantinople that the history of the Ottoman navy begins, but the Admiral (*kaptan-i darya*) was a fairly low-ranking office until Suleiman's day, when the navy won command of the Mediterranean and scourged the Christian coasts off Catalonia, Nice, and Otranto, before being beaten off at Malta (1565) and suffering a spectacular but inconsequential defeat at Lepanto in 1571. This great era is associated with and due to the genius of the Barbarshy pirate Khayreddin, known to Europe as Barbarossa. Under Spanish attack, Barbarossa asked for and received aid from Suleiman, thereby recovering Algiers. For this he was given the post of *beylerbeyi* of the Islands of the Mediterranean, with *ex-officio* membership of the Imperial Divan. In 1534 he was appointed 'Grand Admiral', fighting running battles with the Imperial admiral, the Genoese Andrea Doria, and scoring a decisive victory at Prevesa in 1538 which guaranteed Ottoman control of the eastern Mediterranean until Lepanto.

The headquarters was the great naval dockyard at Istanbul, housing both the fighting personnel and the shipwrights. The latter were formidable: after the crushing defeat at Lepanto, when the Ottomans lost nearly half their fleet, Barbarossa's successor, Uluj Ali, constructed eight new docks and laid down no less than 158 galleys during the winter, and continued to build more ships in the two years following.[39]

Most ships were galleys, whose complement consisted mostly of oarsmen and soldiers. The former came to consist entirely of criminals and, above all, of the famous 'Turkish galley-slaves', Christian prisoners-of-war. The fighting forces were Janissaries or even *sipahis*. Galleys did not need many experienced mariners since they rarely used sail. For all that, the Ottomans had difficulty in recruiting trained seafarers. At the beginning they used the so-called *levends*, experienced sailors of Greek, Dalmatian, and Albanian origin. Later they replaced them with paid troops, recruited *ad hoc* from the islands and coastal districts, and called 'Standard Troops'. But they were really little more than a list of lawless resolutes who did not necessarily have experience of either seafaring or fighting.[40]

---

[38] Hale, *War and Society*, 62–3.   [39] Gibb and Bowen, *Islamic Society*, 94, n. 4.
[40] Ibid., who call them 'nothing better than a rabble', 98–101.

5. THE TERRITORIAL FRAMEWORK

At bottom, this Ottoman Empire was a patchwork of territories and societies overspanned by the Ruling Institution whose function was purely architectonic. It was a conquest empire like the Achaemenian and the Arab empires, but much more akin to the former of these. The Arab conquerors Arabized, Islamized, and homogenized their subjects into one ubiquitous type of social structure, value-set, and way of life. Indeed, they themselves soon lost their identity in their creation. By contrast, all the ancient Persian ruling class seems to have done was to take tribute, maintain order, and otherwise leave things alone. By and large this sums up the Ottoman Empire too. The charge against it is not so much that it was harsh and oppressive, though in decay it could be that; the complaint is that, after the innovations of Mehmet II and Suleiman, it was unimproving, ultra-conservative, and lethargic: an obscurantist dead weight, a great blanket on society. The only subjects it succeeded in Ottomanizing were those it drew into its Ruling Institution. Everybody else went on with their own religion, language, and social customs as before.

5.1. *The Vassal States*

At first most of the Ottoman conquests subsisted as vassal states, but the sultans found that this was a precarious condition and, bit by bit, converted them into directly administered provinces—*eyalets*. Nevertheless great tracts of territory persisted to the end as vassal territories enjoying internal autonomy but recognizing the suzerainty of the sultan. The Tartar and Muslim Khanate of the Crimea, ruled by the Giray dynasty, was particularly useful to Istanbul. It supplied excellent cavalry, which were needed to make good the declining numbers of *sipahis* in the seventeenth century. It was a great source of Christian slaves. It was strategically important once Trebizond had fallen to the Turks, since it allowed Istanbul to turn the Black Sea into a Turkish lake, and to concentrate its naval energies in the Mediterranean and Red seas. It also served to open a flank against pressures from Poland and, later, the Russians. For this reason the Porte maintained its own paid garrisons in the Crimea, and Azov was long a thorn in the Russian side.

Moldavia and Wallachia were ruled by their *hospodars* or *voivods* who were elected by the countries' boyars, at first from the royal house of Bessarab (hence 'Bessarabia'), but then, after 1716 (the Bessarabs having proved disloyal), by Phanariot Greeks. Of course the elections were all fixed by a mixture of bribery and intrigue, but the provinces did enjoy their own brand of government, secured the exclusion of all mosques, and any interference with their religion. In return they paid a tribute and provided military contingents. Transylvania was also a vassal kingdom. It proved an unreliable one which was able, for quite considerable spans of time, to assert an effective independence. Finally among these Christian dependencies one ought to notice the curious status of Ragusa or, as it was until recently known to the tourist trade, Dubrovnik. Originally a dependency of Venice, Ragusa made a peace treaty with the Turks and became a 'free city' recognizing Ottoman suzerainty but receiving valuable trade concessions.

5.2. *The* Salyane *Provinces and Egypt*

Salyane means a fixed annual sum. The *salyane* provinces were those where the governor—the pasha—sent Istanbul only a fixed annual sum and kept the balance of the revenue to pay himself and his administration. This effectively turned the province into the governor's tax-farm, since in return for his guaranteeing Istanbul its fixed sum, he was free to squeeze as much as he could from the province. This was singularly true of Egypt.

This province provides a powerful example of the *quieta non movere* attitude of Ottoman rule. Its administrators and society itself were completely unchanged. The Ottomans did indeed supplant the Mamluk emirs at the outset, but their efforts gradually faded and by the eighteenth century the emirs (now Ottomanized as beys) were effectively in power again.

The province was in the hands of a pasha but to control him the *defterdar*, the chief mufti, and the commander of the six-regiment force of Janissaries were all appointed directly by the capital. He was further constrained by a divan composed of all his officials, chief military officers, and religious dignitaries which met four times or more in the week, but which he was not permitted to attend, though final executive power rested with him.

However, Suleiman allowed the surviving Mamluk emirs to go on buying Circassian slaves, so perpetuating the Mamluk order. Their troops constituted a standing force of cavalry which counterbalanced the governor and the Janissaries. By custom certain offices had to be held by Mamluk emirs and so their influence in government was perpetuated. Over the seventeenth century the local power of the governor and the Janissary regiments waned while that of the beys increased, so that at the beginning of the eighteenth century the chief bey held the post of governor of Cairo with the unofficial style of *Sheikh el-Beled* (Leader of the City). Istanbul might order governors to execute such over-powerful beys but, by a curious quirk, the beys had acquired a traditional right to depose the governor without consulting Istanbul first, so that governors who tried to carry out the executions were quickly but duly deposed. In this way, after perhaps a century, the effective government of Egypt returned to the Mamluk oligarchy, but under Ottoman suzerainty.

Arguably, all this turbulence was so much froth, no more, in that really Egypt was still being governed in the same way and by the same personnel as it had been since the Arab conquest and, indeed, somewhat earlier. Egyptian society was stationary. Its members' social and economic status and activities were hereditarily determined and expressed through numerous perpetual corporations. Over the centuries it had become 'an independent organism, so solidly based and yet so resilient that its stability was never in danger. The foreign slaves, foreign rulers and administrators, and foreign merchants formed only the superstructure.[41]

This stable traditional society was insulated from the successive sets of foreign overlords by its real rulers, that is to say, the age-old bureaucracy.

The new masters stepped into the places vacated by their predecessors; the titles to assignments of land were redistributed, but the relations between landlord and peasant, official and artisan, remained on the whole unchanged . . . the respective functions of the Moslem accountants, the Jewish gold-dealers and book-keepers, and the Coptic tax-assessors and collectors in the eighteenth century were practically what they had been in the tenth.[42]

5.3. *The* Timar *Provinces*

The preceding forms of provincial government were exceptional: the standard form in the provinces proper (*beylerbeylik, eyalet*) was based on the *timar*. Though not a 'feudal system' in the proper sense,[43] this is the analogy to which we must look to envisage the general government in the countryside. The key figure was the knight or *timariot*, who resided in the village where his *timar* was situated, where at the closest of quarters he saw that the peasants respected the land laws, paid their taxes, and behaved themselves. In brief, in the core territories of Rumelia and Anatolia government at village level lay in the hands of some 37,000 petty knights.

These knights came under the military control of the *sanjak bey* who held a *ziamet* or a *has* fief, and these under the *beylerbeyi*—a *has-holder* with the dignity of pasha. A pasha held his own divan, modelled on the sultan's, which had the right to issue orders, hear petitions, and punish illegalities committed by officials and soldiers. He was assisted—but also counter-

---

[41] Gibb and Bowen, 211.   [42] Ibid. 210.

[43] See the discussion in Bk. III, Pt. 1, Ch. 1, *The Feudal Background*, and also in Bk. IV, Ch. 1, 'Tokugawa Japan'.

checked—by two *defterdars* (treasurers), one handling *timar* matters and the other administering the revenues pertaining to the central treasury. These men were independent, having been appointed by the government, and worked to their superiors in the respective *defterdar* departments in Istanbul.

In addition to the military jurisdictions a province was also divided into judicial ones. These were the *kadas*. The *kadis* themselves lived in the towns and sent their assistants into the countryside. The Ottoman *kadi* not only dispensed justice but also supervised the way the sultan's decrees were being carried out. As such he became the comptroller of financial affairs with the duty of informing the central government of any irregularities. A chief *kadi* was often called on to mediate in disputes between rival factions or officials, or might have to deputize as governor of a city or the province where the regular governorship was vacant. He was the local civil administrator *par excellence*, and many *kadis* rose to become *beylerbeyis* themselves, and competition to become a *kadi* finally became so fierce that many indidivuals had to wait for years before receiving an appointment.

The *kadis'* sentences were enforced by the *subashi*. *Subashis* were police chiefs residing in the larger towns or capitals of the province. Like the governor and the *sanjak beys*, the *subashi* subsisted on their own fiefs and, like *timariots*, had to supply the corresponding number of *jelebis*, retainers, to the army. The *Subashi* stood immediately above the ordinary *sipahis* in the hierarchy.

A third major provincial official was the *hazine defterdari* (the treasury *defterdar*). Like the *kadi* he was appointed by the central government. He was wholly independent of the governor. His task was to protect the interests of the treasury and in doing this he was free to communicate directly with his superiors in the capital. There was, however, a limit on these constraints on the governor, since he could dismiss both a *kadi* or a *hazine defterdari*—but had to inform the government if he did so.

It must be reiterated that, as an immensely rich *has*-holder, the governor not only did but was under an obligation to maintain a large body of retainers, so that in effect he had a private army. In time this was to strengthen the general drift towards disintegration that set in in the eighteenth century. For the moment, however, any temptations to use these troops against the central government might well be offset by the presence of Janissary garrisons in the towns and fortresses of the province. For these were independent of the governors, serving under their own commanders.

It is well to note again the outstandingly 'shallow' penetration of Ottoman government. These provincial administrators touched the local inhabitants only in so far as taxes, law, and order were concerned. Perhaps the most invasive of all its activities was the cull of young Christian children, but this only took place in the Christian provinces. For the rest, as Gibb and Bowen frequently point out,

the ruled . . . were all organized into bodies such as trade guilds . . . and it was to these bodies rather than the state, or even the Sultan that they were inclined to accord their most vivid allegiance . . . All, guilds, village councils, and tribes, were to a great extent autonomous though naturally they were supervised by the local governors . . . Any wider allegiance that the individual members of these units might entertain was religious rather than political . . . For these reasons the corruption of the Ruling and Learned Institutions was slow to affect the ruled.

The authors sum up these characteristics as: 'The *superficiality* of Ottoman rule.'

Rycaut devoted an entire chapter to the question: 'What care [do] the Turks take to preserve the body of their Empire free of faction and rebellion? For [he continues] there [are] many Provinces in the Sultan's gift, which are remote rich and powerful, and so administer temptation to the Governours to throw off the yoke of their dependence, and make themselves and their Posterity absolute.'[44]

The first part of the answer is that the governors, as we have just seen, shared some of their authority with the *defterdars*, the chief *kadi*, and the Janissary commanders. Also, the *timars* were now allocated by the palace, so governors could not build a local power-base.

Secondly, whereas the earliest governors were Turkish noblemen, they were now *kapikulu* recruited through the *devshirme* and educated in the palace as we have described. This, according to Rycaut, was the prime reason for their obedience: 'the destruction of an ancient Nobility; and admitting no succession to Offices or Riches but only in the Ottoman line.' Nobody but the sultan enjoyed the hereditary possession of office and property. He continues by pointing out that the *devshirme* governor was brought up in the palace without knowing his blood or family, had no relatives to support him, was briefly appointed to a distant land—and for all these reasons, lacked both the opportunity and the means to advance his own interests at the expense of the sultan's. Rycaut admits that some pashas had indeed taken up arms to try to make themselves independent but explains that the sultan did not need to fight them because they so much lacked local connections that intrigue sufficed to betray them. 'They are but strangers and foreigners in the Countries they ruled.' Rycaut's words, 'without knowing his blood or family', need some modification, however, in the light of the example, by no means unique, of

[44] The topic absorbs the whole of ch. 16. The quotation is at Rycaut, *English Consul in Turkey*, 196.

Mehmet Sokollu, grand vizier from 1565 to 1579. His original surname was Scholovic, and in the days of his greatness he remembered his family back home in Bosnia. He appointed his brother as patriarch of Pec, and a cousin as governor of Buda.

Nor could pashas pass on their wealth for, as we have already said, since a governor was a *kul*, the sultan inherited from him; 'and by this means', says Rycaut, 'all ancient Nobility is suppressed'. Again, whereas earlier governors normally served long terms (twenty- or thirty-year tenures have been reported), from 1574 appointments were reduced to three-year terms, and later on were made annual, though often renewed.[45]

6. THE ACTIVITIES OF THE STATE

6.1. *A Limited Role*

The Ottoman state restricted itself to war, taxation, and the dispensing of justice, with one or two notable exceptions. For one thing, 'not since the fall of the Roman Empire had any state in Europe devoted such care to its system of roads'.[46] There were state arsenals and the great naval yards at Constantinople. Another state enterprise was the system of *medreses* which the sultans set up to train the *ulema*. For the rest, however, private individuals or corporations, not the state, supplied public works and amenities. One characteristic form was the construction of *imarets* in the towns and cities. An *imaret* was a complex of public-service buildings endowed by some private benefactor as an autonomous institution under the law of *vakifs* (*waqfs*, i.e. religious mortmains). Characteristically, an *imaret* consisted of a mosque, a *medrese*, a hospital, a water point, roads, and bridges. Other support organizations like a *bedestan*, that is to say a huge covered market or *souk*, an inn, a caravanserai, a *hammam*, dye-house, slaughterhouse, and the like would be grouped around the *imaret*. These *imarets* served as the focal point of, effectively, a town quarter or *hara* (a term not used in Turkey itself) which grew up around it. As charitable organizations these centres were fiscally autonomous, immune from state confiscation, and administratively independent under their own boards of trustees. Each appointed its own sheikh who had his local police-force and represented the *hara* to the authorities. Similar private provision obtained along the great highways, where sultans or private individuals endowed the provision of wayside inns, caravanserais, *hammams*, roads, fords, and bridges.

---

[45] Rycaut, *English Consul in Turkey*, 69–71. Gibb and Bowen, *Islamic Society*, 145.
[46] Inalcik, *Ottoman Empire*, 46.

But as Gibb and Bowen say,

> The social organization was one of dislocated, self-contained and almost self-governing groups, subject . . . to the overriding authority of the temporal and spiritual power, represented by governors, police officers and the *kadis*. Its characteristic feature was the corporation . . . Not only the artisans and merchants, but all who were engaged in any occupation were members of a recognized corporation, with regular statutes, chiefs and tax assessments. There were, for example, corporations of students and teachers, of domestic servants, of water-carriers—even . . . of beggars, thieves and prostitutes.[47]

This was the subjects' field of 'citizenship', little-interfered-with by governors. These guilds and corporations were almost always affiliates of one or other of the numerous religious orders (*tarikats*) with which the entire Muslim population of the empire was seamed. The guild maintained the members' professional standards and acted as a friendly society; it took care, for instance, of sickness and burials, and provided for the destitute and widows and orphans. From the rulers' point of view these organizations kept order among their members and their sheikhs acted as go-betweens, and indeed allocated the tax-burden among the membership and were personally responsible for its payment.[48]

6.2. *Warfare*

This has already been described in a number of connections: an appraisal of its role in the Ottoman state will follow later.

6.3. *Law and the Judiciary*

6.3.1. THE *MILLETS*

The *sharia* only applies to Muslims, except in so far as non-Muslims have relationships with them, or agree to be tried according to its terms. These non-believers are the *dhimmis* or the protected people; and so not just the Turks but the Arabs before them left the internal relations of the *dhimmis* to be regulated by the religions to which they conformed. The Ottomans, though not inventing this arrangement, regularized and systematized it so that it became one of the most striking features of the empire. These communities were called *millets*—originally 'religions', later 'nations'—and each *millet* established and maintained its own communal institutions for education, religion, social assistance, charity, and justice. The largest and

---

[47] Gibb and Bowen, *Islamic Society*, 277.   [48] Ibid. 278.

most important one was that of the Orthodox Christians—'the Great Church in captivity'. Before the conquest, these Orthodox Christians had been divided into a number of independent patriarchates. The Ottomans abolished these and brought all their adherents under the rule of the patriarch of Constantinople. He could only be installed after the sultan's confirmation, whereupon he became a very important dignitary indeed: a pasha of three horse-tails, with his own court and prison in the Phanar district of Constantinople, and the right to apply almost unlimited civil jurisdiction over the members of his Church. He was even responsible for apportioning the amount of tax due between its various communities and individuals and for collecting and forwarding it to the authorities.

Almost simultaneously with the recognition of this Orthodox Christian *millet*, the Jews were similarly recognized. Mehmet II the Conqueror was favourably disposed to Jews, and they were accorded a dignity and tolerance that stood in striking contrast to the persecutions and expulsions they were suffering in Bohemia, Austria, Poland, and—in 1492—Spain. Jews from all such countries began to flock to Turkey and Mehmet II allowed them to settle in Istanbul under a chief rabbi (*Haham Bashi*)[49] with powers over his co-religionists similar to those of the Orthodox patriarch. The chief rabbi was even given precedence over the patriarch, next to the head of the *ulema*.

A third non-Muslim *millet* was the Armenian, established in 1461. The patriarch's role and powers were like those of the Orthodox patriarch and the chief rabbi but they extended beyond his fellow Armenian Christians to the scatter of other denominations like the Assyrians, the Monophysites of Syria and Egypt, the Bogomils of Bosnia, the Maronites of the Lebanon, and the Latin Catholics of Hungary and Croatia.

6.3.2. OTTOMAN LAW

Sharia

The tension which had arisen in the Caliphate between the *sharia* and the exigencies of secular life was repeated in the Ottoman Empire, but in a somewhat different shape and reached by a different route. Ancient Turkish tradition related the ruler's sovereignty to the establishment of a royal code of laws, *törü*. This tradition had somehow to accommodate to the Divine Law which bound all Muslims, ruler and ruled alike. The Sultan issued his own decrees as *kanun*, and juristic theory ran that such a decree was valid provided it did not run counter to specific provisions in the *sharia* that were generally recognized and in force in the country. In fact many such *kanuns*

---

[49] He was elected by his flock but had to be confirmed by the sultan.

are clearly contrary to the *sharia*,[50] but in such cases the *sharia* was simply 'stretched' to embrace it, which was achieved by the sultan demanding and receiving a *fetva* from his Sheikh ul-Islam which confirmed its agreement with the *sharia*. The influence of the sheikh waxed and waned with the power of the sultan and the political situation. The sheikh's political opposition to the sultan is a feature of the declining empire, not of its prime.

Kanun

So, alongside the *sharia*, which confined itself in practice to its traditional concerns with family, religious, and civil matters, the sultans issued law-codes known as the *kanunname*, which applied throughout the empire. Codification on this scale was without precedent in Muslim states, and indeed was unknown in the Europe of that time. The first such *kanunname* was promulgated by Mehmet II the Conqueror immediately after the fall of Constantinople in 1453, and laid down a criminal code for the *re'aya* and the fiscal obligations of the *dhimmis* and of the Muslims. Much of this related to the *timars*, land registers and surveys, tithes and labour-dues, and so forth. Many of these laws had been traditional before the codification. Mehmet's second *kannuname* of 1476 concerned the chief officials, and laid down their powers, ranks, salaries, and the like. Suleiman, who is known to Europeans as 'the Magnificent' was called 'the Lawgiver' by his subjects for it was he who perfected this codification and reorganized the judicial system. The *kanunname* laid down new penalties for crimes, ranging from amputation to fines and capital punishment. The regulations for the *timariots* and their military duties were redefined and the entire fiscal system was systematized and institutionalized. Suleiman also made strenuous efforts to purify the administration of justice, by prohibiting confiscations and punishments without due process of law. All these momentous codifications were carried out, it might be added, with the active assistance of Suleiman's Sheikh ul-Islam (Ebu 's-Suud), who reconciled the *kanuns* with the *sharia* through a series of *fetvas*.[51]

6.3.3. THE PRACTITIONERS OF LAW: THE *ULEMA*, THE *MEDRESES*, AND THE RELIGIOUS HIERARCHY

The Islamic polity required teachers and preachers, muezzins and prayer-leaders, legists and judges. In the Ottoman Empire all such occupations were in principle interchangeable, for all were part of the Learned Profession, the *ulema*. In the Arab polities the *ulema* was a loose configuration of

---

[50] R. Levy, *The Social Structure of Islam* (CUP, Cambridge, 1957), 267–8 for examples.
[51] Shaw, *History of the Ottoman Empire*, 103–4.

private individuals. The grand innovation of the Ottomans was to organize it into a regular hierarchy. To obtain any public post such as any of those mentioned above, the learned man must have studied and also taught in a *medrese* and possess a certificate making him eligible for employment. The *medreses* of Bursa, Adrianople (Edirne), and Istanbul enjoyed especial pre-eminence. To obtain any of the most important official posts the candidate would have to have taught in one of these royal cities and to obtain the top posts must have been trained in a succession of *medreses* in Istanbul. In Suleiman's time the *ulema* who aspired to the highest office had to pass through at least eight of the *medreses* in a fixed order. This might take them as many as forty years and compels comparison with China's examination system, all the more so because, like the Mandarinate, the Learned Profession was formed into so many grades. The principal dignitaries formed the summit; below them came an echelon of grand *mollas* which was itself divided into fixed classes; then an echelon of lesser *mollas*, and so forth down to the ordinary *kadis* and, below them, the various learned men who could make no grade higher than perhaps schoolteacher or muezzin and the like.

Thus the judges were the top members of the Learned Profession, and themselves formed a regular hierarchy. The chief post was that of the Sheikh ul-Islam; next came the two *kadiaskers* (literally 'army judges'), who were succeeded by the three 'great' *mollas* who filled the posts of *kadi* in Istanbul and the two Holy Cities; below these were ranked the other great *mollas* who were the *kadis* in great centres like Bursa, Edirne, Cairo, and Jerusalem; below these came the 'lesser' *kadis*; and at the bottom the ordinary *kadis*, those who would render justice in a *kada* in the provinces.

In practice things were not as tidy as this. There was little trace of this regularization in Egypt and the Holy Cities. For instance, in Egypt, the most independent of all the provinces, the direct intervention and control of the Sultanate was limited to the judicial service; in all other branches occupied by the learned profession the traditional institutions, personnel, and methods continued to prevail.

6.3.4. THE ADMINISTRATION OF THE LAWS

It will be recalled that in the Caliphate there had been two separate jurisdictions, *sharia* and caliphal, which were embodied in two sets of courts, the *sharia* and the *mazalim* courts. But in the Ottoman Empire the *kadi* courts administered both the *sharia* and the *kanun*.[52] It might be thought therefore that the familiar tension between the secular arm and the religious institu-

[52] U. Heyd, *Studies in Old Ottoman Criminal Law* (Clarendon Press, Oxford, 1973), 216–19.

tion had been dispelled. But this was not so. The local military or the police or even petty officials would order punishments and executions without even the semblance of a trial. A sixteenth-century *kanunname* orders *kadis* to carry out the laws of the *sharia* but to refer matters relating to public order, the protection and defence of the subjects and the capital, or severe corporal punishment of criminals to the local representatives of the sultan, 'who are the governors in charge of military and serious penal affairs.'[53] These were the *beylerbeyis* and the *sanjak beyis*, and they were supposed to judge these referred cases according to the *sharia*. In fact they were often arbitrary and oppressive.[54] 'In the field of justice the Men of the Sword always tended to overstep the bounds of their authority and infringe that of the *kadis*.'[55]

6.4. *Taxation.*

The Arab provinces were treated differently from the rest and Muslims were taxed somewhat differently from non-Muslims. At the risk of a mighty oversimplification we can, effectively, dispose of the Arab third of the Empire by saying that it retained its traditional tax regime: every one paid *kharaj* (land tax) and *ushr* (tithe). *Dhimmis* paid the *jizya* (the head tax) but no *zakat* (alms tax), and the Muslims paid the *zakat* but not the *jizya*. And, as we saw earlier, Egypt's administrative structure and personnel had remained unchanged from caliphal and indeed pre-caliphal times.

By contrast, the Ottomans completely revolutionized the tax regime they found in their conquered European provinces. That had resembled the West European manorial regime, with the peasants *adscripti glebae* and owing two or three days' boon work to their landlords. The Ottomans swept this away, substituting direct imposts instead. This brought the European provinces into line with the Anatolian ones. The resulting system embodied two sorts of taxes, those contemplated by the *sharia* and those imposed by virtue of the Sultan's prerogative powers (his *örf*).

The *sharia* taxes were as enumerated in connection with the Arab provinces; necessarily so, for they were based on the distinction between Muslim and non-Muslim which was empire-wide. Of the *örfi* taxes the most important at this particular time was the basic land tax, which in effect replicated the *kharaj* of Arab lands. It applied to the peasants in Rumelia and Anatolia and was called *chift* or *ispenje*. The *chift* was the basic unit of agricultural land—the area that could be ploughed by a pair (*chift*) of oxen—exactly like the Roman *iugum*. It varied from about 15 to 40 acres according to the fertility of the soil. Another tax, light at this period and

---

[53] U. Heyd, 209.   [54] Ibid. 211–12, and the examples there given.   [55] Ibid. 220.

collected only at irregular intervals, was the *avariz* or household tax first imposed on villages to help pay extraordinary expenses of soldiers and official visits in the area, campaign expenses, or assistance to neighbouring lands that had suffered devastation. This particular tax was destined to become regular and extremely heavy as the state fell into its chronic fiscal deficits at the beginning of the seventeenth century.

To carry out the assessments and often the collection of the taxes, these provinces were divided into so many *mukata'as*, a word cognate with the *iqta*, of the late Caliphate, that is, the usufruct of a given area of land. *Mukata'as* fell into three categories. At one extreme were the *timars*. Here the total usufruct of the lands went to the *timariot* in return for his services. At the other extreme was the *emanets*, so called because they were run by commissioners (*emins*). Here the taxes were collected by salaried officials and all went to the central treasury. By the beginning of the seventeenth century the central treasury (for reasons that will be noticed below) experienced an ever-increasing need for currency rather than services and taxes in kind. From this time onwards the practice of tax-farming, which had certainly been in use here and there in earlier times, became widespread. The *mukata'a* was assigned as a tax-farm (*iltizam*) to tax-farmers who paid an annual fixed sum to the treasury, keeping the balance as their personal profit.[56] This system was destined to have the most disastrous effects on the peasantry.

7. APPRAISAL

7.1. *Justice*

Under Suleiman the judicial system was at its best. Its chief problem was the arbitrariness of the governors, police-chiefs, and the military, as noted above. For instance, the law required that if legal proofs were necessary or legists differed, the defendant could not be convicted except by a *kadi*, but the secular authorities hardly ever observed this rule.[57] Governors would unjustly imprison their subjects and condemn them to exorbitant fines without even a trial. One governor ordered a prisoner to be impaled, unless his father bought his pardon with 400 pieces of gold.[58] Suleiman's *kanunname* for Egypt explicitly denounced the 'barbarity of *kashifs*,[59] Arab sheikhs, and other persons who without reasonable cause put cultivators to death and seized their property'.[60] True, the rule that the *kashif* must inflict no penalty on the peasant without the consent of the local *kadi* and that the governor of

---

[56] Gibb and Bowen, *Islamic Society*, ii. 21–4.   [57] Heyd, *Studies in Old Ottoman Law*, 211.
[58] Ibid. 212.   [59] The district governors in Egypt.
[60] Gibb and Bowen, *Islamic Society*, ii. 129.

Egypt was to investigate breaches of this rule, was reiterated; but nobody knows quite how long it stayed in effect. What is certain is that in time it fell into desuetude.

But despite all such defects, the Ottoman judicial system was an admirable one for its day. Because the sultans made the smallest unit of their civil administration coextensive with the *kadi's kada*; put the *subashi* under his authority; provided a uniform training grading and promotion system for scholars and *kadis*; organized a regular judicial hierarchy and established empire-wide codes of laws—for these reasons Schacht has uncompromisingly declared that 'the legal order in the Ottoman Empire in the sixteenth century was far superior to that prevailing in contemporary Europe, if only because of its uniformity'.[61]

7.2. Order

The Empire was frequently rocked by revolts or civil wars. Although they were conducted by different kinds of leaders, all pursuing diverse causes, they testified to great pockets of simmering discontent. Many popular risings in Anatolia, whose basic causes were social and economic, took the form of heretical religious movements, as they had in the Caliphate: the famous revolt of Sheikh Bedreddin in 1420 would serve as an example. A sufi of Shiite leanings, a mystic and esoteric whose interpretation of Islam seems virtually pantheism, Bedreddin claimed to be the Mahdi. Other popular risings were nominally to support a pretender to the throne but provided the opportunity for thousands of disaffected elements to join his banners. An example is provided by the war of the pseudo-Mustafa in 1555 in Rumelia. He was quickly joined by thousands of peasants, many *ulema*, and a number of *timariots* and border commanders (anxious to resume *ghaza* attacks on Christendom). Enthused by a populistic mysticism akin to Beddreddin's, these followings soon began looting officials' houses and government treasuries and distributing the proceeds as part of a communistic millenarianism. Thousands and thousands of these followers were executed when the revolt was finally put down. Again, for something like 200 years Anatolia was affected from time to time by revolts called 'Jelali' after the first, which was led by yet another self-styled Mahdi named Jelal. His sufistic beliefs found a ready welcome among the disaffected Turcoman tribesmen. Though Jelal's revolt was crushed in 1519 and thousands were executed, another similar sort of revolt, and hence called after him a 'Jelali' revolt, flared up among the Turcomans, this time provoked by the govern-

[61] J. Schacht, *An Introduction to Islamic Law* (OUP, Oxford, 1965), 92.

ment's efforts to survey their lands for tax purposes. Yet a third Jelali revolt took place in 1605–8, this time in central Anatolia and Cilicia–Syria.

By the late sixteenth century lawlessness had become endemic. There were several concomitant reasons for this—overpopulation, which drove peasants into towns which were not equipped to deal with them, unemployed auxiliary troops roving for plunder, peasants fleeing their farms to avoid the suddenly increased burden of taxation. Thus occurred what became known as the Great Flight, with mass uprisings of peasant bands, ex-soldiers, and the so-called *levends* or *levants*, best translated as bandits. It was to cope with these that Janissaries came to be regularly rotated through the greater towns, and later, that the *beylerbeyis* were permitted to recruit their own local forces.

7.3. *Warfare*

War was the operative principle of the Ottoman Empire. The orderly government and light taxation of the peasantry of its core areas depended on 'systematic and determined predation on similar communities lying just beyond its territorial limits'.[62] Most empires were and are gigantic plunder machines, but 'few if any matched the thoroughness and deliberation with which the Ottomans pursued this policy'.[63] We have listed its incessant wars, described its military forces, and have pointed out how its polity arrangement was a military structure subserving civil functions.

There can be no question of the technical and moral superiority of the Turkish military at the time of Suleiman. By any kind of criterion it was the most efficient fighting-force in the whole of Europe. This was evidenced in several ways: by the professionalism of the Janissaries, the specialized corps of gunners and of engineers, the tireless and efficient commissariat. It wisely entrusted tactical control to the local *beylerbeyis* who would know the terrain. It was officered and generalled by nobodies who had risen simply by their talents. Giovio[64] wrote: 'The Turks surpass our soldiers for three reasons: they obey their commanders promptly; they never show the least concern for their lives in battle; they can live a long time without bread and wine, content with barley and water.'[65] Rycaut commented on the severe discipline of their march and especially their camp. Although soldiers who have fought the Turks claim that they win through sheer force of numbers, in his own view: 'the Conquests they have made on the parts of Christendom is a

[62] Paul Coles, *The Ottoman Impact in Europe* (Thames Hudson, London 1968), p. 62.
[63] Ibid. 154.   [64] Paolo Giovio (Paulus Jovius), Florentine historian (1483–1552).
[65] Quoted in Lord Montgomery, *A History of Warfare* (Collins, London, 1968), 248.

demonstration undeniable of some supereminent Order in their army which recompenses the defect of knowledge on the true Mystery of War.'[66]

Cato told the Roman Senate: 'War must support war.' The Ottomans went beyond this—war had to support still more war. For the *timariot* forces wanted to conquer new *timars* for themselves and the *kapikulu* troops looked to campaigns for loot and plunder. The cycle of war and then more war could not cease without destabilizing the entire imperial system. Peace behind stable frontiers would terminate the restless roving life of the *timariot*, who normally was away from his *timar* more often than he resided there, and struck no local roots. Left to himself he would do just that, and soon become akin to the territorial squirearchies and aristocracies in the West. As to the *kapikulu*, if deprived of their opportunities of plunder they would certainly try to replace the existing sultan by another who would resume raiding. Even Suleiman the Magnificent experienced this in 1525 when the Janissaries kicked over their cooking pots (the signal for mutiny) because there had been no campaign for three years. The stability of the imperial system demanded an inexhaustible supply of captured slaves, booty, and lands, so that the Turks were, in Gibbon's words, on a perpetual search for 'new enemies and new subjects'.

There were three flaws in this scheme. We have mentioned that the actual battle season was restricted to only two months or so. There was therefore a definite logistical limit to the Ottoman area of expansion. Once that was reached—and Vienna proved to be the limit—the supply of slaves, booty, and lands which fuelled the system was cut off.

This led to the second flaw. We have developed elsewhere the concept of 'the extraction–coercion cycle'.[67] Troops extract the taxes or the forage or the carts, and this contribution keeps them in being. More troops—more extraction—more troops. Now the rationale of imperial predation is precisely to coerce-and-extract from foreigners, not one's own subjects. But once this predation is checked abroad it has to be carried out at home. In other words, in order to maintain the army it became necessary to raise the hitherto light taxes on the common people, and when they resisted, to browbeat and extract even more to cover the cost of such police operations. This is precisely what was to happen within decades of Suleiman's death.

The third flaw was exacerbated by both the former two, but will exist in any polity which maintains standing armies: they may prove politically unreliable. The *timariots*, who were mostly Turks, envied the upstart eth-

---

[66] Rycaut, *English Consul in Turkey*, 205.

[67] S. E. Finer, 'State and Nation Building in Europe: The Role of the Military', in C. Tilly (ed.), *The Formation of National States in Western Europe* (Princeton UP, Princeton, 1975), 96. See also the Conceptual Prologue, pp. 19–20 above.

nic-European *devshirme* troops. Indeed, it went further than that; at this period it is fair to say that one could never attain any high position in the Ruling Institution of a Turkish empire if one had had the misfortune to be born a Turk! Consequently the *timariots* were restless and unreliable in the provinces while the *kapikulu* troops, being stationed in the capital, were in the perfect position to riot, rebel, and even force the deposition of the sultan, once the campaigns faltered or their pay fell into arrears. In this they behaved liked all mercenary forces in all polities throughout history.

But all this was for the future. In the period we are describing the Ottoman forces on land and sea continued to expand the boundaries of the empire.

7.4. *Fiscal Functions and Standard of Living*

Precisely because of these military victories and the surplus that sustained the *timariots*, the Janissaries, and the court, the peasantry was not hard done by. In the European provinces the abolition of the former feudal dues and of corvée, and the effective guarantee of the peasant-tenancy seems to have led to a considerable lightening of the tax burden. In Egypt, although the tax regime remained unchanged, it may well have been less oppressive because the administration was now firm and stable. Unlike many imperial fiscal systems the Ottoman regime neither imposed conscription nor exacted a corvée. It was not till the fiscal crisis at the end of the sixteenth and in the seventeenth century that the peasantry really began to suffer and deserted their farms in the Great Flight. Indeed, there is a simple enough proof that living standards must have improved during this period and that is the uncontestable explosion of population. In this sixteenth century the population increased by 40 per cent in the villages and 80 per cent in the towns.[68]

Until the 1580s the Ottoman state seemed to have reached an equilibrium. It was, writes Inalcik, a society 'interested not in change but in preservation of the existing order', and he goes on to catalogue its numerous strengths.

The empire's ruling classes—the military and the *ulema*—had secure, lasting and sufficient sources of income. Their consumption of luxury goods increased. Not only sultans and viziers but even less wealthy persons, commissioned great works of architecture and created *vakifs*. The preservation for seventy years of the ratio between the silver akçe and the gold coinage is an indication of this economic and social stability. In 1510 one gold piece was valued at 54 akçes, in 1580 at 60. Thousands of people in government service—courtiers, soldiers, teachers, kadis

---

[68] Inalcik, *Ottoman Empire*, 46.

and bureaucrats—received regular salaries or timar incomes within a clear system of promotion. This society looked to the future with optimism. The productive class knew exactly what taxes were due and effective central authority gave protection from local abuses. Government registers had for centuries recorded the members of all classes, and the state was able strictly to control this class structure. The empire was, at the same time, self-sufficient in all basic commodities, the main imports being luxury goods such as European woollens, Indian textiles and spices, Russian furs and Persian silk.

And then Inalcik adds:

Yet twenty or thirty years later the whole magnificent edifice was shaken to its foundations. Amidst turmoil and confusion, and fearing for their livelihood and future, these same rulers began to oppose the sultan's authority, disregard the law, rob the state Treasury and plunder the property of defenceless people. As violence, profiteering, bribery and other abuses spread, civil disorders increased . . . [69]

How did this come about? And how did it affect the characteristic institutions of the state as we have described them in its glory?

8. A NOTE ON THE DECLINE OF THE OTTOMAN EMPIRE UNTIL c.1750

The basic cause of the Empire's decay was that it stopped being able to pay its way, and for this there were three chief reasons. One was overpopulation. The classical solution to this problem had been to settle the landless people in newly conquered territory. This no longer sufficed, and the state records more and more frequently make mention of landless and unemployed young men, the people we have mentioned as *levends*, and the increase, too, in banditry. The second reason is more important: a considerable inflation caused by the inflow of American silver. By the end of the eighteenth century prices had quadrupled. The third reason was the end of expansion and of booty—hence less revenue.

The conjunction of these three factors provoked a desperate financial crisis and imposed a strain on the traditional institutions with which only the most resolute leadership might have coped. But after Suleiman the sultans who tottered to the throne from their lifelong confinement in the 'cage' were, with one or two exceptions like Murat IV, physical and mental degenerates. The result was what was called 'the Sultanate of Women', which was to be followed by the 'Sultanate of the Aghas' when the troops

---

[69] Inalcik, *Ottoman Empire*, 45–6.

mutinied against incompetent sultans who no longer led them in battle but presided over defeat from the seclusion of their seraglio.[70]

The central Ottoman institutions had been the *devshirme* and the *timar* system. After the wars in the Caucasus and Hungary, which by 1605 marked the end of large-scale conquests, the military imperatives were seen to have changed. The *timariots'* resistance to firearms had made their formation obsolete, while the losses in the late wars demanded great new drafts of infantrymen, and for this the *devshirme* could no longer suffice. As thousands of ex-*timariots* (or their dependants) were recruited into the infantry the distinction between the *devshirme* and Turk infantry was broken down. The *devshirme* system was abandoned, while the number of ethnically Turkish Janissaries rose incessantly, one might say almost in proportion to the abandonment of their strict training, discipline, celibate status, and restriction to everything save the profession of arms.

The disappearance of the *timariot* cavalry was hastened by economic as well as military causes. The court was obsessed by the need for cash to pay the increasing numbers of stipended Janissaries and other forms of infantry. Since it now disposed of the *timars*, it now began to turn them into *iltizams*, tax-farms. As this arrangement spread it revolutionized the social structure of the countryside, for it enabled richer individuals to acquire very large estates—*chiftliks*—and to reduce the peasantry to dependency. At the same time, the disappearance of the *timariots* signified the disappearance, too, of the administrative-policing arrangements that had kept the countryside quiet in the Empire's heyday. To some extent they were replaced by Janissary garrisons in the large towns, but for the most part by forces recruited locally by the *beylerbeyis*, such as the *segmen* infantry. This right to raise their own troops enabled some of the beys to accrete such enormous local power as to become virtually autonomous. Such beys were called the *derebeys* and their emergence attests to the slow process of decentralization which took place between the death of Suleiman and the end of the eighteenth century.

If the Turks managed to stand their ground against the Europeans in the first half of the seventeenth century, this was at least as much due to European distraction in the Thirty Years War, as to Turkish military superiority. This was proved at the end of that war for this not only enabled Austria to re-engage the Ottoman forces but to do so with the new skills that had been developed during the Thirty Years War, and notably the use of mobile field artillery. The Turkish defeat at the hands of Montecuccioli in 1664 marks the end of Turkish technical superiority on the battlefield.

---

[70] A picturesque account of this is given in N. Barber, *Lords of the Golden Horn: The Sultans, their Harems and the Fall of the Ottoman Empire* (1973).

The cash crisis therefore became more pronounced than ever, and with it the measures to raise money ever more desperate—and fatally damaging. The government resorted to arbitrary confiscations of private fortunes.[71] It delivered the *timars* and similar properties over to tax-farmers but, with its weakened administrative reach, could not protect the peasants from their rapacity. The result was the exploitation of these taxpayers by that battery of illegal means and fraudulent exercises with which we are now familiar from over-frequent repetition in connection with other such polities.[72] The peasants fled the land, so that even in the early seventeenth century it was reported that most of Thrace was depopulated and waste. Another and equally familiar effect of the cash crisis was the widespread sale of offices. This in turn engendered the same corruption cycle that we have met with among the mandarins in China. That is to say, the candidate who bought the post of say, *kadi*, had to recoup the purchase price by accepting bribes. 'So that justice in its common course is set to sale, and it is very rare when any lawsuit is in hand, but bargains are made for the sentence . . . and it is no wonder if corrupt men exercise this kind of trade in Trafiquing with Justice; for having before bought the office, of consequence they must sell the Fruit.'[73]

In such wise perished the most characteristic—and administratively formidable—of the empire's institutions: the *devshirme* and the *kapikulu* army, the *timars* and the *timariot* administrative-policing system, the integrity of the judicial system and the enforcement of the great *kanunname*. Power passed from the centre to the pashas, the *derebeys*, and other local magnates.

The radical weakness of the Ottoman administration at this late stage, was to be found, according to Gibb and Bowen in this:

Lacking any real consideration for the welfare of the subjects, losing little by little any moral ideals which might have inspired them in the earlier stages, the officers of the administration were, by their very virtues, led insensibly to adopt a cynical view of their functions and responsibilities. Their world was divided into *hukkam*, 'governors', and *re'aya*, 'subjects', the latter of whom existed, by divine providence, to supply the needs of the former . . . By the beginning of the eighteenth century it had become the established practice to give promotion by favouritism and bribery, and to put up to auction offices (not only administrative, but also judicial and theological), lands, and concessions of all kinds. Cynicism had taken such root that it had ceased to be immoral and become second nature. To maintain discipline over the Turkish soldiery, when its natural foundations in respect for superior ability were absent, became an all but impossible task. The impotence of the Pashas to

---

[71] Rycaut, *English Consul in Turkey*, 71.   [72] Gibb and Bowen, *Islamic Society*, 255–6.
[73] Rycaut, *English Consul in Turkey*, 76. But Gibb and Bowen think this is overstated and that by and large justice was done: *Islamic Society*, ii. 126–8.

prevent abuses, and the probability that they would be condoned at a price, encouraged lawlessness and rebellion, which gradually became more violent and widespread. Yet such was the natural talent of the Turkish governing classes, and so ingrained the conviction of their superiority, not only among themselves, but also in the minds of their subjects that (apart from the turbulence of the Janissaries) it was not until the middle of the [eighteenth] century that the system began seriously to be challenged and to show alarming symptoms of breakdown.[74]

[74] Rycaut, i. 207.

4

The Indian Experience and the Mughal Empire,
1526–1712

1. THE INDIAN EXPERIENCE

S ome historians choose to take Indian civilization as commencing with the riverine cultures of Mohenjo-Daro and Harappa (2500 BC); others with the Aryan invasions (c.1500 BC). Either way the fact remains that it is thousands of years old. Furthermore, Hindu religion, its unifying and unique characteristic, is the oldest continuous religious tradition in the world, such that Hindus are still using some of the hymns of the *Rig Veda*, of c.1500 BC.

Yet during these three millennia before the Mughal period (1526–1739) there was no single Indian polity congruent with Indian civilization. The so-called empires that commence with the Mauryas in 321 BC were loosely articulated, short-lived, and few; and in any case their detail is largely unknown to us. Instead there was a multitude of minor kingdoms whose existence was fluid and short-lived. These do not, except for the one or two exceptional cases mentioned below, deserve analysis, in so far as they do not conform to any of the four criteria of selection I have adopted for this *History*. To repeat these in this context: first, these minor states are not outstanding by virtue of their durability or their populousness or by their contemporary power. Secondly, none of them would serve as archetypical of the rest, since not one can be taken as representative of the class. Thirdly, none were responsible for any significant innovation or invention in the sphere of government; on the contrary, they represent a wholly unoriginal form of polity for, leaving aside for the moment the scatter of tribal oligarchies whose life-span was in any case comparatively short, the norm was autocratic, even despotic, monarchy. Finally, it can hardly be said that any of them are what I have called 'vivid variants' on this general autocratic theme. Yet this verdict must be qualified: there did exist a handful of kingdoms that were extensive, wealthy, and powerful, and whose life-spans exceeded many of the ancient empires we have hitherto explored. Such, for example, was the Chola kingdom and the great state of Vijayanagara. These will be described when we come, later in this chapter, to characterize the nature of pre-Turkic Hindu statehood.

It is not with this, however, that this chapter is primarily concerned. Its central interest is the Mughal Empire, and this for two most powerful reasons. Unlike any of these other states it created a stable administrative structure that held together three-quarters of the subcontinent for over 150 years. Secondly, the ruins of this structure served as the basis for the first successful and durable unification in history of all India as we now conventionally think of it. This was British India, the *Raj*. The Mughals founded an imperial ideal and the Raj took it up and bettered it.

The fact is that until Mughal times India was a geographical expression. It was not like the monocultural and for the most part politically united China. Studying it is more like studying Europe, with its diverse languages, religions, and peoples, and its many states which, like those of India, were continually at war. The India of today is half the area of the USA. It is 2,000 miles from Kashmir to Cape Cormoran, 2,200 from Baluchistan to the eastern frontier of Assam. Eighty-three per cent of its population are Hindu: only 11 per cent are Muslim (though before partition they accounted for 25 per cent). But in addition there are substantial minorities of Jains, Buddhists, and Christians. No fewer than fifteen languages are officially recognized as such, but if the dialects are considered they number (according to Sir George Grierson's researches, 1903–28) no fewer than 225. It is perfectly true that linguistic and/or ethnic uniformity are not sufficient or even necessary conditions for statehood: but they do help it along mightily.

Moreover, in addition to the divisions of language and religion, Hindu society is subject to a hierarchical principle which is unique: that of *caste*. It is impossible to estimate how many castes and sub-castes existed in Mughal times—significantly fewer, one surmises, than today, for they have proliferated steadily—but today their number exceeds 3,000, with a median population of 5,000–1,500, but a variance of a few hundreds to millions of population per caste. While this may not in itself have obstructed the formation of the state, it certainly had the most profound effect on how the state was constituted and governed. For caste was not only the most immediate but also the central concern of the common man, receiving, as has been well said, 'most of the loyalty elsewhere felt towards king, nation, and city'.[1]

It would be false to say that the regions of this subcontinent were never politically united before the Mughal conquest, but exact to say that its highly infrequent unifications were all incomplete, short-lived, and discon-

[1] A. L. Basham, *The Wonder that was India*, 3rd edn. (Sidgwick & Jackson, London, 1985), 151.

tinuous. The elaborate urban civilization of Mohenjo-Daro and Harappa, (in any case, highly localized along the Indus) came to an abrupt end *c.*2000 BC for unknown reasons. It was a dead end, and what happened in the ensuing centuries we do not really know. By contrast the Mauryan Empire (321–185 BC) extended over the entire subcontinent except the far south and reached its height under the reign of the benign Asoka (273–232 BC), one of the two great kings in Indian tradition (significantly, the other is the Mughal Akbar). The conventional wisdom about Asoka's empire describes it as highly centralized, being divided into four great provinces under his sons, with salaried royal officials supervising every activity in the rural localities and the towns; a well-organized fiscal network of royal officials and a central treasury; and good communications and a host of secret agents who provided intelligence. In brief, Asoka's empire was held to be a centralized, patrimonial despotism where the emperor ruled through a host of officials appointed by and responsible to him. For a wide variety of reasons, some self-evident, this could not have been and was not so. I fully share the critical views of Tambiah. It was what he himself likes to call the 'galactic empire', and which the Indians themselves called a *mandala*, that is, a circle.

At its apex was a king of kings subsuming in a superior ritual and even fiscal relation a vast collection of local principalities and regional clusters. Asoka's genius (and that of his forebears) was that he brought such an empire under one umbrella, an achievement that was given concrete expression by the king's officials and missions sent to the farther provinces, including the border regions . . . Such a political edifice was not so much a bureaucratized centralized imperial monarchy as a kind of galaxy-type structure with lesser political replicas revolving around the central entity and in perpetual motion of fission or incorporation.[2]

The next empire, that of the Guptas (AD 320–647, but effectively 320–480), was both smaller and far looser than the Mauryan. Its core territory was, basically, the Indo-Gangetic plain; other parts of the empire were either vassal kingdoms or ones where Gupta 'influence' was strong. Little more than half the area of what was to be British India came under any degree of

---

[2] S. J. Tambiah, *World Conqueror and World Renouncer: A Study of Buddhism and Polity in Thailand,* Cambridge Studies in Social Anthropology, 15 (CUP, Cambridge, 1976), 70. Among my reasons for rejecting the conventional 'centralized' model (I regret I have no space to make the critique in detail) are the following: the self-evident absurdity of assuming so high a degree of centralization when the area was half that of the USA, communication slow and uncertain, and the populations had never been politically united; the absence of central appointments below the provincial levels where such posts were staffed by locals, while the central bureaucracy itself was patrimonial and was dissolved and replaced at each new reign; and the paucity of hard evidence about the running of this empire.

control by the dynasty. The Gupta state perfectly illustrates the Indian conception of empire up to Akbar. An empire was a *mandala* or *chakra*, the emperor was a *chakravartin*, that is, a King of Kings. He administered his own domain in a centralized fashion; the circle of tributary kingships that surrounded these domains were run in a similarly centralized way but enjoyed full autonomy. The duties of their monarchs were to attend on the *chakravartin*, discharge duties for him, and bring him gifts. Their allegiance was highly volatile.[3]

The Delhi Sultanate ran, nominally, from 1206 to 1526, but effectively it crumbled after 1334. Even at its widest extent it could get no further south than the Deccan which it annexed in 1323, only to disintegrate twelve years later.[4]

The importance of this Delhi Sultanate does not lie in its extensiveness, limited as that was, but in the revolutionary fact that it was founded by Turks and Afghans as a Muslim state within which the native Hindus were reduced to *dhimmi* status. It marks the beginnings of the Muslim dominance over India which was not to fade till after Aurungzeb (1707) and the coming of the Raj. Henceforth India was to contain two religions and ways of life, one syncretic and adaptive, one rigidly exclusive; at some times and in a few places mutually hostile, elsewhere symbiotic; in a few places the Muslim rulers persecuting their Hindu subjects and looting their temples, but the great majority encouraging the study of Sanscritic learning and endowing Hindu temples.

In brief, if we add together the span of effective unity under the Mauryan, Gupta, and Delhi dynasties it amounts in total to little more than 362 years. Nothing more dramatically demonstrates that in the Indian subcontinent empire was very much the exception and transience the norm. Furthermore, its turbulent and fluid states never settled down into a 'states-system'; a moving equilibrium like the Chinese kingdoms in the Warring States period, or like those of classical Greece, medieval Italy, or modern Europe as a whole. In these, the rise of one state was immediately countered by a coalition of its rivals, so that the most important states persisted as political entities even if perchance with truncated territories. Here in India,

---

[3] N. K. Sinha, *Economic History of Bengal*, vol. 3 (Firma K. L. Mukhopadhyaya, Calcutta, 1962), 206–16.

[4] Parenthetically, the Sultanate is interesting to this history in quite another way. For about a century, under the so-called 'Slave Kings', the Sultanate was ruled like Mamluk Egypt: the Turkish Mamluk slave corps provided the military leadership, the provincial governors, and the great dignatories of the court. They were only extruded as the number of free-born Turkish nobles and soldiers who were fleeing the Mongols began to accumulate; and in 1290, when the throne was taken over by the Khalijis, the leaders of free-born Turkish immigrants, the power of the Mamluks waned—though it did not disappear.

however, states could and usually did go out of existence altogether. All of them were engaged in incessant warfare with their neighbours. It was the ambition of every vassal king to emancipate himself and become *chakavartin* himself. The *métier* of every monarch was *digvijaya*—'conquering the four quarters'.

Until the Mughals, then, the efforts at political unification of the subcontinent were few, short-lived, and territorially wanting. By contrast the Mughal Empire was longer-lived and, at its height, embraced more territory than Asoka's. But unlike that, it was no 'galactic empire', no *mandala*, but a truly unitary state held together by (for its time) a sophisticated administration. This was the precursor of the unity imposed by the Raj, which was so much more complete that it led to the emergence of what may truly be called an Indian nation.

The Mughals were Muslims. Babur's conquest of the Delhi Sultanate in 1526 confirmed the continuance of Muslim overrule. This 'overrule' must not be taken as signifying the Islamization of the overwhelmingly Hindu population. The Mughals depended on a host of vassals who were indifferently Hindu or Muslim. Also, in the south, there were powerful Hindu states like Vijayanagara and it was not long before native Hindu dynasties re-appeared elsewhere; and all emperors till Aurungzeb made close allies of the powerful Rajput chieftains (Hindu) against the Hindu Mahrattas: indeed autonomous Rajput chieftains acted as generals of the empire.

CHRONOLOGY

The Indus Civilization

*c.*2500 BC	The Harappan culture

The Coming of the Aryans

*c.*1500 BC	Migration of the Aryans
*c.*800	Use of iron. Expansion of Aryan culture

Pre-Mauryan States

*c.*600 BC	Magadha (capital at Patna), hegemonic state
*c.*519	Cyrus the Persian conquers part of north-west India
486	Death of the Buddha
*c.*486	Death of Mahavira, founder of Jainism
327–325	Alexander the Great in north-west India

The Mauryan Empire, 321–185 BC

321 BC	Chandragupta, founder of the empire
268–231	Asoka
185	Collapse of the empire

An Age of Invasions

c.90 BC	Shakas invade north-west India. Fragmentation into many states
c. AD 25	Kushans invade north-west India

The Gupta Empire, AD 320–540

320	Chandragupta I
335	Samudra Gupta
375–415	Chandragupta II
c.454	Hun invasion of north-west India
c.495	Second Hun invasion
c.540	End of Gupta dynasty
606–47	Temporary revival under Harsha
712	The Arabs occupy Sind

The Advent of the Muslims, 712–1206

647 onwards	Proliferation of Hindu states
997–1030	Mahmud of Ghazni's raids in north-west India. Plunder of Hindu temples and persecution of Hindus
1150–1	The Turkish Ghurid dynasty defeats and displaces Ghaznavides
1179–86	Ghurids take Peshawar, Sialkot, Lahore
1186–1205	Continual Ghurid battles against Rajputs. A Ghurid empire in North India
1206	Assassination of Muhammed of Ghur. The empire disintegrates
1206–90	The 'Slave Kings' (Mamluks) take over the empire
1211	Accession of Shams-ud-din Ilutmish
1229	Ilutmish invested by caliph as sultan

The Delhi Sultanate

1236	Death of Ilutmish
1236–66	Instability—Mamluks versus non-Mamluks, and inter-Mamluk rivalry
1266–86	Balban restores unity
1290–1320	Khalji dynasty—freeborn Turks
1320–1413	Tughluk dynasty
1334	The Sultanate begins to disintegrate
1398	Timur sacks Delhi
1451–89	Modest revival under Bahlul Lodi, founder of the Lodi dynasty
1504	Babur (The Tiger) (1483–1530), the first Mughal, takes Kabul

1517–26	Ibrahim Lodi
1526	Babur's decisive victory over Ibrahim at Panipat. Delhi captured
1527	Babur defeats Rajputs at Khanua. Beginning of Mughal Empire (1526–1857; effectively to 1739) (For a dynastic list, see below at p. 1230.)

2 . INDIAN POLITICAL TRADITION

The areas conquered by the Mughals comprised two different traditions of statehood: Muslim and Hindu. As Muslims themselves, how would they treat their Hindu subjects? In the past a number of Muslim rulers of north India—indeed one must go back as far as Mahmud of Ghazni—had oppressed the Hindus, imposed the *jizya* (poll tax) on them, and plundered or even closed down their temples. Others had not interfered with them.

It all depended on the character and the fanaticism or the sheer greed of the Muslim ruler, for in respect of the last-mentioned, the temples provided fantastically rich plunder. Yet the political outlook of a Muslim ruler in India was much the same as those we have already encountered. He would, normally, work within the limit of the *sharia* and listen to the advice of his mullahs in applying it. Alauddin Khalji's rejection of the *sharia* as the basic law of the state was not often met elsewhere. (Nor for that matter was an Alauddin, a treacherous and murderous despot who conquered and pillaged far and wide, a veritable *lusus naturae*, who stopped at nobody and nothing: 'whatever I think to be for the good of the state, or suitable for the emergency, that I decree.'[5]) How far sultans and princes followed their mullahs' advice depended on their own personal piety qualified by the practicalities of ruling over a vast and often armed mass of non-Muslims. But the guiding principles of government in the Caliphate and the Ottoman Empire were the same as those of the Muslim rulers of north India and indeed of any more southerly state where a Muslim ruler had, in one way or another, become installed.[6] To repeat once more, these rulers did not Islamize their kingdoms, for there was the native tradition of statecraft with which these Muslim rulers—especially the Mughals with their numerous and powerful Hindu vassals—had had to come to terms. In so far as Hindus formed a majority of a state's subjects (and *a fortiori*, when the ruler was himself a Hindu), this native tradition profoundly affected the way the ruler conducted his affairs. Yet the Hindu state was in turn itself profoundly affected by—one might even say strait-jacketed by—Hindu social structure.

[5] A good account of this man's vicious career can be found in R. C. Majumdar, *Medieval India* (Tauris, London, 1951), pt. ii, 297–311, esp. the passages quoted from al-Barani.

[6] See n. 4 above for the peculiarities of the 'Slave Dynasty' of the Delhi Sultanate.

This was almost entirely unyielding in the face of political authority, whether Muslim or Hindu. Since this social structure was a function of Hindu religion something must be said about this religion and its reflection in society before we can profitably discuss the traditional Hindu state.

2.1. *Hinduism and Social Structure*

The traditonal Hindu polity was centrally affected by *caste*, which itself is part and parcel of Hindu religion. This is usually termed 'Hinduism', but this usage gives rise to a serious misunderstanding.The reason is that 'the mass of religious phenomena that we shelter under the umbrella of that term is not a unity and does not aspire to be . . . Hinduism refers not to an entity; it is the name the West has given to a prodigiously variegated set of facts. To use the term at all is inescapably a gross oversimplification.'[7]

It is so protean as to defy exact description. It accepts, *inter alia*, the notion that God is omniscient and omnipresent, indeed in some measure it might well be called pantheistic. But the paths to the Ultimate (*Brahman*), which, we must note, is not *isvara* (God) but beyond, are many and none is invalid.

Indian religion has always been hospitable, absorbent and syncretistic. Hence within Hinduism as it exists there is an almost unbelievable tolerance of varieties of both belief and practice. Inside the social structure of Hinduism can be found philosophical mystics, who have no belief in a personal deity, pluralists ranging from crude animists mainly interested in local godlings (such as the village-mother or the jungle spirit) to polytheists of the type familiar to students of Greek, Roman and Egyptian antiquities; and between these two extremes fervent monotheists who address their devotion to a single personal god, conceived in terms superficially akin to those used by many Christians.[8]

Superficially, Hindus will—so an Indian Christian remarked bitterly to me—'worship anything or anyone'. They may worship at the village phallus—the *lingam*—that stands in the middle of the *maidan*; or any one or a number of village or local deities; or belong to any one of the many cults of Vishnu or of Shiva, and indeed other members of the Hindu pantheon such as the goddesses Lakhsmi and Kali and that much-loved god Krishna. Or they may withdraw from all these and live the life of the wandering ascetic, in search of the Absolute. The syncretism of the religion can be and often is rationalized by the concept of Incarnation: *isvara* (God) and Vishnu rein-

---

[7] W. Cantwell Smith, *The Meaning and End of Religion* (Mentor Religious Classics, 1964), quoted in W. Foy (ed.), *Man's Religious Quest: A Reader* (Croom Helm/Open University, London, 1978), 49–50.

[8] A. C. Bouquet, quoted in K. M. Sen, *Hinduism* (Penguin, Harmondsworth, 1961), 37, fn. 1.

carnate in various human or non-human shapes. Observant Hindus, for instance, believe in 'the One or Whole with three forms', that is, the three great figures of Brahma, Vishnu, and Shiva (though there has been no cult of Brahma since very early times), where Vishnu is seen as the preservative and Shiva as the destructive aspect of the Supreme. Now, these great gods and the many others worshipped can and do incarnate themselves in human shape so that in the *Mahabharata*, for instance, the charioteer of the hero, Prince Arjuna, turns out to be the god Krishna.

But certain common elements underly this teeming variety. The Hindu religious outlook has a body of sacred scriptures that go right back to the Vedas, and which have developed and commented upon one another through the centuries. The 'bearers' of the Vedic scriptures are the Brahmins, a class possessing spiritual supremacy by birth, and considered to be the ideal of ritual purity. It has its own great epics, the *Mahabharata* and the *Ramayana*, episodes of which may be acted out in village festivals which help to project their ethical message, while the sophisticated 'educated classes' search the texts and give them profound religious interpretations. Its plastic arts and architecture revolve round a basic model which is recognizably Hindu and unrecognizable as anything else. One common thread of doctrine runs through all manifestations of the religion, and it is this that is critical to the political outlook and behaviour of the Hindus: the transmigration of souls.

The soul of man is caught on a wheel of existence. At death it migrates to yet another body. That body may be that of a lowly caterpillar, or it may be that of a human sweeper or warrior or scholar. The particular body one inhabits at a given moment is the consequence of the soul's deeds or misdeeds in its previous incarnations—and so on: it is his *karmaphala* (the results of his *karma* or action). The wheel of existence never winds down. It goes on for ever, so that the soul is condemned throughout infinity (save in the instance given below) to live out its life in one shape or another. This is *samsara*. By acts of merit (*punya*) the soul may be reborn in a higher-placed category than before. Conversely, the wicked man's soul sinks back to a more lowly place. In this way it might be possible for a human soul to have progressed over countless generations so far up the ladder of incarnation as to be at the point where the wheel of existence stops and the soul becomes one with the Absolute. There are a number of 'ways' (*marga*). One of these is the 'path of duties' and involves the important concept of *dharma*.

Dharma is, essentially, a natural attribute: it is the *dharma* of rivers to flow, of stones to fall, and of humans to fulfil the duties of the station in which their body and soul find themselves. In this sense *dharma* becomes duty, but a duty that flows from one's life-situation. *Dharma*, as duty, is Kantian. It must be pursued for its own sake.[9]

Now this doctrine obviously implies hierarchy: the animal kingdom, then humankind, and then—within humankind[10]—the four great Orders of society and, within each of them, the castes. The Orders are *varna* (literally, 'colours'). The castes are the *jati*.

The *varnas* go back to Vedic times. There is a scholar-priest Order, the Brahmans. Below them are ranked the warrior Order, the *kshatriyas*. Below them comes the great Order of traders, farmers, and the like, the *vaisyas*. The lowest Order is that of the *sudras*: artisans and peasantry. But this is not the lowest class of humanity. Some people are literally outcaste. They perform all the dirty or ritually impure jobs in society. In practice, the *jati*, that is, the castes which are to be found inside all these Orders rather than the Orders themselves, have been the active agents in society, with the exception of the first two, the Brahmans and the *Kshatriyas*. Brahmans played priests to *Kshatriya* kings. The fighting princes of Rajastan, the Rajputs, claimed (though of immigrant origin) to be *Kshatriya*.

Caste has proved an immense puzzle to anthropologists and sociologists and its origin, nature, and function are immensely controversial. Today there are some 3,000 castes which are ranked (though not clearly) in ascending order until one comes to the topmost Brahmans. (This is not to be understood as saying that there are 3,000 rungs in the ladder: in any particular region the number of *jatis* would be much smaller and many of them would have equal status.) The caste has the following main characteristics. First, it is endogamous, that is, one may only marry inside the caste. Often members bear a common name and sometimes claim a common descent. Secondly, and largely a corollary of the above, it clings to the same customs particularly those relating to ritual purity, so that it determines such matters as whom to take meals with and what utensils to use, all the way to marriages and births, no less. Finally, the caste holds a rank in a

---

[9] The classic exposition of this is to be found in the *Bhagavad-gita* ('The Lord's Song'), an interpolation in the gigantic epic, the *Mahabharata*, usually attributed to the 2nd cent. AD. As the two immense armies of the contending royal families line up for the battle to win the throne, Arjuna, the leader of the Pandava host, quails at the thought of the awful carnage he is about to unleash. His charioteer is, however, the Lord Krishna. Krishna tells him, effectively, that it is not for him so to reason: he is *kshatriya* and it is the *dharma* of the *kshatriya* to fight, and 'if thou wilt not wage this lawful battle, then wilt thou fail thine own *dharma* and honour, and get sin . . . Holding in indifference alike pleasure and pain, gain and loss, conquest and defeat, so make thyself ready for the fight; thus thou shalt get no sin' (ii. 33, 38), trans. and interpreted F. Edgerton (Harvard Univ. Press, Cambridge, Mass., 1972).

[10] Strictly speaking the Orders are *jati* too, but I have followed a common convention since it makes exposition clearer.

(somewhat irregular) social hierarchy, the chief criterion being its degree of ritual purity. Social mobility is, consequently, very low. It is permissible for a higher-caste male to marry a lower-caste female but, though nominally permitted, in practice not the other way round.

The members may believe or disbelieve any creed or doctrine, religious or philosophical, without affecting their caste position. That can be forfeited only by a breach of the caste regulations concerning the *dharma*, or practical duty of members belonging to the group. Each caste has its own *dharma* in addition to the common rules of morality as accepted by Hindus generally, and considered to be the *dharma* of mankind. The general Hindu *dharma* exacts among other things reverence to the Brahmans, respect for the sanctity of animal life in varying degrees, and . . . preeminently the cow. Every caste man is expected to observe accurately the rules of his own group, and to refrain from doing violence to the feelings of other groups concerning their rules. The essential duty of the member of the caste is to follow the custom of his group, more particularly in relation to diet or marriage . . . [11]

A very large number of these castes are numerically quite small, geographically circumscribed, and occupationally specialized. If one looked at a village, overwhelmingly the preponderant political form in India even at the present day, one would see these castes interacting by doing to others what their *dharma* orders and receiving from others what, in turn, those castes are mandated to offer. The castes in the village are ranked. Brahmans, if they hold land, are clearly the top caste. Families in a particular *jati* provide goods and services to other families and receive in return perhaps a fixed amount of grain. The kind of services that are rendered back and forth in the village are the change of land-use for the common folk to till, priestly rituals especially at marriages, the carrying of water, sweeping, scavenging, and so forth. Each *jati* performs its particular service to all the others, who reciprocate, forming a tight network of interdependence. And the institution is all-pervasive. [12]

Caste is obviously both cause and consequence of the most extreme social conservatism and it was just this which preserved the Hindu way of life under the Muslim overlordship. But it had important political consequences too. In a country of villages, caste and sub-caste village relationships—along with the guilds and village councils—performed much of what one would normally expect the central power to provide. These caste interrelationships were much more important to the villagers than the dynasty. This is why the Hindu kingdoms were so labile. Their populations had no sense of the state. Their loyalty was towards the social order. Accordingly, one quite central function of the ruler was to preserve the ordering of the castes, and

[11] R. Segal, *The Crisis of India* (Penguin, Harmondsworth, 1965), 35.   [12] Ibid. 35.

the duty to do this and to act within the limits of social custom was the major, perhaps the only significant constraint upon his authority. It is to this that we must now turn.

2.2. *The Hindu Polity*

Earlier in this *History,* when we were dealing with ancient Greece, we singled it out as the beginnings of a unique and enduring innovation in government, the *republic*. We said that this was the only part of the globe up to that time in which such a form of polity had appeared. This was not quite true. In ancient India the prevalent form of polity was indeed the monarchy, but till quite late times—we might put their demise at the time of the Guptas— there existed a number of republics. Indeed, it was in one of these that the Buddha formed his resolve to turn his back on the world and so founded his new religion. The difficulty here is that we know very little about the working of these republics. It looks very much as if they were founded by proud and rebellious aristocrats—*kshatriyas*—who were not prepared to put up with being the underlings of the new monarchies that were becoming more and more autocratic. These *kshatriyas* are thought to have fled the monarchies and established their own oligarchical form of government in the mountainous regions of the north, rather like those Norwegians who exiled themselves to Iceland rather than obey kingship. But it may have occurred the other way round: tribal oligarchies developing into monarchies. At all events, it seems that these oligarchies consisted of a number of noble families, that they were governed by an assembly of the heads of such families who rotated, after election by the rest, into the office of raja: effectively, the presiding officer of the assembly. This oligarchy ruled the local population, who possessed passive rights but not active (participatory) ones.

The earliest monarchies were ruled by a raja (cognate with the Latin *rex*) assisted by a council similar in composition to that of the republics; but by *c.*900 BC the latter had disappeared and had been replaced by the great courtiers and relatives of the king, called the *ratnins,*[13] and after 700 BC even the *ratnins* had gone and the only check on the authority of the king was that of religion. There had been a period in Vedic times when the Brahmans claimed divinity and prestige equal to the monarch's. But their excessive ritualism provoked a reaction in the form of breakaway sects like the Jains and the Buddhists and the rise of *bhakti*, devotional cults like Vaishnavaism with its belief in a personal god. A monarch was always assisted by a high

[13] Basham, *The Wonder,* 42.

(Brahman) priest, the *purohita*, and had to accept his lead in ritual matters. But for the rest he was a despot. Thus, in a certain lawsuit, 'the king made no inquiry but only said "off with him, impale him on a stake"'.[14] The Brahmans, following the *smrti* text[15] known as the *Laws of Manu*,[16] even attributed divinity to him; but, as Basham ironically points out, in a country which could worship stones and trees among other things, 'divinity was cheap in ancient India'.[17] The *purohita* remained equal in dignity to the king,[18] but the latter was in the stronger position for only he wielded *dandaniti*, laws of governing or punishment, which we may roughly equate with sovereignty. Assisted by some eight ministers, a number which could rise to as many as thirty, the king used his *dandanati* to enforce the common law, which was tantamount to the local usages, *plus* the Sacred Law.

This was roughly the situation when the Hindu kingdoms entered their Middle Ages (AD 700–1200). The kingship was hereditary and the succession was governed by primogeniture. However, the king made the selection during his lifetime and if the heir was defective the succession went to other members of the family, such as a younger brother. The succession was by no means always smooth and tranquil; many were the wars fought between uncle and nephew for the throne, and indeed in the early days of the East India Company it was the widespread family quarrels over the succession that enabled its agents to mix in and impose their own candidate. The royal divinity we have touched on earlier was by now disputed. Certainly the raja's coronation was surrounded by the most elaborate rituals: ritual bathing, a fire-sacrifice, the symbolic rubbing of the royal body with twelve different kinds of earth. Then, after worship of the gods, the raja was duly enthroned by receiving from the Brahman priests his weapons and the royal umbrella.[19]

A raja was not supposed to act arbitrarily, but there was no constitutional mechanism whatsoever to prevent him doing so. For all that, he was constrained in three ways: first, because he was expected to observe the Sacred Law, that is, the common *dharma* (as, for example, in *Manu*) and it was not always wise to quarrel with the *purohita* and the Brahmans who were its custodians; secondly, local custom, the rules of the castes, and the regula-

---

[14] Sinha, *Economic History of Bengal*, 88.

[15] *Smrti*, i.e. 'remembered': a class of religious literature comprising lawbooks especially, but also epics and Puranas (sacred texts).

[16] *c.* AD 200 (?), with twelve chapters which range over juridical law, the laws of religious observance and rituals, and domestic morality, and which also presents the doctrines of *karma*, *dharma*, and punishment in hell. Its influence was enormous, and through the various commentaries on it it became virtually canonical.   [17] Basham, *The Wonder*, 86.

[18] Sinha, *Economic History of Bengal*, 170.

[19] P. B. Udgaonkar, *The Political Institutions and Administration of Northern India during Medieval Times* (Varanasi, Delhi and Patna, 1969), 39, 47, 58. I have relied very heavily on this source in what follows.

tions of the craft and merchant guilds had to be observed and indeed enforced where necessary; and thirdly, because the elaborate centralized bureaucracy boiled down in the end merely to an organization that kept order, fought the wars, and collected the money for both. Practically all other socio-economic functions[20] in the state were carried out by the non-official councils in the villages. The people had no sense of state. Hindu society was independent of this and transcended it. The 'state' was simply an extension of the person of the raja whose sole task was to preserve the social structure intact, and this amounted to maintaining the castes and their relativities, suppressing robbers, upholding the local cults, and fighting foreign foes.[21] Was there a tradition of resistance to misrule? Some modern authorities think not.[22] The classical texts differ on the matter. For instance, the *Mahabharata* in one place sanctions revolt against a king who is oppressive or has failed to protect his people ('he should be killed like a mad dog'), while in another place it argues that any king was better than none.[23] Rebellions, however, did take place but here again the traditions conflict. There are texts in the *Dharmashastra* (a work that lays down the codes of conduct) which purport to describe the circumstances in which rebellions could be considered just; the king was presumed to be a 'servant' maintained by a sixth of the taxpayer's income. As a servant he could be sacked for failure to do his duty. Other sources, however, speak of the king as the owner of all land and water in the kingdom. In that case the peasantry are a kind of tenantry and their tax is really the rent they pay. This was the majority view and it certainly does not lack for evidence.[24]

The central bureaucracy of such medieval kingdoms seems imposing; but it must never be forgotten that the agents that actually carried out their decisions were the village headmen and their councils and, in the urban settlements or cities, the leaders and the like who were their functional equivalents.[25]

The bureaucratic machinery could be most elaborate, so that what follows here is the simplest of outlines. The chief ministers were the *purohita*, the high priest; the *pratinidhi*, who was the deputy to the king; the *pradhana*, a kind of grand vizier; the *pandita*, who advised on changes in socio-religious matters; the *sumantra*, or treasurer; and the *amatya* or accountant-general. We do know that the system was patrimonial, that ministers were shuffled around from function to function, and that each minister had to send a

---

[20] Irrigation, temples, and roads might be, selectively, provided by the court.
[21] Basham, *The Wonder*, 88.   [22] Udgaonkar, *Political Institutions*, 65.
[23] Basham, *The Wonder*, 87–8.   [24] Ibid. 109–10.
[25] *Cambridge Economic History of India*, vol. I (1982), 448 [hereafter referred to as *CEHI*]. More will be said about the government of the cities below.

written report to the king who must countersign his approval. But apart from these things we have no idea how the ministry functioned. 'It is difficult', we are told, 'to say how the secretariat and its various departments were organized and how they used to function.' Though we possess a long list of officials, it does 'not throw much light upon their powers and functions'.[26]

There were other high officials as well as the ministers, but generalization is difficult; so that there were numerous exceptions to what is now described. Mention must necessarily be made of the commander-in-chief at the head of the military department, along with his subordinate commanders of the three chief armed services—the infantry, the cavalry, and the elephants. As to the police, they were not distinguishable from the soldiers.[27] In the Revenue Department a chief accountant supervised the collection of taxes and other revenues, controlled the land grants which paid the services of ministers and other officials (the *jagirs*, which are simply benefices), and looked after the state granaries. This department had a chain of officials at the provincial and town levels.

Kingdoms were organized into provinces responsible for tax-collection, law and order, and control of the lower echelons, the *bhukti*; and the districts, the *vishaya* (though the precise connotation of these terms is doubtful). The towns and urban settlements were governed not dissimilarly from most towns throughout the Orient and the Middle East. They lacked any corporate or municipal institutions, rights, 'liberties', or legal personalities. They were governed by a *purapati*, usually a soldier but sometimes a man chosen for literary or administrative abilities. In fortress towns a commander took charge of the garrison and fortress while the *purapati* confined himself to civil functions. From the days of the Muslim Delhi Sultanate the city chief of police (see later) was the *kotwal*, a very senior official with a force of soldiers at his command. But since government looked after little but law, order, taxation, and a few economic matters (e.g. market regulation) the internal life of the towns was carried out by its leading citizens. Cities (we have met this many times before in eastern parts) were divided into wards (*mahal, mahalla*), consisting variously of a single caste or occupation, and in many cases these *mahallas* were walled off from each other, with gates that could be closed at night or during disorders. Inside such *mahallas* disputes would be handled by an 'elder'—a *panchayet*—and appeals beyond him to the *qazi*, the central government's own official at a higher level, were uncommon.

However, a significant development in the centuries up to *c.*1200 com-

[26] Udgaonkar, *Political Institutions*, 92–101, 107.   [27] Ibid. 121.

plicated these formal governmental structures. It was the royal practice of granting away villages. They were made over to officials such as we have mentioned in payment for their service; to vassals who would in return bring a certain number of troops to the field; and to the Brahmans, in recognition of their religious status and activities. Consequently one must perceive these kingdoms as units which not only had fluid borders—which often collapsed entirely—but as pockmarked with areas where lords of various degree exercised important governmental functions, especially fiscal ones. This is a feudalistic but not a feudal system—the grants were not fiefs but benefices—and were effectively a fiscal device. Furthermore, the vassal was not bound like his western counterpart to give counsel to the king, nor did he and his fellows form a council.

Villages were usually granted in multiples of ten, twelve, or sixteen. The grantee was entitled to subinfeudate: a *rajaputra*, say, applied to a *ranaka* (a high-ranking noble) for a benefice. This might be a single village. He was responsible for collecting its revenues and to do this might put out part of it to merchants and accountants. These were not 'tax-farmers' in the usual sense, but the *rajaputra's* agents who were bound specifically to provide the amount specified in the contract made with them.[28] The grantee had not been granted just the income from the village: he *owned* it. Sometimes the grant covered trees, mines, and so on. In some cases artisans or even cultivators were granted, so that they were effectively serfs.[29] In fact, it has been suggested that even in villages where they were not specifically transferred to the owner, the latter probably exercised a general control over them to obey his orders and to pay him all dues.[30] The peasant response to too tight a control was to migrate, and this was a regular feature of the medieval economy.

Whether in one particular kingdom or its successor states, within the same borders or in altered ones, whether granted out to vassals and the like or directly subject to the ruler, the one fixed element throughout the ages was the village. Some have seen the political history of Indian states as little more than the unceasing incorporation and re-incorporation of numbers of villages inside altered sets of boundaries which had been militarily imposed. The boundaries changed all the time but the villages and their functioning remained constant. The village preserved its law and order, defended itself in the event of civil war or depredations, collected and paid over taxes, and settled local disputes. It was run by a headman, usually hereditary, who kept

---

[28] R. S. Sharma, *Indian Feudalism: c.300–1200* (Calcutta, 1965), 200–2. All the foregoing is based on Sharma's work.   [29] Ibid. 226, 228, 234.
[30] Ibid. 235.

records of the tax assessments and a register of land-ownership. He was remunerated by rent-free land and petty dues. By no means was he usually a Brahman. Much more often he was a *kshatriya*, sometimes even of a lower Order. He was the local 'big man'—one of the rich. He worked from an office and might have an accountant to help him, but the records of the southern states and the northern ones differ here.[31] He was assisted by a council, and this was important for it was not restricted by caste. We have no particulars as to how it was brought into being in north India but in the south it was elected on the basis of candidates' property, education, and moral qualifications. These assemblies represented the rich or ruling stratum in a village.[32] In the Tamil lands they threw off subcommittees to look after the water-tanks, the temples, and the roads; but not so in the north. Most importantly, perhaps, the village council acted as a court of first instance and only if it had failed to agree could appeal be made to the raja's court.[33] However the arrangements were more untidy and less well-structured than this description suggests.

Before moving on to discuss the Mughal state, it might be as well to point to the fragile and loose articulation even of some of the wealthiest and most powerful Hindu kingdoms. Despite the lability of their frontiers and incessant warfare with their neighbours, some of these proved fairly long-lived. The Chola state, for instance, persisted with many ups and downs from the early tenth century to its collapse in 1257 and the extinction of its dynasty in 1279. This was a very wealthy kingdom whose core territory was Tanjore and Trichinopoly, and at its greatest extent was overlord to all the lands south of the Kaveri River, not to speak of its overseas possessions which included Ceylon, the Nicobar and Maldive Islands, and parts of southern Malaysia. Its wealth came from the carrying trade; it had ports on either side of the peninsula. It built ships in all shapes and sizes, the largest able to carry 700 passengers. These ships traded as far as Hormuz to the west and China to the east, so that the kingdom possessed prosperous merchant cities.

The relationship of the king to the subject lands was not based on effective administrative or military power, however, but on his ritual, divine status and, as such, his being the source of honours and legitimacy. It was not, therefore, a 'centralized monarchy'.[34] On the contrary, it lacked bureaucratic penetration and by the same token its villages enjoyed a 'remarkably'

---

[31] Udgaonkar, *Political Institutions*, 164.

[32] Evidence from West India indicates that all castes were represented in the Panchayat.

[33] Udgaonkar, *Political Institutions*, 166–9.

[34] So B. Stein in the *CEHI*, i. 32–7. *Contra*, R. Thapar, *A History of India*, vol. 1 (Penguin, Harmondsworth, 1966), 200–11, who thinks it was centralized, with an effective bureaucracy.

wide autonomy.[35] The royal officials were more participant-observers than administrators. Village assemblies were of three kinds. The *ur*, found in ordinary villages, consisted nominally of the taxpayers but effectively of the rich. In the Brahman villages, the assembly (*sabha*) was chosen by sortition. In the trading cities the assembly consisted of the *nagaram*, roughly translatable as 'guilds'. These assemblies collected the assessed revenue, passing on the Crown's share and raising levies for their own local use. In the villages, certainly, the temple was the centre of social and economic life.

We can turn from the Chola state to a successor, the mighty 'war state' of Vijayanagara. This city was founded by a conqueror, Harihara, in 1343, with the Krishna River as its boundary. Here again, trade brought immense wealth. Its rulers were not Tamils like the Cholas, but warriors from the north who overran the petty chiefdoms that had proliferated after the fall of the Chola dynasty. Surrounded by enemies, the rulers needed large sums to pay their soldiers and the Brahman castellans of their fortresses. Like their Chola predecessors they did not extract such resources via a bureaucracy, that is, by regular remittance of taxes from the localities to the central court. Vijayanagara was no more centralized than the Chola state and indeed it may well be regarded as much less so. Through conflicting descriptions, it would appear that some 200 or so warrior-chiefs—*nayakas*—paid tribute: but whether, as the Portuguese Fernão Nuniz[36] reported, these were mere 'renters' from the king and paid their 'rent' by raising troops, or whether they were squireens, landowners in their own right, who were at times associated with the dynasty's military campaigns, is disputed. Bit by bit these *nayakas* prevailed over the assemblies, and these—including even the Brahman ones—were withering away by the time the state was overrun and conquered by the Mughals. A rump kingdom did survive till the late seventeenth century but gradually its members merged into the Indian population, just as the Normans had done in England.

3. THE MUGHAL EMPIRE

To the Europeans, Mughal India was a marvel. India spelt riches, and the empire enormous power. For Indians, Mughal India represents the golden age before the British came to take over their country (for all that the Mughals were aliens and Muslims to boot). But, for sure, this was the golden age of Indian music, painting, and above all architecture. It was an age when fabulous concentrations of gold and silks and jewels were being squandered without limit by the noble class in an orgy of stupendously

---

[35] Thapar, *History of India*, 200.   [36] Quoted in ibid. 328–9.

conspicuous expenditure. The Europeans staggered at the sight and looked on in amazement.

All this—the gaudy trappings of the polity—we have to disregard. In the perspective of a history of government the Mughal Empire's claim to attention is simply this: for the first time in South Asian history there was created an empire which was not of the traditional *mandala* type but, on the contrary, was a unified, unitary, and centralized *state*. This was a massive achievement. What is more, at its greatest extent this state covered nearly the entirety of the area of what was to be 'British' India, as well as significant portions of what was to be modern Afghanistan.

But that, so far as we are concerned, is as far as we can go. Its institutions were unoriginal, it was a conquest state that lived on continuous plunder of enemies, and it was entirely exploitative—a revenue-pump which diverted the produce of the cultivator and the merchant to the exclusive use of a narrow and wasteful ruling circle. Short descriptions of this empire give it the appearance of efficient administration carried on by institutions of a remarkable symmetry. This is not my view at all. That symmetry is contrived. It did not exist on the ground. As we might expect, from the agrarian empires that we have so far encountered (with the exception of the Tokugawa's Japan), administration was slack, ill-organized, confusing, and corrupt. In brief: in not one of the other great Asian polities is the gap between the display of wealth and leisured culture, as contrasted with the slovenly and corrupt administration, so marked. Of all of them the Mughal Empire is the worst. This will be the upshot of the following sections. We must begin, however, with a brief account of the founding and then the chronology of this empire.

3.1. *Chronology*

The Mughal Empire was put together by Babur, lost and finally regained by his son Humayun, and cemented into a state by his son, Akbar. Princely rebellions and wars of succession threw up three powerful autocrats, Jahangir, Shah Jahan, and Aurungzeb. Each of them expanded the empire somewhat, culminating with Aurungzeb's conquest of the southern kingdoms of Golconda and Bijapur, which left only the deep south-eastern corner to its native dynasties. But while he did so, Aurungzeb embroiled himself on his western flank, in the Deccan, in a fruitless effort to subdue the native Indian Mahratta chieftains. After the brief reign of his successor (Bahadur, Shah Alam), civil wars and the short reigns of effete wastrels destroyed central authority and the empire disintegrated.

Babur was a princeling by inheritance and a soldier of fortune by profession. He had a prodigious ancestry: he was fifth in the direct line from Timur and thirteenth, but in the female line, from Chinghiz Khan. He spoke Turkic and properly ought to be regarded as Turkish. But Turks and Mongols were much intermingled in these Central Asian areas and the Indians regarded him as a Mongol. Hence the appellation *Mughal.*

His father had ruled Ferghana and Babur's early campaigns were fought to recapture Samarkand, in which he finally failed; but he did succeed in taking Kabul and Kandahar. It was then that he turned his attentions to the south. The Delhi Sultanate had fallen to pieces but its core area had come under the control of the able and warlike Lodi family. One of the usual succession disputes having broken out, one of the contenders invited Babur's help. Babur made four unsuccessful raids before the fifth in 1525 when, using Turkish artillerymen whose assistance proved decisive, his 12,000 troops routed the 100,000-strong obsolete formations of Ibrahim Lodi in the Battle of Panipat, eighty miles north of Delhi. His possession of the capital and evident intention to stay on there as emperor (he had assumed the title *padishah* much earlier, in Afghanistan) provoked the Hindu Rajput chieftains into battle. Though again outnumbered, his new tactics paid off once more. He broke the enemy at the Battle of Khanua, just west of Agra. In the next couple of years he drove raiding Afghans north again and finished off the final rally of the Lodi dynasty. By 1529 he was master of the Indo-Gangetic valley. He had gained an empire, though it was only a congeries of quarrelling chieftains, and then all that he had gained was lost by his son Humayun. The latter was driven from his throne and into the Persian Empire by a rebel nobleman, Sher Shah, who established a brief dynasty which lasted until 1555 when Humayun returned with an army from Persia and retook his throne, only to die in an accident six months later, leaving the succession to his 14-year-old son Akbar. But the latter's interests were well looked after by his prime minister, Bairam, and the conquests were held together until the time when, at the age of 20, Akbar began to govern personally.

Akbar is one of the great rulers in all history. The empire was first staked out by Babur, to be sure, but its founding was the work of Akbar and this consisted in three things. In the first place, he greatly extended it. He incorporated Rajasthan (home of the Rajputs), Bengal, Orissa, Sindh, Bihar, Kashmir, and Gujarat. Secondly, he endowed the whole of these dominions with a uniform administrative and fiscal system, culminating in himself. And thirdly, though a Muslim, Akbar, having once defeated the Hindu Rajput princes, incorporated them into his ruling circles while ending the religious and fiscal discrimination (at times a veritable persecution) of his Hindu subjects, such as had been practised by his Muslim predecessors. For the first time the Hindu could feel he was at one with his ruler. The social and political solidarity so created was the bedrock of Mughal success, and some argue that its shattering at the hands of the uncompromisingly Muslim Aurungzeb heralded the empire's demise, a view that will be discussed at a later point.

CHRONOLOGY

1526	BABUR
1530–9	HUMAYUN
1539–55	The SHUR DYNASTY: four emperors
1555	Demise of Shur dynasty. Humayun resumes the emperorship
1556	Death of Humayun in an accident
1556–1605	AKBAR ('The Great'). Aged 14 at accession
1556–60	Dominance of Bairam Khan, guardian of Akbar
	Decisive repulse of Afghan invasion at Panipat
1560–2	Dominance of the harem party. Conquest of Malwa
1562	Beginning of Akbar's personal rule. Marriage to Hindu Rajput princess (Amber), mother of Jahangir
1564	Akbar abolishes the *jizya* on Hindus
1568	Rajput stronghold of Chitor taken
1572–3	Conquest of Gujerat gives access to the western seaboard
1576	Bengal conquered
1601–4	Rebellion of Prince Salim (known later as Emperor Jahangir)
1605–27	JAHANGIR
1628–57	SHAH JAHAN (d. 1666). Builder of the Taj Mahal
1647–53	Shivaji founds kernel of a Mahratta state
1658	Civil war among the four sons of Shah Jahan
	Victory of Aurungzeb, a devout Muslim
1658–1707	AURUNGZEB. Conquers down to the Carnatic
1665	Reimposition of the *jizya* tax on Hindus, and selective persecution of their religion
1669	Aurungzeb forces peace treaty on Shivaji
1670	Shivaji resumes the Mahratta offensive
1674	Shivaji crowns himself
1679	Alienation and defeat of Rajputs; Marwar annexed
1680	Death of Shivaji
1681	Rebellion (unsuccessful) of Prince Akbar
1681–8	Aurungzeb leads armies to successful subjugation of Bijapur (1686) and Golconda (1687). Capture and subsequent humiliating execution of Shivaji's heir, Sambhaji. The Mahratta War of Independence against Aurungzeb. After twenty years of fighting, Mahrattas still in arms

1707   Death of Aurungzeb
1707–12   Civil wars of succession. Triumph of Shah Alam, who takes throne
                name of BAHADUR

4. THE GOVERNMENT OF THE EMPIRE

4.1. *Overview of the Empire*

At its largest extent the empire contained twenty provinces (called *subahs*),
themselves divided into sub-provinces, districts, and at the bottom, the
villages. Each was ruled by a governor who was a veritable viceroy, except
that he was shadowed by a Treasury official, the *diwan*, who to some extent
acted as a check on his activities. At each level down to the village every
echelon was staffed by officials in charge of the state's very limited functions: army, police, justice, and the assessment and collection of taxes. Any
established official was a *mansabdar* (an office-holder) and on paper no
distinction existed between those engaged in civil and military activities.
At the apex of the imperial structure, that is, at court and its environs, the
interchangeability of military and civil functions was a reality. At lower
echelons a *de facto* distinction of functions existed. The upper ones were
rewarded (at least, after Akbar's reign) by benefices called *jagirs* which
correspond to the Turkish *timars* and the late-Arab and Egyptian *iqtas*.

The activities of the state were strictly architectonic. Its functions only
concerned warfare, order, criminal and civil justice, and taxation to pay for
all this.[37] Despite the *qazis* (that is to say, *qadis*), the empire never had any
written codes, such as the Ottomans had in the sultan's *kanuns*. The
penetration of the state's officials and activities was very shallow indeed
and most of what happened happened in the cities (many of them densely
populated) and, above all, in the villages. As one has now come to expect,
here at the interface of officialdom and the people the local 'big-men', the
zamindars, acted as the intermediaries.

The apex of this territorial-service pyramid was the *padishah*, the emperor.
He was both the driving force and the supreme co-ordinator of policy.
There was no Vizierate as in Turkey. The Mughal emperor was more
unrestrained in his powers than any of the Asian potentates we have so
far encountered. A Muslim by birth and upbringing, he could if he so
wanted—as did Akbar—quite disregard his mullahs.[38] Surrounded by a

---

[37] Selective irrigation projects form a partial exception, along with highways; and there was
considerable support for religious and scholarly activities.

[38] In 1579 the mullahs incited rebellion in Bengal and Bihar and declared Akbar deposed. Akbar
was easily able to override them. On at least two occasions Akbar dismissed his chief religious officers
and replaced them with more pliant ones. Cf. J. N. Sarkar, *Mughal Polity* (Delhi, 1984), 70, for
examples.

service aristocracy of miscellaneously foreign and domestic ancestry which was his very own creation, the emperor was the supreme animator of the entire polity to a degree unmatched in China, Japan, or the Ottoman Empire.

4.2. *Central Government: Emperor and Court*

Babur and his successors took the designation of *padishah*, Persian for 'Great King', hence emperor, but what was their claim to legitimacy? It seems to me useless to look for a 'political formula'. The Delhi sultans had a better entitlement than the Mughals inasmuch as their status had been conferred by the caliph. The Ottoman sultans, however they had begun, acquired legitimacy as great *ghazis* and subsequently as the symbol and the protectors of Muslims everywhere. Babur and his line did indeed vaunt their descent from Chinghiz Khan and Timur, but while this gave them enormous prestige it did not confer a title to rule. Akbar, it is said—a man disabused of orthodox Islam—claimed to rule by direct divine intervention; how many believed this is highly debatable.[39] But did anybody really require a political theory to justify the Mughals' emperorship? It looks much more like a matter of charisma or, at least, heroic leadership. We ought not to seek for the *credenda* of power but rather its extraordinary *miranda*. To begin with, long habituation to change of ruler by reason of conquest had inured the populace, Hindu and Muslim alike, to recognize in an obscure way a certain *right* by conquest. It exists to this day among Arab peoples. In any case the village communities continued their immemorial activities while the battles rolled about them, irrespective of who ruled them. But then again, the emperor was magnificent: wonderfully attired, indescribably rich, exercising even at court the right over life and death; and this emperor showed himself off to the people as a matter of routine, when he walked on the walls of his palace in the early morning of each day, in the *jharoka-i-darshan* ceremony. From there he would proceed to his *diwan-i-am*, the durbar or Court of Public Audience, where everybody who was anybody at court was present in his due place. It was precisely to impress the court that Shah Jahan comissioned the fabulous Peacock Throne.[40] We have quoted the passage from Pascal before, but it will not hurt to be reminded of it here: 'It would take a very refined reason indeed to regard the Grand Turk as you would any

---

[39] J. N. Sarkar, discusses this question, 467–8.

[40] It took seven years to construct. It resembled a cot bedstead with four legs whose enamelled canopy was supported by twelve emerald pillars each bearing two peacocks encrusted with gems. It cost 10 million rupees.

other man as he sits in the midst of his magnificent seraglio surrounded by forty thousand janissaries.'[41]

Just as there was no theory of legitimacy, so there was no rule of succession. Every single emperor had to meet at least one rebellion from sons or brothers. The unexpected death of an emperor invariably provoked civil wars. For instance, when Jahangir died in 1627 the throne was contested between Shah Jahan and his brother Shahryar, and the victorious Shah Jahan had all his male relatives put to death.[42] Indeed, civil wars could erupt long before an emperor died: the four sons of Shah Jahan broke into rebellion each claiming the imperial title. Aurungzeb, who was the victor, disposed of his brothers in some way or another, by public or private execution, and imprisoned his father in the Fort of Agra where he survived for another eight years.

An emperor was bridled only by his own conscience. Aurungzeb, a devout Muslim, allowed himself to be influenced by the mullahs and was careful to act within the *sharia*; but his predecessors did not feel so bound and Akbar acted without restraint. The Mughal emperorship is perhaps the closest we have come, anywhere in this book, to pure and simple despotism. A whim sufficed to have a man impaled—or ennobled. There was no written code of laws to which the emperor might even nominally aspire. His attitude towards his Hindu subjects was a matter of prudence, at the very best.

This emperor was the unique energizing element in the political system. There was no council of senior elders such as, effectively, came to govern Tokugawa Japan. There was no corporation of mandarins such as restrained the emperor of China. There was no vizier and writers' guild who could get on with things irrespective of an inanimate sultan. There was just the emperor. Nor did the nobility—the *omrah*—provide any substitute for his personal involvement. It was mostly alien; it was his own creation, entirely dependent on him and which he could unmake at pleasure.

4.3. *The Imperial Household*

The palace swarmed with courtiers, officials, generals, Hindu princes, and the like, for it was the centre of government; but this aspect of the palace will be described later, when we turn to the chief officials and to the service nobility—the amirs or *omrah*. For present purposes we confine ourselves to two important components of the household proper: the harem and the

---

[41] Pascal, *Pensées* (Dent, London, 1932) iii. 82; see above, Bk. II, Ch. 1, p. 294 and n. 17.
[42] *Oxford History of India*, 4th edn. (OUP, Oxford, 1981), 376.

guards—dispensing with such officials as the Master of the Elephants, the Tent Master, the Keeper of the Wardrobe, and the Master of Horse.

The harem was known as the *mahal*. It was said to contain 2,000 women at the time of Aurungzeb.[43] Each lady had her own apartment and these were grouped into so many sections, each of which was managed by a female *darogha* with staffs of superintendants and clerks. As in China, the ladies were graded into ranks, the highest receiving as much as 1,028–1,610 rupees, as contrasted with the servants' pay of 20–51 rupees per month. When ministers had to get in touch with the emperor in the *mahal* they sent written reports which the highest ladies would read over to him and then convey his reply to the outside. Interestingly, the Mughal emperor's immediate bodyguard did not consist of eunuchs but of Amazonian women— 'women slaves, very brave and highly skilled in the management of the bow and other arms'.[44] The harem enclosure and its women guards were in their turn set about by eunuchs, and these in turn by Rajput guardsmen. The palace swarmed with eunuchs of every description: Manucci numbers them in thousands. They were directed by the chief eunuch who was very grand and very responsible indeed, since he looked after the entire domestic side of this teeming household. He was responsible for its expenditure, for its jewels, clothing, and entire stock of articles. To discharge this responsibility he had to carry out a laborious stock-taking. It may be added here that this same chief eunuch was also responsible for the state magazines and factories inside the palace compound and elsewhere in the empire. Indeed, his duties went far beyond this brief description—he was responsible for workmen, for paying and auditing all bills, for the kitchens and for cattle food, and for all related duties. This chief eunuch and head of the household held the official title of *mir saman*.[45]

The Imperial Guard consisted of picked members of the noblest families to the number of 4,000. It was commanded by the 'Officer of the Chosen Sentinels', the *darogha* of the *khas chouki*.

4.4. *The Political Process*

4.4.1. THE ROUTINE POLITICAL PROCESS

The best way to approach this is to give a brief account of the daily routine of Akbar, *mutatis mutandis* for later emperors. Akbar attended to business on three occasions during the day. The first was his public appearance on the

---

[43] Sinha, *Economic History of Bengal*, 537. But earlier, describing it under Akbar, this author puts the number at 5,000 (p. 487).

[44] Quoted, from the traveller Manucci, in Sinha, *Economic History of Bengal*, 538.

[45] Ibid. 537–40.

walls of his palace just after sunrise. This was 'giving *darshan*'. The practice was discontinued by Aurungzeb who, as a very pious Muslim, maintained that it amounted to human worship. Very likely, for the multitudes of Hindu commoners who gathered to gaze, it was.

His next appearance was in the *diwan-i-am*, the Hall of Public Audience where he held his durbar. Here officials and all others who had business with the court would be standing in their order of rank, waiting for the emperor to appear on his throne at the rear of the hall. One day in the week, this durbar was devoted to justice: to folk arraigned or, alternatively, presenting their petitions. But the main work of the durbars was to make appointments and hear departmental and provincial reports. Generally speaking, the departmental chiefs read out notes on matters concerning them, to which he responded by giving his instructions. These would chiefly relate to matters like revenue and finance, appointments, and awards of *jagirs* or of cash salaries. Such instructions were noted by clerks and presented to the emperor the next day for his approval. After all the foregoing, the emperor turned his attention to petitions from princes, governors, and the more important officials in the provinces.

The emperor then retired to his private quarters, but not to relax. Obviously, high policy could not be discussed in the open durbar. Akbar began the practice, which became institutionalized, of admitting a few intimates to the apartments situated near his bathroom and later the more important officials and nobles were admitted. Because it took place near the bathroom the gathering was called the *Ghusal Khana*; but Shah Jahan called it the *Khana-i-khas*. Aurungzeb turned this restricted council into a formal state body. Nevertheless, as early as the reign of Shah Jahan, the *Ghusal Khana* was felt not to be private enough for the most important and secret affairs of state. So Shah Jahan would withdraw to a still closer apartment, the *Shah Burj*.

By this time it was noonday and the emperor now betook himself for a meal within the harem. Then, after a short siesta, he dealt with those matters brought to him from officials by the ladies of the harem, as described above. At 3 p.m. he went to the mosque for afternoon prayers, returned to the *Ghusal Khana* for more administration, and only then terminated an exhausting twelve hours on the go. He took supper, and was in bed by 10 o'clock, where he listened to books being read out to him.[46]

---

[46] The foregoing is based on I. Hasan, *The Central Structure of the Mughal Empire and its Practical Working up to 1657* (OUP, London, 1936; repr. Lahore, 1967), ch. 2. Cf. also U. N. Day, *The Government of the Sultanate* (Kumar Publishers, New Delhi, 1972), 16–25 and B. Gascoigne, *The Great Moghuls* (Cape, London, 1987), 184–91.

It was obviously a most exhausting routine and the principal reason the empire held together from the time of Akbar to the death of Shah Alam was that all the emperors followed it; whereas after Shah Alam they never did, and the empire lost its prime mover.

4.4.2. PATHOLOGY OF THE POLITICAL PROCESS

This is similar to what we have found in most Asian empires: plots and threats to the throne from various quarters. In this particular case the great exception is that, apart from the two years 1560–2, the emperor never came under the control of a harem faction, although both Jahangir and Shah Jahan (husband of the beautiful Mumtaz Mahal, for whom he built the Taj) were certainly considerably influenced by their spouses. Nor were eunuchs ever a significant factor. Rather, the threats to the monarch came from the usual quarters: from the disaffected or impatient princes in fratricidal wars or open rebellion against their father. And since there was no fixed rule of succession, the court nobles formed factions to support one or other of the possible heirs to the throne. Another potential threat came from the mullahs. They detested Akbar who, in truth, departed ever increasingly from Muslim orthodoxy even to the extent of forming his own private cult of the Din Ilahi (a little like Akhnaton), and who seemed to them to be favouring the Hindu religion. As we noted above, Akbar was too strong for them. Both Jahangir and Shah Jahan conformed more closely to the orthodox Muslim line, while Aurungzeb completely reversed Akbar's policy of toleration and embarked on sporadic persecutions of the Hindu religion. But none of this signifies that the *ulema* openly confronted the emperor. Their pressure was silent and continuous, but it was up to an individual sovereign to yield to it or not.

4.5. *The Ministers and the Public Services*

4.5.1. *MANSABS* AND *JAGIRS*: RECRUITMENT AND PAYMENT OF THE SERVICES

In earlier chapters we usually began by describing the principal ministers, then their departments, and left the recruitment and background of the bureaucracy till last. In the case of the Mughals it is desirable to invert this order and begin with the structure of officialdom as a whole.

It is essential to understand two things at the outset. First, all land in India was divided into *khalsa* lands, which were the Crown lands and were directly administered by the imperial officials, and the remainder, which consisted of fiefs or *jagirs* and is often described as the 'assigned lands'. (In fact there was a third class which we might call 'zamindar land', and this will be explained later.) The Crown lands formed only a small proportion of the whole. Second, every man styled mansabdar was a civil or military official of some kind or another, but not every official, that is to say not the humbler, was a mansabdar. Furthermore, a high proportion of mansabdars were paid from the revenues of a benefice called a jagir and resembling the Arab iqta; they were, therefore, called jagirdars. But while every jagirdar was a mansabdar, not every mansabdar was a jagirdar. He might be paid in cash. Again, every mansabdar was an official but not every official was a mansabdar.

There is copious information about the mansabdars but reason to suspect estimates of their numbers. On the authority of one respected author these grew from 1,650 under Akbar to 8,000 in 1637 and 11,456 in 1690, partly because the empire greatly expanded during this period, partly because local rajas' domains were nominally treated as jagirs, but mostly through bureaucratic expansion.[47] Another and later authority, however, puts the number in 1648 at 8,000 and almost the same in 1690.[48] Compared with the total number of officials—that is, the clerks and accountants who seem to proliferate through the pages of any account of the Mughals—even the figure of 11,456 is small, the more so because most would have been military officers. So we have to apply the analogy of the Chinese Empire, where the established civil servants formed a thin layer over a very numerous lowly class of clerks, accountants, policemen, and the innumerable and ever-increasing multitude of unpaid and unofficial 'runners'.[49]

It appears, first of all, that the 'established' posts, the appointments made directly by the emperor, did not reach further down than the half-dozen or so most important officials in a pargana (see below). At that point, it seems, lower appointments were made by local officaldom, most probably the governor, similarly to China. So what we find is a narrow group of mansabdars reaching as far down as the parganas, and beyond that appointments were made locally—in short, the standard pattern in all these agrarian empires. The 'established' civil service was located in the towns and highly urbanized, but these lower ranks were not part of the regular bureaucracy. They played the role of the linkman between the authorities and the villagers: that individual variously referred to as headman or

---

[47] Sri Ram Sharma, Government of the Sultanate and Administration (Bombay, 1951), 110.

[48] A. Ali, The Mughal Nobility under Aurungzeb (Asia Publishing House, 1966). This contains a detailed list of the greater mansabdars, i.e. those of over 1,000 zat, for 1658–78, and for 1679–1701. But these tables are not comparable to Sharma's figures. Chapter I of this work is a detailed discussion of the numbers of the mansabdars and it is from p. 1 that the figures in the text derive.

[49] See above, Bk. IV, Ch. 2, 'The Golden Century of the Ch'ing'.

muqaddam or, perhaps, *chaudhari.*[50] (The term *muqaddam* is revealing because it is the Arabic for 'foremost', hence the 'big' man.) These offices were only semi-official in the sense that the emperor neither created nor filled them but recognized them.[51]

We can now return to the established public service, the *mansabdars.* It must not be thought that this was confined to what we should call 'senior appointments'. On the contrary, it included anybody touched by the imperial favour and so it ran from the princes of the blood down to humble cooks. The eccentricity of the Mughal arrangement was that it made absolutely no formal distinction between civil and military but, just the reverse, gave every single official a military rank: like, says one authority, 'the appointments in the Army Medical Service in India who had military ranks'.[52] It was not a unique system—Diocletian had introduced it in the Roman Empire—but it was highly unusual and certainly not found in this form anywhere else among the Mughals' contemporaries.

Under Akbar about 70 per cent of these *mansabs*, particularly the highest ranks, were filled by foreigners: usually Mongols, Turks, Afghans, and Persians. Of the remainder 22 per cent were Hindu and 78 per cent Indian Muslim.[53] By Aurungzeb's day the proportion of foreigners had fallen to about one-half, and Hindus (Rajputs and Mahrattas) made up the majority of the remainder.

So far we have talked of *mansabs* and *mansabdars* as an undifferentiated mass. But *mansab*, means a rank. And what has fascinated students of the Mughals in respect of what they call the '*mansabdar* system' is, precisely, its gradation and the way duties were related to this. The *mansabdars*—which, really, means the corps of established office-holders—were divided into thirty-three ranks. Each rank was supposed to bring to the field a stipulated number of horsemen. The *mansabdar's* salary was paid accordingly. These thirty-three ranks were, grossly, divided into three. Those who had to provide from ten to over 400 horsemen were the *mansabdars* proper. Those responsible for 500 to over 2,500 were *amirs* or, to use the Arabic plural, the *omrah.* Those who were expected to bring great contingents of upwards of 3,000 (the limit was at first 5,000 but this was later extended in one or two cases) were the grandees, the *amir-i-azam* or *amir-i-kiba*, the 'Great Noble-

---

[50] These titles are confusing. They varied from place to place, often varied over time, and are used with wide connotations. But the identifications in the text are based on the authority of P. Saran, *The Provincial Government of the Mughals, 1526–1658*, 2nd edn. (Asia Publishing House, London, 1972), 70, 421; I. Habib, *The Agrarian System of Mughal Empire, 1605–1707* (Asia Publishers, London, 1972), p. 129.

[51] For the headman, see Habib, *Agrarian System* 129–35.

[52] T. Raychaudhuri: private communication.

[53] Ali, *Mughal Nobility*, 35, gives the proportions as 78% Muslim and 22% Hindu.

man'. Now as we have seen, military and civilian rankings were interchangeable in this system, and some *mansabdars*, such as writers or painters or cooks, would have had purely civilian duties. That did not matter. A rank was assigned to them which, in principle, but subject to a vital qualification outlined below, carried the salary appropriate to anyone bringing the stipulated contingent of horsemen into the field. In short, salaries were reckoned in units based on the size of a nominal contingent.

Akbar paid his *mansabdars* in cash but his successors found this too onerous and, accordingly, while some continued to receive cash stipends, others were paid by the right to collect revenue from a given area assessed as equivalent to the *mansabdar's* pay: in short, by an *iqta* or *timar*, here styled a *jagir*. Each rank of *mansabdar* (numerically expressed) entitled the holder to a given amount of pay (*talab*). Where this was not paid in cash but by assignment of a *jagir*, the government made estimates of the revenue that could be expected of administrative districts, down to the villages, and such estimates were known as *jama*. The 'overwhelmingly larger portion of the land, lay with *jagirs*'.[54] In 1646 the total number of *jagirdars* was some 8,000.[55] Most of the *jama* of the empire went to a few individuals. Nearly 37 per cent of its total *jama* went to a mere sixty-eight princes and noblemen, and the next 587 claimed another 25 per cent. Many of these greater *jagirdars* made their own fiscal administration to collect their revenue and this was backed by their own military forces, so that complaints against them at court were futile.[56]

This *mansabdar* system seems admirably symmetrical. In practice it became messier and messier as time went on and complications developed. At the risk of anticipating matters to be related later, we may point out the most important complications. For instance, it was soon found that a *jagirdar* could not (or perhaps would not) bring out the full contingent for which he was being paid. In consequence, a distinction was drawn between the rank (order of precedence) of the *jagirdar* and how many horse he had to bring to the muster. The first was called his *zat* rank, the latter his *sawar*. Sometimes they coincided. More often they did not. Another complication arose out of computing the worth of the actual output of the *jagir*, since this often fell short of its nominal yield, of its *jama*. The salary (*talab*) had to be adjusted accordingly and this necessitated an adjustment of the area of the *jagir*— which meant adjusting other *jagirs*. It was similar when a *mansab* was altered—either by a promotion or a demotion—since the *talab* had to follow this and *talab* derived from the size of the *jagir*. Then there were the difficulties attendant on the rotation of the *jagirs*. The *jagir* was con-

---

[54] *CEHI*, i. 241.   [55] Ibid.   [56] Ibid. 242.

tingent on service. To prevent the *jagirdars* striking local root, it was policy to move them around every four years or so. However, since these *jagirs* were all shapes and sizes, to fit the *jagirdars* into new *jagirs* of equivalent worth was like trying to fill a gigantic jigsaw. Then there was the cheating: *jagirdars* successfully trying to bring in ever-smaller numbers to the muster while still drawing the same amount of money; or borrowing troops from a *jagirdar* friend and presenting them at the muster as though they were his own. Changes necessitated by all these various happenings, and many not enumerated here, were governed by strict regulations and accordingly required the services of 'an enormous number of scribes and accountants'.[57]

The *mansabdars* who were men of the pen and would never be anything else, did not receive the doublet of *zat* rank and *jagir* quota. They were treated as entitled to the amount due from a *jagir* of a certain size and paid in cash.

One final question: what independence had these *jagirdars*? The usual answer is that, until the eighteenth century when *jagirs* tended to become hereditary, they had none. They could be deprived of their *jagirs* at any time, they were rotated from one to another, and the *jagirs* escheated to the Crown at their death. They were noblemen solely by reason of the emperor's will or whim, with one not-unimportant qualification. For, after defeating the Hindu Rajput chieftains, Akbar, as we have seen, took them into his service and indeed they formed a prominent part of his court nobility. But these chiefs were still chiefs: they had their own lands and called on primeval popular loyalties. They were brought into the system as *jagirdars* for the sake of symmetry, but they represented a true landed nobility of independent means not, like the others, mere creations of the monarch.

4.5.2. THE CENTRAL MINISTRIES

Both Babur and Humayun followed the ancient tradition of working through a grand vizier. In Akbar's tutelage this officer was eclipsed by a *wakil* (deputy). But once Akbar began to rule in person the latter became a mere titular office and the Vizierate disappeared altogether. The central characteristic of the central administration was, precisely, that the emperor did not operate through a vizier but handled the affairs of state himself. We have seen that this is what Yüan Chang, the founder of the Ming dynasty, did and that this resulted in so much work for his secretaries that in the end they came to form the Grand Council and effective centre of government. But this never occurred under the Mughals and this is why, when the energy

---

[57] Habib, *Agrarian System*, 258–70. This is a mine of scholarly information.

and will of an emperor failed, as it did after Shah Alam, the imperial system collapsed with it.

Revenue was the province of the *diwan*. 'He had his eye upon every officer of the State who drew his salary from the *jagir*. As the chief executive officer of the State, in addition to his revenue powers, he had control over provinces and provincial officers from the Governor to the *amil* and the *pattwari*. As finance minister he had his finger upon [*sic*] every pie that reached the royal treasury and went out of it.'[58] He had enormous patronage: he nominated the *Subahdars*, the governors, as well as their finance officers (provincial *diwans*) and general police commandants (the *faujdars*) and some lesser officials. Below provincial level he nominated, *inter alia*, such officials as the collectors (*mushrif*) and assessors (*amins*) and some of the *zamindars* (but for these, see below). He was empowered to despatch on his own account a vast mass of routine business such, for instance, as certificates of sanctioned appointments and orders for payments to subordinate officers. By the same token his counter-signature was required for the validation of most papers and orders for appointments. It is worth noting that one of the sections into which his ministry was divided acted as a public records office where all official records came for storing.[59]

The *mir bakhshi* was the military paymaster and adjutant-general rolled into one. He recruited, maintained the registers of the *mansabdars*, laid down the rules for pay, and controlled all military accounts. For the *diwan* proper (the *diwan-i-kul*, or *diwan* of the whole, i.e. the chief *diwan*) did not handle the grants of *jagirs* or cash made for military purposes. The *mir bakshi* was responsible for these. And when an important battle was pending it was he who assigned the posts to the senior commanders in the van, centre, rearguard, and so on. Sometimes he took command himself.[60]

The *sadr-i-sudur* was at once the chief *qazi* (*qadi*) and as such the putative guardian of the *sharia* vis-à-vis the emperor, and also the administrative head of the entire corps of *qazis* in the field. The free-thinking Akbar was not the man to put up with the tutelage of any cleric and downgraded the status of the *sadr*. He also took rigorous measures to cleanse the department of corruption which (as will be seen) seems to have been particularly widespread among the *qazi* courts.

The fourth and final grand officer was the *mir saman*, best described as the minister in charge of state supplies and economic enterprises. Almost none

---

[58] Hasan, *Central Structure*, 205–6.   [59] Day, *Government of the Sultanate*, 44–7.

[60] Sinha, *Economic History of Bengal*, 481–2, relying mostly on the *Ain Akbari* of Abu Fazl, Akbar's confidant, and author of the *Akbarnama* and the *Ain Akbari*, which is a manual of government and administration. Cf. Day, *Government of the Sultanate*, 47–51, Sarkar, *Mughal Polity*, 111–14, Hasan, *Central Structure*, 210–33.

of the empires so far discussed—including the Roman and Byzantine—were market economies. In every single one merchants and financiers were looked on with suspicion and contempt and regulated as far as possible. Not so in the Mughal Empire: this was highly monetized, had numerous large and thriving cities and a significant commercial community. The Mughal emperors treated these with respect and their relationship was one of mutual dependence. But side by side with this private sector the emperor owned about a hundred magazines and workshops, as well as arsenals. Clearly, the financial and administrative responsibility for stocking, stocktaking, and controlling the balance sheets of these enterprises was very considerable.

4.5.3. THE FIELD OFFICES OF THE MAIN DEPARTMENTS

The essence of Mughal administration was simply this: its four departments of finance, war, judiciary, and supply were replicated at each echelon in the territorial hierarchy until they came to their stop at the maid-of-all-work of Indian government, the village. Gascoigne has caught it very well: 'There was in each province a complete hierarchy of administrative officers, repeating exactly the administrative structure at the centre and responsible only to their counterparts at the centre.'[61]

The Province (*Subah*)

The chief official of the province was its governor, often called the *subahdar* but, more properly, the *sipah salar*. He held durbars in exactly the same way as the emperor, and was second only to him in pomp and conspicuous display. Perhaps the most important section of his remit was that one which empowered him to control the numerous 'big men' who lived in his province: such personages as, for instance the *omrah*, the lesser *jagirdars*, and *zamindars*. All these were ordered to obey him and he had authority to punish any who defied him or acted so as to obstruct his administration, with the important exception of rajas, who had direct relations with the imperial court.[62] All troops came under his orders. He was the principal judicial officer (apart from *sharia* matters) and could resort to any means he thought fit to extract the truth. He could go as far as amputating limbs by way of punishment but could not carry out the death penalty—such cases had to go to the emperor—except where rebels or bandits were the culprits. These he could execute without mercy or appeal. He guarded the roads and, by association, commanded the (very important) local intelligence agents

---

[61] Gascoigne, *Great Moghuls*, 105.

[62] Day, *Government of the Sultanate*, 74. But this did not apply to native rajas (p. 73).

who, as in so many of the empires we have described, acted as postal couriers as well.[63]

Distances and poor communications with the central government gave the governors considerable discretion yet they were controlled by a number of institutional checks. They were shunted around, enjoying only brief tenures in any one locality. They were spied on by a host of secret agents of the imperial court. They might be inspected in the course of one or other of the emperor's imperial progresses or, sometimes, by imperial inspectors.[64]

And finally, the governor had no control over his shadow, the local *diwan*, the treasurer, who was appointed directly from the centre and was responsible only to the *diwan-i-kul*. His job involved preventing any money being drawn except by proper warrant, seeing that subordinates did not extract forbidden dues and tolls, controlling the expenditure of the various departments, keeping financial records relating to all the Crown lands and the *jagir* lands. He was allowed a considerable staff. Some were centrally appointed—notably his *peshkar* or personal assistant, his *darogha* or office superintendent, his head clerk, and his treasurer. But he himself had extensive patronage.[65]

The *mir bakshi* was served by a similar number of provincial *bakhshis*: they recruited soldiers, maintained them in good order by inspecting the horses and equipment, and placed their own agents in the lower echelons (the *sarkars* and the *parganas*) to report duly all information that had a bearing on such duties. There is little to say about the provincial *sadr* or *qazi* (usually the same man held the two offices) except that he recommmended the names of local *qazis*.

The *Sarkar*

Again we find officials representing law and order, revenue, and judiciary. The *sarkar* was headed by the local equivalent of the *subahdar*, namely, the *faujdar*. His principal task was to enforce law and order. There is some doubt over the extent of his magisterial powers but it is clear that he was a court of first instance in revenue matters. He commanded a force of soldiers acting as armed police. He was required to come to the aid of the local equivalent of the *diwan*, namely the *amil*, in collecting taxes. He was forbidden to attack villages in Crown or *jagir* lands without the authority of the officers in charge. As the empire wore on it became increasingly difficult to deal with these matters by force alone and a code of instructions exists which explains

---

[63] Ibid. 72–5.

[64] P. Saran, *Resistance of Indian Princes to Turkish Offensive: End of Tenth Century A.D.* (Punjabi University, Patiala, 1967), 184–8.

[65] Day, *Government of the Sultanate*, 75–9.

how the *faujdar* is to handle difficult *zamindars* when his own forces are inadequate.[66]

The revenue officer of the *sarkar*, which functioned under the direct supervision of the provincial *diwan*, was the *amil*. His principal tasks were, first of all, the tax-assessments and next, collecting the tax from the Crown lands. (On the *jagirs*, the *jagirdars* were responsible for collecting the tax, either through their own men or more likely through tax-farmers or the *zamindars*.) He was also responsible for paying in and out of his treasury and sending monthly accounts of such transactions to the provincial *diwan*. Also, each month he had to send the imperial court an intelligence report, recording local prices and rents, the condition of the people and the *jagirdars*, and such like. The *amil* was not a local appointment. He was nominated by the central government but he worked under the supervision of the *subahdar*, who had the right to dismiss him.[67]

The important towns and the cities in the *sarkar* were ruled by a prefect called the *kotwal*. He was effectively the *faujdar*'s equivalent in the towns. He combined the old censor-of-morals duties of the Muslim *muhtasib*, including the regulation of the markets,[68] with the functions of police chief and judge in all criminal cases. He was officially encouraged to maintain an army of undercover agents and to learn everything that every citizen did and how much he spent. The *kotwal* was assigned summary criminal jurisdiction and, indeed, he exercised this throughout the entire *sarkar*, in this respect coming under the direct orders of the *subhadar*. More will be said about him later but it is worth noting in passing that, if he failed to catch the thief, he was supposed to make good any losses a citizen had incurred, and this led naturally enough to there being a host of false accusations. As judicial torture was permitted, it was not difficult to secure convictions.

We have already mentioned how towns were divided into so many quarters or *muhallas*, to each of which the *kotwal* appointed a headman as a *mir muhalla* who had to report daily on all arrivals and departures. The *kotwal* derived further intelligence from the garbage collectors who used to go to every house twice a day. He commanded a large force of cavalry and infantrymen, deploying one horseman and twenty-to-thirty foot-soldiers in each *muhalla*. As in China and notably Japan, each ward or lane was fitted with gates at either end, which were shut during the night or during alarms or tumult. Indeed this practice lasted till the Indian Mutiny. At night the entire town was under curfew and nobody was permitted to

---

[66] Day, *Government of the Sultunate*, 81–2.   [67] Ibid. 83–5.
[68] For the *muktasib*, see Bk. III, Ch. 2, 'The Caliphate'.

enter or to leave it, while posses of troops patrolled the streets three times per night.[69]

The *Pargana*

Sarkars were divided into so many *parganas*. The *pargana* was a cluster of villages. Here again the main functions of the administration at central, provincial, and *sarkar* level were replicated. Assistant to the *sarkar's faujdar* was the *shiqdar*, its executive head and magistrate, responsible for law and order. The *amil*, like his superior at *sarkar* level, was responsible, in the main part, for assessments. The *bitichki*, or chief accountant and registrar, was indispensable to the *amil*. All matters respecting tenure, schedules of assessment, and records of tax collected were kept by an official called the *qanungo*.

We have now reached the interface between the official and the semi-official and non-official administration, the realm of intermediaries, of village 'big men', of bargaining and compromises.

The Mughal bureaucracy . . . was a highly urbanized institution. Its influence was limited to capital cities and hardly filtered down to levels below district headquarters. The lower orders of the hierarchy including *amils*, *tahsildars* or *mamlatdars*, for instance, were probably for the most part non-Muslim, functioning in *tahsils* or *taluks* as local landholders, not as part of the regular bureaucracy but as a subordinate instrument of local administration. These low-graded subordinate officers were the kind of functionaries who were in immediate touch with the villages. Their offices were often farmed and in the backward state of communications they tended to be independent of the regular bureaucratic control of the king, often undistinguished from the private landholders, the farmers of government revenue, and the chief proprietors of joint villages who had all the management of local affairs in rural areas. The power relations of local functionaries varied according to the strength of the central authority and the local influence either of a village community or an individual *zamindar*.[70]

And thus we come to the village itself and to that mysterious entity, the *zamindar*.

Villages and *Zamindars*

The government was city-oriented and city-centred. The Mughals (Emperors, courtiers, officers, upper and middle classes) were essentially an urban people [who] neglected and hated or disliked villages. The government was indifferent to village interests . . . The villages also were uninfluenced by and indifferent to the government.[71]

[69] Day, *Government of the Sultanate*, 85–7; Sarkar, *Mughal Polity*, 222–30.
[70] B. B. Misra, *The Administrative History of India, 1834–1947* (OUP, Oxford, 1970), 640.
[71] Sarkar, *Mughal Polity*, 161.

We have already had occasion to mention the village headman, the *muqad-dam*. He was most important—the man who led the villagers by way of religious prestige and/or wealth. He exercised a general supervision over the village affairs; settled disputes; kept law and order; and above all, collected the taxes. In this he needed the assistance of another village functionary, the *patwari*, who was the man who kept the relevant records in respect of who held what land and what it grew, the rent due for it, and so forth. This *bahi* was accepted by the authorities as the most authentic fiscal record available.

What, then, were the *zamindars*? The word was a term of art rather than a legal category.[72] The word itself, of Persian origin, means control over land.[73] Such an expression might be held to apply to local rajas or ranas—native princes who provided a military contingent to the imperial army but were otherwise autonomous; and indeed, so it was. But in the areas under direct imperial control the *zamindaris* were a class of individuals, some strongly associated with some particular caste (usually by the course of long historical evolution) and others who were successful adventurers of no particular caste who had carved out a tract of territory, and had a title to a part of the produce of the *zamindari*, that is, the area this jurisdiction covered, which might be several villages or as few as one and indeed, in some cases, fractions of one. The sum the *zamindar* exacted was of two possible kinds. Where the peasantry were taxed directly by the imperial government, which collected the land revenue, the *zamindar* was entitled to levy extra rates or dues upon them. Where the *zamindar* acted as tax-farmer, his income was the difference between what he was contracted to pay the imperial treasury and the amount he exacted from the peasantry. Some *zamindaris* were divided into two fiscal parts, the one where the *zamindari* acted as the tax-farmer and the other where the imperial authorities themselves collected the land tax.

The general rule was that the possession of a *zamindari* was hereditary. As such it could be subdivided between the heirs, was saleable, and was generally recognized as 'private' property. For all that, it could be confiscated or conferred by the imperial authority. The reason for this derogation from the general principle that the *zamindari* was a private right or title lay in two features: the *zamindars'* role as tax-collectors—wherein they might not satisfy the imperial authorities—and their command of substantial armed forces, which gave them the opportunity for sedition or resistance. Command over armed force was the first prerequisite for establishing a *zamindari* and then for retaining it. These retainers consisted of both horse and foot.

---

[72] Cf. W. H. Moreland, *The Agrarian System of Muslim India* (Cambridge, 1929), 8, 178, 225, 279. Day, *Government of the Sultanate*, 137–43.　　　[73] *CEHI*, i. 244. Habib, *Agrarian System*, 138–9.

Documentary evidence has suggested an aggregate figure of no less than 384,558 cavalry and 4,277,057 foot-soldiers for the whole Empire—not short of the total claimed for the imperial troops. It is suggested that the bulk of the *zamindaris'* foot-soldiers were peasants impressed for some special action together with a hard core of retainers belonging to the same caste as the *zamindar.* However this may be, I find both sets of figures unbelievably high.[74]

These retainers were used to maintain law and order and to watch out for thieves and bandits; to assist the local *amin* in his tax-assessments; but also to suppress disorderly or mutinous peasants. Not surprisingly, many villages regarded the *zamindar* as their master, while for their part many *zamindars* resented the imperial authorities to the point of armed resistance. Here they could rely on the support of their caste.[75]

5. THE ACTIVITIES OF GOVERNMENT: DESCRIPTION AND APPRAISAL

5.1. *The Army*

Like the Ottoman Empire, Mughal India was a plunder state. It throve on conquest, tribute, and booty. The army was where the taxes went, and where the surplus revenue came from. Its total strength included some 200,000 cavalry plus over 40,000 matchlockmen or gunners,[76] and Bernier—a contemporary witness—put the total number of infantrymen at 300,000.[77] Half-a-million men was by no means an impossible burden for a population of 100 million to sustain—the Roman Empire kept 600,000 with a population of some 60 million. In addition to these troops, we ought to add the uncountable numbers of the local militiamen in the *parganas*, formed for local defence.

The army was basically a cavalry force. The numerous infantry were, as we shall see, of poor quality. There was a contingent of elephants just as there had been in Alexander's time. They were used to seat the raja or commander so that he could be seen by his troop commanders; a good idea, except that it made him an excellent target. Also they were often armoured and used to batter down the gates of fortresses. But they were not a serious factor in battle. The musketeers ought to have been, but according to Bernier their weapons were inferior and also, he says, they were frightened

[74] Habib, *Agrarian System*, 137–57, 163–6.
[75] Sarkar, *Mughal Polity*, 307–13; Day, *Government of the Sultanate*, 137–43.
[76] According to R. Mousnier, quoted in Braudel, *Civilisation and Capitalism*, iii. 512.
[77] F. Bernier, *Travels in the Moghul Empire*, ed. A. Constable (Constable, London, 1891), 219–20.

of them in case they exploded.[78] On the other hand, the park of mobile light artillery pulled by bullock carts excited this traveller's admiration,[79] but rarely does one find any praise for the heavy artillery. This was used for sieges, and the Mughals had a passion for making cannon as long in the barrel and as heavy as they could: the largest were 40-pounders. But they were overwhelmingly cumbersome, requiring trains of twenty yoke of oxen and travelling at only 2 miles an hour. Aurungzeb owned seventy such cannon. They and the field artillery tended to be manned by foreigners.

The basic arm, the cavalry, consisted of the royal regiments, those of the princes, and those of the *mansabdars*. The emperor kept 4,000 horse-guards about his person, many of whom had served him before he came to the throne. Additionally, he had a force of about the same number of *ahadis*, volunteers who may be regarded as gentleman-troopers. The rest of the army was stationed in various theatres of war so that one should talk of armies rather than 'army'. Of these theatres, the most dangerous was the north-west frontier, the traditional route of invaders. Under Aurungzeb a larger part of the forces was stationed down in the Deccan, fighting what turned out in the end to be an unwinnable war against the nascent Mahratta confederacy.

These field forces consisted of the contingents of native rajas, for example, the Rajput princes and, of course, the *mansabdar* troops. Little is known with certainty about their formations—whether they were formed into regiments, for instance. It looks as if each component fought under its immediate superior who was grouped under some *amir*. This immense army could with justice have been described as the 'Ever Victorious' until the second half of Aurungzeb's reign when it was fought to a standstill by the Mahrattas. It had consolidated the north-west, taken Kashmir, and expanded the Indo-Gangetic core of the empire southwards until only a tiny strip, in what we should nowadays call the Carnatic, remained independent. For certain, it was the best army in all India. But it suffered from massive defects which grew in time, and it was vastly inferior to the Turkish army in its prime.

To begin with, it became costlier and costlier to maintain, owing to the fraudulence of the *mansabdars*. What follows is highly simplified. The essence of the situation was this: the *mansabdar*'s pay, based on his *jagir*, was supposed to correspond to the number of troops he brought to the muster. Obviously, if he could bring less than the quota without notice being taken, he would be receiving the same stipend for a lesser expenditure. That is what the *mansabdars* aimed at. One obvious way to cheat was to borrow horses from

[78] Bernier, *Travels*, 217.   [79] Ibid. 218.

one's neighbour. Akbar tried to avoid this by having all horses branded, but this proved too onerous. The same went for the troopers; they could be borrowed for the muster, too. To avoid this, a description of the man was introduced on the nominal roll. But irrespective of such cheating—which was a commonplace in most pre-industrial armies anyway—a process of cost inflation began, rather similar to what had occurred, curiously, in quite different circumstances under England's King Richard I and King John,[80] which was boosted by the great inflation that took place in the sixteenth century.[81] Over time the *mansabdars* brought fewer horsemen than their quota demanded to the musters. Except in dire emergency, this seems to have been tolerated by the authorities. To cut a long story short, by Shah Jahan's day the average contingent brought to the muster was 25 per cent short of the number the *mansabdar* was being paid for. The emperor finally regularized the matter by settling for one-third or one-quarter only of the force the *mansabdar* should legally have mustered, but continued to pay him as though he had brought 100 per cent![82] This was to have the gravest effects when Aurungzeb's armies were fighting the Mahrattas for, as a near-contemporary author says, the Mughal commanders were not maintaining their contingents up to the standards required by the regulations. As a result the 'malefactors' did not entertain any fear of the Mughal *faujdars*, and the *mansabdars* therefore received no revenue frrom their *jagirs*.[83]

Furthermore, the army was technically very inferior. Cavalrymen were not given drill or training, though this itself did not matter inasmuch as they would have learned to ride and wield their weapons before enrolling; the point was that, once enrolled, they were never drilled to fight in formation. As for the infantry, they

consisted of a multitude of people assembled together without regard to rank or file; some with swords, and some with lances, too long or too weak to be of any service even if ranged with the utmost regularity or discipline. To keep night watches and to plunder defenceless people was their greatest service. It was more a rabble of half-armed men than anything else, consisting of levies brought to the field by the petty *zamindars*, or hired men brought by the *mansabdars* to fulfil a certain part of their quota of contingents.[84]

Moreover, the individual trooper or foot-soldier was expected to make his own way to the front, and to pay for his own provisions. For troopers, who rode, this was no hardship, but the infantryman found it arduous and, unless he received his cash pay promptly while in the field, he had nothing

[80] Cf. Bk. III, Ch. 6, p. 911.   [81] Habib, *Agrarian System*, 320.
[82] Day, *Government of the Sultanate*, gives a clear account, 169–71.
[83] Habib, *Agrarian System*, 346.   [84] Day, *Government of the Sultanate*, 146.

to eat. Great caravanserais of camp-followers sprang up who accompanied the army to sell the food and other necessities the troops required. This was not all: the nobility and their followers—musicians, jugglers, harems— along with those of the emperor all moved along with the army. So it wound for miles and miles along the road, at a snail's pace; effectively, a moving town.

5.2. *Taxation*

We have already mentioned the chief revenue officers, from the *diwan-i-kul* in the capital, to the headmen and the accountant—the *patwari*—in the villages. We have also distinguished sharply between assessment and collection of tax. Broadly speaking, the former was always performed by government officials. These also collected the tax on the Crown lands, the *khalsa*. But on the *jagirs* the *jagirdar* collected the taxes, usually using a tax-farmer to do it for him; and elsewhere there were the lands where the *zamindar* collected, as noted already.

The story, then, concerns the assessment system. Taxes were numerous in Mughal India. There were dues, tolls, customs, and many other levies on commerce and manufacture, but the land revenue exceeded their sum total. And, as we have seen in the case of other agrarian states, it was no easy matter to assess the value of a crop.

Before the Mughal conquest the traditional modes of assessment had been: crop-sharing between the officials and the peasants; appraisement (*kankut*), where various methods of estimating yield per unit of area were made; and strict measurement, where the land was measured and the yield fixed on a given unit. Akbar is often credited with having formulated a definitive tax system. In fact he changed his methods again and again for some twenty-four years until he reached his own solution in 1580, but within eighty years, under Aurungzeb, this too had been entirely swept away.

The method Akbar settled on was called *zabti*. A cadaster was carried out registering all holdings and these were divided into three broad categories: good, middling, and bad. On this basis the yields per area-unit were estimated and the tax-rate, fixed on these, became the assessment. But in 1580 Akbar developed what we might call the 'ten-year rule' and this is what is held to be his great claim to fame. Still working on the foregoing principle, the officials recorded the average cash price of the crops over the last ten years. (These details were available from the *qanungos* and *amils* in each *pargana*.) Then—though Abu Fazl's text is ambiguous on this crucial point—it is supposed that the sum arrived at was divided by ten, and this is what the taxpayer was assessed at, irrespective of the current produce in prices. Akbar fixed the rate at which tax was paid at one-third of the yield as estimated by the method above. The Mughals insisted that this be paid in cash, though in certain areas crop-sharing went on as before. But on the whole the cash system prevailed and started the decline of the independent peasantry. They were usually strapped for ready money and had to have recourse to the village money-lender.

This system was never applied all over India, which was far too diverse for that. And in the course of time the very principle fell away, chiefly because it made such heavy demands on the officials. Under Aurungzeb it was replaced by two alternatives: either the *amins* based the revenue on the produce of an optimum year *plus* that of the previous year or, if the peasants objected to this, they had recourse to measurement. The former method was known as *nasaq*, and effectively was based on peasant acceptance of past records as being accurate. The effect was to substitute for Akbar's arrangement sums arrived at not by measurement or valuation but through bargaining. This bargaining was all the fiercer because Aurungzeb raised the tax-take from Akbar's one-third to one-half of the produce.

For the people of India never pay without being forced, and to collect half the total quantity of supplies that they are under obligation to pay to the crown, it is necessary to tie up the principal husbandmen. It is the peasants' habit to go on refusing payment, asserting that they have no money. The chastisement and the instruments are very severe. From time to time they pay a trifling sum and the punishment being renewed again and again, they begin to pay little by little . . . This habit is much honoured among husbandmen—that is, never to pay readily: and to undergo these torments and this disgrace is among them an honour.[85]

One effect of this heavy taxation was—as in China—a flight from the land. Or rather it was a flight to other lands, particularly virgin areas which had to be cleared, for at that time there was a surplus of land over the numbers of the population. The emperors devised a wide range of measures designed alternatively to make the peasant stay and cultivate his land or to go and colonize the waste areas.

But there was another reason too for this flight from the land—the effects of the *jagir* system. For, as in the *iqta* in Mamluk Egypt, the *jagirdar* enjoyed the usufruct of his estate for only four or five years before being moved elsewhere. So, like the Mamluks, he had every inducement to exploit the land and the peasantry as far as he could go. The peasant asked himself why he should labour for a local tyrant who might come upon him the next

---

[85] Manucci, quoted Z. Faruki, *Aurungzeb and His Times* (Delhi, 1972), 462.

day and despoil him of all he possessed, while the *jagirdar* himself reacted—
so says Bernier—in the following manner:

Why should the neglected state of this land create uneasiness in our minds? And
why should we expend our own money and time to render it fruitful? We may be
deprived of it in a single moment, and our exertions would benefit neither ourselves
nor our children. Let us draw from the soil all the money we can, though the
peasant should starve or abscond, and we should leave it, when commanded to
quit, a dreary wilderness.[86]

5.3. *Public Order and State Security*

As in the Roman, Byzantine, and Caliphal empires, Mughal road-building
was not just for military purposes but was connected with the postal service,
which was connected with intelligence and espionage, and these, in turn,
with repression and public order. As the Emperor Aurungzeb said: 'The
main pillar of government is to be well-informed in the news of the
kingdom.'[87]

General information about all that went on in every field army, large
town, and province was provided by a network of official 'writers of events'.
Their reports were seen by the provincial governor and were 'public'—
which is much like our saying 'unclassified' today. But there were two
additional corps who only served in politically sensitive areas: the 'recorders
of events', whose presence was known to the governors, and the 'secret
letter-writers', who were known to no one. The reports of the former went
to the *subahdar* and then on to the emperor; those of the latter to the
emperor alone. These corps were headed by a Chief (*darogha*) of Posts and
Intelligence, whose postal functions were the usual ones of providing
couriers, runners, and relays of horses along the highways. But quite apart
from all these intelligence officers, India swarmed with spies. In 1708 it was
reckoned that the emperor disposed of at least 4,000 of them, but every
great prince or great *amir* had his own corps of spies as well.[88] The
subcontinent was a gigantic whispering gallery where nobody could feel
quite safe. The imperial intelligence service was not always reliable: sometimes either by neglect or by deliberate intent the intelligence agent
imparted false information, or failed to report true information concerning,
for instance, the misdeeds of the governor. But the evidence of European
travellers suggests that on the whole these systems kept the emperor very
well-informed.[89]

---

[86] Bernier, *Travels*, 227.   [87] Quoted in Sarkar, *Mughal Polity*, 243.   [88] Ibid. 243–53.
[89] Ibid. 254–8.

The village was corporately responsible for petty crimes committed within its boundaries and had to make good the loss suffered by any villager or traveller. To this end the headman organized a watch and ward. In urban areas, as we have already seen, the town was controlled by an all-purpose chief executive—police-chief, military chief, chief magistrate—namely the *kotwal*. But it is in the *sarkars* that one notices the close connection between the police authority, the roads, and repression. Here, as we have already said, the *faujdar* was the deputy governor, with jurisdiction over civil, criminal, and military matters. He maintained control of his district through a set of outposts—*thanahs*. The *faujdar* and the local *zamindars* had to escort officials with important messages across their district and hand them over to the next, as well as giving them board and lodging. The *faujdar's* duties included policing and guarding the highways, dispersing and arresting robber gangs, preventing the private manufacture of matchlocks, and helping the *jagirdars* and the collectors in the Crown lands to extract their taxes from the villagers. The expression that was used for the non-payment of taxes was 'smaller rebellion',[90] and it was their duty to suppress it.

It is hard to judge how safe the roads were. Travelling in a caravan which might begin on a modest scale and pick up numbers as it moved, until it reached as many as some 1,700 persons and 300 carts, was common practice.[91] Some European travellers reported that the countryside they passed through was 'swarming' with robbers. On the other hand some individuals who travelled alone found their journeys pretty tranquil; for instance, Terry travelled 4,000 miles and only came under attack once.[92] European merchants' losses by way of robbery were no more frequent than on the roads in the European countries.[93] The contradictions in these travellers' accounts is partly explicable by the vast expanse of the empire, where—as in the Roman Empire—some parts were more deeply guarded than others, and some terrain was highly favourable to robbers. Gujarat, for example, was very peaceable and secure, but the sea-routes off the west coast were threatened by pirates and Gujarat suffered serious depredations in the Mahratta wars. As for highway robbery, this was especially prevalent in the jungle and hill country of central India and Malwa, which provided rich pickings because it lay across the caravan routes from the coast.

For graver rebellions the central government itself intervened, or sent in its own commanders. In one case the outlaws were slaughtered wholesale. It was not uncommon, either, to build towers stuck full of decapitated heads while the bodies were impaled along the road-sides.[94] By these methods and

[90] Quoted in Sarkar, 232.   [91] *CEHI,* i. 356–7.   [92] Sarkar, *Mughal Polity,* 238.
[93] *CEHI,* i. 357–8.   [94] Sarkar, *Mughal Polity,* 236.

those already described, a rough-and-ready peace was kept in this extensive area, half the size of the USA, despite the difficult communications and the terrain. As we shall have occasion to mention, local peasant disturbances and *zamindar* resistance to the central authorities were endemic but, leaving aside princely rebellions which occurred regularly throughout the era, it was not until the reign of Aurungzeb that major regional disorders began. The Jats rebelled in 1669 and 1685, the Satnamis in 1672, the Sikhs *c.*1672, and then the Mahrattas, though theirs was not, strictly speaking, a rebellion since their territories were not part of the empire. But they were the most formidable of all, and their rebellion was the one the emperor could not crush.

5.4. *The Judicial System*

Since we are already somewhat familiar with the background here, this section can be quite short. There were four categories of courts. To begin with there was the emperor's court. One durbar in the week was reserved for judicial cases. These were initiated by petitions, and on one occasion, Akbar had to employ seven officials to process them, but in later reigns the numbers fell away. Shah Jahan heard only some twenty cases per durbar and, when he asked his courtiers why, they replied that it was because justice was being dispensed so satisfyingly at the lower levels. In point of fact few would take a case to the emperor and the majority of such petitioners must have come from the immediate vicinity of the capital. This was an appellate court as well as one of first instance. But that was the full extent of the appeal system. There were courts in every territorial jurisdiction but each stood on a juridical par with the others.

The second category of courts were the *qazi* courts, whose judges, the *qazis*, were nominated by the *sadr* at the imperial court. They had a particularly bad reputation for taking bribes.[95] They were to be found in the capital town of each province, and in each of its *sarkars* and their *parganas*, and a plaintiff could take his case to whichever one he liked, but he could not appeal from a *pargana* court to the *sarkar* court and so forth. These courts were urban institutions. The rural 75 per cent of the population were not touched by them since the emperors left the villages to themselves. These *qazi* courts were of course Muslim courts, and the Muslims were very much in the minority. Nevertheless they used *sharia* procedure only slightly modified by one or two of the emperors, and it will be recalled how restrictive this procedure was. The *qazi* would apply the *sharia* to Muslim

---

[95] Bernier, *Travels*, 237–8.

suitors, and would apply the decrees or *qanuns* of the emperors to both Muslim and Hindu; but when the case involved the personal or religious law of the Hindus he was advised in it by a Brahman *pandit*. This was the maximum concession allowed to the Hindu majority.

However, a very great deal of business was not done by these courts at all, and to tell the truth the office of *qazi* was not greatly esteemed or richly rewarded in Mughal India. The criminal cases which the *qazis* dealt with would have been, almost entirely, the minor offences. For the full range of secular criminal—and an admixture too, of secular civil cases—the courts were what we might call the 'police courts' held by the governor or the *faujdar* or the *kotwal* and so forth. These men—it was the same in the Roman and the Chinese empires, for instance—exercised police power, military power, administrative power, and the judicial power. They did not have to follow a fixed procedure, and were empowerd to and did use judicial torture to secure a confession. In this way, in the administrators' courts, the executive and judicial powers were combined; no distinction was made between the way a criminal or a civil case was handled, nor were the cases ranged in orders of seriousness. The one principal restriction on these courts was that they could not impose capital punishment (except in cases of open rebellion); capital cases were, as we saw, reserved for the emperor.

Outside the towns, cases which did not involve capital punishment or even imprisonment were often handled by the *zamindar*. Elsewhere they were dealt with by the village institutions: the headman, the caste councils, the guild councils, the *panchayets*. The sanction here was degradation and social ostracism and these were exceedingly hurtful in such confined communities where every caste had its place and its own *dharma*, and the entire social and economic life of the individual was situated within this context.

European visitors like Terry approved the rapidity of justice in India as compared with the long-drawn-out proceedings of the lawyers in Europe.[96] (It will be remembered that Kaempfer took the same view in Japan.)[97] We should not dismiss this lightly. It may well have commended itself to the population. Lord Cornwallis (1786–93) reformed civil justice by transferring all civil suits to the district judge, who followed elaborate rules of procedure based on the English model. It was a disaster. So complex was the procedure that no suitor could hope to plead his own cause. He had to have recourse to a lawyer and so a court action cost much more.[98] 'Hitherto . . . the Nawab's revenue officials had decided in a simple, summary fashion disputes between *zamindars* and cultivators regarding their rights and the payment of

---

[96] Quoted in Sarkar, *Mughal Polity*, 216.   [97] Cf. Bk. IV, Ch. 1, 'Tokugawa Japan', p. 1118.
[98] P. Moon, *The British Conquest and Dominion of India* (Duckworth, 1989), 240.

rent; and if this crude but well-established system had been continued, the
ryots might have enjoyed better protection.'[99] All the new arrangement did
was to make the lot of the peasant harder and that of the money-lender
easier. But much should be made of another of Cornwallis's innovations, his
'valuable principle' that was novel and surprising to a people accustomed to
despotic rule, and that in time came to be greatly appreciated: 'all the
officers of Government shall be amenable to the courts for acts done in
their official capacities, and Government itself in cases in which it may be a
party with its subjects in matters of property shall submit its rights to be
tried in these courts under the existing laws and regulations.'[100]

6. THE MUGHAL EMPIRE—AN APPRAISAL

To Europeans, Mughal India was by far the most glamorous of the four
great Asian powers dealt with in this book, and remains so today. What
so attracts them is its art and literature and architecture, the gorgeous
colourfulness of its courts, the exquisite inlay and fretwork and mosaics in
the palaces and shrines and mosques, and not least the fascinating
characters of its emperors, whose every deed and happening was recorded
in their own private diaries or by the court diarists. But rarely has there
been such a contrast betwen a rich and gorgeous artistic culture and a
threadbare political culture. It is impossible not to approach it with a
depressing sense of *déjà vu*. Not one single institutional feature in it is
original. All the main components—the royal autocracy, the ambiguity of
legitimate title, the contestable rules of succession, the service nobility,
their payment by land-revenues, the feudalistic mode of raising the army,
the combination of legislative judicial and administrative powers in a
single officer, and so forth—are features we have met with many times
before.

Likewise with the shortcomings of this empire: it was riddled with
corruption, especially in the courts. The ruling and extracting classes were
the tiniest fraction of the total population, but between one-third and
one-half of the total GNP of the 100 million population was engrossed by
the imperial court and the 8,000 or so *mansabdars*—61 per cent of the take
going to a mere 655 of these.[101] Extraction on such a scale could only be
secured by coercion, and so we return to the now familiar extraction–
coercion cycle: in 1647 the 445 highest-ranked *mansabdars* spent 77.2 per

[99] P. Moon, 238.
[100] Ibid. 242. Cornwallis's words as quoted in the text come from his Report to the Court of
Directors of the East India Company, 1793, and can be found in A. B. Keith, *Speeches and Documents on
Indian Policy 1750–1921* (OUP, London, 1922), i. 177.   [101] *CEHI*, i. 178–9.

cent of their income on their armies.[102] With an 'unlimited'[103] appetite
for resources, the ruling élite could only acquire these by continued
conquest-cum-plunder, and the harshest exactions from the peasantry
compounded by the oppressive methods and the illegalities of the tax-
collectors, and the arbitrary seizure of merchants' wealth.[104] Thus the
monies extracted from the working part of the population went to
support the very forces that took them.[105] This is all a commonplace:
it simply repeats what we have so frequently had to describe in respect of
other polities. Furthermore, in few previous examples was the purely
architectonic character of the administration so marked; for after military
expenditure the ruling clique spent most of the remainder on 'a truly
fabulous life-style', exemplified not only in its town-houses, palaces, and
the like, but in such matters as, for instance, the employment of fourteen
specialized categories of servants in the imperial stables.[106] Very little was
spent on infrastructure: trees were planted along some of the roads to
provide shade, some bridges were built and, similarly, irrigation canals and
paved water-tanks: but when the court and nobility built, it was principally to construct Lahore, Agra, and Delhi, and raise palaces, fortresses,
and mosques. Except for its tax-collectors and policemen the empire,
which soared above and around, was detached from the life of the villages,
the guilds, and above all the castes. It was in these and the rapidly
burgeoning towns that day-to-day government took place.

Yet, despite all this and more the Mughal Empire compels admiration for
being there at all. It is like Johnson's 'dog walking on his hinder legs. It is
not done well; but you are surprised to find it done at all.' It represents the
most substantial feat of political consolidation that India had so far
experienced. It brought together under one head and uniform administrative
structure virtually the entire subcontinent: the largest single state ever seen
in India before the British conquest. And it held it together for 150 years.[107]

Yet its huge size was one important element in its weakness. We began
the chapter by pointing out the diversity of India—how it resembled a
continent, not a state at all. The Mughals conquered and pieced the
conquered states together but did not homogenize them. The Hindu
Mahrattas and the Sikhs both rose against Aurungzeb, the fundamentalist
Muslim emperor.

The ruling class—the *omrah* and the *jagirdars*—were mostly foreign adven-
tureres or native princes whom the emperors had found it inexpedient to

---

[102] Ibid.   [103] Ibid. 173.   [104] Ibid. 186 for extensive illustrations of this.
[105] In the words of Ernest Jones's Chartist hymn: 'The steel shines to defend | What labour
wrought and labour raised | For labour's foes to spend.'   [106] *CEHI*, i. 180–1.
[107] I count from the accession of Akbar (not before) to the death of Bahadur (Shah Alam) in 1712.

destroy: effectively *condottieri*. They served for the emoluments of their *jagirs* but these, they knew, escheated to the Crown on their demise and the emperor moved them around constantly so as to prevent them striking roots in the soil, forcing them to exist solely by and for his favour. The emperors succeeded only too well. 'The nobles, who should have acted as pillars of the state . . . developed into a selfish band of adventurers and fortune-seekers, more interested in securing their own power, position and welfare than that of the people. As the limits of the expansion came to be reached, rebellions, intrigues, murders of kings and pernicious succession disputes became the order of the day.' They quarrelled so incessantly that they were called *hasad-peshah*, that is ' professional quarrel-seekers'.[108]

The empire began to disintegrate after the death of Bahadur (Shah Alam) in 1712. Aurungzeb had left him a poor legacy. He had alienated the fighting Rajput princes by his arrogant treatment of the succession at Jodhpur. It is significant that they did not assist him in his subsequent war against the Sikhs. He was running down the state's financial resources in his interminable war with the Mahrattas. He had pursued a religious policy which is intensely controversial to historians today but which, whether it did or did not raze Hindu temples and so forth, unquestionably reimposed the discriminatory *jizya* on the Hindu population, who reacted with rage. Bahadur patched up the quarrels with the Rajputs and made some kind of arrangement with the Mahrattas also. It was not till he died that the empire started to crumble.

One theory of its collapse is that, like the Ottoman Empire, it had to expand or perish. At best, this theory would have to be qualified. The expansion did unquestionably pay for the wars up to Aurungzeb's reign and left a comfortable surplus of gold and precious stones to be distributed among the emperor and nobles as booty.[109] But this was no more than redistributing the accumulations of specie from the previous princes and kings to new owners. It might therefore be more exact to say that the constant expansion was required for the *omrah* and *jagirdars* to be able to go on living the *dolce vita*. It is also true that the adventurers who flocked to the imperial court were anxious to receive *jagirs* and that only conquests could satisfy their demands. And, certainly, during the Mahratta war, when liquid resources had run short, Aurungzeb found that he had not enough land to

---

[108] Sarkar, *Mughal Polity*, 480; and cf. also Braudel, *Civilisation and Capitalism*, iii. 514–15.

[109] *CEHI*, i. 184–5, gives some striking examples. Akbar's treasure at his death was estimated at 522.4 million florins. A governor of Bengal is said to have accumulated Rs. 380 million of treasures in his thirteen-year tenure.

provide new *jagirs* to pay his *mansabdars*.[110] But expansion was not—as it was in the Ottoman case—necessary to keep the empire functioning, for India was far richer and the taxation of the peasantry could, with due regard to economy, have well sufficed. After all, it was taxes that had provided those immense treasuries of gold and jewels which the emperors despoiled.

It might well be thought that the oppressive taxation of the peasantry was the cause of collapse, and in a highly qualified sense this can be said to be so. We have already pointed out two of the qualifying factors. The first of these is that the *jagir* system, like its *iqta* counterpart in Mamluk Egypt, tempted the *jagirdar* to extort as much as he possibly could from his *jagir* without concern for the future of the land, because he would only be in post a few years before moving on. The second was that 'sacred lust for gold' which sprang from the desire for lavish living and the necessity of paying large numbers of troops to extort the taxation to pay for it. In this way, the more that had to be raised in taxation, the more of it that had to be spent on the soldiery, necessitating still heavier exactions, and so on and on in a vicious cycle. Taxation was indeed exceedingly heavy and the penalties for non-payment savage: the forced sale of wives, children, and cattle; beatings, starvation, torture. This was not universally true, since there were well-off peasants as well as the very poor, but in some areas the taxes deprived the latter of the very means of survival.[111] Some peasants, usually so patient and unwarlike, were goaded into rebellion. More often they fled to *zamindars* who were resisting the *jagirdars'* extortions—the *zortalab zamindars*, signifying those who were seditious or who 'went into rebellion or refused to pay taxes'.[112] In this way the refugee peasants became associated with a widespread *zamindar* struggle against the imperial system. It formed a significant element in the Jat and the Satnami revolts in the reign of Aurungzeb, as well as in many other minor rebellions.[113] But these *zortalab zamindars* made their most significant contribution in the great Mahratta revolt against Aurungzeb, which he never succeeded in quelling. They supplied what the Mahratta hero Shivaji described as his 'Naked, Starved Rascals'. 'Thus was the Mughal Empire destroyed.'[114]

[110] Sarkar, *Mughal Polity*, 319. After Bahadur had recklessly granted *jagirs* in order to win political support, his short-lived puppet successors brought the entire system into decay. The *jagirs* were increasingly granted for political motives, not for military ones. As in later Tokugawa Japan, rich merchants and bankers moved in to acquire *jagirs*. Soon the *jagirdars* were not qualified *mansabdars* nor would they undertake military duties. The emperors had to distribute their own Crown lands. Many efforts were made to save the old system but they were useless (cf. the decay of the *timariot* system in the Ottoman Empire), and by the mid–18th cent. the system was defunct. Sarkar, *Mughal Polity*, 320–1.

[111] Habib, *Agrarian System*, 322–3.   [112] Ibid. 173–4, 283, nn. 59, 331.   [113] Ibid. 345–6.
[114] Ibid. 351.

But the proximate cause of the collapse of the empire was neither the limit to its expansion nor its economy, but one simple political factor: the disastrous run of transient and effete phantom-emperors that succeeded Bahadur.[115] More than any other of all the contemporary grand empires of Asia, the Mughal Empire was the one that depended *uniquely* on the character of the emperor. There was no vizier, however incompetent, to take his place and at least co-ordinate the administration. There were whole armies of accountants and junior clerks but no trained and permanant higher civil service such as developed in the Ottoman Empire. And the nobility did not owe true loyalty, but were there for what they could get.

The steps in the disintegration of the empire followed one another apace. In 1722 the chief minister, Asaf Jah, finding it impossible to bring order into the central administration, retired to Hyderabad province of which he was the *subahdar* and became independent from 1724, founding the dynasty of the *Nizam*.[116] In the same year Saadat Khan took over the rulership of Oudh. Bengal's *subahdar*, Alivardi Khan (1740–56), made only irregular payments of tribute and in practice ceased to recognize the emperor as sovereign. Meanwhile the Mahratta Confederacy, now independent of the empire, suffered a change in government when the chief minister, the *peshwa*, like the Carolingian mayors of the palace, became the real ruler and the raja merely an ornamental figure.

The Mahrattas had already seized Gujarat, Malwa, and Bundelkhand when from out the north-west passes there suddenly arrived the Persian adventurer, Nadir Shah. He seized and looted Delhi and carried off the fabulous Peacock Throne. This was in 1739. It was only a raid but it broke the empire's back. From then on Delhi was fought over, captured, and recaptured by the Mahrattas, by Pakhtuns, and others, while the empire was disintegrating all around it. The emperorship, ever-more nominal, hung on until in 1862 the British extinguished it. But the effective date for the demise of the Mughal Empire is, really, 1739: the year of the raid of Nadir Shah.

---

[115] They fell under the control of a court faction led by two nobles, the Sayyid brothers. The dates and causes of death speak for themselves. Jahandar Shah, 1711–13, assassinated by the Sayyids. Farrukhsiyar, 1713–19, also assassinated by the Sayyids; Rafi-ud-Daulat, 1719, deposed; Shah Jahan II, 1719, also deposed; Nikusiyar, 1719, deposed and assassinated; Muhammad Shah, 1719–20, deposed puppet of the Sayyids. These short-reigning emperors were, without exception, weak, pleasure-seeking voluptuaries, with the backbone of a louse.

[116] *Nizam* is the Arabic for 'governor'. The title was borne by several Indian princes.

PART II

The Re-Creation of the State in Europe

5

The 'Modern State'

I. BACKGROUND AND CHRONOLOGY

*T*he sixteenth century forms the watershed in the political development of Europe and via Europe, of the entire world, for Europe is the birthplace of the modern state. Here, in short compass, a number of diverse developments came to reinforce one another.

Before describing these it is well to recall the chronology of the long-established imperial structures of Asia. In the Ottoman Empire the key dates are 1453, the seizure of Constantinople, and 1566, the death of Suleiman the Magnificent. In China the Ming dynasty rules untroubled. In India Babur has defeated the Lodi Sultan at Panipat (1525), but the Mughal Empire is not really in being until 1556—the accession of Akbar—and collapses after 1712—the death of Bahadur.

During the period covered by these events a number of seminal developments were unfolding in Europe. The first was the discrediting of its two over-arching institutions—the Empire and the Papacy. To this the great papal–Hohenstaufen feud was but a prelude. A further landmark was reached when Boniface VIII (1294–1303) failed to impose his will on the kings of England and of France, and indeed died of shock at the hands of the latter's soldiery. Then followed the so-called 'Babylonian Captivity' (1305–78), when the popes, installed at Avignon, were controlled by France. But the real degradation of the Papacy did not occur until the Great Schism in which two popes, and finally three, each claimed the papal throne. The universalist claims of the Papacy were shattered when Europe's rulers were free to recognize the claimant who best suited their particularist interests. But there was more than that; it was the patent depravity of these rival popes. Urban VI was a sadistic torturer, John XXIII a former pirate-captain.[1] Meantime the empire was de-natured by the Golden Bull, 1356, which effectively turned it into an aristocratic confederation.[2] The combined effect of these two developments was to leave the way open for kings and princes to assert what we would today call their 'sovereign independence' of both emperor and Papacy—and to permit them to assert, with truth, the jurists' tag that 'kings are emperors within their kingdom'.

Two more developments that marked off this century as a turning-point were the Renaissance and the Reformation. The former introduced secularism into the conduct of state affairs, accelerated the movement from clerical counsellors to laymen (usually lawyers), and turned these into the beginnings of a bureaucracy in our modern sense.[3] Of this secularism and the abandonment of the medieval notion of natural law, Machiavelli is the supreme exponent.

'To Machiavelli, the state, that is, Italy, is an end in itself. The restraints of natural law seem mere moonshine to a man of his *positif* habit. He substitutes the practical conceptions of *reason of state* as a ground of all government action, and the *balance of power* as the goal of all international efforts . . .'[4]

A similar conclusion came to be underwritten by the Reformation but by an entirely different route. The Christian unity of the past 1,300 years was shattered from the moment Luther posted his theses at Wittenberg in 1517. The states and statelets of the empire took sides for and against, and fought one another in leagues like the Schmalkaldic (Lutheran) League, until they reached a temporary peace at Augsberg in 1555. The Protestant cities and states had won their freedom of worship, the right to introduce the Reformation into their territories, and (effectively) the principle that the population followed the religious persuasion of their ruler. With this, 'roughly speaking, what Luther did in the world of politics was to transfer to the temporal sovereign the halo of sanctity that had hitherto been mainly

---

[1] M. Gail, *The Three Popes* (Hale, London, 1969), 105–7. A group of cardinals tried to get Urban deposed whereupon he subjected one to the *strappado*, and kept the others in cells too short to lie down in. When forced to flee from Nocera, Urban took these tortured cardinals with him, lashed to pack animals like a baggage train. In the course of this flight the aged bishop of Aquila was kicked to death by the soldiery and left to die. John XXIII was, *inter alia*, the pope who first took to issuing Indulgences on a grand scale.   [2] See above, Bk. III, Ch. 6.

[3] Chabod, 'Was there a Renaissance State?', in H. Lubasz (ed.), *The Development of the Modern State: Readings* (Macmillan, New York, 1964), regards this bureaucratization as the distinguishing characteristic of the Renaissance state.

[4] J. N. Figgis, *Churches in the Modern State* (Longmans, London, 1931), 75.

the privilege of the ecclesiastical, and to change the admiration of men from the saintly to the civic virtues, and their ideal from the monastic life to the domestic'.[5] But the triumph of the secular monarch over the Church, the Erastianism of the new Protestant dispensation, did not stop at the Protestant states. Francis I of France and Ferdinand and Isabella in Spain contrived to establish such a control over their states' Church establishment that, though remaining thoroughly Catholic in doctrine, they were quasi-national in character.[6] This 'transference of the halo of sanctity to the temporal sovereign' gave a fresh impetus and interpretation to the 'divine right of kings' doctrine. With the Papacy out of the way these monarchs claimed to hold their authority directly from God, to be His vicar on earth, and accountable to Him alone. It followed that resistance was sin:

> 'There's such divinity doth hedge a king
> That treason can but peep to what it would.[7]

Another corollary was the principle of indefeasible hereditary succession: it was this that legitimated. This exaltation of monarchy was accompanied by the increasing extravagance of royal styles, for example, 'your Majesty', and the conspicuous expenditure at court.[8]

Combined together, the Renaissance and Reformation formed a most explosive mixture. They ruptured traditional Latin Christianity which had been the European mind-set for 1,300 years and confronted it with a counter-culture, an anti-tradition: in place of ecclesiastical universality, religious particularism; in place of Catholic, other-worldly sanctity, this world of the here and now, the humanist premises and the fleshly, pagan worlds of Greece and Rome and what went with them—'mistresses with great smooth marbly limbs', as the Bishop at St Praxed's reminisces.[9] As we have already indicated, the cultural-religious traditions of China, Japan, India, and Islam were immemorial and no disruption of this nature ever occurred in them. Hence the restlessness of Europe as the counter-tradition upset all the old, familiar assumptions and opened the way for the advances in secular thought, especially in scientific thought and thereby the new technology that was to make the Europeans the masters of the world.

Alongside this cultural disruption, two related developments combined

---

[5] J. N. Figgis, 72.
[6] See below under 'France' and 'Spain' respectively at p. 1282 and p. 1294ff.
[7] Shakespeare, *Hamlet*, IV. v.
[8] Cf. N. Elias, *The Court Society*, trans. E. Jephcott (Blackwell, Oxford, 1983).
[9] R. Browning, 'The Bishop Orders his Tomb at St. Praxed's Church' (first published in *Hood's Magazine*, Mar. 1845, as 'The Tomb at St. Praxed's'), *Browning: Poetical Works, 1833–1874*, ed. I. Jack (OUP, London, 1970), 432–5. A masterly evocation of the worldliness of the Renaissance popes and their courts.

to alter the political contours of the continent: the collapse of military feudalism alongside the growth of commerce and exchange, the money economy, and the finance-houses and international bankers. An earlier chapter has already stated how the first was already collapsing in the reign of Edward I in England[10] (though France lagged behind by at least a half-century). Yet for all the collapse of military feudalism as such, a sort of 'bastard feudalism' remained which was potentially more lethal to the kingly power than true feudalism. Commerce, together with the new alienability of land, prompted the nobility to accumulate vast estates which formed veritable mini-states, able and sometimes over-willing to compete with the central power. Moreover, though they could no longer demand military service of their tenants, the latter were prompt to enter their service as paid retinues or liveries.

These trends waxed stronger with the advance of currency and credit. A war required ready cash. How many times has one read of medieval monarchs pawning their crown jewels? Now, in the fourteenth and fifteenth centuries Italian finance houses were at hand in such cities as Lucca, Siena, Pisa, and *par excellence*, of course, in Florence.[11] In the sixteenth century these Italian houses were far overtaken by the bankers of Antwerp—at its apogee *c.*1550—where little currency was exchanged and most transactions went by bills of exchange. This was the great Age of the Fuggers.

In these new circumstances the duel between the periphery and the centre, between the king as *rex* and the king as *dominus*, renewed itself. It ended in the triumph of *rex*. In the process the Crown enormously strengthened itself—hence the term the 'New Monarchies'—in the Atlantic states of Spain, France, and England.

And all this time technology and particularly military technology was advancing in ways simply unheard of in the Asian states.[12] The uninter-rupted continuity of the latter's cultural and religious traditions produced an intellectual torpor so profound, that—to take one example—it was the Jesuits who had to construct telescopes and other celestial instruments for the Chinese who had themselves discovered or invented them over a century before—and completely forgotten them since! In Europe this was the age of Copernicus, Tycho Brahe, Kepler, and Galileo.

It was also the age of printing. Gutenberg invented for Europe (the Chinese had had it since the ninth century) movable type. Its political, no less than cultural and religious, impact is incalculable. Gutenberg's Bible

---

[10] Cf. Bk. III, Ch. 6 above.   [11] See Book III, Ch. 7 above.

[12] I certainly except hand-guns and cannon. In Tokugawa Japan the harquebus was copied by the Japanese from three imported weapons; and Suleiman the Conqueror built up his formidable park of siege-artillery by using the services of a Hungarian master-gunner.

appeared in 1456. Within a generation printing was established in practically every country in Europe.[13] Initially it catered for much the same clientele as had bought manuscripts: for school-primers and books on religion. But they were so much cheaper and more accessible that governments began to view their dissemination with much the same fear that they regarded popular access to firearms—hence the censorship, where the Catholic Church took the lead (the Index was formulated in 1559, some forty years after Leo X began to proscribe certain works) and was closely followed in some Protestant communities, like Calvin's Geneva. Religious wars were fought by pamphlets as well as swords: the French Wars of Religion (1562–98) were the first of these frequent revolutions and rebellions in which press, pamphlets, and propaganda played a vital role. It is estimated that between 1585 and 1594 the Paris printers to the Catholic League printed over 1,000 publications.[14] Printing began to create something that might justly be called 'public opinion'.

It was the age, too, when the galley gave way to the ocean-going, fully-rigged ship with a stern-post rudder. Guns had been employed as long ago as Crècy, with little effect. But the French used them to drive the English out at the battles of Castillon and Formigny in 1453, and in that same year Mehmet II, with a Hungarian master-gunner, had used them to breach the walls of Constantinople. In 1509 the Venetians caught on to the uses of such cannonry at sea. England's defeat of the Spanish Armada was a matter of gunships.

And of course it was such gunships that brought the Europeans and their ocean-going craft into India, South-East Asia, and the Philippines, and even to China and Japan for a short sojourn. But for the moment these excursions were no more than reconnaissances; the paramount and irreversible consequence of these early armed voyages was not in them, but in the discovery of America, and the consequent Spanish and Portuguese Empires in its south and the European settlement-colonies in the north. The point is that America was totally unknown, not merely to the Europeans but to the Asian empires as well. It was a virgin continent, sparsely inhabited and yet very rich. It positively invited conquest. With these new and fertile acres Europe obviated some of its economic, religious, and insurrectionary problems.[15] Europe was on the point of becoming very, very rich.

[13] *The New Cambridge Modern History*, 14 vols. (CUP, Cambridge, 1957–9), vol. II (1958), 362 [hereafter referred to as *CMH*].
[14] P. Zagorin, *Rebels and Rulers*, 1500–1660, 2 vols. (CUP, Cambridge, 1982), ii. 59.
[15] 'Ghost acreage' is what Jones, *The European Miracle* (CUP, Cambridge, 1981), calls it; see his discussion, 82–4.

2. THE RE-CREATION OF THE STATE IN EUROPE

Territorially, the medieval state was *differentiated*. By contrast the public and the private *functions* were consolidated in one and the same office or individual. As opposed to this, the modern state consists of formerly differentiated territories which have been brought together and whose populations have become *consolidated* under the same common organ of rule. At the same time, a distinction has long been drawn between public and private rights and duties, and by that token, between public officers and private individuals. In brief:

	Territorially	*Functionally*
Medieval	Differentiated	Consolidated
Modern	Consolidated	Differentiated

The twin processes—from consolidated service to differentiated service and from differentiated territory to consolidated territory—constitute the 'development of the modern European state' and began in the Atlantic countries from *c.*1450. They were bound up with the increased size and professionalism of a lay bureaucracy and of the military forces. The details will be discussed later, but the point to be made here is that 'consolidation' entailed a contest between king and magnates. Now this was not unilinear, nor was the outcome predetermined. On the contrary—this consolidation was not consummated in the Holy Roman Empire or Italy, for instance. The consolidation process, however, is in many cases a race; a race between the king with his bureaucracy and his new-type army and a number of magnates with *their* professional bureaucrats and *their* paid soldiery. Just as the king tried to 'round off' his lands into one contiguous territory and bring the magnates within it to recognize his supreme authority, so the magnates were themselves laying field to field and rounding off their territories in the same way and for the same purpose. It was a desperate race where sometimes the king but often the magnates got ahead.

The victory of the monarchy was greatly assisted by what I have else-where called the coercion–extraction cycle. By reason of novel techniques of warfare—of what has been styled the 'military revolution'—war had become prodigiously expensive. Ready cash was needed. It could be bor-rowed, as we have already seen, but only against the security of an enhanced revenue of the Crown. The heavy taxation which this demanded provoked resistance and revolts, and the army put them down. So was created the cycle: the army used coercion to acquire the tax-revenue which enabled it to continue to use coercion; and so on.

The Atlantic seaboard states did not, on the whole, invent new taxes but adapted and, above all, improved the collection of medieval ones. In England the mainstay of state income (leaving aside the Crown's feudal revenues) remained the land tax and the customs. But England was not typical because she used a militia, not a standing army, for home defence and in so far as cash was required—as indeed it was—it was for coastal defence, ships, and the pay of expeditionary forces.

France provides an excellent example of the adaptation of ancient taxes. The *taille* was a tallage such as any feudal lord was entitled to levy on his serfs. In 1439 (see below) the Crown secured the monopoly on this tax—the 'royal taille'—which became the most important source of Crown revenue. The *gabelle* was equally medieval: in its fourteenth-century guise it denoted any indirect tax on goods. In the fifteenth century, however, it came specifically to denote a tax on the consumption of salt. It was administered with varying degrees of severity, sometimes by Crown agents and sometimes by tax-farmers. It was constantly being eroded by the activity of smugglers—the *faux sauniers*. Between them the *taille* and the *gabelle* provided well over 80 per cent of the Crown's revenue and the global amount shot up enormously by the end of the century, a development to be pursued below.

Castile also illustrates how a medieval tax was expanded to meet the insatiable demands of warfare. It was called the *alcabala*, and was an indirect tax chargeable on the selling price of commodities as often as they were sold or exchanged. It had been imposed as a royal tax in 1341 as part of the effort to defeat the Moors, and throughout the fifteenth century was being collected as a tax for which the consent of the Cortes was not required. It accounted for between 80 per cent to 90 per cent of the Crown revenue by the end of the fifteenth century, by which time it was much more productive, as the Crown improved its administration.[16]

The cash-costs of war had increased so enormously not only because troops now served for pay but by way of changes in military techniques and bigger armies. The age of heavy cavalry was passing. The mid-fifteenth century ushered in the age of pike and hand-gun, of heavy artillery for sieges and somewhat lighter, though very unwieldy guns for the battlefield. To counter the artillery the tall, thinnish ('curtain') walls of the medieval castle or city had to be replaced or girdled by low and thick ones, forerunners of the bastion (the 'Italian Trace'), at enormous expense.

In their Italian wars (1503–38) France and Spain tried out all manner of combinations of infantry phalanxes, harquebusiers, and the heavy French cavalry and each had its decisive moment in one or other of the battles, but

---

[16] J. H. Elliott, *Imperial Spain*, 1469–1716 (Penguin, Harmondsworth, 1970), 202.

one formation was indispensable—the infantry phalanx. The Swiss phalanx (the original model) was by now a square of 6,000 men, armed with eighteen-foot pikes and with halberds—later with muskets also. It attacked by hurling itself at the enemy infantry with a greater shock than even feudal cavalry. This formation became the favourite of continental Europe and was copied by the German Swabians, who called themselves *landsknechten*. For more than a century after 1480 (the Battle of Guinegatte), French foot armies were always composed of two elements, Swiss or *landsknechten*, and native mercenary *bandes*. Then, from his own experiences against them in the Italian wars, Spain's *Gran Capitan*, Gonzalvo de Cordoba, evolved a more flexible formation—the *tercio*, composed of only 3,000 men. It was a hollow square whose sides were made up of deep formations of harquebusiers, later replaced by the much heavier musket. The *tercio* proved unbeatable until it was shattered by Condé at Rocroi in 1643.

Meanwhile, the size and hence the cost of such mercenary formations rose inexorably. For instance, the French army that invaded Italy in 1498 numbered about 6,000. In 1635 the number of French troops deployed against Spain was approaching 100,000.[17] In 1678 the number of French campaign troops attained 279,000.

The ultimate development in making the secular ruler an 'emperor in his own kingdom' was his increased control over the Church. One must cast the mind back and recall the extent to which the Church had hitherto led its own life with its own Canon law, its own hierarchy and discipline, and its own immense endowments, to realize how much power the Crown gained in controlling it. As we have already pointed out, in the still-Catholic lands like France and Spain, this control was obtained without secession from Catholicism and the Papacy. But the effects were most pronounced in the Protestant states. Figgis commented thus on Luther's political significance:

The practical abolition of benefit of clergy, the substitution of the ideal of the good householder for that of the saint and the monk, the unification of all powers within the State, the ascription of all coercive authority to the civil ruler, and the inculcation of the duty of absolute non-resistance are not Luther's sole work, even in politics; but they are the most salient features of the whole movement, of whose spirit his career was a symbol. The Church had, in fact, been the first and greatest 'immunist'; as it was the first, so it was the last . . . Had there been no Luther there could never have been a Louis XIV. In fact, the religion of the State superseded the religion of the Church. Its first form was the Divine Right of Kings . . . Its purport is to deny all theories of ecclesiastical superiority . . .[18]

---

[17] The figure usually given is 155,000 but recent research has revised it downwards.
[18] Figgis, *Churches*, 62–3.

3. INDIVIDUAL CASES

Our earlier chapter on the expansion of regalian powers and the consequent unification in the hitherto unarticulated *Regnum Francorum* showed that it did not occur solely by unremitting warfare. Warfare there certainly was—witness, for instance, Philippe Auguste's seizure of the Angevin possessions from King John and the subsequent rape of the Midi. A quite usual way was by purchase. But the method *par excellence* was by marriage. We are in Jane Austen country. The demesne was built up by adding field to field. 'As was once said of the American pioneer: "he didn't want all the land; he just wanted the land next to his".'[19] Owing to its early unification and the subsequent Norman conquest, England forms a partial exception,[20] but France and Spain, Brandenburg–Prussia, the Austrian Empire, and Lithuania–Poland, for instance, were pre-eminently created by the dynastic alliance. The supreme example—but we shall find several others—is the Empire of Charles V: *tu, Felix Austria, nubes.*

This creation of consolidated territorial states by testamentary succession stands in total contrast to the way they were created in Asia—and this includes Muscovy. This author can think of no example where an oriental empire was extended by a marriage alliance. Certainly it is not unusual to find the alliance or support of another state sought or guaranteed by the offer of a daughter or son in marriage. This was very common in the Byzantine empire, to name but one example The Chinese practised this kind of diplomacy also, and, as the last chapter reminds us, so did Akbar when he won over the Rajputs by marrying the princess of Amber. But this is as far as the marriage alliances went. From ancient Egypt and Mesopotamia to China, Mughal India and the Ottoman Empire and even the Roman Empire, all were created in one way alone: by wars of conquest and subjection.[21]

---

[19] Quoted in N. Elias, *State Formation and Civilisation* (Blackwell, Oxford, 1982), 160.

[20] England, yes; but not Great Britain. This was brought about, for the long period 1603–1707, by a union of crowns just as on the Continent.

[21] I have not seen this point remarked on elsewhere. To the extent that it is true the interesting question is 'why?' I can suggest a plausible guess but no more. It is that the dynastic aggregation of empires in the East was prevented by one or both of two factors. The first is that few of these countries recognized the right of a woman to rule. Queen Hatshepsut of Egypt, and the Empress Wu of China are conspicuous exceptions that prove the rule. Some Indian states, however, did certainly recognize the legitimacy of rule by a *rani*. The second reason would lie in the differences between the laws of testamentary succession in the East as compared to those of Europe. This alone would wipe out any of the Muslim cases, since the daughters' share of their father's estate was, under the *sharia*, set at a small fraction of its total worth. And no Muslim state would tolerate a woman ruler anyway. Compare Isabella of Spain's designation as *reina proprietaria*—'queen and owner'.

3.1. *England*

In principle, England ought not be reckoned among these powers that had
to pursue territoriality because she had it even prior to the Conquest. Yet it
was so; and the reason was that whereas in France the dynastic marriages
and claims flowing from them led to the unification of the great principalities under the Crown, in England similar marriage alliances and their
consequences acted to *disaggregate* the kingdom. Some two dozen earls or
dukes with immense incomes, great local concentrations of land and
influence, and their own private armies indulged their ravenous political
and economic appetites.

In the end the kingship did prove itself the stronger. Not only did it re-
aggregate the kingdom, but in its enhanced power it went much further.
The 'New Monarchy' of the Tudors, for all that it had no professional
forces of its own and that local government was in the hands of private
gentlemen, not only suppressed the magnates and disarmed them but took
control of the Church, consolidated its grip on Wales and Ireland, smashed
Scottish invasions, and established a set of powerful prerogative councils
which enforced the law in a summary fashion beyond the capacities of the
courts of common law.

3.1.1. THE PACIFICATION OF THE NOBILITY

In the later fourteenth century land could be alienated more easily and
magnates were pursuing dynastic marriages so that some, like Lancaster or
Neville (Warwick), became inordinately rich.[22] Furthermore, whereas the
king's 'indentured' companies were raised (usually) only for one year at a
time, many magnates retained their servants and soldiers for their lifetime.
These were their 'retinues', and the richer the magnate the larger the retinue.
In 1399 the richest and strongest of these magnates, Lancaster, usurped the
throne. Later the Lancastrian dynasty he had founded was challenged by the
house of York—who had a better hereditary claim to the throne. So, in 1455,
there broke out the Wars of the Roses, spread over thirty years but
consisting really of only a few weeks of actual fighting during all this
period. They came to an end in 1485 when a Lancastrian pretender, the
obscure Henry Tudor, chanced his arm against the Yorkist Richard III at
Bosworth Field, and happened to win. Unlike his predecessors he hung on
to his throne. So was inaugurated the great House of Tudor. It is significant
that Henry (Henry VII) immediately married Elizabeth, the heiress to

---

[22] V. H. H. Green, *The Later Plantagenets: A Survey of English History between 1307 and 1485* (Edward
Arnold, London, 1955), 95.

York—so uniting the two 'Roses' (the symbols of the rival houses of Lancaster and York) in the usual dynastic compact we have discussed.

By this time the number of magnates had greatly declined. This was only partly due to the wars; most can be accounted for by the normal biological failures in the male line—a process that went on all the time. Lawrence Stone has calculated that in 1487 there were only twenty magnates (that is, dukes, earls, and marquises) out of fifty-seven lay peers. Furthermore, as victory swung to one house and then the other, so attainders and executions not only weakened the number of magnates but, since their lands escheated to the Crown, expanded the latter's riches and power. From these sources, it is claimed, Henry VII was able to double his demesne revenues. The Crown became justifiably wary of endowing great or rising families with more lands or even creating new ones: after 1572 no dukedom was created until the reign of James I.[23] Moreover the Crown preferred to rely on lesser *novi homines*. In Edward VI's Council the only son of a peer was Arundel, eleven others were sons of gentry, and another nine stemmed from the lesser gentry. At this date only twenty-six of the fifty-seven noble families had been ennobled before 1509, and only nine of these went back to the Middle Ages.[24]

Also, their estates were smaller.[25] Most damaging, however, was the loss of their fighting capacities. Certainly, they held on to their armed retinues which continued to be the most important component of the Tudor armies, whether for home or expeditionary service. But they were smaller and firmly subordinated to the Council; private castle-building ceased after 1521; and by 1600 their private armouries had disappeared and weapons were everywhere stockpiled in the county armouries.[26] Above all, in the long periods of peace they lost the experience and the appetite for battle. Stone has calculated that in the 1540s three-quarters of the peers had had battle experience; in 1576 this was down to a mere quarter, and in the early seventeenth century only one-fifth. The situation in France was quite the opposite.

3.1.2. THE TAKE-OVER OF THE CHURCH

Devout they may have been, but the English were profoundly anti-clerical, and with good reason. The Church—in Europe generally, not just in England—had so overrun its financial capacities by engaging in 'fringe'

[23] L. Stone, *The Crisis of the Aristocracy 1558–1641* (Clarendon Press, Oxford, 1967), 129. It is argued that this was a particular example of Elizabeth's reluctance to promote anybody unless she had to.
[24] W. K. Jordan, *Edward VI, The Young King: The Protectorship of the Duke of Somerset* (Allen &; Unwin, London, 1968), 79, 94. [25] Stone, *Crisis of the Aristocracy,* 129.
[26] This is what made the Great Rebellion differ so sharply from all previous assaults upon the Crown: the protagonists on both sides did not ride out from castles with their own men and their own weapons, but raced their opponents for the county magazines. Ibid. 133–4.

activities like education or alms-giving that it did not have enough to pay its parish clergy who were, after all, responsible for its core function, the cure of souls. So the parochial clergy were so impoverished that some became absentees while others would hold many posts at once. Then again there was a constant drain of English Church revenue to Rome in the shape of *Peter's Pence* and *Annates*. The public perception was that the parish clergy gave poor value for money. The over-extension of the Church's fringe activities resulted, also, in a very considerable increase in its bureaucracy and it was to pay this gross establishment that it resorted to the selling of indulgences and of special licences to evade Canon law. As a consequence the Church became resented for its 'avarice, its apparent obsession with pursuing its own material betterment by accumulating as much as possible'.[27] It is no wonder then that the English perceived the Church hierarchy as absentee or idle, the monasteries as little but *rentier* landlords, while malpractices like the sale of indulgences aroused disgust as did, above all, the fact that the whole organization was subject to a foreign power whose incumbents had long proved themselves to be little more than the princes of a petty Italian state.

Henry VIII 'backed into' the Reformation. What started him off was an entirely secular desire for a male heir, which required a papal annulment of his marriage to Catherine of Aragon. When this was not forthcoming he turned from the Papacy to his Parliament, and through it (the Reformation Parliament which sat from 1529 to 1536), embarked on a series of anti-papal measures that one by one transferred the extraterritorial powers of the Papacy to the Crown. No more is needed here than to recite the main Acts. In 1531 Convocation was forced under the ancient statute of *praemunire* to acknowledge Henry as the Supreme Head of the Church, 'as far as the law of Christ allows'. Next he menaced the Papacy by the Annates statute of 1532, which threatened to sever its revenues. He blocked the possibility of his divorce case being transferred from England to Rome by passing the Act of Restraint of Appeals—it is this Act that declared: 'This realm of England is an Empire.' Since no appeal now lay beyond the archbishop it fell to him to consider the annulment which, unsurprisingly, he granted. The breach with Rome was completed by the Act of Supremacy, 1534, which announced that Henry was and always had been 'Supreme Head of the Church of England'; note that the previous qualification, 'as far as the law of Christ allows', had now disappeared.

---

[27] E. Cameron, *The European Reformation* (OUP, Oxford, 1991), 36. This is an admirable brief analysis, but Cameron too frequently uses the word 'apparent' (as in the above) when he should be writing 'the perceived'. The former word is ambivalent, half-suggesting that things were not really as they were believed to be.

Now Henry decided to make money out of what he had done. By 1539 all monasteries had been dissolved and their property, valued at £2 million in the day's prices, went to augment the Crown lands. (It did not remain there. Three-quarters of it was to be dissipated into the hands of the landed gentry. This acquisition of monastic property gave these gentry so great a vested interest in the royal break with Rome that even Mary Tudor, the dedicated architect of a Catholic revival, did not dare to try to disturb this aspect of the Reformation.)

Henry had once won from the Pope the designation of *Fidei Defensor* (Defender of the Faith) for his pamphlet attacking Luther. As Supreme Head of the Church it now fell to him to specify its doctrine. He never worked out a consistent religious alternative to Catholicism. Earlier enactments were mildly Lutheran, whereas the later enactments (e.g. the King's Book of 1543) were somewhat Catholic. The country did what the king told them; the wild swings of doctrine that were to last until 1660 only began in the reign of his son, Edward VI.

That all this enormously aggrandized the power and authority of the Crown is too obvious to need demonstration. In a sense the king had become a sort of human, living idol. He was the head of a national Church, with supreme control over its revenues, its appointments, and its doctrine. Church had been made over to State; and in this roundabout, crab-like way Henry had become as Erastian as the religiously self-conscious Protestant princes of Germany.

3.1.3. CONSOLIDATION OF THE TERRITORIALITY OF THE STATE

In All Souls Old Library, Oxford, an Elizabethan overmantel shows the royal coat-of-arms supported by the customary English Lion and—instead of the now-familiar unicorn of Scotland—by the *Draeg Goch*, the Red Dragon, of Wales. The Act of Union it symbolizes is not the one between England and the northern kingdom but between England and Wales.

England's immediate neighbours in Tudor times were, first, Scotland—its hereditary foe, wrapped in its 'auld alliance' with the kingdom of France—hence the saying, 'England is half an island'. Then, across the sea lay Ireland, nominally one of the king's dominions, but largely run by rival Anglo-Irish leaders allied to Irish chiefs and captains. Finally, to the west of Chester lay Wales.

Tudor relationships with Ireland were febrile and fragile. Throughout history the English could never make up their minds whether Ireland was the furthest province or the nearest colony. Henry VIII tried to assert firm control over the island and in 1536 put down a serious rising and in the wake of this, in 1540, he adopted the title of 'King of Ireland'. But the Irish resisted his heirs and in her last years Elizabeth I endlessly expended blood and treasure in trying to subjugate them, with only partial success. What made the matter the more intractable was that the Irish remained loyal to the Catholic Church and this served as a national rallying-point. Not till 1800 was Ireland actually incorporated into the United Kingdom—and even then not for long.

The Tudors were militarily much more powerful than the Scots, but the notion of incorporating this kingdom into England had died the death at Bannockburn (1314). Scotland was dangerous because of her French alliance. Henry VII reacted in a way that will become overwhelmingly familiar when we come to France and, above all, Spain—by a dynastic alliance. He married off his daughter Margaret to James of Scotland, a tie which did not prevent the latter from invading England in support of the French in 1513. The outcome was the annihilation of the Scottish host at Flodden, with 10,000 dead. A later invasion in 1542 ended in another Scottish defeat at Solway Moss. This time Henry VIII did contemplate annexation but did not pursue the idea. In the end, the two countries were to be united as a purely personal union of the two Crowns (1603). Not till 1707 were the two countries united in the same Parliament.

Wales was different. It had been conquered long ago, by Edward I. This king had 'shired' its westerly parts (to speak broadly) but left the wide strip between them and England under the control of the warlike, predatory, semi-independent and rebellious lords-marcher. It was from here that sprang the great rebels of the Lancastrian period. Under Henry VII these areas were overseen by a Council of Wales. Henry VIII incorporated Wales in its entirety into England: the Acts of Union, 1536 and 1543, organized it into English-style shires, and thenceforward it elected thirty-one MPs to the Parliament at Westminster. In this way it was swallowed up, and to this day 'England and Wales' is treated as one of the two constituents of Great Britain, Scotland being the other.

3.1.4. THE REINFORCEMENT OF THE ROYAL POWER

The precise role of the Parliament, its relationship to the populace and to the king, are matters of acute controversy.

The conclusions seem to be as follows. The Tudor way with the Parliament established for good and all the supremacy of statute. This is the same as saying that it established as the sovereign authority the institution we have come to know as the Crown-in-Parliament. The wide new powers which Henry VIII acquired were made to rest, not on the whim of the monarch himself, but on the statute which was made by Parliament and administered through the courts. But Parliament and especially the Commons was not then the free-standing, free-thinking body (we must never forget that a rigid censorship existed) that we think of today. Among the MPs sat an inner ring of Crown servants, who sat around those privy councillors who were MPs. What is more, Thomas Cromwell, Henry VIII's remarkable chief secretary of state, made it his business to try to procure dependable individuals as parliamentary candidates. Further, he took enormous pains in the drafting of legislation and steering it through. The Reformation statutes of 1529–36 enhanced the stature of the king but, by sharing in the passage of these Acts, Parliament also had its stature enhanced.

Side by side with this proceeded a reorganization and bureaucratization of the central administration. Henry VII, a vigorous monarch, was still using the medieval councils as his personal instruments of rule. Under Henry VIII the prerogative courts such as Star Chamber and the Councils of the North and of Wales continued to exist, but Cromwell added new ones like the Court of Augmentations (to superintend the disposal of the confiscated monastic lands). In the end the central financial administration consisted of six specialized courts, each with its own officials.

But the most important change during this reign was that the king's principal secretary replaced the chancellor as the first servant of the king, a change which implied an enhanced role for the Council. Through it the secretary acquired control over revenue, foreign affairs, and religion—to name the most important. And its thrust was made the keener when, in 1534–6, Cromwell brought nineteen of the councillors together and formed them into the Privy Council, with its own secretariat. This was the age of councils—all rulers were governing through them—but the English Privy Council was odd and perhaps unique in Europe in this respect: 'unlike the Councils of France and Spain (able only to advise action which itself could never occur except on the signified authority of the king), that of England *did* things, had full executive authority, and by its own instruments (those letters signed by councillors for which there seems to have been no equivalent in the other national monarchies of the west) produced administrative results throughout the realm.'[28] It used to be thought that the Council virtually collapsed as an instrument of rule when the strong hand of Henry disappeared to give way to the falterings of his son and then his daughter Mary. In fact the reverse may be said to have happened; the realm was kept

[28] G. R. Elton, 'Tudor Government . . . The Council', *Transactions of the Royal Historical Society* (1975), 197.

together in these troubled reigns precisely because of the existence of the executive Privy Council.[29]

Was the Tudor monarchy absolute? This is a much-agitated question. The case for it is that the monarch exercised enormous discretionary powers through his control of all appointments (even in the Church), and hence a vast patronage; that he alone conducted foreign policy and made war or peace; that he possessed a personal dispensing and suspending power that permitted him to set aside the application of a statute; and above all, perhaps, in that the Parliament regarded itself and acted as an agent of co-operation, 'doing the King's business' together with him. But others distinguish the Tudors from the monarchs of France and Spain, denying that it was absolute. They would regard England as a special case. The two contemporary criteria for 'absolutism' were the king's personal right to tax and to legislate. The Tudors—even Henry VIII—could do neither on their own; they had to do them by and with the consent of Parliament. Even supposing Parliament was submissive, it was another and separate body with whom the monarch had to co-operate in order to get subsidies and make laws. Queen Elizabeth would have had an easier time of it getting subsidies for the interminable Irish wars had she been able to impose taxes at will.

Zagorin, who maintains that the English monarchy was absolute, obviously feels uncomfortable about it. Consequently he speaks at one point of its being a 'relative absolutism'—but, we must ask, relative to what or whom? And a few lines later he abandons even this when he says that the English Crown was 'both absolute and limited'.[30] I have defined the absolute monarch as 'a regularly constituted and conferred office whose holder is legally (procedurally) unconstrained, but not necessarily uncon-strained by powerful conventional understandings on matters of substance'. The Tudor monarchy was very strong indeed but it did not conform to the terms of this definition. It was not absolute.[31]

3.2. *France*

A basic difference between France and England was that the French Crown immeasurably increased its powers at least fifty to eighty years before that of England. On the other hand, the country itself still remained disunited, and even when it was (largely) re-aggregated under Louis XI, its administration remained diversified and highly particularistic, so that the outcome was not,

---

[29] My views have been heavily influenced by Elton's work, e.g. his *England under the Tudors* as revised in 1972, but I have taken into account the ducking and weaving of Professor Joel Hurstfield, and the other works cited here below.   [30] Zagorin, *Rebels and Rulers*, i. 91–2.

[31] Cf. Elton, 'Tudor Government', 168–9.

as in England, a reasonably homogeneous political community under the Crown[32] but, on the contrary, a network of dyadic relationships between the Crown and a multitude of local communities. England had been fused as early as the tenth and eleventh centuries, but France during the twelfth to fourteenth centuries had been no more than soldered. The consequence was that in France certain fault-lines persisted (e.g. Brittany, Normandy, Languedoc), and under strain the Grand Monarchy fell apart again during the Wars of Religion, under Richelieu, and finally, the Fronde.

3.2.1. THE PRECOCIOUS ACQUISITION OF POWERS BY THE MONARCHY

The French Crown, all but extinguished by the English until its victory at Orleans (1429), went from strength to still greater strength in the Hundred Years War and, with the expulsion of the English (except from Calais) in 1453, wound up as easily the most powerful monarchy in all Europe.

Its power arose out of the war effort. This war was fought on French, not English soil, and in the eyes of the court and its generals desperate plights required desperate remedies. The verdict of history—at least European history—is that war calls out a superabundance of military, administrative, and fiscal overkills which largely remain in place when peace returns. War has an administrative/fiscal ratchet effect. In this French case the process was assisted by the fact that warfare was intermittent fighting punctuated by truces, so that one was always expecting the battles to flare up again. There never was a peace treaty formally bringing this war to an end. Consequently war-emergency measures stayed on—just in case—until, by the time *de facto* peace existed, they had become part of the political scene.

As we have pointed out in an earlier chapter, the Hundred Years War was a kind of civil war, an alliance of great feudatories against the centralizing tendencies of the Crown. The feudatories were Aquitaine (whose duke was also the king of England), Burgundy, the semi-autonomous Brittany, and the rebellious towns of Flanders. By its victory over England the French Crown had acquired all the wealth and manpower of Aquitaine, but Brittany, Burgundy, and the Flanders towns were still outside the royal demesne. Furthermore, this demesne was itself a mere fraction of geographical France, since this was mostly parcelled out among the princes of the blood who, according to custom, were given apanages to maintain them in the regal style to which it was thought they should be accustomed, and which

---

[32] J. S. Morrill has portrayed England in the 17th cent. as a federation of partially independent county-states and communities (*The Revolt of the Provinces* (London, 1976)). This is going much too far. For criticism see e.g. Zagorin, *Rebels and Rulers*, ii. 132–3.

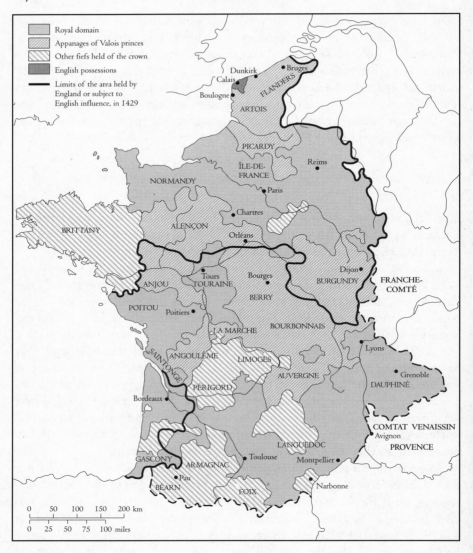

Royal domain
Appanages of Valois princes
Other fiefs held of the crown
English possessions
Limits of the area held by
England or subject to
English influence, in 1429

France c.1453

were in fact so many all-but-autonomous principalities. Other areas were great fiefs belonging to ancient and powerful families like the d'Albrechts and the Foix. Only a map does justice to the administrative divarication of the Kingdom of France.

Now although these great principalities for the moment escaped the direct control of the Crown, the latter had acquired great powers capable of overcoming them. The first was fiscal absolutism. When the war started in the mid-fourteenth century, the French financial system was a chaos and money was raised by hand-to-mouth methods. For France, unlike England, did not enjoy the advantage of a single and representative assembly which had the authority to grant subsidies and was recognized as the source of the main regular taxes. Also, the doctrine of *n'impose qui ne veut*, current in France as in England, was taken in the former to signify that one should pay in conditions of 'evident necessity' (usually taken to mean open warfare), but not during truces, for instance. In brief, taxation was thought of as irregularly spaced *ad hoc* contributions.

By 1370 it was evident that both indirect and direct taxes were required even during peacetime. The direct tax was the *fouage* or *taille*—the hearth tax. The indirect taxes were the *maltote* (a sales tax on materials, metals, clothing, etc.) and the *aides*, of which the *gabelle* or salt tax was the most important. After 1383 the *gabelle* became a standard form of taxation (despite a desperate popular revolt), although it was abolished for a brief moment.

The nobility would not pay the *taille*. They claimed that the tax was to help the war-effort but they themselves *were* the war-effort. The tax fell exclusively on the commoners. Charles VII tried to raise it by negotiating consent from the various provincial Estates, but in the French offensives after 1429 he began to tax first and ask afterwards. The military commanders applied any needful coercion. For instance, in 1425 the Connetable de Richemont levied a *taille* of 120,000 livres two months *before* the Estates convened.

From this it was a mere step not to ask at all. But this raised a political complication. The seigneurs naturally resisted the king levying *taille* on all his subjects at large since every sou he exacted from the seigneur's tenant *pro tanto* diminished the amount the seigneur could raise for himself. In 1439 Charles VII forbade the nobility to oppose him levying taxes and equally, to retain or impose any taxes without his consent. In short, he claimed a royal monopoly of taxation. A nobiliar revolt having failed to shake it, the noble Estate when it met in 1422 demanded that the king levy *taille* only with the consent of the Estates. Charles took a very high line indeed. He claimed that he had the legal right to levy the *taille* on all his subjects and that 'n'est besoin d'assembler les trois États pour mettre sus les dites taille' because it was expensive for poor citizens to send deputies all across France to the Estates. 'They are content that the commission be sent to the *élus* [see below] according to the King's good pleasure.' So, from 1451 he began to levy *tailles* and *aides* on his own authority alone. By 1500, to quote Lot and Fawtier: 'The King had succeeded in extending taxation to the entire body of his subjects and exercising the monopoly of this. It is the essential fact for the reconstitution of public authority. It marks the decisive turning-point in the Crown's march, hesitant at first, towards absolutism.'[33]

But how could this have been done so easily, and irrevocably ? It was achieved through the exigencies of war, the forcible extraction of tax by commanders in the field, and the understanding that the taxation would stop when peace came. But since no peace treaty ever ended the war, the taxation did not end either. In this way, without any individual having deliberately decided this should be so, the taxation became permanent by the force of events.

This outcome had, however, been facilitated by two major differences from contemporary England. The first was the nature of the French Estates-General. This has often been compared with the English Parliament. In fact it was quite a different animal. The very real obstacles of size and linguistic variations could have been surmounted.[34] The crucial difference was that deputies evinced no desire to convene and the reason for this was their regional particularism. 'Even if they attended they thought regionally, their quota of taxation had still to be granted and suitably modified by local assemblies. Local assemblies still granted taxes not, apparently, authorized by a general assembly.'[35]

But just as the kingdom was vertically divided, region alongside region, so it was divided horizontally by social stratification. Once they were (almost) completely exempted from taxation in the fifteenth century, the French nobility had lost the strongest motive for opposing the Crown. So, even when convened, which was not often and only spasmodically, the Estates-General had the narrowest of social bases. It could not rely on the court, which detested it, nor on the nobility, which at this time was more prone to violent resistance than to constitutional opposition, nor on the Paris population, which had run amok in 1357–8. It could rely only on the Third Estate but this was separated by a legally unbridgeable gulf from even the pettiest of the nobility.

Instead of a body like Parliament and a network of local knights of the shire to bear the burdens of local government, France acquired instead ever-larger numbers of paid professional administrators. In the course of this change the ancient, all-purpose administrator, the *bailli* or *seneschal*, lost his functions to new, specialized personnel: for instance, receivers of taxes, masters of water and forests, *lieutenants-généraux* and *lieutenants-particuliers*. The fiscal administration was developed with a sophistication that now

---

[33] F. Lot and R. Fawtier, *Histoire des institutions françaises au moyen-âge*, 2 vols. (Paris, 1957), ii. 265–6.
[34] P. S. Lewis, *The Recovery of France in the Fifteenth Century* (Macmillan, London, 1971), 302.
[35] Ibid. 302.

far outran England's. It consisted of two hierarchies. One looked after the 'ordinary', the other the 'extraordinary' income of the Crown; the former meaning, roughly, the ancient feudal income from the demesne. This was divided into four charges in each of which a *receveur ordinaire* and a *controleur des finances* reported upwards to a *changeur du trésor*, and downwards to petty officials in each *baillage*. Little tax-collection was carried out by state officials; most of it was farmed.

The other hierarchy administered the rapidly expanding field of taxation proper. Local assessments were made by so-called *élus*, though they were in fact appointed by the Crown. Two such *élus* served an area called an *élection* (thirty-one in 1380, eighty-five by 1500). They were served by officials called *receveurs des tailles* and *receveurs des aides*. The *gabelle*, however, had its own staffs, the *grenetiers*, who manned the official salt depots from which the population were made to buy their salt. The customs also had its own staffs. Heading these hierarchies, were (in 1449) four local *généraux des finances* who, sitting together, made up the *Collège des généraux des finances*. Sitting with their counterpart for the demesne revenues, these two bodies were able to establish a rough-and-ready budget.

But one must also recognize that this fiscal absolutism was both occa-sioned by and made possible the continued existence of the second great accretion of royal power—a standing army. We hesitate to call it a military monopoly of power because (to anticipate), outside the demesne the local commands were in the hands of the very feudatories and apanagists that were quartering France. In principle they were no more than the king's appointed commanders, in practice they frequently used the nominally royal troops against him.

Nevertheless, this quasi-monopoly of military power was clearly of the first importance and it came about, once again, by way of the intermittency of battle and truce in the last thirty years of the Hundred Years War. By this time warfare had become professional, and the formations that fought it were the mercenary *bandes*. Very effective militarily, they were loyal only as long as their pay was met. Otherwise, like the *écorcheurs* who raided Burgundy even after the Treaty of Arras in 1435, they would plunder and pillage the very population they were supposed to be defending. This happened unfailingly at the end of a campaign or during a truce, because they were only employed when fighting arose and were dismissed as soon as it was over.

In 1445, although there was no fighting for them to do, Charles VII decided it was too dangerous to let these ruffians loose, and instead put them on 'an unemployment dole' instead. The cost was prodigious—which is why this simple solution to otherwise inevitable disorders had never been used before. But the cost was met by levying the *taille*—supposedly granted only for the year 1445—year after year until it became a recognized impost and therefore he never had to stand down these *bandes*. They became, simply by the inertia of events, a permanent professional standing force. They were called the *compagnies d'ordonnance*, and were the first standing army in Western Europe since the fall of Rome. Their strength became fixed at twenty *compagnies*, and numbered 12,000 cavalry and 8,000 fighting men, a very large force for the times: for instance, at the Battle of Formigny in 1450 the English troops were only some 4,000 strong. Once this force had been constituted the coercion–extraction cycle was institutionalized: the companies enforced the payment of the taxes which maintained them and so, *da capo*. To quote the Russian saying: 'One hand washed the other.'

On top of its fiscal absolutism and standing army, the French Crown obtained a third great power: control of Church patronage and wealth. To plunder the Church was not new to the French Crown—witness Philip the Fair's destruction of the Templars. The tradition of the royal right to tax and control the French clergy now mingled with that very powerful current of theological opinion which, at Basle (1431–49), wanted to subject the Papacy to the authority of a council. In its specifically French form this emerged as what may be summarily if somewhat inexactly described as a claim that its Church should be administered as a territorial unit according to its own local traditions, by its own councils and under the direction of its own bishops. The Papacy was to lose all jurisdiction and no tithes, annates, or other sums were to be paid to the Curia at the conferral of benefices. In 1438, therefore, Charles VII unilaterally promulgated the Pragmatic Sanction of Bourges, creating a 'free Church' somewhat along these lines. We might as well jump to the end of this story, to the Concordat which Francis I agreed with the Papacy in 1516. The pope received French recognition of papal superiority over the General Councils of the Church; Francis gained the suppression of the right of chapters and religious communities to elect the abbots and bishops, and in their place himself put up nominees to the pope.[36] At one stroke Francis had acquired the patronage over 620 preferments with which to reward his political friends.[37] This Concordat vastly increased the royal paramountcy inasmuch as it made over the former role of ecclesiastical elections, councils, and consent to the will of the Crown. The settlement strengthened the theory that the king ruled by Divine Right. This French arrangement was not as radical as the English; but it was effective politically, almost as effective financially—and far more elegant.

---

[36] The king retained the income of the sees as long as they were vacant.
[37] *CMH*, ii. 211.

But though the French Crown had obtained formidable new powers, in practice it could only exercise them in the areas it directly controlled and these were not very extensive. The royal power was intensive but not extensive. It did not embrace the whole kingdom: territorially, France was still a patchwork. To become a modern European state it would have to be territorially consolidated. This task fell to Charles VII's son, Louis XI: 'King Spider'.

3.2.2. THE CONSOLIDATION OF THE TERRITORY

A glance at the map of France in 1453 (see above) shows the smallness of the area directly governed by the king—his demesne: and even that map exaggerates, because it includes newly reconquered Aquitane; a map for the year 1450 would have shown the royal demesne as far smaller.

The map shows also the great fiefs and above all, the apanages of the princes of the blood. Such apanagists and other great feudatories disposed of revenues and military forces which, collectively at least, rivalled the Crown's. The latter had rationalized and centralized administration on its demesne but so had the apanagists, and just as the Crown began to retain permanent or semi-permanent forces, so likewise did great apanagists like the dukes of Burgundy or Brittany. Once again, what we are observing is a race between the realm and a set of rich and powerful principalities. The territories of Anjou, of Orleans, of Bourbon—and above all the conglomeration of lands which made up the great apanage of Burgundy—were all regular states. They had their own administrative machinery and staffs of officials, they had councillors, chancellors, *baillis*, and *seneschaux* just like the king. Often the prince had his own Estates and in consultation with them raised his own taxes. Some might demand and receive the 'gift of Aide' by which they were, effectively, allowed a third or even a half-share of the royal taxation raised on their lands; Burgundy and Flanders paid no royal taxes at all.[38]

These principalities resisted the Crown's efforts at centralization to the point of making war on it. For instance: though each leader of the Praguerie Revolt of 1440 had his own personal reasons, they had a common grievance in respect to two of Charles's centralizing measures. These were his reservation of the *taille* to himself, and his ordinance forbidding all but the king to levy and maintain troops. The rebels, who included the Dauphin Louis, were defeated, but Charles VII never proved able to control the activities of Brittany or of Burgundy, nor for that matter of his dauphin, who in the apanage of the Dauphiné minted his own currency, maintained his own

[38] E. Perroy, *The Hundred Years War* (Capricorn Books, New York, 1965), 221.

army of five companies of men-at-arms and archers, and in effect pursued his own foreign policy.[39]

The League of Public Weal of 1465 was headed, like the Praguerie, by the heir-presumptive to the throne: this was the erstwhile dauphin, now Louis XI. It was more formidable than the Praguerie because it included both the duke of Brittany and the heir to the Duchy of Burgundy. It may well be asked why, at this date, when the king disposed of twenty *compagnies d'ordonnance* he was unable to defeat it. The king had many troops of his own, from Savoy and Normandy particularly, along with the majority of the *compagnies*;[40] but he did not dispose of all of them. His military monopoly was more nominal than real. The duke of Brittany's 6,000 troops included 500–800 captains and men of the royal *compagnies* who had deserted their king for the duke their overlord.[41] Other great lords like Armagnac and d'Albrecht also took the *compagnies* which they commanded into the field against the king.[42] The fact was that, though a king owned the *compagnies d'ordonnance*, the magnates actually commanded them. *Mutatis mutandis* this was to be so until the destruction of the Fronde in 1652.

With foes like these, how, one may well wonder, could the reconstitution of the ancient Regnum ever be brought about? Certainly, it would seem, not by force of arms, for the magnates stood between the royal authority and the practical command of the troops on the ground.

The re-aggregation of the kingdom occurred by a reversal of the basic reason for its falling apart. That reason was the family policy of the Valois which handed out these great apanages as virtually autonomous petty states to the king's immediate family. But a completely incontestable feudal rule attached to any apanage: on the death of the apanagist it reverted to the Crown. The realm came to be re-aggregated by the same means by which it had been dismembered: the effects of family policy. The suddenness of the reversal is extraordinary. At the beginning of Louis XI's reign only one-quarter of France was royal demesne; at its close the only areas outside it were Brittany and Flanders.

In this reconstitution of the kingdom Louis's 'most faithful ally was death'.[43] The sequence is astonishing. The duke of Berry—Louis's brother—had benefited from the League of Public Weal to get Normandy. He died in 1472 and the entire apanage reverted to the royal demesne. The

---

[39] E. Champion, *La France d'après les cahiers de 1789* (5th edn., Paris, 1921; English trans. 1929), i. 192, 194, 196.
[40] P. de Commynes, *Memoires: The Reign of Louis XI, 1416–1483*, trans. M. Jones (Penguin, Harmondsworth, 1972), 69, 91.   [41] Ibid. 67, 81.
[42] Ibid. 63.
[43] P. Wiriath, 'France, History of' (in part), *Encyclopaedia Britannica*, 11th edn. (1910), x. 825.

following year the incestuous count of Armagnac was vanquished and killed and his lands reverted to Louis's daughter Anne. The year 1477 was a true *annus mirabilis*. That redoubtable rival, the great Duke Charles the Bold of Burgundy, was defeated and killed while besieging Nancy. Louis had no entitlement to the County of Burgundy, but the Duchy—a different entity—was an apanage which therefore reverted to him along with Picardy and the Bouillonnais. In 1475 the extensive fief of Anjou had fallen in. René, the count of Anjou, had no direct heir so that when he died in 1480 the other provinces that belonged to the Angevin line (Maine and Provence) went to a nephew. He died the next year and so the entire inheritance reverted to the Crown.

This re-aggregation continued after Louis's death. Brittany was united to France by personal unions between its heiresses and successive kings of France until in 1532 a treaty of union was signed which bound Brittany to France but contained weighty guarantees of its local autonomy. The Bourbonnais had just been annexed in 1531. Thus, Flanders apart, the ancient Regnum was territorially complete.

But territorial completeness did not signify that France had become a homogeneous, fused, political community. On the contrary, as these provinces reverted to the Crown they were not treated to a uniform administration. Indeed, this did not exist even in the Ile de France, the ancient heartland of the royal demesne. Normandy retained its famous 1315 Charter which guranteed its ancient Estates, its own administrative system, and its own *coutumes*. Languedoc retained its local law (*la loi écrite*), its own *parlement* (High Court of Justice), a limitation on the taxes and military service it owed, and its Estates which had the power to control those taxes. The Dauphiné retained its own Estates and *Chambre des Comptes*. One could continue and recite the local particularistic arrangements for Burgundy, Provence, Brittany. In all of them the province retained its Estates and most retained—or obtained for the first time—their own sovereign law-court, their *parlement*. France was a centralized state in that all the subjects in the provinces recognized the authority of the king of France; but this in no way implied uniformity in government, law, or administration. France was still a welter of diverse authorities, particularisms, and immunities. Its centralization consisted of a multitude of individual contracts between the Crown, as the one universally recognized political superior, and the provincial Estates, the towns with their charters, the commercial guilds, and the ecclesiastical establishments. The regime was a web-work of dyadic ties.

It was a fragile artifice and three generations after the end of the sixteenth century the entire arrangement split apart again. In the meantime, however, France passed for the most powerful absolute monarchy in Europe.

3.3. *The Spains*

The Spanish case illustrates the limits to what dynastic marriages and personal unions could achieve; briefly, that they were necessary conditions for the unification of certain territories but by no means at all sufficient ones. If the various political entities—what at the time were called 'the Spains' (Spain or Ispania being a geographical expression)—had not all owed allegiance to a single Crown, they could never have united. If they had not been united, the territory of what we call Spain today could never have been consolidated. Yet the period that elapsed between the first and the second (from 1474 to 1714) was no less than two-and-a-half centuries. Only from the later date were all the diverse political units regulated by one single and uniform administrative system under the centralized rule of an absolute monarch. In the matter of administrative and territorial consolidation Spain was a late starter; and this shows today in its fierce regionalisms which extend, indeed, in Vizcaya and Catalonia, to separatism.

For all that, the reigns of the *Reyes Catolicos*, Ferdinand and Isabella, and their grandson Charles of Flanders, achieved much more than simply presiding over the states that then comprised *las Espanas*, that is, Navarre, Castile, the threefold Crown of Aragon, and Moorish Granada. The Two Crowns of Castile and Aragon conquered and annexed Granada in 1492 and Navarre was annexed to Castile in 1515. This left only Castile and the threefold Crown of Aragon. Castile was much the larger, wealthier, and more dynamic of the two. When Ferdinand and Isabella turned its anarchical late-feudal polity into a 'New Monarchy' they made it the leading power in the peninsula and through this hegemony were able to turn this into some kind of political entity.

How far 'Spain' (anachronistic term) was a 'New Monarchy' is debatable. Elliott, a foremost historian of this period, rejects it.[44] Others, like Batista i Roca, for instance, seem to favour it.[45] The matter can be decided either way or in both: it all depends on how one wants to look at it. Looking only at the ensemble, it is a collection assembled by the accident of dynastic inheritance in which each constituent part maintained its separate identity, citizenship, and institutions. 'The monarch who keeps all these countries together is sovereign of each rather than the king of all.'[46] But when one looks at it in another way one sees that of the two distinct polities encased in one geographical boundary, the hegemonic one (Castile) acquires all the

---

[44] Elliott, *Imperial Spain*, 77–8.   [45] 'A Renaissance State' is the term he uses: *CMH*, i. 328.
[46] Solzano Pereira, quoted in ibid. 322.

distinctive features of a 'New Monarchy'. The other, the lesser and declining one, still clings to all the characteristics of the medieval *standestaat*.

England and France have been extensively discussed in previous chapters, but Spain has not figured at all so far, and so it seems to require a brief chronology.

CHRONOLOGY

456	Visigothic kingdom of Spain
711–18	Muslims from North Africa conquer all Spain except Asturias, Navarre. Territory is called al-Andalus (i.e. Vandal-land)
756	al-Andalus an independent Emirate
801	Louis, son of Charlemagne, takes Barcelona: County of Catalonia free of Muslims
914	Christians established south of Cantabrians, capital at Leon
928	Abd-al-Rahman proclaims al-Andalus a Caliphate
*c.*950	The southerly County of Castile, capital Burgos, breaks away from Kingdom of Leon
987	Catalonia independent of Frankish Empire
1031	Caliphate disintegrates into thirty-odd petty principalities or *taifas*
1035	Death of Sancho the Great of Navarre: Castile and Aragon as independent monarchies
1118	Alfonso I of Aragon takes Saragossa
1143	Leon and Castile recognize Portugal as sovereign kingdom
1146	Almohide Moors invade from Africa. In reaction:
1156–66	Foundation of the Military Orders of Calatrava, Santiago, and Alcantara
1162	Dynastic union of Aragon and Catalonia in the 'Crown of Aragon'
1179	Treaty delimits Castilian and Aragonese interests in the *reconquista*, Valencia for Aragon
1212	Decisive Christian victory at Las Nevas de Tolosa, leading to:
1236–48	Recapture of Cordoba, Seville, Valencia
1230	Merger of Leon and Castile
1267	Castile yields claims to Algarve, completing territorial unification of Portugal
1385	Portuguese victory over Castile at Aljubarotta secures her independence from Castile for 200 years
1469	Isabella of Castile marries Ferdinand of Aragon
1474	Isabella accedes to throne of Castile
1478	The Inquisition installed in Castile (Aragon in 1485)
1479	Ferdinand accedes to throne of Aragon
1487–94	Crown takes over the Grandmasterships of the three Military Orders

1492	Capture of Granada completes the *reconquista*. The expulsion of the Jews from both Castile and Aragon. Columbus discovers the New World
1494	Treaty of Tordesillas: the world divided by pope between Spain and Portugal. Pope Alexander VI grants to Ferdinand and Isabella the title of *Reyes Catolicos*
1502	Muslims of Castile given choice between conversion or expulsion
1512	Ferdinand annexes Spanish Navarre (ruled by a French dynasty since 1234) to Castile
1513	Balboa discovers the Pacific
1516	Accession of Charles, grandson of Ferdinand of Aragon, unites Crown of Castile and Aragon with rulership of the Netherlands and Habsburg lands in Austria
1519	Charles V elected Holy Roman Emperor
1519–22	Cortés conquers Mexico. Added to Castilian Crown
1520–1	Revolt of the *Comuneros*, and *Germania*
1527	Charles's troops sack Rome
1531–4	Pizarro conquers the Inca Empire of Peru
1545	Discovery of the silver mines at Potos
1555–8	Charles abdicates, leaving Netherlands and Italian dependencies to Crown of Spain and the German territories to his brother

3.3.1. THE TWO KINGDOMS

Castile was larger than Aragon, and had some $4\frac{1}{2}$ million inhabitants as against Aragon's 800,000.[47] Castilians were largely agriculturists or nomadic shepherds but wool was far more economically and politically important than cereals, so that Castile became a great exporter of wool (to Flanders) and an importer of cereals. The shepherds, who exerted great political and financial power through their guild, the *Mesta*, prevented the change-over to arable. Aragon, in contrast, had been a great trading kingdom, a veritable thalassocracy, whose monarchs ruled Majorca and Sardinia and Naples. This is why its towns were much more politically significant than in Castile. The hub of this commmercial activity had been Catalonia but her economy was struck down by the Black Death (1347–51) and continuous recurrences of the plague into the fifteenth century. Her 1497 population was only about half that of 1356.[48] Hence the financial capital had shifted to Valencia, which possessed a rich agriculture. So, whereas the Castilian economy was finding its wings, Catalonia's was in full decline.

The social composition of the two countries also differed. In the process of the *reconquista* it was natural that the conquistadores should acquire the lands they conquered from the Moors, and never more so than when

---

[47] Solzano Pereira, 316.   [48] Elliott, *Imperial Spain*, 37.

Andalusia was retaken. Hence arose a grand Castilian nobility, exempt from taxation, which owned vast latifundia—the *ricos hombres* or grandees. These noblemen were in a state of incessant discord among themselves and always in contention with the Crown which, by 1474, they had extensively under-mined. In the Crown of Aragon matters were more complicated. One-third of the Catalonian peasantry were *remecs*, that is, tied to the soil and subjected to what were called the 'six evil customs'. They were in chronic rebellion against their landlords here and elsewhere in the kingdom. At the same time the urban patriciates were under challenge by the lesser traders and artisans (in Barcelona known as the *biga*).[49] These and other social conflicts were compounded by the devaluation of the coinage in 1458 which set the landowners and *rentiers* against the merchants. One result was a Catalan revolution (1462–72) led mostly by the Barcelona merchants. The entire Crown of Aragon was still in chaotic self-division when Ferdinand acceded in 1479. These diverse economic and social conditions were reflected in the very different political institutions of the two kingdoms.

In fifteenth-century Castile, the product of a 700 years' warfare with the Moors, a land of shepherds and peasant farmers, and orientated towards war rather than trade, the most potent check on the power of the king was the turbulence of its mighty grandees. The kingdom did indeed possess its assembly, the Cortes, like most European countries at that time,[50] but compared with the Aragonese counterparts it was handicapped. For, as in England, the king was not obliged to summon it at specified intervals. And, again like England, it did not have legislative initiative; this lay with the Crown. Nevertheless the contrasts with England were more significant than these similarities. First, no individual, not even among the clergy or the grandees, had a right to attend. Secondly, the nobility and the Church were largely tax-exempt, and therefore hardly ever attended the Cortes. For practical purposes this last consisted of two deputies (*procuradores*) from each of eighteen privileged towns.

It was far otherwise in Aragon. Each of its three component states possessed representative assemblies whose powers against the Crown were so extensive as almost to overwhelm it. In this the states were very pre-cocious: Catalonia's Corts dates from 1218, Aragon's from 1274, and these two states endowed conquered Valencia with her own assembly in 1283. Certainly these last two dates are contemporaneous with Edward I's nascent parliaments in England, but the powers of these Cortes or Corts (in Catalan) went far beyond anything to be found there.

Each such assembly held its own meetings, though on occasion they

---

[49] Ibid. 38–41.   [50] See Bk. III, Ch. 8, 'Representative Assemblies'.

might all be summoned together and hold a joint session. Aragon's Cortes consisted of four chambers, not the more usual three: for the Church, for the towns, and one each for the two classes of nobility, the *ricos hombres* and the *caballeros*. In theory, at any rate, unanimity was required in each Estate. These assemblies all met at regular intervals.[51] The Cortes deliberated, voted subsidies to the king, and had acquired legislative initiative. In addition, Aragon possessed an official unknown to the other two states: the Justicia. He was a sort of attorney-general or procurator with the duty of ensuring that no body, high or low, infringed the laws or invaded the liberties of the subject.

The Catalonian assembly, the Corts, was organized into the more usual three estates. It too had the power to vote or withhold subsidies. But its general capacity was extended by a peculiar institution, the *Generalitat* (otherwise *Diputacit*). This acquired permanent form in the latter half of the fourteenth century when it became the standing committee of the Corts. It was made up of three *diputats* and three *oidors* (auditors), one for each of the three estates. They served for three years at a time, and their chief task was to control the fiscal system and then pay out to the Crown the sums agreed by the Corts. Its powers went wider than this, however: it became the watchdog of constitutionality, and the spokesman for the Catalan people *vis-à-vis* the Crown. Elliott comments that at times the *Generalitat* was 'in all but name, the Principality's government'.[52] These Catalonian practices were, by and large, followed in Valencia. All these thoroughly medieval arrangements were a compelling constraint on the Crown: the king had to ask not just one but each of the three assemblies for subsidies—and was quite likely to be rebuffed.

It was this medieval kingdom of Aragon that was now yoked to what was about to become the 'modern' kingdom of Castile: medieval monarchy versus New Monarchy. In less than a half-century the government of Castile underwent profound modernization, whereas Aragon's medieval structures were to persist almost unchanged until they were forcibly abolished by the Bourbon Philip V in 1714.

3.3.2. THE UNION OF THE TWO CROWNS

Isabella of Castile and Ferdinand of Aragon were married in 1469. Isabella did not accede as queen of Castile till 1474, and Ferdinand had to wait until 1479 to accede to the throne of Aragon. Nevertheless, by the terms of the

---

[51] Something not attained in England until the Triennial Acts, 1641, 1694.
[52] Elliott, *Imperial Spain*, 29, 30.

marriage contract Isabella and Fedinand became respectively queen and king of Castile from the moment she acceded.

The contract provided that Ferdinand must live with Isabella in Castile and might not leave it or take his children out of it without her consent. All letters and deeds must be signed jointly in both the realms. The Castilian cities and strongholds were to pledge allegiance to Isabella alone. The king could not wage war or make peace without the advice and consent of the queen. This said, both kingdoms retained their own political institutions, laws, courts, fiscal systems, and currency. They did not share common citizenship. There were customs barriers between the two states and the Indies were declared part of the possessions of Castile, and all 'their trade and traffic' were confined to Castilians, the Aragonese being totally excluded. Thus 'Spain' was a loose confederacy held together purely by the personal union of the monarchs of its two great constituents.

3.3.3. THE REMAKING OF CASTILE

The two Crowns made no significant changes in the institutions of Aragon, despite Isabella's occasional petulance at having to chaffer with the various Cortes for money and even then to receive very little.[53] Indeed in 1480–1 Ferdinand accepted the Catalan Cort's traditional role and procedures, and rounded this off with the *Observanca*, which specifically recognized the limitations on the royal power and laid down the procedure the *Generalitat* should follow in the event of infringements. Thus, the Crown of Aragon went its own, time-worn, medieval way. But the two monarchs transformed Castile into a New Monarchy.

They did it by similar methods to those their fellow monarchs were using in England and France: that is, to amass wealth and patronage, to bridle the grandees, to curb and then control the towns, and to appropriate the emoluments and the presentments of the Church. But they also introduced a new weapon, which took a unique form—the Inquisition; and significantly, this was the one institution which applied over the whole of Spain.

Enriching the Crown

The Crown enriched itself by resuming grants made to nobles without sufficient cause (Cortes of 1480). This brought in 80,000 gold ducats (but compare this with the nobility's estimated total income of 1,400,000 ducats).

---

[53] Cf. Isabella's reputed comment: 'Aragon is ours and we must go and conquer it', quoted in *CMH*, i. 325, and her declaration in 1498 that 'it would be better to reduce the Aragonese by arms than tolerate the arrogance of the Cortes', quoted in Elliott, *Imperial Spain*, 80.

Additional sums were handed back after Isabella's death, in accordance with a clause in her will.

Another new source of income came from the royal take-over of the three Military Orders, patterned on the Knights Templars. The Order of Cala-trava had originated in 1158 as an improvised force of monks and laymen to defend that city from approaching Moors. It then established itself on a permanent footing, the monks withdrawing and the brethren taking vows. The Order was recognized by the Papacy, and shortly afterwards the two other Orders, of Santiago and Alcantara, were founded. As the *reconquista* succeeded, so the military importance of these Orders declined although they were no mean troops and played an important part in the siege and capture of Ronda in 1485. But by this time the Orders had become appurtenances of the very high nobility. A 'Grand Master' enjoyed a vast patronage to numerous appointments, commanded what were effectively private armies, and controlled the Orders' financial resources which were massive; the annual rental of the lands of the three Orders was nearly double the amount brought in by the resumption of alienated Crown lands (see above). In addition, the Grand Masters disposed of some 1500 dignities, and exercised jurisdiction over more than 1 million vassals.[54]

On the death of the Grand Master of Santiago (1476) Isabella compelled the Order to offer the vacancy to Ferdinand and, though he temporarily declined it, he accepted it somewhat later, along with the Grand Mastership of Calatrava and Alcantara in 1487 and 1489. In 1523 the pope institution-alized such royal control by incorporating all three Orders in the Crown.

Bridling the High Aristocracy

When the two Crowns acceded, Castile was alive with banditry and violence. In the normal way a monarch would have relied on the local nobles. Instead, the court ordered the destruction of all nobiliar castles not deemed essential to the country's security and bypassed their owners by reshaping the medieval institution of the *hermandad*. In the Middle Ages the towns had organized popular militias or brotherhoods—the meaning of *hermandad*—to protect their privileges and maintain the peace. In 1476, with the approval of the Cortes (that is, the eighteen privileged towns as described above), the Crown reorganized these local *hermandades* by placing them under the control of a central junta which answered to the Crown alone. This new *hermandad* combined police and judicial functions rather like the local administrators in the Asian empires. Its job was to repress banditry

---

[54] Elliott, *Imperial Spain*, 88–9. D. Seward, *The Marks of War: The Military Religious Orders* (Paladin, St Albans, 1974), 139–86.

and to patrol the roads, and its tribunals had exclusive jurisdiction over the violent crimes : robbery, arson, housebreaking, rape, murder, and inevitably, rebellion. Its manpower was made up of contingents from each town, and in addition there was a standing force of some 2,000 men commanded by Ferdinand's brother. Its rough-and-ready way of dealing with malefactors and rebels, not to speak of the barbarity of its penalties, was so effective that in 1498—only twenty-two years after its inception—its central junta was abolished, and the *hermandades* reverted to their original status as municipal forces.

The joint monarchs, from an early date, excluded the grandees as the 'natural advisers'—and administrators—to the Crown. The reform took place in 1480. The *Consejo Real* was intended to advise the monarchs on appointments, act as supreme court of justice, and supervise the local authorities and it was not composed of noblemen but mainly of *letrados*, which is as much to say, trained jurists. Interestingly in this connection medieval-type Aragon had been far in advance of Castile: its administration had been in the hands of a trained bureaucratic chancery since the fourteenth century.[55] Parenthetically it might be observed that the 'law of proximity' operated here. The royal secretaries naturally saw much more of the monarch and were on more intimate terms with him than his councillors. In any case it was they who prepared the council agenda. Consequently, the sixteenth century is marked by the ascendancy of the secretaries who were not uncommonly major political figures in their own right.

Curbing the Towns

Castile was a country of little walled towns, for these had been established in great numbers in the course of the *reconquista*, and many had been granted wide *fueros* (privileges, charters) and extensive areas of common land. Ordinarily their institutions somewhat resembled those of the early Italian city-states: a general assembly made up of the heads of families which chose the municipal officials. The judicial officers so appointed were the *alcaldes*, the administrative ones the *regidores*. Numbering anything between eight to thirty-six, these formed the effective government of the town. Beneath them were a great variety of minor executive officials such as the *alguazils* (principal police officers) and so forth. Increasingly these little towns were influenced or even controlled by the local magnate. And like many little 'city-republics' they were racked with internal feuds.

The Crown's first step towards controlling these towns was to furnish them with a *corregidor*. He was a small-scale governor, for he combined

---

[55] Elliott, *Imperial Spain*, 90.

judicial and administrative responsibilities. In theory he remained in office for only two years—in practice it was longer—and he could not be a native of the town he was governing. The duties of these *corregidores* were codified in 1500, and by Philip II's reign they numbered sixty-six. However, they did not supplant the council of *regidores* which continued to be very influential, even though it was the *corregidor* that presided over its meetings. On the other hand the formerly freely elected *alcaldes* were now frequently appointed by the Crown, and even where still independently elected, had lost much of their civil and criminal jurisdiction to the *corregidores*. Similarly, in the very extensive feudal jurisdictions that still persisted and where the seigneur's court dealt out justice, the Crown, demanding very high standards of justice, intervened where these were not being met, so that by 1600 the *corregidores'* influence was ubiquitous.

Fleecing the Church

Ferdinand and Isabella were dubbed *Reyes Catolicos* by the Papacy. Both were indeed fervently Catholic and Isabella may even be thought of as a religious fanatic. But this did not prevent the two of them from getting their hands on the Church's material resources. Their interest lay in curtailing its immunities and tapping its wealth. The joint income of Castile's bishoprics and four archbishoprics was some 400,000 ducats, and its total income is estimated at the enormous sum of 6 million ducats per annum, compared with the estimated 1.4 million ducats of the nobility![56] Among its privileges was exemption from taxation, the exercise of temporal jurisdiction over its demesne lands, and its own armies and fortresses.

The Church was therefore too powerful to attack frontally, although it was made to surrender its castles to royal castellans. But though the Church was powerful inside Castile, the Papacy which controlled it was highly vulnerable outside it, in Italy. Sixtus IV (1471–84) was the first of the 'political popes' who subordinated everything to the preservation and expansion of the Papal States and behaved like any other ruler of a petty Italian state. Whenever they got into trouble—which was often—they turned to Castile for armed support. This support was bought at a price.

The Castilian Crown did not, in fact, get the *patronato*, the right to nominate to the bishoprics, until 1523 and long after that there was still litigation between it and the Papacy. But it did obtain the right to nominate in conquered Granada in 1486, and most momentously, full control over Church appointments and a monopoly of evangelization in the New World, in 1493. Imagine the patronage involved in that! The year 1493 was also that

---

[56] Elliott, *Imperial Spain*, 99.

in which the Spanish Borgia pope, Alexander VI, published the two Bulls which divided the globe between Portugal and Spain.[57] The Crown was able to exert even more control over the Church after 1494 when Alexander VI gave it full powers to reform the Spanish religious communities.

These concessions not only brought the Crown a degree of control over the Church hierarchy, but money as well. This cash element was further increased by two other measures. When the war with Granada began in 1482 Sixtus IV deemed it a crusade and permitted the sale of indulgences to finance it. Only a quarter of the receipts went to the Church, the rest to the Crown, and great pressures were brought on everybody to buy an indulgence. In 1520 the Papacy made their purchase a permanent commitment. It is reckoned to have brought in some 450,000 ducats per annum to the Crown. Furthermore, in 1494 the compliant Alexander VI made permanent the arrangement by which the Crown took one-third of the Church's tithes. But the greatest exercise of royal control, of prime political significance, was the establishment of the Spanish Inquisition.

The Inquisition

The Inquisition as such was of long standing. Inquisitors were used against the Albigensian heretics in the early thirteenth century. They were put on a systematic, regularized footing in 1231 and in 1233 were formally drawn from the enthusiastic Dominican Order: hence the pun, *domini canes*, 'the hounds of the Lord'. And so they proved. Their task as inquisitors was to search out heresy, try the accused, give him the opportunity to recant, and if not hand him over to the secular power for punishment—which, at its most extreme, was to be burned alive. Their procedure was inquisitorial. The accused was interrogated with the testimony of witnessess, and in 1252 Paul IV authorized the use of torture to extract confessions. (This use of torture was in no way confined to the Inquisition. It was widespread in such secular tribunals as used inquisitorial procedures and for an identical reason: that they could only find an accused guilty on the strength of a confession.)

Inquisitions were set up in many countries—in England, France, and Italy, for instance, as well as in Spain. But until the Catholic Kings, Spanish monarchs had been tolerant. Castile was a multicultural, multi-religious, and polyethnic society, with its large and wealthy Jewish communities and its Moors, as well as its Christians. But if the rulers were tolerant, the populace

---

[57] It is argued that 'it is folly to speak of a donation of lands which did not belong to the pope . . .' The expression 'donation' simply referred to what had already been won under just title; the decree contained a deed of gift but it was an adjustment between the powers concerned and other European princes, not a parcelling out of the New World and its inhabitants. Louis Duchesne, 'Papacy' (to 1087), in the *Encyclopaedia Britannica*, 11th edn., xx. 687–91.

was not, and fanatical Christian preachers easily whipped up hatred against the Jews and provoked horrible pogroms, particularly in 1391. To save their lives many Jews converted to Christianity—and numbers of these *conversos* began to flourish greatly, moving in the best court circles and wielding great economic leverage.

Isabella—pious or fanatical, according to one's fancy—desired a political community that obeyed 'one king, one faith, one law'.[58] She—among others—wondered how many *conversos* were genuine Christians and how many crypto-Jews. Hence the distinction between 'old Christian' and *converso*. To stamp out crypto-Judaism required investigation and, if proved, some terrible penalty; for to apostasize after conversion (or even *forcible* baptism) carried the death penalty.

Isabella requested papal permission to establish an Inquisition in Spain which differed in one vital particular from the tribunals elsewhere. Whereas those were subject to the bishops' authority, she wanted this Spanish Inquisition to be subject to the Crown alone. Caught in the toils of his Italian policy, Sixtus granted the request and the Inquisition was established in 1478. As reports of its ruthlessness reached Rome Sixtus revoked Crown control and restored the former ecclesiastical control. Furious, Ferdinand replied that the Inquisition must be established *secundum beneplacitum et voluntatem meam in his Regnis et terris meis.*[59] By 1483 Italian policy had once more forced the pope into dependency and he capitulated. In this wise was the Inquisition introduced into Castile. Aragon, however, refused to have it, and indeed in 1485 the Grand Inquisitor was murdered in Saragossa Cathedral. But the opposition of the Papacy and the persistency of Ferdinand finally made the three Cortes surrender so that the Inquisition, uniquely, became an institution common to all Spain.[60]

This 'New Inquisition' was a duly constituted court, with a supreme *Consejo* presided over by the Grand Inquisitor, and inferior tribunals in the larger towns. Its procedure encouraged delation and torture and was used for political as well as religious purposes, for it could and did strike at any person or class of persons in the country, and it could intimidate even by mere threat. Furthermore, its remit ran further than heresy, for it encompassed cases involving apostasy, witchcraft, bigamy, usury, and blasphemy—a terrifying list when backed by the threat of torture. It could be and was used to destroy personal enemies; for instance, Torquemada, the first Grand Inquisitor, took action against the bishop of Calahorra in 1498, while the

---

[58] W. H. Atkinson, *A History of Spain and Portugal* (Penguin, Harmondsworth, 1960), 110.

[59] Quoted in *CMH*, i. 336. 'According to my will and good pleasure in these my lands and realm.'

[60] It was also introduced into all Castilian or Aragonese possessions, e.g. Sicily, Sardinia, and the Indies.

greatest of the grandees were kept under constant supervision. Often the convicted got off with a fine or confiscation of his goods; but for all that, under Torquemada alone 2,000 persons were burned alive at the stake.

To revert to the *conversos*, the purported *raison d'être* of the Inquisition: if crypto-Jews were evil, why not any—or indeed all—Jews? When Granada fell in 1492 the *Reyes Catolicos*, ecstatic at the final triumph of Christianity on Spanish soil, decided on a wholesale solution: all professed Jews were given four months to leave the country. The Moors of Granada suffered a similar fate. The Catholic Kings had spared themselves casualties by promising that, if the garrison surrendered, the Moors would be free to practise their religion. The promise was almost immediately dishonoured by enforced conversions. In 1499 the Moors embarked on a hopeless rebellion and were offered the choice of conversion or expulsion.

One verdict on this religious policy is that it served the highly political purpose of unifying diversity through a common faith. 'At least in the eyes of Ferdinand and Isabella', writes Elliot (suggesting that he himself would not necessarily take this view?), the conquest of Granada and the expulsion of the Jews helped to 'impose a unity which transcended administrative, linguistic and cultural barriers, bringing together Spaniards of all races in common furtherance of a holy mission'. In the same place he says it 'laid the foundations for a unitary state'.[61] But the Iberian lands of the Spanish Crown did not form a unitary state at all. For the Crown of Aragon persisted with its ancient institutions and was recalcitrant in granting the subsidies which Charles V and his successors demanded to fight wars on all fronts—against the French, Dutch, English, and Turks. Huge sums flowed into Castile from the New World, but not nearly enough, and this kingdom had to bear more and more of the costs. Olivares, the chief minister from 1623 to 1643, wrote to his king, Philip IV: 'You should not be content to be King of Portugal, of Aragon and Valencia and the Count of Barcelona, but you should direct all your work and thought to reduce these realms to the same order and legal system as Castile.'[62] This was not to be. In 1640 Portugal broke away,[63] and the Catalans rose in revolt and put themselves under French allegiance until reconquered in 1652. It was not till 1713 that a Bourbon prince, victor in the War of the Spanish Succession, acceded to the throne and as a conqueror, abolished the *fueros* of the Crown of Aragon and

[61] Elliott, *Imperial Spain*, 110.

[62] Quoted in J. Read, *The Catalans* (Faber and Faber, London, 1978), 130.

[63] It had entered the personal union in 1580, when Portugal had lost its king in the battle against the Moors at Al-Kasr al-Kabir (1578); Philip II of Spain sent in an army that defeated the opponents of his candidacy at the Battle of Alcantara, 1580.

introduced a French-type centralized uniformity into the administration of the entire country.

4. THE MODERN STATE

In such ways did the Europeans, after a millennium of breakdown, then near-anarchy, and then feudalism, *re-invent* the state. But what they re-invented was in many respects unlike any antecedent—or contemporary—state-form anywhere else in the world, and it is impossible to overestimate its importance, for this particular state-form is today the world-wide unit of affairs. It was original in three major respects.

4.1. *Legalism*

In this kind of state: (1) law had a particular, indeed a paramount, sanctity. Bit by bit, customary law was assimilated to or absorbed into a single legal *corpus*, and this embraced private civil suits as well as state criminal and administrative ones. The power relationships between individuals and the public authorities were all founded upon and bounded by predetermined legal provisions and norms by means of some established judicial process. (2) The individual was not a mere subject but a citizen in the following sense. Athenian citizenship involved active and direct participation in public policy-making and administration, while Roman citizenship conferred the active right to choose one's magistrates. These forms of citizenship are what the French Revolutionaries came to call *active* citizenship. However, in these newly emergent European states, *c.*1500, only a few enjoyed such active citizenship; but all free men did enjoy certain traditional inherent rights to, notably, life, liberty, and above all, property. In this sense they were not just subjects (i.e. mere objects to be administered) but *passive* citizens. (3). Culpability was personal: that is, the penalty for a crime was visited on nobody but the criminal himself, not his family or his village or (except for a brief period in Norman England) a 'tithing' group.[64] (4) Particular respect was shown for the principle of private property. It was this that under the feudal slogan of *n'impose qui ne veut* resisted rulers' appetite for fiscal absolutism for such a long time. (5) Lawboundedness, respect for private property, and passive citizenship together imply that rulership was in some senses limited. This limitedness of government was strongly reinforced by two other legalistic characteristics, the first being that (6) a distinction came

---

[64] See e.g. J. E. A. Jolliffe, *The Constitutional History of Medieval England* (A. & C. Black, London, 1937), 59–61.

to be drawn between public law and private law, between private ownership and state power, and the distinction re-surfaced between the private person of the monarch and the *res publica*, which came to be conceived as an abstract and faceless nomocracy. This distinction had been elaborated in the Roman and Byzantine empires where the *fiscus* and the emperor were two different things and the former could be sued even if the latter could not.[65] This Roman distinction came back into continental Europe with the revival of Roman law. England, repugnant to the civil law, evolved a common law distinction between the king as a natural person and the Crown as an abstraction. For, underlying both the civil- and the common-law formulations was the common concept of legal personality as opposed to natural personality; a distinction absolutely unknown anywhere else. (7) A corollary was that the individual—or a corporation—could sue the agents of the abstract 'Crown' or 'State' as they would sue a natural person and this meant—owing to feudal practice—suing them in a *lis inter partes*. The right to sue the servants of the sovereign power for alleged wrongdoing was, again, unparalleled elsewhere, and served to confirm the notion that the free individual's status was that of a citizen (albeit a passive one) and not a subject.[66] (8). Except for about half-a-dozen city-republics and the Swiss cantons, all these states *c*.1500 were monarchies (this term includes principalities) and their rulers strenuously and ceaselessly aspired to become *absolute*. By 1660 most of them were.[67] Despite monarchs' unceasing efforts

---

[65] The matter is mentioned in Weber, *Economy and Society*, ii. 710–13, and the critical and bibliographical notes to these pages, at 747–9.

[66] See the previous note for references. In the English case it was more difficult than Roth and Wittich seem to think, though it could be and was done. Monarchs put all kinds of impediments in the way. In 18th-cent. France, for instance, such suits against the state were normally pursued through one of the thirteen 'Sovereign Parlements', irremovable by the monarchs since the judges (of whom Montesquieu was one) had purchased their posts. The monarchy responded by setting up all manner of special tribunals to draw suits away from these *parlements* and resorted, also, to a great deal of sharp practice and collusion to protect their interests. A vivid picture is drawn by Alexis de Tocqueville, *L'ancien régime* (OUP, Oxford, 1957), 60–5 on 'Administrative Justice'. All the same it is clear that these devices were meant to thwart what was the established practice. But as in all the states mentioned, the subject could only sue the Crown in its own courts by grace, not of right, e.g. in England by the royal approval of a Petition of Right. Cf. Sir W. Holdsworth, *A History of English Law* (London, 1922), vol. X (1938), ch. 6, pp. 3–44.

[67] Some historians, e.g. Mousnier, Hinton, and Marxist historians like Christopher Hill, all reach, albeit by very different routes, the conclusion that in the 16th and earlier 17th centuries the English Crown was just as much an absolutism as that of, say, France or Castile. Our own view is that, if only by reason of the powers of the English Parliament and its alliance with the common lawyers, the English constitution was less than an absolutism and, pursuing its idiosyncratic path, established a parliamentary tradition sharply different from the absolutisms of kings of France, Spain, Prussia, Denmark, and many others. I have stated these views at pp. 1274–6 above. The claims of Mousnier *et al.* have been carefully examined only to be refuted, by J. P. Cooper, in J. S. Bromley and E. H. Kossman (eds.), *Britain and the Netherlands* (London, 1960), 62–90: 'Differences between

to abolish these restrictions, they were upheld by the power of the numerous corporate bodies into which society had formed itself (due to the weakness or the absence of strong central government in the anterior period, a condition not met with in Asia), for instance, the guilds, corporations, Estates, and the like, not to speak of the Catholic Church—a ubiquitous hierarchical and authoritarian structure with vast possessions, highly sophisticated legal and governmental techniques, and the most profound hold over the hopes and fears of the common people.

It is necessary to state firmly that these principles were nowhere implemented fully or fairly, and that many were more honoured in the breach than the observance. They do not amount to *Rechtstaat* or constitutional monarchy—*yet*. They were not the sufficient conditions for such state-forms; but they were, perhaps, the necessary ones. For although some of these characteristics could be found in other polities at this time, nowhere else in the entire world were all of them found together.

Neither China nor Japan, for instance, thought of law as a seamless system of legal principles, where every judicial decision flowed from applying the abstract principle to the particular case; or as a set of rigidly fixed laws, whether customary or statutory, that predictably and ineluctably governed the situations they provided for. Justice was envisaged as the effort to mediate or harmonize the interests of the parties (unless one of these parties was the state, in which case implicit and total obedience was expected and exacted.)[68] Neither country had a civil or commercial code

English and Continental Governments in the Early Seventeenth Century'. If taken literally as *ab legibus solutus* this should have allowed them to abrogate or ignore those individual rights talked of above. That such rights survived in England is obvious from the victory of Parliament in the Great Rebellion and the 1688 Revolution. How they came to survive in Europe (with increased difficulty as the 18th cent. wore on) is more problematical and the answer lies in the specific connotation which 'absolutism' acquired in this Western European context and nowhere else. As expressed by Bodin and Loyseau, it did not mean the monarch's unfettered right to do as he pleased whenever he pleased. He was absolute in only a Pickwickian sense: though he had no legal superior he was still circumscribed by the divine law as interpreted by the Church, by 'natural law', which specifically confers the absolute right to private property as well as to life and liberty, and finally by the customary fundamental laws of the state itself. See, *inter alia*, R. C. Mousnier, *The Institutions of France under the Absolute Monarchy, 1598–1789: Society and the State*, trans. B. Pearce (University of Chicago Press, London, 1979), 659–65. This contains the relevant passages from Bodin and Loyseau. For a perceptive comment on the meaning of absolutism and sovereignty at this time cf. B. de Jouvenal, *Sovereignty: An Inquiry into the Political Good*, trans. J. F. Huntington (CUP, Cambridge, 1957), ch. 2.

[68] For the Ch'ing period, see Bodde and Morris, *Law in Imperial China*, esp. the Introduction. For earlier periods, Johnson, *T'ang Code*; A. F. P. Hulsewé, *Remnants of Han Law*, vol. I (Brill, Leiden, 1955). For Japan, D. F. Henderson, 'The Evolution of Tokugawa Law', in J. W. Hall and M. B. Jansen (eds.), *Studies in the Institutional History of Early Modern Japan*, vol. I (Princeton UP, Princeton, 1968), 203–29; I. Henderson, *Conciliation and Japanese Law* (Association for Asian Studies, University of Washington Press, Seattle, 1965).

(as Islam certainly did). Such matters were the subject of local custom and were settled by local notables or divines. In fact the rulers did everything they could to drive private litigants away from the courts. In Ch'ing China it was an offence even to help a private person draw up a petition, let alone help him plead his case.[69] The passive right to real property did indeed exist almost everywhere, and perhaps it was all the more secure for being founded on custom and local conciliation, but movables were more precarious; in the Caliphate, China, and Japan, for example, merchant capital could be decidedly at risk of expropriation. In addition to the threat to property, the harsh criminal codes of all these countries and the extensive procedural discretion allowed to magistrates threatened the life and liberty of everybody. In these criminal cases collectivities and not just individuals might be held to share the guilt; in such cases the idea of a *mens rea* seems to be totally absent. For instance, in China and Japan families, legally bonded together in groups of ten, had to go bail for one another's conduct, share the penalties for law-breaking or absconding, and make up any member's failure to pay his share of tax.[70] Even more, punishments were quite frequently extended to the immediate family of the criminal, and in some cases even to its collateral branches also.

Neither China nor Japan entertained any but the haziest and most moralizing notion[71] of limitations upon the ruler's absolutism. In sharp contrast, the Muslim countries did indeed affirm a clearly articulated principle of limitation, but this took quite a different form from the European one. The caliph or sultan would never interfere with the *qadi* jurisdiction which looked after family, religious, and civil matters. Here he fell in with the elaborate procedural and substantive provisions of the sophisticated *sharia*. But within the nominal limits of the *sharia* he was entitled to invoke the doctrine of *siyasa* (necessity), and this gave him unlimited power in his own *mazalim* courts in all the matters which we deem 'political': taxation, police, conscription, and the like, and by exten-

[69] The K'ang-Hsi Emperor issued an edict in 1692 ordering the magistrates to make their courts so dreaded that the people would not take their quarrels there (van der Sprinkel, *Legal Institutions*, 76–7). For the criminalization of helping litigants, Bodde and Morris, *Law in Imperial China*, 413–17).

[70] In China these institutions were (police) the *li-chia* (taxes) the *pao-chia*. In Japan the (police) unit was the *goningumi*. For the extension of punishments to entire families, etc. see the literature cited above, *passim*.

[71] It is only fair to say that the influence of Confucianist morality, as projected by the emperor's senior ministers and the bureaucracy, was sometimes so suffocating as to reduce the Chinese emperor to political passivity. That an emperor ought be passive and confine himself merely to picking good ministers was one highly influential (because self-serving) strand in the Confucianist canon. The Ch'ing emperors were themselves Confucianists but they were active and brooked no such interference as just described.

sion over life, limb, and property involved therein.[72] Hence the Sunni doctrine of passive obedience—that 'any Muslim ruler, whoever he was and however he came to power—who was able to protect the territories of Islam and impose civil peace was entitled to obedience. Obedience to such a ruler, whether bad or mad, was a religious duty.'[73] So, whereas the western state ruler's authority was circumscribed, that of the Muslim ruler was *bisected*, and in his own sector—the public-policy sector—he was as unconstrainedly despotic as he dared to be.

His power—and this was true of all Asian states—was reinforced in so far as none of them developed the concept of legal personality. No distinction could be made between the person of the ruler and the state. Rulership was essentially personal as against the notion of rulership via an abstract nomocracy. The absence of this concept of the state as a legal person made it the more difficult (though it did not make it impossible) to entertain the idea of the individual suing the ruler or his agents for misconduct. But what really aborted the institution of private suits against the government and its agents was the whole complex of the matters described above: the absence of any notion of civil rights (there was no equivalent word in either the Caliphate[74] or the Chinese or the Japanese polities); the concept of the individual as simply an *administré*, a subject; the consequent conception of the law as simply that which the superior imposed over inferior; the absence of the contractual texture which was the prevalent mode of juristic thought in Europe and which permitted the *lis inter partes* practice of private law to be carried over when the individual took the governmment agents to court.[75] It hardly needs saying therefore that the meaning of 'absolutism' in Asia did not incorporate those restrictions on the rulers' right to invade the liberty and the property of his subjects which Bodin and Loyseau had noted as what distinguished it from the despotic absolutism conferred on the ruler by right of conquest, and tyranny, by which term was meant an equally despotic absolutism which, in defiance of

---

[72] Cf. e.g. Schacht, *Introduction*, 54, 86 ff, 1, 187.

[73] E. Kedourie, 'Crisis and Revolution in Modern Islam', *Times Literary Supplement* (19–25 May 1989), 549. Al-Mawardi (d. 1058), Baghdad (*The Ordinances of Government*) was one of the most influential exponents.

[74] For Islam, W. M. Watt, *Islamic Political Thought* (Edinburgh UP, Edinburgh, 1968), 96–7.

[75] This view, stressing the virtual absence of courts of law in Tokugawa Japan and the despotic powers of its authorities, has been expressed strongly by J. R. Strayer, in Hall and Jansen, *Studies in the Institutional History*, 7–8. Note his contrast between the European Middle Ages with its 'authority based on law' and Japanese authoritarianism; and his statement that 'nothing in the religion, the mores, the political theories, or the habits of thought of the [Japanese] people justifies resistance', whereas in Europe 'the symbol of authority was the right to hold a court'.

tradition, convention, and natural and divine law, the ruler conferred on himself.[76]

This central notion that the relationship of the government to the individual must be based on law, that the individual possessed certain inherent rights, and that consequently he could be deprived of these only by due process, marked the essential difference between these newly arisen European states and those of Asia. It would be quite wrong to think of the latter as lawless—far from it, they were very highly regulated indeed. It was simply that their enacted law was criminal and administrative. It would be wrong to stigmatize all of them as despotic in the sense that the ruler could at will take away the life, liberty, and property of his subjects, but some were such. It would be wrong to say that in none of these polities were rulers constrained by certain conventions; the Chinese emperor certainly had to work within the Confucian consensus. It would be wrong to say that these polities were less well administered than those of Europe, for some were run much better. Tokugawa Japan, for instance, compares favourably with most European states of the eighteenth century. But Asian absolutism knew almost none of the legal restraints that existed in Europe, and few if any of the practical ones. There were no natural aristocracies, no counterbalancing Church, no autonomous guilds, corporations, cities, and the like; in short, no *corps intermédiaires* which formed the bulwark against absolutist pretensions in Europe. And furthermore, the local traditions went with this absolutist grain. The nascent absolutists of Europe had to struggle long and hard before they established fiscal absolutism; of the Asian populations it can fairly be said, in the light of their 2,000 year-old histories, that they were 'born taxpayers'.

4.2. *Mutability*

It is fashionable to mock Tennyson's 'Better fifty years of Europe than a cycle of Cathay'. Sinologists rightly declare that in fact China underwent continuous and considerable changes. But there is absolutely no comparison at all between the enriched but otherwise unchanged format of its imperial regime through some 2,000 years and the breakneck transition of state forms in Europe through barbaric German kingdoms, feudalism, New Monarchy, absolutism, and parliamentarism, democracy, and representative government.

Societies attain stability when the social structure, the political structure, and the prevalent belief system all mutually reinforce one another, and

---

[76] Bodin called the former 'Seignorial monarchy' and the latter 'Tyrannical monarchy'.

become mutable when one or more of these gets out of kilter with the others. The stable, or rather the stationary condition had been attained in Islam by the fourteenth century, in China by the fifteenth, by which time intellectual and technological creativity had ceased in both. Henceforth, their belief systems, unequal and authoritarian social structures, and absolute monarchies so buttressed one another as to produce almost total socio-political immobility, even stagnation.

The reason is that, unlike Europe, their culture was seamless and continuous. Islam and Confucianism were both 'closed' systems; their tradition was whole, uninterrupted, and self-reinforcing. These two great belief systems were precisely the ones that underpinned the mutually reinforcing social and political institutions of the states within their persuasion. But just while the great Asian polities were falling asleep, Europe was jolted by an aggressive revolutionary counter-culture to the one in being, Latin Christianity. The latter's intimate symbiosis with social structure and the political institutions of medieval Europe does not need further recitation here.[77] That Christian belief system was now challenged on two fronts at once. The first, religious nonconformity as expressed in various forms of Protestanism, pointed towards markedly different political structures than those upheld by Catholicism; notably congregationalism which, by powerful analogy, sign-posted some kind of popular control over governments.[78] The other was the exhumation of Graeco-Roman culture, and so, the Renaissance. George Eliot's *Romola* (a failed noved, admittedly) is little read nowadays but it marvellously conveys how secular, this-wordly, man-centred, fleshly, in fact how *pagan* the Renaissance was.[79] The Renaissance ran counter to everything that Latin Christianity preached and stood for; that is the significance (as the novel proceeds to show) of Savonarola and the religious reaction. The point here is that the Renaissance did NOT signify a 'Europe re-discovering its origins'. It represented an entirely new way of thinking and living in complete contradiction to tradition.

These two counter-cultural movements destroyed the unity of the belief system that had underpinned the medieval political and social structures. Equally important, this breach also opened the way for entirely new modes of thinking about the state while it liberated natural science from the shackles of religion and received opinion. With new state forms and new

[77] I do not know any short book that expresses this with greater elegance, clarity, and authority than Southern, *Western Society*.

[78] To take just one, but conspicuous, example, the French Huguenots: J. E. Neale, *The Age of Catherine de Medici and Essays in Elizabethan History* (Cape, London, 1943; paperback edn., 1963), 11–29.

[79] So too, Browning's poem 'The Bishop Orders his Tomb at St. Praxed's Church'; see above, n. 9.

technology, the path was clear for that extraordinary restlessness of Western thought, institutions, and social structure from those days to our own.

4.3. A Multi-state System

In Asia the traditional form of the state was empire. Though country-states emerged when these broke down, they were sooner or later re-absorbed into an empire. The nearest to 'balance-of-power systems' are found in China and in Greece. In China one such 'system' ran through the 'Spring and Autumn' and the subsequent 'Warring States' periods (722–221 BC), and a second during the fourth-century 'period of disunion' at the fall of the Han Empire. In both cases these numerous succession states were ultimately swallowed up by one of their number and empire was restored. In the Greek cases the mutual balance between, first, the city-states and then the Leagues, was ended by the Macedonian and then the Roman conquests.

Not so in Europe, where the immediate successors to the Roman Empire were transient, barbarous proto-states which were ultimately cobbled into feudal systems. Now European-type feudalism is trans-territorial,[80] it knows no 'national' frontiers, since political allegiance was man to lord no matter what country the lord resided in. Equally, the Catholic Church was in its own words catholic and universal and neither knew nor wanted to know anything of 'national' borders (even if that concept had been extant at that time). So Europe did not think of itself (as the Greeks and Romans had thought of it) as 'Europe' (an area) but as 'Christendom', a united, seamless *oikumene* whose being culminated in the authority of the pope and the emperor.

But the re-created state in Europe, like all previous states, rested on the definition of its territory. And the rulers of each such state wanted to be (again in their own words) 'emperors in their own domains'. The state that emerged was therefore a 'sovereign' state, one whose ruler insisted on total control over all the population in his territory and was prepared, in return for reciprocal recognition, to recognize a similar right in other rulers. So arose a number of competing independent sovereign states.

But the ensuing multi-state system stayed in being (as will be shown below) and developed into one of competing country states in a way that did not and indeed could not occur in Asia. In the Arab world even to this day the notion of territoriality is fatally compromised by the sense of being part of the Muslim (or at least the Sunni) *umma*. Ch'ing China was the

---

[80] In Japan no man could serve two lords, nor could the lord of one man be the vassal of the lord of another man. Both were permitted and prevalent in Europe, hence the trans-territoriality.

master of a vast territory with nothing but petty proto-states beyond it. The multi-state system of Japan was destroyed in 1600 by the hegemony of Tokugawa Ieyasu, not to be shaken for another 250 years. In the Indian subcontinent neither Hinduism nor Islam made for a language-cum-religion basis for particularistic territorial allegiance such as was on offer to the European states, and in any case, the two belief systems competed for supremacy.

The European state, then, was a sovereign, territorially delimited political unit, facing other similar units, each striving for supremacy but never achieving it owing to their rapidly adopted skill of forming combinations that would defeat such a purpose, that is, the techniques of the 'balance of power' first developed by the Italian city-states in the fourteenth and fifteenth centuries, and very similar to the shifting 'horizontal' and 'vertical' alliances that characterized the Warring States period in China.[81]

[81] The classic Chinese work is the *Chan-kuo-tse* (= 'Ways of the Warring States'), trans. J. I. Crump (2nd edn. revised, Chinese Materials Centre, San Francisco, 1979). See R. L. Walker, *The Multi-State System of Ancient China* (Shoe String Press, Hamden, Conn., 1953). Ching Ping and Dennis Bloodworth, *The Chinese Machiavelli* (Secker & Warburg, 1976) is also of interest.

6

The Two Traditions:
Absolute versus Parliamentary Monarchy

1. THE TWO TRADITIONS

Some historians consider that the latter half of the seventeenth, rather than the sixteenth, century is the seedbed of the 'modern state'. This is to confuse the generation of the state as such with the perfection of its forms. Since by now nearly all Europe's states were monarchies—of the republics only the Netherlands and Venice were of much international significance—it is with the former that this chapter is concerned. By 1715 monarchy had bifurcated into two forms—unlimited or limited—which, in European parlance are called absolute and parliamentary monarchy. Nearly all were of the former kind. Of these France was regarded as the archetype. The second, the parliamentary category, included Poland and (for a time) Sweden, and a small number of the German states; but its archetype was England.

According to Bodin and Loyseau,[1] the French monarchy (to choose the prime example) was absolute in the sense that it could not be legally overridden. True; but it could be strenuously impeded. It did not operate on a *tabula rasa*. On the contrary, the political landscape (this was true for all the Renaissance monarchies) was littered with medieval survivals in the shape of Estates and Diets, municipalities, corporations, *parlements* and other lawcourts, civil servants, and so forth. An absolute monarch could indeed overbear these—that was true by definition—but, possibly, only after strenuous and sustained effort. The bifurcation of the European governmental tradition into two main categories—unlimited and limited monarchy as indicated above—turned on whether the newly powerful Renaissance kings were able to eliminate these impediments or whether they had to accept and adapt to them. The apposition of France and England shows this very well for Western Europe, that of Prussia and Poland for Eastern Europe. The question which has to be addressed before embarking upon the details of the French and English polities is a genetic

---

[1] See Ch. 5, p. 1300 n. 67 (cont.) above.

one. In the last chapter I took the view that though France and Castile could be regarded as absolute monarchies, England could not. But Bodin had lumped them together and modern historians, such as Zagorin,[2] are prepared to do the same. Even an essay like that of J. P. Cooper,[3] which compares English and French experience, only narrowly reaches the conclusion that England was indeed different. It is common ground, therefore, that the Renaissance monarchies of England and France shared important characteristics. But by 1714 they were so different from one another that one might almost call them mirror-images. Herein lies a most profound paradox. The functional equivalent of the French monarchy, vested in one man, was in Britain the collective tripartite body collectively called the Crown-in-Parliament. There the political process consisted in getting the three organs to work together: in so far as government was 'limited', it was by reason of its own internal checks and balances. In France, on the other hand, where the government was completely unitary (i.e. the person of the monarch), it was limited by reason of a multitude of outside checks and balances: those various regional, municipal, corporate, sectional, and judicial organizations of which France was a great mosaic. In the one, a self-divided but absolute body with little or no obstruction from external forces; in the other, a unitary absolute monarchy which was always having to face them down. Compared with 'practically any other European monarchy of the same period, the striking fact that emerges is the comparative effectiveness of the limitations on royal power in France'.[4]

How then did these two not-dissimilar Renaissance monarchies come to diverge so much in the course of the seventeenth century as to make the polities categorically antithetical?

2. THE FRENCH ROAD TO ABSOLUTISM

2.1. *Impediments to the Monarchy and the Politics of* Marchandage

We left France with a re-aggregated realm and a king who was fiscally absolute, the source of all new law, and served by a standing army and extensive bureaucracy. His kingdom was rich and the most populous in Europe. Francis I was powerful and self-confident enough to challenge Charles V of Spain for the imperial title and to engage Spain in continual warfare for the control of Italy, and his successor, Henry II, followed suit.

[2] Zagorin, *Rebels and Rulers*, i. 89–93.
[3] J. P. Cooper, *Differences between English and Continental Governments in the Early Seventeenth Century: Britain and the Netherlands* (Chatto & Windus, London, 1960), 62–90.
[4] A. Cobban, *Aspects of the French Revolution* (Paladin, London, 1971), 68.

Yet after the Peace of Cateau-Cambrésis in 1559 the entire edifice collapsed, and from then until 1661—when Louis XIV began his long personal rule—the state was for most of the time being violently forced apart and then forced together again. Clearly, then, this absolute monarchy must have contained flaws that made it much more fragile than its outward splendour ever intimated, and indeed, so it did. What were they?

The first was the uselessness of the Estates-General as a central source of taxation. In about one-quarter of the country, mostly on the periphery of the kingdom, the provincial *États* had survived and the Crown was forced to negotiate piecemeal with them. Perhaps even more importantly—'as the early history of the English parliament shows—[in France] the consolidation of royal power and the development of national unity would have been well served by the existence of a single representative institution'.[5]

The second was what we are entitled to call the permanent civil service, especially in the localities: the staffs of the *trésoriers*, *élus*, and *receveurs* who assessed and collected taxes, as well as all those specialized corps of foresters, river-comptrollers, road-surveyors, and the like. In 1515 the persons serving the state (including clerks and minor *commis*) numbered 8,000; in 1665 this total had risen to 80,000.[6] Such an extensive bureaucracy was supposedly one of the foundations of absolutism but it was also a dead weight, a strait-jacket. For one thing they—and in particular the local finance bureaux—were extremely corrupt. But in addition they were legalistic, circumlocutionary, and slow. They had been intended and were only effective for the raising and disbursement of peacetime revenues, being too costive to meet the sudden exigencies of a war. Yet warfare was fast becoming the norm: in 1515–98 France experienced thirty years of warfare (of which sixteen were the Wars of Religion), and in 1600–1713 the total was no less than sixty-five years (of which the Fronde accounted for five).[7]

But this was not the worst of it, for the Crown could not sack any delinquent *officiers* (except for proven criminal offences). They *owned* these appointments. They had *bought* them from the Crown and could only be deprived of them by the Crown buying them out, which it could never afford to do. The practice of selling offices was an old one, sure enough, but to finance his Italian wars Francis I actually created new offices simply in order to sell them. By the mid-seventeenth century their number is estimated at 40,000/50,000. By buying the office the purchaser enjoyed freedom from the *taille personnel* (one, at least, of the indispensables for *noblesse*) and

[5] D. Parker, *The Making of French Absolutism* (Edward Arnold, London, 1983), 15.

[6] A. Jouanna, *Le Devoir de révolte* (Fayard, Paris, 1989), 80.

[7] Derived from app. 3, in Luard, *War in International Society*.

received the fees and emoluments of the appointment. It was, in brief, an investment. By the end of the sixteenth century a government department existed to handle buying and selling such offices—the *Recette Générale des parties casuelles*—at the cost of a 10–25 per cent tax. Bequeathing the property to one's posterity was commonplace and soon became general, and the entire matter was systematized by the arrangement called the *Paulette*, in 1604. This set a rate of tax for the transfer of an office. The conditions were reviewed and could be altered at nine-yearly intervals. This hereditary transmission of offices was particularly significant in the case of the *parlements*, the 'sovereign lawcourts' of the realm, whose judges formed a wealthy, highly conservative, and obstructionist oligarchy which the Crown might intimidate but not remove.

These *parlements* presented yet another obstacle to the Crown. A number of the provinces had their own *parlements*, but the *parlement* of Paris was pre-eminent, its jurisdiction embracing nearly half the entire kingdom. *Parlements* were an enormously important part of the state organization. They had a general civil and criminal jurisdiction, acting as courts of appeal from all the inferior courts in the land and also as courts of first instance for certain categories of offences. In the second place—in an age where, as in England, administration was more often than not carried out through judicial forms and organs—the *parlements* issued 'regulatory decrees' which in effect gave detailed administrative form to its own judicial decisions and the decrees of the government. But for present purposes their significant role was the political. Since the fourteenth century the *parlements* had been accustomed to register the edicts of the king as conformable with the ancient laws and customs of the Regnum (whatever these might be). But did this imply, also, a power *not* to register? In which case the royal law or decree would have no legal standing? Hotman during the Wars of Religion, and Joly during the Fronde both claimed that the Paris *parlement* was the essential core of the feudal *curia regis* and as such could re-examine and modify any royal edict. Undeviatingly hostile to any alterations in the ancient formulae, processes, and precedents, it embarked on a running battle with the Crown over the administration of justice, foreign and domestic policy, and even over taxation. In time of war—which as we saw was most of the time—all these were intertwined, and all were matters where the royal authority was supposedly supreme. The Paris and the provincial *parlements* expressed their views through 'remonstrances', and in the last resort might defy the royal wrath and decline to register the edict. There were a number of ways by which a king could legally override this: he could send it *lettres de jussion*, orders for immediate registration, or hold a *lit de justice* which legally overrode the *parlement*. In the last resort he could exile recalcitrant members (not a severe penalty) and, if he really dared, abolish the courts altogether. (This is what a minister of Louis XV did in 1771, but to no avail since they were reinstated in 1774.) They were an encumbrance, especially in wartime. Significantly, the two occasions when Louis XIII imposed harsh restrictions on their power to remonstrate and delay were in 1629, when hostilities with Spain began, and 1641, in the full heat of this struggle.

Over time, the hereditary bearer of a high office such as a *parlementaire* would be ennobled. So arose the 'nobles of the Robe'. In the eighteenth century these came to adopt all the manners and customs of the *noblesse de l'épée*. Whether, as some say, they came to be the spearhead of an 'aristocratic resurgence against the Crown'[8] is a matter of dispute.

But what dominates the political process of early absolutism and gives it its fundamental and distinctive character is the relationship of this ancient *noblesse de l'épée* to the monarchy. The political process consisted of clientelism, patronage, and the king's use of them to 'manage' his great subjects. This Renaissance absolutism was not monolithic but cellular, a honeycomb of dependencies. The grand nobility had not 'gone away' with the New Monarchy but had adopted the policy of: 'if you can't beat 'em—join 'em'.

2.2. *The* Noblesse de l'Épée *up to 1624*

Not all grandees were governors, but all governors were certainly grandees. With their great landed possessions (e.g. Montmorency owned 600 manors) the high nobility exercised a dominant influence over the petty nobles of their *pays*, their tenants and townsfolk, and all those dependent on them in their turn. France was a strongly hierarchical society and by the same token a society of clienteles. It was also, as we have repeatedly had to say, a country of multifarious and powerful corporations and fierce, deep-rooted particularisms; though all three sometimes coincided, they sometimes crossed, but it was by using these forces that the political system operated. The king kept his nobles sweet by grants of honours, lands, pensions, appointments, and the power to distribute minor appointments to their followings. In their turn these great nobles dispensed these favours to their dependants, high and low, like so many Mafia 'Godfathers', and so guaranteed the Crown their allegiance and service.

Clienteles consisted, first of all, of the nobleman's immediate household. The *Maison du Roi*, for instance, numbered 4,000 persons, the duke of

---

[8] For the *nobiliaire*, see F. L. Ford, *Robe and Sword: The Regrouping of the French Aristocracy after Louis XIV* (Harper & Row, New York, 1965). *Contra*, J. H. Shennan, *The Parlement of Paris* (Eyre & Spottiswoode, London, 1968).

Anjou's over 1,000.[9] A second component was the military one: officers were exclusively noble.[10] The captains of the *compagnies d'ordonnance* were not simply noblemen; they were the most eminent personages in the kingdom, including the princes of the blood, the high officers of the Crown, and the very marshals themselves. (The latter handed over their tasks to lieutenants, but these too were noblemen of rank).[11] *A fortiori* the constable, marshals, and the colonels of regiments were all of the highest nobility also. The office of colonel deserves further notice because it illustrates how deep the roots of dependency could be sunk into the army itself. Whenever a new regiment was to be established the Crown commissioned a nobleman as colonel, and he in turn appointed captains to recruit the men and was then responsible for their arms, uniforms, and provisions—at the royal expense. In this sense, though, the regiment 'belonged' to its colonel and the system produced a closer affinity between the ranks and the captains and the captains and the colonel than between any of these and the king. It produced what in effect was yet another clientage or *fidélité* carried from the social into the military sphere.

Thirdly came the train of persons who owed their posts or honours or pensions or favourable marriages and the like to the grandee, whether through his intervention on their behalf at Court, or because he had given them money to buy their office or afford their dowries. Where tracts of the royal demesne had been alienated to a grandee (as in the apanage of a prince) he could dispose of all the offices.[12]

The king could not dispense with these great noblemen for he simply did not have nearly enough officials to run the country without their co-operation. In return, he offered them titles and honours and gifts of money—which he well could since he was by far the richest man in the land. The relationship was a finely balanced one, for while the king depended on the high nobility for their followings, so these followings would fade away if the king denied their noble patron the wealth, titles, and so forth that he could distribute to them as largess.

Politically the most important of these great noblemen were the provincial governors. This office is first attested in 1330, but it was not until 1561 that the entire country was divided into *gouvernements*.[13] Their origins were 'varied and complex' and their remits could differ widely, some specifying

---

[9] Jouanna, *Le Devoir*, 37.

[10] D. Bitton, *The French Nobility in Crisis* (Stanford UP, Stanford, 1969), 31.

[11] R. Doucet, *Les Institutions de la France au XVIᵉ siècle*, 2 vols. (Paris, 1948), 623.

[12] Jouanna, *Le Devoir*, 38.

[13] R. R. Harding, *Anatomy of a Power Élite: The Provincial Governors of Early Modern France* (Yale UP, New Haven, Conn., 1978), 8.

certain detailed powers, others forbidding them; but the heart of the matter was that the governors represented the king's authority in the province and their general commission would run 'to represent our person in all the affairs of the said province and do all you can that you recognize as necessary for the good of our service and the security, peace and tranquillity of the same province'.[14] In principle the post of governor was a *commis*, not an *office*; but bit by bit governors were permitted to bequeath their posts and the definitive change-over to venality occurred in 1584 when Henry III required payment for all governorships. Thus governors were not necessarily irremovable—as we shall see, Richelieu removed several—but the more usual practice was for the king to buy the governor out or get him to change places to a less prestigious province. For 1515–1650 the average tenure of a governor was some eleven years and an average 28 per cent of the governorships were inherited in the same family.[15]

The governor was of immense political importance, especially if he resided in his province (many did not). He controlled military affairs . . . 'He had a major, indeed often a decisive say in local appointments, whether to offices, the governorship of fortresses, or to municipal administration. This military power and patronage gave the Governors overwhelming authority . . .'[16] Where the monarch was strong, resourceful, and politically skilful he could balance the interests of this or that governership against others'. But things were not always as simple, and this was particularly true where the king was a minor and there was nobody authoritative to dictate the division or rotation of these spoils of office, only a power vacuum—and into it would rush the great competing houses like those of Lorraine or Montmorency or Bourbon. The one matter on which all these competitors concurred was that no individual or house should secure a monopoly of distributing the royal largess at court. In such circumstances some governors could turn and become formidable opponents of the Crown.

In 1559 all the potential foes of absolutism—local *États*, governorships, municipal authorities, *parlements*, and corporate bodies of all kinds—were galvanized by an adventitious explosion which took them way beyond their customary limited objective of preserving and enlarging their privileges. It is possible to accommodate clashing interests, but not religious passion. Lutheranism had entered France in the 1520s and had been ruthlessly persecuted. The 'Burning Court' (*Chambre Ardente*) of the Paris *parlement* was established in 1548. However, by this time Lutheranism had given way to Calvinism and in 1561 a very considerable number of

[14] Ibid. 14. [15] Ibid. 121 (for tabulation).
[16] R. J. Bonney, *Political Change in France under Richelieu and Mazarin, 1624–1661* (Oxford, 1978), 286.

Calvinist congregations existed.[17] It made rapid gains among the great nobles but even more among the petty nobility. The reformed doctrine of course made a great appeal to the townsfolk also; as they came under government threat, they put themselves under the protection of their local seigneur. So was forged the novel religio-military machine of the Huguenots. Each congregation had its own consistory of ministers and lay elders; these were grouped into 'colloquies' in every *pays*; these were then grouped into synods in each province; and these came together at the top in the national synod. The Calvinist nobility recognized their own social hierarchy, as was to be expected, but from 1562 it was made to coincide with the Church hierarchy, with Condé as the recognized 'Protector-General of the Churches of France'.[18] The resulting religio-military structure constituted a veritable state within the state.

Up to 1559 the Crown had succeeded in the necessary balancing of the noble houses against one another without offending them all—the ancient royal mission of 'baron-management'. The bottom fell out of this arrangement in 1559 when, hard on the Peace of Cateau-Cambrésis with Spain, which filled France with the dissatisfied petty noblemen who had formed the French cavalry arm and were now unemployed, the new king, Henry II, was killed by accident during a tourney, leaving the conduct of government to his widow Catherine de Médicis as regent for three young sons. Francis II, the eldest, was aged 15 at accession and married to Mary, Queen of Scots. Mary was a niece of the ardently Catholic Guises and their ensuing monopoly of court patronage immediately incited other great houses to challenge them. But the young Francis II died within the year, leaving his mother Catherine de Médicis in control since the new king—Charles IX—was only 10 years old.

There now ensued a thirty-year period of strife between the rival noble factions and this was lifted out of the customary neo-feudal frame by becoming a war of rival confessions, each filled with murderous religious rage. Houses or branches of houses which had suffered under the Guise associated themselves with the Calvinist 'Huguenot' cause and a variety of clients clustered around them, notably the largely unemployed French petty nobility. *États* were torn apart; families like the Montmorencis were divided against themselves; each municipality chose its side. This was the first revolution in which the press, pamphlets, and propaganda played a vital part. Huguenot writers tended to stress the limitations on royal authority

[17] *CMH*, ii. 224 puts the number at 2150 but this is now thought to be greatly exaggerated and a piece of Calvinist propaganda.

[18] L. Romier, 'Les Protestants français à la veille des guerres civiles', *Revue Historique*, 129 (1917), 254–63.

even to the point of legitimizing resistance. Hotman's *Franco-Gallia* (1573) argued that royal absolutism was of recent growth and historically unfounded, since it had always been shared with the Estates-General. Du Plessis Mornay's *Vindiciae contra tyrannos* (1579) asserted a contractual basis to the royal authority and that in certain circumstances it was not merely a right but a duty to oppose it. Catholic writers went further—the Jesuit Bellarmine, for instance, justified tyrannicide. In between such extremists stood the *politiques*, appalled by the civil war and seeking a political solution to the situation. Of their works the most famous is the renowned *Six Books of the Republic* of Jean Bodin (1576), a plea for a royal absolutism tempered by respect for the law of God and the property and liberty of the subject.

The Wars of Religion, which began in 1562, ushered in a period of strife and breakdown which went on for 100 years until 1661, when Louis XIV began his fifty-four years of personal rule. It is no business of this chapter to recount the disturbed history of France during this tormented century. In very brief compass: the entire period was a dialectic between aristocratic violence and monarchical *marchandage*. The latter was abandoned in favour of royal counter-violence at only one point—between 1624 and 1642—in the ministry of Cardinal Richelieu, and even then with an important qualification.[19] Richelieu's victory over the Huguenots in 1629 and the defeat of provincial rebellions in 1630–2 may be seen as beginning the expansion of royal power which proceeded inexorably, despite the 'blip' of the Fronde (1648–53) until its high point under Louis XIV, *c.*1680.

What prompted the nobility to enter the wars? It was by no means just religious conviction: that confessionalized an already existing state of hostility. Instead, one might discern, *inter alia*, family pride, a very touchy sense of personal honour, and efforts to acquire the royal favour and so maintain a numerous clientele. A common theme was a traditional concern for what was called 'the Common Weal'; by which was understood a sovereignty divided between the king, the nobility, and the Estates-General. In short, there was a twofold set of motives, one self-serving, the other *la patrie*. 'Seen this way', a recent historian observes, 'revolt appears as a means of expressing political opposition, an archaic method characterized by recourse to violence and even to alliance with the foreigner, but a "normal" method given the absence of institutional means able to play such a role.'[20]

Such sentiments were sparked into confrontation by the adventitious disappearance of their customary 'arbitrator'—an adult and politically street-wise king. Given a power vacuum at the top, the struggle between

---

[19] This being Richelieu's creation of a clientele of his own. See p. 1317 below.
[20] Jouanna, *Le Devoir*, 9–10.

the houses was over who should control the spoils of office, but owed its particular viciousness to the infusion of religious fervour: to use Jouanna's phrase, 'the confessionalization of the nobiliar strategies'. Horrible things were done in the name of Huguenot and Catholic. There is one print that shows a man, supine, his belly slit open and filled with oats, and a horse eating them from amongst his entrails. These wars—campaigns punctuated by various 'pacifications'—went on till 1598.

The question is why they ever ended. And what is said about these wars is true, *mutatis mutandis*, even of Henry IV's reign and that of his son, Louis XIII, up to the ministry of Richelieu (1610–24), and is true, again, of the period after the cardinal's death in 1642 up to 1661, when Louis XIV announced his personal rule. To make war the grandee contenders had to raise troops. To pay them they relied on foreign aid (England, Spain), on their own personal fortunes, and most considerably, on the 'seizure of royal taxes in the Provinces controlled by the rebels'.[21] They would take over the *bureaux des finances* and the royal treasure in all the *généralités* they happened to control. As it strengthened them, it *pro tanto* weakened the Crown. Peace was made when the Crown amnestied the magnates and their followings for all the illegalities they had committed and especially their seizure of the royal treasure, and bought them off by conferring governerships, offices, titles, and pensions. Even the great Henry IV of Navarre concluded the pacification in this way; as he sourly said to Sully, France had been *vendu, pas rendu*. The pensions he had to grant alone amounted to some 24 million livres.[22] Yet there is good reason to believe that these nobiliar revolts were not financially profitable—that at most they paid only the military expenses the rebel had incurred.[23]

Henry IV's widow Marie de Médicis, now the regent, tried to follow his advice: 'satisfy the magnates and the *officiers*.' But first one then another courtier became a 'favourite' and engrossed the royal patronage (Concini, then Luynes) with the predictable consequence that the great nobles revolted—perhaps it would be better to say demonstrated in arms—five times in the next fourteen years, receiving the usual amnesty and gratifications for calling their action off. These great nobles were not anti-royalist. On the contrary. Just as the peasants shouted for *le roi sans gabelle*, the nobles demanded the king without jumped-up favourites.[24] The rebellious grandees (it is important to distinguish them from the petty nobility) were not seeking to weaken the power of the throne but to get a share of its power.

---

[21] Jouanna, *Le Devoir*, 388.
[22] J. B. Wolf, *Louis XIV*, Panther edn. (Norton, London, 1970), 218–20. E. Lavisse, *Louis XIV: Histoire d'un grand règne, 1643–1715* (R. Laffont, Paris, 1989); Parker, *Making of French Absolutism*, 47.
[23] Jouanna, *Le Devoir*, 389.   [24] Cf. ibid. 232–7.

2.3. *The* Noblesse de l'Épée *under Richelieu*

In this context, Richelieu's great ministry was an untypical interlude. He became Louis XIII's chief minister in 1624 with the determination, as he put it, 'to destroy the Huguenots' party, to humble the pride of the grandees, to compel all subjects to their duties'.[25] He fulfilled this programme completely. He defeated the Huguenots and took over their *places fortes*, but allowed them to retain liberty of worship. They were reduced, in fact, to a religious minority. And also, by force if necessary, he did compel the common people to 'their duties'. And, as we are going to see, he certainly humbled the pride of the grandees.

But there is as much continuity as innovation in the way Richelieu handled them. Not unlike the former favourites Concini and Luynes, Richelieu established himself as a 'favourite'—hence the numerous conspiracies against him: the Chalais Plot of 1626, the 'Day of Dupes' of 1630, Gaston d'Orleans's rebellion in 1632, which ended in the defeat of his ally, Montmorency and his capture and execution; the plot against his life in 1636, the war of the Count of Soissons which was terminated by his mysterious death at La Marfée, and finally the assassination-plot of Cinq Mars. To all these Richelieu reacted with calculated terror. No *marchandage* here: some nobles were executed—Chalais, Montmorency, Marshall Marillac, Cinq-Mars. Others were imprisoned or exiled. In his *Succincte Narration* Richelieu catalogues his victims: the dukes of Bellegarde, of Elbeuf, and of Guise ejected from their governorships, the imprisonment of Puylaurens, of Marshall d'Ornano, of the king's two half-brothers, the Vendômes, of the marquis of Chateauneuf, and so on. Eleven governors were removed from their posts.

It is this ruthlessness towards the grandees that makes Richelieu's regime 'untypical', but his mode of replacing their influence was not. Into the gaps he had created Richelieu built up a clientele of his own. In this sense he continued the *marchandage* tradition but with himself, with the assistance of Condé, as the patron. He appointed some of his relatives as governors, and with his huge fortune made dependants in every important province with gifts of pensions, presents, government posts, and the like. The alliance with Condé, the first prince of the blood, brought him, too, the support of the extensive Bourbon 'connection'. It has been said that the subordination of the secretaries of state to Richelieu 'was a consequence of his patronage rather than of his formal superiority as chief minister'.[26]

[25] A. J. du Plessis, Cardinal Duc de Richelieu, *Testament Politique* (Edn. André, Paris, 1947), 95.
[26] Parker, *Making of French Absolutism*, 86.

But it was in this official capacity that Richelieu expanded and reinforced the royal authority by establishing a network of *commis* (not *officiers*) to work alongside the governors. His reason sprang from France's plunge into a war with Spain in 1635 that was to go on until 1659. The war needed money on a greater scale than ever before, since armies had trebled in size since the last century and might now rise to some 150,000 men. Getting the populace to accept royal authority was horribly violent; recalcitrants were imprisoned, their property sequestrated, and 'special brigades' of troops were sent into the villages to enforce payment. Richelieu's ministry has been described as a 'war dictatorship' where everything was subordinated to the need to raise money. At the beginning of the century war expenditure was less than 5 million livres per annum; in the 1620s it averaged 16 million; by 1635 it was 33 million; and after 1640 had risen to over 38 million per annum.[27]

This is what led Richelieu to develop the old post of *intendant*, in the gift of and immediately revocable by the Crown. Some manner of *intendants* there had been since the mid-sixteenth century but Richelieu expanded their duties. From 1628 their commissions began to include the triune power over 'justice, police and finance', and after France was at war they increasingly acquired powers over the military.

As Richelieu intended, the *intendants* came to control the local fiscal apparatus. Here the *trésoriers* in their *bureaux des finances* allocated the global sum the government demanded among the *élections*, and then told the *élus* to assess in their parishes. Thus the *trésoriers* were key officials in the provinces.

This fiscal system proved far too slow for wartime. In 1637 *intendants* were empowered to levy forced loans on the towns, in 1638 to levy the *subsistence*, in 1639 the tax *des aises*, in 1641 the sales tax, and then, in 1642, the most important tax of all, in fact the basic tax, the *taille*. They were to preside over the *bureaux des finances*, visit the *élections*, and carry out the parish assessments. In short, the entire fiscal apparatus run by privileged irremovable fiscal *officiers* was now answerable to the king's own personal commissioners.

At the same time the affairs of the army demanded increasing attention. Villages where troops were billetted suffered the *terreur des troupes* who were little more than looters, thieves, and rapists, so that villagers were forced into buying exemption from their attentions if they were not to endure their savagery. Moreover, the troops were in a permanent state of indiscipline because their pay and rations were always in arrears. Large numbers of officers were indulging in the usual corrupt practices—for example, the *passe-volants*—that made them money at the government's and the troops' expense. Then, on a different plane, was the problem of getting supplies to

[27] Parker, *Making of French Absolutism*, 64.

these armies. It was to deal with matters such as these that *intendants* of the army were commissioned with the main task of 'maintaining the rule of law in the army, and giving advice to the military commanders in the Council of War'. They were required also to maintain a certain rough justice in the 'contributions' exacted by the troops, and gradually acquired a role in recruiting and in supervising the payout to the army during the winter period.[28]

It is entirely understandable that these innovations outraged the fiscal *officiers*, the *États*, and the Paris and many local *parlements*. Their membership had cost them money and was a property, so that the control powers of the *intendants* both demeaned them and affected their incomes. These were all 'men of the robe', many of them ennobled, and all had a strong corporate sense as to where they fitted in the state. Richelieu overrode them all. Local *États* might be suppressed or at least, remodelled (as in the Dauphiné and Provence). In 1641 the increasingly fretful and obstructive Paris *parlement* was forbidden to 'meddle with affairs of state' and told that if its remonstrances, having been duly heard, were rejected by the king it must register royal edicts forthwith.

In short, when the cardinal died in 1642 there was no longer a feeble un-self-confident monarch desperately trying to buy off rebels to his authority, but an imperious Crown striking out in all ways at any impediment to its authority: using exile, banishment, imprisonment, and capital punishment as its means and propaganda, secret police, *intendants de l'armée* and *intendants de justice, police, et finances* as its principal instruments.

It used to be thought that the Crown set up the *intendants* in order to diminish the governors who, it was said, were the Crown's great competitors.[29] This seems nowadays to be almost the reverse of the truth. The governors' military patronage was still vast: it was they who raised troops via commissioned colonels, who in turn appointed the captains; they helped to select mayors and town councillors; they acted at Court as intemediaries on behalf of their dependants for pensions and official posts and so forth. Furthermore, the Crown depended on them for nominations; how else could the ministries know which persons were suitable candidates for the many posts that came up?[30]

In hidden respects, however, their clienteles had diminished. To some extent this was due to the war and its changing character. Richelieu razed all castles in the interior that were of no strategic importance.[31] The heavy cavalry, the *compagnies d'ordonnance*, which they had commanded, was now

[28] Bonney, *Political Change*, ch. 12, *passim.*
[29] Cf. Doucet, *Les Institutions*, i. 231, 233.
[30] Parker, *Making of French Absolutism*, 26–7.
[31] Ibid. 105.

outmoded and was quietly phased out. Then again, once at war with Spain it would have been impossible for the *haute noblesse* to call out the petty nobility because these were all in the field. The governors felt the lure of Paris, the centre where marriages were brokered, credit obtained, legal affairs best handled, and of course the place to solicit pensions on behalf of oneself and one's dependants. Of those governors appointed 1627–50, two-thirds were in Paris when they died.[32]

Were the *intendants* indeed set up as watchdogs over these governors? They were by no means self-made men. All Richelieu's and Mazarin's appointments were noble. Their fathers were largely *maîtres de requêtes*, some were treasury officials, and there had been a huge increase in the number who were members of a *parlement*. Most of them in fact belonged to the now fast-expanding *noblesse de la robe*. The value of the *intendants* to the government lay in the fact that most had received a uniform training in law.[33]

Unlike the governors who, as we noted, averaged some ten years in office, *intendants* were normally appointed for only three. Few were *fidèles* of the governor but many would have had long-standing ties with him.[34] Governors, for their part, liked having their own nominees as *intendants* and regarded them—as in fact they were—as useful collaborators.[35] On their side, the governors gave the *intendants* the military escorts they often needed. The *intendants*, seized of sovereign judicial authority, offered the governors a way of superseding recalcitrant local courts, something that they themselves did not have the audacity to do. *Intendants* helped them repress military indiscipline, which threatened any governor's regime; for the *intendants* acted as martial-law judges and toured the camps more thoroughly than ever a governor did. Again, as the demands for war-finance grew, ever-more rapacious governors were happy to see outsiders rather than themselves carrying out forced loans and confiscations.

2.4. *Mazarin and the Frondes*

In 1643 Richelieu was dead, and so was the king. The wily Italian, Cardinal Mazarin, took the place of the former, the 5-year-old Louis XIV succeeded the latter. Government was effectively in the hands of the cardinal and Anne of Austria, the queen-mother. Their personal relationship was so close—indeed, from Mazarin's letters, touchingly so—that some historians believe that the two went through a marriage ceremony.

Mazarin continued his late master's style but far less abrasively. Like

---

[32] Parker, *Making of French Absolutism.*   [33] Bonney, *Political Change,* 82–91.
[34] Harding, *Anatomy of a Power Élite,* 80–2.   [35] Bonney, *Political Change,* 300.

Richelieu he had amassed an enormous fortune and, given his relationship to the queen-mother, acquired the monopoly of court patronage. With these behind him he pursued the policy of *marchandage* with a certain relish. Yet after a mere five years a storm burst over him and France was once again plunged into civil war.

Three matters combined to create this crisis, and all were connected with war finance. The inevitable attempts to screw more taxes out of the population precipitated widespread tax rebellions and revolts which had to be put down by the *intendants* with the special troops assigned to them. This violent unrest formed the background of the Fronde.

The continued sale of offices and the *Paulette* tax on transfers had been a great financial resource under Richelieu when, in 1630–4 for instance, it provided nearly 40 per cent of the Crown's total income. It had now (1645–9) fallen to only 8.1 per cent, but this was still some 50 million livres as against 125 millions from the *taille*. Nevertheless, the continued sale of offices and ratcheting upwards of the *Paulette* infuriated the *officiers* (since the more posts created, the less their own were worth) at a time when they were increasingly resentful of their subordination to the royal *intendants*.[36]

The third ingredient in this heady brew was the bitter resentment of the grandees at their exclusion from court patronage—especially by an Italian. The street rabble of Paris and the common people at large also hated Mazarin for the crushing load of taxes.

What made the Crown helpless, however—perhaps even more so than Charles I of England's recent case in 1640—were two immediate disasters. The first was that the Spaniards concluded a peace treaty with the United Provinces of the Netherlands and thus freed themselves to continue the war against France with greater strength than ever before. The second was the plight of the public finances whence, in 1648, since creditors would lend it no more, the state became effectively bankrupt.

The 'Fronde'—'a sling'—was so called from the Paris mob's stoning Mazarin's windows. It is conventional to talk of three Frondes: the Fronde of the *parlement*, which began in 1648 and ended in the Peace of Rueil, 1649; the first Fronde of the Princes, which began in 1650 and was defeated by 1651; and the third Fronde, of Condé, opened in 1651 and defeated by the royal troops in 1652–3. Different considerations weighed with the protagonists in each case.

The first Fronde began in a fierce money dispute between the *parlement* and the court which, mishandling it badly, drove the former to an assault on

[36] R. J. Bonney, *The King's Debts: Finance and Politics in France, 1589–1661* (Oxford, 1981), Table V. B. in app. 2, p. 313.

royal absolutism. Encouraged by Parliament's defeat of Charles I in England, it drew up a charter for reform which would have turned France into a limited monarchy. It demanded, *inter alia*, that the *intendants* must be forthwith abolished; this was on behalf of the 3,000 or so financial *officiers* who had been turned into mere subordinates. The second demand was also self-serving: the Crown must not create any *new* offices. But the third and fourth were true blows against royal absolutism. No taxes were to be levied without the consent (i.e. the 'verification') of the *parlement* and no subject was to be detained for more than twenty-four hours unless brought before a court.

The court had to accept the charter and this 'parliamentary' or constitutional phase of the Fronde lasted from August 1648 to March 1649, with little bloodshed, but then degenerated into a serious war between the court and various magnates. The first Fronde of the Princes began when the Grand Duc du Condé was making intolerable military and political demands and clearly intended to become the master of the court. Mazarin arrested him and two other nobles, only for them to be released after France's second great commander, Turenne, also on the eastern frontier, threw in his lot with them. This Fronde was over by 1651. Turenne now came over to the Crown but Condé pursued his vendetta assisted by Spanish aid and money, and the third Fronde was his own. Beaten by Turenne and the royal armies, he finally fled to the service of the king of Spain. Mazarin was fully restored to power in February 1653.

The first reflection that may be made upon this shabby war is that it shows the immaturity of the French state; what Lavisse happily calls 'l'inachèvement de la France': the state could only work harmoniously if the king could 'manage' these magnates. This immaturity is evidenced also by the frivolity of the magnates' behaviour. It is hard to find a single one who had any other purpose than the most narrow and frequently trivial self-interest. Personal feuds altered the temporary and ever-shifting alliances and so did the vanity and ambition of a flock of aristocratic tarts like the duchess of Longueville or the duchess of Chevreuse. Swapping lovers among the magnates, urging them to make war, make peace, change sides; no wonder this is what was called 'the war of the chamber-pots'.

Another reflection relates to the discord among the various opponents of the *intendants*. The Paris *parlement*, in demanding their withdrawal and an end to the sale of offices, had united all these elements, but no sooner did the Crown give way on this than they fell to quarrelling. The provincial *parlements* would not join Paris in a political defiance of the king; they had no wish to be subordinated to this great *parlement*. The Paris *parlement* itself did not see eye to eye with some other courts, such as the *Cour des Aides*. In the provinces the *trésoriers* and *élus*, liberated from the *intendants'* dominion, disputed amongst themselves.[37] Thirdly, the *intendants* did in fact return, but under different hats: for instance, the Crown would send down *maîtres des requêtes*.[38] A royal declaration of 1652 effectively annulled the *parlement's* proposals of 1648, although these were never officially revoked. From 1654 the *intendants* were once more permanant administrative agents, first, to extort the taxes, secondly, to assert the authority of the king, and in the third place, to deal with the tax revolts which were spreading everywhere. The peasants had taken the activities of the Paris *parlement* as amounting to the abolition of taxes and they rose in fury when collection was resumed.[39] But from 1654 onwards the *intendants* dominated the *élus* and thus wrought 'a momentous political change' in finance, since all its aspects now fell to them.[40]

The third reflection is that, despite a superficial similarity, this was not the same as previous nobiliar risings. Clientelism was no longer a military resource. For one thing this was due to the great gap between the grandees and the petty nobles, the former being enormously wealthy, while many of the latter could barely scratch a living from the soil. And since the grandees now thronged the court, the petty nobility associated them with the taxation and other unfavourable actions of the government. On the other hand, without these grandees' intermediation at court, these petty nobles had no way to advance themselves and this served to embitter them the more. In their being abandoned for the court, they saw the grandees as abandoning also the old ideal of the *Bien Public* which had united them in the past. The petty nobility were marginalized, and indeed in some instances they sided with their peasants (though never to the point of revolt).[41] And—since we are talking about clienteles—nor were the urban patriciates any longer inclined to rally to the support of the grandees' ambitions.[42]

Another difference from the old 'clientelist' rebellions lies in the changed pattern of warfare, for if the nobles were not being backed by their clienteles, where did their armies come from? From two sources, and the first of these does indeed continue to be clientelist, and that is *military* patronage. We showed how the grandee raised an army at the king's command and expense, by nominating colonels who in turn nominated captains. These commanders were far closer to the troops than was distant Paris. So a good deal of the fighting went on between the different armies of the kingdom—Turenne's command, for instance, or Condé's. For the rest, the grandees hired foreign mercenaries—the duke of Lorraine made a fat living out of this, for instance—and again, when Mazarin went into exile, which he had to do on two occasions, he returned at the head of mercenary forces.

Where did the troops' pay come from, then? Some was foreign, Spanish gold. For the rest it was a similar story as before; the local grandee would raid the government's' *caisses* in his province and make do with that. In the end, when peace was restored the Crown would amnesty the now-reconciled nobleman for his illegalities and compensate him for his expenses.

A fourth reflection bears on the role of the Paris *parlement*—and indeed of the *parlements* in the provinces, too. These defended the customs—especially the financial ones—of their own provinces as well as looking after their own interests. They still had the right to remonstrate and they could do this on the same or related matters not once only but several times. Nor had they ever formally abandoned their claim to be able to refuse to register royal edicts. For the moment the matter rested—the king had won, after all. But the claims were not dead, merely dormant. They would be revived in the last years of Louis XIV and become the greatest qualification to the absolutism of his successors.

One final reflection concerns the difference between France and England. In the latter Parliament won, in France it was the Crown. This was only the necessary and not the sufficient condition for the realization of absolute monarchy, but the personality—and the long reign—of Louis XIV made up that deficiency and set the pattern of royal absolutism that was to last till 1789.

2.5. *Louis XIV Makes himself Absolute*

2.5.1. THE 'SUN-KING'—A MYTH?

After the darkness and turmoil of the last half-century came Louis the God-given, the Sun-King, and the mists immediately dispersed. He took personal charge of government and overrode all obstructors; extended his grip on the provinces through strengthening his *intendants*; and domesticated a huge and modern standing army that was the terror of all Europe. His sweeping royal powers now knew no obstacle that he could not and did not by his fiat overcome. In this way he constructed for himself a Palace-type polity where decisions were taken by him and his court, and which served as the classical model of continental Europe.[43] Such, until very recently, was the accepted version. The reality was considerably different.

There is no doubt that when Louis spoke of his 'personal rule' he meant

---

[43] It is accepted, for example, in Perry Anderson's beautifully written and concise chapter on France in his *Lineages of the Absolutist State* (NLB, London, 1974, repr. Verso, 1979), 100–2.

this literally. From the outset he meant to show everybody that he was master. It is also true that while in full vigour he did overcome all those groups that had been impediments to the royal power in previous reigns. Thirdly, and also true, he greatly extended the range of his *intendants'* duties and so achieved better surveillance and control of these groups, and furthermore not merely enlarged and modernized the army but thoroughly civilianized it by bringing it under his ministers' control. But—and this is where modern interpretations would differ from the old—he did not do so by supplanting the grandees nor by treating them as an opposition. There was always a hard core of eminent noblemen to whom he turned for advice and, as for the *noblesse* as a whole, his strategy was to balance the families' claims and interests against one another and create an equilibrium both between them and him, and amongst themselves. In this, he was playing the ancient, respected, and welcome role of the royal 'arbitrator'. It represents a continuity with the past, not a break with it.

In so far as Louis got his own way with the institutions and corporate bodies that had thwarted his predecessors, it was due less to peremptory commands (though these were not always lacking) than to his own over-powering mystique, and to blandishments, persuasion, and pressures. Nor did Louis abolish any of these bodies or institutions. As soon as he died they began to revive their old pretensions and become a thorn in the side of the regime he had bequeathed.

> We have scotch'd the snake, not killed it:
> She'll close and be herself, whilst our poor malice
> Remains in danger of her former tooth.
> (Shakespeare, *Macbeth*, iii. ii)

Louis's absolutism was the product of his overpowering personality, not new institutions, and its juridical status was heavily qualified in practice. Why and how the version of Louis as the omnipotent Sun-King should have arisen and his monarchy have been regarded as the very classical model of European absolutism is the puzzle that we shall address by way of our conclusion.

2.5.2. LOUIS: PERSONAL RULE

From the very outset Louis made clear that he alone would rule. Here is his comment on the period when Mazarin died, in 1661:

Disorder was rampant everywhere . . . The men of quality, accustomed to deals with a minister who himself had no distaste for these, and for whom they were sometimes necessary [*sc.* Mazarin], were always inventing imaginary rights over anything that affected their sense of seemliness. There was not a governor of a fortress who was not difficult to govern: not a demand which was not mingled with some reproach about the past or some hint of disaffection, foreseen and to be feared for in the future: favours exacted and seized rather than awaited, one always being the consequence of another so that, in fact, nobody any longer felt under an obligation for them.[44]

'Monsieur,' Louis formally told the Chancellor, 'till now I have been pleased to entrust the government of my affairs to the late Cardinal. It is now time that I govern them myself.'[45] Louis's brutal demotion and destruction of that great and talented *surintendant des finances* Fouquet under-lined this resolve. 'I determined', he said, 'on no account to take a First Minister and allow anyone else to fulfil the function of the king as long as I bore the title. To the exact contrary I wished to divide the execution of my orders among several persons so that all the authority for the same should reside in me alone.' And again—reflecting his mistrust of the high nobi-lity—'I believed it was against my interest to seek out men of superior station because my prime need being to establish my personal reputation, it was important for the public to recognize by the rank of those I utilized that I had no intention of sharing my authority with them.'[46]

2.5.3. WHAT LOUIS DID

No sooner was the second Fronde over than Louis, just 14 years old, convoked the Paris *parlement* and settled his scores with it. By a *lit de justice* he decreed all its acts annulled. Ten *parlementaires* were exiled, the rest forbidden to have any dealings with or accept money from such gentlemen as Beaufort or Rohan who had abetted them in the usurpation of power. For the rest, the *parlement* was expressly forbidden to interest itself any longer in the affairs of the kingdom, in finances, or the activities of the adminis-trators. 'I was convinced', he wrote, 'that it was pertinent to usher in my administration by this act of severity . . . Sure enough the *parlements* which had till then made difficulties about complying with the *arrêts* of my Council accepted with all the respect I could hope for the *arrêt* by which I forbade them to continue this abuse.'[47] In 1661 he issued the famous decree which stipulated that decrees of his Council took precedence over those of the *parlements*. In 1667 he ordered the Paris *parlement* to register a number of edicts immediately without delaying for remonstrances, and when a number of the judges asked for a plenary session to consider this requirement Louis exiled some of them and ordered three to resign office. In 1673 he issued the most

---

[44] Louis XIV, King of France, *Mémoires de Louis XIV, écrit par lui-meme*, 2 vols. (J. L. M. de Gain-Montagnac, Paris, 1806), ii. 375–6.   [45] Wolf, *Louis XIV*, 180.
[46] Louis XIV, *Mémoires*, ii. 385–6.   [47] Ibid. 399–400.

important edict of all. The *parlements* must register his edicts on the spot. They might remonstrate *only after* they had done this. Furthermore, if Louis rejected such remonstrances, no further ones would be entertained. The provincial *parlements* were less prepared to co-operate than that of Paris, but 'even for these more distant tribunals there were fewer overt challenges to the government'.[48]

The provincial *États* posed a more difficult problem. It is not possible to generalize about their composition except that they were organized into the three Orders of Clergy, Nobility, and *Tiers État* because the composition of the second and third of these Orders varied. What can be said, however, is that everywhere it was the high ecclesiastics and the nobility who predominated: in Burgundy (and Brittany too), for instance, every gentleman whose nobility went back four generations had the right to sit and the *Tiers* was made up of the mayors of some towns and the deputies of certain others. They appointed their own officials and channelled the regional sentiment, laws, customs, and privileges which had prompted their establishment *qua* new provinces recently attached to the Crown. There was therefore no way of either suppressing or dictating to them. They provide an admirable example of the point which has been hammered home in respect to the agrarian empires of Rome and the East, namely, that the local functionaries of the central government were relatively few, they only reached down so far in the countryside and were therefore reliant, in carrying out the government's orders, on the co-operation and good pleasure of the local notables.

Consequently in this case the Crown, even Louis, was forced to haggle. For all that, he was able to get them to part with substantial sums: for instance, in Languedoc Louis had begun the reign asking for 2 million livres and receiving only 1 million, but by 1676 had got them to pay 3 million livres without demur.[49]

Another of the battery of measures that Louis used to domesticate the grandees (including the enhancement of the 'court society' mentioned below) concerned the governors. 'It was from then [*sc.* 1661]', wrote Louis,

that I began to reduce the excessive powers which for a long time past had been exercised by the governors of the frontier towns . . . And since what had made them most absolute in their fortresses was the latitude allowed them in the way of raising money by taxes and the freedom to make up the garrisons with troops who were their dependants I resolved to deprive them imperceptibly of both. So, from day to day, I arranged that troops who were my own personal dependants should

[48] R. Mettam, *Power and Faction in Louis XIV's France* (Blackwell, Oxford, 1988), 209. He pooh-poohs the 1661 decree (p. 208). [49] Parker, *Making of French Absolutism*, 121.

enter the most important towns . . . What I carried out at that time without difficulty or clamour could not even have been suggested a few years before without danger.[50]

The duties of the *intendants* were widened, especially after Colbert (who had persistently bridled them) died in 1683. Their ever-widening range of duties will be related below.

The towns also came under closer royal control, though for fiscal rather than political reasons, perhaps. Their mounting debts were investigated by the *intendants* and new regulations made to prevent them accumulating any more. By a 1673 decree extraordinary expenditure had to be authorized by a meeting of the inhabitants (which itself required the *intendant*'s approval). In 1691 the *intendants* were required to verify the municipal accounts. The edict of 1692 ended the election of mayors; instead the office was put up for sale and very soon the office of councillor, also elective, suffered the same fate. A 1699 edict transferred the municipalities' regulatory powers over crafts and trades, hospitals, prisons, and the like to lieutenants of police or official inspectors, both of them answerable to the Intendancy. Some towns which had enjoyed an autonomous position were summarily dealt with. Marseilles was an example and one of Louis's first acts in 1660 was to march on it with his army and suppress its ancient constitution. The constitutions of Aix and Arles were remodelled at the same time.[51]

Louis was intricately involved in affairs of the Church, which was unsurprising given that he himself was a fervent believer who became even more devout in his last years; that the Church hierarchy stretched downwards to the *curés* and the village pulpits in a way that the civil administration, for all its *intendants*, could never pretend to; and that, thirdly, it was a considerable source of finance. The king's reactions to the religious currents inside the Church are far too tortuous even to be outlined here, given that it was divided into many schools of thought which combined or contended according to the issue in question.[52] But in respect of finance the Church, like the bodies we have just been reviewing, proved no obstacle. The Assembly of the Church met every five years and was accustomed to chaffer with the Crown over the size of its *don gratuit*. It had actually refused to make one at all during the Fronde and even in 1655, despite months of niggling negotiation, donated a mere 600,000 livres. Ten years later, however, it gave 2.4 million livres and, furthermore, transformed it into a customary gift.

---

[50] Louis XIV, *Mémoires*, ii. 401.   [51] Parker, *Making of French Absolutism*, 122.
[52] Mettam, *Power and Faction*, 245–8, 252–6. R. Briggs, *Early Modern France, 1560–1715* (OUP, Oxford, 1977), 166–211.

Three things remain to be reviewed—the machinery of administration, that is, the *intendants*, the condition of the army, and—what is intimately bound up with both—the position of the grandees in the light of this personal rule.

The *intendants* were fully restored, their commissions were made more or less uniform, and their remit

came to include every stage in the distribution and allocation of the various taxes; the distribution of wealth among the population; the condition of roads, rivers and bridges; the levying of local tolls and duties; the regulations for the military and luxury industries; the provision of supplies and quarters for troops; the efficacy of the legislation against immorality and subsequently against the Huguenots; the integrity and behaviour of local officials; and the many provincial practices and traditions on which the government hoped to impose some national unity and rationalization.[53]

As a consequence the *intendants* began to appoint staffs of *sub-delegués*, usually natives of the locality, to assist them.

Whereas the field armies had been almost private preserves of their grandee commanders (who were often governors) because they appointed the colonels and through them the captains, Louis got control of officer appointments (by means to be described), and within a short time turned the forces into the docile instruments of himself and his war ministers. The army was at once domesticated, civilianized, and nationalized.

The growing powers of the *intendants* and the subjection of the royal commanders—all grandees—to the monarch's personal will would suggest at first sight their extrusion from their former pre-eminence, and currency has been given to this by the well-known fact that Louis expected them to appear at court and cut them off from their local influence and clienteles. This was not the way of it. It is true that one of the king's first acts was to ban members of the royal family from his *Conseil d'en Haut*, and to rely upon ministers who were by no means *noblesse de l'épée*. But Louis depended on the latter as they did on him. To get at the notables in the localities, the members of the *États*, the *parlement*, the towns, and so forth so as to co-operate with the officials who carried out his wishes, he had to work through them. In return they needed—or coveted—pensions, places, and honours which could only come from him. The *haute noblesse* was still in being and still powerful and he was part of them, albeit their head. It has been shown that there was a small group of noblemen who consorted and gave advice to

the king whose names we know, and others, anonymous, but whose existence can be confirmed.[54]

The court—and by this I include the great secretaries of state—was the
centre of government where policy was decided: a European-style Palace
polity, in effect.

2.5.4. LOUIS'S STYLE

Louis's style was polite but peremptory and overpowering. Officials and
courtiers would tremble when called to the royal presence. When occasion
demanded it—as in his 1657 confrontation with the Paris *parlement*—he
could thunder, but to suggest that all the changes we have described were
effected by his personal fiat would be quite wrong. Most, in fact, were
brought about by a mixture of pressures, persuasion, blandishments and
rewards, and so forth. There was much more give-and-take in his regime
than the 'Sun-King' formulists believed.

With popular riot and rebellion breaking out every year through famine
or extortionate taxation, with the lesser nobility sinking ever deeper into
indigence and later, as his wars opened, with French disaffection (e.g. the
Camisards) inviting foreign fomentation, the king had to manage his *haute
noblesse* as all previous monarchs had, by dispensing favours. The great
difference was that now everything had to come through him. He and
nobody else would grant the favours, and they had to be asked for. It is not
true, as the received wisdom had it, that Louis insisted on the magnates
attending his court: as we saw, the high nobility had been drifting towards it
of their own accord for some time. But those who did not attend could
expect nothing. When somebody asked him to favour an individual who had
failed to court him, his reply would be: 'I never see him . . . . Everything that
is a favour must be asked for personally.'[55]

Again it was not sheer royal *diktat* that made the *parlements* so unusually
docile. In the Paris *parlement*, at any rate, bribes and favours were freely used;
in the provinces the *intendants* supervised the *parlements'* activities, reported to
the king on their members, presided, if they so wished, over their inferior
tribunals, and removed special cases (*évocation*) from their jurisdiction to go
straight up to the king's council.

Likewise with the provincial *États*, though this often proved a more
difficult operation. The *États* were a vital source of finance; their jurisdiction
covered one-quarter of the kingdom. Here there might be endless chaffering
admixed with pressures, favours, bribes, and persuasions of all kinds, till at
last a bargain was struck. In these assemblies the *intendant* was at a dis-

---

[54] Mettam, *Power and Faction*, 86–96.   [55] Lavisse, *Louis XIV*, i. 128–9.

advantage; he was of relatively lowly status compared with some of the noble and ecclesiastic members of the *États*, and it was the governor who in fact conducted the protracted negotiations.[56]

The way Louis remodelled the army and brought it under his direct control is an excellent example of how he went about politically sensitive business. As we saw earlier, he had begun to infiltrate the governors' garrisons with his own household troops from the first moment he assumed personal rule. Now, he took pains to control the appointment of officers. 'I also took trouble to make all appointments myself, down to the most inferior ranks, in the infantry as well as the cavalry: something my predecessors had never done before, having always relied on the Grand Officers to whom this function had come to belong as an attribute of their dignity.' These 'Grand Officers' were the colonel-generals of the infantry and of the cavalry and the grand master of the artillery. Between 1661 and 1669 Louis bought them all back.

Having taken over the appointment of officers, Louis then infiltrated his own household *fidèles* into the rest of the army. 'For a long time past', he wrote in 1666, 'I had taken pains to train household troops and it was from them that I took nearly all the officers for the new companies raised.'[57]

He could not but leave the colonels and the captains in place because they had bought their posts, but he had his two redoubtable ministers of war, Le Tellier and Louvois, create intermediate ranks—lieutenant-colonel, major, and lieutenant—which were in the free gift of the king.

Le Tellier and Louvois brought the army under an exclusively civil administration which inspected and controlled them. At the top were *inspecteurs-généraux*, below them the *intendants de l'armée*, and at the base the war commissioners and *trésoriers extraordinaires*. Among other things, this administration confirmed whether the due number of troops had been enlisted, looked out for cheating on the muster-rolls, stopped officers taking unauthorized leave, and so forth; but its most important task, performed by Tellier, then Louvois (to 1691), and then by the king himself, was to subordinate the entire conduct of war to this civil authority. The supreme direction of war lay in the hands of the secretary for war and the quartermaster-general. Nor were these secretaries of war themselves soldiers. They had served their apprenticeship as *conseillers d'état* or *maîtres de requêtes* or *intendants*. In his *Mémoires* Louis would have one believe that the machinery of warfare was as precise as the movements of a clock of which he was the prime mover.[58] Certainly, the War Ministry meticulously organized the

[56] Mettam, *Power and Faction*, gives many examples.   [57] Louis XIV, *Mémoires*, ii. 237–8.
[58] Ibid. 277.

logistics of a campaign and its correlated activities and there are some instances of Louis's personal interference with the course of the campaign.[59] But by and large he and his ministers left tactics to the field commander and concerned themselves with planning and organizing objectives and strategy, giving the commanders a general 'intention'. With this the latter had no choice but to comply since the War Ministry allocated their troops and supplies with specific relation to the projects assigned to them. There are some examples to the contrary, for example, Louis could not make Vendôme send troops across the Alps to reinforce the armies in Italy. The *Mémoires* make everything look tidy. 'Haphazard', however, is what one historian calls Louis's interventions and adds that the king's power was certainly real but rarely used.[60]

2.5.5. TO WHAT EFFECT?

The case for 'royal absolutism' was this. In law, he was the supreme lawgiver; justice was royal and in the last resort the king could 'evoke' cases from the ordinary courts or use his powers of *justice retenue* to override their decision, just as he had means to override the sovereign courts, the *parlements*; the army was the royal army with the king himself as commander-in-chief; he was head of the Gallican Church; and he was the supreme executive. And—to give effect to his status he had at his command an administraive network of *commis*, the *intendants*, and a regular army. So the notion is born of a supreme potentate whose wish was law.

It was not like that. Consider first the dead weights on his activities. The first that springs to mind is the 60,000 or so inferior officials who could not be sacked and at their low-lying level were, really, independent of the king. Then there follow the *parlements*, the local *États*, and the *haute noblesse*.

The *intendants* have been seen as the instruments that got rid of these albatrosses. This was not quite the way of it. The *intendants* did certainly supervise that inferior bureaucracy and to that extent rationalized it and limited (they could never abolish) corruption. But they had to work in close conjunction with the two other powerful forces, the local nobility and the *États*. In both of them the high nobility played a key role embodied in the office of the governor. For all the attention we have bestowed on the *intendants*, the governors still 'governed' their *gouvernements*—they were in general charge of all that took place in it. As we have seen, the *intendants* tended to be *personae gratae* with governors—collaborators rather than watch-dogs. But as this implies, the governors could have their way just as much if not more than the *intendants*. These governors, it must be remembered, were

---

[59] For instances, see Wolf, *Louis XIV*, 548, 555, 560, 561, 566–7.   [60] Ibid. 645.

from among the very highest stratum of the *noblesse* and *intendants* were by comparison middle nobles. Governors were not necessarily sinecurists; on the contrary, many governors conducted detailed inquiries into economic and social conditions and took a local view whereas, it would be fair to say, the *intendants* represented a Paris view of the provinces. It was in the *pays d'états* that the three-cornered relationship between the great aristocratic governors, the middle-ranking *intendants*, and the *États*, with their complement of high-flying ecclesiastical and aristocratic notabilities, took place. *Intendants* were really of no social stature to bargain with such bodies. This was the governors' role and it was they who acted as the intermediaries when the issue was one of how much tax the *États* should offer.

We come to the *parlements*. Note that they had not *lost* their right to remonstrate; it had been truncated, so that willy-nilly the king's command was to prevail. However, the king not infrequently made use of the Paris *parlement* to give juridical support to some particular claim or action, while the *parlement* itself could still summon up enough audacity to resist the king on a matter it felt very strongly about. This is the lesson to be drawn from the conflict between Louis and the *parlement* in 1713 over the papal Bull *Unigenitus*. The background is both political and theological. As to the first, the *parlement* was rock firm on the 'Gallican' status of the Church in France and on some occasions, in fact, backed Louis in his resistance to the Papacy over this matter. Secondly, however, this Gallican Church contained many *tendances*, ranging from the Jansenist position at one end to the Jesuit position at the other, and from those dedicated to its independence of the pope in matters of doctrine to those—the ultramontanists—who looked to the pope for its definition. In his old age Louis had become more and more devout (or bigoted, as suits one's taste). He had got the pope in 1705 to issue a Bull condemning Jansenism, a highly unpopular move. In 1713 he returned to the matter and, much against the pope's will, got another Bull which condemned a long list of propositions and practices which it claimed were Jansenist. This aroused a tumult from many quarters. Numerous devout Catholics were shocked to find that beliefs and practices they had always deemed orthodox were 'Jansenist' after all. The *parlement* not only reflected these feelings—it felt that the king has betrayed Gallicanism by inviting and trying to enforce the pope's right to lay down doctrine. For the first time since 1673 it demanded to remonstrate, and this was followed by a long series of remonstrances, *lits de justice*, and exile for some parliamentarians. In the end the *parlement* gave way but not before adding as a rider to its act of registration that the Bull should be accepted only so far as it did not violate the Gallican liberties of the French Church.

In one respect, certainly, Louis did succeed in removing a powerful obstacle and turning it, at the same time, into an enormously powerful instrument of administration. This was the army. However much all the other policies might be unpicked in subsequent reigns, the army continued to be regular, professional, and subject to the civil power.

What is striking, and arguably more significant than the things Louis did, is the things he did *not* do. Basically what he did was to create instruments for taxation, military power, domestic order, and—a topic we have not mentioned—economic growth. But he left the country in the same juridical, economic, and social state of fragmentation as he found it.

Juridically, for instance: setting Canon law apart, the southern regions were subject to the written Roman law whereas the north was governed by a medley of regional and local customs. This broad division is an enormous over-simplification because in various areas seigneurial *ordonnances*, royal legislation, and the decrees of seigneurial and municipal courts had modified the law. Moreover, it does not take account of the multiplicity of courts. There were 80,000 seigneurial courts which, technically inferior and subject to appeal to the royal courts, dealt, as courts of first instance, with a wide variety of civil and criminal matters; and some seigneurs even dispensed 'high justice' which gave them powers of capital punishment. Nor should we forget that the various executive agencies of government, such as the *greniers* or the administrators of the royal waterways and forests, the admiralty, the customs, the royal mints, and so forth all heard cases in courts of their own.[61]

Nor was France a politically solid unity. It housed several independent enclaves such as Avignon, Mulhouse, Orange, and others. The boundaries of the jurisdictions of the *généralités*, the *parlements*, the ecclesiastical dioceses, and the thirty-nine *gouvernements* all differed from one another.

The fiscal system was similarly fragmented. The *gabelle* varied from those areas called the *pays de grande gabelle* to those of the *pays redimés*, and the price of the salt varied quite enormously between these areas. There was a similar fragmentation in the customs system. The country was criss-crossed by internal tolls, customs barriers, and seigneurial dues, and much of France found it freer to trade with the foreigner than with a very large part of French territory.[62]

In short, there was a great gap between the juridical claims of French absolutism and its actual exercise. What is more, a good deal of it was unpicked in the subsequent reigns. Not the Intendancies nor the regular army, certainly; but the *parlements* regained their powers to delay royal

---

[61] Parker, *Making of French Absolutism*, 22–3.   [62] *CMH*, vii. 215–16.

legislation through remonstrances (and were to use them to far-reaching effect during the eighteenth century), and the *États* became ever-more self-assertive. As Cobban puts it: 'If we compare the French monarchy in the eighteenth century with practically any other European monarchy of the same period, the striking fact that emerges is the comparative effectiveness of the limitations on royal power in France.'[63]

Yet this regime was taken as the classical model of absolutism in Europe. Why? One reason lies in the very size, wealth, and military power of the kingdom and what at times appeared its near-domination of Europe. France had 20 million inhabitants and was by far the most populous unitary state on the Continent. Next, the grandeur with which Louis surrounded himself: it is no accident, for instance, that Frederick II's palace of Sans-Souci was built to emulate Versailles. The king's power was attested—and adulated—by a string of teams of propagandists as well as by many of his courtiers, and by historians like Voltaire in his *Siècle de Louis Quatorze*.

But having said all this, let me stress that the fact that the French monarchy found itself thwarted and obstructed does not detract from its claim to be absolute. The point was made earlier in this *History* that all European absolute monarchies, and for that matter most of the Oriental ones, were expected to operate within traditional laws and customs of their countries. Had Louis had no such obstacles to surmount, had he indeed governed by simple fiat, then he would have been, in our definition, not an absolute monarch but a despot. This is indeed what many writers and intellectuals were beginning to call him in his last years. They were wrong. Louis was an absolute monarch. He was not a despot.

In England, however, in contrast to France and all the European absolutisms that imitated her, there evolved a limited and parliamentary form of government and, also, the prototype of the competitive political party. So, against the absolutist trend emerged an antithetical political tradition.

3. THE ENGLISH ALTERNATIVE

3.1. *The Line of March*

The English monarchy travelled in the very opposite direction to that of France in respect of what follows. Both exercised very wide personal discretionary power. It is true that the king of France had the advantage of the Tudors in so far as he was fiscally absolute, could legislate at pleasure, and possessed a corps of professional officials and a standing army. For all

---

[63] Cobban, *Aspects of the French Revolution*, 68.

that, the discretionary powers of a king of England were not small. He was 'His Majesty'. He held his throne by divine right. He was head of the nation's Church. Though he could not make statutes or impose direct taxes without the assent of Parliament, most times he simply did not need to. It was *his* Parliament. It met only when he called it and sat only as long as he wanted it to. Intervals of several years elapsed between one Parliament and another. It was there to do the king's business, with no legislative initiative.[64] A king could do without it for long stretches at a time because certain revenues could be raised through his personal prerogative, for example, new customs duties ('impositions'), benevolences, and 'forced loans'; and likewise, the prerogative allowed him to issue proclamations, that is, wide-sweeping administrative ordinances. He could even bend existing statutes quite a lot: in part by dispensing particular persons from their application or by a general suspension (the *non obstante* clause), in part through his power to appoint or dismiss his judges. Moreover, he had courts outside the ancient common law courts: the Council and the Court of Star Chamber acted by summary inquisitorial procedure, could impose fines (and, sometimes, 'unusual' punishments), and by these means could and did control local administration in the person of the lord-lieutenants and the justices of the peace—all of whom were in any case appointed and dismissed by him. The law, the prerogative, and the courts all combined to restrict civil liberties: by enforced religious conformity, censorship, and a highly elastic definition of treason which extended beyond overt acts to what were held to be seditious words.

As we have already said, both the French and English monarchies were cluttered by medieval survivals: the former by *États*, *parlements*, and the like, the English monarchy with its Parliament, medieval-type militia-army, and so forth. But whereas the seventeenth-century French trend was to concentrate the powers of these encumbering institutions in the person of the king, in England it was just the reverse. There were at least two periods when the king appeared to be able and willing to follow the French example and, by neutralizing or abolishing Parliament, take all legislative and taxing powers to himself, but this did not in fact happen. On the contrary: the general direction in which England moved was to *dismember* the Tudor concentration of powers, and scatter them between a number of discrete and largely autonomous organs. What was still, say in 1603, a concentration of powers in the person of the monarch ends, in 1714, in a flexible and complex system of 'checks and balances'. From a near-absolute monarchy, England became a crowned nobiliar republic.

---

[64] Compare it in these respects with the various Cortes in Aragon, see pp. 1289–90 above.

3.2. *The Course of Events, 1603–1714: A Teleological Guide*

This guide is avowedly teleological and has to be because it openly sets out to highlight the incidents and developments that, with hindsight, are seen to be significant in the movement towards a *telos* that I want to describe. That *telos* is the so-called 'balanced constitution' of 1714 or, as some historians prefer, 1727. I am not averring that the actors in this century were motivated by a clear—or even an obscure—intention to arrive at this kind of constitution. I do not say that these developments were necessary. I am simply saying that such is the *telos* at which those developments happened to arrive.

Just as in the case of France, so with England we have to begin with a statement of the social composition of the Stuart machinery of administration. The four great differences between the absolutism of the king of France and the relative limitation of the English monarchy were, we may recall, that the former could strike taxes and make laws at pleasure and was served by a standing army and paid professional bureaucracy.

At this time, it has been estimated, there were some 20,000 *officiers* in French local government. But in England there were almost none except a few paid parish clerks or overseers of the poor.[65] The lord-lieutenants, the JPs, the local tax-commissioners, the officers of the unpaid shire-levy that passed for the army, all came from a limited class, the nobility and gentry, and they were *lay* administrators. Even so, a fair proportion of them had studied law and about a quarter of the JPs had actually been called to the Bar. Moreover, Quarter Sessions required a quorum of lawyers. Furthermore, lawyers attended the Sessions more regularly than the other members,[66] appointed and removable by the Crown but serving honorifically. In each shire some eighty families regularly filled the posts of JP or tax-commissioner, while some twenty or thirty of the more influential among them would provide the lord-lieutenant and deputy lieutenants and the MPs. They were united by marriage alliances; they regularly met and socialized with one another at the Quarter Sessions and the Assizes; and they dominated the House of Commons which became their 'peculiar institution', their national headquarters, so to speak. Thus the parliamentary class dominating Parliament, the national paymaster, were the assessors of tax in their localities, and the officers of the shire-levy.

Now once the King of France 'domesticated' the grand nobility, as we

---

[65] 'Most of the lower officials were paid, and even if they only worked part-time in public affairs they certainly were not honorary officials like the Justices of the Peace themselves.' W. Fischer and P. Lundgren, 'The Recruitment and Training of Administrative and Technical Personnel', in C. Tilly (ed.), *The Formation of National States in Western Europe* (Princeton UP, Princeton, 1975), 479.

[66] Ibid. 478.

have just described, he was left in direct and unimpeded command of his army and paid local officials. In short, he had a machinery of government. But a king of England could not dispense with his gentry at all, because this would leave him facing his subjects without any local services or army whatsoever.

The plain truth was the law, as they [*sc.* the gentry] practised and understood it, and the local administration of England, had made the ordinary life of the country depend at every point on them and hardly at all upon the Crown. The entire machine—law-courts, parishes, poor law, city and country—could run very well without the King; but it could not run without the gentry. In other words the gentry were essential to the power of the King, but he was not essential to theirs.[67]

Why did he not establish a paid army and bureaucracy like his French counterpart? The answer is obvious: he had no resources that would remotely have made this possible, because they lay in the hands of the House of Commons, that is, the gentry. The King could not force it to grant him supply because he had no standing trained army, and the reason for this was that Parliament refused him money. At the beginning of the seventeenth century, then, the gentry are central to any explanation of what was to happen.

3.2.1. THE FIRST MOVE TOWARDS ABSOLUTISM: 1629–1640

We are not called on to pronounce on the causes of the Civil Wars, about which a most ill-tempered controversy rages. It suffices to say that the Commons and King Charles I quarrelled over a number of things which included foreign policy, commercial policy, taxation, and civil liberties (and the liberties of the Commons). One of these issues was outstanding enough to play the decisive role in the events of the second half of the century too, and this was religion. Charles I was very High Church, so much so as to provoke fears that this was a mere prelude to Roman Catholicism against which the country and the large Puritan component in the Commons were obsessively opposed.

After increasingly bitter disputes between the Commons and himself, King Charles decided to do without Parliament and rule by his prerogative powers alone. He was surprisingly successful. He cut his expenses by a policy of peace and increased his revenue by using prerogative forms of taxation that lay outside Parliament's authority. They included the scrupulous collection of antique feudal dues (e.g. wardship), benevolences, and forced loans, and above all the constitutionally 'grey' area of tonnage and

---

[67] C. V. Wedgwood, *The Great Rebellion: The King's Peace, 1637–1641* (Collins, London, 1956), 367.

poundage. In 1634 he imposed ship-money on the coastal shires and this was another unquestionably extra-parliamentary prerogative tax whose antiquity went back as far as the Anglo-Saxons.[68] In 1635, when the writ was addressed to all the counties and not just the coastal ones, the parliamentary class decided that it was going to be a permanent impost. The judges found for the Crown against Hampden's legal challenge to it.

Meanwhile Charles was making the JPs do more and do better. Through his Council and his Court of Star Chamber, he tightened up their administration of the poor law and other social measures. He also designed to improve the militia by making the gentry-officers enforce training-drills and musters and the like, in order to form what was called a 'perfect' or an 'exact' militia. Similarly tough action by the prerogative Court of High Commission enforced the detested Arminian Church policy. Things appeared to be going exactly as Charles wished—the euthanasia of Parliament.

Nemesis came in 1638 when his attempt to enforce a new Prayer-book on the Presbyterian congregations of his other kingdom, Scotland, provoked rebellion. Charles abandoned his 1638 campaign owing to the inadequacy and reluctance of the shire levies. In 1639 he began a second campaign, but the shire levies wanted no fight and indeed sympathized with the religious views of the Scots. These promptly occupied the six northern shires and charged Charles £860 per day occupation-money until and unless he made peace. The king had no alternative but to fall back on Parliament. To the abortive Short Parliament of 1640 there succeeded the Long Parliament in November of the same year. Here the Commons was unanimous on a wide programme. The prerogative courts of Star Chamber, the provincial councils, and the Court of High Commission were swept away, leaving justice exclusively to the Common Law courts. The Triennial Act made Parliament a permanent, not an intermittent feature of the constitution. And they blocked (so they imagined) every modality of extra-parliamentary, prerogative taxation.

In November 1641 the Irish rebelled, massacring the Protestant settlers. The king asked Parliament for money to fund an army but the Commons would not trust him with one and drafted a bill (1642) to transfer the control of the militia from the king to itself. Charles refused assent and Parliament split. A slender majority passed a bill, which lacked the necessary royal assent, to raise an army which should be under its control. Charles responded by raising his standard, supported by some half of the gentry—the Cavaliers. Civil war broke out, Charles was comprehensively beaten, and,

[68] *Scip-socn.*

having reopened the war in alliance with the Presbyterian Scots (1648) and lost it, was publicly beheaded by the decision of the Long Parliament in 1649. A parliamentary republic, the Commonwealth, was proclaimed.

3.2.2. COMMONWEALTH AND PROTECTORATE

Until 1653 the country was run by a set of parliamentary committees but, these proving ineffective, it was replaced by the Protectorate—a kind of surrogate monarchy—of Oliver Cromwell. Throughout the entire Interregnum, however, the real political power was the New Model Army which Cromwell commanded. It assured the government of a tax-revenue five times greater than that which the gentry had reprobated under Charles, most of it spent on the expanded navy and large New Model Army. It strikingly demonstrates the basic technique of absolutism: high taxation enforced by a standing army which in turn is maintained by the high taxation it enforces—the 'coercion–extraction cycle'. It was especially visible after 1655 when Cromwell divided the country into eleven districts each supervised by a major-general, not unlike French *intendants*. But this absolutist government lacked one essential quality: legitimacy. It was regarded overseas and by increasing numbers at home as an unmitigated tyranny, and when Cromwell died its illegitimacy caused it to crumble. The dominant faction in the army invited Charles II to return, which he did in 1660. All legislation of the Interregnum from 1641 was declared null and disappeared from the statute books.

3.2.3. THE RESTORATION, 1660–1685

The revisionist historians are wrong to argue that the Civil War was constitutionally indecisive in that the 1660 Restoration simply restored the 1641 *status quo*. Not so: the prerogative courts—Star Chamber, High Commission, and the provincial councils—were not restored; the laws precluding the Crown from raising taxation and legislating except through Parliament were maintained. Secondly, hatred of Catholicism—associated with French absolutism ('no Popery, no wooden shoes')—had become fanatical. Again, the experience of the Interregnum had intensified a number of popular and/or gentry attitudes, among which were an abiding hatred of a peacetime standing army, abhorrence of Puritanism and the dissenting sects, a passionate devotion to Anglicanism, and a fervent popular royalism which fused together the divine right of kings, Anglicanism, and passive obedience.

Moreover, politics, hitherto centred on the Court, shifted into a parliamentary mode. Charles II tried to do without Parliament by taking undercover subsidies from Louis XIV, and when the customs and excise picked up with the rise of British commerce after 1679, he dispensed with Parliament and ruled by his prerogative powers alone. But the vigour and irrepressibility of Parliament was enhanced by the furious controversy that broke out over the prospect of a Catholic monarch, since the heir-apparent (James, duke of York, the king's brother) was a self-confessed Catholic. The parliamentary classes divided into those who wanted an Act to exclude James from the succession (hence 'Exclusionists') and the court faction, which stuck firmly to the doctrine of the divine right of kings and passive obedience. The former, led by Lord Shaftesbury, repeatedly tried to get Parliament to pass an Exclusion Act and were just as frequently thwarted by Charles. The two sides in this Exclusion crisis vigorously—and corruptly—contested the elections and can fairly be viewed as the prototype of political parties; for, though their formal organization was rudimentary and their local adherents scarcely saw beyond county horizons, they were brought together on a 'cry' and on 'instructions' they were to force upon their candidates in return for their votes. Embryonic, they yet served to give organization to the electoral contests that occurred more and more frequently because of the steady increase in the size of the electorate and the realization that almost the only way to wealth, honours, and office was now through Parliament. The elections were conducted with bribery and fiddling of the electoral rolls, with the result that the court party and the Exclusionists party—which at this time called itself the Whigs—alternated in the control of the Commons. Each strove to destroy the other and rule *alone*, and to this end every change of majority led to a massive purge of offices which became the spoils of the victor.

3.2.4. THE SECOND DRIVE TO ABSOLUTISM: JAMES II

James II was a confirmed Catholic whose devotion to that persuasion was unbudgeable. Whether he tried to Catholicize British institutions in order to become absolute or tried to become absolute in order to Catholicize those institutions, or whether as some apologists aver he was doing neither, but simply trying to introduce religious toleration, is very hard to say—and it does not much matter. The irreducible historical facts are that a large number of highly placed personages *believed* he was trying to Catholicize and that in pursuit of his aim (whatever that might have been) he adopted clumsy and highly suspect methods that, unchecked, could have, and many say would have, led him to become as absolute as Oliver Cromwell but more dangerous because, unlike Cromwell, James was legitimate.

James was capable of threatening to undermine nascent parliamentarism because, unlike his predecessors, he had enough money to pay for a standing army, and once in that position a king or prince could carry on and use the one to enlarge the other, as the later case study of Prussia demonstrates so well. His now ample supply of money derived from the tonnage and poundage which, by custom, were voted for life on a king's accession and had now become highly productive owing to the sharp upturn in British commerce. So James did not depend on Parliament for supply. With this extra-parliamentary revenue he could maintain and expand the tiny standing army which Parliament had voted Charles II in 1660: three or four thousand garrison troops and a personal bodyguard, to which two regiments of the New Model Army (now demobilizing) were added when Parliament was terrified by the Fifth Monarchy Man Venner's rising in 1661. In 1663 Charles II's army numbered 4,878 garrison troops and 3,574 regimental ones.[69]

James's intention was to surround himself with Catholic officers and ministers. This entailed breaking the Anglican monopoly of public office and hence the repeal of the Test Act (1673) which obliged all office-holders to have taken communion in the Anglican mode. Parliament refused to repeal this Act, so James prorogued it—and Parliament never met again under his authority. To evade Parliament's refusal, James fell back on his undoubted prerogative power to dispense with the law in particular cases, and used this to commission a Catholic officer. He then hand-picked a bench of judges and brought a collusive case before them to determine whether his action was legal. They duly found for him (*Godden* v. *Hales*, 1686), whereupon he promptly replaced numerous Anglican JPs with Catholics (and Dissenters), admitted some highly dubious Catholic ministers to his Council, and appointed the Catholic Tyrconnel to govern Ireland, where he proceeded to overthrow the Protestant supremacy with a view to repealing the land settlement Acts and return the lands to their original Irish owners. Is it surprising that many Protestants saw these actions as deliberate moves to establish a Catholic supremacy? More of such actions were to follow. James ordered the bishop of London to suspend a controversial preacher and, when he refused, revived the prerogative Court of High Commission to discipline him—but then went on to use it to punish attacks on the Church of Rome. He also made use of this court to break the Anglican monopoly in the universities. In 1687 James issued a first Act of Indulgence which granted freedom of worship to both Catholics and Dissenters, and in 1688 a second one which he now ordered the entire clergy to read from their pulpits. Seven bishops petitioned the king to excuse the clergy from this duty. In reply James brought them to trial on a charge of seditious libel. The case turned on whether the dispensing power could be used not only to dispense

---

[69] C. Barnett, *Britain and her Army 1509–1970* (Penguin, Harmondsworth, 1974), 113–15. The New Model Army had been 40,000 strong.

particular individuals but also to suspend an entire class of statutes. The jury found against the king, amid wild and widespread rejoicing in which, ominously, the soldiers joined.

Plumb has said that the universality of the opposition that James had now aroused sprang not just from the individual measures recited above, but from 'his outright onslaught on the very basis of political power which if successful would have made the Stuarts as absolute as their French and Spanish cousins'.[70] The dramatic sequel was precipitated by the birth of a male heir, for this guaranteed that the Catholicizing policy would be perpetuated. But fear of his now 30,000 strong army was too great for political opponents to consider resistance except with the aid of an outside power, for they trembled at how brutally the king had crushed the Protestant duke of Monmouth's rising only three years before. Finally a small group of Whig notabilities turned for help to the Dutch and fiercely Protestant Prince William of Orange and Mary, his equally staunchly Protestant wife, who was James II's own daughter. William landed his army, key officers of James's army defected to him, and risings broke out in the north. Overcome with panic, James fled the country, leaving to a new, 'Convention' Parliament the task of deciding what to do in this extraordinary situation.

3.2.5. THE REVOLUTION SETTLEMENT, 1688–1701

Parliament declared that James had abdicated and recognized William and Mary as king and queen, and accompanied this by passing the Bill of Rights: a much watered-down version of a Declaration of Rights. For all that the Bill of Rights made parliamentary consent necessary for the Crown to use the dispensing and suspending power or maintain a standing army in peacetime, these have appeared to some revisionist historians to be very insignificant consequences.[71] In fact, as we shall see, the Revolution and the Bill of Rights opened the way for a series of Acts which widely extended civil liberties as well as definitively transforming Parliament into a permanent and central organ of the constitution. One further consequence was the Act of Union, 1707, which dissolved both the English and Scottish Parliaments and created instead a single Parliament of Great Britain in which both were represented. In this way the two distinct kingdoms ceased

---

[70] J. H. Plumb, *The Growth of Political Stability in England, 1675–1725* (Macmillan London, 1967), 62.

[71] Amazing people! First they maintain that the Civil Wars were constitutionally indecisive in that the *status quo ante bellum* was restored in 1660. Now they claim that the Bill of Rights was insignificant too. If both these propositions are true, the constitutional situation in 1689 is identical with that in the 1630s—which is manifestly absurd.

to be united only by a personal union, and became a single constitutional unit.

The period ushered in party strife of a frequency and intensity that would never be repeated in the entire period 1714–1830. The Whigs were the party of the court, of Dissent, of the monied interests and Bank of England, and of the Continental wars, especially the protracted War of the Spanish Succession. The Tories were the party of the country squires, of the Anglican Church, of the landed interest, and of peace. The frequent elections were fought with gerrymandering and the spoils system, so that the majorities veered from one party to another and the Crown had to tack and veer after each election in order to maintain its policies. Parliament was a loose cannon and not surprisingly it was at this period that, through its control over supply, it was able to investigate the conduct of the executive branch, call for accounts, and influence the royal prerogatives of war and diplomacy. This is the moment when it most nearly resembles what the American 1787 Constitution would be.

3.2.6. THE 'CROWNED (AND NOBILIAR) REPUBLIC': 1701–1714

In 1701 a new Act of Settlement was passed excluding the descendants of James II (fervent Catholics) and vesting the succession in the next heir (very distant in line), to wit, Sophia, duchess of Hanover and her heirs (if Protestant). The initiative came from William III, but the bill was drafted by a Tory-dominated Commons largely opposed to William. Hence the clauses that, *inter alia*, restrict the Crown's freedom in foreign policy (Act of Settlement, 1701, section III), define the status of the Privy Council, and as so often before, restrict the right of office-holders ('placemen') to sit as MPs: all of them were thinly veiled Tory censures on William. (The clauses concerning the judges and impeachments are commented on further below.)

Not all Tories were enamoured of this Hanoverian succession. They regarded hereditary descent as indefeasible but realized that if strictly followed it must lead to the Stuart pretender, a Catholic, ascending the throne. Some—the 'Jacobites'—dickered with this alternative and a minority espoused it. By the time Anne was dying, in 1714, her successor under the 1701 Settlement was George, the son of the deceased Princess Sophia. In 1714 the succession passed peacefully to him. His Council of Regency was composed almost entirely of Whig lords: not unsurprisingly, since he bore the Tories a terrible grudge for having pulled out of the Continental war against France (in which he too was engaged) by the Treaty of Utrecht in 1713. The Whigs were able to taint the Tories with the Jacobite brush and the indiscretions of a few Tory rank and file associated them with the Jacobite rising of 1715. The Whigs took advantage of the 1715 election to sack Tory appointees and give their posts to Whigs on an unprecedented scale. This ushered in a half-century of undiluted Whig majorities, something that enabled Robert Walpole to form the first 'one-colour' administration in 1721. The role of ministers was to act as middlemen between the Crown, with its remaining prerogatives of appointing and dismissing ministers and conducting foreign policy, and the Commons, with its own undoubted monopolies over finance and legislation. Unlike the future American 1787 Constitution, the Commons had largely failed to exclude 'placemen' from its membership. The placemen were in the gift of the Crown. The Crown could support its minister with this vast patronage, who used it to influence the elections and likewise the House of Commons. Thus, for the first time in a century the executive and the legislative branches were brought into harmony, and a long period of constitutional stability ensued.

3.3. The Deconstruction of the 1603 Constitution

3.3.1. DECOUPLING LOCAL GOVERNMENT FROM CENTRAL GOVERNMENT

The basic units of local government were the parish, county, and the municipal corporations. The latter were all incorporated (or legally deemed to be so) by Charter. By this time town government rested mostly (but not always) with certain narrow groups with powers to co-opt, a tendency accelerated by the machinations of all governments to control the House of Commons, since the boroughs returned four out of every five MPs. Hence the multiplication of boroughs, the amendment of their Charters, and the reallocation of their voting-rights. These contributed to their general demoralization and corruption. The party interventions also help explain the wide variety of borough franchises.

Outside the municipal boroughs the parish had become the maid-of-all-work after the Elizabethan Poor Law Act of 1601 imposed on it the duty of electing 'overseers of the poor' who were to strike a rate and disburse it in the interests of the poor. Thereafter further tasks relating to roads, watch and ward, and an entire miscellany of social services were heaped on them. The overseers, the surveyors of roads, the petty constables, and the posses whom they could call out, served obligatorily and without pay. Originally these parishes were open: that is, the elections of the Church authorities and the civil officials we have named were made by the entire body of parishioners. Latterly, legislation had often restricted this power to a narrow select group: such were the closed vestries.

General control over the parishes vested in the JPs. Some powers could be exercised by a single JP. Sitting probably in his own house, he could summarily order the punishment of any individual for swearing, being drunk, or poaching; could exact security from parish officers on mere suspicion of defalcations; could order the punishment of unmarried mothers and vagrants. Petty Sessions of two Justices appointed the overseers of the poor and surveyors of roads, fixed the poor rate, and audited the parishes' accounts. But the Quarter Sessions was a powerful court of the entire bench, surpassed only by the royal judges coming down in Assizes. They ordered the striking of rates for such matters as repair of bridges and upkeep of jails, they could fix wages, license trades, and were the court of appeal from petty sessions. That purely administrative functions should be carried out by judicial magistrates was a carry-over, of course, from the practice of the Middle Ages. It singularly refutes Montesquieu's view that in England the two were kept strictly separate.

Now up to 1641 these magistrates had been kept up to the mark and subjected to ever-stricter controls by the Council and notably the Court of Star Chamber. These could deal summarily with what they regarded as disobedience or negligence. With their demise in 1641, central administrative control lapsed altogether. Only the common law courts could now act. The procedure for doing so was very cumbersome[72] and actions were few and far between. As Basil Williams put it, 'instead of being mainly agents of an almost autocratic government, they [the JP's] acquired virtual independence as the local oligarchies of the districts'.[73] The Justices, as he rightly adds, were so many 'local despots'.[74]

In this way and in complete contradiction with what was happening in the absolutisms of Europe, the entire local administration of the country was dissociated from central control. When one remembers that the scope of central government was confined (except for a service like the post office, perhaps) to defence, justice, and the taxation to pay for them, and that everything that touched day-to-day life was carried out through the local authorities, one comprehends the magnitude of what this grand decoupling signified.

[72] Holdsworth, *A History of English Law*, x. 156–7.
[73] B. Williams, *The Whig Supremacy, 1714–1760*, The Oxford History of England (Clarendon Press, Oxford, 1962), 51.   [74] Ibid. 52.

3.3.2. DECOUPLING THE JUDICIARY FROM EXECUTIVE AND/OR LEGISLATIVE CONTROL

The judiciary too was decoupled from the main apparatus of central government. This was done in two ways. One was the triumph of the common law courts over the prerogative courts. When dealing with matters like conspiracy the prerogative court judges were apt to think in terms of public policy. In contrast, the common lawyers put their emphasis on the private rights of individuals and especially on their property rights. In its zeal for the safety of the state the Star Chamber summoned the accused to answer not only to matters specified in the bill issued against him, but to other unspecified matters, too; whereas the writ, as issued in common law practice, required the defendant to answer only to the charges specified therein. Finally, unlike the common law courts, the Star Chamber did not use juries. In resisting the Star Chamber's encroachments on the protective procedures of the common law, these common law judges were at one with the House of Commons in its self-assertive mood of the 1630s. This alliance of common law courts and the legislature contrasted with the position in France where the *parlements* were the main check on royal legislating. Thus the first way in which the judiciary were decoupled from the executive came about by the abolition of all the prerogative courts by the 1641 Act. All suits were now adjudged by one single set of courts strongly assertive of the property rights of the individual.

The judiciary was decoupled from the executive in another way, also. The early Stuart judges were dismissible by the Crown, and that power was actually exercised, for example, in the dismissal of Chief Justice Coke. The judges' dependency continued after the Restoration and was certainly responsible for upholding James II's right to the dispensing powers in the case of *Godden* v. *Hales* (1686), where James hand-picked the bench. The independence of the judges was not enacted in the Bill of Rights, and it was left to the Act of Settlement, 1701, to lay down unambiguously that 'Judges' Commissions be made *quamdiu se bene gesserint* [for as long as they act well] and their salaries ascertained and established; but upon the address of both Houses of Parliament it may be lawful to remove them'. (This provision was only once invoked, in the case of a drunken Irish judge in 1830.)

From now on the judiciary was entirely free-standing, bound only by statute. This decoupling of the judicature from the executive and for that matter from the legislature was, again, unique in Europe and it is not surprising that Montesquieu, himself a lawyer and member of the Bordeaux *parlement*, should have made its independence a central feature of his conception of the British constitution.

Another decoupling of the judicature fits logically here, though it had taken place long before, in 1670. Till then juries had to follow the directions of the trial judge under pain of a fine. *Bushell* had been a member of a jury that had acquitted the Quakers, William Penn and William Mead, and for its pains this jury had been fined 40 marks and then, in default, thrown into prison. The judge's reason was that they had acted 'against the plain and manifest evidence and against the direction of the court in respect to the law'. The Chief Justice struck down this reason as altogether insufficient and from then on juries were free to acquit or not as seemed right to them. And here one must remark that the very notion of trial by jury was virtually unknown to continental Europe. It was a very material safeguard to civil rights, as was proved by the jury's acquittal of the Seven Bishops in 1688, and it is no wonder that the Liberal revolutionaries of the mid-nineteenth century all made jury trial a central demand. The legal expression for opting for jury trial is 'throws himself upon the [verdict of the] country'. It was an important popular element in any constitution.

3.3.3. DECOUPLING THE SUBJECT FROM THE STATE

It would be pointless to guarantee the independence of courts and juries if there were no civil rights to defend. But judicial independence combined with civil rights created a ring-fence around citizens, so decoupling them from the state.

The many civil rights enacted after 1670 were not a royal *ex gratia* dispensation but neither did they all spring from some deep-seated and unremitting commitment of Parliament to 'liberty'. Most were enacted, in fact, for somewhat discreditable party reasons.

The first of these rights—to religious toleration—only looks good if it is contrasted with most of the continent of Europe, and especially France where, after the revocation of the Edict of Nantes in 1685, there was none whatsoever. In the Republic of Holland the laws discriminated severely against some Protestant sects, and particularly harshly against Catholics, who were denied all citizen rights and were permitted to hold religious services only if they paid a fine. However, the laws were not enforced and the country enjoyed the reputation of being the most tolerant in Europe.[75] In this the Republic was not altogether dissimilar from England, where religious discrimination and persecution were far stricter in law than in actual practice.[76]

All the same, Catholics were treated quite abominably. They were still, in law, subject to the Elizabethan fines and penalties for saying Mass, for

---

[75] See e.g. *CMH*, v. 142–3.   [76] Williams, *The Whig Supremacy*, 74–5.

recusancy, and for teaching school. Restoration laws prohibited them from sitting in Parliament or on any municipal corporation, and from holding any office under the Crown.

Dissenters were treated marginally better, but the Corporation and the Test Acts obliged all holders of office in municipal corporations or holding any office of trust to take communion according to the Anglican rite. The Toleration Act of 1689 allowed them to build conventicles and worship the way they pleased, but the concession was partly reversed by the Tories under Queen Anne and, really, matters only began to improve at the Hanoverian succession. In 1728 Walpole's Indemnity Act (annually renewed), curiously, indemnified those holders of offices who had failed to take the requisite oath or to receive the sacrament. In short, the law was not repealed but those who failed to obey it were indemnified. This was, in effect, toleration. But efforts to repeal the Test and Corporation Acts outright failed. They were to remain in force till 1828, and the disabilities of Roman Catholics until the Catholic Emancipation Act of 1829.

Leaving this rather shabby story aside, the subject was in other important respects quite dramatically decoupled from the state. Arbitrary arrest was one such respect. The Habeas Corpus Act of 1679 restricted the executive's power to keep a subject in prison indefinitely. By granting the writ, the courts were ordering anybody who was unlawfully imprisoned or otherwise detained to be brought before them in person to face examination. The writ could be used against private persons—kidnappers for instance—but also against the king's officers. As Clark says, the 'contrast with the irresistible force of the French *lettres de cachet* was sharp'.[77]

Habeas Corpus did *not* apply to persons held on charges of treason or felony where, up to the Revolution, a suspect could be summarily arrested and face a trial with almost no procedural safeguards. The Bill of Rights of 1689 somewhat liberalized the Statute of Treason by providing that the charge must be supported by two witnesses, that the defendant must receive a copy of the indictment against him and, at the trial, be permitted the help of counsel. He was also to receive the names of all the jurors two days before the trial so that he could challenge. These important concessions greatly softened the impact of the non-applicability of the writ to cases of treason.

[77] G. N. Clark, *The Later Stuarts*, The Oxford History of England (Clarendon Press, Oxford, 1934), 95. But see J. R. Western, *Monarchy and Revolution: The English State in the 1680s* (Problems of History Paperbacks, Blandford, London, 1972), 64–5, who thinks it made very little difference—at this time, at least. His main case seems to be that 'the law defined political offences so widely that arbitrary powers of arrest were hardly necessary'. But this objection must fall for the period after 1688 once the law of treason was amended as described in the text.

The censorship of printed materials was frequently connected with the matter of treason: for example, an author or printer might be accused of publishing a seditious libel. The censorship was effectuated through confining publication to the presses of Oxford, Cambridge, and the London Stationers' Company. The Act which prescribed this monopoly was due to expire in 1695 and the Lords certainly wanted to renew it. However, it was unpopular for rather ludicrous party reasons: each of the two censors—one Whig and the other Tory—had in turn given offence by refusing to ban a work that especially annoyed their political opponents. What is more, the Commons resented the commercial monopoly of the London Stationers' Company. They refused to renew it, and since the two Houses could not agree the Act simply lapsed.

By this curious sequence of intentional, non-intentional, and inconsequential actions the liberties of the subject had been protected against arbitrary arrest and failure to bring to trial; against charges of plotting or practising treasonable activities; and against prior restraint. A fourth liberty, the liberty of domicile, was protected by the common law of trespass. Packaged together, these four freedoms added up to a liberty of person, domicile, and expression that surpassed anything in any other country of Europe except, perhaps, the Dutch Republic.

3.3.4. DECOUPLING THE EXECUTIVE FROM THE LEGISLATURE

Does this ring strangely—the *decoupling* of the executive from the legislature—when it is an elementary fact that the two are intimately linked through the presence of royal ministers in Parliament? This linkage is, indeed, held to be one of the most distinctive features of the British constitution. But whether king or Parliament had the upper hand in this linked—one might almost say *merged*—dyarchy is the central puzzle about the eighteenth-century constitution. But we must walk before we can run and that means distinguishing between the things that were the executive's and those that were the legislature's.

The Crown

The executive was (and still is) the Crown. This is not the same as the 'natural person' of the king or queen and herein lies the first difference between the character of the Hanoverians and the French Bourbons: the latter ruled in their own persons whereas the kings of Britain could personally do very little without the assent of Parliament. Clark asserts that the power of the monarchy increased after 1660;[78] but this is because he

---

[78] J. C. D. Clark, *Revolution and Rebellion: State and Society in England in the Seventeenth and Eighteenth Centuries* (CUP, Cambridge, 1986), 70.

fails to distinguish between the person of the king and the office he holds. It may well be that the monarchy was stronger, but if so that was because it had to work through a Parliament which itself was stronger. As an individual the monarch could effect far less on his own account than ever before. By 1701 he could not, as an individual, levy any tax, or legislate, or issue ordinances, or dispense or suspend the operation of laws, or dismiss his judges.[79] Indeed there were other, more personal restrictions on him: for instance, he had to be an Anglican, could not leave the country without Parliament's permission, and so forth.

The efficient secret of this chief executive was that it was free-standing and irremovable. There are lots of constitutions where the chief executive is elected and removed by the legislature at its pleasure, but the British monarch was a life executive and irremovable short of revolution. As far as administration was concerned this hereditary monarchical element gave as great a stability to the British polity as the strong monarchy did in France or Prussia.[80] By contrast, consider our remarks elsewhere on the debilitation of government in Poland because of its elective monarchy.

'Government' was unquestionably the king's government—the ministers were the king's ministers, the army His Majesty's Army, the navy the Royal Navy, and so forth. The practical reality of this was evidenced by the fact that it was still the king who paid the salaries of his major officials. They were borne on the 'Civil List'. Fees and percentages were one part of the pay of exalted public servants, but their regular salaries were charged to the Civil List. This was (and is) the annual income granted the sovereign to meet certain charges. It was supposed to bear the full cost of the royal household (as it is today) but also—and more importantly—the salaries of the judges, ambassadors, and ministers, as well as pensions granted in his and his predecessors' reigns. As it was a fixed sum for life (although it often got into debt and Parliament had to bail it out), these administrative salaries were a matter for the king and independent of parliament. Furthermore, the ministers of the Crown appointed their own subordinates who were sometimes paid fractions of a salary from the Civil List but, for the most part, were remunerated by fees and percentages in the course of their duties. Here again, Parliament had no say.[81]

---

[79] Cf. the extent of the personal powers of Louis XIV as described in the preceding pages.

[80] See R. Pares, *King George III and the Politicians* (Clarendon Press, Oxford, 1953) and *id.*, *Limited Monarchy in Great Britain in the Eighteenth Century* (Routledge & Kegan Paul, London, 1957).

[81] It did not acquire one till 1816. By then, as a consequence of the many administrative changes that had been brought in after Burke's Economical Reform speech of 1780, the various fees in each department had been pooled into what was called a fee-farm, in an attempt to pay the officials more equitably. In 1816 Parliament undertook to make up any deficiency in the fee-farm—and thus acquired a (then-unwelcome) toe-hold on the payment of the public service.

It followed from this conception of the executive that the way it got on with its business was no affair of Parliament except that, now and again, if a major scandal erupted Parliament might set up a Select Committee to inquire into the matter. Such incursions, frequent under the later Stuarts, ceased almost entirely after 1714, as ministers finally 'managed' the legislature so that they and it were brought into conformity.

In addition to being chief executive, the sovereign still retained a group of truly vital prerogatives. It was he who laid out the lines of foreign policy, including war, and chose as ministers the politicians who could deliver a parliamentary majority for providing the legislation and finance to make his policy effective. All the same, though he could certainly make foreign policy in a vacuum without Parliament, in a vacuum it would remain. To begin with, the sovereign could no longer dispense with Parliaments and parliamentary elections. In 1694 the definitive Triennial Act was passed and Parliaments ceased to be temporary accessories to kings in embarrassed circumstances, to be convened and dissolved at will. They became as permanent an organ of the constitution as the monarchy itself.

Again, for all that the prerogative gave the sovereign the right to make war, he could not, under the Bill of Rights, maintain a standing army in peacetime without the consent of Parliament, and the sanction was provided by way of the Mutiny Act, 1689. This Act assured the discipline and indeed the continued existence of the British army both at home and abroad by decreeing the death penalty for mutiny. Without this Act the soldiers could refuse orders or desert at will. As the Act ran for one year at a time it had to be renewed annually. (Parenthetically, this compelled the sovereign to convene Parliament at least once every year.)

The Legislature

The relationship between king and Parliament passed through three phases. In the first, already described, Parliament was the ancillary of the sovereign. The second was a phase of confrontation, and ran from 1689 till the Hanoverian settlement in 1714. It was due to the rapid alternation of mutually hostile party majorities in the House of Commons. The Crown had to manœuvre to get Parliament to provide the gigantic sums needed for fighting the Continental wars which engaged the country from 1689 to 1697 and, again, from 1701 to 1713. The electorate was comparatively large and growing. It is estimated that under William III it numbered some 200,000, or one-thirtieth of the population;[82] and an absolute figure as great as that at the opening of the nineteenth century. The two parties that sprang up in

[82] Plumb, *Growth of Political Stability*, 29.

the Exclusion crisis, though rudimentary, fulfilled the minimum definition of a party as a connection that competed with one or more others to put up candidates for election to the legislature and mobilize electoral support for them. 'More general elections, and more contests at these elections, took place between 1689 and 1715, than for the rest of the eighteenth century. Indeed more general elections took place between 1688 and 1714 than at any other comparable period in the history of Parliament, excluding medieval times.'[83]

Whigs and Tories were not merely in conflict over ideological matters. They fought for power in the constituencies.[84] They competed for the patronage, property, and the like that came with control of the municipal corporations. Under William the ideological issues widened. The Tories stood for peace, the Anglican monopoly, and the landed interest; the Whigs were the party of war *à outrance*, of more toleration towards Dissent, and of the Bank of England and the monied interest generally.

So, Plumb continues:

Every manœuvre to bring Parliament to heel had failed; in 1689 the Commons enjoyed a freedom and an independence that they had not possessed since 1641. As well as freedom, they had acquired a certain, continuing place in government; no year was to pass without their meeting, and this they knew would be so. And after the execution of Charles I and the flight of James II, few could dispute where sovereignty ultimately lay . . . Control was impossible. Parliament it seemed, was free to harry monarchs, topple ministries, cut supplies, refuse taxation, concern itself with peace and war, formulate those constitutional changes that it felt necessary for its protection, and generally ride roughshod over the administration.[85]

The third phase, which began in 1714—some would say 1727—and ran through till 1830 was one of harmony only occasionally disturbed by, historically, minor frictions. How did this come about and which—Crown or Parliament—was the dominant partner?

The first question admits of a more clear-cut answer than the second. The politico-religious atmosphere was more favourable to civil harmony than for the last 100 years. For one thing, 1715–39 were years of peace. For another, rationalism had begun to invade religion so that the Anglican–Dissent antagonism was far less acrimonious. Thirdly, the Tory interest—one of the two antagonists of the last century—disqualified itself for any role when a few of its members became implicated with the Jacobites. A 'one-party' situation had emerged (always remembering that the Whig party was a quasi-party, a loose confederation of great Whig families and their

[83] Ibid. p. xv.   [84] Ibid. 64.   [85] Ibid. 64–5.

connections). What is more, the great Whig families exercised a patrimonial sway over their tenants in the counties and could nominate MPs at will in the 'rotten' boroughs. Finally, both George I and George II relied on the Whigs, who had engineered the Hanoverian succession, just as they owed no thanks to the Tories.

This was the background to the process through which the 'decoupled' Crown and Parliament were 'recoupled': the process which came to be called 'the old corruption', or the 'influence' of the Crown. The sovereign alone appointed ministers and other high officers of state, and once appointed, these disposed of the patronage that went with their posts—the Treasury in particular, which had control over departments like the Customs and Excise Office, or the Post Office, with thousands of jobs at their disposal. The Admiralty had hundreds of jobs as dockyard workers to dispose of, as well as dozens of contracts. In this way a huge fund of influence was opened, via the king, on behalf of the ministers whom he chose to carry out his policy. That influence was used by ministers (or, as we shall note, by a particular self-designated minister) to rig elections, and it is a fact that from 1715 to 1830 no minister in power *ever* lost an election.

However, winning a parliamentary majority was a necessary but not sufficient condition for stability. Parties were little more than loose 'connections', so that the MPs, though they might call themselves Whigs—for example—were very much individual and private persons. An assembly of some 500 persons cannot be brought to any sense of order, whether in the agenda, the conduct, or the conclusion of its business, without some mechanism to organize them. In those days—and right up to the 1850s— this was supplied by still more ministerial influence and patronage. Influence might be reflected in honours and awards. The patronage might be a power which the minister delegated to the MP to nominate a constituent for appointment as a postmaster.

As we have seen, under the later Stuarts the control of the House fluctuated between Whigs and Tories, each using their term of office to try not merely to win the next election but to extinguish the rival party altogether. This was never successful until the Hanoverian succession, when the Tories were extinguished as a political force. Some 150 Tories continued to be elected to each Parliament, but their political influence was marginal. In short, 1715 saw the instauration of single-party domination. The Whigs were in complete control. The Whig ministries could henceforth rely on the Crown, and in return the Crown could select the ministers it wanted in the full expectation that the election would again return a court majority and that this in turn would prove amenable to the measures presented to it. This arrangement was made the more secure by the Septennial Act, 1715, slipped through in the panic over the Jacobite rising of that year on the pretext of greater security. It meant, *inter alia*, that ministers could live with the majority they had procured for seven years and not a mere three.

Now that the executive and the legislature were *re*-coupled, who controlled whom? The interrelationship was subtle: the one certain thing is that Crown and Parliament worked together; there were no more confrontations such as had shaken the entire seventeenth century.

The monarchy was a *limited monarchy*, but as Sir Richard Pares gnomically remarked, 'It was (and still is) hard to say exactly what were its limitations'.[86] Somewhat perhaps like 'Bottom's Dream'? 'I have had a dream . . . but past the wit of man to tell what dream it was.' 'Despite a 'payroll vote' of some 200 MPs and a sturdy bunch of some 150 'country party' MPs, the Commons was by no means subservient. On matters that stirred it deeply it was prepared to vote down legislation. It did so on the Peerage Bill (1719), which would effectively have confined the peerage to its existing families. Likewise it voted against the Excise Bill but in favour of the War of Jenkins' Ear (1739). And it was, again on great occasions, prepared to vote against unpopular ministers; for example, contrary to the wish of the king it forced Walpole to resign in 1742. By the same token, ministers who felt confident of its support could insist that the monarch accept a minister whom he himself wished to exclude; for instance, over the elder Pitt crisis in 1757. In this instance the party manager—Lord Newcastle—effectively told the King that if he did not give way the entire ministry would resign.

What ought one to conclude? Pelham used to say that when Parliament was against him he might get his way by royal support, when the king was against him he might sometimes get his own way by relying on Parliament, but that if the king and the Parliament concurred he had to give way.[87] In 1780 Lord North, usually regarded as a blind servant of George III, told this king: 'Your Majesty is well apprized that, in this country, the Prince on the Throne, cannot, with prudence, oppose the deliberate resolution of the House of Commons.'[88]

The first conclusion is that the executive and legislature were in counterpoise, one might even say in counterpoint: in that *the Parliament could certainly stop the king from doing what he wanted to do but was unable to compel him to do what it wanted done*. The second, more comprehensive conclusion is that, without the slightest doubt, this was a *limited* monarchy, at the opposite end of the scale from that of the Bourbons.

[86] Pares, *Limited Monarchy*, 8.   [87] Williams, *The Whig Supremacy*, 21.

[88] Quoted in P. Langford, *A Polite and Commercial People: England, 1727–1783*, The New Oxford History of England (Clarendon Press, Oxford, 1989), 687.

3.4. *The Unity of the Constitution*

The British constitution as we have described it so far must seem to be not much more than a set of disconnected bits and pieces or (to quote what Bentham was to say about the common law) 'a shapeless heap of odds and ends'. The extensive activities of local government which regulated and provided for the day-to-day needs of the common people were disassociated from the central government. At the level of this central government, the judiciary were wholly independent of the legislature and/or the executive. The citizen himself—under the protection of those courts—enjoyed freedoms in respect to domicile, property, free speech and expression, and to a degree of religious toleration: freedoms that, beneath the law, put him at arm's length from the executive. Even the executive and the legislature were distinct entities, mostly in harmony but occasionally in opposition, connected by the umbilical cord of the several ministers. And yet these parts fitted into a harmonious unity, so stable as to earn the wonder and respect of all Europe.

Why did it hang together and why was it so stable? In my view, because it was possessed, dominated, and operated by members of a homogeneous social class: the greater aristocracy in Parliament, the lesser gentry—the squirearchy—in the countryside.

One of the most striking—and still rather mysterious—social transformations of the later Stuart period is the resurgence of a vastly wealthy landed aristocracy. Whereas under the early Stuarts the gentry had made the political running, now it was the aristocracy. How this had re-emerged is problematic. It has been suggested that it was partly due to favourable changes in the land laws, the increased survival rate of peerage families, and their leading role in the 1688 Revolution—their 'moment of glory' on which they were to live for the next 150 years and which gave them the incumbency of the highest positions of state from which, once seated, they were never ejected.[89] At all events, this wealthy peerage increasingly squeezed the minor gentry out of the electoral contests. Those fast and furious and frequent elections under the later Stuarts had driven up the costs of elections, and the aristocrats could outbid the gentry by distributing favours, or money, or by granting constituents such things as hunting rights or the patronage to church livings. And with the Septennial Act of 1715 the cost of the elections shot up sharply, since the successful MP had seven years and not a mere three in which to exploit his position to enrich himself. This is why fewer and fewer elections were contested as the eighteenth century wore on.

[89] J. Cannon, *Parliamentary Reform* (CUP, Cambridge, 1982), 431–54.

The aristocratic extrusion of the lesser landowners left the latter as JPs and the like, while it transformed the Parliament into an aristocratic preserve. The Commons was largely an annex of the Lords: the number of MPs who were the sons of English peers in 1690 was thirty-two, but in 1754 it was seventy-seven. In addition, there sat seventeen Irish peers, six sons of Irish peers, thirteen sons of Scottish peers, forty-five grandsons of peers—and so on and so forth.[90] This is to reckon without the numerous commoners who, like Burke for instance, sat there by virtue of the patronage of some aristocratic borough-holder.

But the other branches of government were also held by members of this same class. The highest Court of Justice in the land was—the House of Lords. The officers of the army, although they were commissioned by the king, were gentlemen who bought these commissions, very often the elder sons of peers; just as the higher positions in the Church were filled by the younger sons of peers. Ministers were almost always peers.

In short, the judicature, the legislature, the executive, and the counties were all in the hands of the same social class. This gave a remarkable unity to the constitution. Any quarrels were family quarrels. And in the deferential, overwhelmingly agricultural society of that day this landed class, whether the squires or the great aristocrats, commended itself as the natural leader of the people.

In his famous chapter 'On the Constitution of England', published in 1748, Montesquieu, having—as we know—averred that the judiciary and executive and legislature were all in different hands, states that one would expect them to fall into immobility or inaction. But, he goes on, 'since the necessary movement of business forces them to move, they will be forced to move in concert'. He was wrong. They might well have brought the conduct of government to a standstill—witness the turbulence under the later Stuarts. The reason they did indeed operate in concert owed nothing to the compulsion of events. It was owing to the political cement provided by the unity of the entire governing class.

'Balanced constitution', 'mixed constitution'—what are we to make of these as descriptions? Something; but the central point is, surely, the pluralism, the collegiate nature of this form of government. It is not concentrated in one man as in France but is distributed among many men and, indeed, many organs of government. As we have seen in very early chapters, a collegiate government of this kind, embodying—as this one did—numerous checks and balances, qualifies as a *republic*. In this case, however, the executive power resides in a monarch. Hence it is a 'Crowned

[90] Ibid. 447 for the full list.

Republic'. And since the electorate returned aristocrats as their representatives, a republic of the nobiliar kind. The most apt description of the British polity after 1714 would be, therefore, 'a crowned, nobiliar, republic'.

4. TWO EAST EUROPEAN VARIANTS OF ABSOLUTISM AND LIMITED MONARCHY: PRUSSIA AND POLAND

An earlier chapter ('Representative Assemblies')[91] showed how Estates and other representative assemblies mushroomed throughout Europe, as far east, indeed, as the confines of Muscovy. Some of these exercised immense, indeed controlling, power over their king or prince. In and around 1650 the Estates in the various lands of the elector of Brandenburg were roughly on a par with those of the Polish *Sejm* and both of these were considerably more powerful than the Parliaments of the early Stuarts. But a century later the former was a more thoroughgoing absolutism even than France while the latter had developed its parliamentarism to such excess that the state, its central executive having been eroded, fell an easy prey to its predatory (and absolute) neighbours.

4.1. *Brandenburg–Prussia*

Presentation of the Prussian road to absolutism poses some difficulties in that the three main processes in its constitutional development, to wit, the elimination of the Estates, the building up of a professional standing army, and the creation of an intrusive, territories-wide bureaucracy are intertwined and what is relevant in one of these respects may also be relevant to another. This unavoidably entails some shuttling back and forth between them.

4.1.1. THE DESTRUCTION OF THE ESTATES

In 1619 there was no *state* of Prussia—just a clutch of distinct territories, petty states if one wishes, which by the accident of hereditary descent had come to George William, of the Hohenzollern line. Society and economy in these three territories varied greatly, but in all three the Estates were very powerful. On the lower Rhine lay Cleves and Mark which were Catholic, relatively prosperous, with a free peasantry and noblemen who were not exempt from tax as was common elsewhere. Here the Estates had attained almost complete control of finance, administration, and—when the occasion arose—of troops. Seven hundred miles east, on the Vistula and Baltic, stretched the Duchy of Prussia, with its one big town, the port of Koenigs-

---

[91] Bk. III, Ch. 8.

berg. Prussia was the land conquered by the Teutonic Knights in the fourteenth century. This was a sparsely populated, poor, agricultural region, exporting beer, grain, and timber to the west. It was primitive and non-monetized. Here the nobles—the Junkers—dominated the countryside and they dominated the Estates. They possessed total control of taxation, had to be consulted in all matters of foreign policy, and even the levying of troops came under their authority. Finally, in the central area around Berlin (15,000 inhabitants) lay the ancient Mark of Brandenburg. Its princes were electors of the Holy Roman Empire. They had frittered away their domain revenue and got into severe difficulties from which the noble-dominated Estates rescued them only at the price of complete control and administration of finance, joint consultation in foreign policy, and a joint committee with the elector which was vested with the executive power to raise troops.

The road to absolutism starts with the Thirty Years War and the accession of the Elector Frederick William I in 1640. The territory had been occupied, exploited, and heavily taxed by Swedish troops of occupation and when peace came in 1648 the elector had no more than 1,300 soldiers—barely enough for garrison duties. Frederick William convened the Brandenburg Estates in 1650 and asked it to grant additional taxation in order to expand the number of his troops. Now the standard tax was the land tax called the contribution. In the rural countryside—and the population of all the territories was some 80 per cent agrarian at that time—this tax was organized and administered by the local nobles. In each district (*Kreis*) they appointed one of their number as *Kreisdirektor* and apportioned the tax between their estates, for they themselves paid no tax; they levied it on their peasants. In the towns, however, this contribution was levied at a traditional standard rate. The elector wanted the nobles to abolish this land tax in favour of the new Dutch invention, the excise. The nobility refused to accept a tax which would bear on them equally with commoners.

But in 1653 the elector and the nobles struck a bargain. He got his tax, and some money; and they got the control of the countryside. He received half-a-million thalers, to be spread over the next six years. In return, not only were noble lands protected from falling into non-noble hands, but the law relating to peasant status was changed. Hitherto the onus of proving that a peasant was servile had rested on the nobleman. Now the onus of proving that he was free was to rest on the peasant—and how many peasants would have the records to prove their freedom? So the arrangement effectively opened the door to the wholesale enserfment of the peasantry that followed. This was to make Prussian absolutism much more far-reaching than that of France, because from that point on the Junker came to control the whole life-span of the peasants on his estates. He judged them, appointed the village schoolmaster, exercised (in effect) the presentment to the church living, and—once a man was declared a serf—could exact whatever dues he chose to set. This agreement is known as the Recess of 1653.

With his new revenue the elector increased his troops—mercenaries—to 4,000. But then, in 1655, the Great Northern War broke out between Sweden and Poland, and threatened the interests of his Duchy of Prussia. The Estates refused to give him more money for more troops: what had the nobles of Brandenburg to do with his ambitions in Prussia? Frederick William responded by using his tiny army to collect tax from the peasants nevertheless. He was able to pay for 22,000 troops at the height of the war. When it ended he acted as Louis VII of France had—he retained some troops in service. The peacetime (1660) strength was now 10,000 men.

Frederick William made another unsuccessful try in 1660 to get the Estates to authorize the excise. They responded by leaving the land tax as before, but made the excise permissive in the towns. In 1680 he made it compulsory and appointed paid officials, the *Steurräte*, to administer it. The subsequent extensive bureaucratization of Brandenburg was raised on this basis, but that will be dealt with below. The point here is that as the excise was indefinitely expansible, the elector no longer had any interest in convening the Estates. With adequate revenues, his new officials in the towns, and his expanded army, the elector was absolute.

But this was only in the Mark of Brandenburg. The Estates of Cleves and Mark rejected a demand for more money. *That* was settled by the elector's soldiers. They agreed to make him the generous grants he required. He, for his part, recognized their privileges, so that these Estates remained active well into the eighteenth century.[92] But politically these Estates were now neutered and offered no obstacle to the princely absolutism.

There still remained the Duchy of Prussia. A sort of Cleves situation repeated itself here. The grand duke quartered 2,000 troops there and got his money after promising to reconvene the Estates in six years' time. He was anticipated by the re-emergence of the opposition faction supported by adjacent Poland. The grand duke captured its chief men and executed its leader. The Prussian Estates collapsed and indeed, after 1715 it met only on ceremonial occasions.

In these ways the elector became fiscally absolute and much more. None

[92] The regime always had difficulty in collecting the taxes, though, because the Cleves citizens detested the Prussians. H. C. Johnson, *Frederick the Great and His Officials* (Yale UP, London and New Haven, 1975), 23, n. 30.

of these Estates now dared intervene in his foreign policy or his control and deployment of the army.

4.1.2. ROYAL COMMAND OF A STANDING ARMY

This extensive tax-gathering exercise had been undertaken with one paramount objective: to expand and maintain a permanent force of paid professional troops. In the Thirty Years War the electors had followed the prevalent practice of commissioning colonels to raise, equip, and appoint junior officers to a fighting force at the elector's expense, and in return for pay and emoluments. The contract between them and the elector was known as a *Kapitulation*, and the elector appointed officials—*Kriegskommissaren*—to check the arrangements and the proper fulfilment of the contract. The army became a permanency between the Recess of 1653 and the death of the great elector in 1688, by which time its numbers had risen to 30,000. Consequently the office of *Kriegskommissar* acquired permanency also. But all through his reign the elector kept modifying the contracts so that he could, for instance, veto appointments of junior officers. Furthermore, the *Kriegskommissaren*—a local one in each district supervised by an *Oberkriegskommissar* in every province—took over the logistics: for example, he organized forage, billeting, transportation and supplies, all of which bulked particularly large in a rural, non-monetized economy. So, increasingly, the *Kriegskommissar* interfered in the economic life of the district.

We have, then, a set of *Oberkriegskommissars* in the provinces, each controlling a number of *Kriegskommissars* in their separate districts. The wars of 1655–60 and then of 1679 led the elector to establish a field marshal to command the troops in *all* his territories along with a Supreme Council to control and co-ordinate the various *Oberkriegskommissars* throughout the provinces. The Council was known as the General War Commissariat.

The great elector's son was not a militarist. But he did succeed in acquiring the title of *king* in 1701. His successor, Frederick William I (1713–40), was by contrast a military fanatic and a ferocious organizer. He expanded the army from 30,000 to 80,000 men, so creating (as we shall shortly see) a most serious manpower shortage, and he also abolished the *Kapitulationen* system: he himself took over the recruitment and appointment of all officers.

But where were these officers to come from? The Junkers were at that time quite different from the later reputation they acquired. They were pacific, beer-swilling and beer-producing landlords, owners of great estates, serf-masters, entrepreneurs, traders; who exercised seigneurial jurisdiction over their tenants and serfs and acted as the local police chief, prosecutor, and judge. They saw the king as their rival—he had curtailed their power.

They had no interest in soldiering. But William I forced them to send their younger sons to his *Kaddettenhaus* (established in 1722) and had them dragged there by the police if they resisted. But at the same time he invested soldiering with unprecedented honour and glamour—such as prominence in the table of precedence, regular employment, and high rates of pay. By the end of his reign in 1740 the nobility were responding enthusiastically and acquired the conventional reputation of the Junker. Nine-tenths of the officers were by then the sons of the nobility.

It will be remembered, however, that this same nobility supplied the *Kreisdirektors*, the men who apportioned the land tax among their Junker peers in each district. By now, with the Estates in desuetude, the *Kreisdirektor* was usually the *Kriegskommissar* as well, organizing the army logistics in the rural areas.

These officials were now brought in to solve the manpower problem caused by the rapid expansion of the army. Very few free men would volunteer to be a soldier in those days! William sent recruiting officers to scour his lands and even those of his neighbours to beg, borrow, or even steal 'volunteers', but this did not suffice. Therefore, in 1732 he divided his state into so many cantons, each large enough to supply the replacements for a regiment of infantry or of cavalry as the case might be; 5,000 families in the former and 1,200 in the latter. From then on the local Junkers co-operated with the state by providing the services of their own peasants. A regimental recruiting officer was stationed in each canton. Every male birth was notified to him by the local pastors. He would visit and inspect the male children when they attained 10 years and if he passed them had them wear a red tie to signify that they were destined for the army. The list of exemptions pretty well cut out the townsfolk and virtually the entire burden fell on the peasant. In this way, the noblemen who were the officers in the army (or whose sons were) delivered their own serfs and led them into the field for their military service; trained them; and controlled them. Yet the needs of this nobleman's farm could not be neglected. So, after two years induction and training under the control of his noble landlord, the serf was returned to the farm to work for him and supply his servile labours for ten months of the year. Then, when the spring came he would have to don his uniform again and be led into the field by his proprietor for the spring manœuvres. Only in wartime or during these two months of the year was the Prussian army at full strength. Under Frederick the Great the size of this army was to reach 150,000 men.

Let us glance at the chain of command. At the top, the General War Commissariat exercised control over the *Oberkriegskommissars* in each province, who in turn exercised control over the *Kriegskommissars* (now called *Landräte*) in the rural districts, and the *Steuerräte* in the towns.

In this way a Prussian king exercised complete and immediate control over a vast army made up of a core of trained professional troops and a huge draft component. There was no irremovability of officers here as in lands like England and France where commissions were purchased. The entire corps was at the sovereign disposal of the monarch. In this way was the second of the attributes of absolutism acquired: the complete monopoly of the armed forces.

4.1.3. ERECTING A MILITARIZED BUREAUCRACY

The third component of absolutism was a trained and obedient bureaucracy; but in Prussia this served yet another purpose. Given that the state consisted of three separated territories, a common bureaucracy was required to bring them together into a single political unit. In this poverty-stricken sand-box of a country the basis for this bureaucracy was the army itself. In this respect the translation from one to the other resembles not a little what took place in Tokugawa Japan.

To understand how this common administration evolved it is first necessary to know that over a long period there were not one but three administrative structures side by side, and that only by 1740 were these all fused together at central and local level. The first of these structures administered the royal domains, which were extremely important since they provided about half of the total revenue. The second was the military administration of the districts and provinces. The third was the excise administration in the towns, that is, the jurisdiction and duties of the *Steuerräte*.

The *Steuerräte* had at first exercised the simple duty of adjudicating local disputes over the application of the excise tax. But such a tax is a very intrusive one. The government continually extended its base so that the *Steuerräte* had to supervise weights and measures, toll-gates, and suchlike. Within twenty years of their inception the *Steuerräte* were appointing the town mayors, there were no more councillors, and they themselves had taken on a truly vast range of functions. Decrees of 1684 and 1689—which is a goodly time before the office reached its apogee—are revealing. The *Steurrat* decides on complaints and claims that fall outside the regular procedure of the courts. He controls food prices. He inspects weights and measures, reports on defraudment and embezzlement. He also acquires police duties in the sense of looking after the well-being of the towns: hence he controls the building of houses, fire precautions, and regulates streets and rivers. The *Steuerrat* was no petty official in one of the hamlets that passed for 'towns' in these primitive lands. He had to inspect and take responsibility for about twelve of them. This wide range of tasks demanded a specialized staff: clerks, cashiers, accountants, tax-collectors, city-gate controllers, and a quasi-police force to control mills, breweries, bridges, and the like. He was perhaps the most important official in the entire bureaucratic hierarchy.

Side by side, the domain lands were being administered by *Amtskammeren*—Administration Councils—which answered to the *Hofkammer*—the Superior Council—which was a section of the prince's Privy Council.

Finally we come back to the third of these administrative structures, the military one which we have already examined. By 1688 it had come to include and to control the taxation and other functions of the rural districts (the *Kreise*) and the towns. The General War Commissariat in Berlin was served by the *Oberkriegskommissaren* in each province who in turn were served by the *Kriegskommissaren* (later called *Landräte*) in each *Kreis*; and its *raison d'être* and that of these subordinate offices was to organize logistical support for the army. And we saw also how the post of *Kreisdirektor* and that of district *Kriegskommissar* were vested in the same person. He was no longer chosen by his Junker peers but appointed by the government.

When obligatory military service came in after 1713 as described, these same *Landräte* were responsible for organizing the drafts. Thus the rural administration of the *Kreise*—the districts—fell under the jurisdiction of the provincial war commissioner who in his turn was responsible to the General War Commissariat in the capital.

But the *Steuerräte* were also military officials, sent down by the government to sort out all the problems connected with the excise, yes, but also to organize the logistics of the army. So these officials, too, answered to the provincial war commissioners. In short, by 1688, and—as far as the draft is concerned—by 1732–3, there was *one* overall military board in Berlin served by provincial military boards which themselves were served by Junkers in the *Kreise* and by the *Steuerräte* in the towns. As this occurred, this supreme military board in Berlin, which was originally responsible only for military logistics, had become responsible for rural and town revenues, then for the draft, and finally for administration *generally*.

But the vast expansion of the army after 1732 entailed far more taxation than before. Hence the final screw in the extraction–coercion cycle and the completion of the administrative structure. The General War Commissariat had three divisions—for the army, for taxation, and for general administration, and its local officials were always colliding with the *Amtskammern*. Their constant bickering, especially in the royal courts at the royal expense, led Frederick William I to a final step: merging the two revenue-raising circuits at both the local and the supreme level. To this end the *Amtskammern* were merged with the *Steurrätte* into what can be translated as War-and-Domain Chambers; while at the top the General War Commissariat now took the title of the General-Supreme-War-and-Domains-Directorate which, mercifully, was called the General Directorate for short. By 1740, the year Frederick William died, the construction of the state was, according to one trustworthy authority, complete.

The Directorate was divided into four geographical sections. A minister was in charge of each and was expected, apart from his territorial responsibilities, to be the expert on a specific field of administration: posts and mint, army supplies, land utilization, state boundaries.

Now, unlike France which entrusted its local direction to individuals—the *intendants*—Prussia worked throughout, at central and provincial and rural level, through *boards*. These central-government ministers presided over their board and it was their collective decision that carried matters. When Frederick II (the Great) succeeded in 1740 the initiatives for their decisions usually came from him; who, it should be noted, worked from his palace at Potsdam, whereas the ministries were in Berlin, so that he did not normally meet his ministers, but worked on documents. He received their reports (as well as many from other quarters) and then finally sent the ministers their instructions. Frederick was another of those workaholic monarchs who, like Louis XIV, intended to run their entire state in person. His energy was enormous. He would take only five or six hours sleep, rose early, read all the reports from ambassadors, ministries, and the nobility before breakfast, and had annotated all these reports and petitions before his midday meal. Furthermore, in his urge to be ubiquitous, he would enter into direct correspondence with the field-officials in order to verify their statements, arrange for secret conduct reports to be made and brought to him on a regular annual basis and, as he travelled throughout the kingdom, would make personal inspections on the spot.[93]

Thus what had begun as simply the War Commissariat had now absorbed all administrative functions in the state. Moreover, the king extended its jurisdiction to Prussia and to Brandenburg alike and, with some modification, to the Rhenish territories also. In this way all his territories, geographically separated as they were, nevertheless fell under one common superior and one uniform administration.

The size of this civil service was much smaller than used to be thought. The best estimates put it at between 2,100 and 3,100 officials in the mid-eighteenth century[94] or about one civil servant for every 800 subjects. This is somewhat surprising given the scope of government activity, which

---

[93] *CMH*, vii. 309, 311–12.   [94] Johnson, *Frederick the Great*, app. I, pp. 283–8.

included the Post Office, the finance offices and Customs and Excise, and the administrative boards for forests, salt, and mines; the schools[95] and the Church also required large numbers of officials.

It was dominated by aristocrats at the top, whose number decreased to zero as one moves downwards. All the ministers were aristocrats (1740), and so were ten of the eleven Provincial Board presidents (1754.) But only a quarter of the councillors on these War and Domains Boards were aristocrats, the rest commoners. The subaltern officers in all the above were, with hardly any exceptions, commoners. When one turns to the local government, the *Landräte* were all aristocrats, as one expects: they were, as we have stressed, the local Junker class. On the other hand *Burgermeisters*—the mayors—were all commoners.[96] One noteworthy feature is that many of what we might describe as the middle-management posts in the bureaux were filled by retired subaltern officers—fairly mediocre administrators[97]— while the lower posts were by preference filled by disabled NCOs and rank-and-file.[98]

The king set the greatest store on his officials' probity and the councils that supervised their activities were expected to plant spies to report on them. Instructions rigidly settled their hours and conditions of employment and they suffered heavy fines for breaches, while any expenditures beyond the budget limits was surcharged on the official. They were subject to the strictest obedience to hierarchy.

By 1713 most judges—certainly the superior ones—were admitted only by competitive oral and written examinations in the law. For the non-judicial posts, however, former administrative experience was deemed better than formal training; though by 1740 candidates had to produce evidence of this, for example, by providing written answers to statistical problems, or drawing up a mock budget.[99] Yet in general the requirements for generalist civil servants were much less rigorous than for the judicial ones, where a university qualification was essential.[100]

The quality and effectiveness of this bureaucracy is today open to serious challenge. Until fairly recently Schmoller's views, published in 1898, held the field.[101] One gleaned the impression of a Prussia with a numerous bureau-

---

[95] Teachers are not included in the figures given above. Perhaps they ought to be—for instance they are civil servants in today's France. Were they included in the Prussian totals the figures would increase dramatically—perhaps as much as doubling the total.

[96] Johnson, *Frederick the Great*, 288.   [97] The revisionist view of ibid. 57.

[98] Fischer and Lundgren, 'The Recruitment and Training of Administrative and Technical Personnel', 520.

[99] H. Finer, *The Theory and Practice of Modern Government*, 2 vols. (Methuen, London, 1932), ii. 1, 198–201.   [100] See the remarks at p. 1367 below.

[101] G. Schmoller, *Das Brandenburgisch-preussiche Innungswesen von 1640–1896: Hauptsächlich die Reform unter Friedrich Wilhelm I* (Berlin, 1898).

cracy of trained and fully professional civil servants who were inspected, appraised, and supervised to ensure that they worked long hours, never flagged in their duties, and were of the utmost official probity and rectitude and mechanically did exactly what their superiors told them. That principle of harsh, exacting, inflexible discipline that Germans, not to speak of other Europeans, associated with the word 'Prussian' found its origin here. Nor were they extravagantly paid. Just the reverse. *Travailler pour le Roi de Prusse* is still a French expression for working your fingers off for peanuts.

In practice, so it would seem, the administrative system was hidebound and unimaginative. Frederick II loathed almost every sector of it except the noble Junker *Landräte*.[102] The General Directorate were *Dummkopfen*, the Councils of the Provincial War and Domain Boards were 'idiots', 'indolent', and 'careless', and the *Steuerräte* were 'lazy and incompetent'. But these views probably only reflect the impatience of a hyperactive monarch and his somewhat paranoiac conviction that the members of the Directorate and the Provincial Councils ganged up against him. The chief defect of the senior officials at all levels seems to be simply that they were routine-ridden, fearful of taking initiatives, and not very imaginative. The Provincial Boards acted as a passive counterweight to the king in that they could obstruct, delay, and falsify reports: but they could not assume active leadership at all—that lay entirely with Frederick.[103] Yet he did very little to alter the structures he found in place, except to strip the General Directory of certain powers, notably the administration of the excise. His efforts to galvanize them by his 'spy system' failed, though it is true that between 1740 and 1786 Frederick did cashier no less than eleven out of the forty-one presidents of the Provincial Councils.[104]

We remarked earlier on the lack of training of the administrative personnel. Each Provincial Council followed its own pattern. But Johnson shows how miscellaneous were the origins of the councillors. Out of eighty-six Councillors, eighteen were former army quartermasters and fifty-one were former excisemen, domain contractors, merchants, inspectors of works, or members of the diplomatic corps. Only seventeen of them were the administrative interns known as the *auscultatoren*, who were the then-equivalent of today's 'fast track' or 'high-fliers'. They served a year's internship and on the strength of their performance (as adjudged by the council they were serving) could move on to higher posts. The highest of the high-fliers were those who served in the General Directory. Because the internship could prove so valuable—and was also a scarce resource—it is not surprising that nominations for such posts were made by noble patrons.

[102] Johnson, *Frederick the Great*, 61–2.   [103] Ibid. 39, 43–5.   [104] Ibid. 45–8.

Altogether, the main charge against this administrative system is bureaucratic inertia and mediocre personnel. For all that, it compares favourably with the other states of Europe. Bribery certainly existed, mostly among the excisemen; but bribery was endemic throughout Europe at that time and the Prussian bureaucracy appears to have been far less subject to it than that of other states.

4.1.4. THE CHARACTER OF THE PRUSSIAN ABSOLUTISM

For all these qualifications, it seems to me that the Prussian absolutism was not only different in kind from that of France, the supposed model state for this kind of monarchy, but altogether more intense. Seeley overstates his point, but if we are looking at Prussia in a comparative perspective, it is the central point. That is to say: the army.

Let us, then, compare the army of Frederick William I with other Continental armies. It was nearly equal to that of Austria, which had a population about six times as great. It was half as large as that of France, whose population was about nine times as great. But if we wish to estimate correctly the effect which this incredible military force must have had upon the state which maintained it, we must take several other facts into consideration. We shall find that, both as increasing the absolute power of the government and as a burden upon the people, the army of Frederick William was much more formidable than could be inferred from its greater proportionate numbers. For about one-third of it consisted of foreign mercenaries, and of the rest the rank-and-file consisted not in any degree of the educated classes, who might be capable of some regard for liberty and some jealousy of arbitrary power, but of agricultural serfs, who even in their own homes lived under a subjection as complete as in the camp. Moreover, overwhelming as is the force which a vast, unintelligent standing army gives to a government even at the present day, there are nowadays in every state counteracting influences, some shadow of a parliament, some pretence at a free press. In Prussia the local parliaments had almost everywhere passed into insignificance—there was no Mutiny Bill—and in the time of Frederick William the press had no freedom. Nothing counteracted the brute force of this mass of armed slaves, ruled with iron severity and officered by their hereditary masters, the noblesse, who had made themselves in turn, as it were, serfs to their king and commander-in-chief; for the Articles of War bound the officer to obedience 'even against his own honour'. If we reflect on all this, we shall still recognize that Frederick William, when he organized the army, achieved a work no less important politically than in a military sense. He created not only a new Great Power in Europe but also a new form of government. For in resting it so thoroughly upon his army and in drawing from it such unlimited power, he contrived a new variety of monarchy; so that the Prussian state from his time does not resemble the model of the France of Louis XIV but anticipates modern military bureaucracies and furnishes a model to Napoleon.[105]

4.2. Poland

Adjacent to Prussia—and indeed exercising suzerainty over its duke until 1701—lay the vast state of Lithuania–Poland. From 1572 the history of Polish government is that of Prussia (or for that matter France) in reverse. Like England, it espoused parliamentarianism; but the quintessential difference lies in the fact that from 1572 the Polish monarchy became elective by the nobility in fact as well as in name, and the fixed, free-standing executive that acted as the spinal column of the British state was missing. Unlike what occurred in Britain, the king became subservient to the assembly, then its puppet, and finally little more than a transient and embarrassed creature of a foreign power.

The history of the *Sejm* to the sixteenth century has been noted already in an earlier chapter.[106] In 1493 there existed a completely organized political structure. The central *Sejm* worked towards the Provincial *sejms* and the even more local *sejmiki* (thirty-seven in Poland, twelve in Lithuania). Their chief task was to elect paid representatives and mandate them strictly on the items of the agenda (which had been circulated in advance). These representatives assembled in the six Provincial *sejms* to concert their policy for the *Sejm* itself. Once this had disbanded, these same representatives reported back to their *sejmiki*, which then took all the necessary administrative steps, such as assenting to a tax and arranging its collection.

The national *Sejm* itself (in fact there were two, one for Poland and one for Lithuania until the Union of Lublin, 1569) consisted of an Upper House, the Senate, as the direct descendant of the former Privy Council and made up of the Catholic prelates, the provincial governors, the castellans, the crown marshal, the chancellor, vice-chancellor, and the treasurer. In

---

[105] J. R. Seeley, *The Life and Times of Stein, or Germany and Prussia in the Napoleonic Age*, 3 vols. (CUP, Cambridge, 1878), 172. O. Hufton, *Europe: Privilege and Protest, 1730–1789*, Fontana History of Europe (London, 1980), 219, adheres to the revisionist view. According to her this 'formidable despotism' was 'more apparent than real'. Admittedly Prussia was a unitary state but—she says—'it lived with social privilege, provincial particularism, social prejudices which could defeat government pronouncements on toleration and educational reforms . . . control was far from total and only existed at all because he [Frederick the Great] never flew in the face of his true supporters, the Prussian nobility'. Such limitations were true of every single state in the world at that time and indeed right into the 20th cent. until the advent of totalitarianism in Russia and Germany. We can grant the criticism; but that does not negate the verdict of Seeley.   [106] Bk. III, Ch. 8, 'Representative Assemblies'.

1529 they numbered eighty-seven; in 1569, after the Union of Lublin, 140. All were mighty magnates. The Lower House, the Chamber of Deputies, was also composed of noblemen except for representatives of Cracow, the then-capital and, after the Union, of Vilna too; but these had no vote. (It should not be inferred from this that the towns were voiceless. In matters of taxation the Crown consulted them separately.) In principle every one of the 150,000 noblemen, many of them as poor as some of their peasants, was entitled to attend this House; and indeed, it was because time and expense kept them away that the system of election was introduced. Estimates of the nobility's ratio to the rest of population range from 8 per cent to 12 per cent; much higher than in England and France, where only some 2 or 3 per cent of the population were reckoned noble. Indeed, they formed a ruling stratum about as wide as the active citizens of Florence and much wider than the noble class of Venice.[107]

With their now-exclusive command of the legislature, these minor noblemen, the *szlachta*, quickly proceeded to strangle the towns and enserf the peasantry. As to the former, by 1600 their representation in the *Sejm* had disappeared, they had lost their autonomy, and as townsmen, were (after 1496) forbidden to acquire land. Thus, outside the towns themselves, all proprietors were noblemen.

These measures made the *szlachta* enormously prosperous in the sixteenth century and this new-found wealth was the foundation for the brilliant Polish Renaissance. For the enserfment enabled the large landowners to go over to commercial farming and there was a vast market in the west for Poland's grain and other agricultural products. By now Poland was the second largest state in Europe, with a population of some 8 million, and the wealthiest of all the countries of Eastern Europe. She was enjoying her golden age.

In 1505 the Ordinance *Nihil Novi* confirmed all the privileges of the *szlachta* and established the principle that new laws could be made only in the *Sejm*. In 1538 Sigismund I promised never to infringe the existing laws nor issue new ones at will. There was by now a conscious recognition that the government consisted of a condominium of the king, the Senate, and the Chamber of Deputies, both of these last being exclusively noble. And indeed in the Union of Lublin of 1569, which formed one single state out of Poland and Lithuania, this was formally styled the *Rzeczpospolita Polska*—the *Republic* of Poland! It might be remembered that, at that moment, the only great extant republic was Venice. The affinities between what the Polish nobility had achieved against their kings and what the Venetian nobility had

---

[107] See above, Bk. III, Ch. 7, 'The Republican Alternative: Florence and Venice'.

achieved against the doge are compelling, whether or not they were so seen at that time.

When the Jagiellon dynasty died out in 1572 and the elective principle came into force, the *szlachta's* hour had struck and from then Poland passed under the absolute dominion of the *Sejm*. Candidates for the vacant throne came forward from many foreign realms. In 1573 40,000 noblemen gathered together and elected Henry of Anjou as their new king. This inexperienced young man abandoned his new kingdom only a few months later to claim the throne of France as Henri III; but not before he had conceded to the *szlachta* the Henrician Articles which sealed the doom of the executive power. These Articles confirmed that the throne was elective, and henceforth every election became an auction from which the *szlachta* extracted new concessions. The Crown was forbidden to dismiss its officials, all noblemen of course. It was not empowered to enlarge the diminutive army of 3,000 men. It had to convoke the *Sejm* every two years and the latter's consent was necessary for all important decisions. A king could not even rely on his own demesne as a counterpoise against the greater magnates; many of these possessed estates, notably in the Ukraine, that were as big as his, and maintained private armies that equalled his in size also. The kingdom had become, effectively, a nobiliar republic with a royal figurehead. No dynasty was ever to rule the kingdom again—instead, the kings were individuals from all over Europe, sometimes—but only sometimes—from Poland itself.

The middle of the seventeenth century saw a gradual decline in prosperity, and then a catastrophe when the country was simultaneously overrun by Russians, Swedes, Prussians, and Cossacks while the peasants rose in a *jacquerie* against their landlords. The devastation wiped out more than one-third of the population. Yet it is precisely then, in 1652, that we hear of the *szlachta's* final act of politicide—the *liberum veto*. By an extension of the notion that all nobles were juridically equal, it was maintained that every single member of the *Sejm* must concur for any decision to be valid, as noted in Book III, chapter 8. In other words, one nobleman, by crying out 'I object', could not only veto the proposition before the legislature, but *ipso facto* brought about its dissolution. From then onwards it was used frequently; and naturally the power of one petty nobleman to paralyse the entire business of the state brought its own nemesis. The magnates were not going to have their carefully concocted plans disrupted in this way. They began to form clienteles among the gentry, so that soon the entire country was dominated by some thirty great magnate families. At the same time foreign powers realized how easy it had become to intervene in the election of a new king in Poland, or to alter its foreign policy. From now on, vetoes were bought and sold.

Unsurprisingly, therefore, Poland became defenceless against her powerful neighbours; Russia to the east, Prussia to the west, Austria to the south. In 1772 they moved in concert and hacked three slices, one apiece, off the defenceless royal republic. At last the alarm sounded: the *Sejm* appointed a Council of thirty-six to advise the king, but this did little to restore a central executive power. Not until 1791 (two years, be it noticed, after the French Revolution), did a Patriot party, along with the king, terrified of further invasion, persuade the *Sejm* after long, long last to accept a hereditary monarchy, a strong executive vested in its hands, the renunciation of aristocratic privilege, and the end to the *liberum veto*. The interesting thing about this catalogue is that (apart from French aristocratic privileges) England and France had never lacked any one of these from their very beginnings.[108]

There are weedkillers which operate by making the plants overgrow their strength, whereupon they perish. The unrestrained growth of the parliamentary principle in Poland killed the state in exactly this way.

5. THE TWO TRADITIONS REVISITED

Of Prussia and Poland little more needs be said here than that, by 1715, the Prussian monarch was absolute in theory and practice whereas in Poland it was the bicameral legislature (the *Sejm*), composed exclusively of the nobility, that was absolute, the monarchy being elective and *pro tanto* dependent on it.

The contrast between France and England in 1715 is more complex. One outstanding difference relates, surely, to central–local relationships. In France the localities were administered by a multitude of paid civil servants supervised by the royal *commis*, that is, the thirty-two *intendants*. In England the local administrators, the JPs, lord-lieutenants, and so forth were appointed by and removable by the Crown but that was the limit of central control over them. They administered the Acts of Parliament with almost complete independence from the centre. Unlike the French local officials, they were the local notables giving honorary service, and the personnel they controlled in the parishes in connection with roads and police and poor law were mostly unpaid laymen also.

The second outstanding difference—but some might rate it above the former—is that in France the judge of last resort was the king personally

---

[108] The decision came too late to have any effect. The second partition of Poland took place in 1793 and the third, which extinguished it altogether, in 1795.

(hence *lettres de cachet*) or his tribunal, the *Conseil*. The sovereign lawcourts, the *parlements*, were certainly highly influential but the Crown could override them or remove cases from their jurisdiction to his own. In England, by contrast the courts were the ancient common law courts, trial was by the adversary system, and—in the appropriate types of cases—the verdict was delivered by a jury which was independent of the judges, who themselves were completely independent both of the monarchy and the legislature.

The third difference lies in the unlimited *personal* authority of the king of France in all matters—the fiscally absolute head of the executive, commander-in-chief of the armed forces, supreme judge, and unique legislator—by comparison with the limitation of the monarch in England (or, rather if we are speaking of 1715, of Great Britain). Here the king still possessed important prerogatives in his own right, but had to carry Parliament with him to exercise them. The real issue here is, which of the two—Parliament or king—was uppermost? The general consensus—the 'Whig' version— used to hold that Parliament was supreme. Nowadays it is recognized that the Hanoverians exercised control over the elections and MPs by their 'influence', and some revisionists therefore claim that the Crown was as supreme as it ever had been.[109] It must surely be obvious that any such supremacy was contingent on retaining control of the MPs and that in itself is an utterly different situation from the French monarch's ability to say, at his own pleasure, *sic volo sic iubeo*. In 1715 the French and British systems of government differed in almost every significant feature.

6. THE FATE OF THE REPRESENTATIVE PRINCIPLE

Until the eighteenth century Poland was the only state in which the executive was fully responsible to the legislature; in Britain the pattern was one where a free-standing executive was *balanced* by the elected and representative legislature. This pattern is evident even in the American Constitution of 1787, in so far as the president is elected by an entirely different constituency from that of the Congress and cannot be removed by it except by impeachment.

Now the parliaments or Estates of most of the important countries of Europe were extinguished in the seventeenth century, so that some Anglocentric historians have assumed that only the English, later British, Parliament remained to carry forward the theme of representative government. But parliaments and Estates did in fact survive in many parts of Europe; we have seen how they did so in Poland and the same would be true of

---

[109] For instance, Clark, *Revolution and Rebellion*, 80.

Hungary, of many of the German statelets (particularly in the south), and in Sweden also; not just in England. What occurred in the eighteenth and early nineteenth centuries was a *general revival* of the representative assembly. But here the Anglocentric vision does contain a certain truth. For it was not via Sweden or Bavaria or Wurtemburg or Poland (above all not via Poland) that the revival took place. It took place via the English example and was based, directly or indirectly, on its model.

Other countries' adaptation of the English constitution was highly idiosyncratic. Apart from Latin America—which never adopted this model—the global adoption (and adaptation) of the representative system of government took place via the contagion of England in the continent of Europe, and the subsequent contagion of Europe in the rest of the world. It is in this respect that the Anglocentrism which sees England as 'the Mother of Parliaments' has stated a great truth. But this grand future for English parliamentarism was not due to its superior techniques or wisdom in medieval times compared to very many of the Cortes or *parlamenti* or Riksdag and the like. Its peculiar formation, its survival and supremacy over the executive and then, by historical accident, its export to the thirteen American colonies, were none of them foreordained—very much the reverse.

7

The Transplantation of the European
State-Models, 1500–1715

1. THE GREAT DISCOVERIES, 1480–1607

T he events of the last two chapters had taken place against a momentous background: Atlantic Europe had discovered a completely new and vast continent and by conquest and colonization was replicating itself there. Adam Smith exclaimed: 'The discovery of America and that of a passage to the East Indies by the Cape of Good Hope, are the two greatest and most important events recorded in the history of mankind . . .'[1] As it stands, this statement is not true; alter it to refer to the history of *government* and it becomes so.

The last chapter concluded with the year 1715. So for the Discoveries we have to retrace our steps. The earliest American colonies, which were overwhelmingly Spanish, reflect the Spain of Ferdinand and Isabella, Charles V and Philip II, and the *siglo de oro*. The English colonization of North America reflected Stuart England. These two national traditions were completely antithetical.

The momentous sea-voyages known as the Great Discoveries took place at the end of the fifteenth century. At that time the lucrative traffic that brought spice from the 'Spice Islands' was monopolized by the Arabs, the Egyptians, and the Venetians. Portugal's Prince Henry the Navigator (1394–1460) questioned whether it was not possible to bypass this Red Sea route by circumnavigating Africa and reaching the Indian Ocean that way. The Portuguese already knew the African coastline and had discovered the great Atlantic islands. So when Bartholomew Diaz rounded the Cape of Good Hope in 1447–8 and sailed north up part of Africa's eastern coast, they had good reason for thinking that their hunch was correct. But it was commonly understood (justly, as it turned out) that this sea route to the Indies was very long indeed.

[1] Adam Smith, *The Wealth of Nations* (Encyclopaedia Britannica edn., Chicago and London, 1952), bk. 4, ch. 7, p. 271.

In that same year, 1482, a Genoese seaman who had much pondered the matter[2] presented himself to the court of Lisbon with a disarmingly simple proposition. In Adam Smith's words: 'The longer the way was by the East, Columbus very justly concluded, the shorter it would be by the West. He proposed therefore, to take that way as both the shortest and the surest';[3] but the Portuguese backed their eastward route and it was not until Isabella of Castile sponsored him in 1492 that Columbus and his three ships sailed to find Asia by the west. On 12 October, 1492 he landed at San Salvador (Watling Island), discovered Cuba, which he thought was the land of the Great Khan, and finally Santo Domingo, or Hispaniola as it came to be called (nowadays housing the Dominican Republic and Haiti). In his three subsequent voyages Columbus found more islands, touched the mainland near the Orinoco, finally reached Honduras, and died in 1506 still completely convinced that he had found the outlying lands of Asia.

But by this time the Portuguese actually had their eastern sea-route in active service with annual expeditions bringing back spices, and this was because a full five years *after* Columbus discovered America, Vasco da Gama had doubled the Cape of Good Hope, reached Mozambique and, finally, Calicut. From then on the Portuguese methodically planted a string of forts and trading stations all the way between Ormuz, in the Persian Gulf and Macao (not reached till 1557).

The Castilian court had to hope that Columbus's discoveries were indeed the East Indies, but after Amerigo Vespucci had followed the coastline (1499–1500) and Nunez de Balboa on the Isthmus of Darien 'stared at the Pacific' (1513), it was clear: not only was this new land not the Indies but it was an obstacle to reaching them. Was there a passage through it? Magellan found it but it lay far to the south, at Straits named after him. America was proved to be a huge land-mass blocking Europe from the Indies. But by that time the Spanish court was far from caring, for in 1520 Cortés had discovered and conquered Mexico.

England did not dare challenge the Spaniards in their seas. Instead she tried to find her own sea route to the Indies by a north-east or a north-west passage. In 1497 Cabot, in the service of England, rediscovered Newfoundland—and thought it the land of the Great Khan. In 1567 the Muscovy Company failed to find a north-east passage. In 1576 Frobisher tried the

---

[2] Consulting (and believing), *inter alia*, a number of Biblical texts and prophecies.

[3] Smith, *Wealth of Nations*, bk. 4, ch. 7, p. 240. The principle underlying both Columbus's and the Portuguese navigators' approach was basically identical and is aptly summed up in Lewis Carroll's 'The Lobster Quadrille': '"What matters it how far we go"? his scaly friend replied. "There is another shore, you know, upon the other side. The further off from England the nearer is to France."'

north-west route but all he found was the Hudson Strait, Baffin Land, and Frobisher Bay.

In the meantime the Spanish and Portuguese were completing the exploration of Central and South America. Portugal had made a landfall in Brazil—not that this land was much regarded except for its timber—and Pope Alexander VI had negotiated the 1494 Treaty of Tordesillas which drew a line which separated the Portuguese dominions from the Spanish dominions to the west.

The Spaniards explored in all directions. Mexico was conquered between 1519 and 1521. From 1525 there were explorations into what became Peru, Ecuador, and Chile which culminated in Pizarro's conquest of the Inca Empire (1529–35). What became Panama and Venezuela were penetrated by 1532, Colombia by 1536. La Plata was reached in 1535. In Chile, Valdivia founded Santiago and advanced as far as the Magellan Straits. Meanwhile numerous expeditions advanced north from Mexico into what is now the United States in search of the fabled Seven Cities of Cibola. In this way Florida, Oklahoma, Texas, and California were visited by the conquista-dores—and later, by the missionaries.

The rest of North America was neglected. Its coasts were inhospitable and the only attractions seemed the teeming cod fisheries (which were indeed of immense importance to Spain, France, and England) and the fur trade. It was not till the seventeenth century that the newly arrived French and English began to explore the interior. By 1673 the French had explored the St Lawrence River to Lake Ontario, while in 1682 La Salle conceived the grand notion of seizing the entire Mississippi valley. As for the English, their first successful colony was established in Virginia in 1607, and the next in 1620 when the Pilgrims landed at Plymouth Rock in New England.

Many places that these European incomers traversed and 'claimed' were left unoccupied, and a large number of settlements perished by starvation or Indian attack. But by the seventeenth century one could map out five broad areas of successful colonization. The far north of North America, along the St Lawrence River and taking in 'Acadia' (Nova Scotia), was French and they had extended themselves in forts down the Mississippi to its mouth, where they founded Mobile (1711) and New Orleans (1717). The rest of the eastern seaboard from Acadia down to Georgia was English. The Dutch, as befitted a sea-power and little else, settled in the interstices, in Manhattan and Brooklyn. They did seize Curaçao from the Portuguese, and made it of huge trading importance. They seized Surinam also. Later in the seven-teenth century the English took Manhattan and Brooklyn ('New Amster-dam', thenceforward called New York) from the Dutch.

In the Caribbean the Spaniards were firmly ensconced in the larger islands such as Cuba, Jamaica, and Santo Domingo (Hispaniola), but as their military power declined in the seventeenth century the French and English were quick to descend on the area. The Spaniards had neglected the lesser Antilles and in this group the French settled Guadeloupe, Tortuga, and Martinique, and the English settled Barbados, Bermuda, the Bahamas, and in 1665 seized Jamaica. With their semi-tropical climate they were called 'the sugar islands' and were far more highly regarded by the French and English than their colonies in North America.

South of the English and French areas of North America the territory was—excepting for the three Guyanas (English, French, and Dutch Surinam)—divided between the Portuguese in Brazil and the Spaniards in the rest of the subcontinent, up through Central America and Mexico to what is today New Mexico, Texas, and California. They held Florida, and had launched out of Central America and Peru to found Buenos Aires in Argentina.

2. COLONIES

2.1. *A Variety of Forms*

There were five different kinds of colony.[4] First come the *settlement colonies*, like the English and the French-Canadian. Here, communities had come out and worked the land. The second type were also settlement colonies but differed from the former ones in that the colonizers certainly came to live and work in the new lands, but as proprietors and rulers rather than as farmers. Fieldhouse calls them 'mixed' settlement colonies but it might be better to call them *settler-domination* or *settler-ascendancy* colonies. The Spanish and Portuguese colonies were of this type. The third kind were also 'ascendancy' colonies, but differed in that the settlers formed a very thin upper crust of planters who oversaw servile labour on the plantations. These then were *plantation colonies* like the sugar- and tobacco-raising islands of the Caribbean and Gulf of Mexico. The name for the fourth type speaks for itself: *trading-post colonies*. Dutch Curaçao and New Amsterdam exemplify this type. Fifth and finally there were some colonies with a function akin to the posts on a Roman *limes* or an America-style 'frontier', where no hard-and-fast line divided *meum* and *tuum*. The colony was set up to patrol and exercise general surveillance over its hinterland: the Portuguese settlements

---

[4] In this I have followed D. K. Fieldhouse, *The Colonial Empires: A Comparative Survey from the Eighteenth Century*, 2nd edn. (Macmillan, Hong Kong, 1982), 11–13, while partly altering his terminology.

in Angola and Mozambique can stand as examples. Fieldhouse calls them *occupation* colonies, but one might equally use a term like *surveillance-colonies*.

2.2. *Colonizing: The Spanish and the English Models*

Although the French and the Dutch and even the Swedes at one time planted colonies in the Americas, their presence was either eliminated or absorbed by the eighteenth century. North America (Quebec apart) became English-speaking, and Central and South America (Brazil apart) spoke Spanish.[5]

Spanish and English colonization in America were forms of colonization where the immigrants had left their native countries in order to live, work, build their houses, and raise their children there, yet they differed from one-another in virtually every other respect.

2.2.1. PSYCHOLOGICAL DIFFERENCES

The Spanish and the English settlers had different motives. The English colonists came out to escape religious or political persecution or simply to try to improve their lot or both, and to do this by working the land, by—as John Locke might have put it—'mixing their labour with the soil'. The first Spaniards to emigrate, in the period of the conquistadores (1500–50) were *hidalgos*—second sons, soldiers, and officials.[6] For their ventures the Crown authorized them to stake their fortunes (sometimes with the help of a subsidy) on condition that they shared whatever they got with the Crown. The advance agents were the *adelantados*, following the precedent in the *reconquista* in Spain. Their mentality combined 'greed for gold, for land, and for slaves; their passionate longing to strike down the heathen and win souls for Christ; and, more subtle, but no less compelling, their love of great deeds for their own sake'.[7] '"I came to get gold, not till the soil like a peasant," said young Hernan Cortés when he first landed in Cuba. But the Spaniard came to win not only gold but also land—for land meant power,

---

[5] Why not Portugal, too? Present-day Brazil covers almost half the land-mass of South America and in Latin America as a whole for every three Spanish speakers there are two who speak Portuguese. For the moment let it suffice to say that the country colonized late (1530–2) and ineffectually, that its ties with the mother country were not clearly defined until the second half of the 16th cent., and that initially its area was limited to the line set out in the 1494 Treaty of Tordesillas. It was by encroachment that it gradually moved to claim and colonize the enormous area that lies west of the Tordesillas line—a good deal of it between 1580 and 1640 when Portugal was united to Spain, so that such encroachments did not seem to matter.

[6] A. D. Ortiz, 'The Golden Age of Spain, 1516–1659', trans. J. Casey, in J. Parry and H. Thomas (eds.), *The History of Spain* (Weidenfeld & Nicholson, London, 1971), 288.

[7] J. H. Parry, in *CMH*, i. 440.

prestige, and a new home . . . But the will to labour was not in them, for the great majority . . . regarded themselves as gentlemen . . . and Spanish gentlemen did not dirty their hands.'[8]

All the other enterprises of the Spaniards in the new world, subsequent to those of Columbus [observed Adam Smith] seem to have been prompted by the same motive. It was the sacred thirst of gold that carried Ojeda, Nicuessa, and Vasco Nugnes de Balboa to the Isthmus of Darien, that carried Cortés to Mexico, and Almagro and Pizzarro to Chile and Peru. When these adventurers arrived upon any unknown coast, their first inquiry was always if there was any gold to be found there; and according to the information which they received concerning this particular, they determined either to quit the country or to settle in it.[9]

The two peoples' attitudes to the natives was strikingly different too. After their initial brushes with the West Indian populations, whom they enslaved and who died out under ill treatment and the impact of the European diseases to which they had no immunity, the mainland Spaniards in Mexico and Peru attempted to safeguard their natives. The fact that they died in millions—Mexico's native population is said to have fallen from some 30 million to, perhaps, 3 million,[10] before subsequently rising again— was a source of grief to them but also of deep concern; for they depended on such labour to exploit the lands they had acquired. Furthermore, they needed the women—since only one-third of the emigrants were female.[11] And it is quite improper to neglect, as Adam Smith certainly did, the Spaniards' self-imposed mission to evangelize the Indians. The neo-*hidalgos* imposed themselves and the Spanish way on the Indians in the new cities they had built, but it was the massive and self-sacrificial missionary activities of the friars that Hispanicized the Indian masses in the remote countrysides where they lived. Certainly the Indian was forced into dependence; but he had been dependent before, upon his Aztec and Inca lords; it was simply that the Spaniards had now taken their places.

---

[8] A. Herring, *A History of Latin America* (Knopf, New York, 1965), 188–9. The 'plantocracy' of Virginia does not at this period present a true analogy at all. It began as a colony of, generally, smallholding planters, and did not develop into the 'plantocracy' until the 18th cent.

[9] Smith, *Wealth of Nations*, bk. 4, ch. 7, p. 242. Smith is occasionally very funny. See, for instance, his mocking description of St Domingo and the quite hilarious description of the procession to display the products Columbus had brought back after his first voyage. Ibid. 58–9.

[10] W. H. McNeill, *Plagues and Peoples* (Penguin, Harmondsworth, 1979), 189. McNeill points out that the early estimates of the Amerindian population (some 8–14 million) have been dramatically revised, so that it is now thought to have reached about 100 million. Demographers whom I have consulted think this far too high, and put the maximum figure at 40 million.

[11] J. H. Elliott, *Spain and its World: Essays* (Yale UP, London and New Haven, 1989), 11.

But the Spaniards were not colour-conscious like the English, and a huge miscegenation took place.[12] In fact the Instructions of Governor Ojeda in 1503 actually encouraged intermarriage. The English (it is customary nowadays to say 'Anglo-Saxon') attitude to the North American Indians was wholly different.[13] Very little effort was made to evangelize them. They were too wild or too dangerous to become servile labourers. Marriage with them was unthinkable, common-law unions rare, and 'half-breed', the term applied to the offspring of such unions, acquired a contemptuous, pejorative sense. Most of the North American Indians either died out through the White Man's diseases or were killed off and, at the end of the day, in the far south and far west, were penned into Indian reservations.

Spanish and English attitudes to authority were different, also. The English colonies were open to any who wished to immigrate and, in New England especially, attracted numerous religious and political dissidents who were cantankerously resentful of the mother country. The Spaniards, however, restricted immigration to those of Iberian descent, and took good care to weed out any potential trouble-makers. And whereas the English immigrants had internalized their basic civil liberties, the Spaniards were more in tune with the smack of authority.

Even the *mode* of settlement differed. A Spanish colony started up with the founding of a town, a *ciudad*, which like its ancient Roman ancestors incorporated the surrounding countryside. It was in such towns that the conquistadores and the great landowners had their palaces. The chief functions of these towns in the early days were administrative and military, not economic. By contrast, the English settlers lived in their own homesteads at first, and only when these were numerous enough did they grow together into a town.

2.2.2. LOCAL CIRCUMSTANCES

The native populations in (most of) Central and South America consisted of docile Indians, accustomed to work the land for their political masters, and they passively accepted the same status when the Spaniards took over. So the conquistadores found it easy as well as convenient to live off them in the noble way of life they had coveted. Not all Indians were docile and not all areas contained large number of Indians. The Araucaunian Indians of Chile were fierce and indomitable—fighting did not cease till about 1880. In

---

[12] For instance, in 1988 mestizos made up 55% of the Mexican population as against 29% Indian and 15% pure-blooded white. In Peru only 12% of the population are pure-blooded white as against 32% mestizo, the rest being Indians. In Colombia the mestizos form 58% of the population, the whites only 20%. Chile's population is 92% mestizo. Source: *Encyclopaedia Britannica* (1989).
[13] See pp. 1394ff below.

Argentina the Indians were so few that they could be driven out or exterminated in the third or fourth decade of the nineteenth century, leaving this temperate and fertile land open to the hordes of hungry immigrants, Italians and *gallegos* notably. But the North American Indians were very different from those of New Spain and Peru. Unlike them, they were incapable of and hostile to uninterrupted and heavy servile labour on the settlers' farms. In those areas such as Virginia and the Carolinas where economics dictated plantation agriculture in tobacco or sugar, the absence of native Indian labour was made good by importing Africans as chattel slaves. The Spaniards had no need for such imported labour except, to a limited extent, in the coastal areas of Venezuela and Peru. (On the other hand the Portuguese in Brazil were huge importers of African slaves to work the sugar plantations of Recife and Bahia.) The English colonies (the plantation ones aside) were countries of small and middling freeholding farmers; whereas the characteristic Spanish colonies were or soon became the province of landlords whose *latifundia* were worked by the native Indians.

The economic potential of the English and the Spanish colonies differed accordingly. The English colonies were agricultural. But much of the Spanish economy was extractive, as witness the great Mexican silver mines at Zacatecas and Guanajuato, and (now Bolivian) San Luis Potosi, the greatest silver mine in the world. In what is Chile and the La Plata region, however, where no such mines existed, the settlers found that cattle were breeding in myriads and they became great cattle-ranchers, raising the herds not for meat but for hides which supplied a multitude of needs, from soldiers' armour to tallow for candles.

So also the social structure of the two kinds of colonies reflected these economic differences. Though both were colonies of settlement, the Spanish immigrants were a self-selected batch of, for the most part, adventurers, soldiers, and officials, in short, a ruling stratum; and that is precisely the role they took on possessing the land. In contrast, most of the English (and subsequent European) immigrants came out in entire communities, running the gamut of social status and economic skills. The fact that a goodly proportion came as indentured servants and even convicts was also not without significance in the social mix.

2.2.3. TIMING

It is easy to forget that the first English establishments, of 1607 and 1620, were founded over 100 years later than the Spanish. The point is not that the latter were fully and durably established while the English colonists were still scrabbling at the bare soil, but that the two types of colony reflected the political conditions in Spain and England at the time of their foundation (and indeed continued to do so throughout their history. It must *never* be lost to mind that they all of them were always in communication and communion with their mother countries). Spanish colonies reflected the political conditions and aspirations of the New Monarchy of Ferdinand and Isabella: Castilian absolutism, the curbing of the higher nobility, the religious conformity; in short, an authoritarian and missionary mode. Furthermore this New World was treated, juridically, as so many other *Españas*, that is, as so many other kingdoms: juridically coequal with all the others, a dependency of the Crown alone; all of whose inhabitants, Indian, mestizo, or white, were subjects of the Crown and protected by the laws that this enacted. The English colonies, by contrast, reflected the tension between Crown and Parliament, leaning to the parliamentary side. The colonies were certainly the Dominions of the Crown and yet not one colony lacked a legislature whose minimalist function was to set the taxes. Furthermore, these colonies began as and remained so many separate entities. They were founded under different charters or, alternatively, were split off from a parent colony, their new political status being recognized by the English Crown.

These remarks bring us to the heart of what we are about to explore: the quite different traditions, one authoritarian and holistic; the other libertarian, semi-autonomous, and politically fragmented; but both European and representing the two traditions in that continent. By 1776 Adam Smith could say in his *Wealth of Nations*: 'In everything except their foreign trade, the liberty of the English colonists to manage their own affairs in their own way is complete . . . The absolute governments of Spain, Portugal and France, on the contrary take place in their colonies . . .'[14]

3. THE SPANISH EMPIRE IN AMERICA

3.1. *Salient Characteristics*

The Spanish American Empire was a complete novelty in world history. Not because it was vast, for so also were the Persian, Roman, and Arab empires; not because it consisted of conquered states, for so did the Roman, Persian, and many others; not even because its metropolis lay thousands of miles away, since the same can be said of the Mongol Empire, for instance. What was utterly new was not just the remoteness of the metropolis but that one could not, as in every previous case, reach it overland. The Spanish

---

[14] Smith, *Wealth of Nations*, bk. 4, ch. 7, pp. 252, 253.

Empire was separated from Spain by some seventy days' good sailing.[15] It was the first sea-borne empire.[16]

Despite the great distance and the hazardous nature of the sea-journey between Spain and America, the Spanish Crown was able to exercise comprehensive control of its new lands. The empire was as real and solid as any land empire had been in the past. Its kernel was New Spain (Mexico). North of this province Spain certainly claimed New Mexico, California, and Florida but, except in California, only a few officials and missionaries lived in those places. South of New Spain the kernel of the empire was the former Inca Empire of Peru, and this was intensively settled. Finally, Spain held most of the Caribbean islands: Cuba, Hispaniola, Puerto Rico, and Trinidad.

The empire was a symmetrically organized and holistic political system. It was hierarchical and politically authoritarian, commands emanating in principle from the king. Yet it was law-bound, some might say excessively so, and a cat's cradle of institutional checks and balances. It was socially authoritarian also, the pure-blooded whites forming a ruling class of some 0.25 million, in control of 9 million native inhabitants.[17] And it was religiously authoritarian: conformity to the Roman Catholic Church and only to that Church was actively enforced. A final characteristic was that, after the universal European custom of that time, its economy was made to conform to the interests of the mother country.

3.2. Evolution of the Political Arrangements, to c.1600

It took about fifty years for the imperial edifice to be completed. Progress was faster in Mexico and its neighbours which were incorporated as New Spain than in the south, where Peru had to wait till 1542 before receiving a viceroy. A twofold development occurred, of controlling councils in Madrid, and their agents, who were variously known but for the moment may be called governors, who were sent out (or given authority on the ground) to take over from the unruly adventurers, the conquistadores. The imperial structure in New Spain was completed in 1535 when the court appointed a viceroy (the highly successful Mendoza) to administer it.

In Peru the conquistadores were far more turbulent than they had been

---

[15] In his first voyage, Columbus (who had a favourable crossing) left Spain on 3 Aug. 1492 and sighted Santo Domingo on 12 Oct. The *Mayflower* that carried the Pilgrim Fathers to Plymouth Rock in 1620 made the crossing in 66 days.

[16] It consisted of a great land mass and not merely a string of trading posts as the Portuguese sea-borne empire did in the 16th cent.

[17] C. McEvedy and R. Jones, *Atlas of World Population History* (Allen Lane, London, 1978), 275.

even in New Spain. Pizarro secured the Crown's assent to go to Peru as *adelantado*, governor, and captain-general of the as-yet unconquered Peru. But when he had subdued it he was soon embroiled in ferocious wars with his deputy and civil wars between his supporters and those of his rivals continued for another ten years. The appointment of a viceroy in 1542 proved ineffectual, and only in 1551 could viceregal rule and a completed administrative system be said to have been installed.

Three features stand out: the conquistadores' usual custom was to grab and hold first, and seek legitimation afterwards; to defy the authority of the royal officials and to fight one another. Left to themselves they would have formed quasi-feudal principalities, such as were by now obsolete in Spain itself, and given the Crown little but lip-service. The Crown, which had warred down its own grandees and then subdued the towns in the *comunero* revolt (1520–1), had no intention of letting them do this, but its early efforts to control the conquistadores via its governors were often ineffectual. It was, however, establishing institutions of central control. These were the *Casa de la Contratacion* as early as 1503 and the Council of the Indies in 1524; the former being a sort of board-of-trade and shipping, the latter the supreme governing body for the entire American Empire, under the king.

3.3. *The Organs of Government*

The government of Spanish America, then, was subject to the directions of the Council of the Indies in Spain and of the *Casa de la Contratacion*. In America itself, hierarchical tiers of authority were established. Their coping-stone was the viceroys. The first and most important Viceroyalties were New Spain and Peru, but in the eighteenth century their jurisdictions were further divided into New Granada and La Plata. The Viceroyalties in their turn came to be divided into lesser government units administered by presidents, so that they were called *presidencias*, and by governors. Providing the base were the governing bodies of the towns—the *cabildos*—formed on the same pattern and with the same object as the town-*cabildos* of Spain. They were supervised by the powerful royal official called the *corregidor*. But another kind of *corregidor* was later established: the *corregidor de Indios*, set up originally to look after the interests of the native Indians. Their jurisdictions were usually rural and remote. These *corregimientos*, therefore, were also a basic unit of government.

From this sketch it may well seem that Spanish America was unmitigatedly authoritarian, but it was not. The most important institution to mitigate this was the *audiencia*, of which, at the close, there were ten. An *audiencia* (described more fully below) was a regular court with administrative duties, a common form of the day throughout Europe. These *audiencias* put limits on the activities of all administrative bodies, but on the viceroys in particular and, as they had direct access to the Council of the Indies in Madrid, they were a powerful check and balance on viceregal power. Furthermore, this authoritarianism was neither arbitrary nor unaccountable. On the contrary, it was tightly law-bound. This is not to say that there was no arbitrary and capricious government in Spanish America. There was lots of it, but this was an abuse of the laws, not their product.

3.4. *The Metropolitan Councils*

In accordance with the views of the time, colonies existed for the benefit of the metropolitan country, and at its very best for the mutual advantage of both. This was to be guaranteed by establishing commercial monopoly and regulation of the colonial economy; in short, it was 'mercantilist'. This was supposedly effected by excluding all foreigners from the colonial trade, by channelling this trade through one single Castilian port, and by making the economies of the colonies complementary to that of Spain. The first regulatory body in Castile was set up to ensure just this. The *Casa de la Contratacion*, established in 1503, quickly acquired such functions as licensing ships, ordering their activities on the high seas, and safeguarding the transportation of the royal treasure. It was also the supreme court to try all cases arising out of the American trade. In addition, it maintained archives of maps, charts, ships' logs, and maritime lore.

The *Casa* acted as the agent of the Council of the Indies. This was an offshoot of the original Royal Council which was made an independent body in 1524, by which time the Indies clearly demanded their own central directing agency. Like the other councils that surrounded the Spanish Crown it was advisory, and like them it consisted of trained lawyers. It was the supreme court of justice for the empire, it controlled its finance and trade, and it made laws and decrees. We have drawn attention to the law-bound nature of Spanish colonial rule. In this it was following in the steps of Spain itself. The nobility of Spain had long since complained that the *Reyes Catolicos* put justice and public affairs in the hands of the *letrados*: one nobleman calculated that the number of law students at the universities numbered 70,000.[18] The Council fairly showered the Indies with laws and regulations. They numbered over 400,000 by 1635, reduced, with great labour, in the Compilation of 1681 to a mere 6,400.[19]

---

[18] F. Braudel, *The Mediterranean and the Mediterranean World in the Age of Philip II*, trans. S. Reynolds, 2 vols.; 2nd edn. (Collins, London, 1973), ii. 682.   [19] Herring, *History of Latin America*, 157.

3.5 *The Viceroyalties*

In law, the Viceroyalties were the Crown's kingdoms beyond the seas, on a par with Castile, or Aragon, or the Italian lands, or Flanders.

We drew attention, earlier, to the fact that a Spanish colony began with the founding of a town. The town councils, the *cabildos*, were the building-blocks of the administration. A town consisted of its *vecinos*, legally enrolled householders. From these were drawn the dozen or so *regidores* who formed the *cabildo* and this elected two *alcaldes*, chief magistrates. It was not long before the Spanish Crown treated these *cabildos* as it had those of Spain. Their power to raise local taxation was cut down. (In effect, most of their income came from property—for example, from dues for the use of the common pasturage or the establishment of a stall in the market—and it rarely sufficed for the town's essential needs.) In Mexico, where the *regidores* were used to electing their successors, the Crown began to make life-appointments, the *regidores perpetuos*, and by 1528 there was no other kind and elections ceased except for that for the two *alcaldes*. Later the Crown put the office of *regidor* up for sale, often with the right to transmit it to heirs.

Finally, the affairs of the municipality were controlled in the interests of the central government by importing the Spanish office of *corregidor*. That office had been generalized in Spain in 1500 and the description given earlier[20] will bear repetition. The *corregidor* was a Crown appointee in every city, usually a trained lawyer, for a two- or three-year term; and—effectively—a local governor who combined judicial and administrative functions. He monitored the affairs of the municipality, maintained public order, and was the most important of the local judicial officers, outdoing the town's own *alcaldes*.[21] Anybody looking to the *cabildo* as evidence of popular government in Spanish America must look again. 'As a repository of the people's liberty, a training school for the democratic system, the *cabildo* possessed no potency at all.'[22]

So much for the base of the Viceroyalty. At its apex stood the viceroy, the 'stand-in' for the king himself, and as such treated with regal pomp and ceremonial. He was the head of the administration, and also the president of the great supreme lawcourt, the *audiencia*, to be described below, but by and large his local patronage was limited as was the armed force at his disposal, nor could he spend money from the colonial treasury without the prior approval of the king. In fact—as will become evident—his notional powers were very circumscribed. Certainly, if the Crown's object was to

---

[20] See pp. 1293–4 above.   [21] See pp. 1293, 1385 above.
[22] Herring, *History of Latin America*, 159.

make it impossible for viceroys to become independent, the arrangements were a total success.[23]

The two greatest Viceroyalties were New Spain and Peru, though subsequent ones were carved out of them. Even so they were still immense, and tiers of intermediate officers were necessarily interposed between the viceroys and the *cabildos* at the base. Such were the presidents, and the captains-general, who enjoyed very great discretion. They did not take their orders from the viceroy as one would expect, but directly from the Crown which appointed and removed them, and it was to the Crown that they reported; so that they often acted in disregard of the viceroy. Below these officials and on a par with the *corregidores* of the towns were the *corregidores de Indios*, arguably the most important class of officials in the empire, but we shall defer a description until we come to the Indian question.

All these offices and their chains of command were enmeshed in a host of checks and balances. For instance, nearly all the senior appointments were made by the Crown, not the viceroy; many of them had the right to appeal past the viceroy straight to the Crown (effectively, of course, the Council of the Indies). And we have already noticed that the governors and captains-general were direct Crown appointees who, again, could appeal directly to the Crown. Also, at any moment the Crown might send an inspector (*visitador*) to inquire into the viceroy's management, and at the end of his term every viceroy had to submit (like most high officials) to an intensive and protracted inquiry into his administration: the *residencia*. But the greatest check on his powers—and for that matter those of the governors and captains-general—was that exerted by the *audiencias*. They reported to, or their decisions could be appealed to the Council of the Indies, The first *audiencia* was set up in Santo Domingo in 1511, and their number increased to ten by the end of the sixteenth century. They were at once courts of appeal and cabinet councils with political and administrative powers. They were wholly independent. Since their decisions had final authority under the king, they acted at times like a legislature. *Audiencias* also exerted a general supervision over the conduct of the inferior magistrates, and had to sit regularly to review administration and make recommendations. The supervision of Indian affairs was an especial care laid on them.

In New Spain and Peru the viceroy was president of the *audiencia*, but without a vote. He was required to consult it on all major decisions. In his prolonged absence or an interregnum it temporarily exercised all viceregal powers. It could hear appeals against the viceroy and report to the Council

[23] J. H. Parry, *The Spanish Seaborne Empire*, 'The History of Human Society' series (Hutchinson, London, 1966), 202–5.

of the Indies. On the other hand, the viceroy might himself appeal against its decisions and also complain against the conduct of any of its *oidores* ('auditors' or judges). It should be noted that, like all high officials in the New World, its personnel were all *peninsulares*, natives of old Spain.[24]

So, for all the outward appearance of hierarchy, the viceregal system was anything but that. Here is one of the supreme examples of the legalistic character of the nascent modern European state, the point we have been stressing repeatedly. But it was not necessarily efficient. Parry expresses the general consensus very concisely when he writes:

This cumbrous system of checks and balances might make for impartiality and respect for law—respect, at least, for the forms of law. It certainly did not make for administrative efficiency or speed of action.[25] All important decisions and many unimportant ones, were made in Spain. In the Indies, there was no decision which could not be reversed and no jurisdiction which could not be inhibited. Appeals and counter-appeals might hold up essential action for years, until the occasion for it was forgotten. 'Obey but do not enforce'[26] became the administrative watchword of an empire whose legislation and basic policy were, in many respects, models of enlightenment for their time.[27]

3.6. *Social Stratification and Skewed Government*

In practice, as is usual, the strict letter of law was skewed to suit the interests of the dominant political class. From the beginning a highly stratified class society developed which 'set' within only a few years of the Conquest. At its top the *peninsulares*, Spaniards sent out from Spain, occupied all the most senior posts: for instance, there were 170 viceroys between 1535 and 1813 and only *four* were American-born. Similar ratios prevailed among the governors and captains-general and the bishops.[28] The second stratum was the dominant socio-economic class: the *creoles*. This word—*criollos* in Spanish—is used in some contexts, for example, in the southern United States, to signify somebody of mixed blood and is often used pejoratively. In the Spanish-American context it bore the exactly contrary connotation: the creole was a person of Spanish blood but born

---

[24] Ibid. 197–9.

[25] Elliott, *Spain and its World*, 15, quotes a *residencia* of the viceroy of Peru which began in 1590 and, having consumed 49,553 sheets of paper and the viceroy having died, was still unfinished in 1603.

[26] *Obedezco pero no cumplo*. Again and again one comes across examples of disobedience by the colonial authorities: they could argue, for instance, that the decree was not workable, or (like the New Laws of the Indies, 1542) likely to provoke revolt; and so forth. And it took at least two months sailing in each direction for the simplest message to come and go between Old Spain and the New World.   [27] J. H. Parry, *Europe and a Wider World, 1415–1715* (Hutchinson, London, 1949), 71.

[28] Herring, *History of Latin America*, 187, n. 1.

in America. The persons of mixed Spanish and Indian blood comprised the third stratum, the *mestizos*. The Indians formed the fourth class, and at the very bottom there were the outright chattel slaves brought from Africa.

The bending of the laws involved three parties: the creoles, the Indians, and the Church. The interests of the two former groups came into collision, into which the Church intervened very actively. We have, then, to say something more about the nature of the creole stratum, and then address what we have so far barely discussed, the question of the native Indian population. In between these two strata there lay the economic institution known as the *encomienda*, which effectively entitled settlers to tribute and labour from the natives. The *encomienda*, even in very principle, actively engaged the Church's evangelizing role, and so the Church must also be discussed.

There were no creole peasants and almost no creole manual labourers in these societies. The heirs of the conquistadores now included *encomienda*-holders, ranchers, and mine-owners, some of whom soon became very rich. The clergy was numerous in absolute terms (albeit a mere fraction of the Indian population). There were lots and lots of creole officials, lawyers, clerks, and the like; and in the larger towns numbers of merchants and craftsmen. Altogether in 1600 the *peninsulares* and the creoles numbered about 250,000, as against some 9 million Indians.[29]

By no means were all these creoles wealthy: Herring estimates that only 4,000 of them held *encomiendas*, the rest taking the humbler occupations mentioned.[30] But the *encomenderos*, the cattle- and sheep-ranchers and the mine-owners, were often the same individuals. They lived away from their sources of income and spent it in the capital towns, and these towns were effectively under their control, for the *cabildos* were in their hands. Their councillors were unpaid but controlled extensive patronage, much of it self-serving. For instance, the settlers required land: they, as *regidores*, were responsible for distributing it; the towns needed meat: they, as ranchers, produced it and as *regidores* fixed the price of it. They could be sued in court, it is true, but it was they who elected the *alcaldes*, the town magistrates! Finally, as *regidores* they influenced or actively carried out the administration of native labour under the *encomienda* system. So it is necessary to consider the Indians and the labour problem.

The problem arose because the settlers were not numerous enough to work the land themselves, while, under law, the Indians were free subjects of

---

[29] McEvedy and Jones, *Atlas*, 275. But Herring, *History of Latin America*, 188, n. 2, gives a lower figure of only 160,000 creoles and Spaniards for the year 1574.

[30] Herring, *History of Latin America*, 188, n. 2.

the Crown and therefore enjoyed freedom to move, change residence, occupation, and employer, own property, sue and be sued, and have easy access to the courts. In the islands in the earliest period of the Conquest the settlers' response to labour-shortage was the *repartimiento*, that is, a conquistador's allocation of the natives of Hispaniola among his followers as, effectively, slaves. From this developed a compromise between the freedom of the Indian, the economic needs of the settlers, and the duty on which the most Catholic kings of Spain insisted, of evangelizing the Indians. So began the *encomienda* system, the right to command tribute (in kind) and labour services from an Indian village or group of villages in return for which the *encomendero* gave it protection and promoted and assisted missionary activities there.

Thus the Church was centrally involved. We have talked of the conquest and the conquistadores, but in a more profound sense Spanish America was colonized by the Church. Its priests reached into villages and areas too remote for the soldier to bother about and in a short time it exerted a profound ascendancy over the Indians, for reasons that are still not really explicable. The missionaries regarded the Indians as their charges and they were not prepared to stand by and see them oppressed. They thus became the denouncers of the *encomenderos*, and the opposition of these two parties was sharpened by their contest for labour services, for the missionaries also needed native labour for building their mission stations and continuing the communal agriculture that maintained them. The first great waves of missionary activity occurred in 1524–5 with the coming of the Franciscans and the Dominicans, the Jesuits coming later. They had been hand-picked and highly trained, and they held radical ideas about human liberty. From as early as 1511 churchmen began to complain to the Court about the injustices perpetrated on the Indians, and indeed Fray Montesinos succeeded in this way in getting the Crown to issue the Laws of Burgos, the first colonial code in Europe, in 1494.

These laws laid down three clear principles: the Indians were free men and not slaves, they were to be converted by persuasion and not by force (they did not come under the Inquisition), and they were to be made to work. In return, the demands the *encomendero* could make on them were limited, and other rules were set to prevent ill treatment. In fact there were no means of policing these laws. Of the missionaries who protested the most famous was Las Casas, whose *Concise Narrative of the Destruction of the Indians* went through numerous editions in many European languages, especially the Protestant ones, and became the solid foundation for the so-called 'Black Legend' of Spanish oppression in the New World. In 1542 Las Casas, who was in the habit of frequenting the Spanish court, finally got

King Charles I (the Emperor Charles V) to promulgate the New Laws of the Indies. Had these been enforced they would have terminated the *encomienda* system within a relatively short space of time, but settler revolts, especially in Peru, forced their modification: the *encomendero* could demand tribute in kind—foodstuffs particularly, of course—but might not exact labour services. Subsequently and consequently, the amount of tribute came to be regulated by the *audiencias*, and resulted in fixed incomes which, at a time of inflation, began to shrivel away. By 1600 the *encomienda* had almost disappeared.

But Indians were still expected to work, and the discovery of the silver mines at Zacatecas and Potos created an urgent demand for their labour. So, having eliminated by law the *private* duty to compel labour, the Crown now authorized the *authorities* to requisition it—in effect the corvée. Every Indian village had to detail a fixed proportion of its population for public work for so many weeks in rotation throughout the year. The local magistrates then allocated them to tasks like repairing roads and bridges, public buildings, and the like. However, included in such 'public' undertakings was the working of the silver mines (in some cases the cultivation of sugar, too). Wages were indeed paid. Naturally they were very low. In New Spain this system was called the *repartimiento*, in Peru the *mita*. The abuses were enormous, so that it is only right to signal that the Indian did have a mode of redress which was not always ineffectual. In New Spain a special court called the *Juzgado General de Indios* dispensed summary justice and assessed the liability of the villages to provide labour. Unfortunately for the Indians no similar court existed in Peru, and suitors had to go through the slow, cumbersome procedures of the *audiencia*.

But as the *encomienda* fell away, a new class of officials emerged to control the Indians and see that they did their corvée. These were the *corregidores de Indios*. They became a vital tier in the hierarchy—one authority regards them as the 'foundation of colonial government'.[31] They were often creole, though appointed by Madrid. The term was short but renewable. They combined judicial and administrative authority. But there really was little or no effective check on their behaviour and their rule was, in theory, one of exploitation and repression, although in practice they often did not exercise their power. The *corregidor de Indios* was tax-collector, policeman, and magistrate all in one. He could collect whatever sum he was able to extract, and pocket as much as he pleased; he could call up the 'public' labour of the Indians only to farm it out to private individuals; he could name his own price when buying from the Indians and make compulsory sales to them at

---

[31] Fieldhouse, *The Colonial Empires*, 19.

the price he himself set. He could even get Indian lands for himself and cheat the Indian out of his water rights. Even worse were the *alcaldes mayores*, lesser officials with much the same functions as the *corregidor* but assigned to minor communities and often receiving no salary; in which case they were even more corruptible.

It seems only fair by way of comparison to point out that the North American Indians enjoyed no rights at all as subjects of the British Crown and that those who were not exterminated were herded on to reservations where, parenthetically, the Indian agent was frequently as tyrannical as any Spanish *corregidor*. It is also fair to draw attention to the plight of peasants in Eastern Europe at about this time: the *serfs* of Prussia, Denmark, Poland, Austria, and Russia. They enjoyed no freedom of movement, no right to choose their occupations, and had no legal recourse against the exactions of their landlord.

3.7. *Summary*

The New World colonies then, were treated as distinct kingdoms subject to the Crown of Castile. They were organized accordingly as coherent hierarchical entities, many of their most characteristic institutions being imports from Castile. As in Castile, the government was strictly authoritarian—in so far as any self-governing or representative bodies as might exist either lay in the grip of a narrow, wealthy oligarchy and/or were very restricted in their duties. But the hierarchical arrangements consisted of an intricate pattern of checks and balances which made revolt or even autonomy quite impossible, yet made for interminable delays and counter-orders, exaggerated by the effects of distance from Madrid.

A second major characteristic of the government was its intense legalism: laws and edicts were showered upon the colonies and it was expected that all would be done with due process of law. But this was contradicted by a third major characteristic: the social structure, which subjected the 9-million strong Indian communities to the rule of some quarter-million creoles, of whom some 4,000 were very rich *encomenderos*, ranchers, and mine-owners who controlled the municipalities, and the *corregidores* who sometimes worked the Indians in the rural communities on their own private account. This societal polarity set most of the legal safeguards at nought. The new kingdoms were, meanwhile, thoroughly evangelized in the Roman Catholic faith, and were as uniformly conformist as the mother country. Together with the use of Indian craftsmen in church architecture, this exhaustive evangelization did more perhaps to 'colonize' the native populations than the deeds of arms and conquest, for through it the Indians received a faith, a philosophy, and a new language. In practically every one of these respects the kingdoms of Spanish America differed from the British colonies in the north of the continent.

4. THE ENGLISH COLONIES

4.1. *Colonization, Colonies, and Colonists*

The *Recopilación de las leyes de Indias* (1680) contains a statement of a consistent policy of the Spanish Crown since the reign, at least, of Philip II:

> Inasmuch as the Kingdoms of Castile and of the Indies are under one Crown, the laws and manner of government of the one should conform as nearly as possible to those of the other. Our Royal Council, in establishing laws and institutions of governments in the Indies, must ensure that those Kingdoms are administered according to the same form and order as Castile and Léon, in so far as the differences of the land and peoples will allow.[32]

The aspiration was largely realized. England also transmitted to its American colonies its own legal and governmental tradition but hardly by design. It emerged, was unforced, and was incremental.

4.1.1. COLONIZATION

Since in the early seventeenth century the Spaniards were too strong to evict from Central and South America, the English were forced to look to such Caribbean islands as were not already occupied—notably the lesser Antilles group, which they then partitioned with the French—and to the North American mainland. The islands produced sugar and tobacco, rich cash crops. The plantations were worked with imported African slaves. They were, therefore, 'plantation colonies'. The nearest to approach their model on the mainland were Virginia and the Carolinas. Of all the colonies in America, Westminister's favourites were these 'Sugar Islands' and after them these southernmost mainland colonies. Indeed, the further north the colony, the less enthusiasm did Westminster entertain for it, and for the northernmost, in New England, it felt a positive distaste.

It is with the mainland colonies that we are concerned here. The country north of Spanish Florida was being claimed in the name of the English Crown, which did not mean that nobody else laid claims to it—for the French and the Dutch certainly felt free to settle there—but that no Englishman could go there and take land to settle without some express authorization from the English Crown.

---

[32] Quoted in Parry, *Spanish Seaborne Empire*, 197–8.

The first permanent English settlement was made at Jamestown in 1607 by the newly formed 'London' joint-stock company. Its object was to colonize and Christianize. Its directors in England (elected and controlled by the shareholders) appointed the colony's governor and his council. The next permanent settlement was planted in 1620 at Plymouth, not far from today's Boston. This was largely the work of religious dissidents who obtained this right to colonize from the same 'London' Company. Thus the colonization of English North America began at its northern and southern extremities. From that time on new colonies were formed, filling the empty space between, until a long but narrow strip along the entire coastline from Maine to Georgia had been colonized.

4.1.2. THE THREE CONSTITUTIONAL FORMS OF COLONY

Far from the British American Empire being a single unity under a viceroy, it came to consist of thirteen separate governments, each with its own currency, own trade laws, and very often, its own religious attitudes. They were politically interrelated only by common subjection to the British government. Furthermore they were of diverse constitutional forms. Although each foundation had to be authorized by the Crown, the latter could do this by making an outright gift of lands to a given individual or set of individuals, the 'proprietaries'; or the would-be colonizers could be a joint-stock company who persuaded the Crown to give them a Charter to proceed. In either case, it will be noticed, the initiative did not come from the government but from private individuals—dissimilar from Spain or Portugal or France, where the state was involved in the colonization.

From such beginnings there emerged three constitutional forms. The first, which embraced the colonies of New England, was what we may call the 'corporate' (sometimes the 'chartered') colony, the second the 'proprietorial', and the third the 'royal' colony.

The 'corporate' colonies followed a pattern set by the Massachusetts Bay Company in 1629. This was a joint-stock kind of colony but, in 1629, by some legal chicane or other the colonists received permission to buy out any objecting English shareholders so that the company became effectively America-based and administered, conveying the company's seat of government with them to America. In this way the provisions of the joint-stock company became the constitution of the colony: that is, it was administered by a governor and eighteen 'assistants', annually elected by the stockholders or the freemen (who did not have to hold stock in the company). The point here is not the detail of the constitution, which in any case changed considerably. It is the doubt that now hung over the relationship of the colony to the British Crown. In physically transferring the company to

Massachusetts, had the colonists effectively become independent of the Crown? Certainly this was sometimes claimed, especially during the English Civil Wars. Massachusetts was a persecuting colony, exercising a total religious control over its members. Dissidents fled it to form their own little governments in Connecticut and Rhode Island and so, as offshoots of the original colony, they too shared this ambiguous relationship to the English Crown. Apart from this, the distinctive feature of these 'chartered' or 'corporate colonies' was that none of its officials were appointed by the Crown and they neither had nor had sent intermediaries to England to represent them there.

The 'proprietary' colony's constitution was an archaism. Conceived at a date when there was still a palatinate in Durham, it transferred this kind of authority to a named individual or group. Thus, in 1632 Maryland, a tract of country carved out of the colony of Virginia, was granted by Charles I to George Calvert (later Lord Baltimore). He, his heirs, and assigns were made 'the true and absolute lords and proprietaries' of the territory in return for one-fifth of any gold or silver found, and two 'Indian flint arrow-heads'. As proprietary, Calvert became captain-general of the armed forces and disposed of all offices, clerical and lay. He had the right to create and grant manors to vassal lords, but the laws of the colony had to receive the consent of the freemen or their representatives. New Jersey and the Carolinas were proprietary colonies, too. The most distinguished one is Pennsylvania, a vast territory which in 1681 Charles II granted to the Quaker, William Penn, who wanted it as a haven for this much-persecuted sect. Penn made a principal feature of complete religious toleration. The definitive constitution of 1689 (the 'Charter of Privileges') provided what had by now become the standard arrangement of a governor and council appointed by the proprietaries, and an assembly of four representatives for each county.

What distinguished the proprietary colony from the royal colony was that it was the proprietary, as both landlord and head of the government, who appointed the governor and high officials. He stood between the Crown and the colonists; but the characteristic feature of the *royal* colony was that here the Crown itself appointed. The first such colony was Virginia, originally managed—as we have seen—by a joint-stock company, the 'London' Company. Mismanaged and all but bankrupt, it was judicially dissolved at the behest of James I in 1624. Thereafter its governor and council were appointed by the Crown and subject to royal instructions; but the assembly, the lawcourts, and the organs of local government remained in place as before. This pattern was to be much followed. In 1685 only two colonies were royal, but by 1763 only Maryland and Pennsylvania were proprietarial, and only Connecticut and Rhode Island were 'corporate'; all the others were royal.[33]

4.1.3. COLONISTS

In 1660 the European (and largely British) population of the English colonies was only 70,000 (though in all French Canada there resided a mere 3,000 Frenchmen); but in 1700 there were 250,000 and by 1763 no less than 2,500,000 (including blacks). This was about one-third of the then-population of Great Britain.[34] The English immigrants were not self-selected *hidalgo* types, come to rule and exploit conquered races. It is true that the first colonists in Jamestown in 1607 were 'gentlemen' who knew no manual crafts and had come to find bullion lying about the woods. There were almost no manual labourers or artisans in the first two shiploads of immigrants and it was this that accounted for the great mortality in the colony's first five years. But the colonists learned their lesson, and instead of mining gold fell to planting tobacco. Compare them with the Pilgrims and the 'Great Migration' of Puritans (*c.*1630–40) to New England. The men who migrated there came with their families to flee from religious persecution and set up their own chapels, or to escape what they regarded as intolerable tyranny at home. Maryland was established for persecuted Catholics, and the Quaker origins of Pennsylvania have already been touched upon; but both colonies soon enacted religious toleration, so that they attracted Huguenots and persecuted German sects, followed by the Scots and Irish. Thus, unlike Spanish America, the English colonies were open to all comers and as such positively attracted dissidents.

Again unlike the Spanish immigrants, where the larger number of impoverished minor nobles encouraged migration, few English noblemen went to America: the immigrants were of the middle and artisan strata of English society, not to speak of indentured servants and convicts. There was no 'feudalism' in the colonies—the abundance of land and the shortage of labour made this impossible.[35] The social structure of the colonies consisted of a dominant socio-political class, then a stratum of freeholder farmers, next a layer made up of free artisans and labourers. Below all of these were the indentured servants, who were virtual serfs until they had

[33] This extension of the royal type of constitution was not always due to the Crown's wish to exercise direct authority, but was done to meet the behests of substantial interests in the colonies themselves. Particularly was this true of the Carolinas (1725) and Georgia (1752).

[34] R. C. Simmons, *American Colonies from Settlement to Independence* (1976), 74; J. Miller, *Origins of the American Revolution* (Faber, London, 1945), 43. McEvedy and Jones, *Atlas*, suggests 1 million whites in all Latin America in 1700, and 0.3 million whites in North America (p. 279).

[35] C. A. and M. R. Beard, *The Rise of American Civilization*, 1 vol. edn. (Cape, London, 1930), 52–5.

worked out their time. And at the very bottom of the pile were the black slaves. But though such a stratification was common to all the colonies, the composition of its layers could differ greatly. New England, for instance, was dominated by rich merchants and their dependants, very superior and distinct from the common run of farmers, artisans, and the servile elements. On the other hand, south of the Potomac the upper class were landed gentry, using the laws of entail and, often, primogeniture, and who despised merchants and 'trade'. They were slave-owing barons who cowed the free-holders in open-air elections, and indeed called themselves cavaliers. Yet this was no closed hereditary class like the English aristocracy. A dirt farmer could work his way into being a great landowner and as such join their ranks. As for the middle colonies, their governing classes were a mixture of landowners and traders, like the Dutch-descended patrons of New York.

In all colonies the ruling orders demanded and got obedience and deference. In churches, for instance, 'the congregations were seated accord-ing to their age, social position, and estates'.[36] Below them the bulk of the population in the north-east and middle colonies consisted of the free-holder farmers: industrious, ambitious, poorly housed, and often illiterate. But they had the franchise and when popular or populist parties formed, it was they who provided their basis. The third layer, of artisans and labourers, could not vote unless they could meet the property qualification for voting, an arrangement that in some shape or form existed in all the colonies.

So there should be no question of these colonies being 'democratic'. They were in fact highly oligarchical. But for all that, the colonists brought with them the common law and parliamentary tradition of England.

4.2. The Imperial Framework

In the decade or so before the American Revolution of 1776 some colonial publicists were beginning to question the sovereignty of the English Crown-in-Parliament, or at least its extent. Till then, the constitutional status of the colonies was, broadly speaking, as follows. The colonies were akin to Ireland or the Isle of Man; they were 'Dominions', dependencies of the Crown, not sister kingdoms like the Viceroyalties of Spanish America. They had their own political institutions and the Crown, by itself, had to work through these if it wanted to tax them or make laws for them. The power of the Crown-in-Parliament, on the other hand, was unlimited. It had always claimed power to bind the Dominions of the Crown, could legislate for them, and could tax them.

---

[36] C. A. and M. R. Beard, *The Rise of American Civilization*, 129.

In practice it chiefly used this sovereignty over the American colonies to regulate trade matters, although from time to time it might intervene, in a special case, to reshape a colony's Charter (e.g. the Charter of Massachusetts in 1726). For, as regards internal affairs of a colony, the assumption was that effective authority was exercised by the Crown rather than the Crown-in-Parliament. If colonial charters had to be abrogated or reshaped, the Crown was left to do this. It was supposed to control the activities of the colonies through its instructions to the governors it appointed (or the proprietary governors who had to be approved by it). They were supposed to be the agency which pushed the Crown's legislation through the colonial legislature or, alternatively, vetoed such local laws as it opposed. Furthermore the Crown could itself disallow such laws via the Privy Council. In fact about 2.5 per cent of laws passed by colonial legislatures were disallowed, for instance, discriminatory legislation against religious minorities. On the other hand, laws restraining the slave trade were also disallowed.[37]

In practice, for reasons that will be explored shortly, the governors proved a feeble transmission link, and Rhode Island and Connecticut actually elected their own governors. By and large, English imperial interference with the internal affairs of the colonies was minimal except in one area: trade and industry.

No single British ministry was responsible for imperial policy. In principle it was a matter for the Privy Council but this became more and more honorific and, as it did so, the Privy Council came to rely on the specialized advice of a Board of Trade and Plantations. Its remit permitted it to scrutinize colonial legislation, recommend the disallowance of colonial laws which conflicted with imperial trade policy, propose the names of governors and draft their instructions, recommend laws affecting the colonies to Parliament or the Privy Council, and hear colonial complaints. But the Board was purely advisory and never managed to acquire a Cabinet minister to head it; it lacked any executive or legislative powers.

In short, the British government regarded the empire as little more than a trading association, and in so far as it did interfere with the activities of the colonies, it was almost entirely with those affecting the unity of this trading association. This last rested on two sets of policies. The first consisted of the Navigation Acts. All trade to and from the colonies had to be carried in British-owned and -manned ships. All goods, irrespective of their place of origin, had to be transshipped via a British port. And certain designated colonial products had to be exported direct to a British port. The second

---

[37] S. E. Morison, H. S. Commager, and W. E. Leuchtenberg, *The Growth of the American Republic* (OUP, Oxford, 1969), i. 84.

set of policies was designed to ensure that the colonies should not compete with the mother country. Some of their products were banned or restricted: wool, wool yarn, and cloth, for instance. Sometimes one industry was discouraged and another encouraged: for instance, the 1750 Iron Act forbade the colonies to establish new slitting and rolling mills, or to produce steel, but encouraged them to produce bar- and pig-iron for export to England.

There has been much controversy over the effects of this 'old colonial policy'. Adam Smith in his *Wealth of Nations* did point out that the disadvantages were not all on one side. The tobacco- and rice-planters suffered because they had to sell to Britain and were forbidden to sell direct to Europe, but the producers of items like indigo, timber, or sugar benefited from bounties on their exports to Britain. On balance it would seem that the colonies came off worse and one estimate puts the cost to them, in the early 1770s, at between £500,000 and £1,500,000. On the other hand it was Britain who bore the cost of their defence.[38] It was, of course, precisely this trade-off between the British government's desire for colonial contributions to the cost of defence and its pursuit via this mercantilist system that first agitated and finally provoked the colonies into resistance in the 1770s.

4.3. *Government in the Colonies*

Despite their differing constitutional origins, a similar pattern of government emerged in all of them: a governor, a council, and an elected legislature. The ubiquity of the elected legislature is truly noteworthy. It actually antedated the Pilgrim Fathers! For, while Virginia was still the property of the 'London' joint-stock company, this body directed the establishment of a representative assembly to make local laws subject to the Company's consent, so that in 1619 twenty-two 'burgesses', two from each settled district, met with the governor's council. When in 1624 James I made Virginia into a royal colony, so that it was the Crown which now appointed the governor and his council, he nevertheless confirmed the planters' right to elect their assembly, to make laws, and vote taxes. The original Massachusetts constitution was, as we have seen, the joint-stock company's charter transplanted to America. It provided that its governor and his eighteen assistants were to be elected annually by the stockholders and/or freemen, and that, furthermore, these latter were to meet every quarter to conduct the elections and pass laws and regulations. Maryland was supposed to be ruled by its proprietary, Lord Baltimore, but in 1642 a freeholder assembly emerged here also. The Civil Wars and the Puritan triumph in England gave a great boost

---

[38] Fieldhouse, *Colonial Empires*, 68.

to colonial assemblies, and from 1660 it may be said that the Crown stipulated assemblies as a matter of course. There is one great exception to this, however, which proves the general rule—and that is the royal 'Dominion of New England'. Under James II all Puritan New England, New York, and New Jersey were incorporated as a single 'Dominion of New England', to be governed by a governor and a council but, specifically, without a representative assembly. This, of course, was consistent with James's authoritarianism and distaste for Parliament. But when in 1689 the colonists heard that he had fled the throne they rose in revolt, imprisoned their royal governor, and ended the experiment by resuming their original charters.

Let us then turn to the three components of the colonial governments: governor, council, and assembly.

The governor's commissions, issued under the Great Seal of England, were the highest expression of royal will. As chief executive he might grant land; he enforced customs and trade laws. He was also the commander-in-chief and (by a separate commission) vice-admiral. He appointed the minor judges, JPs, and inferior officials. Although the king's representative in the colony, he had greater prerogative powers over the assembly than the king did over Parliament, for he was under instructions to exercise actively his right to summon, dissolve, and prorogue the assembly, to redistrict the constituencies, to decide where the session should be held, and above all, to veto legislation.

Associated with the governor was the council of about a dozen men. Now this had multiple roles. It acted as the Upper House of the assembly. Together with the governor it constituted the colony's highest lawcourt. And it had to concur with the governor in a number of executive matters, such as granting land, appointing minor officials, and summoning the assembly. In some colonies the council acted as a check on the governor but as it was he who nominated them for office and could suspend them for opposition, they were for the most part compliant.

In British eyes, the governor was the royal representative who vetoed objectionable legislation and got the assembly to pass the laws the Crown wanted; but it did not work this way at all—in fact, just the reverse. The reason for this was that these colonial assemblies, supposedly feebler *vis-à-vis* the executive than the British Parliament, were in most cases very much stronger. This progressive strengthening of the powers of the assemblies against the governors is the most striking characteristic of colony government, exploding, finally, in the Revolution of 1776. We have said that the colonists transplanted British institutions to their own soil; in time they outdid them.

The electorates of the various colonies were, on the whole, extensive. The franchise was based on a property qualification. In New England this was the old English 40-shilling freehold and so, very liberal. The most onerous qualifications were in New York (a freehold of around £40) and South Carolina, where it was progressively steepened after 1745, so that in 1759 it required the ownership of 100 acres or the payment of 10 shillings per annum in tax.[39] It has been suggested that, in New England at least, these qualifications would have permitted as many as 50–80 per cent of white adult male colonists to vote. But this was not reflected in the composition of the assemblies, which consisted largely of the landed and well established.

These assemblies steadily increased their powers vis-à-vis the governors, and they did it through using the one power that even the Crown regarded as their irreducible minimum, control over public finances. In Virginia and Maryland the governors' salaries were beyond assembly control because they derived from taxes on tobacco exports, but everywhere else it was for the assemblies to grant—and this meant also to withhold. The Crown did its utmost to insist that they paid the governors regularly, but had no means of enforcing it.

But the assemblies often went even further. In this respect they resembled those German Estates of the fifteenth and sixteenth century where the prince had dissipated his income and the Diets took power to appropriate sums for particular purposes, and even to set up their own commissions to audit the accounts. Thus in Virginia the assembly came to acquire full control over money bills and over fees of public servants. It also acquired control over the creation of new towns and counties and the apportionment of their representation—a power of formidable political importance, as will be seen. For all that, Virginia did not often see many collisions between the governors and the assembly, because in that colony governors identified themselves socially with the dominant gentry class who made up the assembly.[40] Just the reverse occurred in South Carolina. Its Commons House acquired control over the same political functions as the Virginia assembly and also established commissions to carry out local public works. But in this colony incoming governors struggled to cast off these shackles and in this way precipitated sharp conflicts.

In both the Carolinas the assemblies resisted, also, all gubernatorial efforts to influence the outcome of elections. For instance, Governor Boone of South Carolina failed in his attempt to challenge the validity of an election (1762) and the assembly fought hard and long to block the

---

[39] Simmons, *American Colonies*, 247–8.   [40] Ibid. 249.

governors' efforts to re-district the electoral constituencies.[41] North of Virginia, the Massachusetts assembly obtained control over the governor's salary, and likewise in New Jersey and New York. In the latter the assembly also obtained control of appropriations and the audit of accounts. As for Rhode Island and Connecticut, these corporate colonies had, as we have seen, acquired the right actually to elect their own governors and these were not bound by British instructions, either. It was no wonder, then, that Governor Belcher of New Jersey, for instance, exclaimed, 'I have to steer between Scylla and Charybdis . . . to please a King's ministers at home and touchy people here; to luff for one and bear away for another', or that in similar vein Governor Dinwiddie of New York chided his Assembly as 'obstinate, self-opinionated: a stubborn generation'.[42]

How had this come about? How is it that these assemblies overran their governors, while in Britain the House of Commons allowed the king's ministers to exert firm and stable rule, rebelling only in rare and especially fraught situations? The answer lies in the very reason that the Crown was able to govern through the Commons in eighteenth-century Britain, and that reason has already been described in the preceding chapter. It was by the use of the Crown's extensive and all-pervading 'influence', that is, its patronage, that the Crown's ministers were able to control the constituencies, determine the outcome of the elections, and 'manage' the House.

Now these were precisely the powers that the colonial governors lacked. The previous paragraphs have shown how the assemblies prevented them gerrymandering the constituencies. In addition, their lack of patronage prevented them from influencing the electors. This lack of patronage was due to the combined effect of the policies of Westminster and of the assemblies. The latter, in many cases, took over the nomination of the minor officials and the higher officials were appointed by the British ministers.[43]

It should not be thought that these colonial assemblymen stumbled by sheer accident or trial and error on the consequences of executive interference with free elections and how to prevent it. They were acutely conscious of all that went on in England and this is a point that must never be forgotten: the continuous and continuing British connection and the tremendous impact of the British constitution upon their own perception of the constitutional order. The colonists accepted the British model, but in doing so they came to view their assemblies as replicas of the Westminster Parliament and inferred that their powers should be the

[41] Ibid. 248–9.   [42] Beard, *Rise of American Civilization*, 117.
[43] Simmons, *American Colonies*, 246.

same; whereas in fact they knew that the governor could and did exercise powers which the Crown had lost in Britain such as the power to veto, to summon and prorogue Parliaments at pleasure, even to dismiss judges. Bolingbroke had described Walpole's 'system' as the control of a Parliament by the manipulation of 'honours, titles and preferments . . . with bribes which are called pensions', and so forth.[44] This had not escaped the colonists. The British pamphleteers who subscribed to such views and their American counterparts who adopted them were published and republished throughout the Thirteen Colonies.[45]

This continuing British connection and the overwhelming influence British thought and institutions had in the colonies is what accounts for the colonists' ever-increasing attachment to the niceties of the common law. The common law, in the interpretation of Chief Justice Coke, was capable of binding Parliament itself. This view had been rejected by his fellow-judges in his own time. We mention this because of a widespread belief that this was one of the principles of the common law brought over by the Pilgrim Fathers and accounts for the present-day American practice of judicial review of the Constitution. In fact, the 'common law' which the pioneers brought with them was little more than an assortment of rude though enormously powerful principles—trial by jury, the protection of property by due process, a rudimentary form of habeas corpus, and the provision that no man should be compelled to witness against himself. In the beginning this was as far as 'common law' went. Its archaic procedure, which required specialized lawyers, and even its substantive legal rules were unsuitable and indeed remote from the problems that arose in opening vast virgin territories. Indeed some of the colonists actually disliked the common law, since it was under this that they had been persecuted and forced to flee.[46]

The common law of England was, in fact, not really known, and the law the authorities applied was probably primitive. In the absence of lawyers to expound the law some colonies permitted litigants to plead their own cause; for instance, the Massachusetts 'Body of Liberties' did so. But as American society became complex there arose the need to have a full, complex body of law and hence also the need to understand it—which implied trained lawyers. The public showed ever-increasing interest in it. The common law was now seen as able to protect civil liberties against arbitrary executive power on the one hand, and on the other as a distinguishing mark of

[44] Quoted, Simmons, *American Colonies*, 258.   [45] Ibid. 258.
[46] R. David and J. E. Brierley, *Major Legal Systems in the World Today: An Introduction to the Comparative Study of Law* (Stevens and Sons, London, 1985), 399–400.

Englishness against the menacing French.[47] English legal treatises were extensively published, and the number of lawyers in American public life rose rapidly.

In the first colonial conference held in New York in 1690, two of the seven members were lawyers; of the twenty-four men who attended the Albany Congress of 1754, thirteen belonged to the legal profession; in the first Continental Congress that launched the Revolution, twenty-four of the forty-five delegates were lawyers; in the second Congress, that declared Independence, twenty-six of the fifty-six delegates were of that class; and in the Convention that framed the federal constitution thirty-three of the fifty-five members were lawyers.[48]

4.4. *The English Model Overseas*

Here then was the English parliamentary model writ large: 'no foreign colony had comparable legislative powers in the eighteenth century', writes one commentator,[49] but goes on to add, 'In fact the colonists were considerably more self-governing than the English intended them to be'; and we have explored why. In a similar way, the lawyers who studied and practised the common law became tribunes of the people and supplanted the preachers who had hitherto been the great opinion-leaders of their congregations. These two powerfully reinforcing notions of limited government via parliamentarianism and law-boundedness expanded as the American population grew. By 1760 it was a third the size of Great Britain's. The subsequent independence of the United States and its rise to world power represented also the rise of parliamentarianism and law-boundedness, the basic components of the liberal-democratic state, to world power.

5. WESTERNIZING RUSSIA, 1682–1796

To the far east of the Atlantic powers lay a state that was in Europe but not part of it. Its people called it the 'lands of Rus'; the western European states knew it as 'Muscovy'. Apart from some infrequent and miscellaneous contacts such as its diplomatic negotiations with Rome and Vienna in the later fifteenth century and England in the sixteenth century followed by burgeoning encounters in the seventeenth century with Poland, Sweden, and Austria, it was insulated from Western Europe until, effectively, Peter I, 'the Great'. But even by the death of Catherine the Great in 1796, westernization remained very limited. Indeed it amounted to little more than a

---

[47] Ibid.   [48] Beard, *Rise of American Civilization*, 101.
[49] Fieldhouse, *Colonial Empires*, 62.

reshaping of the aristocracy in the western mode and a highly limited role for the patriciates in the (very few) towns; the bulk of Russian society remained largely untouched. It had to wait until the latter half of the nineteenth century before beginning to be restructured.

5.1. *The Russian Political Tradition*

To the western states Russia was a remote, marginal place where Europe and Asia join, which from the time of the Mongol conquest could be called 'European' only by a kind of courtesy until the eighteenth century. It had lived a life of its own. It was isolated from the west of the continent. All the great movements and experiences that created the new model European state had passed it by. It was not Christianized, even superficially, until 987, (500 years behind the Franks) and, even then, in the Orthodox form which cut it off from the European Catholic mainstream, the more so in that, after 1054, the two Churches were in schism. Its isolation became almost absolute for two centuries after its conquest by the Tartars (Mongols) began in 1237. The European west was further cut off by the pagan Lithuanians. These only began to be Christianized in 1387, but since they were Catholic this made matters worse; for Orthodoxy as against Catholicism supplied the principal if not, indeed, the solitary sentiment for regarding oneself as Russian and not Polish–Lithuanian.

So, after the Mongol conquest Russia's historical evolution ran on quite different lines from the western states. For a start, she was hardly yet a territorial state since her frontiers were open, disputed, and fluid. Ukraine and the Don Basin fell to Lithuania; south of them roamed the wild Cossacks, runaways from oppression and bondage; still further south lay the Tartars, who had split into three Khanates (1350–1400); and to the east stretched the Siberian steppeland which went on seemingly for ever until it reached the Pacific Ocean.

The primary intellectual and religious influence was that of Byzantium, but Greek was not commonly used because the liturgy had been translated into Old Church Slavonic. The country had never used Latin, never entertained the equivalent of western scholastic philosophy, never experienced the Protestant Reformation, the Renaissance, or a native Enlightenment. Rather the reverse: for example, when a Church versus State controversy did arise, as it did in the seventeenth-century schism between Orthodoxy and the Old Believers, it was no conflict between closely reasoned rival theologies. It originated in ecclesiastical obscurantism and generated millenarian and antinomian sectaries, but was never at any time conducted along the rational lines of the Reformation and never produced theologies that pointed towards republicanism, as did so many varieties of Protestant dissent. The Orthodox Church—the Church of Byzantium, it must be remembered—had always yielded precedence to the secular power and indeed provided it with its absolutist and caesaropapist ideology.

In any event, the country could never have undergone the European Reformation and Renaissance since it was illiterate. There were priests so ignorant that they could believe—and teach—that there were *four* persons in the Trinity (the last being St Nicholas) and others unable to repeat the Lord's Prayer. There were almost no schools. Whereas Western Europe had had universities since the eleventh and twelfth centuries, Russia's first university was not founded till 1755.

But the most striking and important contrast between Russia and the rest of Europe was that the country had no tradition of what we have called 'law-boundedness'. Roman law (i.e. the law of Byzantium) was available, but what little of it found its way into indigenous Russian law came via the Canon law of the Church. The earliest law-codes were like the western barbarian codes such as the Lex Salica or Lex Friesionum, and there was never a feudal system to introduce a contractual element into ruler–ruled relationships. The barbarian codes of Western Europe were transformed by the revolutionary legal developments of the twelfth and thirteenth centuries, but no such thing occurred in Russia (under the Mongols from the thirteenth to the fifteenth centuries), whose primitive laws persisted until the Court Manuals of 1497 and 1550 and, finally, the more comprehensive code of 1649. But the state of law at this time can best be judged by two simple facts: there was no systemic body of private law, nor any trained jurists or advocates. In any case, new laws accumulated faster than they could be codified: between the 1649 code and 1832 they numbered over 30,000. Between 1700 and 1815 no less than ten commissions were set up to codify them, but none succeeded, though a number of partial codes were drafted such as the Military and Naval Codes, General Regulations (for civil administration), and so forth. Not until 1832 did Russia possess a complete collection of its laws. A legal code was promulgated only in 1833 and this (though it consisted of Russian laws) merely followed the definitions and the classificatory system of the *Code Napoléon*.[50] In effect, until as late as the mid-nineteenth century, Russia did without systematized laws, a legal profession, and the law-boundedness that was the essential characteristic of the western state tradition.

[50] See H. J. Berman, *Justice in Russia* (Harvard Russian Research Center Studies, Harvard UP, Cambridge, Mass., 1950), 122–59 (ch. 6, 'The Spirit of Russian Law'), on which I have relied for the above.

Some historians believe that Russia's theory and practice of law was inspired by a quite different and very alien source from that of the west, that is, the Mongols.[51] Others disagree, furiously. The 'Tartar' case rests on the ground that from the mid-twelfth century Russia consisted of a number of separate principalities (albeit ruled by members of the same families); that the first undisputed overlord that all Russians experienced was the Mongol khan; and that the despotic authority he wielded was the primary element in Russia's political tradition.

The Mongols did not occupy or settle but left the princes in being and simply levied tribute from them. But before each tributary prince could assume authority he had to go in person and obtain his investiture—the *iarlyk*—from the khan, who played prince against prince and, this condition met, would give preference to those princes who promised most tribute. In this way they became, effectively, the tax collectors for the Mongols. So (it is argued) when Ivan IV, the 'Terrible', proclaimed himself Tsar of All Russia in 1547 his model was not the Byzantine emperor (long extinguished, anyway) but the Tartar khan (who also called himself 'tsar' in Russian). Here, it is claimed, was the first centralized authority the Russian princes had had to face and it was from this source that they learned all about absolutism, unconditional obedience, the imposition of household taxes, the conduct of diplomatic relations, and how to deal with insubordinate subjects.[52] Ivan regarded elective western monarchs as limited or 'contracted' (*uriadniks*), whereas he was the sovereign (*samoderzhets*). Only two monarchs met his standard of unconditional authority and power over persons and property: the Russian tsar and the Turkish sultan.[53] This was also the view of Giles Fletcher, an English observer of Queen Elizabeth's day: 'The manner of their government is much after the Turkish fashion . . . The state and forme of their government is plaine tyrannical, as applying all to the behoofe of the prince and after a most open and barbarous manner.'[54]

Other historians argue just as fiercely the other way: the model for Ivan III and Ivan IV, they maintain, is definitely the emperor of Byzantium and of the Holy Roman Empire, not the Mongol khan. The Russians learnt about conducting diplomatic relations from Byzantine and papal negotiations and envoys. They learnt about politics through the Greek metropolitans who were appointed by Constantinople throughout the Mongol period.

The difficulty here is to know what is meant by 'politics'. The metro-

[51] Otherwise, Tartars. This was what the Russians—among others—called the Mongols. So, in the text, the two terms are to be treated as interchangeable.

[52] R. Pipes, *Russia under the Old Regime* (Weidenfeld & Nicholson, London, 1974), 74–5.

[53] Ibid. 77.

[54] G. Fletcher, *Of the Russe Commonwealth (1591)*, ed. E. A. Bond (Hakluyt Society, London, 1846), 26.

politan and the bishops were hardly the people to teach rulers about administrative techniques, chancellery practice, taxation, and military organization.[55] Certainly, the Church introduced Canon law, but secular law shows 'little sign of direct Byzantine influence', and 'the concept of a direct continuity between Byzantium and post-medieval Russian political ideas finds little support in the history of Russia during the century and a half that followed the fall of Constantinople'.[56] On the other hand, the tsars did derive from Byzantium their theocratic notion of the sacred monarchy in harmony with and protective of the Church, together with the model of a great autocracy. It would seem to me that the Mongol legacy to the Russian princes consisted of techniques for carrying on political activities, but that Byzantium provided the grand ideology and model of a sacred absolutism over a single, united, and vast territory.

5.2. Reclusive Russia: Ivan the Terrible, 1533–1584

Ivan, aged only 3 when he inherited the throne, was subjected to the thraldom of the great barons (the boyars) at court, often going in fear of his life. At the age of 13 he asserted his independence by ordering the seizure and murder of the leader of one of these factions. Many and varied are the opinions about his personality, but to me he seems a psychopath: mercurial, murderous, sadistic, and at the same time a shrinking coward, steeped in Orthodox piety to the point of superstition. He killed his son and heir in a fit of rage. He massacred the population of the city of Novgorod. And we know of a list of 3,000 nobles whom he had had executed, which he sent to the monasteries with orders to pray for their souls.

The reason for spending this time on a personality is because under Ivan (not necessarily true of Vasily III and Ivan III or later monarchs) Russia appears as the extremest example of arbitrary and capricious despotism to be found anywhere in this History. Ivan's Russia shared few of the traits which characterize the modern European state. Russia's frontiers were unstable. Its origin lay in a quite tiny principality of Moscow, under the Tartar yoke. Bit by bit this conquered or absorbed its neighbouring Russian principalities. When Ivan IV conquered the Tartar Khanates of Kazan and Astrakhan (1552–6) and then began to penetrate Siberia, Russia became the largest state in the world. But for two centuries or more its modern

---

[55] Berman, Justice in Russia, 129; E. L. Keenan, 'Union of Soviet Socialist Republics: History of Russia and the Soviet Union: From the Beginnings up to c.1700', Encyclopaedia Britannica, 15th edn., (1989), xxviii. 968–78. [56] Obolensky, The Byzantine Commonwealth, 411, 413, 468.

southern frontiers were fluid and held by Lithuanians or Tartars or Cossacks.

Certainly, like the Western European absolutisms, the tsar's absolutism knew no legal limits, but at this stage it was nevertheless subject to certain *extra*-constitutional limitations. This arose from the nature of the nobility at that date. It consisted of princes, that is, descendants of Rurik or the Lithuanian princes or of the Tartar khans; the boyars; and—later—the military servitors of the tsar to whom he alloted land for military service. The boyars were, originally, retainers of the princes, but they held allodial lands, that is, held them outright with no service obligations. They were *votchina* ('patrimonium') and hereditary. As the grand dukes of Muscovy absorbed the other principalities so they took over the latters' boyars. However, as freeholders boyars had the right to quit the service of their prince and transfer their allegiance to another. In the 1420s departure to another prince began to be regarded as treason and eventually Ivan III forbade it. But this prohibition became redundant once the Muscovite prince had absorbed all the other principalities, because there was no other orthodox prince to whom they could go.

The mixture of all the different elements that made up the nobility led to tensions which came to be regulated by a table of precedence. This was the *mestnichestvo*, an important element in Muscovite rule. Together with the fact that being a boyar was not hereditary, it prevented the emergence of an 'Estate' of the nobility such as obtained in the West. Later Peter the Great was to establish a table of ranks—the *mestnichestvo* was its ancestor.

The boyars were most powerful when the tsar was a minor or perhaps a mental defective. By tradition a tsar ruled with the advice of a Council (Duma) of boyars. He selected its members and it met when he decided, but Ivan IV took his decisions before he met them. Its composition fluctuates and it disappeared altogether in 1711 when Peter I replaced it by the body he called the Senate. However, a new institution was established in 1598, the *Zemski Sobor*, an assembly of the members of the Duma, the higher clergy, and provincials (but there were no election procedures or quotas for selecting the last). Its Golden Age was the aptly named Time of Troubles (1598–1613) when the Russian throne was rocked by Polish–Lithuanian (i.e. Roman Catholic) invasions and civil wars fought in the name of two successive royal pretenders each claiming to be Dmitri, the dead (but supposedly murdered) son of Ivan IV. It was the *Zemski Sobor* of 1613 that elected Michael Romanov as tsar. This *Sobor* comprised all categories of freemen—not just the nobles and Church hierarchs but townsmen and even peasants.[57] Once the royal

---

[57] R. O. Crummey, *The Formation of Muscovy, 1304–1613* (Longman, London, 1987), 149, 165, 230–1.

absolutism had stabilized, however, the role of such an assembly was reduced and it finally died of inanition: the last authenticated *Sobor* met in 1653.

However, it is important not to exaggerate the influence of the boyars. They never formed or fought for their privileges as a corporation, but as families or clans.

The Orthodox Church provided a second constraint, but much feebler than the Catholic Church in the west of Europe. The Orthodox Church, unlike Roman Catholicism, was headed by five patriarchs. It decided matters of doctrine by synods, and—by this time at any rate—the Church in a number of the states which had embraced orthodoxy was autocephalous: that is, it was headed by its own metropolitan. (In Russia in 1589, this role was taken over by the patriarch of Moscow.) In full Byzantine tradition the Church hierarchy was alone responsible for holy doctrine but the monarch was responsible for Church administration. This did not prevent individual churchmen from sometimes exerting a considerable restraining influence on the tsars, but this was a matter of personalities, not an institutionalized relationship. Ivan IV's metropolitan, Makary, was able to admonish and restrain him, but his successor, the metropolitan Philipp Kolichev (also appointed by Ivan), who fell out with him, was tried, condemned, and exiled to a distant monastery, where subsequently Ivan's agents murdered him.

Thus the boyars and the Church hierarchy posed no such restraints on Ivan IV as the landed nobility and the Catholic Church did in the West, and there were no towns, guilds, and corporations to cope with, either.

Western absolutism was restrained, in addition—and perhaps even more effectively—by its inherent and widely understood duty to respect life, liberty, and property. As to the last, the idea of private ownership—the *votchina*—was accepted. Not only the nobility but the freeholder farmers also held their land as an alod (that is, as free estate as opposed to land held on a service tenure). But in practice the property of the former was at risk; on one pretext or another Ivan IV would judge, condemn, and then expropriate the properties of noblemen on a vast scale. He seized the properties of noblemen in the Moscow area and recompensed them with lands in distant territories, often charged with some service obligation. In fact, Ivan IV's main 'revolution' was precisely to carry forward the more limited policy of Vasily III and Ivan III, of exacting service obligation for all land whether it was allodial or granted in service tenure (*pomesty'e*).

As for liberty, up to the 1490s both the boyar and the allodial peasant were free to change their masters and to move about. But war and famine at the end of the fifteenth, in the early sixteenth, and the early seventeenth centuries provoked a crisis: the service-obligated lands could only provide their quota of soldiers and their horses and equipment and at the same time maintain their owners and their families if there was enough labour to work the land. So the 1490s saw the peasants' right to quit an estate restricted to the period two weeks before and after St George's Day, and the Law Code of 1649 completed the enserfment of the peasant. It set no limit to landlord powers, recognized the serfs as so many chattels, forbade them to complain against their landlords except for state security matters, and deprived them of the right to testify in civil cases.[58] So, just as serfdom was being extinguished in Western Europe it was being consolidated in Russia. Such enserfment but complemented and completed a universal system of bondage, for all trades and professions were hereditary; traders and artisans were fixed to their places of residence, travel was controlled by internal passports, and the frontiers were tightly sealed.

Nor did due process of law exist. Cases were tried by the local administrator with no qualifications in law. No system of private law existed. In the sixteenth century the procedures were unbelievably archaic: where there were no witnesses the magistrate chose one party or the other to kiss the cross, and the one who did so was considered to have won his case.[59] And this at a time when France and Spain were staffed with the *noblesse de robe* or the *letrados* and the English Inns of Court were turning out common law lawyers like Chief Justice Coke. In the seventeenth century procedures were slowly improved but they lagged far behind the (over?) complex systems of Western Europe.

5.3. The Opening to the West: Peter the Great, 1682–1725

'It has been said that under Peter Russia learned western techniques, under Elizabeth[60] western manners, and under Catherine[61] western morals.'[62] In fact Peter introduced a little more than techniques: he tried to enforce western manners on his subjects, particularly on his court. To this belong the striking gestures associated with his reign, such as his personally shaving off the beards of his courtiers, forcing the citizenry to shed their ancient caftans and wear western dress, bringing the court ladies out of purdah by making them and their menfolk attend state balls, and so forth. Hence the importance Peter attached to building his new capital, St Petersburg, as a window on the west. But these enforced changes of manners were extremely artificial. They aped the west; they did not enter into its spirit.

More enduring and important were the industrial techniques imported

---

[58] Pipes, *Russia under the Old Regime*, 104–5.   [59] Fletcher, *Of the Russe Commonwealth*, 66–7.
[60] 1741–62.   [61] 1762–96.   [62] Quoted, Pipes, *Russia under the Old Regime*, 132.

and his efforts to expedite the industrialization[63] of this benighted and backward country where townsfolk (even where 'town' means any settlement of over 1,000 people) formed less than one in twenty of the population and the only large towns were St Petersburg and Moscow (which was indeed very big, even by Western European standards: 150,000–200,000 population).[64] There is something terrifying but also pathetic in the way he sent his own chosen associates into Holland to learn one specific technique apiece in shipbuilding,[65] as though these few men could turn around Russia's vast sluggish society of wooden huts, forest and wilderness, dirt, illiteracy, and black superstition. But he encouraged the settlements of foreign merchants and offered huge inducements to tempt anybody, Russian or foreign, to set up a factory: subsidies, interest-free loans, and—typically Russian and non-western—a supply of forced labour, especially to the state-owned factories, which were numerous. By the end of his reign more than half of Russian exports consisted of goods like sail-cloth, canvas, and iron.[66]

Till Peter's reign Russia's hermetic reclusion had been chiefly tempered by large numbers of foreign troops and their officers left over from the Thirty Years War. Peter definitively ended that reclusion. Foreign merchants and others were established in a Moscow suburb. He injected his country firmly into the mainstream of European diplomacy, and of course from that point the contact with foreign courts, foreign nationals, and above all foreign armies created a momentum towards westernization that was irreversible and cumulative. The impetus behind this was quite simple: *war*. Peter was above all a warrior. His ambition was to drive Sweden out of the Baltic Provinces and open for Russia a seaboard on the west. He aimed, too, at taking Russia down to the Black Sea—at that time a Turkish lake—against the resistance of the hardy Crim Tartars and their Turkish allies. To do all this he required an army and navy. The latter he had to create from scratch. As to the former, the efforts of his predecessors to copy western armies were incomplete and even though Russia had replaced Poland by 1686 as having the most powerful army in Eastern Europe, Peter's own reorganized and westernized forces were defeated by a much smaller number of Swedes at the first siege of Narva (1700). All but one of Peter's years as sovereign were spent in warfare. The protracted war with Sweden necessarily involved Russia with Poland, Denmark, and Prussia as northern and Baltic

---

[63] In the 17th cent. Russia was exporting timber, naval stores, and potash to the English and the Dutch, and the government was deeply involved in the promotion of trade and commerce. This was particularly true of metallurgy so that by 1700 Russia was Europe's leading producer of pig-iron.

[64] M. S. Anderson, *Peter the Great* (Thames & Hudson, London, 1978), 12–13.

[65] R. K. Massie, *Peter the Great: His Life and World* (Cardinal, London, 1989), 165–86.

[66] Ibid. 100–3.

states. From this point onwards the country was caught in an ever-widening gyre of European great-power politics.

But in domestic rearrangements (and these were numerous and far-reaching) Peter was not a westernizer, except perhaps in that he reorganized and restructured the central administration on the Swedish model and improved the territorial organization of the country. But in no way did he abolish the widespread restrictions on individual liberties; rather, he twisted them still tighter and brought them into a coherent system.

Peter was in theory as much an absolute ruler as any of his predecessors, and more in practice; and proclaimed himself to be. His 'Military Service Regulations' of 1716 state: 'His Majesty is a sovereign monarch [*samoderz-havnyi*] who is not obliged to answer for his acts to anyone in the world; but he holds the might and the power to administer his states and lands as a Christian monarch, in accordance with his wishes and best opinions.'[67] Furthermore, there were no *extra*-legal constraints on his autocracy. The powers of the boyars and of the Church to restrain him as (albeit feebly) they had restrained Ivan IV had now disappeared. The autocracy was all-powerful in practice as well as in theory.

The old Duma of boyars had just disappeared. Peter phased it out of existence by simply not summoning it. There had been a twofold development. While Ivan IV imposed service obligations on their land, he and his successors built up their own military servitors known as *dvoriane*, servitors of their court (*dvor*). This class of servitors was supplemented by landless gentry, the so-called 'sons of boyars'. The tsars retained the services of these *dvoriane* by grants of land that were held as *pomest'e*, that is, carried a service obligation. By Peter's day the distinction between the *votchina* and the *pomest'e* was disappearing. Both were heritable but the cavalry levy serving from the land was being phased out. Both types of allodial and *pomest'e* land-holding owed service to the Crown.

Peter reorganized service in the 'Table of Ranks' devised in 1722. This table, based on foreign models, ranked posts in the military, the naval, and the court service in parallel columns (thus establishing correspondences), and grouped them into fourteen ranks, the highest number one, the lowest, fourteen. The holder of a post listed in the table was entitled to the rank that pertained to it in much the same way as, say, the commander of a company would have the rank of captain. Peter wanted every *dvorianin* to

---

[67] G. Vernadsky, *A Source Book for Russian History from Early Times to 1917*, vol. II: *Peter the Great to Nicholas I* (Yale UP, London, 1972), 365. It has been pointed out that this formula is a straight quotation from the definition of the king of Sweden's powers under Swedish law. That seems to be neither here nor there. In making it part of his own Military Service Regulations it was as much Peter's as if he had formulated the words himself.

start at the bottom rank (fourteenth) and work his way up, so all began as privates in his two Guards regiments. Clerks in the civil service and rankers in the military services were not considered *dvoriane*, but if they had risen to fourteenth rank in the army or eighth rank in the civil service they became hereditary nobles (if they were not so already). The acquisition of the rank which carried privileged social status and the right to own land and serfs became a national obsession[68] (though nobles who had no *rank* did not lose their noble status). In the event, there was a small commoner entry at the bottom of the Table of Ranks: in 1730 93 per cent of the four highest ranks came from the families that had held high office in Muscovy, but between the fourteenth and the tenth ranks there were numerous promotions of commoners to noble rank in the army and the provincial administration.[69]

The system imposed prodigious restrictions on the landholding classes. All sons of the *dvoriane* were officially registered. If over 10 years old they had to present themselves for periodic inspection. Up to 16 years of age they were obliged to study elementary mathematics, and then entered the state service for the rest of their lives! *Dvoriane* tried to avoid these intrusions in multifarious ways but, broadly speaking, compliance was ensured. This Table of Ranks has justly been called 'the keystone of Russian absolutism'.[70] Few decrees of Peter's reign had been so carefully researched and prepared for. The experience of Venice, Austria, Spain, Poland, France as well as Sweden, Denmark, and Prussia were all drawn upon, and even the British Queen Anne's table of ranks was consulted.[71]

The landholders were now thoroughly subjected to the wishes of the Crown and such restraints as they had ever been able to impose on the tsars from Ivan IV up to Peter's time had entirely disappeared.

Despite former tsars' 'shortest way with Metropolitans (or Patriarchs)', the seventeenth-century Church, *qua* corporation, still enjoyed a considerable autonomous power: it administered and taxed itself, it had jurisdiction over family suits, wills, and inheritances and suits between laity and clergy, and it was—including the 557 monasteries and convents with their 14,000 monks and 10,000 nuns[72]—immensely wealthy. The dissolute, free-thinking, and westernizing Peter endured the enmity and incessant nagging of the Patriarch Adrian, but on the latter's death in 1700 the autonomy of the Church was doomed. Peter left the post of patriarch vacant and turned the administration of the monasteries over to a new state organ, the Monastery

[68] Pipes, *Russia under the Old Regime*, 125.   [69] Ibid. 125.

[70] P. Dukes, *The Making of Russian Absolutism, 1613–1801* (Longman, London, 1982), 79.

[71] Prussian experience proved paramount. For the provenance of the decree see ibid. 82–3.

[72] Massie, *Peter the Great*, 788.

Office. This reformed the monasteries and 'managed' all their money and property.

Though the land was returned to the Church in 1721, the Ecclesiastical Regulation of that year applied what had befallen the monasteries in 1700 to the entire Church. The Patriarchate was abolished. In its stead a 'Holy Governing Synod' was set up on the model of a civil administrative department. Its chief task was to oversee church administration, settle disputes, and deal with lapses such as absenteeism. Though consisting of churchmen it was headed by a chief procurator—its effective driving force—who was usually a layman and not infrequently an army officer. Thus the Church had become little more than another department of state. Like the *dvoriantsvo*, it was the servant, not the watchdog, of the autocracy.

What other quarters might pose constraints on or offer resistance to the tsar's authority? Certainly not the puny towns. But popular uprisings were widespread and frequent. There were Cossack risings in 1598–1613, and in 1672 the legendary rebellion of Stenka Razin. The Cossacks rose again in 1707 and many, many peasants joined them: the disturbances spread through sixty districts (*uezd*) in unrelated outbreaks. There were also smaller-scale revolts among peasants drafted for work in state factories between 1703 and 1710. In the 1720s bands of runaways ran riot, often attacking the land-lords.[73] Sometimes these movements were joined by groups of Old Believers who had betaken themselves to the forests and cut themselves off from the state and the tsar whom they regarded as the Anti Christ. But these out-breaks, scattered and divided as they were, never posed a threat to the regime.

There was before 1700 the possibility of conspiracies to depose him by a combination of court noblemen and the *streltsi* regiments, usually in favour of some plausible pretender such as, for instance, Peter's ex-regent half-sister Sophia whom he had confined in a convent. The *streltsi* were a corps of musketeers which had been established in the mid-sixteenth century as a permanent professional standing force, and by Peter's day were a hereditary military caste who lived in their own separate quarter of Moscow and who, like the Janissaries at this date, took to trades and professions when not on active duty. In 1698, when Peter was absent, the *streltsi* mutinied. Peter hurried back to find the revolt already suppressed, but in his suspicion that it had been engineered by Sophia with a view to her restoration, he tortured the mutineers to extract confessions and finally had hundreds of them deported or executed. In 1700 the *streltsi* were disbanded, and replaced by Peter's own two regiments: the Preobrazhenskii and Semenovskii regi-

[73] Dukes, *Making of Russian Absolutism*, 85–7.

ments. (This did not eliminate the threat of military intervention; on the contrary, these Guards regiments were the instruments by which, for instance, Peter's widow Catherine and her successors, Elizabeth, Anne, and Catherine II were all proclaimed empress.)

Court conspiracies did not necessarily involve the military. Peter despaired of his pacifistic, idle, and pietistic son Alexis, who finally renounced the succession and then, one day, absconded to Austria. When Peter finally got his son back he pursued a ruthless and ferocious interrogation under torture of all who might have knowledge of a conspiracy. In the end evidence was procured that did seem to prove that Alexis had still entertained the ambition to become tsar despite his renunciation. He was knouted, then tried and condemned by a specially convened civil and ecclesiastical court and confined to prison to die in mysterious circumstances.

The tsar, then, suffered no external constraints at all: the landholding class was shackled, as was the Church, the towns were of no account, and the popular disturbances were never a serious threat. Subject to no legal or extra-constitutional restraints, was Peter's tsardom bound by the inherent limitations characteristic of the western absolutisms—the duty to respect the life, liberty, and property of the subject under due process of law? Peter did not and never wished to strike off the heads of those subjects to whom he had taken a dislike. Certainly, he did set up a special police department, but this worked through denunciation and delation, not by a constabulary force; and he carried out the merciless repressions of conspiracies and revolts, as already mentioned. But all these were in accord with the very harsh laws relating to treason and crimes against the state; and as we have had frequent occasion to remark, this area was always one where the judicial protection of the individual was very weak indeed. State security was paramount.

Peter did not abolish private proprietorship in land, and indeed did the reverse. When he introduced salaries for state service in 1714 the land remained in the hands of the owner, whether it was *votchina* or *pomest'e*. Service was certainly exacted, but not in return for the land but for belonging to the class of the nobility. Private peasant land did not exist any more. One might argue that all this made for the security of landed property; but it would be the security of the prison-house.

As to liberty, the balance is uniformly negative. The peasants needed for working the land were in flight to the black lands of the south, especially as these were opened up by advance towards the Black Sea. This exodus was countered, therefore, by an ever-increasing restriction of the peasant's right to leave his village. Russian landlords had acquired a customary right to control the lives of the population on their estates: manorial justice did, in fact, precede enserfment and it was generally recognized that what the landlord did with his peasants was his own private concern. Add this right of manorial control to adscription—the latter being specifically recognized and defined in the Code of 1649—and the peasants' serfdom was completed. But under Peter the landlord acquired even greater rights over the peasantry, since he was made responsible for collecting the poll tax from them and also, when Peter introduced conscription in 1699, for organizing the draft. The poll tax was the single most powerful instrument in keeping the population tied to one place. Clearly, if individuals could move about they could evade the tax and leave the rest of the community to pick up the bill. All villagers and townsfolk were registered in a particular place and watched over by the local taxing authority, which might be the landowner or the village elder or the town authorities. A townsman could not leave his town even on business unless he was certified by his colleagues as having paid his taxes. (Nobles and soldiers did not pay the poll tax—it was raised for their upkeep.)

The conscription was perhaps the cruellest burden the peasant had to bear. Every twenty households had to furnish one soldier, who had to serve for his entire active lifetime. When he returned to his village—if he ever did—it would be as a decrepit or invalid old man, remembered by no one and with no share in the communal land. The *Recruit Laments* which were sung when the young conscript departed for his service resembled funeral dirges.[74]

Nor was this all. The peasants on private estates—serfs proper, as it were—could not, for the reasons given, move from their place. But there were also the peasants on state land and these did have a certain mobility; they could travel outside their village, but only with an official passport. Among fiscal duties, state peasants had to supply free labour—in short, were subject to the corvée—but this was not limited to specifically local purposes such as the upkeep of roads and bridges and the like. Great drafts of state peasants were herded into state factories to provide a labour force and St Petersburg was notoriously built on the bones of thousands of state peasants who had been directed and kept there by the authorities. As far as 'proprietarial' (privately owned) serfs were concerned, too, the landlord had the right to sell them to other landowners, and a decree of 1721 implicitly condones this by prohibiting the sale of serfs away from their families; it says that if such sales cannot be altogether prohibited then they must comprise whole family units.[75] And finally, the peasant had no right to complain against his landlord.

[74] Pipes, *Russia under the Old Regime*, 122.   [75] Vernadsky, *Peter the Great*, ii. 354.

The rule of law had made a little progress, in that Peter promulgated collections of laws—codes—pertaining to certain policy areas. Such, for instance, were the Military Code, the Naval Code, and the General Regulations. Though state courts were presided over by judges who were administrators, efforts were being made to introduce accusatorial as well as inquisitorial procedure in the courts. A code or system of civil and commercial law had still not developed, nor had any class of jurists or lawyers. Precisely because there was no professionalized judiciary, and notably none who could control maladministration, Peter established the Procuracy. The procurator-general (who was secretary of the Senate and controlled its proceedings) was served by a network of local procurators charged to check the legality of administrative activities. This was an administrative department set up to watch all the other administrative departments and it testifies to the lack of any possibility of independent 'juridical defence' against the administrators. In this it forms an exact parallel to the Chinese 'Censorate', described above, which was brought into existence for identical reasons.

Thus, Petrine absolutism was emphatically not European absolutism. It had almost none of its attributes listed in the Conclusion of Chapter 5 above. On the contrary, it had brought into a coherent and far more efficacious system all the strands of unfreedom which existed in the sixteenth century and which had been twisted tighter and tighter ever since. It was a system of universal bondage, unrestrained by any inherent limitations based on sacred or natural law.

Madariaga characterized the Russian state in 1762 at the opening of Catherine II's reign thus:

Bondage, in one form or another, extended all the way through Russian society; the individual was bound to serve a person or the state; he was bound to a particular community which he could not leave without the permission of the corresponding authority; and he was bound by a system of collective responsibility to the other members of the community he belonged to . . . Russia had thus become a society in which activity did not depend on the free initiative of the individual but on the permission of the government. Everyone was assigned to a particular legal category or status (*sosloviye* or *sostoyaniye*), most conveniently translated by 'estate' and could only carry out the activities proper to that estate, or enjoy its privileges . . . the one exception to the rule of physical immobility was the estate of the *dvoriane* or nobility.[76]

---

[76] Isabel de Madariaga, *Russia in the Age of Catherine the Great* (Weidenfeld & Nicolson, London, 1981), 79.

5.4. *The Beginnings of Convergence: Catherine the Great, 1762–1796*

Catherine was the German wife of the worthless drunkard tsar, Peter III. She became empress by a *coup d'etat* of the Preobrazhenskii Regiment, through the machinations of her lover Orlov, who was one of five brothers serving as officers in that regiment. (Peter III himself perished soon afterwards.)

Catherine is one of the characters beloved of popular historians and historical novelists because of her romantic love-life. As well, she was the heroine of the French Enlightenment *philosophes* of France who were then at the height of their glory; she corresponded with and entertained them, and they in return hailed her as the 'Semiramis of the North'. There can be no doubt that she took the court, and the court in its turn took aristocratic Russian society, into the mainstream of the European Enlightenment. Let us give a few illustrative examples only. She encouraged the theatre. She enormously stimulated translations of foreign books into Russian and founded a society to sponsor them. She not merely tolerated but supported the publication of satirical journals like Novikov's—and so forth. She lifted the age-old restrictions on the nobility travelling abroad, and the impressions and views they brought back with them were more important at the end of her reign than the influence of her court. One might fairly say that this was when the Russian intelligentsia was born. This ferment of publications and important ideas lent powerful support to the emulation of western political institutions, while making the Western European writers and politicians think of the 'Russians' (i.e. its *dvoriane* really) as part of the European intellectual community.

Hardly so, in truth; and even at the end of Catherine's reign the Russian polity (with some marginal exceptions to be picked up later) remained the old Russian polity except in respect of one class: the *dvoriane*.

To begin with, the government remained as unrestrained by law and institutions as ever. The Senate belies its Roman overtone. Peter had grouped the numerous departments into a number of colleges and the Senate, which he nominated, acted as their co-ordinating council, strictly subordinated to him. Catherine grouped most of the 'colleges' into six divisions each dealing with a number of fields of administration. The procurator-general acted as a co-ordinating director and remained strictly subordinate to the empress. One could argue that the government was now stronger than ever before because it could give much greater effect to its commands. Catherine also reorganized Peter's arrangements for local government. Peter had divided the country into *guberniyas*, great provinces headed by governors, but below them there was only a skeleton staff to implement policy. For instance, there was no police-force, just a universal system of delators and informers.

But under Catherine the ability of government agents to penetrate into the population greatly improved. She split Peter's huge *guberniya* into smaller units, divided in turn into districts (*uezd*) of some 20,000–30,000 male heads, and she abolished the institution of the province, which had formerly lain between the *guberniya* and the districts (1775). Each *guberniya* had a governor, plus a deputy governor in charge of finance. The governor did not himself issue orders. In the fashion of the day, he presided over a collegiate board which did this—the governor, his deputy, and two appointed councillors. The new system of lawcourts came under this board, a system that ran from the Senate as ultimate court of appeal through civil and criminal high courts down to the lower land courts in the countryside and their equivalent in the towns. The judicial and administrative functions were united in the 'lower land court', which was in fact controlled by its presiding officer, the land commissar, who was a noble elected by his fellows but a paid agent of the government. (The borrowing from Prussia and Austria is very clear.)[77] This 'lower land court' was responsible for public order, fire, roads, and bridges. Though executive action lay with the commissar, punishment had to be authorized in the full court.[78] The town equivalent of the land commissar was the provost (*gorodnichi*), again not a judge but a police chief with a small armed detachment at his disposal. He was appointed directly by the Senate and was placed (if he did not already have it) in the eighth rank—the one at which the recipient became a *dvorianin*. One innovation needs to be stressed and that is the considerable role of election in local government. The governors were assisted by officials who had been *elected* from the nobility and the state peasants in the countryside, and from the urban patriciates in the towns. These took care of such matters as routine police work, law-enforcement, security, and tax-collection. The nobility also elected a marshal to represent their collective interests, as will be mentioned below, and nobles, townspeople, and state peasants also elected officials to administer institutions such as schools and orphanages. These initiatives gave considerable scope but, in practice, were not pushed very far.

The role of the town provosts must be seen in the general context of policing. Peter had made the St Petersburg chief of police responsible for police throughout the empire. Catherine decentralized by handing the function back again to the governors. The town provost presided over a board which itself was responsible to the governor. The 1782 Police Ordinance divided towns into 'quarters' of some 200–700 households. In each

---

[77] See Bk. IV, Ch. 6 above.   [78] de Madariaga, *Russia in the Age of Catherine the Great*, 283.

'quarter' commissioners were appointed. The constables in the wards of these quarters were locally elected every three years. Such town police-forces had a very wide general duty of supervision and control and had summary jurisdiction over minor offences.

Unhappily, we have absolutely *no* knowledge of how this Ordinance worked in practice,[79] but of the local government organization in general we can certainly say this: there was a huge increase in the number of officials. In 1773 the total in central and local government was 16,500. In the following year there were 12,712 in local government alone. In 1781 the figure was 22,000, in 1796 an estimated 27,000. And the cost of local administration rose accordingly. In 1774 it was 1,712,465 roubles; in 1785 5,618,957 roubles; and in 1796, the end of the reign, 10,921,388 roubles.[80] Even if there is no one-to-one correspondence between the number and/or the cost of the local civil servants and an increase in their activities, it is obvious that there must have been an increase and that it would have been considerable.

The government, then, was powerfully reinforced. What constraints did it meet? Catherine had the longest reign in the century and was, broadly speaking, undisturbed by military coups and/or court intriguers such as those which had troubled her predecessors. But the absence of any fixed rule of succession and in particular the mysterious circumstances in which her husband, Tsar Peter III, had met his death did expose her to challenges by a train of pretenders. The tragic farce of the—not just one but—*two* pseudo-Dmitri's in the Time of Troubles was played out several times during her reign. Pretenders provided a focus for popular discontent, of which there was plenty. Klyuchevsky, the classic Russian historian, had shrewdly written: 'When the Russians are unhappy the way is open for a pretender.'[81] During Catherine's reign there were no less than seventeen pretenders.[82] Their claims were preposterous and their stories totally incredible to any reasonably informed person[83]—which, of course, the peasantry were not. All they saw was the *good* tsar or tsarina who had at last returned to take the place of the imposter-tyrant. These pretenders posed no threat to Catherine with one great exception: the revolt of Pugachev. A Cossack ex-soldier, Pugachev claimed to be Peter III, back to take his throne. His revolt was to spread over a vast territory of 4.5 million inhabitants and, at times, Pugachev had 30,000 men under arms. They swept north towards Kazan, pillaging, burn-

---

[79] de Madariaga, *Russia in the Age of Catherine the Great*, 295.   [80] Ibid. 290.
[81] Quoted, Hufton, *Europe*, 238.   [82] Ibid. 238–9.
[83] See e.g. the case of the female pretender Tarakanova: and note the extraordinary way in which she was trapped and disposed of, in Troyat, *Le Prisonnier no. 1: Roman* (Flammarion, Paris, 1978), 209–10.

ing, robbing, raping, torturing, and murdering the landlord families in their path. The revolt was only finally put down when regular troops were released by the signature of peace with the Turks.

Apart from these popular uprisings, extra-legal constraints on the autocracy could be looked for, as we have seen, only in the towns, the Church, and the landholding classes. Whether the towns were strictly subordinated to their provosts as many maintain must be left in doubt, for there is no evidence either way. However, Catherine's 'Charter of the Cities' (1785), which allowed burghers to set up their own Duma and form a corporation, used to be thought a dead letter, but recent research shows that some town Dumas were quite active; of course, the full realization of the *zemstvos* had to wait until the decree of 1864.[84] As for the Church, Catherine satisfied both the logic of Russian history and the deist or secularist outlook of her favourite *encylopédistes* by reducing the number of convents and monasteries and putting all their inmates and churchpeople on a salary. Monastic and Church lands were administered by the Crown, and the Church's peasants now became state peasants (1764). The Crown received 7 million roubles from this transaction but returned a mere 400,000. As for the landholders, the *dvoriantsvo*, they were not a corporate restraint on the monarchy as they were in the West. Most of them entered service because they needed the money, the provincial gentry declined to follow the grandees of the metropolis, and such personal liberties as they won from Catherine and of which we shall speak below, related to their economic and social privileges, not to political rights, apart from an extension (1785) of the privilege of local assembly already granted in 1775. Some of these assemblies were not entirely inactive, and they were useful vehicles for making representations on local needs through their elected marshal to the Senate or even the empress.

There still remains the question as to whether the Russian monarchy had developed those inherent limitations in respect to the life, liberty, and property of its subjects that were present in the European concept of absolutism.

As we noted, under Peter the *dvoriane* were dedicated to state service and that service began after the inspection of youths at age 10, from the age of 16, and was for life. After Peter there ensued a steady emancipation of the *dvoriantsvo* which brought it closer and closer to the European model. In 1730 Peter's wildly unpopular edict requiring landowners to bequeath their estates to a single heir was repealed. In 1731 the Empress Anne founded a Cadet Corps in which noblemen's children had preference. In 1736 the age at which the *dvoriane* youths had to enter state service was raised from 16 to 20, and

---

[84] For the text of the Decree see Vernadsky, *From Peter the Great to Nicholas 1*, 415–18.

instead of running for life it was limited to twenty-five years. Furthermore, families with a number of sons could keep one at home to manage the family property.

The underlying reason was because of the years Russia was at peace and neither needed nor could afford so large an army. The *dvoriane's* emancipation culminated in Peter III's edict of 1762 'Concerning the granting of freedom and liberty to the entire Russian *dvoriantsvo*', which abolished compulsory service and was *de facto* observed by Catherine and confirmed in 1785 by her 'Charter to the *Dvoriantsvo*', a document which brought them into parity with their European counterparts. Their dearest wishes— material ones, be it noted, not political—were now confirmed, especially the lifting of their lifetime obligation to serve. In the 1762 Charter it was enacted that nobles in service could remain there or leave as they thought fit; that they might travel abroad and take service there; but that the Crown hoped that whenever they were needed they would rally and respond 'to the first summons of the autocratic power'.

Complementary to that, they were 'confirmed in the rights of private ownership . . . not only over the surface of the land that belongs to each of them', but also over its mineral and water resources. They received the right to buy villages and conduct trade and manufacture on or from their estates. They were granted the full protection of due process of law: they could not be deprived of their dignity, rank, property, or life 'without trial' by their peers, nor could they be subjected to corporal punishment. Finally, their exemption from paying personal taxes and billeting soldiers in their own houses were affirmed.[85] Thus ended the age-old principle that nobles were allotted serfs to enable them to serve the Crown in the armed forces. Now, the nobles no longer served, but they kept their serfs! And the serfs took great exception to this.

The 'Charter to the Towns', also promulgated in 1785, repeated the privileges granted the *dvorianstvo* as recounted above: notably trial by their peers to the members of the merchant estate and townsfolk, security of property, and immunity (to the patriciate only, however) from corporal punishment. But while the *dvoriantsvo* were brought into the European mainstream and could glitter at the Congress of Vienna alongside the grandest and most ancient of the European nobility, the lot of the Russian serfs became more servile than ever before.

Nevertheless the majority of Russian peasants were *not* serfs. In fact there were proportionately fewer serfs in Russia than in Prussia and Denmark. In the 1858–9 census only 37.7 per cent of the country's 22.5 million population

---

[85] For the text of the Decree see Vernadsky, *From Peter the Great to Nicholas 1* 413–15.

were proprietary serfs, that is, serfs belonging to the private domains of individuals. There were indeed a vast number of 'state' peasants who, like the proprietary serfs, were bound to the land—but who were otherwise free to make their own living. However, these figures and ratios change considerably over the period. At the end of the eighteenth century the two groups were roughly equal. In the nineteenth century, however, the proportion of serfs declined.

Dues exacted from serfs were of two kinds. Quitrent was concentrated around the barren north-east, labour dues around the black-earth provinces, but they were not divided in any clear-cut way: sometimes both would coexist in the same village or estate. In Catherine's reign many greedy landowners pushed their peasants into ever-more intensive labour services by a variety of forms of exploitation.

Yet one of several British travellers of the 1820s maintained that in the crowded parts of English towns or the poorest villages of the countryside the inhabitants were far worse off than the serfs; their wretchedness was such that in comparison 'the condition of the Russian poor is luxury', and in parts of Scotland some folk were lodging in houses 'which the Russian peasant would not think fit for his cattle'.[86] But this did not mean, he said, that the Russian serf's lot was 'on the whole, more enviable than that of a peasant in a free country like ours. The distance between them is wide— immeasurable; but it can be accounted for in one single word—the British peasant has rights; the Russian has none.'[87] For the proprietorial serf was completely under the domination of his landlord, who was at once the recruitment agent and tax-collector, judge and jury.

In all these respects the state peasant was better off. He had the strength of the commune behind him, where his elected elders played a more considerable role in administering peasant common law in the village than the local official. For instance, a peasant commune had the right to banish an unpopular member to Siberia without consulting the official. Again, if the state peasant paid his taxes and poll tax in the village and in a town, he could move to the town and become a townsman. Furthermore, the state peasant could not be bought or sold.

Many of the greater landowners laid down their own codes of 'law'.[88] The landlords were the great beneficiaries of Catherine's liberalization policy. The proprietorial serfs, on the other hand, were its greatest victims. A decree of 1767 runs: 'the landlord's serfs and peasants . . . owe their lord proper submission and an absolute obedience in all matters according to

---

[86] Pipes, *Russia under the Old Regime*, 149–52.   [87] Ibid. 154.
[88] Vernadsky, *From Peter the Great to Nicholas 1*, 441–9.

laws that have been enacted from time immemorial.' Delinquents were to be taken to the nearest government office for sentence—'without leniency'. And then it goes on to quote from the Code of 1649 that if they 'should make bold to submit unlawful petitions complaining of their landlords, and especially to petition Her Imperial Majesty personally', both the originators and the composers of the petitions were to be knouted and condemned to penal servitude for life.[89]

It is true that, outside serfdom, Catherine did rationalize the administration of justice and made it approximate more to western conditions. A system of summary courts which handled both civil and criminal cases was set up at the lowest level. Above them was a set of courts for each separate 'estate' in the area and above them, once again, a high court which entertained civil and criminal suits from all 'estates' alike. The distinction between the civil and the criminal law was recognized, though there was still no comprehensive system of civil law and certainly—as we have seen—no civil or criminal code. Apart from the *dvoriantsvo*, privileged by the Charter of 1785, and the townsmen in the Towns Charter of 1785, the subject could not engage the state authorities in any kind of *lis inter partes*. Hence the Procuracy as a guardian of procedural legality. But its limitations can readily be imagined when we learn that most of the local appointments were military men, lower in rank than governors, and with their tradition of deference to a superior rank reinforced by their tradition of military discipline. The best that can be said is that their numbers grew and that in course of time they did begin to dare to complain against their superiors more often than in the past,[90] especially since Catherine brought them under the control of the procurator-general who was very powerful. Yet there is absolutely no comparison whatsoever between this and the effect on maladministration of a free press, public court hearings, and the right to sue the agents of government in a *lis inter partes* before trained, professional judges and through the agency of professional advocates.

To sum up: in administration and the judicial system Catherine's Russia made advances that paralleled, but in an etiolated form, the common practices of Europe. The nobility (and Court), now thoroughly westernized in dress and in manners, enjoyed the freedoms of trial by their peers and the right to own property and to travel freely, such as had existed in the West for centuries, as did the professional classes. Townspeople too, under the 1785 Charter, were allowed to travel abroad and to own property in real estate and in goods. The serfs were almost outside the pale of public law

---

[89] Vernadsky, *From Peter the Great to Nicholas 1* 453.
[90] de Madariaga, *Russia in the Age of Catherine the Great*, 57–9.

and wholly in the hands of their landlords, yet they benefited from the 1775 decree which authorized anybody, of whatever social estate, to set up an enterprise: and on some estates the serfs did set up such enterprises and became exceedingly rich, with serfs of their own (in the landowner's name). State peasants, as we have seen, were not wholly in the hands of the state-stewards because the commune was very powerful. Though the *dvoriantsvo* was empowered (as we saw) to call assemblies in each province, we cannot pass judgement on them because there has not been one single study of any of them. Putting this possibility aside for want of any knowledge, it can be affirmed with conviction that the *dvorianstvo* as such was not a political restraint upon the monarchy. The absolutism was as complete as ever and was to prove the most durable in all Europe. One would have to wait until 1833, when the first codification of existing valid law since 1649 was promulgated; to 1861, when the serfs were emancipated; to 1864, when the local *zemstvos* and local self-government was inaugurated, jury service and new courts were founded (and the Russian Bar established); and 1883, when the peasants were made to buy out their land, before one could seriously talk of the 'westernization' of Russia. At the time of Catherine it was just opening out in these directions.

8

The Apogee of Absolute Monarchy:
Europe, c.1770–1780

1. THE ANCIEN RÉGIME

*B*y 1770–80 Europe felt it was coming of age; perhaps, indeed, that it had actually attained the *age de raison* which can also be translated as 'years of discretion'. The Quarrel of the Ancients and the Moderns and Swift's *Battle of the Books* were over and the moderns had won. Europe felt equal, if not indeed superior, to the ancient Graeco-Roman world, which had intimidated and dwarfed it till then. Four great, interconnecting developments were in movement, developments which seemed to be putting the seal on that drive to absolute monarchy that had begun in the sixteenth century.

The first was the completion of a European *oikumene* of sovereign territorial states. The Empress Catherine II of Russia had declared in 1762: 'Russia is a European State' which stretched between 32 degrees of latitude to 165 of longitude.[1] With this the territorial ambit of the European state-form was complete: it stretched from Russia to the Atlantic and from Norway to Sicily. This entire area was now filled by states which had attained at least the first and essential pre-conditions of modernity, in that by now all of them were territorial states in which—with only two or three fairly marginal exceptions, such as Switzerland, for example—the central power (usually a monarchy) rested upon a professional bureaucracy and a standing army. If we look back on our chapters about European polities after the fall of Rome, they will be seen to begin with the states in the west, then extend to the city-states of the middle belt, and only in Chapter 6 above do they begin to consider the East European states of Prussia and Poland. Now Austria and Russia have to be studied as well. All the spaces have been filled up,

The second notable development concerns the aristocracy. In the medieval feudal *regna* the king and the aristocracy were the inseparable elements of the ruling class and there was no way a king could govern except through

---

[1] Quoted from Catherine's 'Instructions to the Commissioners for composing a new Code of Laws', in T. G. Barnes and G. D. Feldman (ed.), *Rationalism and Revolution, 1660–1815: Readings. A Documentary History of Modern Europe* (Little, Brown, and Co., 1972), 56.

his nobility. Though their political relationships had greatly changed, king and aristocracy still formed the ruling élite in the eighteenth-century monarchies, and though one party might tame the other, neither could do without the other. They were symbiotic; they were at the same time antithetical. In some places at some times they resembled those marriages where, as the saying goes, the two partners cannot live together—and cannot live separately, either. There can be no doubting the overwhelming political and social hegemony of the nobility in this eighteenth century. Except in a mere handful of states and principalities they were the great landowners, the ministers, the higher clergy, the officer class, and the dispensers of all the patronage these roles carried with them. From the sixteenth century onwards the royal thrust to absolutism meant curbing and controlling (*not* sweeping away) all intermediary bodies that came between them and the common people. These intermediary bodies were principally aristocratic (with their strongholds in local Estates and their own seigneur-ial courts), but we must remember and mark that there were, also, the Church, the urban patriciates, the guilds and corporations, and—on a wider scale altogether—the particularistic institutions of historical regions, espe-cially in such so-called 'composite states' as the Habsburg lands, where conglomerates of quite diverse political units recognized the same sovereign dynasty. Unchecked, these bodies were formidable obstacles to royal power as the case-history of seventeenth-century France has already illustrated. Curbed and controlled, however, they were indispensable to the monarchs as the interface between their local officials, of whom there were never enough, and the mass of common folk. Thus, for instance, the Church penetrated right down to the village pulpit, indeed, to the individual home. The city councillors and the syndics of guilds and corporations controlled the affairs of their memberships. Local Estates, comprising aristocracy, Church digni-taries, even (sometimes) urban patriciates, held sway throughout the pro-vince or dependent kingdom. Montesquieu called them the *corps intermédiaires* but they were also, to use a favourite modern French expression, the monarchs *interlocuteurs valables*. They are of a piece—and for the same reasons—as Roman decurions, Chinese 'gentry', or Islamic 'notables'.

In the West, during this eighteenth century, the assault on the inter-mediary bodies faltered or came to a full stop. In contrast, it was hyperactive in the continent's eastern extremities, in Russia, Prussia, and Austria, and in some degree in one or two statelets in Italy such as Tuscany, where territoriality and/or centralized authority had come relatively late. None of these states even began to be regularly centralized until the later seven-teenth and the eighteenth centuries. Furthermore (Tuscany excepted) their frontiers had been undefined and fluid, they did not have standing armies, and had precious little in the way of bureaucracies either. In short, they were late developers, and this highlights the importance of royal absolutism in these lands. In contrast, the sovereign bodies of England and France—Parliament or King—showed no similar reforming zeal at all. Institutionally their states marked time. These had been the earliest territorial, law-bound sovereign entities served by standing armies and professional civil servants. Their rulers no longer needed to embark on state-building, like their eastern counterparts. Less legislation was passed in the British Parliament in the half-century after 1714 than at any time before or since; fewer elections were held; fewer constituencies were contested. As to France, the great reforming efforts had taken place under Louis XIV, but with him, in Sorel's words, 'the monarchy reached its apogee'. It was succeeded by 'chaotic despotism, irresolute omnipotence, centralized anarchy'.[2] After him it was downhill all the way.

The third and notable development of this era—many would say the greatest—was the revolution in ideas and world-outlook expressed in the 'Enlightenment', otherwise called *le siècle des lumières*, or the *Aufklarung*. More will be said about this remarkable current of beliefs later. Here it is enough to note the following. This was the (so-called) *Age of Reason* and—whatever Reason might be—it was by Reason that all institutions were to be appraised. This was an implicit and sometimes explicit challenge to the sedulously inculcated belief that kings ruled by Divine Right. That doctrine was still being professed, but how far was it believed and indeed how far could it be believed if, in line with the *philosophes* (and even with certain monarchs like Leopold of Tuscany) regal authority was grounded on Reason and Nature, on an implicit contract between the ruler and his subjects?

Not only that; the *philosophes'* often widely diverse points of view nevertheless added up to a hardcore or programme of reforms that any self-respecting 'enlightened' monarch could be expected to carry out. Now to a large extent the 'programme' of the Enlightenment publicists coincided with the state-building process, so that the royal reforms can well appear to be kings' conscious adoption of the Enlightenment blueprint. In fact many of these reforms follow in a straight line those which kings had initiated since the sixteenth century. They were being expressed in Enlightenment terms but were not directed by them: anti-clericalism, curbs on the aristocracy, extrusion of the Estates, internal free trade. But it seems impossible to deny an independent force to much of the Enlightenment philosophy. It did not

---

[2] A. Sorel, *Europe and the French Revolution—The Political Traditions of the Old Régime*, ed. A. Cobban and J. W. Hunt, trans. A. Sorel (Fontana Library; Collins and Fontana Press, London, 1969; trans. 1885), 230–3.

control but it *influenced* these reforming monarchs. This is what accounts for their espousing religious toleration, the softening of the penal code, the extension of popular education. None of these are inconsistent with unencumbered absolutism, but none are strictly necessary to it.[3]

The Enlightenment programme was in no way democratic. It propounded the betterment of the people but certainly not *by* the people. Rousseau's *Du contrat social* (1762) contains the memorable phrase about forcing a man to be free, but that sentiment was widespread. Charles Frederic of Baden was determined to make his subjects 'free, opulent and law-abiding citizens, whether they like it or not'.[4] 'Turgot yearned for five years of despotism to set the people free . . .'[5] The *philosophes* who would not look to the people to set themselves free could not look to the ancient 'intermediary bodies' either. On the contrary, these aristocracies, these priests, Estates, municipal corporations, guilds, and the like were the resistant strongholds of conservatism: indeed the very institutions that made the people unfree. For action it was necessary to turn to the monarch, but for liberating action it was necessary that he be 'enlightened'. The *philosophes* were there to enlighten him. This being so, the more active and the more absolute this monarch, the greater the chance of success for the *philosophe* programme. Hence their advocacy of the most extreme form of such absolutism: 'legal despotism' or 'enlightened despotism'.[6] Hence too the consequence that the greatest hopes for the carrying-out of their programme and the greatest enthusiasm were placed in those monarchs who seemed to be the most 'despotic'—the rulers of Russia, Austria, and Prussia.

2. THE CHIEF STATES OF EUROPE

The political map of *ancien régime* Europe defies any facile generalization. This age has been called, among other things, the Age of Absolutism or the Age of the Enlightened Despots, but the expressions are misleading. Cer-

[3] This matter has been the subject of fierce controversy among historians, some of whom adhere to the 'blueprint' model of the Enlightenment as a set of beliefs that dictated rulers' activities, and others, the *raison d'état* model, which argues that this, *not* the ideas, was the motivation for the reforms. As my text indicates, I consider both these positions are extreme. See H. M. Scott, *Enlightened Absolutism* (University of Michigan Press, Ann Arbor, 1990), 1–4.

[4] Quoted in H. S. Commager, *The Empire of Reason: How Europe Imagined and America Realized the Enlightenment* (Weidenfeld & Nicolson, London, 1978), 114.

[5] L. Gershoy, *From Despotism to Revolution, 1763–1789: The Rise of Modern Europe* (Harper & Row, New York, 1944), 49.

[6] F. Venturi, *Italy and the Enlightenment: Studies in a Cosmopolitan Century: Selected Essays*, ed. and with an introduction by S. Woolf, trans. S. Corsi (Longman, London, 1972), 44. Scott, *Enlightened Absolutism*, 4–10, for the vicissitudes of these different terms. He himself plumps for 'Enlightened absolutism' which is in line with my own definition of absolutism, *vis-à-vis* despotism.

tainly, most states were monarchical (this includes principalities), but a number of republics persisted and even among the monarchies a fair number were 'limited' in law as well as practice.

2.1. *The Republics*

There were a few rare traces of democracy in some of the Swiss cantons, but the rest were ruled by patriciates—an upper class, usually intermarried and hereditary, but not 'noble' in that the usual privileges of European nobility such as apparel, fiscal immunities, and the like did not apply to them. Three Italian republics conform to this description: Genoa, which was now run by a doge and two assessors; Lucca, a patriciate-aristocratic oligarchy; and Venice, whose constitution had not changed from what we saw it was in Chapter 7 of Book III.[7] The most dynamic and important of all the republics was unquestionably the United Provinces, that is, the Dutch Republic, but here again power resided in the hands of a small number of wealthy families.

2.2. *The Limited Monarchies*

All the remaining states of Europe were monarchies, but by no means were they all 'absolute'. 'Germany' did not exist, but the largely German-speaking Holy Roman Empire comprised no less than 294 statelets and 2,303 territories or jurisdictions,[8] so that it would be otiose—and painful—to have to categorize them all. Most of the larger states had by now become absolute monarchies, but the Estates had managed to hold their ground in some of them like Württemberg, Saxony, and (rather faintly) Bavaria.[9]

Poland, as we have seen, was not just a limited monarchy but was so limited that some writers prefer to place it among the republics. Britain was, of course, a limited monarchy, but the popular elements in its electorate must not be underestimated. Sweden swithered between a strong monarchy up to 1722 and a merely decorative one up to 1772, at which point Gustav III seized back the royal prerogatives. Even so, the *Riksdag* survived with not-inconsiderable powers; the balance between king and legislature was not unlike that in Britain. In brief, Sweden was always a limited monarchy but exceptionally so between 1722 and 1772. Finally, there is what most histor-

---

[7] Y. Durand, *Les Républiques au temps des monarchies* (Collection SUP; Presses Universitaires de France, 1973), 119–20. R. R. Palmer, *The Age of the Democratic Revolution*, 2 vols. (Princeton UP, Princeton, 1959), 35–7.   [8] Hufton, *Europe*, 143.

[9] F. L. Carsten, *Princes and Parliaments in Germany from the Fifteenth to the Eighteenth Centuries* (Clarendon Press, Oxford, 1959).

ians call the 'Habsburg lands' but what is more conveniently referred to here and later as Austria or the Austrian Empire. Because of the efforts of Joseph II (1780–90) this is sometimes thought of as an absolute monarchy, but nothing could be further from the truth. At every turn and in every domain the emperor was trapped and obstructed by constituted bodies which for the most part were manned by the nobility.

2.3. *The Absolute Monarchies*

The absolute monarchies comprised the greater states of France, Prussia, Russia, Spain, Portugal, and Denmark (which then included Norway); the smaller ones were German statelets like Hesse, Hanover, and the Palatinate, and the Italian principalities and so on of Modena, the Papal States, Parma, and Tuscany, and the kingdoms of Piedmont (i.e. Savoy) and the Two Sicilies (i.e. Naples). But these themselves fall into three different groups (which incidentally, points up the main argument of this chapter). In the first, the monarchy is in full vigour and fighting a strenuous battle with ancient law and custom and traditional social bodies such as the aristocracy and the Roman Church. Their rulers were fully engaged in something much more than 'reform', which term suggests simple improvements; they were state-building, that is, forming the modern territorial state with its bureau-cratic and military machinery out of the fluid materials that were still in place in the seventeenth century. They were, in effect, trying to catch up with the already completed state-form of the West. We have already considered Russia and Prussia. Austria forms the third of such states.

In contrast, states of a second group may be said to be vegetating. Here the accumulated interests and structures of the past are not swept away, indeed, they wax in vigour—the resurgence of the French *parlements* provides the best example. As time passes, these static state structures prove less and less adapted to the rapidly advancing complexity of their societies. France is the supreme example. Britain, as a limited monarchy with popular elements in its state structure and a considerable potential for even more of the same, avoided petrifaction, but even so, by the century's end it lay far behind the 'enlightened' governments of Europe in such matters as, for example, religious toleration and the harshness of its penal code.

Finally there is a small group of states that catch refreshing whiffs of enlightened absolutism but relapse after a relatively short time. Spain enjoyed a burst of creative improvements under Charles III (1759–88) and so did the Kingdom of the Two Sicilies, where he reigned as king before becoming king of Spain. The extensive reforms of Peter Leopold, grand duke of Tuscany (and brother of the Austrian Joseph II) were *not* effaced by his successors. But the efforts of Gustavus III of Sweden after 1772 mostly perished with him after he died from the assassin's bullet at the masked ball which gave rise to Verdi's opera of that name. Similarly, the strenuous efforts of Pombal, chief minister in Portugal (1750–77), were swept away when he fell from power.

3. THE ENLIGHTENMENT 'PROGRAMME'

The tensions and transactions between the 'enlightened' monarchs and the customary bodies—nobility and Roman Church to the fore, but extending to all nodes of privilege such as the guilds, the town corporations, the legal profession—are largely explained by the political charge the 'enlightened' monarchs carried. Without expounding the full philosophical basis, we can easily produce a check-list of the practical changes that these monarchs wanted to introduce, because they are highly uniform as between the different schools of *philosophes*, and spring from the basic tenets of Enlightenment philosophy. In expounding this, however, the work of these 'enlightened' monarchs must not be disparaged.[10] They have a lot to be said for them. Some created states out of what had been agglomerations—as in Prussia and the Austrian heartland. They introduced humane and sensible policies where these had been lacking, they improved administrative efficiency and, despite their aristocratic bias, they did not depress the condition of their subjects. On the contrary, they improved it, if only marginally. It can hardly be said that equality before the law or the curtailment of servile obligations or the abolition of torture were inimical to the masses.

French Enlightenment philosophy is shallow. It was heavily dependent upon Locke, whose influence preponderated all over the Continent throughout this century. The *philosophes* who followed his path were not what we would call philosophers but, rather, publicists: one thinks of such writers as Voltaire, d'Holbach, Helvétius, d'Alembert, Diderot, and so forth. It will be noticed that all these names are French, and this is no accident. The roots of Enlightenment philosophy lie in Britain but French language and literature was the overwhelming and universal literary and cultural influence throughout Europe, so that it is not surprising that once Lockean ideas had taken root in Europe it should mainly be through French writers and thinkers that they were propagated. But this should not be taken to mean

---

[10] Cf. Commager, *The Empire of Reason*, 115–17, which is, precisely, such an exercise in disparagement. Commager's argument is encapsulated in the subtitle of his book, *How Europe Imagined and America Realized the Enlightenment*. This is a splendid book, marvellously written, and imbued with rare pace and passion, but in its nature it has to disparage the work of the enlightened monarchs—in order to make out its thesis that it was not Europe that realized the Enlightenment ideals but America.

that the Enlightenment was a purely French phenomenon and France an epicentre which radiated its views to the rest of Europe. On the contrary, similar or consistent ideas often developed autonomously elsewhere. There was a Scottish Enlightenment of very great power, in which the names of David Hume, Ferguson, Miller, and Adam Smith are outstanding. The German *Aufklarung* spanned a great range, from the acutely rational to the near-romantic. Among the former Kant is outstanding, but it is right to invoke Pufendorf also—for all that he was a product of the previous century—because his ideas attained great prominence in Germany and Austria owing to the recommendation of thinkers as diverse as John Locke and J. J. Rousseau. Pufendorf expounded a theory of natural law which became a textbook in Protestant institutions of higher learning in both the North German states and Scotland. At the other extreme lay what I regard as the lachrymose outpourings of Goethe, Schiller, and Lessing.[11]

Another important and almost entirely independent centre of Enlightenment views was Italy. Here Venturi opened up a great field of study by exploring beyond Muratori and Beccaria into the multitude of second- or even third-rate thinkers, molehills to their mountains.[12]

The relative influence of all these thinkers was greater in some places than in others. For instance, Pufendorf's natural-law theories were highly influential in parts of Germany and in Austria. I do not regard Cameralism as an Enlightenment idea, though many 'enlightened' historians choose to call it such for all that it originated long before, in seventeenth-century Germany; but it too was highly influential in the German statelets, Prussia, and Austria.

What Locke had propounded, and the *philosophes* thence publicized, in his *Essay on the Human Understanding* and the two *Treatises of Government* was based on two concepts: Nature and Reason. In the former work Locke had denied all 'innate ideas' and held the mind to be a *tabula rasa*. This being so, it could be written on. Hence the importance of education in the recommendations of the *philosophes*. What was written on it should be the product of Reason. To enlightened men Reason was a sort of sharpened and honed common sense and it was held to work in much the same way in all human beings. Reason had been corrupted by the abuses of the Middle Ages, which had been carried over into the eighteenth century and institutionalized in the Church, social and economic classes, prejudice, and similar environing impediments. (Of these the Roman Church was held to be the most corrupting influence of all.)

[11] See e.g. Sorel, *Europe and the French Revolution*, 132–5 for characteristic outpourings from Goethe, Schiller, and Lessing.   [12] Cf. Venturi, *Italy and the Enlightenment*.

Nature was closely involved with this concept of Reason. Nature worked according to knowable principles or laws, but these were hidden under the corrupting and distorting layers of ignorance, superstition, religion, and the like. Reason then was invoked to unfold the true, the pristine—that is, Nature as such. Since there was Nature, so there were 'natural laws' (as opposed to man-made laws which might be very oppressive and nefarious). Reason could establish what these natural laws were. Hence the extremely important political application of these contentions as set out in the *Second Treatise of Government*. The fact that Reason tells us what are the natural laws enables us to compare them with the man-made ones, and to demand that government makes them conform to the former, under pain of loosing the people from their allegiance: the celebrated notion of the Social Contract. This notion dissolved away the old idea of proprietary divine-right monarchy. Hence Frederick the Great's aphorism that 'the King was the first servant of the state', and Duke Leopold of Tuscany's political testament where he states that 'a ruler, even a hereditary ruler, is only a delegate, a servant of the people whose cares and troubles he must make his own'.[13]

It was from their desire to free mankind from the shackles of the supernatural and the unnatural by the application of Reason that the *philosophes* propounded a menu. The menu is not *à la carte* but it is not *table d'hôte* either. To change the metaphor, what is propounded here is an 'identikit' of the Enlightenment attitude. Some thinkers attached greater importance to this rather than to that, some omitted various items listed here while others might add new ones. The following check-list is therefore incomplete, but can fairly be said to encapsulate *most* of the reforms sought by *most* of the *philosophes*.

To begin with, there was a package of anti-Catholic Church measures.[14] This Church was held above all other institutions to be the corrupter of humankind. Some *philosophes* went beyond attacking the Church to espouse deism (like Voltaire) or even atheism (Holbach, La Mettrie), but all of them wanted to reduce the number of monasteries and to impose heavy taxes on or even expropriate their wealth; they approved of concordats to increase state control of Church activities and nominations to livings; and they heartily approved the movement against the Jesuits, begun by Pombal in Portugal in 1759–61 and followed in France in 1764 and 1767, culminating in the pope's dissolution of the Order in 1773. The pretexts were various but the chief motive was that they (the Jesuits), being fervent Ultramontanists,

---

[13] Quoted, Scott, *Enlightened Absolutism*, 19.

[14] Here is a case in point. Maria Theresa is often regarded as an 'Enlightened Despot', for she unquestionably carried out a wide range of the essential Enlightenment reforms. Yet she hated the Enlightenment, and was a fervent Catholic and an enemy of religious toleration.

constituted a challenge to monarchical insistence on sovereign independence.

Measures like these could and perhaps would have been taken by any
Renaissance monarch had he been powerful enough. But this was surely not
so for other of their anti-Church doctrines. How many monarchs and
princes of the Reformation and Counter-Reformation and the Thirty Years
War would even have contemplated religious toleration? Yet some of these
'enlightened' states (notably, Prussia) went far beyond what had already
been attained in Britain and the Dutch Republic, the paragons of religious
freedom. The abolition of the censorship and the free play of ideas was
another cause they espoused (Prussia again). In both cases, the intention
was to un-cocoon Nature and its laws from the web of ignorance which
religion and state censorship had cast over it.

A second cluster of items related to justice and the law. These are not
merely important for their state-building role; they reaffirm and strengthen
the claim of the European states—and only they—to be law-bound in
comparison to the Asian states, in the sense we formulated previously.[15]
The *Rechtstaat* ideal could not be realized as long as there was no equality
before the law, no common law of the land, no rational self-consistency to
it, only enclaves of private justice instead. Such are some of the hallmarks of
the fully developed modern European state; so the Enlightenment proposals
mark a most important stage in its departure from the fragments of feudal
law that were still encumbering the legal processes of the time. In many
states, and certainly in all of those wherein serfdom existed—which is as
much to say, in Denmark and the three great eastern states—the landed
noblemen still dispensed seigneurial justice to their serfs. Hence the
Enlightenment demand for its abolition and the substitution of universalistic codes of state law and sentencing. Here again one might argue that
these demands were logical extensions of the long-standing drive to monarchical absolutism, but this was not necessarily true of other matters
relating to justice. One was the abolition of torture. Its arbitrary irration-
ality was set out with admirable sarcasm in Voltaire's *Dictionnaire philosophique*.
Transcending this particular reform went the demand for a rational penal
code that would balance penalties against offences with the maximum
possible humanity. This element derived from Beccaria's *Tratto dei delitti e
delle pene* (1764) which, among other things, condemned torture, confiscation
of property, and capital punishment, and advocated instead the prevention
of crime by education. Beccaria's work had an enormous impact on the
enlightened monarchs; indeed, it is not much of an exaggeration to say that

---

[15] Bk. IV, Ch. 5 above.

among the greater states it was only in vegetative France and Britain that it failed to affect the laws.

What we are witnessing here is the birth of *humanitarianism*. We have frequently commented on the barbarity of punishments and the indifference to human and animal suffering in all the great empires up to this time. This humanitarian impulse was to spread far beyond the items we have just mentioned and was to be carried forward by individuals far removed from the *philosophes*—by philanthropists and/or deeply committed Christians. It is to such as these that the anti-slavery campaign is due, as well as the effort to have serfdom abolished. Serfdom struck the reformers as the negation of the natural equality of mankind and a denial of the natural right to life, liberty, and property.

Reason being the yardstick of all human activity and the sole, if not the certain guarantee that it would produce happiness, the *philosophes* also pressed for the reform and the spread of education, by way of national school-systems and the establishment of new faculties in the universities.

On the economy, however, these publicists quite failed to agree. Broadly speaking they fell into two camps which were diametrically opposed on most economic issues. The Physiocrats affirmed that the only source of wealth was the application of labour to the soil and hence advocated freedom of movement and manufacture inside the state, and the free play of market forces to determine prices. Hence *laissez faire, laissez passer*. The other school, sometimes called Mercantilism, sometimes Cameralism, or—after the French minister—Colbertism, stood by the tradition that the state must protect itself by external tariffs and continue to intervene to endow the economy with an infrastructure of roads, canals, and a merchant fleet, to build factories, to regulate prices and the movement of artisans from one place to another, and to promote companies for trade and/or colonization abroad. Only perhaps in the matter of tariff barriers could these two schools of economists come together, and so we see, in the various enlightened monarchies, the Enlightenment reform package associated with a hands-off attitude to the internal economy, or alternatively—as in Prussia, for instance—an active intervention in it.

4. THE ENLIGHTENED MONARCHIES

It is not proposed to discuss France or England here. As we have pointed out, they were vegetative, but in any case we shall be saying something about the mid-eighteenth-century British constitution in Book V, Chapter 2, when we come to consider its influence on the USA, just as we shall have regard to developments in eighteenth-century France in Book V, Chapter 3, on the

French Revolution. Here we shall concentrate upon the major enlightened monarchies with the exception of Russia, already considered in the previous chapter.

The principal monarchs and states affected can be compared by the following list:

Austria	Maria Theresa	1740–80
	Joseph II	1780–90
	Leopold II	1790–2
	(grand duke of Tuscany, 1765–90)	
Naples	Charles III	1735–59
Portugal	Joseph I (via Pombal)	1750–77
Prussia	Frederick II (the Great)	1740–86
Russia	Catherine II (the Great)	1762–96
Spain	Charles III	1759–88
	(formerly king of Naples)	
Tuscany	Leopold I	1765–90
	(Holy Roman Emperor)	1790–2
Sweden	Gustavus III	1771–92

We shall take only a cursory look at the smaller kingdoms and principalities here, leaving our major descriptions to Prussia and, above all, Austria.

We can begin by coupling Naples and Spain, since the king of the former left to become the king of the latter. The *Regno* was still in 1735 what we have called an imperfect or uncompleted territorial state. Although its parliament had ceased to meet after 1642, so making it in theory an absolutism, only 384 out of more than 2,000 communes were directly subject to the Crown. The rest were dependants of the aristocracy. In Sicily the monarch was not absolute at all, being checked by the still-vigorous parliament which was dominated by the *bracci* of the Church and the nobility, both of which, of course, were prime targets of the Enlightenment. Charles's efforts to have Neapolitan law codified were not successful, which is forgivable considering that it had to take account of some 1,300 feudal courts. His assault on the clergy was more successful. His Concordat of 1741 empowered him to tax Church property, limit Church jurisdiction, and restrict the number of clergy. He kept the Inquisition out. Charles even tried to permit Jews to settle in Naples but was defeated by popular resistance.[16] In 1759 Charles quit Naples to become king of Spain. When his ignorant and frivolous son, Ferdinand

[16] S. Andrews, *Eighteenth-Century Europe: The 1680s to 1815* (Longman, London, 1965), 155.

IV, reached his majority in 1767 Tanucci, the architect of Charles's reforms, still tried manfully to attack the seigneurial jurisdictions but now received no support. He had a little more success with the Church; he was able in the 1770s to ensure that half the land confiscated from the (expelled) Jesuit Order should go to the small peasants. But power had come to rest in the queen, Maria Carolina, a daughter of Maria Theresa of Austria, and this ignorant bigot secured Tanucci's dismissal in 1776. For all that, a degree of reform persisted. The 1780s saw an attack on guild privileges. Some progress was also made in Sicily, though not till 1789 were the last remnants of serfdom abolished. By and large, however, the Church still maintained its formidable position and the nobility, that other bastion of stagnation, remained almost untouched by all these efforts.

We left Spain with the accession of the Bourbon Philip V (1700–46). His model was Louis XIV's France. To this end he abrogated the privileges of Aragon, thus eliminating the last legal obstacle to absolute rule; divided the entire kingdom into *partidos* under military governors; and reaffirmed that it lay with him to appoint the judges and *corregidores*.[17] He vigorously supported the Church—Spain was singularly priest-ridden. At this time she contained 160,000 clergymen. Philip encouraged the Inquisition: during his reign there were no less than 700 *autos de fe*. The country was dominated by the Church and the nobility via their control of the higher and local positions of state, appointments to the great ecclesiastical positions, their landed and commercial wealth, and their manipulation of seigneurial justice. Nevertheless Charles had better fortune here than in Italy, partly because the country was undergoing a powerful economic revival, but also because he was served by particularly able and enlightened ministers: Campomanes, Aranda, and Floridablanca.

In Spain the Enlightenment was not anti-clerical. On the other hand, the Spanish state was committed to 'regalism', a parallel to French Gallicanism, and it was to serve this that Charles's ecclesiastical reforms were directed. An attack on Church privileges had already begun in the Concordat of 1753, which, *inter alia*, allowed the Crown to tax Church lands. Charles travelled further along this path when in 1761 he declared that royal permission was required before Papal Bulls could be accepted in Spain. The two great pillars of the Church were the Jesuit Order and the Inquisition. Charles had a number of reasons for disliking the Order, among which was their Ultramontanist defence of papal claims which, of course, clashed with

---

[17] See the text of Philip V's reforms, 1711, quoted in Barnes and Feldman, *Rationalism and Revolution*, 30–1.

Spanish 'regalism'. In 1767 he followed the example of Portugal and France (which had expelled the Jesuits in 1759 and 1764 respectively) to banish them.[18] He found it politically impossible to abolish the Inquisition. He is reported as saying: 'The Spaniards want it and it does not bother me.'[19] But its jurisdiction was curtailed and its procedure made more fair. The appointment of less fanatical inquisitors resulted in a decline in the use of torture and the number of public burnings. Its last victim—an old woman—was burned in 1780.

Charles made strenuous efforts to improve education by establishing secondary schools and reinvigorating higher education. He tried—without a great deal of success, it must be admitted—to get the university curriculum revised, desirous that they should teach science and economics. And he destroyed the monopoly of the *colegios mayores*. These had originally been hostels for poor students but were now narrow and highly exclusive clubs. It was in their nature to be extremely conservative, and their great offence in Charles's eyes was that they stuck together to promote their alumni into the plum jobs of the administration. However, their very success had bred a counter-establishment, the *mantéistos*, from students whom they had excluded. Campomanes was a *matéisto*, for instance. In 1771 Charles set about a drastic purgation of the *colegios*, and demoted their candidates for high posts—for example, he cut down their numbers in the Council of Castile.

All this, and Floridablanca's efforts to ban torture and simplify judicial procedure, were standard parts of the Enlightenment 'package', but economic policy proved highly controversial. The first of the economics ministers, the unfortunate Esquilace (whom Charles had brought with him from Italy), was a Physiocrat and his efforts to introduce the Physiocratic single tax on all lands enraged the clergy and the nobility since they would lose their exempt status; his free-trading attempts to strip the Five Grand Guilds of their monopoly over the pricing of textiles, jewellery, and spices made them his enemies too; and his Act which abolished the ancient and highly popular controls on grain prices and relied on market forces instead provoked the notorious rising (the *mutin*) of Madrid, which spread to Saragossa, Cuenca, Barcelona, Bilbao, and Cadiz. Esquilace fell and price-control returned. The rest of the ministers were strongly interventionist.

In 1788 Charles died, to be succeeded by Charles IV. For all the great effort that had been put into reform, it had only dented the surface. Despite

---

[18] Herr, 'Regalism and Jansenism in Spain', in S. Andrews, *Enlightened Despotism: Readings* (Longman, London, 1967), 42–9.

[19] Quoted, M. McKendrick, *A Concise History of Spain* (Cassell, London, 1972), 145.

the Colbertism (or, if one will, Cameralism) of the ministers, the economy had not leapt ahead as anticipated. Regalism was never completely achieved; the 1790s saw a return of the old clerical arrogance. And despite the other reforms Spain still remained a backward country. The French Revolution transformed Floridablanca and Charles IV into arch-reactionaries and all further innovation came to an abrupt end.

In Tuscany the Grand Duke Leopold (1765–90) was the brother of the emperor, Joseph II, and like him a devotee of the Enlightenment. His reforms were extensive and also successful. Leopold might fairly be said to have completed the evolution of Tuscany as a centralized territorial state, since at the date of his accession it was, effectively, a personal union of Florence and Siena along with their respective *contade*, and a number of other municipalities. He created a unitary state structure. Of this he was the absolute monarch, and he used his power to enact the greater part of the Physiocratic-cum-Enlightenment package. His efforts have been described as 'reform in its most radical, sustained and self-conscious form',[20] and it is very significant in this respect that in 1779 he ordered a minister (Gianni) actually to draft a constitution for the state (completed in 1782). This was strikingly innovative, bearing in mind that the American Constitution dates from 1787.

Mortmain and entails were made illegal, the *arti* (guilds) were abolished (1770), internal transit dues were abolished, free trade in grain was gradually introduced, and a new fiscal regime instituted that more or less ensured tax equality between all classes. Leopold admired Beccaria and followed him in abolishing torture and capital punishment and the confiscation of the criminal's property. He rationalized the judicial system and in 1749 fatally undermined the seigneurial jurisdictions by allowing suitors to appeal from them to his own courts. And in 1776 he promulgated a penal code for the entire Duchy.

Leopold also assailed the Church. He restricted the powers of the Inquisition, reduced the number of saints' days, limited the rights to sanctuary, curtailed ecclesiastical jurisdiction, and abolished the tithe. In the end—as he grew increasingly dogmatic and filled his state with swarms of informers and *sbirri*—he went too far. He became a Jansenist and as such redesigned the liturgy, only to be met by a storm of popular protest. A bench of bishops, called in 1787, opposed any continuation of his measures and, when he quit Tuscany in 1790 to become emperor, he left the Duchy in the throes of clerical reaction.

Perhaps the most interesting insight into Leopold's political views is

---

[20] Scott, *Enlightened Absolutism*, 65.

what emerges from a document he addressed to his sister Marie-Christine in 1790. In it he declares that the sovereign, even if hereditary, is still only the 'delegate and servant of the people'; that the relationship between him and his people is contractual, and a sovereign who does not keep to his share of it forfeits his position; that it was his duty to render account and get approval for all new laws; that taxation should not be imposed arbitrarily; and, finally, 'that the sovereign should rule only through law'.[21]

Although the Milanese was now an Austrian province, its governor, Count Firmian (1759–82), imposed on it a transformation similar to Tuscany's. The economy was subjected to a mixture of Physiocracy and Cameralism, so that new roads and canals were built, the guilds abolished, restrictions were placed on mortmain, and the fiscal system reformed on the basis of a cadaster which transferred the tax load to property and land, and reduced it on trade and on persons. After a difficult struggle, tax-farming was abandoned and the collection of the indirect taxes taken over by state servants. As in Tuscany, internal administration was consolidated. The Milanese was divided into so many provinces and communes, and—in order to win over the support of the landowners—local administration was to be carried out by councils of 'deputies' who had to be individuals paying the land tax. And, as one might expect, the Church was also an object of attack. Here education was a great bone of contention. The Inquisition tribunal was banned, many monastic schools and those of the Jesuits were closed, and the Order itself was dissolved. But, though undoubtedly 'enlightened', this absolute government would nevertheless brook no popular resistance and swarmed with the spies and agents who were to form the foundation of Metternich's notorious 'system' some fifty years later.

While so much was stirring in the Italian states, Portugal, an absolute monarchy whose Cortes had ceased to meet since 1697, 'concentrated on devotional exercises and the production of port'.[22] Despite having no industry, scarcely able to feed itself, and with its wine trade in English hands, it was rich from Brazilian gold which, incidentally, gave the Crown an income entirely independent of the Cortes and must be held responsible for the latter's euthanasia and the royal absolutism. The condition of the peasantry was abysmal. The country was the most priest-ridden in all Europe. 'It was said that there were nearly 900 religious houses, that the

[21] For the entire text—even more interesting than the summary given above because of its forceful reference to the imprescriptible rights with which Nature endows the people, in a tone fully reminiscent of Jefferson's Declaration of Independence—see Sorel, *Europe and the French Revolution*, 147–8.   [22] J. O. Lindsay, 'The Western Mediterranean and Italy', in *CMH*, vii. 288.

Church not only accounted for nearly half the population but owned something like two-thirds of the land.'[23]

All this was attacked by Joseph I's all-powerful minister Carvalho e Memmo, later ennobled as the marquis of Pombal, who had conceived two master hatreds: for the grandees and for the Church. A man of unflagging energy, cruel, and of autocratic temper, but possessing great physical courage withal, Pombal forbade the Inquisition to carry out any sentences without official approval, and expropriated the Jesuits' property and expelled them. This was done on the pretext of implication in an aristocratic plot, which also served to strike down the noble opposition, for the grandees involved were found guilty and executed. The attack on the Jesuits was pressed home by a flood of propaganda: one pamphlet which reviled their administration (or exploitation) of the Paraguay Indians reached a circulation of 20,000, printed in five languages.

Having thus struck down his two principal opponents, Pombal was free to execute those items in the Enlightenment package which appealed to him. His economic policy was thoroughgoing Cameralism and he intervened and set up state enterprises with indefatigable vigour. But he also abolished internal trade restrictions, and actually established free trade between Portugal and its American colonies. He continued his attack on the aristocracy and the Church by limiting mortmain, abolishing the aristocratic monopoly of public offices by introducing a merit system into the royal service, secularizing the schools, modernizing the curriculum of Coimbra University, and interestingly, as a true Enlightenment man, he actually extended civil rights to Jews—this in perhaps the most anti-Semitic country of all Europe!

The powers of the Inquisition were curtailed. Slavery in Portugal was abolished. The army was modernized. So, too, up to a point, was the central administration, where Pombal created a single Royal Treasury with the chief minister at its head. To accomplish this Pombal relied on the authority of the king, the protection of a secret police, and wholesale imprisonment. One historian speaks of his term of office as one of 'terrorism and senseless brutality, murder, and torture'; another calls it a monolithic despotism.[24]

Pombal had one outstanding accomplishment to his name. He took command when the great earthquake of 1755 destroyed an entire third part of Lisbon, and it was due entirely to his leadership that the city was rebuilt—beautifully—in two years. But the rest of his reforms ended in nothing. He was dismissed when his king died in 1777, and within a few

---

[23] Lindsay, 'The Western Mediterranean and Italy', 289.
[24] Hufton, *Europe*, 272; Gershoy, *From Despotism to Revolution*, 152.

years of his own death in 1782 the country lapsed back into its clerical–aristocratic torpor.

Gustavus III's absolutism, snatched from the overweening authority of the *Riksdag*, resembled Pombal's in this respect—that it came and it went. His role (1771–92) was for the most part to promote an impressive florescence of literature, opera, and drama (justly known as 'the Swedish Enlightenment'), to engage in some dubious and unsuccessful military ventures, and—in the realm of politics—to have a good deal more to do with technically interesting developments in the Swedish constitution than with the package of enlightened measures propagated by the *philosophes*.

His constitutional innovations were directed at becoming absolute. Far from being in this condition in 1771, the Swedish Crown was little more than a presiding figure in an aristocratically dominated parliamentary system. After one year's vain attempt to govern with the Diet and its executive organs, Gustavus organized a conspiracy in which he tore up the constitutional arrangements of 1722 and made the Diet swear to his own constitutional document, of fifty-seven Articles: the first written constitution of any sovereign state. But the suggestion that this made him 'absolute' is laughable. The new constitution resembled, in fact, that of Britain. The king was head of the executive and only he could propose legislation; but he needed the *Riksdag*'s consent for passing new laws or repealing old ones, and it alone could strike taxes and control the budget.

Gustavus's domestic programme was a far cry from what Pombal or Leopold or Charles III had carried out. His chief measures included reform of the currency and regulation of the national finances, which were irrelevant to Enlightenment principles. More to the point, however, were the abolition of torture, the impeachment of the supreme court for maladministration and misfeasance, the subsequent shake-up of the entire judicial system, the freedom of the press, religious equality, internal free trade, and—in a Colbertian move—the establishment of a national monopoly of distilling brandy.[25] Yet out of these welcome reforms, the freedom of the press was revoked in 1778 and the national distilleries—a grotesque financial failure—provoked such intense peasant unrest that it could only be put down by armed force. This measure too was repealed.[26]

In fact the action of Gustavus that was most relevant to the political ideals of the Enlightenment was his second constitution, the 'Act of Union and Security', which unequivocally sided with the non-privileged Orders and confronted the aristocracy. This document reaffirms in an even more

[25] R. N. Bain, *Gustavus III and his Contemporaries*, 2 vols. (Kegan Paul, London; Trench, Trübner and Co., 1894), i. 161, 163, 173.   [26] Ibid., i. 192–3.

detailed manner the royal prerogatives and fails to specify in any detail at all the powers of the *Riksdag*. Thus he had taken a step which did indeed bring him within an ace of 'absolutism'. But the new constitution also contained provisions that were highly evocative of Enlightenment philosophy, for it declared that 'all subjects enjoy the same rights' and all were to be judged by the same courts. Only the very highest offices of state were reserved for the nobility; all others 'shall be accessible to all subjects of whatever rank or condition'. This constitution, it should be noticed, preceded by six months the French *Declaration of the Rights of Man and the Citizen.* It was popular in Sweden with all classes except the nobility, whose privileges it had almost entirely undone.[27] Hence the notorious aristocratic conspiracy of 1792 in which, during a masked ball, the king was shot and mortally wounded, dying a fortnight later—and, incidentally, throwing the governance of Sweden into chaos.

All the monarchs mentioned so far—perhaps Leopold of Tuscany and even Count Firmian are partial exceptions—might be best described as improvers, whereas the rulers of Prussia and Austria during this period are better described as state-builders. Their pre-eminent role was to gather up and centralize disparate lands and jurisdictions, strengthen and rationalize their administrative structures, and fortify and promote the economy. They would have done this even had there not been an Enlightenment because their intense rivalry and their two great wars forced both of them to increase their tax-intake and to modernize their central administration and defence. Their efforts and the Enlightenment outlook did not necessarily run in tandem. For instance: Frederick the Great and Maria Theresa of Austria both went in for state-building but, whereas Frederick was regarded as the embodiment of the Enlightenment, Maria Theresa, pious churchwoman and virulent anti-Semite, detested it.

In an earlier chapter we saw Frederick as a workaholic, an uncompromising autocrat, a king who preferred and fostered his aristocracy, who despised his ministers and communicated with them from a distance through his private office (*Kabinett*) at Potsdam by means of documents, and denatured the General Directory by distributing some of its functions to new and separate agencies. But his character and activities are a mass of contradictions. He is widely seen as the very model of enlightened absolutism yet, while there is no need to retract one word from the description of Prussian absolutism given in Chapter 6 above, Frederick's status as an Enlightenment hero is much more problematical. As a youth his interests lay in literature, music, and the arts and he despised and loathed his coarse and uncouth

[27] The text of the document is printed in Palmer, *Age of the Democratic Revolution,* i. 512–13.

father, Frederick William I. He had tried to flee the court, only to be trapped and compelled to see his friend and accomplice executed before his very eyes. As crown prince he had in 1736 initiated his correspondence with Voltaire that was to continue for the next twenty years. As king he hosted Voltaire and d'Alembert in his court. He wrote verses (not very good ones) in what spare time he had, he had a real affection for music and played the flute, and he found time to write a good deal. His prose was 'lively, witty and incisive'.[28] His *Anti-Machiavel* is not much regarded but, taken together with a lengthy list of other titles, the quantity and at times quality of his output is more than respectable compared with his contemporaries and, certainly, with the deluge of books that pours from the presses today. For a very active king, it is quite outstanding.[29] To him only the French were civilized. His palace at Potsdam, called Sans-Souci, was modelled on Versailles. He conversed and wrote in French; his German was clumsy. This was the man whom d'Alembert called *le roi philosophe*[30] and who was likened by Voltaire to Caesar, to Augustus, Marcus Aurelius, to Virgil, Pliny, Socrates—to name but a few.[31]

Yet the moment he ascended the throne in 1740 he launched a violent, unprovoked attack on Austria in order to seize Silesia, so initiating a war that did not end till 1748; he launched the 'Seven Years' War in 1756, which ended with his retaining Silesia but at the cost of one-tenth of Prussia's population; and he snatched West Prussia from a helpless Poland in 1772. For all that he was a *philosophe*, he was also an out-and-out militarist. And many of his state measures bore no relationship to the Enlightenment philosophy at all. Peter Gay says the *philosophes* were dismayed and then provoked by his failure to take their advice. And not just that. They

discovered soon enough that the Athens of the North was only a frigid Sparta after all; the philosopher-king was more the militarist king than the pacific philosopher. Frederick's cynical invasion of Silesia, his patent unreliability as an ally, his reimposition of censorship, his shabby and, whatever the provocation, brutal treatment of Voltaire after their friendship began to pall in 1752, his disheartening failure to overhaul the laws and humanize the army . . . all this decisively outweighed his ostentatious affection for French men of letters, his irreligiosity and his diligence.[32]

Nor is this all. The 'revisionists' have struck again. This time it is to claim that most if not all of Frederick's reforms had been anticipated by his

---

[28] Scott, *Enlightened Absolutism*, 273.   [29] His *Œuvres* run to 33 volumes.
[30] P. Gay, *The Enlightenment: An Interpretation*, Vol. II, *The Science of Freedom* (Weidenfeld & Nicolson, 1970), p. 483.   [31] Ibid. 483–4.
[32] Ibid. 484–5.

father Frederick William I. This is true, they say, in the matter of religious toleration, judicial reform (Cocceji was a man of the previous reign), Cameralism (of long standing), and compulsory education.[33] But this does not mean that the king was not an 'enlightened despot'. Indeed, it has nothing to do with the case. Where is it written that a king could be an enlightened despot only if he pulled up what was bequeathed him by the roots and planted an entirely different crop? A king can altogether discontinue what occurred in his father's time, as well as continue it. Frederick did the latter and he did it with an intense and unremitting commitment whose effects were to strengthen, deepen, and widen the reforms initiated by his predecessors.

Furthermore, looking at the detail, the adverse judgements seem to me too harsh in some particulars. To begin with, Frederick affirmed, believed in, and largely acted on the principle: 'I am the first servant of the state.' He was a free-thinker and deist, so that it did not come difficult for him to introduce religious toleration. He went much further than his father: 'All religions must be tolerated. The Fiscal shall only keep an eye open lest one encroaches on the other, for here everyone must be allowed to choose his own road to salvation.'[34] Pagans, deists, agnostics, even the Jesuits were tolerated; and Jews also were left alone—even given a measure of legal protection—though they were never integrated into German society. Frederick relaxed the penal code: he abolished torture and the death penalty for theft (in Britain, even after 1815, there were *three hundred* offences carrying the death penalty!), and eliminated many 'cruel and unusual punishments', such as mutilation. At the beginning of his reign he abolished the censorship of newspapers but later he revoked this. The question is, to what effect? Lessing maintained that the newspapers were sterile, and in another place he compared the freedom of Vienna to that of 'your Frenchified Berlin . . . Don't talk to me about your freedom to think and write. It's just the freedom to market as many insults about religion as one likes . . . [the country] is the most slavish in Europe.'[35] Moses Mendelssohn, who had lived all his life in Prussia, talked of a 'freedom of thought so widespread that their effects [*sc.* of the arts and sciences] reached down to the humblest inhabitant'. The freedom of publication and discussion impressed the British traveller, John Moore. But perhaps the most decisive rebuttal of Lessing was Immanuel Kant: 'Our age is the age of enlightenment, the century of *Frederick*.'[36]

[33] Scott, *Enlightened Absolutism*, 266.

[34] W. Hubatsch, *Frederick the Great: Absolutism and Administration*, trans. P. Doran (Thames & Hudson, London, 1973), 41.   [35] Scott, *Enlightened Absolutism*, 272–3.

[36] Ibid. 287–8.

For all that, a great deal of what passes for his enlightenment can equally be seen as state-building. Religious toleration itself can be seen in this light; it prevented communal strife and, in particular, preserved the unity and *esprit de corps* of the army.[37] Judicial reform partakes of this same ambivalence and it goes together with two other policies as part of his overriding ambition to build Prussia into a great, efficient, and modern state.

The first of these policies was territorial expansion and resulted in the seizure of Silesia, and later, in 1772, of West Prussia. Frederick had no legal claim on Silesia whatsoever, but he coveted it for its rich industrial potential. West Prussia was immensely significant because it united Brandenburg with East Prussia—it was the 'Polish corridor'—and its possession made the entire northern strip of Prussia continuous territory. At the beginning of his reign Prussia's population was 2,500,000; Frederick left it with 5,000,000.

His second great policy was vigorous and unremitting Cameralism. While protectionist tariffs were erected, internal tolls were swept away. Frederick established state monopolies in porcelain, tobacco, silk, and other manufactures. He developed shipbuilding at Stettin, promoted the exploitation of the mineral resources of Silesia, founded a central bank, and by no means neglected agriculture. He carried out extensive drainage projects, built canals, and attracted colonists from the outside to settle in the many waste areas of the kingdom. Consequently, the country's annual revenue of 7 million thalers in 1740 had risen to 19 million at the end of his reign and he had increased the state reserves from 8 million to 51 million thalers.

His third great policy was to systematize and rationalize the judicial system and the laws. At his accession the administration of justice was still largely in the hands of the manorial and municipal courts. The aim of Frederick's chancellor, Cocceji, was to replace this with a centralized and uniform system staffed by trained and full-time professional judges who would administer a single, uniform law-code for the entire kingdom. It is unnecessary to dwell on the significance of a common law and judicature in the establishing of a unitary state; witness the very early development of a common law in Angevin England. Moreover Frederick, though unquestionably an autocrat, firmly believed that its principal civic goal was to establish the strict and impartial application of the laws between subject and subject and, even more importantly, between his own officials and the public. When the Prussian legal system was introduced into (previously Polish) West Prussia in 1772 it was proclaimed that: 'We ourselves or our state ministry

---

[37] Hubatsch, *Frederick the Great*, 197–200.

can give no decisions which have the force of a judicial ruling.' In 1774 Frederick circularized all the provincial chambers to the effect that he did not think that the rights of subjects were being sufficiently protected; the public were complaining that 'they are not listened to or given enough help, while conversely the officials are highly favoured'. (It was this conviction that led him to intervene personally in the Arnold case, where a miller had petitioned him asking protection against the decision of the local *Landrat*.[38]) His intended codification of provincial laws never took place; but at least each province was left with only one central court, judges were better paid and had to pass a merit test, and noblemen had to provide trained judges to preside in their seigneurial courts. Above all, work continued on the uniform legal code. This the king never lived to see. It was not completed until 1794. This was the Prussian *Landrecht* and it remained in force until 1900. Frederick was an unqualified autocrat but he governed through the rule of law. Prussia was on the way to becoming a *Rechtsstaat*.

There is no reason to dissent from the judgement that 'Frederick was less influenced by the Enlightenment as a guideline for action than by *raison d'état* interpreted in an enlightened way. The principle was trimmed to suit the particular circumstances of his own state.'[39]

Whereas Prussia had been composed of several *disjecta membra* but held together by the General Directory and the provincial chambers which worked to it, Austria was nothing more than *disjecta membra* owing allegiance to the Habsburg dynasty. Almost all of these component lands had their own Estates or Diet and, below these, layers of seigneurs dispensing their own justice over their serfs. This aggregation did not even have an official name. It was usually referred to as 'the Habsburg lands'. It is Europe's supreme example of empire via dynastic marriage-alliance, its supreme example of a state based on personal union, a 'mere agglomeration of territories'. There was Hungary with its ubiquitous gentry and nobility and powerful Diet, which may be regarded as the 'Aragon' of the Austrian Crown; with its dependencies in the Slav lands of Croatia, Slovenia, and in Transylvania and the Bukovina. There was Bohemia, conquered at the Battle of the White Mountain in 1620. In between lay the German-speaking heartland, the Archduchy of Austria itself and Styria, Carniola, and Carinthia. At least all these territories were contiguous, but in addition the dynasty ruled Belgium and the Italian Milanese. It was, as Sorel puts it, 'all extremities and no centre'. 'There was no Austrian nation nor the means of making one . . . It was equally impossible to fuse these diverse populations into a homogeneous whole or to govern them together . . . Austria was

---

[38] Hubatsch, *Frederick the Great*, 216–17.   [39] Ibid. 43.

founded on nothing but contracts and laws of inheritance.'[40] The variety of the component lands of this state and the diverse relationships between the ruler and his subjects is captured in the Grand Imperial Title: 'Emperor of Austria, King of Hungary, of Bohemia, of Dalmatia, Croatia, Slovenia, Galicia, Lodomeria, and Illyria; King of Jerusalem etc; Archduke of Austria; Grand Duke of Tuscany and Cracow; Duke of Lotharingia, of Salzburg, Styria, Carinthia, Carniola'. . . and so on.

In each state the sovereign had a lieutenant but had to work with the local Diets, on which all judicial and financial officials were dependent. Power resided in these Diets, which were dominated by the local aristocracies who defended local privileges and, notably, their own right to tallage their serfs at pleasure. The more the ruler took from the peasantry the less there was for the seigneur, hence a veiled battle between the two. In effect these component states were so many dyarchies between Crown and the Diets, since the Crown could not impose but only bargain for taxation and, once the 'contribution' had been struck, the Diets and not the Crown collected the taxes. Furthermore these Diets upheld their own separate legal systems and distinctive laws. Yet it was in this empire that 'the most radical programme of reform from above in eighteenth-century Europe' was carried out.[41] This cannot be explained in terms of the French Enlightenment, though a small number of noblemen and some officials were affected by it. Austria was influenced by its openness to Germany in the north and to Italy in the south. The major influences were Cameralism and the notion of natural law. The root cause or push to reform was military defeat: by the Turks in the 1730s and, more humiliatingly, by the Prussians in the 1740s. The period of reform fell into two distinct phases, the reign of Maria Theresa, who was, as we have seen, an opponent of the Enlightenment, and Joseph II (her co-ruler for some years), who was an out-and-out doctrinaire.

Frederick II invaded Silesia in 1740, which was also the year when Maria Theresa acceded. And it was the need to raise an army and hence to raise money to pay for it that set in train the efforts to standardize and rationalize the administration of the dominions. This was compromised at the start when the young empress, in full retreat from Frederick, had to call on the Hungarian Diet with tears in her eyes, to rally to her support. This they did to the tune of 40,000 men and six cavalry regiments, but they received huge concessions in return. The Diet, like that of Poland, consisted entirely of magnates—300 in its Upper House and (nominally) 25,000 in its

[40] Sorel, *Europe and the French Revolution*, 471–5.   [41] Scott, *Enlightened Absolutism*, 146.

lower; and these seigneurs tenaciously clung to their ancient rights in respect of taxation, serfdom, and seigneurial justice.

Maria Theresa, with her highly intelligent and dedicated ministers Haugwitz and then Prince Kaunitz, authorized measures to centralize her authority. Haugwitz was a confirmed Cameralist and the foe of the territorial Diets. He united the state treasuries of Austria and Bohemia into a single Directory, and their supreme courts into a single *Hofrat*. In the localities he expanded the Crown's fiscal authority by what at first were called Deputations and after 1749 the Representations-and-Chambers, which were increasingly staffed by royal nominees. A reorganized Council of War, the *Hofkriegsrat*, paralleled these fiscal and judicial unifications. (These reforms did not apply at all to Hungary nor to the Milanese or Belgium.) To preside over all these new organs Haugwitz established a Directorium.

But these measures met with only tepid success. The Church was untouched. And, to crown Haugwitz's disappointments, the Seven Years War against Frederick was going very badly and demanded sums far greater than even Haugwitz's reforms could provide. He resigned in 1760 and was replaced by Kaunitz.

Kaunitz dissolved the Directory and replaced it with a Council, the *Staatsrat*, an advisory body, with himself as president. The central Habsburg lands were divided into *gubernia*: administrative boards with special responsibility for raising troops, but which later expanded their functions to embrace price-control and the protection of the serfs from their landlords. Beneath the *gubernium* these lands were divided into districts, each run by a district headman (*Kreishauptman*), originally staffed by local landowners, later by professional civil servants. These men began to resemble the Prussian *Steurrat*—they took on more and more functions: police, roads, schools, hospitals, and the like. These officials were answerable to the Diets as well as to the Crown, but over time their responsibilities to the latter prevailed. 'Not without reason', remarks one well-known authority, 'is Maria Theresa regarded as the founder of the unified Austrian state . . .'[42]

For all her piety, the quest for money, not the Enlightenment, drove the empress to encroach on the Church; the more so since it was the wealthiest in Europe. She authorized restrictions on mortmain and control over the monasteries. For similar fiscal reasons she tried to limit the seigneurs' indefinite right to tax their peasants: their boon work (*robot*) was limited to three days a week and they were promised a minimum acreage for their own use. Great Cameralist efforts went into improving agriculture and

---

[42] O. Jaszi, *The Dissolution of the Habsburg Monarchy* (University of Chicago Press, Chicago, 1961), 62.

introducing root crops, promoting horse- and sheep-breeding, and exploiting forests. And Maria Theresa took a real and constructive interest in education: the General Education Regulation of 1774 was a comprehensive scheme for primary and secondary education, including training-colleges for teachers. At the end of Maria Theresa's reign there were in her hereditary lands fifteen training-colleges, eighty-three high-schools, forty-seven girls' schools, and 3,848 elementary schools training over 200,000 children.[43]

Was this 'Enlightenment'? Not at all—it was *raison d'état*. Her censors tabooed Voltaire, Pascal, Montesquieu, even Gibbon, and Goethe's *Werther*. The bishop of Eger burned 4,000 books of his own free will.[44] And for all her genuine intention to promote the welfare of the common people, she had no intention of letting them get above their station. A firm believer in aristocracy, she is reported as having said: 'Those who are born in boots should not desire to wear shoes.' So it is not surprising that the depiction of Maria Theresa as an Enlightenment figure is widely questioned.

But the same cannot be said of her son and (from 1765) her co-regent. If any ruler was besotted by the ideas of the Enlightenment and if any ruler tried to carry them out to the letter, it was Joseph II; all the more so because of his mounting impatience with his co-regent mother over the whole of fifteen years. When he came to rule alone he was in a hurry. He spared almost nothing. He was an out-and-out absolutist. He loathed the Estates, enforced barbaric punishments in his army, pursued unification, centralization, the supremacy of the German language, the elimination of feudality, and in addition and in the fullest tradition of the Enlightenment, state independence from the Church, freedom of expression, and religious toleration. Joseph did not abolish serfdom as such but he limited the extent of the *robot* and, for the rest, gave serfs unlimited freedom to migrate, marry, go to school, and enter any trade without permission of their landlords. He tried to introduce the Physiocratic land tax, which would be paid (albeit in unequal proportions) by all subjects including the aristocracy, but this met with so much opposition that it was never carried out. In the field of administration he further intensified the centralization commenced by his mother. He tried to reduce the power of the Estates, introduced German throughout his dominions as the official state language, and in Hungary— the hotbed of discontent—undermined the provincial 'congregations', which were the strongholds of the local nobility, by establishing ten artificial local-government units each headed by a state official in charge

[43] E. N. Williams, *The Ancien Régime in Europe* (Penguin, Harmondsworth, 1970), 447.
[44] Jaszi, *Dissolution*, 64.

of all local appointments. The centralization extended to the laws also. He abolished the seigneurial courts in Hungary. Elsewhere, though retaining them for civil suits, he made them subject to appeal to his own higher courts. He introduced a Penal Code in 1787 and a Code of Criminal Procedure in 1788 which, *inter alia*, provided equality before the law, extended opportunities for appeal to higher courts, and restricted the application of the death penalty. Most of his Civil Code was published posthumously in 1790, and was not completed till 1811. After that, though, it enjoyed the same durability as the Prussian *Landrecht*—it lasted till 1918.

At Joseph's hands the Church suffered as much as it had been pampered by his mother. He regarded it as a mere part of state administration. He extended religious liberty to the Protestants and the Orthodox and even to the Jews. (On the other hand, he persecuted deists.) He ordained that the Crown's assent was needed before a papal Bull could be made public, and did away with some 700 monasteries and nunneries and put the rest under state control. Marriage was made a civil contract. The schools were secularized. Censorship, though not abolished, was relaxed.

It all ended in tears. Everything went wrong. For one thing, traditional economic relationships were frequently upset. For instance, when a monastery was suppressed all those who had worked for or supplied it became unemployed. Elsewhere there was revulsion against Joseph's interference with Catholic rituals. Joseph was a Jansenist, or at least something very near it: that is, his viewpoint was that of Muratori's famous work on Christian Devotion. His austere near-Jansenism repelled the common people, enamoured of the colourful processions and rites of the popular Church. The Hungarian nobility in particular were enraged by the inroads into their seigneurial privileges, and above all, by the proposed land tax. As a consequence, in 1789 Joseph was forced to convene the Diet and cancel all his administrative reforms. This did not help in Belgium, however, where all classes united for different reasons, some in opposing the suppression of the monasteries, some the constraints on the Estates and, among the common folk, the Jansenist interferences with their traditional modes of worship. All came together: first in a set of sporadic revolts, then armed confrontation with Austrian troops, and finally the latters' defeat at the hands of the rebels. And at the same time as this revolt erupted Joseph II, who had spent so much effort on building up his army, suffered defeat at the hands of the Turks. Joseph 'would not be told'. His brother, the wise Leopold of Tuscany, observed of him: 'He tolerates no contradiction and is imbued with arbitrary, brutal principles and the most severe, brutal and violent despotism. He despises everything which is not his own idea.'[45]

This remark reveals the fatal flaw of absolutism. As Napoleon said, 'nothing goes by itself'. This driving and improving absolutism was like that of the oriental monarchies in its dependence on the energy of the monarch, the blanketing influence of bureaucracy, the intrigues at the Court, the inability to be everywhere at once. By its apogee, absolutism revealed its limitations.

5. THE LIMITS OF EUROPEAN ABSOLUTISM

5.1. *The Repetitiveness of the Palace-Polity Pattern*

In previous chapters we have described a succession of Asian absolutisms: the 'Palace polities'. In this chapter we have described European absolutism at its apogee. But this differed from the Asian absolutisms in two main ways: the law-bound nature of the European ones and the tenacious survival and even revival of the so-called 'constituted bodies' or *corps intermédiaires*, which resisted (if only passively) encroachment by the monarch. For the rest, the limits and limitations on European absolutism are as in Asia. To work properly they required dedicated and intelligent rulers, preferably enjoying long reigns. Failing that, they required monarchs who were at least 'good pickers' of subaltern ministers. Where these conditions were absent the regime degenerated into the routine administration of a soulless and rigid bureaucracy, or fell prey to court intrigues with weak policies frequently reversed, or, finally, allowed for the revival of moribund 'constituted bodies' whose resistance weakened the monarchy still further.

5.2. *Personal Rule: 'Nothing Goes by Itself'*

In earlier chapters we have seen how eastern potentates like Shih Huang-ti, Mansur, Suleiman II, or Akbar the Great filled their waking hours with the affairs of state and how, as a result, the regimes prospered; and likewise how they fell into a decline the moment the throne descended from these hardworking individuals to incompetent or effete successors. And we have met similar characters in Europe: Philip II of Spain, the Emperor Charles V, Louis XIV, Frederick the Great. These men ran the state as a personal concern, a one-man business. We have already dwelt on the outlook and methods of Louis XIV. The attitude of some of the 'enlightened' monarchs

[45] Quoted, T. C. W. Blanning, *Joseph II and Enlightened Despotism: Readings* (Longman, London, 1970), 43.

of the later eighteenth century can be gleaned from such of their comments as the following.

Here is Louis XIV giving advice to his protégé, Philip V of Spain: 'Never allow yourself to be ruled; be the master; have no favourites or prime minister; listen to and consult your Council but do you decide yourself.'[46] Here again is the oft-quoted comment of Frederick II:

A well conducted government must have a system as coherent as a system of philosophy, so that finance, police, and the army are coordinated to the same end, namely the consolidation of the state and the increase of its power. Such a system can only emanate from a single brain, that of the sovereign. Idleness, pleasure-seeking and imbecility are the causes which keep princes from the noble task of securing the happiness of the people. The sovereign is the first servant of the state.[47]

And finally, this poignant cry from an emperor at the end of his tether, Joseph II amidst the ruin of his handiwork: 'I do what I can and no one can reproach me with neglecting anything; but no one aids me either in management or in details . . .'[48]

Frederick William I and Frederick II, Maria Theresa, Joseph II, and Leopold of Austria, and Catherine the Great of Russia all tirelessly ran the state in their own person. There were also those monarchs who, though too lazy to do this, picked excellent ministers to do it for them: one thinks of Joseph of Portugal who picked Pombal, and Charles III who picked such men as Tanucci (when he was king of Naples) and Aranda, Campomanes, and Floridablanca (when he was king of Spain). But even dedication, whether of ministers or their masters, was of little avail if the reign was cut short. Louis XIV was able to transform the situation in France because his active reign lasted for more than half-a-century. Frederick II ruled from 1740 to 1786, Maria Theresa from 1740 to 1780. Compare this with the short reign of the unhappy Gustavus III of Sweden, murdered in mid-career.

It was when a great monarch like Frederick II was succeeded by incompetent and unworthy ones, or when a court intrigue cut short the career of an able and energetic minister, that the limitations of the Palace polity became as apparent as it had always been in the East. In some cases, where court intrigues had cancelled one another and left no prestigious individual in charge, the outcome was likely to be the unimproving, routine-ridden rule of an anonymous bureaucracy. This outcome was of course the most likely where a well-organized bureaucracy was already in place, as it was in

---

[46] Louis XIV, Instructions to Philip V of Spain, quoted in Barnes and Feldman, *Rationalism and Revolution*, 29. [47] Quoted in Andrews, *Eighteenth-Century Europe*, 119.
[48] Quoted in Gershoy, *From Despotism to Revolution*, 116.

classical China, for instance, or in the Ottoman Empire. We have seen how Chinese emperors carried on a subterranean conflict with the Mandarinate, using the eunuch establishment as an alternative staff for carrying out their personal policy, and how weak emperors succumbed to one or the other or, even, to both together.

In the present context Prussia provides the parallel. It will be remembered that Frederick the Great despised his ministers, never met them, but simply corresponded with them and gave them their instructions. It was through his office *Kabinett* that he exercised his completely personal rule.[49] His successors also worked through it, but they were unworthy men. Frederick William II (1786–97) is rightly described by Stein as ruling 'under the influence of a favourite, of his courtiers, male and female. They came between the throne and its regular advisers.'[50] Among other things (including two morganatic marriages) he was, we are told, 'a gaping spiritualist and surrounded himself with the superstitious and particularly with those who were superstitious and vicious at the same time'.[51] Frederick William III (1797–1840) was, by contrast, 'at the same time the most respectable and the most ordinary man that has ever reigned over Prussia'.[52] Between the regular ministers with their staff of civil servants and this personal Cabinet of capricious monarchs there was a running war, and this was brought into the open when the Prussian state all but collapsed after its disastrous defeat by Napoleon at Jena and Auerstadt in 1806. Stein's consequent memorandum on Cabinet rule and the need to eliminate it so that government should rest in the hands of the monarch and the regular bureaucracy is uncompromising, savage, and total. The insolence of these Cabinet members, he wrote, 'hurts the self-respect of the higher officials; one grows ashamed of a post of which one has only the shadow, since the power itself has become the spoil of a subordinate influence . . .'[53] (Oh, shades of the Chinese experiences!)

So was initiated the 'Reform period' of Stein and Hardenburg: short-lived (1806–12), but momentous in replacing personal rule by that of the ministerial bureaucracy, 'the more impersonal system of bureaucratic absolutism, culminating in enlightened ministerial despotism tempered by the will of the privileged classes'.[54] It was described in a private letter from a Prussian statesman, Otto Camphausen, in 1843 in these words:

---

[49] A good description of this office and the way it worked is to be found in Hubatsch, *Frederick the Great*, 220–5.   [50] Seeley, *Life and Times of Stein*, i. 268.
[51] Ibid. 191.   [52] Ibid. 195.
[53] Ibid. 269. The memorandum, which is published in full, occupies pp. 267–73.
[54] H. Rosenberg, *Bureaucracy, Aristocracy and Autocracy: The Prussian Experience, 1600–1815* (Harvard UP, Cambridge, Mass., 1958), 208.

A system of rulership by career bureaucrats peculiar to the Prussian state, in which the king appears to be the top functionary who invariably selects his aides from the intellectual élite of the nation, recognized as such by means of truly or allegedly rigorous examinations. He allows them great independence, acknowledges thereby their co-rulership and, consequently, sanctions a sort of aristocracy of experts who purport to be the true representatives of the general interest.[55]

When he was not governed by his ministerial bureaucracy, a weak or lazy monarch was likely to be governed by a court favourite. These might well be serious statesmen like Pombal in Portugal, Tanucci in Naples, Aranda, Campomanes, and Floridablanca in Spain, even the unfortunate and short-lived Struensee in Denmark. But their careers could be cut short— as in the case of Pombal and Struensee—by the death of their protector and/or the intervention of the queen mother. At worst, however, these court favourites could be pernicious, foolish, or corrupt—or all of these together—as, for instance, at the court of Frederick William II mentioned above. In these circumstances policy became capricious and inconsistent: the intrigues at court resembled those in the palaces of China, Byzantium, and the Caliphate, and need no further recital here. But one has only to look at the vertiginous succession of ministers in France under Louis XV and Louis XVI, who came to office only to reverse the policy of their predecessors, to understand how and why the monarchs who fell below the intelligence and unremitting dedication of their forebear Louis XIV brought the state to confusion and—in this French case—ultimately to revolution.

The weakening of the monarch's personal power opened up yet a third alternative: the reappearance of obstacles which the strength of, say, a Louis XIV had brushed aside; witness the revival under Louis XV and XVI of three of these antagonists: the *parlements*, the local Estates, and finally, the aristocracy.

So much for the similarities between the Palace polities of the East and those of Europe; but as we have said, the differences between them are, first (a feature already commented in previous chapters), the law-bound nature of the European absolute monarch. This was a characteristic of the European monarchies of the Middle Ages, and that tradition was carried forward under the new monarchies of the Renaissance. But the Enlightenment carried the notion much further by its belief in uniformities in Nature, the logicality of Reason, and correspondingly, the need to rationalize, systematize, and codify the laws under which subjects were to live. Hence the great codes in Prussia and Austria and the sketch of such a code in Russia, which we have already noticed. These codes carry law-boundedness

---

[55] Quoted in Rosenburg, *Bureaucracy, Aristocracy and Autocracy*, 208.

to new lengths. They make explicit the legal, almost contractual nature of the relationship between the government and the subject by demonstrating what protection the latter can expect from the laws: authoritarian to the utmost degree, making no concessions to 'democracy' whatsoever, these Palace regimes nevertheless mark the beginnings of the *Rechtstaat*.

The second difference is the great strength of the 'constituted bodies' in Europe as compared with those in Asia. There the aristocracies were service aristocracies, made or broken by the whim of the ruler; the towns the seat of royal garrisons; the guilds, which were numerous enough, were so many corporations working under government control; and a Christian-type, organized, structured Church was unknown. In Europe, by contrast, the Middle Ages still continued to weigh heavily on the eighteenth century, one reason—perhaps the pre-eminent one—why the French Revolutionaries wanted to erase all traces of this 'Gothick' age and rear a new society on new, rational principles such as would run even to replacing the seven-day week by *decadi*, the ancient names of the months by ones based on their climatic characteristics, the ancient weights and measures by metric ones based (inaccurately, as it turned out) on the measured circumference of the earth . . . and so one could go on. Here in Europe a Louis XIV could dominate such medieval constituted bodies, a Frederick the Great could reach an accommodation with his Junkers; but contrast the different experiences of Maria Theresa, who courted her aristocrats—particularly the Hungarians—and Joseph II, who flouted them only to be faced by open revolt.

Three kinds of obstacles confronted these European monarchies' efforts to make their absolutism effective on the ground. The first was the Roman Catholic Church. It was going through a bad patch in this century. Jansenism had captivated many Catholic monarchs, such as Joseph II or Charles III of Spain; the Jesuit Order had offended them by its Ultramontanism; and the upper ranks of its own hierarchy, like many of the regular Orders, were slack if not corrupt. But for all that, this Church was an organized structure with its own means of mobilizing the people and communicating with them through the pulpit; a faculty that was precious in an age before national newspapers, let alone broadcasting. Furthermore, the Church was a great property-owner, on whose estates and establishments vast numbers of common people's livelihoods depended. So the Church could powerfully affect outcomes. It could do so by actually supporting even an 'enlightened' monarch, provided he was a pious Catholic. In this way and for this reason the Church wholeheartedly supported the devout, indeed bigoted, Maria Theresa. But by the same token it could stir its congregations to revolt, as it did when the monarch was a Jansenist like Joseph II or Charles III.

The second great obstacle was the aristocracy. We have already seen that monarchy and aristocracy were part and parcel of European state-building from the very beginnings of the reconstruction of European governments after the collapse of Rome. They could not be dissociated but the question could never quite be settled as to who was to predominate. 'When two ride a horse, one must ride in front.' The eighteenth-century aristocracy had long ceased to assault the Crown with force of arms. But though they had laid down their weapons, they were not going to surrender their privileges. These included their fiscal exemptions, their seigneurial courts, the owner-ship and government of their serfs, and their right, embodied in their Estates or 'congregations', to police their districts. They were deeply offended by the enlightened monarchs' efforts to curtail or abolish all of these.

The third was the 'composite' nature of many states. All these states had been built up by aggregating smaller political units. Thus, Austria consisted of a score of such units, and the function of the monarchy and its exiguous bureaucracy was, initially, only architectonic. Even France, it might be argued, belonged to this 'composite' category in so far as its provinces, particularly in the *pays d'état*, were still vigorous. Absolutism involved form-ing these disparate units and bodies into 'a more perfect union'. In France this was accomplished, but only by a stupendously convulsive popular revolution, followed by some fifteen years of military dictatorship. The nineteenth-century unification of Germany and of Italy—and the failure of Austria to follow suit—demonstrates how very difficult this was to achieve.

And finally there were the common folk themselves. What the enlight-ened monarchs did, they did for them, but this was not always welcome. The alterations in the liturgy were detested. The unemployment that resulted from suppression of the monasteries caused hardship. Free trade in foodstuffs could mean feast or famine—they preferred the customary state-fixing of prices. The abolition of the guilds was unwelcome for much the same reasons. The Enlightenment was *not* a popular movement any more than it was democratic. Reactionary mobs roamed the streets of Naples and the fields of Spain to attack it.

None of these obstructive institutions existed—or at least none existed with anything like their deep roots, their tenacity, their self-confidence—in the Asian empires. These were Montesquieu's *corps intermédiaires* and they reduced, qualified, even in some cases annulled the practical operation of legal absolutism.

Bibliography

ALDERSON, D., *The Structure of the Ottoman Dynasty* (Clarendon Press, Oxford, 1956).

ALI, A., *The Mughal Nobility under Aurungzeb* (Asia Publishing House, London, 1966).

ANDERSON, M. S., *Peter the Great* (Thames & Hudson, London, 1978).

ANDERSON, P., *Lineages of the Absolutist State* (NLB, London, 1974; repr. Verso, 1979).

ANDREWS, S., *Eighteenth-Century Europe: The 1680s to 1815* (Longman, London, 1965).

—— (ed.), *Enlightened Despotism: Readings* (Longman, London, 1967).

ATKINSON, W. H., *A History of Spain and Portugal* (Penguin, Harmondsworth, 1960).

BAIN, R. N., *Gustavus III and his Contemporaries*, 2 vols. (Kegan Paul, London; Trench, Trübner and Co., 1894).

BARBER, N., *Lords of the Golden Horn: From Suleiman the Magnificent to Kamul Ataturk* (Macmillan, London, 1973).

BARNES, T. G., and FELDMAN, G. D. (eds.), *Rationalism and Revolution, 1660–1815: Readings. A Documentary History of Modern Europe* (Little, Brown, and Co., 1972).

BARNETT, C., *Britain and her Army 1509–1970* (Penguin, Harmondsworth, 1974).

BASHAM, A. L., *The Wonder that was India*, 3rd edn. (Sidgwick & Jackson, London, 1985).

BEARD, C. A. and M. R., *The Rise of American Civilization* (1-volume edn., Cape, London, 1930).

BEFU, H., 'Village Autonomy and Articulation with the State', in Hall and Jansen (eds.), *Studies in the Institutional History*, 301–14.

BERMAN, H. J., *Justice in Russia* (Harvard Russian Research Centre Studies, Harvard UP, Cambridge, Mass., 1950).

BERNIER, F., *Travels in the Moghul Empire*, ed. A. Constable (A. Constable & Co., London, 1891).

BITTON, D., *The French Nobility in Crisis* (Stanford UP, Stanford, 1969).

Bhagavad-gita (The Lord's Song); translated and interpreted by Franklin Edgerton, (Harvard UP, Cambridge, Mass., 1972).

BLACK, C. E., *Comparative Modernization: A Reader* (Macmillan, London, 1976).

BLANNING, T. C. W., *Joseph II and Enlightened Despotism: Readings* (Longman, London, 1970).

BLOCH, M., *Feudal Society*, trans. L. Manyon, 2 vols. (Routledge & Kegan Paul, London, 1962; paperback edn. 1965).

BODDE, D., and MORRIS, C. (eds.), *Law in Imperial China: Exemplified by 190 Ch'ing Dynasty Cases* (trans. from the 'Hsing-an hui-lan'), with historical, social, and juridical commentaries by D. Bodde and C. Morris (Harvard UP, Cambridge, Mass., 1967).

BODIN, J. H., *Les Six Livres de la Republique de Jean Bodin Angevin* (Etienne Gamonet, Geneva, 1629).

—— and LOYSEAU, C. (eds.), *Traité des Seigneuries*, in *Les Oeuvres de M Charles Loyseau* (Paris, 1701).

BONNEY, R. J., *Political Change in France under Richelieu and Mazarin, 1624–1661* (OUP, Oxford, 1978).

—— *The King's Debts: Finance and Politics in France, 1589–1661* (Oxford, 1981).

BRAUDEL, F., *The Mediterranean and the Mediterranean World in the Age of Philip II*, trans. S. Reynolds, 2 vols. (2nd edn., Collins, London, 1973).

—— *Civilisation and Capitalism: Fifteenth–Eighteenth Centuries*, 3 vols. (Collins, London, 1981–4).

BRIGGS, R., *Early Modern France, 1560–1715* (OUP, Oxford, 1977).

BROWNING, R., *Poetical Works 1832–1864*, ed. I. Jack (OUP, London, 1970).

BULL, H., and WATSON, A. (eds.), *The Expansion of International Society* (Clarendon Press, Oxford, 1984).

Cambridge Economic History of India, vol. I, ed. T. Raychaudry, I. Habib, D. Kumar, and M. Desai (CUP, Cambridge, 1982).

Cambridge Modern History, The New, 14 vols. (CUP, Cambridge, 1957–9).

CAMERON, E., *The European Reformation* (OUP, Oxford, 1991).

CANNON, J., *Parliamentary Reform* (CUP, Cambridge, 1982).

CARROLL, L., *Alice in Wonderland*, in *The Complete Illustrated Works of Lewis Carroll* (Chancellor Press, London, 1982).

CARSTEN, F. L., *Princes and Parliaments in Germany from the Fifteenth to the Eighteenth Centuries* (Clarendon Press, Oxford, 1959).

CHABOD, F., 'Was there a Renaissance State?', in H. Lubasz (ed.), *The Development of the Modern State*, 26–42.

CHAMPION, E., *La France d'après les cahiers de 1789*, 5th edn. (A. Colin, Paris, 1921; English trans. 1929).

CHESNEAUX, J. (ed.), *Popular Movements and Secret Societies in China, 1840–1950* (Stanford UP, Stanford, 1972).

CHÜ, T.-T., *Local Government in China under the Ch'ing* (Harvard UP, Cambridge, Mass., 1962).

CIPOLLA, C., *Literacy and Development in the West* (Penguin, Harmondsworth, 1969).

—— *European Culture and Overseas Expansion* (Penguin, Harmondsworth, 1970).

CLARK, G. N., *The Later Stuarts*, ed. C. H. Stuart, 'The Oxford History of England' (Clarendon Press, Oxford, 1934).

CLARK, J. C. D., *Revolution and Rebellion: State and Society in England in the Seventeenth and Eighteenth Centuries* (CUP, Cambridge, 1986).

CLAVELL, J., *Shogun: A Novel of Japan* (Atheneum, New York, 1975).

COBBAN, A., *Aspects of the French Revolution* (Paladin, London, 1971).

COLES, P., *The Ottoman Impact in Europe* (Thames and Hudson, London, 1968).

COMMAGER, H. S., *The Empire of Reason: How Europe Imagined and America Realized the Enlightenment* (Weidenfeld & Nicolson, London, 1978).

COOPER, J. P., 'Differences betweeen English and Continental Governments in the Early Seventeenth Century', in J. S. Bromley and E. H. Kossman (eds.), *Britain and the Netherlands*, Proceedings of the 1959 Oxford–Netherlands Historical Conference, 1959 (Chatto & Windus, London, 1960), 62–90.

CRUMMEY, R. O., *The Formation of Muscovy, 1304–1613* (Longman, London, 1987).

DAVID, R., and BRIERLEY, J. E., *Major Legal Systems in the World Today: An Introduction to the Comparative Study of Law* (Stevens & Sons, London, 1985).

DAVIS, F. L., *Primitive Revolutionaries of China* (Heinemann, London, 1977).

DAY, U. N., *The Government of the Sultanate* (Kumar Publishers, New Delhi, 1972).

DE COMMYNES, P., *Memoirs: The Reign of Louis XI, 1416–1483*, trans., M. Jones (Penguin, Harmondsworth, 1972).

DE JOUVENAL, B., *Sovereignty: An Inquiry into the Political Good*, trans. J. F. Huntington (CUP, Cambridge, 1957).

DE LONGRAIS, F. J., *L'Est et l'ouest* (Institut de Recherches d'Histoire Française, Paris, 1958).

DE MADARIAGA, I., *Russia in the Age of Catherine the Great* (Weidenfield & Nicolson, London, 1981).

DE TOCQUEVILLE, A., *L'Ancien régime* (OUP, Oxford, 1957).

DORE, R., *Education in Tokugawa Japan* (Routledge & Kegan Paul, London, 1965).

DOUCET, R., *Les Institutions de la France au XVI*ᵉ *siècle*, 2 vols. (A. et J. Picard, Paris, 1948).

DUCHESNE, L., s.v. 'Papacy' (to 1087), *Encyclopaedia Britannica*, 11th edn. (1911), xx. 687–91.

DUKES, P., *The Making of Russian Absolutism, 1613–1801* (Longman, London, 1982).

DUNN, C. J., *Everyday Life in Traditional Japan* (Batsford, London, 1969).

DU PLESSIS, A. J. (Cardinal Duc de Richelieu), *Testament politique* (Éditions André, Paris, 1947).

DURAND, Y., *Les Républiques au temps des monarchies* (Collection SUP; Presses Universitaires de France, 1973).

ELIAS, N., *State Formation and Civilisation* (Blackwell, Oxford, 1982).

—— *The Court Society*, trans. E. Jephcott (Blackwell, Oxford, 1983).

ELLIOTT, J. H., *Imperial Spain, 1469–1716* (Penguin, Harmondsworth, 1970).

—— *Spain and its World: Essays* (Yale UP, London and New Haven, 1989).

ELTON, G. R., *England under the Tudors*, 2nd edn. (Methuen, London, 1974).

—— Presidential Address: 'Tudor Government: The Points of Contact: II. The Council', *Transactions of the Royal Historical Society* (1975), 195–211.

FAIRBANK, J. K., *Chinese Thought and Institutions* (University of Chicago Press, 1987).

—— and TÊNG, S.-Y., *Ch'ing Administration, Three studies*, Harvard Yenching Institute Studies, 19 (Cambridge, Mass., 1960)

FARUKI, Z., *Aurungzeb and His Times* (D. B. Taraporevala & Sons, Delhi, 1972).

FEUERWERKER, A., *State and Society in Eighteenth-Century China: The Ch'ing Empire in its Glory*, Michigan Papers in Chinese Studies, 29 (Ann Arbor, 1976).

FEUERWERKER, A., *The Foreign Establishment in China in the Early Twentieth Century* (Centre for Chinese Studies, Univ. of Michigan, Ann Arbor, 1976).

FIELDHOUSE, D. K., *The Colonial Empires: A Comparative Survey from the Eighteenth Century*, 2nd edn. (Macmillan, Hong Kong, 1982).

FIGGIS, J. N., *Churches in the Modern State* (Longman, London, 1931).

FINER, H., *The Theory and Practice of Modern Government*, 2 vols. (Methuen, London, 1932).

FINER, S. E., 'State and Nation Building in Europe: The Role of the Military', in Tilly (ed.), *The Formation of National States in Western Europe*, 84–163.

FISCHER, W., and LUNDGREN, P., 'The Recruitment and Training of Administrative and Technical Personnel', in Tilly (ed.), *Formation of National States in Western Europe*, 456–561.

FLETCHER, G., *Of the Russe Commonwealth (1591)*, ed. E. A. Bond (Hakluyt Society, London, 1846).

FORD, F. L., *Robe and Sword: The Regrouping of the French Aristocracy after Louis XIV* (Harper & Row, New York, 1965).

FOY, W. (ed.), *Man's Religious Quest: A Reader* (Croom Helm/Open University, London, 1978).

GAIL, M., *The Three Popes: An Account of the Schism—When Rival Popes in Rome, Avignon and Pisa Vied for the Rule of Christendom* (Hale, London, 1972).

GASCOIGNE, B., *The Great Moghuls* (Cape, London, 1987).

GAY, P., *The Enlightenment: An Interpretation*, Vol. 2, *The Science of Freedom* (Weidenfeld and Nicolson, London, 1970).

GERNET, J., *History of Chinese Civilization*, trans. R. J. Foster (CUP, Cambridge, 1982).

GERSHOY, L., *From Despotism to Revolution, 1763–1789: The Rise of Modern Europe* (Harper & Row, New York, 1944).

GIBB, H., and BOWEN, H., *Islamic Society and the West*, vol. 1, pts. 1 and 2 (Royal Institute of International Affairs, London, 1950 and 1957).

GREEN, V. H. H., *The Later Plantagenets: A Survey of English History between 1307 and 1485* (Edward Arnold, London, 1955).

GROUSSET, R., *L'Asie orientale des origines au XVe siècle* (Presses Universitaires, Paris, 1941).

HABIB, I., *The Agrarian System of the Mughal Empire, 1605–1707* (Asia Publishers, London, 1972).

HALE, J. R., *Renaissance Europe, 1480–1520* (Fontana, London, 1971).

—— *War and Society in Renaissance Europe, 1450–1620* (Fontana, London, 1985).

HALL, J. A., *Powers and Liberties* (Blackwell, Oxford, 1985).

HALL, J. W., *Government and Local Power in Japan, 500–1700: A Study Based on Bizen Province* (Princeton UP, Princeton, 1966).

—— 'Feudalism in Japan: A Reassessment', in Hall and Jansen (eds.), *Studies in the Institutional History*, 15–55.

—— and JANSEN, M. B., *Studies in the Institutional History of Early Modern Japan* (Princeton UP, Princeton, 1968).

HARDING, R. R., *Anatomy of a Power Elite: The Provincial Governors of Early Modern France* (Yale UP, New Haven, Conn., 1978).

HASAN, I., *The Central Structure of the Mughal Empire and its Practical Working up to 1657* (OUP, Oxford, 1936; repr. Lahore, 1967).

HENDERSON, D. F., 'The Evolution of Tokugawa Law', in Hall and Jansen (eds.), *Studies in the Institutional History of Early Modern Japan*, 203–29.

HENDERSON, I., *Conciliation and Japanese Law* (Association for Asian Studies, University of Washington Press, Seattle, 1965).

HERR, R., 'Regalism and Jansenism in Spain', in S. Andrews, *Enlightened Despotism*, 42–9.

HERRING, A., *A History of Latin America* (Knopf, New York, 1965).

HEYD, U., *Studies in Old Ottoman Criminal Law* (Clarendon Press, Oxford, 1973).

HINTZE, O., *The Historical Essays of Otto Hintze* (OUP, Oxford, 1975).

HODGES, R., *Dark Age Economics* (Duckworth, London, 1982).

HOLDSWORTH, Sir W., *A History of English Law* (Methuen, London, 1923).

HOOK, B., (ed.) *The Cambridge Encyclopaedia of China* (CUP, Cambridge, 1982).

HOWARD, M., 'The Military Factor in European Expansion', in Bull and Watson (eds.), *The Expansion of International Society*, 33–42.

HSIEH, P. C., *The Government of China, 1644–1911* (Johns Hopkins Press, Baltimore, 1925; repr. Frank Cass & Co., 1966).

HSU, I. C. Y., *The Rise of Modern China*, 3rd edn. (OUP, London, 1983).

HUBATSCH, W., *Frederick the Great: Absolutism and Administration*, trans. P. Doran (Thames and Hudson, London, 1973).

HUFTON, O., *Europe: Privilege and Protest, 1730–1789* (Fontana History of Europe, London, 1980).

HULSEWÉ, A. F. P., *Remnants of Han Law*, vol. I (Brill, Leiden, 1955).

INALCIK, H., *The Ottoman Empire: The Classical Age, 1300–1600* (Weidenfeld & Nicolson, London, 1973).

JANSEN, M. B., and STONE, L., 'Education and Modernization in Japan and England', in Black, *Comparative Modernization*, 214–37.

JASZI, O., *The Dissolution of the Hapsburg Monarchy* (University of Chicago Press, Chicago, 1961).

JOHNSON, H. C., *Frederick the Great and His Officials* (Yale UP, London and New Haven, 1975).

JOHNSON, W., *The T'ang Code*, vol. I, *General Principles* (Princeton UP, Princeton, 1979).

JOLLIFFE, J. E. A., *The Constitutional History of Medieval England* (A. & C. Black, London, 1937).

JONES, E. L., *The European Miracle* (CUP, Cambridge, 1981).

JORDAN, W. K., *Edward VI, The Young King: The Protectorship of the Duke of Somerset* (Allen & Unwin, London, 1968).

JOUANNA, A., *Le Devoir de révolte* (Fayard, Paris, 1989).

KAEMPFER, E., *The History of Japan* (J. Maclehose & Sons, Glasgow, 1906).

KEDOURIE, E., 'Crisis and Revolution in Modern Islam', *Times Literary Supplement* (19–25 May 1989).

KEENAN, E. L., 'Union of Soviet Socialist Republics; History of Russia and the Soviet Union; From the Beginning to *c.*1700', *Encyclopaedia Britannica*, 15th edn. (1989), xxviii. 968–78.

KEITH, A. B., *Speeches and Documents on Indian Policy 1750–1921* (OUP, Oxford, 1922).

LANGFORD, P., *A Polite and Commercial People: England, 1727–1783*, 'The New Oxford History of England' (Clarendon Press, Oxford, 1989).

LAVISSE, E., *Louis XIV: histoire d'un grand règne, 1643–1715* (R. Laffont, Paris, 1989).

LEHMANN, J.-P., *The Roots of Modern Japan* (Macmillan, London, 1982).

LEVY, R., *The Social Structure of Islam* (CUP, Cambridge, 1957).

LEWIS, P. S., *The Recovery of France in the Fifteenth Century* (Macmillan, London, 1971).

LINDSAY, J. O. (ed.), 'The Western Mediterranean and Italy', in *CMH*, vol. 7, *The Old Regime, 1713–1763* (CUP, Cambridge, 1957).

LIU HSIANG (attributed to), *Chan-kuo-tse or The Ways of the Warring States*; trans. J. I. Crump, 2nd. edn. revised (Chinese Materials Centre, San Francisco, 1979).

LOT, F., and FAWTIER, R., *Histoire des institutions françaises au moyen-âge*, 2 vols. (Paris, 1957).

LOUIS XIV, King of France, *Mémoires de Louis XIV écrit par lui-meme*, 2 vols. (J. L. M. de Gain-Montagnac, Paris, 1806).

LUARD, E., *War in International Society* (Tauris, London, 1986).

LUBASZ, H. (ed.), *The Development of the Modern State: Readings* (Collier-Macmillan, London, 1964).

McEVEDY, C., and JONES, R., *Atlas of World Population History* (Allen Lane, London, 1978).

McKENDRICK, M., *A Concise History of Spain* (Cassell, London, 1972).

McNEILL, W. H., *The Rise of the West* (University of Chicago Press, Chicago, 1963).

—— *Plagues and Peoples* (Penguin, Harmondsworth, 1979).

—— *The Pursuit of Power: Technology, Armed Force, and Society since A.D. 1000* (Blackwell, Oxford, 1982).

MAJUMDAR, R. C., *Medieval India* (Tauris, London, 1951).

MANN, M., *The Sources of Social Power* (CUP, Cambridge, 1986).

MASSIE, R. K., *Peter the Great: His Life and World* (Cardinal, London, 1989).

METTAM, R., *Power and Faction in Louis XIV's France* (Blackwell, Oxford, 1988).

MILLER, J., *Origins of the American Revolution* (Faber, London, 1945).

MISHRA, B. B., *The Administrative History of India, 1834–1947* (OUP, Oxford, 1970).

MONTGOMERY, B. L., *A History of Warfare* (Collins, London, 1968).

MOON, P., *The British Conquest and Dominion of India* (Duckworth, London, 1989).

MORELAND, W. H., *The Agrarian System of Muslim India* (Cambridge, 1929).

MORISON, S. E., COMMAGER, H. S., and LEUCHTENBERG, W. E., *The Growth of the American Republic* (OUP, Oxford, 1969).

MORRILL, J. S., *The Revolt of the Provinces* (London, 1976).

MOUSNIER, R. C., *The Institutions of France under the Absolute Monarchy, 1598–1789:*

Society and the State, trans. B. Pearce (University of Chicago Press, London, 1979).

NAQUIN, S., and RAWSKI, E., *Chinese Society in the Eighteenth Century* (Yale UP, New Haven, 1987).

NEALE, J. E., *The Age of Catherine de Medici and Essays in Elizabethan History* (Cape, London, 1943; paperback edn., 1963).

The New Cambridge Modern History, 14 vols. (CUP, Cambridge, 1957–59), vol. 2 (1958).

OBOLENSKY, D., *The Byzantine Commonwealth* (Weidenfeld & Nicolson, London, 1971; Cardinal edn., 1974).

ORTIZ, A. D., 'The Golden Age of Spain, 1516–1659', trans. J. Casey, in J. Parry and H. Thomas (eds.), *The History of Spain* (Weidenfeld & Nicolson, London, 1971).

PALMER, R. R., *The Age of the Democratic Revolution*, 2 vols. (Princeton UP, Princeton, 1959).

PARES, R., *King George III and the Politicians* (Clarendon Press, Oxford, 1953).

—— *Limited Monarchy in Great Britain in the Eighteenth Century* (Routledge & Kegan Paul, London, 1957).

PARKER, D., *The Making of French Absolutism* (Edward Arnold, London, 1983).

PARRY, J. H., *Europe and a Wider World, 1415–1715* (Hutchinson, London, 1949).

—— *The Spanish Seaborne Empire*, 'The History of Human Society' series (Hutchinson, London, 1966).

—— and THOMAS, H. (eds.), *The History of Spain* (Weidenfeld and Nicolson, London, 1971).

PASCAL, B., *Pensées* (Dent, London, 1932).

PENZER, N. M., *The Harem: An Account of the Institution as it Existed in the Palace of the Turkish Sultan, with a History of the Grand Seraglio from its Foundations to Modern Times* (Spring Books, London, 1965).

PERRIN, N., *Japan's Revolution with the Sword, 1543–1879* (Godine, Boston, 1979).

PERROY, E., *The Hundred Years War* (Capricorn Books, New York, 1965).

PING, C., and BLOODWORTH, D., *The Chinese Machiavelli* (Secker & Warburg, 1976).

PIPES, R., *Russia under the Old Regime* (Weidenfeld & Nicolson, London, 1974).

PLUMB, J. H., *The Growth of Political Stability in England, 1675–1725* (Macmillan London, 1967).

RAWSKI, E. S., 'Literacy', in B. Hook (ed.) *Encyclopaedia of China* (CUP, Cambridge, 1982).

READ, J., *The Catalans* (Faber & Faber, London, 1978).

REISCHAUER, E. O., *The Japanese* (Harvard UP, Cambridge, Mass., 1977).

—— *Ennin's Diary: The Records of a Pilgrimage to China in Search of the Law* (Ronald Press, New York, 1955).

—— and FAIRBANK, J. K., *East Asia, the Great Tradition*, vol. 1 (Modern Asia edn., Houghton Mifflin, Boston, Mass., 1960).

ROMIER, L., 'Les Protestants français à la veille des Guerres civiles', *Revue Historique*, 124 (1917), 254–63.

ROSENBERG, H., *Bureaucracy, Aristocracy and Autocracy: The Prussian Experience, 1600–1815* (Harvard UP, Cambridge, Mass., 1958).

RYCAUT, P., *An English Consul in Turkey: Paul Rycaut at Smyrna, 1667–1678* (Clarendon Press, Oxford, 1972).

SALMON, J. H. M., (ed.) *The French Wars of Religion: How Important Were Religious Factors?* (D. C. Heath and Co., Boston, 1967).

SANSOM, G., *A History of Japan*, vol. 1, *to 1334* (1958), vol. 2, *1334–1615* (1961), vol. 3, *1615–1867* (1963) (Dawson, Folkestone, Kent, 1958, repr. 1978).

—— *Japan: A Short Cultural History* (1st edn., 1931; Century Hutchinson, London, 1987).

SARAN, P., *Resistance of Indian Princes to Turkish Offensive: End of Tenth Century* A.D. (Punjabi University, Patiala, 1967).

—— *The Provincial Government of the Mughals, 1526–1658*, 2nd edn. (Asia Publishing House, London, 1972).

SARKAR, J. N., *The Mughal Polity* (Idarah-i Adabiyat-i-Delli, Delhi, 1984).

SCHACHT, J., *An Introduction to Islamic Law* (OUP, Oxford, 1965).

SCHMOLLER, G., *Das Brandenburgisch-preussiche Innungswesen von 1640–1896: Hauptsachlich die Reform unter Friedrich Wilhelm I* (Berlin, 1898).

SCHURMANN, H. F., and SCHELL, O., *China Readings*, 3 vols. (Penguin, Harmondsworth, 1967–71), vol. 1: *Imperial China* (1967).

SCOTT, H. M., *Enlightened Absolutism* (University of Michigan Press, Ann Arbor, 1990).

SEELEY, J. R., *The Life and Times of Stein, or Germany and Prussia in the Napoleonic Age*, 3 vols. (CUP, Cambridge, 1878).

SEGAL, R., *The Crisis of India* (Penguin, Harmondsworth, 1965).

SEN, K. M., *Hinduism* (Penguin, Harmondsworth, 1961).

SEWARD, D., *The Marks of War: The Military Religious Orders* (Paladin, St Albans, 1974).

SHARMA, R. S., *Indian Feudalism: c.300–1200* (Calcutta, 1965).

SHARMA, SRI RAM, *Government of the Sultanate and Administration* (Bombay, 1951).

SHAW, S. J., *History of the Ottoman Empire and Modern Turkey*, vol. 1 (CUP, Cambridge, 1976).

SHENNAN, J. H., *The Parlement of Paris* (Eyre & Spottiswoode, London, 1968).

SIMMONS, R. C., *American Colonies from Settlement to Independence* (Longman, London, 1976).

SINHA, N. K., *Economic History of Bengal*, vol. 3 (Firma K. L. Mukhopadhyaya, Calcutta, 1962).

SMITH, A., *An Inquiry into the Nature and Causes of the Wealth of Nations* (Encyclopaedia Britannica Inc., Chicago and London 1952).

SMITH, T. C., 'The Land Tax in the Tokugawa Period', in Hall and Jansen, *Studies in the Institutional History*, 283–312.

—— *The Agrarian Origins of Modern Japan* (Harvard UP, Cambridge, Mass., 1959).

SMITH, V. A, *The Oxford History of India*, 4th edn. (Clarendon Press, Oxford, 1981).

SMITH, W. CANTWELL, *The Meaning and End of Religion* (SPCK, London, 1978).

SOREL, A., *Europe and the French Revolution—The Political Traditions of the Old Régime*, ed. A. Cobban and J. W. Hunt, trans. A. Sorel (Fontana Library; Collins and Fontana Press, London, 1969).

SOUTHERN, R. W., *Western Society and the Church in the Middle Ages* (Penguin, Harmondsworth, 1970).

SPENCE, J. D., *Emperor of China: Self-Portrait of K'ang-shi* (Jonathan Cape, London, 1974).

STONE, L., *The Crisis of the Aristocracy 1558–1641* (Clarendon Press, Oxford, 1967).

STRAYER, J. R., 'The Tokogawa Period and Japanese Feudalism', in Hall and Jansen, *Studies in the Institutional History of Early Modern Japan*, 3–14.

SUMNER, W. G., '*Folkways*' (Mentor edn; New York, 1960).

TAMBIAH, S. J., *World Conqueror and World Renouncer: A Study of Buddhism and Polity in Thailand*, Cambridge Studies in Social Anthropology, 15 (CUP, Cambridge, 1976).

THAPAR, R., *A History of India*, vol. 1 (Penguin, Harmondsworth, 1966).

TILLY, C. (ed.), *The Formation of National States in Western Europe* (Princeton UP, Princeton, 1975).

TORBERT, P. M., *The Ch'ing Imperial Household Department: A Study of its Organisation and Principal Functions* (Harvard UP, Cambridge, Mass., 1977).

TOTMAN, C. D., *Politics in the Tokugawa Bakufu: 1600–1843* (Harvard UP, Cambridge, Mass. 1967).

TROYAT, H., *Le Prisonnier no. 1: roman* (Flammarion, Paris, 1978).

TURNBULL, S. R., *The Samurai: A Military History* (Osprey, London, 1977).

—— *Battles of the Samurai* (Arms and Armour, London, 1987).

UDGAONKAR, P. B., *The Political Institutions and Administration of Northern India during Medieval Times* (Varanasi, Delhi, and Patna, 1969).

VAN DER SPRINKEL, S., *Legal Institutions in Manchu China* (1962).

VENTURI, F., *Italy and the Enlightenment: Studies in a Cosmopolitan Century: Selected Essays*, ed. and with an introduction by S. Woolf, trans. S. Corsi (Longman, London, 1972).

VERNADSKY, G., *A Source Book for Russian History from Early Times to 1917*, vol. 2: *From Peter the Great to Nicholas I* (Yale UP, London, 1972).

WALKER, R. L., *The Multi-State System of Ancient China* (Shoe String Press, Hamden, Conn., 1953).

WATT, W. M., *Islamic Political Thought* (Edinburgh UP, Edinburgh, 1968).

WEBER, M., *Economy and Society: An Outline of Interpretive Sociology*, ed. by G. Roth and C. Wittich (University of California Press, Berkeley and London, 1978).

WEDGWOOD, C. V., *The King's Peace, 1637–1641* (Collins, London, 1956).

WESTERN, J. R., *Monarchy and Revolution: The English State in the 1680s* ('Problems of History' Paperbacks, Blandford, London, 1972).

WILLIAMS, B., *The Whig Supremacy, 1714–1760*, 'Oxford History of England' (OUP, Oxford, 2nd. edn., 1962).

WILLIAMS, E. N., *The Ancien Régime in Europe* (Penguin, Harmondsworth, 1970).

WIRIATH, P., 'France; History of' (in part), in *Encyclopaedia Britannica*, 11th edn. (1910), x. 801–73.

WOLF, J. B., *Louis XIV* (Panther edn.; Norton, London, 1970).

WU, CHING-TZU, *The Scholars* (Foreign Languages Press, Beijing, 1973).

ZAGORIN, P., *Rebels and Rulers, 1500–1660*, 2 vols. (CUP, Cambridge, 1982).

Book V

Pathways to the Modern State

I

Overview

*I*n 1776, which is where we start, the great Asian civilizations were vegetating, even decaying. They had reached the condition with which they were quite consciously satisfied and from which they did not wish to move. Indeed, their governments strenuously resisted any influences which they thought might upset their priceless equilibrium. The Chinese still regarded their country as the hub of the world, the 'central kingdom', and rebuffed the efforts of outside powers like Britain to intrude upon them. Tokugawa Japan had sealed itself off from overseas. The Ottoman Empire slumbered, as did, in fact, all the states of Islam. The Mughal Empire was no more and the Indian subcontinent was in turmoil and decay. The only advances, such as they were, lay in military technology—the use of firearms—and even this was borrowed from the West.

It was quite the reverse in Europe. Its striking characteristic, from the fall of the Western Roman Empire, was precisely that it never stopped moving, was always restless, uncomfortable with itself. In this continent the polities went on developing beyond what we described in the last chapter. It was as if the continent were out on a 'quest'—but on an endless road with no particular, or possibly, several alternative terminals. Terminals, or 'goals' (to use the American expression) seem to be a recurrent obsession in nineteenth-century Europe. Writer after writer produced a 'system' which demonstrated the all but imminent arrival of the terminal stage in world history. History was about to end with them. Comteism predicted the ultimate phase of human society, the Positivist Age. Marx saw the last phase in the triumph of the proletariat, after which the dialectic that moved human society would stop. Herbert Spencer demonstrated that all matter—whether organic, inorganic, or social—proceeded from homogenized lumps to highly differentiated heterogeneity, and that this final term in Evolution was at hand. It was not that Europe was questing some Holy Grail. It was that there were several such Grails to quest for. Europe was always travelling but never arrived. Never did it reach a point of rest or equilibrium.

Not only the formats of the state continued to develop, but so did its techniques. With a little poetic licence one might say that 'government began yesterday': that intrusive, inescapable, and unremitting direction and control, which is how we nowadays regard 'government', began about a century ago on the back of the industrial and then the technological revolutions. From the turn of the century date the techniques of penetration, of surveillance, of information, and the development beyond foreseeable bounds of energy resources and, as one of its results, the production of huge social surpluses. Britain's industrial revolution was extremely precocious, and not till *c.*1870 was industrialization the norm in Europe and its lusty infant, the United States. Industrialization is much, much more than an important element in political development. It is, in truth, the very *cusp* of world history. The long millennia of agrarian society which we began with in our survey of ancient Mesopotamia and Egypt was abruptly terminated and an entirely new age, of incalculable possibilities, had opened.

It is by this route that we arrive at the subject of this 'Overview'—the so-called 'modern' state. Following the crumbling of the European empires after 1945, political scientists contemplated well over 100 non-Western succession states with the utmost sympathy and sought most earnestly to understand them and inform them, but, above all, to help them to 'develop' or 'modernize'. Yet despite numerous academic conferences these two terms defied consensus except that, despite differences, the characteristics of 'modernization' turned out to be indistinguishable from those of the western and westernized states to which these political scientists belonged. This was regarded as insultingly patronizing by the school of cultural relativists who proclaimed all forms of society as of equal value.

The western political scientists' view that their own states were 'modern' was not cultural imperialism or condescension, but the *echo* of the non-West's perceptions of what was so distinctive—and also so very enviable— in the western polities. In every age some states are perceived as more 'modern' than others. In just such a way, no doubt, King Alfred regarded Byzantium as distinctly 'modern' compared with his own rag of a kingdom. A number of the new succession-states chose to regard the USSR as more modern even than the western states—as, in fact, the 'most advanced form of society in the world'—and thought that by copying its traits they would rapidly become 'modern states' too.

The syndrome of characteristics which the self-assumedly 'backward' states of nowadays regard as worthy of their emulation in what they deem to be a 'modern' state consists eminently of six characteristics.

First comes the *nationality* principle as the basis for territorial organization, as contrasted with the 'traditional' bases of dynasty, kinship or lineage, or religious community. The second is the principle of *popular sovereignty* as the legitimizing principle of all political authority, as contrasted with the 'traditional' bases in theocracy, divine right, noble birth, or caste. The third is the *secular principle*: the separation of the political processes from religious distinctions, activities, and values. The fourth is *social purposiveness*: 'the state as a work of art', as against the traditonal unreflecting reverence for pre-existing authority whether cultural or religious or political. The fifth is *economic independence*, not in the sense of autarky but as the construction of an independent and nationally sovereign basis for health, wealth, and power, implying extensive industrialization as contrasted with the traditional rural economy. The sixth is a notion of *citizenship* which goes further than the formal guarantees of civil and political rights, and stipulates economic and social rights such as the right to education, to work, and to social-welfare benefits.

All these features of the modern state are, without any exception whatsoever, derived from the West. To be more specific, they spring from three events or trains of events: the American Revolution (1776–87), the French Revolution of 1789, and the industrial /technological revolution.

1. NATIONALITY AND NATIONALISM

Nationalism is the claim that each ethnic (or religious?) group feeling itself to be a nation has the right to independent existence, ruled by its own nationals and its own laws in its own territory. This notion was never propounded in this uncompromising and universalized form till the French Revolution. Since then it has become one of the great revolutionary inspirations of the world, the grave-digger of empires. It stimulated and justified the revolt of Latin America against Spain and Portugal, of the Balkans against the Turk, of Asia and Africa against Britain and France and Belgium and Holland. It was a new political formula which radicalized populations against their colonial rulers. This is why and how, in the nineteenth century, it exploded the empires of Austria and Turkey, each embracing tens or scores of different nationalities. But, by the same token, where people of the same culture and feeling themselves to be a nation were divided into a number of states, it became a great unifying force which created a new and larger nation-state as, for instance, in Germany and Italy.

2. POPULAR SOVEREIGNTY

This goes under a number of different names. The most common, associated with Pufendorf, Rousseau, and the French Revolution, is 'popular sovereignty' or 'sovereignty of the people'. Palmer, in his *Age of the Democratic Revolution*, paraphrases it as the 'People as the constituent power' in order to stress his argument that it was held to lie with the People and not with kings, gods, or any such things, to ordain the rules under which the People should live.[1] Sir Henry Maine chose to call it 'Popular Government'.[2]

The principle affirms that no government is legitimate and hence obedience-worthy unless it can demonstrate to its subjects that its powers have been conferred by them. This dogma, it must be noted, is neutral—it does not predicate any particular form of regime; it will accommodate liberal-democracy, autocracy, oligarchy, even totalitarianism, providing only that the office-bearers are able to convince the public they have received office by popular mandate—whatever this is (and however contrived). Until Napoleon's accession, the crowned heads of continental Europe had claimed to rule by divine right. Once Napoleon acceded this hoary old political formula was on the defensive. It now appeared that any Tom, Dick, or Harry might come forward and seize the state, provided he had taken sufficient pains to make it appear that he had done so as the result of a call from the People.

Thus this doctrine gave rise to not one, but two main forms of polity which, as may be seen at once, are the Forum or Republican versus the Palace/Forum or Palace. The former is the fruit of the English constitution and the subsequent American Revolution. The Revolution's goal was to provide legal guarantees for civil rights, most of which had long been recognized and exercised in Britain, but which were here clarified and expanded in the full tradition of the European Enlightenment; for instance, unqualified freedom of religion and the prohibition of cruel and unusual punishments.

The main lines of the 'Republican' form were these. Government was, so to speak, of the People but not directly by the People. The latter would have been democracy, still a dirty word, and which was understood to mean direct democracy where every citizen was consulted and the government was the simple servant of their resultant will. In the American Republican form, government was exercised through elected representatives of the people who were chosen in free elections, for short terms, after which they had to meet the electors again in a fresh election: hence they were representative and also accountable. For the rest, all manner of restraints were built in to protect the individual citizen from governmental encroachments. The first of such restraints was a written constitution separating the three 'Powers'—the executive, legislative, and judicial—into three distinct agencies, that is, a version of the 'checks and balances' principle which we have seen was the criterion of republicanism from the classical age. The others were contained within the Constitution, notably a set of clauses, the 'First Ten Amend-

---

[1] Palmer, *Age of the Democratic Revolution*, vol. 1.

[2] H. Maine, *Popular Government* (John Murray, London, 1885).

ments', which is referred to as a 'Bill of Rights' and which guaranteed civil rights. The syndrome of these main features was called, variously, Representative Government, Limited Government, Constitutional Government, or—the phrase we shall use most commonly from now on—liberal-democracy, and the philosophy—or ideology—that underpinned it was liberalism. Until after the Russian Revolution of 1917 this was the form of government that all the non-western states regarded as modern.

But as we have already hinted, popular government could also validate a radically different, indeed, antithetical form of government: a Forum/Palace polity which was the Greek tyranny writ large. In the sharpest contradistinction from the limited government propounded by liberalism, it held that the sovereignty of the People could never and should never be abridged. This of course is Rousseau's main contention and the reason he despised representative government. The People as a whole and the People all the time were the only constituent source of authority. The doctrine comes out very clearly in the writings of the Abbé Sieyès. For him the Nation and the People are the same thing, and he goes on: 'The nation is prior to everything. It is the source of everything. Its will is always legal; indeed, it is the law itself.'[3] Or again: 'All the public authorities without distinction are an emanation of the general will; all come from the people, that is to say, from the nation.'[4] This is given specific formulation in Article 25 of the French 1793 Constitution: 'Sovereignty resides in the people; it is one and indivisible, imprescriptible and inalienable.' In this way any individual, however rough and ready, could be elected to power through a popular vote or plebiscite, or alternatively might seize power violently and have this confirmed by a popular vote. In this way he would unite in himself all the legislative, executive, and judicial powers, with no guarantees except himself for civil or indeed any other rights, and consequently in a position to remain in power until an occasion proved opportune for yet another popular vote of validation. This was the road Napoleon followed and, in our own century, Hitler and Mussolini.[5] These rulers made the law: if they set up

---

[3] Sieyès, *What is the Third Estate?*, ed. S. E. Finer (Pall Mall Press, London, 1963), 124.

[4] Ibid. 17.

[5] I do not cite Stalin and his successors in this context because they were supposedly validated by a liberal type of constitution (the Stalin Constitution of 1936, the Brezhnev Constitution of 1977). Their absolute grip on power was achieved by misinterpreting or ignoring any clauses in these constitutions that did not suit them. They were extreme examples of what in fact has been the usual pattern in the many new states—in which I include the centenarian Latin American ones—that embraced the liberal-democratic form. They were façade democracies, concealing the rule of an individual dictator or of an oligarchy. Nor do I include Cromwell, although Napoleon's dictatorship was denounced by contemporaries as 'Cromwellian'. Cromwell came to power on the back of the New Model Army and, try how he might, he never got a Parliament that was willing to give him absolute power. He just took it.

legislatures these were either subservient or powerless. Once elected they were no longer accountable for their day-to-day actions and re-election was rigged. Any constitution or bill of rights they admitted to was tailored to maximize their powers not to be restrained, and the three powers were not separated but were fused in their person. And all this was perfectly proper in so far as they incarnated the 'Voice of the People', because to re-quote Sieyès, 'its will is always legal. Indeed it is the law itself.' This was the path that led to what Talmon called 'totalitarian democracy'.

3. THE NATION-STATE

The two principles of nationalism and popular sovereignty are difficult to keep apart and indeed their fusion is evident in Sieyès' identification of People and Nation—the entire community within the national territory. Each principle reinforced the other. The 'national state' is one where one people, or at least the vast majority of the population forming this peculiar people, inhabit the territory; as against dynastic or composite states. The nation-state is not the 'national state'; it goes much further because it asserts that this national state does not belong to a dynast or to anything else but to the nation itself, that is, to its people. Anti-dynastic, anti-clerical: it spelled the doom of the Church and/or the aristocracy as rulers, and thereby reduced the number of possible polities to only two: Forum and Palace, the latter dividing into traditional monarchies or Palace/Forum tyrannies (in the Greek sense). The Church and the aristocracy did not die, but were demoted to the role of powerful—in most cases extremely powerful—'pressure groups'. They influenced the rulers; no longer could they rule by themselves, as had happened, in certain cases, in the past.

4. SECULARISM AND CONSCIOUS PURPOSE IN THE MODERN STATE

The twin principles of nationalism and popular sovereignty carry certain negative implications of the utmost importance. Whatever 'popular government' may turn out to be in practice—and Hitler's tyranny was a version of it—there are some things it decidely is *not*. It is *not* compatible with theocracy—the principle that for so long held the Ottoman Empire together and also provided a justification and method for the government of non-Muslims. It is *not* compatible with hereditary absolute monarchy such as justified the kings and queens of Spain and Portugal in their hold over their Latin American subjects. It is *not* compatible with traditional allegiance, such as justified the rule of a sheikh in the Middle East or a chief in Africa. Every one of these forms is 'traditional', and it is precisely because the principle of popular sovereignty is antithetical to every one of them that it is part of the syndrome of 'modernity'. Nor is this all: the implication, indeed the object of popular sovereignty is that the people shall be consulted on and determine their political future. In short, it implies that public policies shall be a matter of CONSCIOUS PURPOSE. It sharply constrasts with the unreflecting loyalty to existing authorities which is implicit in all 'traditionalist' formulae.

By the same token, in overriding religion as a legitimating principle the nation-state implicitly, and usually explicitly, is SECULAR. It is this-worldly; this is particularly explicit in the case of the liberal-democratic states, and 'a free Church in a free State' was a central tenet of liberalism. Equally, secularism can be promoted in popular dictatorships. But theocracy dies a hard death and the history of secularism in Europe, its seed-bed, shows just how hard. It would be pointless to recount all the stages of this secularization in any detail, and we have already discussed it in connection with the Enlightenment of the eighteenth century. The entire nineteenth century in Europe (exceptionally, not the United States, as will be seen) was affected politically by the Church–State controversy; this was true even in Britain where 'free thought' suffered civil and political disabilities until the last quarter of the century, not to speak of social persecution and boycott. In the Catholic states of Europe society was riven by clericalism versus anticlericalism; the *Kulturkampf* in Germany, the Vatican–state controversy in Italy, the division of France into a Right and Left which was, more than anything else, a reflection of secularism versus theocratic notions. In the new secular states created after 1918 marks of the self-inflicted wounds still persist. Italy is still polarized by clericalism and anticlericalism, while the two main German parties represent 'Christian' values versus Social Democracy.

5. INDUSTRIALIZATION: THE QUEST FOR ECONOMIC INDEPENDENCE AND SOCIAL WELFARISM

Industrialization, which is the veritable hinge of world history since Neolithic times and the progenitor of our modern world, is of so vast a significance that an entire chapter is, later, devoted to this theme. Here let us briefly note three immediate sets of consequences.

5.1. *Some Social Consequences*

Industrialization threw up two new classes, capitalists and 'proletarians', whose contest for economic and political dominance became an underlying theme of state evolution and indeed, for Marxists, its unique theme and driving-force. Hence the emergence from the 1860s and 1870s of a variety of similarly inclined·political movements that can ˏcomprehensively be termed 'socialist' which promptly began to spread through the continent of Europe (exceptionally, not the United States). It is no part of this preliminary overview to catalogue and record their vicissitudes. I confine myself to three observations. First, all these movements were premissed on a growing polarization of society between a handful of capitalist proprietors and the great mass of exploited and downtrodden industrial workers. Next, they all demanded, as a pre-condition for improving the lot of the industrial worker, an extensive interference with the free-market mechanism up to, indeed, the complete state ownership of all the means of production, distribution, and exchange. Thirdly, on the grounds that all industrial workers shared a common interest in fighting the capitalists and not, at their behest, fighting themselves in so-called 'capitalist' wars, all these movements espoused internationalism. In short, by one route or another European socialism reacted against both liberalism's market economy and nationalism alike. In 1917 there occurred a decisive break between those socialist parties which espoused representative government as the route to socialism and those, the Bolsheviks—who later took the name Communists—who were prepared to seize and maintain power by coercion and promote the true, socialist interests of the proletariat irrespective of how the proletarians themselves felt about it. A polity on these lines was founded in Russia in 1917 and rapidly expanded to become the Soviet Union. Despite a liberal-seeming constitution, it was in fact a most extreme form of the Palace/Forum polity, a self-avowed 'dictatorship' akin to that wielded by the Jacobins in 1793 but infinitely more oppressive.

5.2. *Some Political Consequences*

The reason for it being more oppressive lies, precisely, in another effect of industrialization. Government's penetrative powers were vastly enhanced. Information could be transmitted fast, in the end, instantaneously; surveillance of the population could be exerted over every individual; conformity to commands could be enforced by the state's own agents at the very grass roots; the transportation of goods and men from one end of a country to the other at speeds and in volumes hitherto inconceivable allowed the 'forces of order' to be moved at speed to the remotest centres of unrest. Hitherto, the agrarian-based state's function had been largely architectonic, confining itself for the main part to defence, law and order, and taxation; and, as we have seen, even these activities could only be carried out with the intimate co-operation of private intermediaries, that is, the local notables. This was no longer necessary. The state would, and—because of the increasing wealth industrialization brought about—the state *could* afford an army of civil servants, whereas hitherto these had always been far, far too few.

6. WEALTH AND WELFARISM

Throughout the eighteenth century there were continual riots over the high price of bread, and great masses of the peasantry were still living on the margin of subsistence. Industralization first enabled wealth to keep pace with the rapidly rising populations; then it overtook population growth and threw up an ever-increasing social surplus. Living standards improved, and then—not without popular pressure—the state began increasingly to make up for certain material difficulties the citizen might be suffering. The point about 'welfare', however, is that it goes beyond this concept: the state undertakes to make up these handicaps to the individual in his capacity as a participant in the community—as a citizen. It is this that distinguishes welfare today from the age-old concept of a 'poor law' where the material benefits were conceded to a defined deprived category rather than accorded as a right to all citizens *qua* citizens. This concept of welfare includes the citizen's right to schooling, to form protective associations, and to receive provision against old age, sickness, unemployment, and the like. In this way WELFARE became the sixth element in the concept of modernity.[6]

7. THE EXPORTATION OF THE MODERN STATE MODEL

Perhaps we should have added even a seventh element to the syndrome of modernity, namely, military power. This too was powerfully enhanced by industrialization and because of their modern equipment the European powers (and the United States) were able to dominate any parts of the world they chose. In the words of the old couplet:

[6] I am well aware that 'welfare' has quite a different connotation in the USA. It corresponds to what Europe calls 'public assistance', i.e. last-resort and means-tested public support, to which certain obligations may be attached ('workfare' in the absurd and illiterate American vocabulary). It has a deeply pejorative significance and in this way is the exact opposite of the meaning of welfare in the European context.

Whatever happens, we have got
The Gatling gun, and they have not.

It was neither Europe's manpower nor wealth that created her vast overseas empires, but arrogance, courage, firearms, and battle-fleets. The disparity in wealth between Europe and, say, Latin America or India, was by no means so marked in the eighteenth century. In the nineteenth century, however, Britain, America, and France became noticeably wealthier and technologically superior. Throughout Latin America and, later, in the Balkan peninsula, the principles on which their states were erected—nationality, popular government, and secularization—and the embodiment of these in the liberal-democratic system, suggested that these were the pre-conditions to national wealth and power, and not simply desirable in themselves. By the last quarter of the nineteenth century this conclusion seemed inescapable in the light of the upsurge of Germany and Japan alongside the former industrial powers, for these too were erected on the 'modernizing' principles and had adopted liberal-democratic constitutions. So, as the French Revolutionary principles began to penetrate British India from the 1880s, even revolutionizing Iran in 1905 and Turkey and China in 1908 and 1911, those principles, along with the parliamentary system, were regarded as a *means* to affluence and power.

But this was not the only route by which the remainder of the globe received the institutions of the modern state. One way in which the exportation of the Western European model took place is almost identical to that in English North America before 1776, and for the same reason: the establishment of British settlement colonies in Canada, Australia, New Zealand, and South Africa. Political institutions followed the flag. All these countries were endowed with some form of British parliamentary government, adapted to the local conditions (e.g. Canada and Australia were federal as well as parliamentary). Yet this mode of transmission was outside the general run. More common and more widespread were a variety of methods premissed on superior wealth and armed might.

To begin with, contact with the well-armed, aggressive Europeans brought a number of non-western states to question their own traditional values. This was very marked in such civilizations as India and Turkey, and in China where Confucianism was beginning to be undermined by the middle of the nineteenth century. This corrosion of their traditional values weakened the morale of these polities and laid them more open to change, whether self-imposed or forced from abroad.

Next, a number of states, alarmed at the West's military power and aggression, hurried to protect themselves by adopting and adapting the

West's own methods. They vaccinated themselves, as it were, with the very poison that was threatening them. One might call this 'preventive anti-colonialism'. The most successful of such states was unquestionably Japan. Turkey, through the *Tanzimat* and the Young Turk movement, went some way but could not avoid dismemberment after the First World War, when, having lost its Arab and European subjects, Kemalism put it firmly on the modernizing road. Thailand and Egypt, to mention only two others in this category, also made strenuous attempts to modernize, in the latter's case without success.

Finally come the effects of Imperialism and the not-so-long delayed anti-colonial reaction. The Europeans quartered up the world betweeen them: by 1900 one-fifth of the land area and one-tenth of the world's population were gathered into the European empires. The conquerors by no means trans-planted the institutions of the modern state in their entirety. They imposed a government by bureaucrats and soldiers and created frontiers, often quite arbitrary ones, to form territorial states out of a congeries of previously tribal governments. There were no representative native assemblies, though there might well be consultative bodies. On the other hand, they did bring with them western systems of law. Their presence provided the natives with a constant example of how to govern and an equally persistent source of resentment and frustration at not being allowed to govern themselves.

The First World War of 1914–18 brought about the collapse of the German, Austrian, and Ottoman empires and therewith established a series of succession states which adopted the liberal-democratic model; but they could not work it for long and, with the honourable exception of Czecho-slovakia, allowed themselves to be governed by a local strong-man or dictator. That war, however, had its effects in the Middle East also, where the Arab states were emancipated from the Turks, given a semi-colonial status under the 'mandate' system, and promptly aspired to shake this off and become fully independent. Here again their goal was to become modern states like those of the West, and here again these new succession states failed at the attempt. The Second World War of 1939–45 broke up the empires of Britain, France, Holland, and Belgium and, as we have already pointed out, created more than 100 new succession states, mostly in Asia and Africa. Some of these opted for the communist model on offer from the USSR, whose record had been consistently anti-colonial and which was claiming to provide the short cut to all but immediate industrialization. Those opting were relatively few because the western powers endowed their departing empires with constitutions enshrining their own representative liberal-democracy institutions. Most of these succession states were multi-ethnic, a problem for even the most mature liberal-democracies and, at the time of writing, quite unresolved in such cases as Northern Ireland, Belgium, and Canada. It was an additional hurdle for these new countries to leap. In practically all cases they failed to make the so-called 'Westminster' model work. Their fate was to fall into military dictatorship punctuated by brief intervals of corrupt and manipulated parliamentarianism.

8. THE EPISODES

The main topics to be covered in this book should now be clear. They are the moves towards the creation of the nation-state and its two main forms; the struggle in Europe to perfect the liberal-democratic form; the impact of industrialization; the subsequent acceptance by the rest of the world that the kind of state which had emerged in Europe and the United States as a result of these factors was the paradigmatic modern state. So, first, we must review the American Revolution and its quite remarkable inventions in government, inventions which, themselves alone, went far to complete this modern state paradigm. There must follow a discussion of the French Revolution and its effects, notably despotic democracy and the Pandora's box of nationalism. The third chapter will show the competition between the conservative, that is, anti-Enlightenment ideologies in Europe and those making for modernity, as the continent gropes painfully towards liberal-democracy. Only then shall we discuss industrialization: partly because its full establishment in Europe and the United States occurs at much the same time as liberal-democracy had become the European norm, but equally to re-emphasize that the American and French revolutions and their consequences antedate industrialization and are not its products, as much vulgar opinion seems to maintain. On the back of the combination of the fall-out of the political revolutions and the industrial revolution, comes the expansion of Europe and America into the non-western world, and with this the exportation of the paradigmatic modern state to these areas. The final chapter begins with the extraordinary—and still continuing—effects of the technological revolution on political life and then traces the vicissitudes of the two major forms of popular government, both in Europe and overseas, up to the collapse of the dictatorshop model, first in its heartland and then throughout the rest of the world. It will be shown that, contrary to Fukuyama, this is not 'the end of history'. It promises simply to be the beginning of a new cycle in the conflict between Forum and Palace forms of polity.

[Editorial note: The author did not live to complete the final two chapters.]

2

The American Revolution

1. ITS IMPORTANCE

*T*he transcendent importance of the American Revolution is that it demonstrated for ever that quality of the Western European government we have called 'law-boundedness'. Here is a government which draws its powers from and can only act within a framework of fundamental law—the Constitution—which is itself interpreted by judges in the ordinary courts of the country. Could law-boundedness go further, could it receive a more striking affirmation?

It is notable too that while its government is elected on a wide popular franchise, its power to act is lost in a maze of channels which dilute it and slow it down:[1] the celebrated 'checks and balances' in the system do not abolish explicit expressions of the popular will but restrain it. In this way the United States stands as the paradigm of what we have been calling the 'liberal democracy'.

But thirdly: in arriving at this, the United States made no less than six governmental inventions, all of which have been taken up world-wide: the deliberate formulation of a new frame of government by way of a popular Convention, the written constitution, a bill of rights within this constitution, the latter's status as paramount law guaranteed by judicial review, the 'separation of powers' along functional lines, and the division of powers between the national and the state governments now denoted by the term 'federalism'.

[1] . . . that for many a league
The shorn and parcelled Oxus strains along
Through beds of sand and matted rushy isles—
Oxus, forgetting the bright speed he had
In his high mountain-cradle in Pamere,
A foiled circuitous wanderer.
(M. Arnold, 'Sohrab and Rustum')

2. SOME CHARACTERISTICS

2.1. *Its Immediate Impact on Europe*

The Revolution made little impact on the countries south of the Alps and the Pyrenees except, perhaps, Italy which hailed Benjamin Franklin as a new Lycurgus.[2] In Britain it caused some militancy but little else, but Ireland, where Grattan affirmed that the Irish looked to America, responded by the formation of the 'Liberty Boys'. In Germany and France, however—particularly France—the result was, in Palmer's words, 'an incredible outburst of discussion, speculation, rhapsody and argument, a veritable intoxication with the *rêve américain*'.[3] Over the period 1760–90 twenty-six books on America appeared in at least three different languages. In addition there was a large increase in periodicals. Apart from this, the American ideals and theories were canvassed throughout salons, reading clubs, Masonic lodges, and the like. And the Americans—particularly Benjamin Franklin—displayed their almost atavistic talent for self-advertisement in carefully contrived propaganda.[4] In Germany and France adulation went to unbelievably foolish lengths which have to be read to be believed.[5] Goethe and Schiller protested at the raising of German troops by Britain (but it should not be forgotten that there were others, like Schlützer and Sprengel, who strenuously defended the British cause and thought of the Americans as a pack of ingrates).[6] In France the Americanism of the war years comprehended sentiments of Liberty, Virtue, Prosperity, and Enlightenment;[7] but side by side there went serious and hard-headed scrutiny of the new constitutional arrangements. What most impressed the French was the very idea of a constituent assembly, one that could draft a constitution as an act of intellect and will. For the rest battle raged between those who did and those who did not see too much of the ancient British constitution in the make-up of the new American one and/or disapproved of the separation of powers.[8] An example was being set for the French themselves when their revolutionary hour struck in 1789: the fact that they freely used the term 'Convention' is one brief but significant support for this view. The first perceived character of the American Revolution was, then, that its very

---

[2] C. W. Toth, *Liberté, Egalité, Fraternité: The American Revolution and the European Response* (Whitston, New York, 1989), 5.   [3] Palmer, *Age of the Democratic Revolution*, i. 242.
[4] Ibid. 242–53.   [5] Ibid. 256–7, quotes a number of examples.
[6] E. Douglass, '*Sturm und Drang*: German intellectuals and the American Revolution', in Toth, *Liberté*, 51, 54–5.
[7] D. Echeverria, 'Mirage in the West: French Philosophers Re-discover America', in Toth, *Liberté*, 411.   [8] Palmer, *Age of the Democratic Revolution*, i. 266 ff.

essence was a fresh start initiated from below despite and in contravention of the 'constituted authorities'.

2.2. *The Trans-Atlantic Enlightenment*

Germany and France were countries where the Enlightenment burned most brightly, and this American Revolution was in the purest spirit of the Enlightenment—to a degree that was doubtless devoutly wished for in Europe but impossible to achieve against the dead weight of an hereditary aristocracy and a formidably wealthy and entrenched Church. America was possessed of neither. Here such ideas as natural rights, the Social Contract, liberty and equality, freedom of speech and conscience, and the like could go into practice with little obstruction. America had its own educated class which had thoroughly imbibed the European Enlightenment—especially, as we shall see, the philosophy of John Locke. Professor Commager, the doyen of the patriotic school of American historians, has put the American case in a book with the revelatory title: *The Empire of Reason—How Europe Imagined and America Realized the Enlightenment*.[9] But although Commager is always either rhapsodizing (America) or parodying (Europe), his main thesis is surely sound: the ideas of the Enlightenment *were* more fully realized in America than in Europe. This is not merely due to the absence of a hereditary aristocracy and established Church, but also because the 'American Tories' or, as they called themselves, the 'United Empire Loyalists' were driven out of the United States into the Canadian wastes and never returned to mount a counter-revolution. In short, the Revolution reflected the European Enlightenment back to its European point of origin, where it served throughout the nineteenth century as an inspiration.

2.3. *The British Exemplar*

An earlier chapter[10] contrasted two traditions in European government: absolute monarchy on the Continent and parliamentary and limited monarchy in Great Britain, which was very much in the minority. The American Revolution gave this latter tradition a powerful push. It not only redressed the balance between the two traditions but, together with its original British exemplar, contested, eroded, and finally overwhelmed Continental absolutism. The new government installed by the United States in 1787 made explicit the British common-law rights of citizens, and added some of its own. It established much stronger checks and balances than in Britain—and,

---

[9] Commager, *The Empire of Reason*.   [10] Bk. IV, Ch. 6.

indeed, anywhere else in the world. And it substituted for the absolute sovereignty of the Crown-in-Parliament a constitutionally limited sovereignty which was further constrained by having its main functions split into three separate departments and by a further division of functions between the national (in this case federal) and the state governments.

Not one of the Founding Fathers would have denied that they owed a debt to the British constitution. Hamilton said so aggressively. Sam Adams declared (in 1759, it should be noted) that it was 'the best model of government that can be framed by mortals', and even members of the Stamp Act Congress were proud to 'have been born under the most perfect form of government'.[11] Until 1775 the sentiment that united the 'patriots' was, in George Mason of Virginia's words: 'We claim nothing but the liberty and privileges of Englishmen in the same degree, as if we had still continued among our brethren in England.'[12] But by 1775 this admiration had turned to scorn: they had become radicalized by British attempts to interfere with them and were nourishing themselves the while on the radical—Whig—views of the British constitution found in such writers as Harrington, Milton, Sydney, and Richard Price.[13] By 1775 they saw it as 'under the hands of bribery and corruption, *rotten* to the core'. It was, it has been remarked, 'an amazing transformation'.[14] They were now claiming that 'they were the true guardians of the British constitution', enjoying it in 'greater purity and perfection' than the English themselves.[15]

But at the same time many of the patriots rested their opposition to the imperial Parliament on a more abstract plane, namely natural law and natural rights. The central theorist of this position was, of course, John Locke. Nature had endowed humanity with certain natural rights, governments existed solely in order to protect these rights, and so, simultaneously, the government was contracted to this course by a social contract with its population and the government, clearly, was constrained to act only within the terms of the same. If it failed to do this, then the contract had been violated and the people could withdraw allegiance from the government and re-establish their rights through a new one. This indeed was the philosophical underpinning of the Glorious Revolution. One of the laws of nature was that no government could take its subjects' property without their consent. Such, according to Locke, 'subverted the end of government'. The American patriots found in Locke's doctrines both the specific argument as to why they should not be taxed without their open assent and, also, the

[11] G. S. Wood, *The Creation of the American Republic, 1776–1787* (University of North Carolina Press, Chapel Hill, 1969), 11.   [12] Miller, *Origins*, 122–3.
[13] Wood, *Creation of the American Republic*, 16.   [14] Ibid. 12.   [15] Ibid. 12–13.

claim that the Mother of Parliaments was not, as Blackstone had it, unequivocally sovereign but, as Chief Justice Coke would have had it in Stuart times, constrained by the law—in short, limited and not sovereign at all. In this sense, then, one might visualize American political thought as 'purifying' the British constitution from its present defects and taking it back to where it should never have strayed from: natural law binding even a sovereign parliament. But, adapted in this way or not, the British constitution was the model on which the colonists built.

3. FORWARD TO INDEPENDENCE

'No document in the world, outside Holy Writ, has been the occasion for such a mass of annotation and exposition as the Fundamental Law of the American Constitution.'[16] I do not know how Hornwill arrived at these figures, but find the general tenor of his remark irresistible. These commentators differ among themselves so often that one is tempted to say, in Kipling's words:

> There are nine and sixty ways of constructing tribal lays
> And every single one of them is right.[17]

The version that follows is mine and from now on the 'intrusive I' will play a much larger role than the editorial 'We'.

3.1. *The Climacteric of 1763*

It will be remembered[18] that the thirteen colonies had experienced a century-and-a-half of self-government along British lines, but with a more democratic franchise, more upward mobility, less-polarized income distribution, and no established Church or aristocracy of blood. It was a homespun government perhaps, but it had deep roots and it suited its people, most of whom were Englishmen (though significant numbers of Scots and England-hating Irish had entered in the last half-century). It is also worth noting at this point that, although its educated class lagged far behind Europe's in letters and art, it contained a considerable number of better-off people who knew their common law even if they were not practising lawyers, were well versed in the classics of European political thought, and whose passion, apart from turning a dollar, was playing politics.

---

[16] H. W. Hornwill, *The Usages of the American Constitution* (Kennikat Press, Port Washington, 1925), 22.   [17] R. Kipling, 'In the Neolithic Age'.
[18] Bk. IV, Ch. 7.

These colonies had been under threat from Spain in the Floridas, from France in Canada and along the line of the Mississippi down to their port of New Orleans, and from the Indians. The colonists were glad to be protected by Britain. But by the Treaty of Paris, 1763, the French threat was eliminated. England had vastly profited from her victory in the war. The French ceded Acadia, Canada, Cape Breton, and all Louisiana east of the Mississippi apart from the island of New Orleans. However, the Indian threat remained. Its danger was highlighted in the conspiracy of chief Pontiac, which initially seized most of the westward British forts and could not be put down till 1765. It is significant that, to the colonists, the Seven Years War was 'the French–Indian wars'.

In the aftermath of her victory Britain drew new frontiers. A proclamation of 1763 established the provinces of Quebec, East Florida, West Florida, and Grenada. At the same time—and this infuriated the colonists—she closed all the conquered Louisiana beyond the Alleghany Mountains to settlement; the land west of this boundary up to the Mississippi was to be an Indian reserve. Britain's sweeping triumph established her as the leading power in America. In short order, however, her victory turned out to be a can of worms.

3.2. *Money, Money, Money!*

Money, it is said, is the root of all evil: it has certainly been one of the most prolific stimuli to revolt, rebellion, and revolution—in western history, at any rate. In England—Magna Carta and the Barons' War and the Civil War in 1642; in France—the nobiliar revolts of the sixteenth century, the Fronde, and finally the great Revolution of 1789; in Spain—the revolts of the Netherlands, Catalans, and Portuguese: all serve as examples. The American Revolution started as a tax revolt too.

The Seven Years War doubled the British national debt from c.£75 million to c.£147 million.[19] She had borne the cost of defeating the French in North America almost on her own.[20] Not only that: her ever-busy merchants evaded the various Trade and Navigation Acts and carried on a profitable contraband traffic in the West Indies—another loss to the imperial revenue. Yet the 'British Americans enjoyed a lighter tax burden than any people of the western world—except the Poles'. It is reckoned that

---

[19] Palmer, *Age of the Democratic Revolution*, i. 153.
[20] B. B. Nye and J. E. Morpurgo, *The Birth of the U.S.A.* (Penguin, Harmondsworth, 1964), 128–9.

it was 1 shilling per capita in America compared with 6 shillings and 8 pence in Ireland and no less than 26 shillings in Britain.[21]

What happened in the ensuing thirteen years was that the British repeatedly made efforts to tighten up the colonial economic laws and to impose taxes on the colonists to help pay to protect the western frontier from Indian attack. The colonists—their tempers frayed by the losses now incurred among the contrabandists and by those who had speculated in the western lands which were now closed to settlement—resisted. The British tried one measure, met resistance, withdrew it and tried another, and so forth, each incident contributing to growing bitterness, radicalization—and a sense of solidarity—among the colonists. The British ministers acted with extreme ham-handedness and insensitivity, while each of their blunders was seized on by the firebrands and revolutionaries among the colonists; such as the ineffable Patrick Henry, Sam Adams, and James Otis, who established a network of Corresponding Societies in Massachusetts, an example soon followed in the rest of the colonies. Exaggeration was compounded. One has only to look at the litany of complaints delivered 'to a candid world' in the latter part of Jefferson's Declaration of Independence to see that half were factitious and of the remainder half were grossly exaggerated. Take the Quebec Act, 1774, for instance. Although this left the province's government in the hands of a royal governor and his council, in all other respects this was a liberal, indeed noble, document. It restored French civil law to the Quebecois, and pledged toleration for their Roman Catholic religion. For their pains the British were accused of extending religious toleration to the Catholics so that they could be used to suppress the liberties of the colonists.

Effectively, there were only four alternative ways of getting money from the colonists. The British government could appeal to each of the thirteen colonies: but this would not produce enough money or men. Or—the colonists could be given representation at Westminster (Adam Smith's solution); but no American would countenance this. Thirdly, there was Franklin's suggestion of an inter-colonial union for defence—but here again, the colonists would have none of it. Finally, there was taxation imposed through the imperial Parliament. The successive attempts at the last were what provoked the colonies into non-co-operation, then into riots and rebellion, and finally into hostilities. British coercive measures through 1775 were met by the skirmishes at Lexington and Concord, followed by Bunker Hill and then the American invasion of Canada. In this heady atmosphere the colonies assembled in the Second Continental Congress.

---

[21] Palmer, *Age of the Democratic Revolution*, i. 153–5.

It voted in favour of the Virginia Resolution demanding independence. The world-famous Declaration of Independence drafted by Jefferson followed, on 4 July 1776.

Its first and memorable part is an inimitable summary of the natural-law and social-contract theories of John Locke, pure and simple. The second part is that string of complaints by which the breach with England was purportedly justified and about which I have already expressed my scepticism.

It is difficult to characterize the War of Independence as a civil war in that the Loyalists were individuals and small groups lacking any coherent organization. They were easy prey to patriotic mobsters who destroyed their houses, tarred and feathered them, and stole their property. They could do little but lie low until a British force seized their area. For all that, it is reckoned that about one-third of the American population were pro-British as against an equal number of 'patriots', the remainder standing apart from both.[22] Furthermore, the rapacity of this war should not be underestimated as it is in so many bland transatlantic 'authorized versions'. The French revolutionaries were indeed to confiscate twelve times as much property as the American patriots but their country was ten times as populous. Again: in the French Revolution there were five *émigrés* per 1,000 population—in America there were twenty-four per 1,000.[23] These unfortunates, the United Empire Loyalists, had to flee to Canada. True, in the Treaty of Versailles, 1783, the victorious Americans promised to pay them compensation for the property they had confiscated. But they never did. It was left to the British government to settle the bill to the tune of some £3½ million.

The British lost the war through *hubris* and *superbia*. In the event, although the Americans never won a decisive battle, neither did the British. The French joined in on the American side in 1778 and by the end of the war Britain was fighting the navies of France, Spain, and Holland. The British surrender at Yorktown was due to a combined US–French land blockade and an effective French sea blockade. This was the battle that terminated the war. It reflected no credit on either British arms or diplomacy.

---

[22] See e.g. John Adams's estimate, in Nye and Morpurgo, *Birth*, 195.
[23] Palmer, *Age of the Democratic Revolution*, i. 188.

4. THE POLITICAL INSTITUTIONS OF THE WAR YEARS, 1776–1787

The Americans, says Wood, had a 'paranoia about power'.[24] They believed that a *libido dominandi* must inevitably corrupt 'men in high stations'. They had no use for governments by the one or the few: only by the people themselves[25] (and even then in a highly qualified way). It was a choice between liberty and despotism.[26] It followed, as John Adams observed, that 'our provincial legislatures are the only supreme authorities in our colonies'.[27] 'Despotism!' Few terms of abuse were so freely used on the republican side. It is true they were used as, very much, the equivalent of 'absolutism' today.[28] But to suggest even that they were subject to an absolutism—they should have been so lucky! Once the war began the royal governors fled and the state legislatures themselves became the government, not just a check on ministerial power as they had been before. This was itself revolutionary because 'for centuries the government had been identified with the executive or the Crown'. 'Legislation was considered exceptional, corrective, and concerned only with the common welfare.'[29] Many of these legislatures—Virginia's is the noteworthy case—formulated Bills of Rights,[30] and all of them paid lip-service to the principle of the separation of powers, but in almost all the states the governorship was reduced to a virtual nullity. In eight states the governor was chosen by the legislature and ten limited the governor's term to one year only. In the Carolinas the governor had no right of veto. Governor Randolf of Virginia regarded himself only as 'a member of the executive'. Jefferson concluded in Virginia, 'all the powers of government, legislative, executive and judiciary, result to the legislative body'.[31] In 1775 practically all the colonists were still protesting their loyalty to the Crown: then they changed almost overnight to fervent and apostrophic republicanism, a form of government identified with a supposed 'public virtue'. Jefferson remarked on the speed of the transition as did John Adams, and even today 'it remains remarkable and puzzling'.[32]

The thirteen sovereign states fought the war under an agreement called the Articles of Confederation and Perpetual Union (1777), in which each state retained its independent sovereignty. Among its most significant

---

[24] Wood, *Creation of the American Republic*, 17.   [25] Ibid. 22.   [26] Ibid. 23.
[27] Ibid. 351.   [28] See Bk. IV, Ch. 8 above.   [29] Ibid.
[30] It is printed, to show its resemblances to the French Declaration of the Rights of Man and the Citizen (1789), in Palmer, *Age of the Democratic Revolution*, i. app. 4.
[31] M. Cunliffe, *American Presidents and the Presidency* (Eyre & Spottiswoode, London, 1969), 28–9.
[32] Wood, *Creation of the American Republic*, 91, 93.

provisions were the following. Each state was to have one vote apiece. A common treasury was established but it was supplied by the several states in proportion to their assessed land. As and when a state raised land-forces all officers under the rank of colonel were to be appointed by the state's legislature. For its part, the Confederation, assembled in Congress, was empowered to regulate disputes and appeals between the states, engage in war, make foreign treaties, control the currency, emit bills of credit, appropriate money, and lay down the numbers of the armed forces *providing* nine states agreed. In the recess of Congress a 'Committee of the States' would manage the general affairs of the Confederation. In short, the raising of troops and the wherewithal to pay for them and its collection lay in the hands of the individual states. It is true that a majority of nine states could pass a resolution, but the Articles were silent as to how it was to be enforced.

Barely adequate to meet the demands of the 'Glorious Cause' when the thirteen States were at least confronting a common destiny, the Articles suffered from the emotional drain and disillusion once the war was over. For the problems of war were not the same as those of the peace, which opened a Pandora's box of quarrels—over the future of the western lands, commercial policy, the slave trade, the redemption of state and confederal bills of credit, the inflation of the paper currency. The state governments provided no model for a new frame of common government—only what to avoid. Almost all the statesmen of any eminence were united in loathing the tyranny of the state legislatures. They were shocked by their confiscations, their wild issue of paper money, their arbitrary suspensions of the recovery of debts. John Adams, even in 1776, called this 'democratic despotism'. Madison said that they had made too many laws, many of them repeatedly unjust, and that they drew to themselves all powers, the judicial and executive as well as the legislative.[33] 'The concentration of all powers in the legislature, in the same hands', wrote Jefferson, 'is precisely the definition of despotic government . . . 173 despots would surely be as oppressive as one.'[34]

But the states liked being sovereign. For a full six months in 1782 Congress could barely summon up a quorum, and the delegates who did attend were strong supporters of republicanism and states' rights. It was being dilatory over a 'nationalist' group's request for a Convention at Philadelphia to reconsider the Articles of Confederation, when it was jerked into action by a pathetic skirmish with some 300 poverty-stricken farmers.

[33] Wood, *Creation of the American Republic*, 407.
[34] R. Middlekauf, *The Glorious Cause: The American Revolution, 1763–1789* (OUP, Oxford, 1982), 610.

Grandiosely called 'Shay's Rebellion', it was put down with no difficulty, but it so frightened the Congress that the requested Convention was duly summoned and met at Philadelphia on 14 May 1787.

5. THE MAKING OF THE CONSTITUTION, 1787

5.1. *Reading History Backwards: The Seductive Influence Of* The Federalist Papers

The *Federalist* is a series of essays by Hamilton, Madison, and Jay, written in 1787, to persuade the New York legislature to ratify the draft Constitution. Let it be said at once that it is one of the truly great classics of political science. Paradoxically, the great prestige it rightly enjoys and the powerful authority it carries are the very things that block an understanding of how the Constitution was brought about and what its contemporaries, especially some of its particularly prominent framers, thought about the document they had signed at that time. This is because, for decades, if not for an entire century and more, shoals of historians and their even more numerous students have seen the Constitution through the eyes of the *Federalist*.

Now, the *Federalist Papers* are pieces of special pleading, designed to justify *every single item* of the draft Constitution. They do this with such persuasive logic, and such self-consistency, that it seems as if the Constitution was drafted with a complete, coherent, rational scheme in the minds of its framers. But this is not how things happened at all. The making of the Constitution was a thing of wrangles and compromises and in its completed state it was a set of seemingly incongruous proposals cobbled together *faute de mieux*. And, furthermore, that is what many of its framers thought. The commentators and historians who have approached the Constitution through the spectacles of the *Federalist*—and furthermore, we may add, in the knowledge that this Constitution has successfully weathered more than two entire centuries, in which time it has been flexible enough to make the transition from the imperatives of an agrarian society to that of the industrial age—have been seeing the framing of the Constitution through the eyes of today; not unlike naïve students who think that the English troops who marched into France in 1338 were shouting 'Hooray! For we're off to the Hundred Years War.' In reality these founders were floundering in a mass of uncertainties and had hopes but no knowledge at all of how their handiwork would fare. A number of American historians have come to understand this.

Professor John Roche is even harsher than I am: Hamilton and Madison were 'inspired propagandists with a genius for retrospective symmetry',[35] the Electoral College for electing the president 'was merely a jerry-rigged improvisation which has subsequently been endowed with high theoretical content',[36] and the completed draft Constitution was a 'make-shift affair'.[37] He dismisses the view that the Constitution was 'an apotheosis of 'constitutionalism', a 'triumph of architectonic genius'. It was, he says, 'a patchwork sewn together under pressure of both time and events'. He concludes with the same indictment of the *Federalist* that we started off with: that 'this volume had enormous influence on the image of the Constitution in the minds of future generations, particularly on historians and political scientists who have an innate fondness for theoretical symmetry'.[38]

5.2. *Preoccupations in the Philadelphia Convention*

Was the central issue at Philadelphia whether there would be a national government at all, or was it a contest between those wanting the maximum independence for the states and others—like Madison, for instance—who wanted a 'consolidated' government in which state powers would become almost residual? Historians disagree.[39] But even apart from this, there were plenty of other things to preoccupy the delegates. They came to the Convention with an understanding that the 'three powers' should be 'separated', but they had seen this principle crippled, if not abrogated, by the behaviour of certain state legislatures. However, they still envisaged this 'separation' as basically between the executive branch and the legislative branch. They gave scant attention to the third, the judicial branch, as an independent counterpoise to the other two. They were still paranoid about power and feared the encroachments of the state legislatures, but whether they favoured the legislative or the executive they must inevitably be jumping from a frying-pan into a fire. This induced them to think that any new government should hold itself aloof from the direct influence of the people as far as was consistent with a democracy. When they settled on indirect elections for various organs, they maintained that this was representative government, and republican, as against democracy, meaning direct democracy which was the bane of the Greek city-states. They did not care for this at all. The arbitrary behaviour of the state legislatures and their engross-

[35] J. R. Roche, 'The Founding Fathers: A Reform Caucus in Action', in J. P. Greene, *The Reinterpretation of the American Revolution, 1763–1789* (Harpers and Row, New York, 1968), 447.
[36] Ibid. 459.   [37] Ibid. 462.   [38] Ibid. 468.
[39] For the first view, F. McDonald, *The Formation of the American Republic 1776–1790* (Penguin, Harmondsworth, 1967), prelim page. For the latter view, Roche, 'The Founding Fathers', *passim*.

ment of the executive and judicial powers was ascribed to the people having far too much say in electing them. Everywhere there were disparaging views of the people. Sherman of Connecticut—a former shoemaker—maintained that 'the people . . . should have as little to do as maybe about the government. They want information and are constantly liable to be misled.' Gerry (Massachusetts) commented 'the evils we experience flow from the excess of democracy . . . the worst men get into the legislature'.[40] Presenting the Virginia Plan, Randolph affirmed: 'Our chief danger arises from the democratic parts of our constitutions . . . the powers of government exercised by the people swallow up the other branches. None of the constitutions have provided sufficient checks against democracy.'[41]

5.3. Framing the Constitution

In my view (and here I follow Roche),[42] the issue at Philadelphia was not whether there should be a national government or not. All parties wanted one. The differences arose over structural issues—how this government should be constructed and what should be its relations with the states. 'States' righters' who maintained that everything must be done through the mediation of the state governments had no use for the Convention.

The problems to be faced were enormous and took the delegates into quite uncharted territory. Indeed, I cannot think of any other single example of a people, or peoples, constructing their polity from scratch. They admired the British constitution, but American conditions made copying it impossible. Substitutes had to be found for the irremovable and heredi- tary chief executive (the king); the absence of a hereditary nobility precluded the formation of a House of Lords; the existence of sovereign states raised the question of their relationships to the national government which did not occur in Britain, where the local authorities were the subordinates of the Crown-in-Parliament, and so on.

The simplest method to relate how the Constitution came to be patched together is, perhaps, to start with the two great rival 'plans', called— somewhat inaccurately—the Virginia or 'large states' plan and the New Jersey or 'small states' plan.

The Virginia plan, presented by Randolph but vigorously supported by James Madison, was for all-out national supremacy. The states would be

[40] F. Lundberg, Cracks in the Constitution (Princeton UP, Princeton, 1980). This is a gimcrack book, written by a journalist to 'debunk' the mystique of the Glorious Constitution. As such it does not succeed but it is full of quotations from the Founding Fathers, properly attributed in the notes. I cite it simply because it is a convenient source for these quotations.

[41] McDonald, Formation, 166.   [42] Roche, 'The Founding Fathers', 437–69.

quite residual. The legislature was to consist of two Chambers. The Lower Chamber would be elected directly by the people and the representation of the states' deputies therein would be proportional to population. The Upper Chamber would be elected by this Lower Chamber from names proposed by the state legislatures. These two Chambers would elect the chief executive and choose the judges. In so far as it was restrained at all, this bicameral legislature would be subject to a Council of Revision, made up of the chief executive and a number of judges, which could exercise a suspensive veto. The scope of this national government was sweeping. Not only would it possess all the powers already vested in Congress but in addition it could veto the acts of state legislatures, and had plenary power to do whatever the separate states were incompetent to do or in which 'the harmony of the USA may be interrupted by the exercise of individual legislation'.[43] And, to crown all, the national government could use force against recalcitrant states.

It seems to have taken a little time for delegates to realize that under this plan Massachussetts, Virginia, and Pennsylvania would virtually dominate the legislature, whereupon the smaller states reacted in the New Jersey plan.

It paid the usual lip-service to the principle of the three separate branches of government. The legislature would consist of one Chamber only which (as in the Virginia plan) would appoint the chief executive and judges, but there would be no Council of Revision. The powers of this legislature were specifically enumerated: it could exercise these and no others. These laws would be paramount to state laws. Above all, however, this legislature, unlike the Virginia plan, would be composed of equal—not proportional—representation of all states.

This plan was rejected and attention turned back to the Virginia plan. One immediate alteration was that the Upper House, instead of being elected by the Lower, should be elected by the state legislatures. Then it was suggested that this one should represent the states as such and the other the people at large but the smaller states still insisted on equality of states both in the Lower and the Upper House. A new suggestion was made—to split the difference. The states would have equal representation in the Upper House, the Lower House would be elected proportionately to population. After wearisome debate this was, reluctantly, accepted. It was the so-called 'Great Compromise'.

But this still left unanswered the problem of the chief executive, and, to a lesser degree, of the judiciary. Some delegates, of 'republican' sympathy, so

---

[43] Quoted in Roche, *The Rounding Fathers*, 448. A power very similar to this was extended to the (unelected!) Commission of the EC under the Maastricht Treaty, 1991, a treaty extolled by Britain's prime minister and foreign secretary as a 'retreat from centralization'. I have seen retreats compared with which this would be a headlong advance.

distrusted the office that they proposed a three-man executive, but this found no favour. The chief executive must be a single individual. Should he be elected by the people at large? The vast spaces and distances of the United States seemed to rule out the possibility of any sizeable vote going for one candidate. Indeed, it would be very difficult if not impossible for this sparse, scattered population even to put a face and a policy to any name proposed. Election by the state legislatures was rejected because of the now massive distrust of their 'fickleness'. Should—as previously proposed—he be appointed by the Congress? If so, then for how long? A short term would subordinate him to the legislature. A long term might prove dangerous unless he were ineligible for re-election.

Bit by bit his powers were defined. The term of office was to be four years, re-eligible for election. He was to be commander-in-chief of the armed forces. By and with the consent of the Senate he would make all major appointments. He could veto acts of the legislature, but this veto could be overridden by two-thirds majorities in both the Chambers.

Much was the alarm in certain quarters. The inimitable Patrick Henry ('give me Liberty or give me Death') declared that it was a 'squint towards monarchy'. The journal entitled *The Freeman* stated that the president was vested with powers 'exceeding those of the most *despotic monarchy* . . . in modern times'. For these reasons the mode of electing this very powerful officer seemed irresolvable. Then as a 'half-baked compromise',[44] 'an awkward, irrational'[45] 'jerry-rigged improvisation'[46] was reached. It was the Electoral College system. The people of the states or their state legislatures would elect electors, their numbers being equal to that of their (two) senators plus others according to the state's population, and these electors would vote, all on the same day, for a president, and a candidate from another state as vice-president. The candidate with most votes became president, the runner-up the vice-president. This at last seemed the best the Convention could do, and the scheme was adopted.

Its importance was capital. By this absurdity the Presidency acquired its own constituency, independent of the Congress, and by the same token took the nomination of the judiciary out of Congress's hands—the Senate must advise and consent to the nominations but it was the president who made them. 'The US Constitution until September 6 would have established a congressional government. On that day the government became a mixed one, for in rendering the President independent of the Congress the delegates rendered the judiciary relatively independent also.'[47]

[44] McDonald, *Formation*, 186.   [45] Ibid. 185.   [46] Roche, 'The Founding Fathers', 459.
[47] Cunliffe, *American Presidents*, 20, 22.

To come into force the draft Constitution had to be ratified by at least nine states, and once it was published it met strenuous resistance from the 'anti-Federalists'. Their most effective argument was that the Constitution lacked a Bill of Rights and they began to demand a second Convention. Although the tally of nine was reached, giving the Constitution the force of law, New York and Virginia withheld assent and without them the new federation would be reduced to a fiction. It was to try to win over the New Yorkers that the *Federalist Papers* were written, but in vain. Finally the 'Federalists', and notably Madison, decided for tactical reasons to give in to the demand for amendment. When the First Congress under the new Constitution met in 1789 Madison set out to formulate the 'Bill of Rights' in the form of amendments. No less that 186 were proposed which Madison reduced by collation to eighty, and then to nineteen. There he left it. But as the amendments made their way through Congress the Senate stepped in and further reduced the number, to ten. These are the famous first Ten Amendments that make up the Bill of Rights.

5.4. *The 1789 Constitution*

Everybody has commented on the elegant style and the conciseness and brevity of the Constitution. Napoleon observed that 'Constitutions should be short and obscure'. This American Constitution bore him out, for some of the major issues had been ducked. What was the qualification for voters? Was not the concept of citizenship ambiguous? Were not some matters overlooked such as, for instance, that scope of the Supreme Court's competence to rule on Congressional Acts? These and a small host of other issues, starting with the meaning of the Constitution's very opening phrase (in the Preamble): 'We, the people of the United States, in order to form a more perfect Union', and so on—what exactly are 'the people'? The variety of issues raised by the words of the Constitution can be gleaned by even the most cursory glance at Corwin's *The Constitution and What it Means Today*, and even this is but a digest of the far more numerous cases that have come up in interpreting the Constitution.

Nor must we see the Constitution of 1789 through the eyes of today, after two centuries of modification by laws, amendments, and usages. It must be remembered that the Senate of those days had a membership of twenty-six and was indirectly elected (as indeed the Presidency was supposed to be), and that the jurisdiction of the Supreme Court was not defined as it was to be after the *Marbury* v. *Madison* case of 1803. Very soon, indeed, usage and convention modified this model. When Washington sought the Supreme Court's advice on the constitutionality of the Neutrality Declaration of

1793, the Court replied that it was not its function to tender advice. Likewise Washington consulted the Senate, which to many contemporaries and possibly to himself must have looked like a Governor's Council of the pre-revolutionary days; but they had no intention of playing such a role. Embarrassed, they muttered they would rather make up their own minds on the matter and from that moment on both sides kept their distance. Both precedents strengthened the principle that the three powers were distinct and independent. How they would work together was anyone's guess. Today we can see that this spatchcocked miscellany of structures and responsibilities proved workable, flexible, and durable. Apart from the immemorial British constitution, this is the oldest constitution in the world, and to have survived almost unchanged across the span of two centuries is a tribute to its adaptability and its almost reverential status among the citizenry.

6. SIX GREAT INVENTIONS IN THE ART OF GOVERNMENT

6.1. *Inventions: A Recapitulation*

Let me briefly recall what I mean by an 'invention'. Some practices in government originated in and have been transmitted from antecedent societies. To rate as an 'invention' it is not enough that it be the first attestation of the practice: the 'invention' is not only an innovation that is transmitted, materially or ideationally, to other societies but is one which comes into general use thereafter. In other words, some first attestations of an innovation are also the last such attestations: they are not 'inventions' because they are 'one-off'. They have no progeny.

Often similar practices spring up at times and places independent of the first attested one. The Mandarinate bureaucracy was a Chinese invention; something very much like it was introduced in Great Britain in the nineteenth century—but there was no direct copying from the Chinese model. So that we have to talk not only of inventions but of re-inventions.

Finally I have selected what I deem the 'inventions' because these are the ones that related to the formation of the 'modern state'. This has now become the global unit of government. The fact that a good many of the later inventions we list in this *History* are of European origin is purely coincidental: there are some 200 independent states in the world at the time of writing (more are being created every year) and all have taken the European state as the model. It is now the global state-form.

The nascent United States advanced the model with six inventions, innovations that have won world-wide acceptance. It is true that the great majority of states honour these innovations in the breach rather than in the observance: but their acceptance that this is how things are supposed to be (though they will not let them be) must be seen as the tribute that, like hypocrisy, vice pays to virtue.

The six inventions the United States introduced into the theory and practice of government were, respectively: the notion of a Constitutional Convention (or Constituent Assembly) to frame a constitution; the written constitution; the Bill of Rights which, *inter alia*, this constitution embodies; the use of the courts of law or specially constituted tribunals to signal breaches of the constitution and exercise powers to obstruct or cancel them; the so-called Separation of Powers on different lines from the 'mixed' constitutions of the past; and, finally, true Federalism.

6.2. *The Constitutional Convention*

This device has been called 'legalizing revolution'. It is also bound up with the second invention, which follows, namely, that of a constitution as supreme law governing and constraining the government's actions, or, to put it another way, recognizing two levels of law, one transcendent and the other subordinate.

Though the general idea was familiar enough to Americans it did not mature till the 1780s. In nine of the ten states that gave themselves new constitutions after the Declaration of Independence, the new constitution was drafted and proclaimed by the state legislature. A constitutional Convention was indeed called in Pennsylvania but it was also the legislating body for ordinary business. (In the three other states the colonial charters remained the basis of government). Now it is true that six of the state legislatures did not draw up their constitutions until they had solicited authority to do so from the voters, and that in two cases there was some measure of popular ratification. The fact remains that these constitutions were the creations of the ordinary legislatures and what the legislature could do it presumably could also undo. Thus the New Jersey legislature in 1777 unilaterally altered the constitution, changing its wording. In Georgia the legislature three times 'explained' parts of the constitution. In South Carolina the legislature became notorious for its 'repeated irregularities' and suspensions of the constitution.[48]

But how—should this course be deemed necessary—new-frame the Confederation of the entire thirteen independent states? How had constitutions emerged in the past? Some had been imposed by outside powers or granted—like charters—by the paramount authority, or simply assumed by

[48] Wood, *Creation of the American Republic*, 274.–5.

the already existing 'constituted bodies'. None of this was of any use to the now independent colonists. They were faced with a *tabula rasa*.

The entire course of the Revolution had been premissed on the view that authority flowed from the people. It was the people, then, which alone could 'constitute' new government. As the people obviously could not all gather together at one place it could only proceed through representatives. Together they formed the Convention and it was such a body—representing the people, let us repeat—that drafted the constitution. This constitution was held to have created the powers of government, the division of authority between its various parts, and the mechanisms and processes by which these were to act together. The next step was to write it down (see below) and, in theory at any rate, get it ratified by the people, its ultimate source. This done, the constitution went into effect and thereafter the government had to work within the bounds that it had delimited. Its work done, the Convention dissolved and a government took its place. The people, having acted as constituent, gave way to citizens who came under the government's authority. The constitution could indeed be changed, but only by a new Convention or a similar popularly based amendment process.

The novelty did not lie in the fact that the Convention was based on the recognized authority of the people. There was nothing new in popular government of one sort or another. The Forum-type polity, the republic, had been invented long ago—but not the Convention way of creating a new constitutional structure. That was the innovation, and in this case the 'invention'. It is no accident that in 1792 the French elected what they called the Convention when set to change their constitution. Since that time the more usual term has been a Constituent Assembly, but it amounts to the same thing: a body that represents the people (or at least purports to) assembles and drafts a constitution, and when this has been done and duly ratified by the people, dissolves itself, leaving government to the institutions that it has laid down.

6.3. *The Written Constitution*

Up to this date the constitutions of Europe were uncodified collections of traditional customs, conventions, and statutes or proclamations of former times. These used to be called 'unwritten constitutions'. The 'written' constitution was taken to signify 'works of conscious art, that is to say, they are the result on the part of the State to lay down once for all a body of coherent provisions under which its government shall be established and conducted'.[49] As far as I can determine the first written, that is, 'codified' constitution in Europe was the one imposed by Gustavus III of Sweden in 1772.[50] In America the new constitutions of the states were certainly written, but drawn up as we have seen by the legislatures. The first attestation of a written constitution drawn up by some form of Convention or Constituent Assembly representing the people is the 1787 Constitution of the United States.

The idea of codified rules for government was not unfamiliar to Americans. They were conversant with Magna Carta, with the Puritan Instrument of Government of 1653, with their own 'Mayflower Pact', and of course the Royal Charters which had been the constitutions of the individual colonies.

As the alternative to the Articles of Confederation was hammered out at the Philadelphia Convention, so it had to be written down. Thus emerged the Written Constitution: so widely adopted that only three countries of the modern world do not have one—Britain, of course, New Zealand, and Israel. These three states have their own arrangements but for purely idiosyncratic reasons their 'organic laws' are not fully codified written constitutions.

The written constitution was an invention in two different respects. The first is that it provides a yardstick against which citizens can gauge their rights and responsibilities. The logic of this is nowhere more concisely expressed than in the Preamble to the French 'Declaration of the Rights Of Man and the Citizen' of 1789. These rights are written down, it says, 'So that this declaration, perpetually present to all members of the body social, shall be a constant reminder to them of their rights and duties', and, 'So that, since it will be possible at any moment to compare the acts of the legislative authority and those of the executive authority with the final end of all political institutions, those acts shall thereby be the more respected.'[51]

The second aspect links with the invention of the Convention, that is, fear of legislative interference with the constitution. Referring to England, one writer proclaimed that the liberties of the people could not be allowed to depend 'upon nothing more permanent or established than the vague, rapacious, or interested inclination of a majority of five hundred and fifty-eight men, open to the insidious attacks of a weak or designing Prince, and his ministers'.[52] Instead, the Americans began to define a constitution as

[49] J. Bryce, *Constitutions* (OUP, New York and London, 1905), 6.
[50] See above, Bk. IV, Ch. 8, p. 1445.
[51] 'The Declaration of the Rights of Man and the Citizen, 1789', trans. and repr. in S. E. Finer, *Five Constitutions* (Penguin, Harmondsworth, 1979), 269.
[52] Wood, *Creation of the American Republic*, 266.

something 'distinct from and superior to the entire government including the representatives of the people'.[53] This implied a distinction between fundamental and statutory law, the former governing the latter. This notion too has been taken up, piecemeal, throughout the entire world and is today implicit in the definition of a constitution. It is a restraining device, a guaranteeing one. The full flavour of the word does not come out in the term 'constitution', which is indeed an odd one, seeing that 'constitutions' were in the Roman Empire ordinances of the emperor. It does come out strongly, however, if we remember the German term; it is the *Grundgesetz*, the fundamental law. Likewise in the former Soviet Union the written document was called 'Constitution (Fundamental Law)'.

The written constitution, interpreted as the higher or fundamental law controlling the institutions of government, is the second of the great American inventions in government.

6.4. *The Bill of Rights*

Here was another and most influential invention but which was not pre-conceived at all in the Philadelphia Convention. There were models for Bills of Rights in some of the new state constitutions, notably Virginia's, but they were not germane to the new national constitution since the states were not shy to alter their constitutions at will. But the 'Bill of Rights' embodied in the Constitution as part of the supreme law of the land emerged in the course of the hurly-burly over ratification between the Federalists and the anti-Federalists which we have already mentioned. 'Where', asked the latter, 'is the barrier drawn between the government and the rights of citizens, as secured in our own state government?' It was necessary to 'reserve to the people such of their essential rights, as are not necessary to be parted with'.[54] For their part the Federalists argued that, since the Constitution enumerated the specific powers of the national government, it followed that every other power was reserved to the people.[55]

As I count them there are nineteen Articles, Sections, or clauses that enshrine specific rights—nine embodied in the original text and ten in the form of amendments. Their common characteristic is that they all relate, one way or another, to 'civil' rights as against what today we would call social rights. They relate, for instance, to due process of law, the rights of the accused, jury trial, habeas corpus—all well established in Britain—along with others, such as the right to bear arms, the right not to testify against oneself, the freedom of conscience and religion, and the prohibition of

---

[53] Ibid.   [54] Ibid. 356–7.   [55] Ibid. 536–43.

censorship, that are more or less indigenously America. The British provenance, however, is unmistakable. These were the rights of Englishmen,
defined and expanded.

Furthermore these rights must be construed in the light of two of the
first ten Amendments to the Constitution (that is, of the 'Bill of Rights' of
1791). Amendment IX says that the enumeration of certain rights in the
Constitution should not be construed to 'deny or disparage' others retained
by the people. Amendment X is the famous one that runs: 'The powers not
delegated to the United States by the constitution nor prohibited by it to
the States, are reserved to the States respectively, or the people.' To put this
positively, the Constitution grants powers to the Federation, it leaves the
residuum to the states, and in some cases it allows both Federation and
states to carry out similar acts of government (for instance, levying taxes).
But certain powers are denied both to the national government and the
states as well. These are the individual rights conceded in the Constitution
and its amendments. They are entrenched rights. If the national government
wishes to interfere with such rights it would have to change the Constitution itself—a laborious and long-drawn-out process. In this sense, the
Constitution follows the tradition of John Locke's 'Civil Government'. It
draws a ring-fence around individuals which no government can touch.

This concept came to be adopted all but universally. (The chief exceptions apart from outright dictatorships are some of the so-called 'Old
Commonwealth' countries which follow the British tradition of the courts
following the common law as amended by statute.) In European states in
particular, in the aftermath of the French Revolution, it became *de rigueur* to
embody similar 'bills of rights' in the constitutions they began to adopt. In
almost every case (the exceptions were very temporary constitutions like the
Spanish of 1812 or the Polish of 1921), bills of rights preceded the grant of
universal suffrage. Austria for instance laid down a bill of rights in 1867 but
did not grant universal male suffrage till 1907. In Belgium the respective
dates were 1831 and 1891–2.[56]

Like the American rights, these were for the most part civil rights. The
great change came as far as I can see in the constitutions of Mexico (1917),
the Soviet Union (1918), and Weimar (1918): these constitutions enshrined
not only civil rights but social ones such as the right to education, social
security, and the like. This was to become the common pattern in practically all of the succession states to the European empires between 1918 and
1960 and thereafter.

---

[56] For a more complete list, see S. E. Finer, 'Notes towards a History of Constitutions', in V.
Bogdanor (ed.), *Constitutions in Democratic Politics* (Gower, Aldershot, 1988), 27–8.

In the latter category of states these rights are simply not honoured, and that raises the fourth great invention of the American Revolution: to ensure some way of signalling any infringement of the constitution and—here was the rub—imposing sanctions on the government if it did not make good. In the American case this was secured by 'judicial review'. But the pre-condition was a court that was independent of the executive and of the legislature. It is necessary, therefore, to come to 'judicial review' by first discussing the fourth great invention: separation of powers by *functions*.

6.5. *The Separation of Powers*

The use of checks and balances is certainly not an American invention, as our explorations of the Roman Republic and the Italian city-states have shown. Two of the sub-varieties of 'checks and balances' were especially prominent in eighteenth-century thought: the notion of the 'separation of powers' and the notion of a 'mixed constitution'. For quite some time the American publicists tended to muddle the two.

Conversant as they were with the British constitution, the Americans took its threefold division into an executive, a legislature, and a judiciary for granted. In their eyes the great virtue of the British constitution did not lie in that, but in the fact that it was *mixed*. This is a doctrine that goes right back to Polybius, the historian of the Roman Republic.[57]

Now the notion of the mixed constitution is sociological. In the British case the mixture was composed of the monarchy, the peers representing the aristocracy, and the commons representatives of the people. Each of their three organs—monarchy, House of Lords, and House of Commons—possessed powers to check the others.

The American invention consisted in substituting for these sociological categories organs or branches of government—the familiar executive and bicameral legislature—distinguished from one another by virtue of the *functions* they performed. The chief executive commanded the armed forces, made peace or war, and carried on the administration: these were the 'functions'—and the inherent nature—of the executive power. The bicameral legislature made laws—the legislative function. And the judiciary adjudged between rival claimants.

It is widely believed (because it appears in the *Federalist*) that this doctrine is due to the 'celebrated Montesquieu'. But Roche maintains that the

[57] It has been followed in painstaking (if not breathtaking) detail in J. G. A. Pocock, *The Machiavellian Moment* (Princeton UP, Princeton, 1975). An admirable work on the topic is M. J. C. Vile, *Constitutionalism and the Separation of Powers* (Clarendon Press, Oxford, 1967).

Convention 'did not propound a defence of the 'separation of powers' on anything resembling a theoretical basis' and that 'the merits of Montesquieu did not turn up until *The Federalist*.[58]

The essence of Montesquieu's famous analysis of the British constitution[59] is this. After defining—or rather illustrating—what pertained to the executive power and the legislative power and the judiciary, he concluded that: 'All would be lost if the same man or body of dignitaries or nobles or commoners exercise these three powers: that of making laws, executing the public will, and judging the crimes and differences of private persons.' They must therefore be *separated*, that is, exercised by different individuals in such a way as to act as checks and balances upon one another. True, 'these three powers might fall into repose or inactivity. But since they are forced to move by the necessary movement of affairs, they will be forced to act *together*.'

In Montesquieu's formula the joker is the word 'power'. In French it is *pouvoir*. But this translates best as 'government', as in *l'homme contre le pouvoir*— man against the government, against the state. Power in the sense of 'might' would translate as *puissance*. Montesquieu was implying that each of these three organs or authorities performed its own peculiar function. In fact a governmental activity does not dictate what department or organ should undertake it, but the other way round: the nature of the department or organ dictates the nature of the function it is performing. Whether a tomato is a fruit or a vegetable may be answered by a department including it in a schedule of fruits or by a court of law in a verdict, or by the legislature passing a law on the matter. In its endeavour to prevent one branch of government from encroaching on another the Supreme Court of the United States has spent many hours deciding whether or not an activity can be properly regarded as a matter for the executive, legislative, or the judiciary.

Such metaphysical considerations did not concern the Convention delegates. Their preoccupation was how to prevent the national legislature they were establishing from swallowing up the other two branches of government just as the state legislatures were doing. They did not arrive at this by meditating on Montesquieu. The Separation of Powers came about in the way already described: by the novel mode of electing the president via the Electoral College, thus rendering him independent of the Congress and making the judges to a large extent independent too. In this almost unpremeditated fashion three mutually independent branches of government had been constructed.

---

[58] Roche, 'The Founding Fathers', 457.

[59] Montesquieu, *The Spirit of the Laws* (1748), bk. xi, ch. 6, 'On the Constitution of England'.

That mutual independence was reinforced by Article I. vi. 2 which effectively precludes holders of offices of profit under the Presidency from sitting in Congress. This made the separation between legislature and executive absolute. It was a deliberate reaction from the British practice where ministers could and did sit in the legislature. It was this provision that made a Cabinet system impossible in the United States and created the 'solitary' or isolated Presidency, with the White House at one end of Pennsylvania Avenue and the Congress at the other.

But these three powers, though independent, strayed from the Montesquieu formula in so far as that assumed each would exercise its own peculiar 'function' and none other. On the way to the consummation of 6 September the Presidency had picked up the right to veto bills of the legislature and the latter in turn was empowered to override such vetoes by a two-thirds majority in both Chambers. The president nominated to high posts but only with the advice and consent of the Senate, and this applied, it should be noted, to the nomination of judges to the Supreme Court. Similarly the president made treaties but, again, by and with the consent of the Senate. The House of Representatives could impeach the president but it was the Senate which acted as the court which tried him. Furthermore, the two Chambers were divided against themselves. Neither could override the other. To be sure, money bills had to emanate from the House of Representatives but this did not preclude the Senate from amending them.

The Federalist, I must repeat, was propaganda. Its authors had no choice but to defend every jot and tittle of the draft Constitution. How was Madison to rationalize these overlaps between the functions of the three powers?

The first point to notice is that Madison conceded that the powers of the executive, legislative, and judicial branches differed *ratione materiae*: 'The several classes of power, as they may in their nature be legislative, executive or judiciary'.[60] How to get over the difficulty, then?[61] Madison did not allege (as most people have) that Montesquieu misunderstood the British constitution. On the contrary, he thought his analysis and description quite correct. But the British constitution did co-mingle the executive and legislative functions. It must follow, then, that such co-mingling did not contradict his theory that the three Powers must be separated. He widened this argument to show that, in any case, most state constitutions (Virginia's in particular) laid down the Separation of Powers but in practice followed the overlapping of the functions of any one with that of the others.[62]

At this point the argument takes an entirely different twist which one can

---

[60] *The Federalist Papers*, no. 48 (Madison). [61] Ibid., no. 47 (Madison).
[62] Ibid., and no. 48 (Madison).

only describe as audacious. Not only does the theory not require that the three branches should not be 'wholly unconnected' with one another, but they positively ought to be connected. They must be 'so far connected and blended as to give to each [branch] a constitutional control over the others'.[63] 'A mere demarcation on parchment' will not do the trick. Nor would appeals to the people, in a Convention or otherwise, provide a satisfactory sanction against breaches of the principle.[64] Then follows the celebrated passage: 'The great security against a gradual concentration of the several powers in the same department consists in giving to those who administer each department the necessary means and personal motives to resist encroachments of the others. Ambition must be made to counteract ambition. The interest of the man must be connected with the constitutional rights of the place.' 'It may be a reflection', he added, 'on human nature that such devices should be necessary to control the abuses of government. But what is government itself but the greatest of all reflections on human nature?'[65]

This was very prescient indeed. This is just how matters have worked out in the United States. But although all governments stand today by the Separation of Powers they do not observe it in the extreme American form: they have an umbilical link, the Cabinet, between the executive and legislative branches. It has to be admitted that the very success of making the three mutually independent departments 'their own appointed limits keep' has been dysfunctional. Montesquieu had presaged that 'the three powers might fall into repose or inactivity. But since they are forced to move by the necessary movement of affairs they will be forced to move together.' Whatever the disagreements on policy, in the last resort basic administration must go on. With three departments blocking one another, however, it is not surprising that 'American government' should be characterized as a 'thing of fits and starts'.

6.6. *Judicial Review*

For all their talk about the 'three powers', the Americans were perfunctory about the judiciary. The pre-independence colonists did not like the courts overmuch. Some disliked them because they regarded their verdicts as too often 'a confused mixture of private powers and popular error and every court assumed the power of legislation'.[66] Such people feared judicial independence and judicial discretion. Others, however, saw the courts as

[63] *The Federalist Papers*, no. 48 (Madison).   [64] Ibid., no. 48 (Madison).
[65] Ibid., no. 51 (Madison).   [66] Wood, *Creation of the American Republic*, 298.

simply an adjunct, an inferior branch, of the executive. The judges were magistrates and the mood of 1776 was to supersede or at least control all magistrates by the panacea of popular government as expressed in their state legislatures. The disillusioned 1780s reacted strongly against the irresponsible state legislatures, not least because they had engrossed powers more proper to the judiciary. Finally there were some who used the courts as a weapon against the British Parliament by relying on Chief Justice Coke's dictum in the Bonham Case, 1610, that 'when an act of Parliament is against common right and reason . . . the common law will control it and adjudge such a law to be void'.[67] In a few isolated cases in the 1780s state judges were applying this view to statutes of their legislature.[68] But such practices were very uncommon—they were thought (correctly) to run counter to the great Blackstone doctrine of the absolute sovereignty of the Crown-in-Parliament. But this notion that 'Will and Law were not synonymous in a free state' resurfaced once the Constitution was recognized as the supreme law of the land: did this not mean that all acts of government were but secondary ones and were controlled by it? For all that, the Convention devoted only one day to judicial review, and since nobody raised the question of whether it extended to review federal statutes, the records throw no light upon this issue.[69] Moreover, once the main lines of the Constitution were settled, its Article III (the judiciary article) was short, obscure, and perfunctory.

There is still enormous controversy as to quite what Article III means and/or what the Founding Fathers wanted it to mean. In view of the fact that only one day of the Convention was devoted to the judiciary and that this did not mention judicial review of federal statutes, the Fathers' intentions must remain, to say the least, moot. When one examines the text of the Constitution itself, again doubts are raised. Article VI states that: 'This Constitution and the laws of the United States which shall be made in pursuance hereof . . . shall be the Supreme Law of the Land.' In Article III. 2 it says that within certain limited exceptions, 'in all the other Cases before mentioned the Supreme Court shall have appellate jurisdiction'. There is no doubt that this confers on the Supreme Court the authority to strike down decisions and actions taken by the *states'* authorities. It is silent on whether it applies to a *federal* statute.

In 1778 Jefferson was arguing strenuously that to allow 'Judges to set aside the law makes the Judiciary Department paramount in fact to the Legislature which was never intended and can never be proper'.[70] Hamilton

---

[67] E. S. Corwin, *The Constitution and What it Means Today* (Princeton UP, Princeton, 1978), 221–2.
[68] Wood, *Creation of the American Republic*, 455. Corwin, *Constitution*, 221–2.
[69] Roche, 'The Founding Fathers', 462, n. 64.   [70] Wood, *Creation of the American Republic*, 304.

had taken the opposite view,[71] and it is to him that we owe the eloquent eulogy of judicial review in no. 78 of the *Federalist*. And here is to be found the unequivocal statement: 'whenever a particular statute contravenes the Constitution, it will be the duty of the judicial tribunals to adhere to the latter and disregard the former.'

In fact the issue was not decided by arguments, but by a judicial *coup de main*. Congress had passed a Judiciary Act in 1798. *Inter alia*, this empowered the Supreme Court to issue writs of mandamus. Marbury was an individual who had been promised a lesser federal judgeship but had been refused it. In 1803 Marbury, relying on the Judiciary Act, 1798, appealed to the Supreme Court for a writ of mandamus to force Madison (the seceretary of state) to grant him the commission. The chief justice (Marshall) expressed no doubt that in right and in law Marbury was entitled to the commission. *But*, the Supreme Court was not empowered to grant writs of mandamus. The Court had scrutinized the section in the Judiciary Act that dealt with mandamus and had found it *unconstitutional and therefore void*. That decision was never contested. The full range of judicial supremacy over the interpretation of the Constitution and the consequent sanction of declaring a statute null and void was a *fait accompli*.

Particularly since the Second World War and as a result of American military occupation, this doctrine of a court which can rule on the constitutionality or otherwise of an Act or statute and (usually) set it aside, so compelling the government either to withdraw it or to take steps to alter the constitution, has been widely copied. The signal difference is that in a few of the cases, Ireland being one of the exceptions, the constitutional court is not the Supreme Court of the ordinary courts of the state but a specially appointed body. In Germany, Austria, Italy, and Japan, for instance, candidates for membership must be legally qualified, but they are appointed or elected in various different ways, usually involving the legislature, as in Germany where the two Houses of the parliament each have the right to nominate to the court.

6.7. *Recapitulation of the Structure of the National Government*

Let us briefly recapitulate the nature of the American national government. It consists of three great branches, the executive, the legislature, and the judiciary. The executive is appointed, nominally via the Electoral College but in fact by popular voting in the fifty states, each of which has its individual quota of votes (based mainly on population). The president thus

---

[71] Wood, *Creation of the American Republic*, 454.

elected holds his office for four years and is re-eligible, but for no more than one extra term. He can be impeached by the legislature with the Senate acting as the trial court but he cannot otherwise be removed nor his constitutional powers shorn or amended by the legislature. This—the Congress—consists of the Senate and House of Representatives, with equal powers so that neither can overrule the other, the concession to the House of Representatives being only that it alone can initiate money bills. Both these two Houses are elected—but for different terms and by different constituencies. Each state has two senators who sit for a six-year term, one-third retiring each year. The House of Representatives is elected through nation-wide electoral districts every two years. In this way both Chambers are completely independent of one another.

The president cannot enact any law. Only the Congress can do so. The president can veto a Bill of Congress. The Congress can override the veto by a two-thirds majority in each Chamber. The president has no access to finance—except what the Congress allows him. The president makes treaties, but with the advice and consent of the Senate, and makes senior appointments under a similar condition. The judges of the Supreme Court are among the senior appointments where the president's nominations require the advice and consent of the Senate. Once appointed they are guaranteed security of tenure. They interpret the Constitution and in the event of finding any statute unconstitutional they thereby make it null and void.

The Constitution, the supreme law of the land, contains, *inter alia*, a number (I count nineteen) of specific rights. These are forbidden to both the federal government and the states. The only way to alter or rescind such rights is by amending the Constitution. This is a long and arduous process, beginning with the adoption of the necessary resolution by two-thirds majority in each Chamber of Congress (or alternatively by two-thirds of the state legislatures, which is then subject to the ratification by Conventions or the legislatures in three-quarters of the states).

Here, then, we have in their connected form the governmental inventions of the United States: to recapitulate, the constitutional convention, the separation of powers, the written constitution and its status as supreme law of the land, judicial review of the constitution by the highest court of the judicial system and its consequent delimitation of metes and bounds to all statutes including those coming under the Bill of Rights and those, whether of the states or the federal government, which involve the division of powers between the two. This 'division of powers' under American federalism is not something we have so far dealt with.

6.8. *Federalism*

'Federalism' is perhaps the most striking of all the American inventions in government. At the time of the Convention the term did not even have a fixed meaning: today the term 'federalism' attaches only to the general form of compound government that was set up by the 1787 Constitution. A Confederation is a league of independent sovereign states which run their own affairs through their own officers, and, in so far as they desire common institutions or actions, arrive at these by delegating the appropriate power upwards to the confederal council, however that may be composed; while for its part this council can do nothing (e.g. raising taxes or an army) except via the institutions of the member states. Madison and Hamilton devoted several interesting pages to examining such leagues, from the Greek Amphyctionic Council to the States-General of the Netherlands.[72] By contrast, the federation pioneered by the Americans divided the spectrum of governmental powers between two tiers of authorities: the 'national' government and the individual state governments, both of which acted directly on the people. The governments, whether the national one or the state governments, were juridically equal. And each government, state or national, was precluded from passing legislation that would have prevented the other carrying out its constitutional responsibilities. In the American case, the powers of the national—I shall call it the federal—government were enumerated. All residual powers were 'reserved to the States respectively or to the People'.[73]

Federalism of this nature was held to be a bold innovation of Madison's. Maybe—but this notion sits ill with Madison's previous record as one of the fiercest and thoroughgoing exponents of the supremacy of the 'national' government and the exiguous and subordinate status of the states.[74] In 1787 he had claimed that the national government should be supreme and that the states should exist 'only in so far as they can be subordinately useful'.[75] Most other delegates were haunted by the shade of Blackstone and the century-and-a-half's experience of legislative sovereignty: anything else was impossible. 'I never heard of two co-ordinate powers in one and the same country before', exclaimed Grayson. Sam Adams intoned that an '*Imperium in Imperio* . . . [is a] solecism in politics'.[76]

---

[72] *The Federalist Papers*, nos. 18, 19, 20.

[73] The US Constitution, Art. X. The point here is that the Bill of Rights and other provisions in the Constitution forbid a range of powers to be exercised by the national and the state governments as well. That situation could only be put right by a constitutional amendment.

[74] Roche, 'The Founding Fathers', 447.   [75] Wood, *Creation of the American Republic*, 525.

[76] Ibid., for other examples of this sentiment.

The truth of the matter was that, as Wood observes, 'Few had actually conceived of [it] in full before the Constitution was written and debated.'[77] But bit by bit the components of such a federal state had been accumulating throughout the Convention. The critical moment was when Paterson, the author of the rejected New Jersey plan, 'made clear his view that under either the Virginia or the New Jersey systems, the general government would . . . act on individuals and not on states'. This was anathema to the states-rights faction for whom the cardinal doctrine was that the federal government's constituents were the states and not the people. But he continued to resist the 'consolidators' cavalier proposition to override the states and to regard them as so many mere municipal assembles. So, he continued, 'But it is said that this national government is to act on individuals and not on states; and cannot a federal [*scilicet* a 'confederal'] government be so framed as to operate in the same way? It surely may.'[78] The moment this position had been agreed, true federalism was born. This core premiss endowed the constitution with a profound originality. It had squared the circle: how to make two sovereignties abide in the same body politic.

Other matters followed. The states *qua* states received equal representation in the Senate—so that they were intimately connected with legislation, treaty-making, and senior appointments. The federal government had lost its right to veto state statutes. It had received enumerated and not general powers, and the residuum of powers was left to the states. Add all these together and it is not hard to construct the scenario for a federal government which would satisfy both the states and the federal government and keep them in equipoise—particularly with a Supreme Court to monitor whether one had encroached on the prerogatives of the other. So, when they undertook to persuade the New Yorkers to ratify the Constitution, Madison and Hamilton were left with no choice but to defend the entire package—much as it fell far short of their original plans for a 'consolidated' government. Madison conducted the defence brilliantly: first conceding that in this, that, and other respects the Constitution was indeed 'national' or consolidated, then turning round and saying that in other respects it was what he called 'federal' meaning what we would call confederal. He concluded that the proposed constitution was 'neither a national nor a federal [*scilicet* confederal] one, but a composition of both'.

As I remarked it is from this date that the distinction between 'federal' and 'confederal', between the *Staatenbund* and the *Bundestaat*, appeared, and it

---

[77] Ibid. 525.

[78] These passages are from Farrand's *Records of the Federal Convention*, vol. I, as quoted in Roche, 'The Founding Fathers', 451.

has had an enormous influence, not only in Europe but throughout the world. India has espoused its brand of federalism, so has Malaysia, so have Australia and Canada, so has Germany, to name but a sample. It is open to all states to conduct their affairs as a federation: the hard thing is for the federation to keep itself together. The number of failed federations is much greater than the number of successful ones. The United States itself teetered on the brink of destruction during the War for the Union in 1861–5. Others, such as the USSR or Yugoslavia, have simply broken down in turmoil of civil unrest or outright war.

Here, then, we complete our account of the major inventions of the American Revolution. It is a most intricate cat's cradle of self-defeating powers: divided three ways at the federal level, then divided geographically between this level and the fifty state governments, which themselves are also divided three ways on the model of the federal government. In practice, the internal checks and balances are even more numerous, for instance (the examples are illustrative, not exhaustive), the bicameralism of the federal Congress, its fragmentation into many powerful functional committees, the extensive use of the referendum at state level. This is the most legalistic constitution in the entire world. In theory it should never have worked, nor should it work today. *Eppure si muove.*

It has provided an armoury of governmental techniques, one or more of which have been taken up by most countries in the world; it has shown how political power may be bridled; and it has stood for two centuries as the ultimate exercise in law-boundedness. This is a formidable achievement and it has carried forward the concept of the modern state into what I think, in the light of the following chapters, we can call its penultimate phase.

3

The Legacy of the French Revolution

*T*he French Revolution is the most important single event in the entire history of government. The American Revolution pales beside it. It was an earthquake. It razed and effaced all the ancient institutions of France, undermined the foundations of the other European states, and is still sending its shock-waves throughout the rest of the world.

In the eyes of its admirers it is an epic, a drama of heroic proportions, full of colour and passion. To others it is a murderous catalogue of bloody insurrection, hysterical mob violence, sadism, judicial murder, and wholesale massacres.

Its sheer destructiveness—compared with the American Revolution—is easy to understand. The American Revolution responded to purely American conditions and these involved little more than fitting out existing viable governments endowed with representative institutions with a new super-structure. This course was not available to the French would-be reformers. The net of privilege, the geographical incongruities in matters of taxation, laws, and local administrations, the hierarchical structure of society, and the presence within it of the First (clerical) Order and the Second (Noble) Order had to be swept away completely before new institutions could be created. American conditions allowed its revolution to stop short at effecting a mere change of rulers. In France it was needful to destroy a whole system such as was common to the rest of continental Europe.

It gave the term 'revolution' a new connotation. In the *Encyclopédie* Diderot had defined this as 'politically speaking, a considerable change that has occurred in the governance of a state'. For later generations and our own a new age began with the American revolution, but this is not how the colonists themselves had seen it. They claimed to be going back to the old, and rightful basis of government. In fact 'revolution' was rarely applied to the War of Independence. The term seems first to have been used by Tom Paine (1783) and Richard Price (1784).[1] But with the French Revolution the idea acquired overtones: a change in government associated with a recasting of the old social order; a new stage in world history (as Condorcet

---

[1] F. Gilbert, 'Revolution', in P. P. Weinder (ed.), *Dictionary of the History of Ideas*, vol. IV (Scribner, New York, 1973–4), 155.

saw it);[2] the characteristic of extreme violence associated with a period of total extra-constitutionality, as in the Convention and the Terror, and the claim that thenceforth the 'Government of France is revolutionary until the peace'.[3]

The very scope of this revolution was unparalleled and, indeed, nothing on its scale occurred again until the Russian Revolution of 1917. It went dramatically further than elsewhere: more radical, more protracted, and extending to classes that the American Revolution had largely left untouched. Condorcet perceived this even in 1794 when he compared it with the American Revolution:

Because the revolution in France was more far-reaching than the American it was much more violent: for the Americans, who were content with the civil and criminal code that they had received from England; who had no vicious system of taxation to reform; and no feudal tyrannies, no hereditary distinctions, no rich, powerful and privileged corporations, no system of religious intolerance to destroy, limited themselves to establishing a new authority in place of that which had been exercised up till then by the British. None of these innovations affected the ordinary people or changed the relations between individuals. In France, on the contrary, the revolution was to embrace the entire economy of society, change every social relation and find its way down to the furthest links of the political chain, even down to those individuals who, living in peace on their private fortune or on the fruits of their labour, had no reason to participate in public affairs—neither opinion nor occupation nor the pursuit of wealth, power, or fame.

The Americans, who gave the impression that they were fighting only against the tyrannical prejudices of the mother country, had the rivals of England for their allies . . . the whole of Europe was united against the oppressor. The French on the contrary, attacked at once the despotism of kings, the political inequality of many constitutions only partly free, the pride of the nobility, the domination, intoler-ance, and wealth of the priesthood, and the abuses of the feudal system, all of which are still rampant in most of Europe, so that the European powers inevitably united on the side of tyranny . . .[4]

'The Revolution' (I have written elsewhere):

was a break with the entire daily pattern of former existence . . . In a few short months the old seven-day week is abolished and 'decades' substituted . . . the familiar names of the months are changed, the customary units of weight, height, distance are all altered to a completely novel system . . . all the ancient provincial boundaries and their proverbial names are abolished and the whole country is re-districted into new units bearing the names of some geographical feature—rivers,

[2] Marie-Jean-Antoine-Nicolas de Caritat, Marquis de Condorcet, *Sketch for a Historical Picture of the Progress of the Human Mind*, ed. S. Hampshire (London, 1955).
[3] Gilbert, 'Revolution', 157–8.   [4] Condorcet, *Sketch for a Historical Picture*, 147–7.

mountains etc. . . . the state religion is not merely disestablished but actively persecuted and its temples turned over to a variety of novel and often bizarre cults. Very few revolutions seek to reach into the humdrum routines of ordinary existence. The Great Revolution did. It was not remote from the popular folk; it reached into the most trivial details of their lives. The Revolution convulsed the entire society.[5]

It is not for nothing that the French history syllabus divides into Modern History up to 1789, and Contemporary History from 1814. The Revolution legitimized—or undermined—many hitherto cherished hopes and beliefs. It represents the intersection of the Enlightenment, the Messianic, and the revolutionary, and the result was that it irreversibly changed what Mosca called 'the political formula', that is, the principle or belief about government that makes the people regard it as duty-worthy. From then on election by the people became the touchstone of legitimacy. Slow to prevail in middle Europe—perhaps we might say not until a century, even a century-and-a-half later—it came nevertheless. Meanwhile, from Europe this formula began to irradiate the entire world—Latin America, Asia, and then Africa. The new succession states of the great European empires, including the Russian, are all based on this political formula: popular election confers legitimacy and nothing else does, and it is the majority of wills that must prevail. This formula was and still is used to generate representative government, but as the close of the French Revolution shows, it could equally well legitimize the populist autocracy of Napoleon Bonaparte.

1. THE REVOLUTION

I must stress most emphatically that the title of this chapter is not 'The French Revolution' but 'The *Legacy* of the French Revolution'. What follows under the consecutive headings of 'The Revolution', 'The Cycle of the Revolution', and the 'Chronology' is only a preamble to *the Legacy*. Such a preamble is necessary in order to know what happened. Also it introduces certain events and personalities referred to in *the Legacy*. It is lengthy, despite the most desperate—and selective—pruning, because this quite extraordinary convulsion is packed with so many abrupt changes in direction in so short a time.

---

[5] This text comes from S. E. Finer, *Comparative Government* (Penguin, Harmondsworth, 1984), 263–4.

1.1. *Revisionism*

I doubt if any historical event has been interpreted and reinterpreted so variously as the French Revolution.[6] No version seems to stick. Fortunately I do not have to join the fray, except for the briefest of glances at the run-up to the revolution and the immediate events that precipitated it. In so far as I have done this, it represents my own personal judgements amid the host of assertions and counter-assertions.

1.2. *Eighteenth-Century Background*

1.2.1. THE DEGENERATION OF THE AUTOCRACY

As we saw, Louis XIV, by way of his immense personal authority, overawed the traditional obstructors of royal policy: municipalities, corporations, guilds, and *parlements*, and likewise ensured that the court nobility as well as those in the provincial *États* gave him ample co-operation.[7] He had, as we also observed, acted as his own chief minister, and though his system was breaking down by about 1700 he still retained enough grip on affairs to provide France with a reasonably coherent central administration. All this was now to change. In adulthood Louis XV proved too indolent to follow the punishing routines of his mighty grandfather. The only periods when France had a coherent administration were under Fleury (1726–43) and perhaps Choiseul (1758–70). For the rest, minister struggled against minister, a prey, moreover, to incessant court intrigues as well as the influence of the Pompadour and the du Barry. It was, in Cobban's words, 'a republic of heads of factions'. As the Crown lost its grip, its erstwhile obstructors crept back on to the scene. The provincial Estates became restive, and, above all, the *parlements* once more acquired the freedom to remonstrate and deny registration (until overruled) that they had enjoyed before Louis XIV. The miserable Louis XVI, who acceded in 1774, made the indolent Louis XV appear like a thunderer from heaven: and it is owing to Louis XVI, personally, that the disaffection which unquestionably existed all over France between 1787 and 1789 turned into full-bloodied revolution.

[6] For the period to 1962, see G. Rudé, *Interpretations of the French Revolution*, Pamphlet No. 47, The Historical Association (Routledge & Kegan Paul, London, 1964) and A. Cobban, *Historians and the Causes of the French Revolution*, Pamphlet, General Series, no. 2, The Historical Association (Routledge & Kegan Paul, London, 1946). Hufton, *Europe*, ch. 12, so flatly contradicts most of the so-called 'traditional' versions, that one is put in mind of a tailor turning a jacket completely inside out. D. M. G. Sutherland, *France 1789–1815*: Revolution and Counter-Revolution (Fontana, London 1985) is fairly revisionist and so is S. Schama, *Citizens* (Viking, London, 1989).

[7] See above, Bk. IV, Ch. 7.

1.2.2. THE DEPENDENCY ON LOCAL NOTABLES

D'Argenson, in his *Mémoires*, makes John Law exclaim that councils and committees could be discounted. This was certainly not the case, and for the very same reason that tempered would-be centralization in every one of the agrarian societies we have met with so far. This was simply that there were not enough bureaucrats to enforce the government's will on recalcitrant local notables. France was ruled by thirty-two *intendants*.[8] The tasks of the *intendant* had enormously multiplied—but his staff had not. In 1787 the *intendant* of Brittany had a mere ten clerks in his central office and his sixty-three *sub-délégués* were very underpaid or not paid at all, and in consequence many were unreliable or inadequate.[9] The result was that the *intendants* had little option but to ask for the co-operation of the local notables. The alternative was damaging confrontation, and this was common: Louis XV's reign was 'plagued by direct confrontations between Intendants and provincial military Governors on the one hand and recalcitrant *parlements* on the other'.[10]

1.2.3. THE RESURGENCE OF THE *PARLEMENTS*

Dissatisfied with the role Louis XIV's will had accorded him in a Council of Regency, the duke of Orléans got the Paris *parlement* to nullify it in return for restoring their rights of remonstrance to their former state. Thenceforth they proceeded to get in the Crown's way. In 1771, therefore, the minister Maupéou confiscated the offices of the *parlementaires*, sent them into exile, and set up an entirely new set of courts. The *parlements* replied by crying 'despotism'. To the regret of Voltaire but the delight of vested interests and the common people one of Louis XVI's first acts was to restore the *parlements*. They did not, however, cease to obstruct fiscal reform.

But obstruction was perhaps the least damaging of the *parlements'* contests with the Crown. Much more important in the longer run were their self-justifications which sapped the very legitimacy of the royal absolutism. Basically, the *parlements* were seeking a constitutional monarchy in which the Crown's absolutism would be shared with themselves. Anything short of this was denounced as 'despotism'. It was the *parlements* rather than the *philosophes* that put into circulation and impregnated the aristocratic class with what one might otherwise surmise to have been the doctrines of Rousseau and the coinages of the Revolution itself: *citoyen, loi, patrie, constitution, nation, droit de la nation, cri de la nation*.[11]

---

[8] R. L. V. d'Argenson, *Journal et Mémoires*, édition Rathery, 9 vols: (Paris, 1859–67).
[9] Schama, *Citizens*, 114–15.   [10] Ibid.
[11] Palmer, *Age of the Democratic Revolution*, 449.

After the mid-century the *parlement* of Paris increasingly insisted that its role was the guardian of the 'Constitution' of the kingdom. Its *Grande Remontrance* of 1753 declared flatly that in conflict between the king's absolute power and the 'good of his service', the courts respected the latter, not the former.[12] The royal view was affirmed by Louis XV in his famous *séance de la flagellation* in 1766. Here he declared that sovereignty derived from him alone, that the authority of the courts derived from this royal authority, and that 'these therefore cannot be turned against it'. 'It is by virtue of my sole authority that the officers of my courts proceed, not indeed to the making of laws but to the enregistering, publication, and execution thereof.'

In 1776 certain edicts proposed to abolish the corvée which was almost obsolete and amounted at most to a week's unpaid work in the year, and substituting for it a simple tax that *everybody* would pay, and to abolish the *jurandes*, the restrictive guilds that limited accession to many industries. The *parlement* of Paris refused to enregister these edicts on the general grounds that the 'First rule of justice is to preserve for everyone what is due to them, a fundamental rule of natural right and of civil government which consists not only in upholding rights in property but in safeguarding rights attached to the person and born of prerogatives of birth and estate'. The commutation of the corvée for a general tax on all was to establish 'an equality of duties', 'to overturn civil society whose harmony rests only on that gradation of powers, authorities, preeminences and distinctions which holds each man in his place and guarantees all stations against confusion . . . The French monarchy, by its constitution, is composed of several distinct and separate estates. This distinction of conditions and persons originated with the Nation; it was born with its customs and way of life.'[13] As Palmer observes, 'the *Parlement* equated a week of peasant labour on the roads with the very essence of the French monarchy, the constitution, the prerogatives of birth, the Three Orders, and divine justice'.[14] They defended the prerogatives of the guilds against Turgot in a similar way—thus the cause of the guilds became that of the Three Orders, the nobility's that of the commoners. The government proposed to open a military school for noble and non-noble youths alike. The *parlement* objected: 'Each Estate has its own occupations, ideas, duties, genius and manner of life, which should not be adulterated or confused by education.'[15] Palmer asks the question: why was the National (Constituent) Assembly so radical from the very beginning?

---

[12] Hufton, *Europe*, 316.   [13] Quoted, Palmer, *Age of the Democratic Revolution*, 450–1.
[14] Ibid. 452.   [15] Ibid.

And he shrewdly responds: 'indeed if everything was abolished together in 1789, it was because everything had been together defended.'[16]

1.2.4. THE SEDUCTION OF THE ARISTOCRACY

Paradoxically, by 1786 or 1787 a number of members of the nobility rejected these arguments. They followed the *philosophes'* general attitudes which were socially and juridically egalitarian and which did not shrink at fiscal equality irrespective of their Order. It is wrong to think of the Order of Nobility as an aristocracy of caste and privilege opposed to the *Tiers*, who are unprivileged and suffer accordingly. An additional reason for this was the material one: that privilege was now affecting a larger number of persons than ever before and entrance into the aristocracy by way of the venality of offices became more and more common. At the risk of exaggeration, one might say that where everyone is privileged then nobody need insist that they are themselves privileged. It was this egalitarian core of noblemen who joined the *Tiers* and formed the first wave of the attack on 'feudalism' and the call for a constitutional monarchy.

1.2.5. THE PRICE OF BREAD

The price of bread was critical. Bread formed some three-quarters of most people's diet and, usually, a family would spend from a third to half their income on it. If the price rose to famine levels, as it did from time to time, these families were on the verge of starvation. There had been a long history of government involvement in the grain trade in France: the setting of prices, for instance, and limitations on freedom to transport grain away to other areas. When prices soared to excessively high levels the people—country-folk or townspeople—would riot: either to punish millers or dealers whom they would accuse of forcing up the price, or to make them break open their stores and put them on the market, or to fix their own price and

---

[16] Ibid. 453. The views I have expressed about the *parlements* are vigorously contested, indeed contradicted, by the 'revisionists'. They do make some good points: e.g. that the monarchs and their councils were not so efficient as to be regarded as paragons of virtue and progress, and that the government could act aggressively against the *parlements*. But at the end of the road the argument seems to boil down to asserting that the Crown over-frequently acted 'illegally' or 'unconstitutionally' in overriding the *parlements* (Cf. Hufton, *Europe*, 303–4). But the *lit de justice*, the *lettres de jussion*, even the exile of refractory *parlementaires* were not illegal, and to say they were 'unconstitutional' is to beg the question: what *was* the constitution of France—was it to be what the *parlements* said it was, like the Supreme Court of the USA except that its judges had bought or inherited their positions? Or was it what Louis XV laid down (quoted above), in his *séance de la flagellation*. Implicit in the revisionists' view, it seems to me, is a dislike of absolute monarchy and delight in seeing it challenged. Certainly, the *parlements* have a case; but as somebody once retorted to a man who maintained that Hitler had a case—'everyone has a case'. And how can anyone nowadays possibly justify their uncompromising resistance to even the slightest change to the established political and social order?

enforce it, or to prevent the movement of grain from their village—or *quartier*—to somewhere else in the kingdom. Nothing could enfuriate them more.

The townsfolk tended to suffer more than the peasants, but the latter had troubles of their own. It has been said that seigneurial dues were being tightened in the last years before the Revolution but this could not have been possible.[17] Furthermore the burden of seigneurial dues varied widely throughout the country. One-and-a-half million people were still serfs and had to pay fees at marriages and funerals, could not move freely, had to pay fees for exit, and faced restrictions on the sale of property. On the other hand, in other parts of the realm the incidence was simply marginal.[18] But they were very poverty-stricken. A small minority did indeed have enough land to require the services of other villagers to help them cultivate it, but for the rest even those that did have land did not have enough to subsist on and made up their income by remittances from their relatives who had found work elsewhere, or by cottage industry, or through seasonal labour.

The larger towns had big 'submerged' groups of the poor, the destitute, vagrants, criminals, and prostitutes, who played little or no part in political riots though they might well have joined in the numerous bread riots that punctuated the 1780s. Not so those who called themselves the sansculottes. These were a mixture of small shopkeepers, petty employers, wage labourers—the *menu peuple*. It was they, not the lumpenproletariat, who formed the revolutionary 'mobs' and who, especially in Paris, became very highly radicalized, and a prime mover in the Revolution.[19]

1.2.6. STATE FINANCE

It was a fiscal—or rather a cash-flow—crisis that, insensibly, brought France to the point of revolutionary confrontation. This is not the same as causing the downfall of the monarchy. The end of absolutism did not necessarily entail the Revolution.

The traditional means of running France's finances were (apart from hidden bankruptcies) taxation and loans. Certainly, the fiscal immunities of the privileged classes diminished the revenues of the government, but even if they had lost these immunities altogether it is 'very unlikely' that the

---

[17] Sutherland, *France 1789–1815*, 70–1.   [18] Ibid. 71–2.

[19] G. Rudé, *Paris and London in the Eighteenth Century* (Fontana, London, 1970), 21, 51, 59. Rudé will have none of 'the legend of the crowd as riffraff or *canaille*, or as a mob' (p. 29). I think this unacceptable. The 'crowd' could and did act with sadistic bestiality: consider how de Launay's head was hacked off with a penknife, or the fishwife screaming for Marie Antoinette's liver for a fricassee. These crowds were extremely volatile: when the fishwives murderously stormed the Tuileries they were cajoled by Lafayette, and began to cheer *Vive la reine*. Lynching individuals from the *Lanterne*, spearing heads on pikes, mutilating corpses—these are hardly the actions of 'respectable' *menu peuple*.

additional income would have made much difference to the deficit.[20] In 1789 lenders lost confidence in France's capacity to meet its obligations and stopped lending. A cash crisis arose. And the French government could respond only by increasing its collateral—and this meant, by increasing taxation.

France was the most populous and rich of all the European national states and correspondingly intent on asserting great-power status. Here lay the source of the fiscal crisis of the 1780s: for this required constant wars and each war left a mountain of debt which every subsequent war added to. Despite the warnings of his financial ministers, Louis XVI allowed himself to be sucked into alliance with the nascent United States, and this was to prove fatal. Altogether it cost France 1.3 billion livres.[21] Necker's famous *compte rendu* of 1781 showed the budget in balance. This was because he was addressing himself to the ordinary, that is, peacetime expenses of the Crown. In 1786 Calonne discovered that the budget was not running a surplus but was, on the contrary, running a deficit of 112 million livres per annum! He met the immediate problem by heavy borrowing on the Amsterdam exchange. Knowing that the *parlement* would, as usual, obstruct his efforts at fiscal reform to increase the Crown income, he resorted to the ruse—not without precedent—of convening an Assembly of Notables to consider his proposals. This turned out to be the beginning of the slippery slope to confrontation and the convocation of the Estates-General.

1.2.7. THE CONJUNCTURE OF 1787–1789

In 1787 three separate crises came together. One, of which we have spoken, was the government's desperation for new money. The second, a response to ministers' efforts to secure this money, was a ferocious running battle with the *parlement*, enthusiastically supported—at this stage—by public opinion, which saw it as a welcome defiance of 'despotism'. The third was a violent economic crisis. The price of bread soared and brought the *menu peuple* of the towns and especially in Paris to near-starvation. At the same time thousands of textile workers were being thrown out of employment. The air became electric as crowds entered on the traditional violent modes of securing cheap bread.[22] In this way, on top of the fiscal and constitutional crises, the crowd suddenly emerged as a prime political force.

Calonne's Assembly of Notables (important names drawn from the great corporations and institutions of the kingdom) met in February 1787. It rejected Calonne's proposals and Brienne, his successor (and himself a celebrated notable), fared no better. The Assembly referred him back to

---

[20] Schama, *Citizens*, 68.   [21] Ibid. 63–5.   [22] See above; Rudé, *Paris and London*, 72–3.

the *parlement*, which thereupon declared that by fundamental laws of the kingdom new taxes could only be levied with the consent of the Estates-General—which had last met in 1614. The king's reaction was to dissolve the *parlement*, exile its members, and set up a new court, the *Cour Plenière*. But the treasury was now empty. Brienne had no alternative but to agree to the convocation of the Estates-General, to meet 1 May 1789. His successor was Necker, the former director-general of finance. Forthwith he reconvened the *parlement* of Paris, which returned amidst delirious rejoicing on 23 September.

Two days later it had cast away its popularity and prestige for ever. For it proclaimed that in the forthcoming Estates-General the three Orders must, as in 1614, vote separately—not by heads. It was in vain that later the king agreed that the numbers of the *Tiers'* deputies would be doubled. This did not mean a thing as long as the three Estates voted by Orders and not by heads. On the other hand, should the government be made to change its mind, the *Tiers* would enjoy parity with the other two Orders combined: it would only need one or two dissident noblemen or clerics to come over and it would have a majority. From this moment on the political struggle changed character. It became a struggle of the *Tiers* against the other two Orders.

2. THE CYCLE OF THE REVOLUTION

2.1. *Some Characteristics*

Here I propose to single out only three characterisics that seem particularly germane to the argument of this chapter. The first concerns the relationship between the Revolution and the Enlightenment, and it follows on from what was said about the latter in Book IV, Chapter 8, above. The Revolution has two faces: individualism and community, the later being exemplified, for instance, in the work of Rousseau. In France the Enlightenment 'package'—as outlined in the chapter cited—is represented by the wholesale reforms proclaimed on 4 August 1789, but in France these acquired the solid backing of the national community, *la patrie*. Hitherto the Enlightenment package had been the programme of an educated and sophisticated well-to-do class, but was not accepted and in most cases was even repugnant to the masses: this is why the *philosophes* pinned their hopes on 'despotism', albeit an 'enlightened' one. In France the package which was put into effect was the attribute of all but the monarchists and crypto-monarchists and became a 'cause', indeed a quasi-religion, for which the republic's mass armies—and those of Napoleon too—would fight. The marriage between the individualism of the Enlightenment and the craving for community is encapsulated in Robespierre's rather despairing cry, as he saw faction after faction arising to destroy his dreams of Reason and Virtue: 'il faut une volonté une.'[23] The tension between the individualism and cool rationalism of the philosophes and the emotional allure of community was to intensify in Europe after 1814.

It is a commonplace that the course of the Revolution moved from the so-called Right—constitutional monarchy—to the far Left and the Committee of Public Safety before returning to a middling position under the Directory in 1795. Two characteristics of this progression are noteworthy. First, the prime movers were the revolutionary governments—which were led to the very end by men from the professional and business classes, what Marxists and Marxisants like to call the *bourgeoisie*—and the Street, consisting of the sansculottes, at first unorganized, then finding their focus in the electoral constituencies into which Paris was divided by the Municipal Law of 1790: the *sections*, and their elected body, the Commune of Paris. The revolutionary progression was moved by a dialectical interchange between the two. At certain times the sansculotte crowds pushed the government into unwelcome decisions while at other times a faction in the legislative body and/or its elected government called out the crowd to intimidate its rivals. Not until 1793–4 were the sansculottes brought under central control, though elements of them rioted in order to try to hold their positions. The leftism of the sansculottes from 1789 was due to two main causes. One was the fear of aristocratic reaction and cancellation of the decrees of 1789 and beyond. (This was not illusory, as witness counter-revolutionary rebellions in the provinces and the intrigues of the king.) The second main reason was war. Popular hysteria called for extreme measures whenever the war was going badly—as it was in the first months of 1792, and then again, even more disastrously, in 1793. In defeat the more 'extreme' and 'ruthless' faction of politicians displaced their rivals on the Right; for instance, the storming of the Tuileries and the subsequent September Massacres in the bad months of 1792, until invasion was halted by the cannonade at Valmy on 20 September; or, when the war went badly in 1793, the fall of the Gironde and the Jacobin Terror, until victory came with the decisive Battle of Fleurus in June 1794. In contrast, when the war went well the pressure was relaxed; thus, after Fleurus deputies saw no point in continuing the Terror and Robespierre, who did, was arrested and guillotined. From that moment the tide of leftism was turned back.

The second characteristic of the revolution's progression is its rudder-

[23] One could almost say that the Revolutionaries were telling the people: 'you will swallow the Enlightenment even if we have to kill you to do it'—and promptly did just that.

lessness. The *ancien régime* had its own logic: it was backed by an age-old tradition, and founded on the hierarchy of the Three Orders, the privileges of corporations and municipalities, the established Church, and so on. Creaky and anomalous as it was, it cohered; it was a complete *system*. The Revolution swept every part of this away. It had created, as it were, a 'level playing field' with the Americans, got to the position of civic equality, the liberty of the subject, the freedom of conscience, and the rule of law from which the Americans had started. But once it had done this—what next? The American colonies were each viable states that might have remained independent: all that was required here was to create a new superstructure to replace the old imperial one. 'Du passé, faisons table rase', runs a line of the Internationale. This is precisely what the revolutionaries had done. They had doomed themselves to the luxury of starting entirely afresh, but they did not know, or rather, they were wholly disunited as to what new governmental institutions they wanted to create. That is the reason for that dismal procession of constitutions—the arrangements for the election of the Estates-General in 1789, and the constitutions of 1791, 1793, 1795, 1799, 1802, and 1804. By the last France put herself and her institutions under the *tutelle* of an imperial autocrat. After 1814 the quest for an agreed form of government was resumed but never concluded. The country can now count no less than sixteen successive constitutions. Burke was very perceptive about this: 'it is with infinite caution', he wrote, 'that any man should venture upon pulling down an edifice, which has answered in any tolerable degree for ages for the common purposes of society, or build it up again without having models and patterns of approved utility before his eyes.'[24]

3. THE COURSE OF EVENTS

CHRONOLOGY

The Constitutional Monarchy

1789	
Jan.	Sieyès, *Qu'est que le Tiers État?*
5 May	Estates-General meets, separate Orders. Food crisis
10 June	*Tiers* invites other Orders to common verification of credentials
17 June	By 491–89 calls itself the National Assembly
20 June	*Tiers* takes oath not to separate until the constitution of the kingdom has been established on solid foundations. This attack on absolute monarchy can be regarded as the beginning of the Revolution

[24] Quoted, Rudé, *Interpretations*.

22 June	The 407 electors of Paris *Tiers* begin regular meetings in City Hall
27 June	Paris electors of the *Tiers* constitute themselves a government
11 July	Dismissal of Necker
12 July	Paris insurrection, government loses control
13 July	The people search for arms. Paris electors form permanent comittee, organize a National Guard of *bonne bourgeoisie*
14 July	Storming of the Bastille. The aristocratic emigration begins. Necker recalled. Paris electors form into a Commune. In provinces *intendants* fade away. Peasant unrest increases—the *Grande Peur*. Chateaux burnt, documents destroyed
4 Aug.	End of serfdom and corvée. Women prominent in bread riots
26 Aug.	Declaration of Rights of Man and the Citizen
4 Oct.	Women, with Lafayette and 20,000 National Guard, march on Versailles
5 Oct.	Court forced to reside in Paris. The National Assembly dominated by constitutional monarchists
2 Nov.	Church property nationalized

1790

21 May	Paris divided into forty-eight sections
19 June	Nobility abolished
12 July	Civil Constitution of the Clergy
16 Aug.	The *parlements* abolished. New judicial system
27 Nov.	Oath of the clergy

1791

2 Mar.	Guilds dissolved
13 Apr.	Pope condemns civil constitution of the clergy
20 June	Royal family's flight to Varennes. Arrested and returned to Paris
14 Sept.	King accepts the Constitution
30 Sept.	National Assembly dissolved. Members not eligible for election to new Legislative Assembly
1 Oct.	Legislative Assembly convenes

The Legislative Assembly

1792

20 Apr.	War declared on Austria. *La Marseillaise*
13 June	Prussia declares war. Brissot (Girondin) ministry supported by Jacobins and Paris *sections* who are a majority in Assembly. Disasters in war, counter-revolution in south: grain riots, food shortages, pillaging. King dismisses Brissotin ministry
20 June	Sansculotte mob invade the Tuileries
22 July	*La patrie en danger* proclaimed
27 July	Brunswick Manifesto threatening Paris *sections* and National Guard with vengeance

30 July	The Marseilles volunteers reach Paris
9 Aug.	Paris Commune broken up, replaced by new (very radical) Commune made up of 288 commissioners from the *sections*
10 Aug.	Left-wing Jacobins (the 'Mountain'), Paris *sections*, and National Guard, directed by new Commune, storm Tuileries. King suspended from duties. Danton heads provisional government
2 Sept.	Prussians take Verdun
2–7 Sept.	The 'September Massacres'
20 Sept.	Battle of Valmy turns back the enemy

The Convention

Elections for the Convention

21 Sept.	The Convention meets. Abolition of monarchy
22 Sept.	The Republic proclaimed
19 Nov.	France willing to help any people against its king
3 Dec.	Decision to try Louis XVI
11 Dec.	Interrogation of Louis XVI
15 Dec.	Decree on treatment of occupied territories

1793
21 Jan.	Execution of Louis XVI
1 Feb.	War declared on Britain and Holland
14 Mar.	Revolutionary revolt in Vendée
29 Mar.	Tribunal set up to judge without appeals
6 Apr.	Committee of Public Safety set up
29 Apr.	'Federalist' anti-Jacobin rising in Marseilles
3 May	First law on the maximum (grain prices)
30 May	Jacobins overthrown in Lyons
31 May	First anti-Girondin uprising in Paris. Central Revolutionary Committee, militia of 20,000, the tocsin sounded
2 June	Convention surrenders to the insurgents. Leading Girondins arrested. Jacobins (Mountain) command majority
10 June	'Federalist' revolts spread, Vendéens take Saumur
24 June	Enactment of Constitution 'of 1793' or of 'Year I'
10 July	Election of the great Committee of Public Safety headed by Robespierre which ruled by Terror until 27 July 1794
17 July	Final abolition of feudalism
27 July	Robespierre joins Committee of Public Safety (Danton having quitted it on the 10th)
23 Aug.	The *Levée en masse* decreed. 1 million men raised
4/5 Sept.	Mass demonstration by sansculottes, dole for the needy. The *armées révolutionnaires* set up to use Terror to regain rebellious towns
17 Sept.	The Law on Suspects. The Terror begins
29 Sept.	General law of maximum (prices)

Oct.	Inflation being curbed, food supplies more regular, drive to consolidate Committee's power in Paris
10 Oct.	Convention declares: 'The provisional government of France is revolutionary until the peace'
16 Oct.	Marie Antoinette executed
24/30 Oct.	Girondins tried
31 Oct.	Girondins executed
10 Nov.	'Festival of Reason' in Notre-Dame
4 Dec.	Law constituting Revolutionary Government. Overriding powers on internal administration and police conferred on Committee of Public Safety. Representatives on Mission under central control, local administration transfered to District and Commune councils reporting to governing committees. Each assigned a 'National Agent' reporting to the central government. The Paris Commune subordinate to Committee of General Security

1794

24 Mar.	Hébert (far Left) attempts insurrection and is executed
27 Mar.	The local Revolutionary Armies disbanded
5 Apr.	Danton and Desmoulins guillotined
8 June	'Festival of the Supreme Being'
June	Paris Commune purged, its *armée revolutionaire* disbanded, 'popular' societies in *sections* closed, *sections* become rubber-stamp for Jacobins
10 June	Law of 22 *Prairial* speeds up 'justice' and denies prisoners aid of defending counsel. The Great Terror (1,300 victims)
26 June	Victory at Fleurus clears France of invaders
27/8 July	Fall and guillotining of Robespierre
29 July	Seventy-one councillors of Paris Commune follow suit
1 Aug.	Repeal of 22 *Prairial* Law
24 Aug.	Committees of Public Safety and of General Security demoted. End of the Terror: executions drop and prisoners released from gaols
22 Sept.	Year III begins
12 Nov.	Jacobin club closed
8 Dec.	Reinstatement of surviving Girondins
24 Dec.	Law of the maximum repealed. Invasion of Holland

1795

21 Jan.	Freedom of worship restored
Jan./Mar.	Free trade in grain, galloping inflation, wages lag, famine in provinces
12 Apr.	Mob (*Germinal*). Riots and protests, march on the Convention, dispersed by National Guard. Paris in 'state of siege', ex-Terrorists and deputies of 'the Mountain' arrested, deportations to Guyana
20 May	(20/3 *Prairial*). Massive Paris uprising, Convention besieged, General Menou and 20,000 regulars attack and disperse. Harsh sup-

	ression of Jacobins. The end of the sansculottes as a political force
31 May	Revolutionary Tribunal abolished
Jan./Oct.	Belgium and Holland overrun, peace with Prussia concedes left bank of Rhine
22 July	Peace with Spain

The Directory

22 Aug.	(5 *Fructidor*) Constitution of the Year III approved. Two-thirds deputies to retain their seats (so as to exclude royalists)
23 Sept.	Year IV begins. Constitution promulgated
5 Oct.	(13 *Vendémiaire*). Every Paris *section* rejects two-thirds law, royalists in arms, 20,000 march on Convention. Napoleon's 'whiff of grapeshot' disperses insurgents
26 Oct.	End of Convention
2 Nov.	Directory constituted
10 Dec.	Economy in ruins. Forced loan

1796	
Mar./Nov.	Napoleon's conquests in Italy

1797	
18 Apr.	Elections: a royalist majority in Legislature
3/4 Sept.	(22 *Fructidor*) Carnot and Pichegru ejected from Directory, army marches in under Augereau (Napoleon's lieutenant), elections for 'royalist' deputies annulled
18 Oct.	Napoleon concludes the Treaty of Campo Formio

1798	
22 Mar.	Elections of Year VI. Jacobin gains
11 May	(22 *Floréal*) Assembly excludes 106 such deputies
19 May	Napoleon leaves for Egypt
24 Dec.	The Second Coalition against France

1799	
Mar./Sept.	Successive heavy defeats of French
26 Sept.	French regain initiative. Coalition begins to fall apart
9 Oct.	Napoleon back in France
10 Nov.	*Coup d'état* of 18/19 *Brumaire*. The Directory overthrown
25 Dec.	Constitution of the Year VIII. The Consulate of Three, Napoleon First Consul

From here the NAPOLEONIC ERA begins.

4. THE WORK OF THE REVOLUTION, 1789–1791

4.1. *The Domestic Scene, 1789–1791*

This is the period of the National Assembly. Basically, all the destructive works of the Revolution were accomplished here; the painful work of construction was to follow and reach completion by the plebiscitary auto-cracy of Napoleon. This period saw the 'Declaration of the Rights of Man and the Citizen' (of which much more, later), its realization by the destruction of the entire past order, the attribution of unlimited power to the state, and yet, paradoxically, the fragmentation of the state administration. It launched its fateful attack on the Church which was to invest the counter-revolution with the characteristics of a Holy War.

Social, provincial, municipal, and guild distinctions were all effaced. Hereditary titles, coats of arms, and even distinct liveries for servants were abolished. Public offices ceased to be a private property, being bought out and their cost charged to the National Debt. Fiscal and other economic inequalities were abolished. This did not mean merely the equalization of the tax burden. When the Assembly, on 4 August 1789, famously declared 'feudalism is abolished', they meant by the term the abolition of all peasant obligations originating from lordship such as serfdom, labour services, hunting rights, game laws, and seigneurial courts. (This did not apply to any historical property relationships: the peasant had to buy these out, until these too were extinguished outright in 1792 and 1793.) Every citizen was equal before the law, there were no longer different penalties for the same offences. The age-old 'intermediate bodies' which had acted so effectively as checks upon the executive were swept away, most notably the haughty *parlements*: at first left in suspended animation, their *parlementaires* were bought out and they were then closed down to be superseded by elected courts. Guilds and corporations of professions, arts, and crafts were abolished.

The one 'intermediate body' which did survive was the Catholic Church. The predatory state abolished tithes, pluralism, and annates but in November 1789 went much further and confiscated all Church property. It was argued that Church property was not like ordinary private property because it was inalienable and held in trust. Therefore there was no reason why the state should not take it over and pay the clergy stipends, so effectively turning them into civil servants. This the clergy emphatically did not want to be. In return the Revolution asserted its right to act as the final judge of public morality: 'The clergy only exists by virtue of the nation', said Barnave, 'so the nation [if it so chooses] can destroy it.'[25] But it was (and

---

[25] Quoted Schama, *Citizens*, 489.

still is) a Catholic axiom that the Church and the state were coeval. Barnave's affirmation was yet another side of the approaching *statocracy*, if we may so term the theory and the practice of the sovereign absolutism of the state. In the face of Church opposition the Revolution pressed its demands still further. On 12 July 1790 the Assembly decreed the Civil Constitution of the clergy. In future the parish priest would no longer be ordained by the bishop but chosen by the elective assembly of the district, and the bishop would no longer be ordained by the pope but by the elective assembly of the department. It seemed to the revolutionaries that since the clergy were now civil servants they should take the same vow to uphold the Constitution as everyone else. They therefore exacted an Oath of Fidelity to the constitution, including the civil constitution of the clergy. In March 1791 the pope condemned the civil constitution leaving the French clergy with the choice of the Revolution or the Faith. Most priests chose not to swear the oath. The Assembly grew more and more hostile to them until, in the end, they came to be hunted down, exiled, murdered, and their ceremonies banished to the woods and to cellars.[26] So began the Holy War between Church and Revolution.

By this raft of measures the National Assembly had wiped the slate clean. Since nothing was left of the past (except the hereditary monarchy), everything had to be built anew. 'All citizens are eligible for office and agency with no other distinction except their virtues and their talents.' Every citizen is guaranteed freedom of movement, freedom to assemble peaceably and to speak and publish his views without prior censorship. A national system of schools open to all would be introduced.[27]

But what eventuated was licence and not liberty, aggravating an already botched constitution and the fragmentation of state authority. The 'Declaration of the Rights of Man and the Citizen' had affirmed that 'the basis of all sovereignty lies essentially in the Nation', and that 'Legislation is the expression of the General Will; all citizens have a right to participate in it either in person, or through their representatives'.[28]

This is very vague. Was there, for instance, to be direct or indirect election, universal or restricted manhood suffrage? But the main thing is that it consecrated the principle of election by or through the People, and this principle was applied everywhere, even for judges and the clergy, except in one case—the monarchy, which was hereditary.

This 1791 Constitution took great pains to put as great a distance

---

[26] C. Brinton, *A Decade of Revolution, 1789–1799* (Harpers & Bros., London and New York, 1934), 51.
[27] The Constitution of 1791: Chapter (*Titre*) 1.
[28] As translated in Finer, *Five Constitutions*, Arts. 3 and 6.

between the legislature and the sovereign People as it decently could. It divided the (male) citizenry into actives and passives—the former possessing incomes of a certain amount, the latter those whose incomes were less. Out of 24 million inhabitants some 4,300,000 were active citizens. Only they could vote and when they did so for the Legislative Assembly they did this indirectly. At the base the active citizens elected electors who then proceeded to elect the deputies. But this principle of election was extended everywhere else. The National Assembly, in abolishing the historic provinces, had substituted eighty-three *départements* (based on topographical features) which in turn were subdivided into districts, cantons, and finally, the basic units—usually the ancient, immemorial ones—the communes. Each of the latter had an elected council, a mayor, and a *procureur*. The district too had an elected council, an executive directory, and a *procureur*. In theory these lesser units were subordinate to the highest, the *département*, which in its turn was an elected body with a council and executive directory. But, with the experience of the royal *intendants* fresh in everybody's minds, no official was appointed from the centre to these local bodies, not even the *département*, so that in practice the chain of command had disappeared. Instead France had become some 44,000 units enjoying almost complete autonomy. The villages were mostly apolitical; but the towns were highly active and very radical indeed. This fragmented France was in effect—and was so called at the time—a 'Federation'. It was thought that because all citizens would sink themselves in the love of the *patrie*, no further cement was necessary, hence the famous national occasions such as the annual celebrations of the fall of the Bastille, where citizens of communes tearfully fell upon each others' necks amid *tableaux vivants* and fireworks. At this point France was considered as one great love-in.

The same principle of election governed the judicial system that replaced the *parlements*. A network of new courts was set up at municipal, departmental, and national level whose judges were to be elected (but had to have legal qualifications), and to serve for six-year terms. Godechot sums up the effect of the new local government and judicial systems: 'The authority of the central government over the administrative agencies was reduced to virtually nothing.' The king could only suspend officials but the legislature could re-install them. The courts were weakened by the division of authority between the chief of police, the president of the presentment jury, the president of the district court, the public prosecutor, and the royal commissioner. Nor could the legislature do any better than the king; it had no means to make the people pay their taxes or respect the law. Indeed, Godechot adds, sometimes these elected local bodies became counter-revolutionaries invoking the 'right to resistance to oppression' against the Assembly itself.[29]

This constitution is incomprehensible unless one realizes that it was a direct carry-over from the Enlightenment's *idée fixe*, that is, to destroy 'despotism'. Its aim was to weaken the central executive as far as it possibly could. It applied the doctrine of the separation of powers in the most literal sense, with a far weaker executive than the American and a judicial system that was altogether prevented from meddling with the other two branches. The legislature—once the Assembly had dissolved and been replaced by a Legislative Assembly—was to consist of one chamber of 745 members elected by that indirect and limited suffrage we have already mentioned. It was entirely independent of the king, who could neither adjourn it nor dissolve it. All his Acts had to be countersigned by a minister and no minister was permitted to sit as a member of the Assembly. On the other hand, by reason of their penal responsibility, these ministers could in effect be attacked for political responsibilities, so making their removal by the king inevitable. The king, for his part, could suspend the promulgation of a law for two consecutive sessions of the Assembly, that is, for four years; notwithstanding this, the legislature could interfere with the executive's powers over war, peace, and treaty-making. The legislature then, was virtually all-important and this went for its relationship with the reformed judiciary. No obstructions by the *parlements* here! On the contrary, and in accordance with Chapter V, Article 3 of the Constitution, 'the courts might not interfere in the exercise of the legislative power or suspend the execution of laws, nor undertake administrative functions, nor summon administrators to appear before it in respect of their duties'.

4.2. *War, and the Restoration of Central Authority*

In April 1792, for convoluted domestic reasons, France declared war on Austria. Its armies met with unbroken disaster. The Paris mob's fury was to revenge itself with blood. On 20 June they attacked the Tuileries. On 11 July the government issued the cry *la patrie en danger*. Volunteers were called for— hence the famous march of the Marseillais. The old Council of Paris was overthrown by radical elements and a neo-Commune formed. On 10 August the mob stormed the Tuileries, massacred its Swiss Guards, and put the king under house arrest. The Assembly had effectively capitulated to the Jacobin club and the Commune, and Danton took charge of a provisional govern-

---

[29] J. Godechot, *Les Révolutions (1770–1799)* (Presses Univ. de France, Paris, 1970). The 'resistance' text is in the 'Declaration', Art. 2.

ment. But in August, when the Prussians took Verdun, the mobs went completely wild: they broke open the prisons, selected their victims, subjected them to a summary trial, and murdered them in droves: the September Massacres.

A fortnight later came the famous cannonade at Valmy. The enemy had at last been turned back. Power was now vested in the Convention, newly elected by universal male suffrage, and it was, now, entirely republican. The monarchists were out. Instead the Convention divided into a huge morass of 'undecideds'—the Marsh or Plain, as it was called—with the Gironde taking the more moderate position on the right of the podium and the Jacobin faction of the Mountain taking up the left. On 21 September, the day the Convention met, it decreed the abolition of the monarchy. France was now the 'single and indivisible *Republic*'.

As the French armies continued their advances the king was put on trial, convicted, and executed. In response, in February 1793, an anti-French coalition was formed that included Britain, Holland, Spain, and the Austrian Empire. Again the tide of war turned. In their turn the Austrians retook Belgium (March 1793) and the Prussians advanced to Valenciennes (July 1793). Meanwhile authority in the provinces had totally broken down: Bordeaux, Arras, Nantes, Lyons, and the Vendée were in full revolt. The Convention established a Committee of General Security with police powers, and a Committee of Public Safety with dictatorial powers over (basically) foreign affairs, warfare, and the security of the interior. It was on this committee that Robespierre, St Just, Carnot, and Danton sat. Their immediate aim was to destroy their Girondin enemies on the Right. They did it by inciting the radicalized and republican Commune against the Convention, which they stormed, forcing the arrest of twenty-two Girondin deputies (subsequently guillotined). But at the same time the powers of the Paris Commune were curtailed. The local communes lost most of their important powers and were made fully responsible to the Convention. In the capital and provinces the Terror ruled: some 1,300 executions were carried out. To quell the provinces special units of dedicated revolutionaries were formed into *armées révolutionnaires*, and with them commissaries, to suppress the city revolts. In this, by way of the most bloody and barbaric terror, they proved successful: horribly so. Fouché could boast of his handiwork: 'Lyons n'est plus.' At Nantes the victims were drowned—the *noyades*. The Vendée population was decimated.

Then, once more, the tide of battle turned. This was due to the new armies, organized by Carnot, of which we shall speak anon. The Coalition forces began their retreat in December 1793. Then followed the French victories at Tourcoing (May 1794), Charleroi (25 June 1794), and the crowning battle of Fleurus (26 June) with the revolutionary armies overrunning Belgium.

The need for the Terror was over. The colleagues of Robespierre feared they might be his next victims, while the general public was sick of the wholesale guillotinings. On 27 July Robespierre was arrested and then executed. From this moment the slow retreat from the 'revolutionary government' began, to culminate in the thoroughly mediocre—and middle-class—government of the Directory. The momentum of revolution was stopped. It would remain for Napoleon to consolidate it and bring it to an end.

5. THE LEGACY: (1) THE RIGHTS OF MAN AND THE CITIZEN

The best way to appreciate the 'Declaration of the Rights of Man and the Citizen' is to read it. A good deal of modern criticism is jejune and parochial: for instance, that it does not include the freedom of association, of education, or of domicile, or that equality does not figure among the 'natural and imprescriptible rights', or that property (*videlicit* private property) is declared 'inviolable'. It is pointed out, too, that many of the Articles are time-bound, reflecting the exigencies of the situation; for instance, the right of 'resistance to oppression' was included to provide an *ex post facto* justification for the storming of the Bastille. It is not designed to protect the poor against the rich (it certainly did not!), but was a weapon of war to smash all the ancient institutions deemed pernicious and a shield to defend its authors against a resurgence of royal 'despotism'.

All perfectly true, but for our purposes beside the point. Here is the text:

The Representatives of the French People constituted in National Assembly,
Considering that ignorance, forgetfulness or contempt of the rights of man are the sole cause of public misfortune and governmental depravity,
Have resolved to expound in a solemn declaration the natural inalienable and sacred rights of man,
So that this declaration, perpetually present to all members of the body social, shall be a constant reminder to them of their rights and duties;

So that, since it will be possible at any moment to compare the acts of the legislative authority and those of the executive authority with the final end of all political institutions, those acts shall thereby be the more respected;
So that the claims of the citizenry, founded thenceforth on simple and uncontestable principles, shall always tend to the support of the constitution and to the common good.

Consequently the National Assembly recognizes and declares in the presence and under the auspices of the Supreme Being the following rights of man and of the citizen:

1. In repect of their rights men are born and remain free and equal. The only permissible basis for social distinctions is public utility.

2. The final end of every political institution is the preservation of the natural and imprescriptible rights of man. These rights are liberty, property, security and resistance to oppression.

3. The basis of all sovereignty lies essentially in the Nation. No corporation nor individual may exercise any authority that is not expressly derived therefrom.

4. Liberty is the capacity to do anything that does no harm to others. Hence the only limitations on the individual's exercise of his natural rights are those which ensure the enjoyment of these same rights to all other individuals. These limits can be established only by legislation.

5. Legislation is entitled to forbid only those actions which are harmful to society. Nothing not forbidden by legislation may be prohibited nor may any individual be compelled to do anything that legislation has not prescribed.

6. Legislation is the expression of the general will. All citizens have a right to participate in shaping it either in person, or through their representatives. It must be the same for all, whether it punishes or protects. Since all citizens are equal in its eyes, all are equally eligible for all positions, posts and public employment in accordance with their abilities and with no other distinction than those provided by their virtues and their talents.

7. No individual may be accused, arrested or detained except in the cases prescribed by legislation and according to the procedures it has laid down. Those who solicit, further, execute or arrange for the execution of arbitrary commands must be punished; but every citizen charged or detained by virtue of legislation must immediately obey; resistance renders him culpable.

8. The only punishments established by legislation must be ones that are strictly and obviously necessary, and no individual may be punished except by virtue of a law passed and promulgated prior to the crime and applied in due legal form.

9. Since every individual is presumed innocent until found guilty, legislation must severely repress all use of force beyond that which is necessary to secure his person in those cases where it is deemed indispensable to arrest him.

10. Nobody must be persecuted on account of his opinions including religious ones, provided the manifestation of these does not disturb the public order established by legislation.

11. The free communication of thoughts and opinions is one of the most precious rights of man; hence every citizen may speak, write and publish freely, save that he must answer for any abuse of such freedom according to the cases established by legislation.

12. [Necessity for a police force.]

13. [Upkeep of police and administration necessitates taxation.] This must be borne by all citizens equally, according to their means.

14. [Citizens' right to query need for taxation, freely accept it and monitor its expenditure.]

15. Society possesses the right to demand from every public servant an account of his administration.

16. A society in which rights are not secured nor the separation of powers established is a society without a constitution.

17. Since property is an inviolable and sacred right, no individual may be deprived of it unless some public necessity, legally certified as such, clearly requires it; and subject always to a just and previously determined compensation.

There are five points to notice. The first is the implicit assumption of 'law-boundedness' which we have pursued throughout this volume as one of the characteristics, perhaps the most important characteristic, of western civilization as against those of Asia. It is particularly noteworthy that the rule of law is specifically referred to in no less than nine of its seventeen articles.

Unquestionably, the American Constitution and the rights it guarantees, which also lie fully in this tradition, preceded the French Declaration but there is a difference between the two cases. The Americans, heirs to the British parliamentary—and one should say feudal—tradition, could identify specific legal rights in the knowledge that these would be operating within a general framework of recognized law. Law-boundedness and the limited monarchy were the characteristic contributions that the British brought to the European tradition of government. In France, however, law-bounded-ness could not be taken for granted. There the very existence of *lettres de cachet* and torture testified to the contrary. So, whereas the American Constitution and its Bill of Rights consist for the most part of the liberties, especially legal safeguards against the state, that the colonists regarded as no more than reclamation of their English birthright, the French Articles are not specific but general, indeed, universal in their applicability. What they lose in specificity they gain in universality. And whereas the American rights are juridically enforceable and could be invoked in a lawcourt against the state, the French rights were declarations of intent.

The second point is that the French Declaration specifically asserts that the 'basis of all sovereignty lies, essentially, in the Nation' (whatever that may be) and that 'legislation is the expression of the general will [even more obscure than 'the nation'] in which all citizens have a right to participate'. Together these two Articles add up to saying that the state is henceforth a 'nation-state': not necessarily a national state, though this would help, as will be seen later in discussing nationality and nationalism; but in the sense that this state, whatever its composition and wherever its boundaries lie, is the property of its own citizens and of no one else. By extension these two Articles signify that a nation can dispose of itself as it wishes—it cannot be disposed of as it had been by dynastic agreements. It has an inherent right of 'self-determination'.

The third point is that in this nation (however this be defined, but here taken as the collectivity or community of citizens) all are juridically equal: equal before the law, equal in fiscal matters, equal in access to public office, and so forth. There are no individuals or corporations or Orders which are privileged. Being a national is all.

The fourth point is that, with the possible exception of the doctrine of the inviolability of private property, the entire document is so obviously the blueprint of virtually all modern states (I except a few Islamic ones, particularly those of a fundamentalist nature) that the proposition hardly requires actual demonstration. Virtually every state today which wishes to make a significant break with its past institutions or—like the succession states to the European empires or the new South Africa—has to create a fresh set of institutions, feels that it must, *mutatis mutandis*, follow the prescriptions in the Declaration in order to be recognized as 'modern'.

The final—and, alas!—bitter-sweet point is that despite all we have said about its prescriptions of law-boundedness and popular participation in forming policy—the essentials of what we would today regard as a 'con-stitutionalist' or 'liberal' state—the Declaration can be and has all too often been read in quite a different way with directly contradictory consequences. This is because it contains an inherent and lethal contradiction. It states that all authority flows from the general will, but it also declares that man possesses natural and imprescriptible rights, and the two are *not compatible*. That is made more than abundantly clear by the actions of the French revolutionaries themselves: the confiscation of the Church properties, the enforced translation of priests into civil servants, the suspension of all judicial safeguards during the Terror, the procedures used in the judicial murder of Louis XVI—all of these were justified on the grounds that all activities emanated from the general will and that the Assembly or the Convention embodied it. Paradoxically this has made the Declaration more universalistic than ever. If it were confined simply to safeguarding the rights of man, it would be much in the position of the US Constitution's guarantees and appeal only to countries which wanted to bridle the power of the public authorities against their subjects. As it stands it gives licence to any petty tyrant to rise to power on the basis, usually factitious, of a supposed general will to see him as its supreme embodiment. So the age-old dichotomy between Forum polities and Palace polities renews itself in its more modern form.

6. THE LEGACY: (2) NATIONALISM

The common view is not so much that France 'invented' nationalism, but that she provoked it in Europe as a reaction to her aggressions, notably in Germany. However, few concepts are as entangled as 'nationalism'. Was it not a French *nationalism* against which the peoples of Europe reacted, and if not, what was it? How is one to describe the intense feelings of fraternal solidarity celebrated in the Feasts of the *Fédérés* which took place not only in Paris but in every commune throughout France? Or the sentiments that inspired the revolutionary armies: 'the great words Liberty and Equality, the Republic and the Nation, the rolling thunder of the "Marseillaise" and the lighter strains of the "Carmagnole". He saw the tricolour every day at his barracks and again, in the battlefield . . .'[30] And the matter is further confused by the compounding of terms like 'the People', 'la Nation' 'la Patrie', the 'General Will'.

The source of confusion is that 'nationalism' is sometimes used to describe a state of mind, a sentiment, and sometimes a theory, even an ideology. It goes without saying, however, that you cannot have this ideology without presupposing the sentiment of nationhood (though the reverse is not true). On the basis of this distinction it will be argued here that until quite late in the Revolutionary and Napoleonic periods what France experienced was an impassioned national sentiment. When this turned into a patronizing arrogance towards conquered peoples and the French began to regard themselves as a superior people this sentiment laid a foundation for what was, much later, articulated as a doctrine or pro-gramme.

But what is this 'nation'? During the Revolution two terms persistently crop up. They are 'la Nation' and also 'la Patrie'. The first will be found everywhere, particularly as an adjective, as in 'the National Assembly', 'the National *Cocarde*', 'the basis of all sovereignty lies essentially in the Nation'. 'La patrie' occurs notably, of course, in the very first line of the *Marseillaise* 'Allons enfants de *la patrie*', in '*la patrie en danger*', in 'The most sacred duty and the most cherished law is to forget the law to save the *patrie*'.[31] 'Everything

---

[30] R. R. Palmer, *Twelve Who Ruled* (Princeton UP, Princeton, 1965), 80–1.
[31] Quoted from Decree of July 1792, in Schama, *Citizens*, 611.

belongs to the *patrie* when the *patrie* is in danger',[32] or 'People, Marat is dead: the lover of the *patrie*'.[33]

Sieyès presents us with a definition of 'nation' which is singularly blood-less. It is not an ethnic entity. It is the idea of 'an equal union of individuals'. France, as an authentic political body, was at root such a union. It was not a union of corporations, or of provinces, or of Estates. These were all 'multiple' unions or unions of unions. The very essence of nationhood was to be *one* union of the very components out of which all other unions were made. Sieyès endlessly repeated the two words in con-junction, 'une nation, une nation une'.[34] Elsewhere he says: 'What is a nation? A unity of combined individuals who are governed by one law and so are represented by the same law-giving assembly.'[35] This definition certainly makes some kind of sense for the earlier years of the Revolutionary conquests in Belgium, the Rhineland, Nice, and Savoy, but its inadequacy soon became apparent. In 1794 we find two members of the Committee of Public Safety attacking 'four languages in the Republic that were not French: German, Breton, Basque and Italian'. The existence of these lan-guages, they declared, produced 'a linguistic federalism, a division in the community, for the people who spoke them could not understand public events'. Barère affirmed that the exodus of 20,000 Alsatians was due to their German language, which 'made them more sympathetic to Germany than to France. No one could be a citizen, obey the laws or participate in the commonwealth without commanding the common medium of expression.'[36] In principle such annexations could expand the Republic indefinitely. Hence Carnot's doctrine of France's 'natural frontiers': they were the natural limits of mountains, rivers, and seas within which the French nation would be defined.

'La patrie' is altogether a warmer word than 'nation'. It is more 'family'. 'As late as 1776 the Academy had defined *patrie* in terms of *pays*: a French-man's country was merely that part of it in which he happened to have been born.' Hitherto the term used to describe the French state had been *royaume*. Now, with the Revolution, 'France was finding itself. Instead of a collection of *pays* she had become a single *patrie*.'[37] It is, in short, one's native land—one's country.

[32] Quoted from Decree of July 1792, 626. [33] Ibid. 741.

[34] M. Forsyth, *Reason and Revolution: The Political Thought of the Abbé Sieyès* (Leicester UP, Leicester, 1987), 72.

[35] J. P. Mayer, *Political Thought in France from Sieyès to Sorel* (Faber & Faber, London, 1943), 10.

[36] Palmer, *Twelve Who Ruled*, 320. Cf. also J. Talmon, *The Origins of Totalitarian Democracy* (Mercury Books, London, 1961), 110–11.

[37] J. M. Thompson, *The French Revolution* (Blackwell, Oxford, 1944), 121.

However, quite soon the meaning of 'patrie' and 'nation' began to overlap. The nation began to be conceived not as a *Gesellschaft* of individuals,
which was what Sieyès' definition came close to, but as a united moral body,
a reification, a *Gemeinschaft* closely bound up with the notion of the Sovereign
People, and this in turn with that elusive entity the general will. 'The great
aim of the Committee [of Public Safety] was to create a nation, a community with a single faith, where men of all localities, all religions, all dialects,
all degrees of education, all stations in society, all variety of private interests,
should co-operate in supreme loyalty to a common country.'[38] This community was not merely a unity: it was *one*. For Robespierre, 'a citizen was not
just everyone born on French soil. Only he was a citizen who was spiritually
identified with the substance that constituted French nationhood, the
general will.'[39] And for Robespierre—and the Mountain generally—this
general will precluded any sort of pluralism in society. As he put it, 'Il faut
une volonté une'.[40] And this notion tied in with other revolutionary
sentiments of the day—the connotations attaching to *La République*, equality,
citizenship. So: one great corporation would replace the hodgepodge of the
Ancien Régime.

Thus the Revolution became a kind of religion, and one that everybody
was supposed to share.[41] On 23 August 1793, the Committee decreed the
levée en masse. Such was what we may safely call 'national sentiment' in
Republican France. In its early phase it was benevolent to its neighbours.
In its first declarations of intent, the National Assembly had in May 1791
declared that 'The French nation renounces the undertaking of any war with
a view to making conquests, and it will never use its forces against the
liberty of any people'. This changed somewhat when the Republic's armies
had overrun Belgium in 1792: now the Convention decreed that the liberated
peoples must raise armies and contribute to the upkeep of the French
occupying forces. By 1795, with the French armies everywhere triumphant,
the formula changed yet again: the laws of the annexed provinces or 'sister-
republics' were, through the agency of their local Jacobin-type puppet
governments, to follow those of France. Princes and foreign governors
were deposed, new revolutionary authorities instituted, national armies
were established, French laws and constitutions were imposed. And the
doctrine that the conquered territory must contribute towards the Republic's war costs had turned into naked exploitation. Whatever France's
government of the day might decree, its local agents 'battened on the
annexed provinces like locusts, and their extortions and requisitions went

---

[38] Palmer, *Twelve Who Ruled*, 385.   [39] Talmon, *Origins of Totalitarian Democracy*, 113.
[40] Ibid. 116.   [41] Thompson, *French Revolution*, 425.

on at such a pace that whole areas were stripped their resources'.[42] With Napoleon's Italian campaigns, the extortions (which gave Napoleon a free rein, of course) were openly avowed. In this way, from its original pacific pretensions, the Republic had turned into a vast plunder-machine and its generals, notably Napoleon, were openly adhering to Guibert's famous maxim that 'war must pay for itself'. Its effect was to build a wall of resentment between the French occupiers, who now began to think of themselves as superior mortals, and the insulted and exploited native populations. It is from such a matrix that there springs the ideology of nationalism according to Isaiah Berlin, who suggests that 'nationalism as distinct from mere national consciousness—the sense of belonging to a nation—is in the first place a response to a patronizing or disparaging attitude towards the traditional values of a society, the result of wounded pride and sense of humiliation in its most socially conscious members, which in due course produce anger and self-assertion'.[43]

Certainly the French provoked such outbreaks of anger and self-assertion in many countries they occupied and Napoleon's conquests and reorganizations in Europe brought the entire matter of national consciousness to the fore, and in the course of this was generated the intellectual doctrine and the ideology of *nationalism*.

Napoleon invaded Spain in February 1808, and occupied Madrid on 3 March. There followed the famous *dos de Mayo*—the uprising against the invaders. At first sight Austria seems a most unlikely candidate for popular rebellion but the dynasty was preparing its revenge. The army was being refashioned, a citizen *Landwehr* was set up, and in a pale imitation of the French *levée en masse* all Austrian men between 18 and 45 who could bear arms were called to defend the *Vaterland*. The population was fired with anti-French fervour; they were inspired by patriotic songs, lays, and proclamations. But the court had sadly miscalculated. The French seized Vienna on 13 May 1809.

None of these rebellions, or others like them (there were others in parts of Italy, for instance) can be said to exhibit anything more than ardent national consciousness; certainly, nothing rational. This fell to the Germanies. 'Germany' was a geographical expression if, indeed, it was even that. Certainly, this German *Volk* was distributed among some 300 principalities, and a large number of free cities as well. The middle class was not estranged. Officialdom was, for its time, relatively honest and efficient. In these circumstances it was the universities—and the secret societies—which

---

[42] Rudé, *Interpretations*, 214.

[43] I. Berlin, *Against the Current: Essays in the History of Ideas* (Hogarth Press, London, 1979), 346.

became politically prominent. The universities were peculiarly detached from considerations of practical politics. Instead, they concentrated on abstract *essences*: of the state, liberty, law, right, and the like. They were not merely not unaware of this—they gloried in it. 'They had had their own revolution as glorious as the French: this revolution is in the country of the mind.'[44]

Then the Germans—or the Prussians, at least—were jolted out of their smugness by the disastrous battles of Jena and Auerstadt in 1806. From this, nationalism, *an ideology*, was born. It was the handiwork of counter-Enlightenment Romantics. In their eyes the Enlightenment had cut off the individual from his social tradition. They preferred—like Burke—that which had grown to that which had been made. But whereas Burke had extensive experience of practical politics, these Germans had none. Instead they looked back on a medieval past, to folklore and legend, to badges of identity. Herder (d. 1803), a precursor, saw language as the most important if not the all-important badge of identity. 'A people may lose its independence but will survive as long as its language survives.' 'What nature separated by language, customs, character, let no man artificially join together by chemistry.'[45] The importance of the notion of nations as language-groups was taken up later by the much more influential philosopher Fichte. Fichte is the father of the German Romantic version of nationalism. It is expressed in his impassioned *Reden an die deutsche Nation* of 1808. He maintained that Germany had a special mission to carry forward the cultural inheritance of Europe. Since this cannot be accomplished without power, then the Germans must create a nation-state. 'Nationalism becomes a religion. Individuals are to sacrifice themselves to the nation, hallowed by history.'[46]

Smith calls this 'the organic version': the subject of history is the nation and this stands over and above the individuals who compose it. These individuals possess common mental characteristics which act as badges of identity. Nature itself is responsible for this cultural individuality, expressed as it is in the manifest differences in language, customs, history, and the like. Hence we can infer a spirit, a *Geist* of a nation which fuses it into an organic whole. In Smith's summary,

The German organic version of nationalism is . . . based on the principle that nations possess the 'capacity to shape history by the workings of the national will'. It embraces three distinct notions: (1) that of cultural diversity, i.e. Herder's idea

[44] Quoted, Palmer, *Twelve Who Ruled.*
[45] Quoted by A. D. Smith, in *Theories of Nationalism* (Duckworth, London, 1971), 181.
[46] H. S. Reiss, *Political Thought of the German Romantics* (Blackwell, Oxford, 1955), 18.

that the world has been divided into unique organic 'nations' or language groups, (2) the notion of national self-realization through political struggle, and (3) that the individual's will must be absorbed in that of the organic state—both of these latter ideas being the peculiar contribution of Fichte.[47]

Generalizing from its many different theorists who succeeded one another throughout the nineteenth and twentieth centuries, Smith gives a blandly abstract but comprehensive definition of what *nationalism* is: 'An ideological movement, for the attainment and maintenance of self-government and independence on behalf of a group, some of whose members conceive it to constitute an actual or potential "nation" like others.'[48] I call this bland because it misses the immense emotional charge of the ideology of nationalism, whereby the individual can feel that everyone owes his supreme loyalty to the nation-state.

Nationalism as here defined is destined to be a continuing theme throughout the rest of this volume and there is therefore no need to pursue its development in any further detail here; but three points might be helpful in clarifying the nature of this 'legacy'.

First, its doctrine is a combination of two of the principles of the 'Declaration of the Rights of Man and the Citizen'. These are, first, that the nation decides its own destiny and, second, that by 'the nation' is meant the People. Together these combine to produce the doctrine of 'national self-determination', that is, that any group considering itself as a nation has the right to its own nationals as rulers and to frontiers coincident with the territorial distribution of its people. It is put with the utmost—almost naïve—simplicity by J. S. Mill in his *Representative Government* (1861):

Where the sentiment of nationality exists in any force, there is a *prima facie* case for uniting all the members of the nationality under the same government, and a government to themselves apart. This is merely saying that the questions of government ought to be decided by the governed. One hardly knows what any division of the human race should be free to do if not determine with which of the various collective bodies of human beings they choose to associate themselves.[49]

Next, the rapid and ubiquitous spread of this ideology. This must surely be, in part at least, due to its versatility in combining with other ideologies that sprang up in the nineteenth century. But, to be brief, the ideology spread into Latin America, where it provoked secession from the Spanish and Portuguese Crowns, and then, from Western and Eastern Europe it spread ever eastward. The breakup of the European empires gave it full

---

[47] Smith, *Theories of Nationalism*, 17.   [48] Ibid. 171.

[49] J. S. Mill, *Representative Government* (Everyman edn.; Dent, London. 1st pub. 1910, repr. 1971), 360–1.

scope in Asia and then Africa, where most colonial dependencies were receiving their independence in the 1960s. Not one single state in the world has escaped the contagion.

Thirdly, its change of tone. Up to the liberal revolutions of 1848 in Europe, nationalism was liberal[50] and internationalist. The world was seen as a variety of nation-states each in harmony with the other. 'The map of Europe', wrote Mazzini, 'will be re-made. The Countries of the People will rise, defined by the voice of the free, upon the ruins of the Countries of Kings and privileged castes. Between these Countries there will be harmony and brotherhood.'[51] Compare this with Treitschke the historian, reflecting the clumsy brutality of the *Kaiserreich*. States exist, he pronounced through 'ordeal by battle'. 'No State in the world can renounce the "I" in its sovereignty.' 'The grandeur of history lies in the perpetual conflict of nations.' His love-affair with the Teutonic Knights and the ancient *Deutsche Volk* was reflected in a gross arrogance towards other peoples, in particular the French and the Poles, embracing on the way the Belgians and Dutch, but reserving his greatest hatred for the English.[52] For on the way, and with increasing vigour after 1870, the ideology of nationalism had ceased to be the cult of the liberals and had passed to the most extreme conservative elements in society: court, aristocracy, army. The huge following that their leadership attracted cannot be seen to better advantage than in the positions taken up by the two sides in the Dreyfus Affair that split France into two bitterly opposed camps.

But by no means were all the populations affected. In the hiatus left by the decline of nationalism-liberalism and the rise of nationalism-militarism there had emerged the ideology of international socialism, which enjoyed widespread support, particularly in Germany with its large and powerful Social Democratic Party. What is more, all such socialist parties were united, loosely to be sure, in the Second Socialist International. But blood proved thicker than water. When, for reasons of state or further desire for *revanche*, the chauvinists of France, Germany, Austria, and Russia declared war upon one another and a reluctant Britain came in, the Socialist International collapsed and the entire populations of the belligerents supported their war-leaders.

Of the last and tragic development, the end-result was an ultra-nationalist Nazi Germany seeking her war of revenge. Hitler's *Mein Kampf*, semi-

---

[50] For a definition of the term see the following chapter.

[51] J. Mazzini, *The Duties of Man (1844–1858)* (Everyman edn; J. M. Dent, London, 1907), 52.

[52] Quoted in J. Bowle, *Politics and Opinion in the Nineteenth Century* (Jonathan Cape, London, 1954), 353–5.

literate though it is, carries racialist militarism to its utmost. The war he launched showed how prophetic Heine had been 100 years back:

There will come upon the scene armed Fichteans whose fanaticism of will is to be restrained neither by fear nor by self-interest; for they live in the spirit; they defy matter like those early Christians who could be subdued neither by bodily torments nor by bodily delights . . . he has allied himself with the primitive powers of nature, that he can conjure up the demoniac forces of old German pantheism; and having done so, there is aroused in him that ancient German eagerness for battle which combated not for the sake of destroying, not even for the sake of victory, but merely for the sake of the combat itself . . . Then will break forth again the ferocity of the old combatants, the frantic Berserker rage whereof Northern poets have said and sung so much. The old stone gods will arise from the forgotten ruins and wipe from their eyes the dust of centuries, and Thor with his giant hammer will rise again, and he will shatter the Gothic cathedrals . . .[53]

7. THE LEGACY OF THE REVOLUTION: (3) CITIZEN ARMIES

The mass religion of The Nation was reflected in equally mass defence. The mass citizen army was the third great legacy of the Revolution. The concept lapsed with it but revived with the Franco-Prussian War of 1870. Thereafter, Britain alone excepted, it became the universal pattern in Europe.

Some idea of the abyss separating the armies of the pre–1789 period and 1914 can be gleaned by comparing their relative size and ethnic composition. In 1740 the peacetime Prussian army numbered 80,000 men, that of France 160,000.[54] In 1914 the peacetime strength of the German army was 750,000, which swelled to 1,700,000 on a war footing. Excess reserves and the *Landwehr* brought the total that could be put in the field to 5,300,000. The peacetime strength of the French army was 800,000, its wartime strength 1,600,000, which, with reserves, totalled 4,400,000 men that could be put in the field.[55]

That was not the only significant change. In 1914 the armies of the Great Powers were all made up of nationals. This was in sharp contrast to the eighteenth century. Around 1789 a quarter of the French regiments were foreigners. Only a third of the Prussian army was native in 1742, but this figure had risen to 50 per cent by 1750, and two-thirds by 1763.[56]

The Revolution and Empire brought about a complete change in the military strategy and tactics of the day. The flintlock and the socket bayonet

[53] H. Heine, *Religion and Philosophy in Germany*, trans. J. Snodgrass (London, 1882), 159–60.
[54] *CMH*, vii. 179.   [55] J. Archer, *The Art of War in the Western World* (London, 1987), 422.
[56] *CMH*, vii. 180, 182.

had made every soldier both musketeer and pikeman. The result was the *ligne mince* formation. The army would march in column of route and was drilled to change immediately into line formation. So came about the long, thin lines of strictly positioned infantry. Battle consisted of forming a long, thin line and then advancing through the smoke of the field artillery to pour a curtain of fire in the advance and then—at about twenty feet from the enemy—to charge home with the bayonet. The cavalry came in to hold or overwhelm or pursue. Soldiers had to be long and carefully trained to follow these tactics, and that made them a scarce commodity and a very costly one.

The armies that France launched against Austria with such supreme confidence on 20 April 1792 were unfit to fight. They had been weakened by the emigration of their most competent officers,[57] were short of men and *matériel*, and were said by one of their senior officers to be 'distrustful, mutinous and ill-disciplined'.[58] They broke and ran and laid the way open to Paris. The government called for volunteers—hence the famous march of the Marseillais—but only sixty incomplete battalions could be raised. They were obviously not fit to meet the invaders, so (on 11 July 1792) the government declared *la patrie en danger* and ordered every able-bodied male to consider himself liable for service. However, it left the communes and districts to make the invidious choice of who should go to the front. Such soldiers were styled the *fédérés*. Their quality was poor, and despite the *patrie en danger* proclamation only 60,000 were raised, of whom only half joined their units. Furthermore the law limited their liability to the duration of only a particular campaign, so that in December they discharged themselves and the work of recruitment had to begin all over again. In February 1793 the government ordered yet another compulsory levy of 300,000 men. Only half that number was raised. Out of this experience sprang the conviction of the need for wholesale compulsory enlistment, and it was this which was embodied in Carnot's decree putting all able-bodied men 'en réquisition permanente'. This decree differed from its predecessors in that it applied *equally* to *all* able-bodied males between certain ages and for this reason proved acceptable. Only the first tranche (18 to 25 years) was needed: it produced 425,000 men, and from that time on, for the next five years, successive annual intakes from this tranche kept the Republican armies up to strength. At the same time the old-time army, the various types of volunteers, and these newly conscripted troops were welded into one by the *amalgame* of 1793. Effectively two new battalions were brigaded alongside

---

[57] Lafayette reckoned that one-third of the officers had resigned their commissions and expected another third would do so soon (Thompson, *French Revolution*, 266–7).
[58] Quoted, ibid. 267.

one battalion of the old regulars. The total personnel amounted to 750,000 men. Along with Carnot's efficient logistical arrangements and the careful selection of those officers who had showed prowess and intelligence in battle, a new army had been forged. This army not only turned the enemy back but conquered in all directions.

Up to this point it had fought with the old tactics of the eighteenth century. All this was to change. The new tactics were dominated by the iconoclastic notions of the Count Guibert. Guibert had served in the Seven Years War, and then wrote two books of strategy and tactics. Among his chief maxims were: that armies should live off the country they invaded— that 'war must support war'; and that the baggage and supply trains should be kept to the barest minimum, relying on foraging and requisitioning to do the rest and abandoning the *ligne mince* for the column: a unit some 300 men across and twenty-eight ranks in depth. Add to these novel tactics the Republican ardour of the troops and in addition, their own large numbers. Hitherto the infantry had been a precious asset not to be lightly squandered. Now the French could afford to take huge casualties. As Napoleon told Metternich after Austerlitz: 'I can afford to expend thirty thousand men in a month.'[59]

Napoleon took over Guibert's doctrines and use of conscription, or, to speak more accurately, compulsory universal military obligation, where he built on Jourdan's Law of 1798. When enemy territory was annexed this law was enforced there, too. Yet for all that the system contained the elements of its own decay. By 1813, 1,300,000 citizens had been conscripted and in the 1813–14 period Napoleon was able to raise another 1,000,000. Up to that date the conscription does not seem to have been too unfavourably received: the proportion of defaulters and recalcitrants did not exceed 3 or 4 per cent. The number of conscripts evading the draft then rose dramatically as it was realized that the Empire was not 'Peace' but brought perpetual war. Furthermore the armies became increasingly non-French. For the Wagram campaign Napoleon raised 300,000 men, but half were foreigners. In the 700,000-strong Grande Armée only 300,000 were Frenchmen.[60]

We have already mentioned the wave of anti-French and anti-'Jacobin' rage that sprang up in Russia, Austria, and above all, Prussia. There, the immediate result of Jena was to bring reformers like Gneist, Hardenburg, and Scharnhorst to the fore. Napoleon had confined the number of Prussian effectives to a paltry 42,000. The Prussians evaded this by filling

---

[59] Maude, F.N., 'Conscription', *Encyclopaedia Britannica*, 11th edn. (1910–11), vi. 971–4.

[60] Finer, 'State- and Nation-building in Europe: The Role of the Military', in Tilly, *Formation*, 151, 146.

the ranks of time-expired soldiers with new men who in their turn gave way to yet another wave of conscripts so that, in effect the tiny army could be expanded immediately war broke out by the army of reservists, the *Landwehr*. The decision to fight Napoleon came too soon for this to take its full effect and the government had to call on volunteers to swell its numbers.

But, after 1815, these French or Prussian mass armies reverted to the standard regular formats for fighting 'limited wars', and only Russia retained conscription. In Prussia the reformed army was still basically the regulars, but supplemented by the men of the first reserve, the *Landwehr*, which had its own units and officers. The king and the nobles who officered the regular army regarded this force as politically unreliable. In 1862 Count von Roon introduced the army reforms which laid the basis for a new kind of mass army. The concept of universal military obligation was retained, but with a difference. It was de-civilized. The recruit spent three years in the army, and then became a reservist—called up for so many weeks' retraining and exercises every year. Behind them stood yet another force of reservists. Europe scoffed at an army of this kind. The other powers believed it was impossible to train a soldier in less than seven years and looked on the Prussian army as being half-formed of untrained militiamen. They could not have been more wrong. This army smashed the Austrians in six weeks in 1866 and went on to destroy the regular army of France in 1870.

This proved a turning-point. Restoration France's military law had permitted conscripts to buy substitutes and this practice became so widespread that in the Second Empire the army consisted almost entirely of volunteers with seven years' service. Immediately after the débâcle of 1870 argument raged between those who insisted in keeping the old regular format and others who wanted to copy the Prussian system. The latter prevailed. With the British exception, every army on the Continent was based on universal military obligation and organized into line and reserve units as in Germany. It was in this form that the 'nation-in-arms' eventuated in the period leading up to the Great War of 1914–18.

The armies, line and reserve, had now reached those enormous totals shown above—in the order of $4\frac{1}{2}$ million–$5\frac{1}{2}$ million. In the old days no state could have supported the cost of paying so many troops. But now they did not have to pay them more than a mere pittance. Here was a complete contrast with the eighteenth century: after all, it was the cost of the American War that had led to the financial crisis in France and thereby the Revolution. This was all turned on its head, and the reason for it was that by now *the ideology of nationalism* had gripped the masses. It no longer seemed exceptional to be a soldier. Every able-bodied man regarded this, now, as a sacred duty. That is how, when 1914 came, so many millions of men went to their graves like sheep.

In a ghastly parody of those sieges of the eighteenth century, in these new nationalistic wars not cities but entire societies were besieged. Whole states were blockaded to deny the enemy the use of what his supply of *matériel* depended upon. So was initiated submarine warfare, the blockade of food and materials, and, as soon as aeronautical technology permitted it, the destruction of the enemy's civilians since they produced the war *matériel*. At home, all civilians were pressed into service. If not in the ranks, they served in the ammunition factories or on the land. When manpower ran out the states turned to women to carry on these activities. No single part of any nation was not concerned directly or indirectly with supporting the war effort. Not only did the state take over the standard logistical requirements of the armies (Napoleon's mass armies had depended on various private *fournisseurs*), but it went further: it nationalized the economy, it took technology into its own service, and it even took in ideology—its great lie-factories that turned out war propaganda and controlled the press and other mass media. All was now swallowed up in a gigantic extraction–persuasion cycle.

So was ultimately realized the full force of the Carnot *levée en masse* decree.

From this moment until that when the enemy is driven from the territory of the Republic, every Frenchman is commandeered for the needs of the armies. Young men will go to the front; married men will forge arms and carry food; women will make tents and clothing and work in the hospitals; children will turn old linen into bandages; old men will be carried into the squares to rouse the courage of the combatants, and to teach them hatred of kings, and republican unity.[61]

The notion of the nation in arms had returned, but on a scale as comprehensive and as total as society itself. So the whirligig of time brings its revenge.

8. THE LEGACY OF THE REVOLUTION: (4) NEO-ABSOLUTISM—THE FORUM-PALACE POLITY

8.1. *The Jacobin Dictatorship, 1793–1794*

8.1.1. 'DICTATORSHIP'?

'Dictatorship' is one of a family of terms which includes, for instance, 'absolute monarchy' and 'despot' which we have discussed a good deal *en passant* throughout this *History*. Unfortunately, these are terms of art. The

---

[61] Quoted, Thompson, *French Revolution*, 425.

precise meanings that scholars have attached to any of these terms tend to overlap so that definitions are extremely *nuancé*. But for present purposes it is important to see what distinction if any lies between a dictatorship and an authoritarian regime.

Definitions here must be stipulative but must not violate common usage. You would not today, for instance, talk of a 'benevolent tyranny' (though you might, if you were an ancient Greek). The genus, of which all the other terms represent species, is 'authoritarian'. (The word is a neologism of *c.*1880.) The characteristics of authoritarianism are that authority over the people derives from the government, not vice versa, and that techniques, voting, and discussion are based on *its will*. 'Authoritarian', then, describes a *style* of government of either an individual or a collegiate council.

The species of the genus, authoritarian rule, comprise: 'absolutism' *vis à vis* 'despotism', and 'absolute monarch' *vis à vis* 'despot'; 'tyranny', and 'tyrant'; 'autocracy' and 'autocrat'; and, finally 'dictatorship' and 'dictator'. Absolutism and despotism have already been much discussed, so let us turn to 'tyranny'. This too has already been discussed, in its ancient Greek context, in Book II, Chapter 2, where I indicated that it is not until the fourth century BC, and particularly in the work of Aristotle, that *monarchos* is defined favourably, while *tyrannos* is given a very pejorative meaning indeed. It connoted the 'irregular seizure or exercise of power, personal rule, autocratic rule, armed intimidation, pomp and ceremony, but also populist policies'. But Aristotle's *Politics* is pretty confused about the definition, and furthermore he conceded that some tyrannies were benevolent and praiseworthy: for instance, he reports that the tyranny of Peisistratus of Athens was spoken of as a Golden Age.[62]

These characteristics overlap strongly with those we attribute—since *c.*1918—to 'dictatorship'. For instance, that famous historian Elie Halévy wrote an article in 1936 called 'The Age of Tyrannies' where he is clearly referring to what others were calling 'dictatorships'.

Autocracy means, literally, 'of itself, ruling'. It connotes self-standing and self-authorizing rule, unlimited by any other legal authority. The 'autocrat' is the one who rules in this way. The term is neutral between legitimate rule (a king could govern autocratically) and usurped rule. The abstract word 'autocracy' can also be used as a collective noun, as in the late Leonard Schapiro's *The Origins of the Communist Autocracy*.[63]

Thus we come at last to '*dictator*' and '*dictatorship*', and here the usage of the

[62] Bk. II, Ch. 2, above.

[63] L. Schapiro, *The Origins of the Communist Autocracy* (London School of Economics/Bell, London, 1955).

term has changed substantially from its original meaning. Dictatorship is simply the abstract noun relating to the office or the regime of a dictator, and it can be used to refer to the rule of one single individual or of a body of individuals. Hence, for instance, the 'Jacobin dictatorship' and the 'dictatorship of the proletariat'.

As we have seen, the original dictatorship was a constitutional device of the early Roman Republic. In this form, therefore, the term connotes the legitimate conferral of supreme authority on an individual for a limited period in order to deal with a state of emergency. It is what Rossiter called 'Constitutional Dictatorship', and it has not escaped attention that this is akin to the 'War Powers' granted to an American president.[64] But this early Republican usage changed under Sulla and Julius Caesar. Under Sulla's pressure the comitia appointed him *Dictator legibus scribendis et republicae constituendae*—a dictator 'to make the laws and reform the Republic'. This was to confer plenipotentiary powers over the Republic; and furthermore, the tenure of the office was not limited in time. In the Civil Wars Caesar was able to pressure the authorities into appointing him dictator for one year; then, after a short lapse of time, dictator for a ten-year period; and in 44 BC he was appointed *dictator perpetuus*. So 'dictatorship' now acquired the connotation of the usurpation of supreme authority in a crisis situation.

After this the term went to sleep until it sprang up again at the Revolution. One thing is certainly plain: it was the Sulla–Caesar kind of dictatorship that was now being referred to. But the terminology was very confused. Various invidious words were used synonymously, for example, 'Despot', Protectorate (after Cromwell), Protector, and also Cromwellia. But it could also be used in a benevolent sense. Thus, in 1792 Marat did not resist the policy of handing power to a strong and wise man who could be called either a tribune or a dictator.

The ambiguity of meaning is made very plain in 1852 by Bagehot's 'Letters on the French coup d'état of 1851': 'Two things are not quite enough kept apart—I mean the temporary dictatorship of Louis Napoleon to meet and cope with the expected crisis of 1852, and the continuance of that dictatorship hereafter—the New or as it is called, the Bas Empire.'[65]

The former meaning was used by Garibaldi when he declared himself dictator of Naples in 1860; he was holding the situation until the future form of the Italian state was decided and once that was done he stepped down. But later in France it was still being used pejoratively, signifying

---

[64] C. Rossiter, *Constitutional Dictatorship: Crisis Government in the Modern Democracies* (Harcourt Bruce and World, New York, 1963).

[65] W. Bagehot, *Literary Studies*, 4th edn. (Longman, London, 1891), 309 ff.

oppression (1871) or despotism (1869). And note its equivalence with Caesarism: 'Le césarisme c'est la dictature convertie en système permanent de gouvernement.'[66] But by the end of the century the word dictator is being used in its modern sense: Bryce, talking of South America in 1912, says that the subcontinent's imitation of the US Presidency 'generally led straight to dictatorship'.[67] However, it is after 1918 that the word came to be universally used in the sense of crisis management + supreme power + permanence = *illegitimacy*.

8.1.2. THE COMMITTEE OF PUBLIC SAFETY

A brief chronology of the Committee of Public Safety will show the sense in which it was a *dictatorship*. Under the 1791 Constitution the central government consisted of a Cabinet of ministers chosen by the king, *vis-à-vis* an independently elected Legislative Assembly. In August 1792 this arrangement lapsed because the king was no longer permitted to exercise his duties. From that date to June 1793 (the expulsion of the Girondins and triumph of the Mountain) France did not have a government in the usually recognized sense. Executive action emerged from the interplay of ministers (elected by the Assembly) and a number of legislative committees. This was no way to run a country in the throes of revolution and with the enemy advancing on all fronts. When General Dumouriez defected to the enemy in April 1793 the Assembly responded by establishing a Revolutionary Tribunal and two committees—the Committee of General Security (police matters, largely) and the Committee of Public Safety (appointing generals, making peace and war, and controlling the interior), and sanctioned 'Revolutionary Committees' in the *sections* of Paris while sending *représentants en mission* to enforce the Revolution in the provinces. In June the ruling Girondin faction established a 'Revolutionary Army'—'a band of patriotic vigilantes, solid *sansculottes*, who would march into the countryside or anywhere else their services might be required, to root out and punish hoarders, traitors, moderates', and the like.[68] The Committee of Public Safety, acting with extraordinary dispatch, suppressed the Vendée revolt, and through its *représentants en mission*, who were later called 'Terrorists', suppressed the revolts in the bigger towns with ferocious and pitiless barbarity.

To expel the foreign enemy the Assembly, on 23 August 1793, ordered the *levée en masse*. Still faced with a fresh wave of opposition in the great towns, it again meted out its now customary sadism and indiscriminate brutality. Its

[66] M. Jourdeuil, *Du Césarisme en France* (Librairie Muzard, Versailles, Paris, 1871), 5.

[67] J. Bryce, *South America—Observations and Impressions* (Macmillan, London, 1912), 538.

[68] W. Doyle, *The Oxford History of the French Revolution* (Clarendon Press, Oxford, 1989), 244.

hand was vastly strengthened by the Law on Suspects of 17 September 1793, where local watch (*surveillance*) committees could arrest anyone who by his contacts, words, or writings and so forth suggested that he was a supporter of tyranny. These suspects were haled before the Revolutionary Tribunal which sent most of them to the guillotine.

On 10 October the Convention declared that the 'Government of France is revolutionary until the peace': in short, could act at its own discretion and stop at nothing to defend the Republic. Simultaneously the new Jacobin Constitution of 1793 was suspended and St Just proposed that the Committee of Public Safety should take control of the entire state apparatus. Meanwhile the bloody repression in the provinces continued—two-fifths of the executions taking place in the three *départements* that made up La Vendée.

The critical date in the evolution of the Committee of Public Safety as a dictatorship was not reached however till 4 December (14 *Frimaire*) 1793 when, subject to the authority of the Convention, it was vested with supreme powers over all committees dealing with internal administration and police. A Council of Ministers did indeed exist but they were a mere channel for the orders of the committees of General Security and of Public Safety. On what did these rely? What or where was their support? In the armed Commune of Paris, which was always liable to rise against the Convention, and in the network of Jacobin clubs that now ran far and wide. The original Jacobin Club had been established in Paris and provincial centres followed suit. These all corresponded with one another, and in Spring 1790 affiliated to the Paris Club. Their numbers had swelled to some 900 in July.[69]

The Committee of Public Safety, from this time on, established the first strong central authority since 1787. The execution of laws at local level was transferred to the districts and the communes, who had to report every *décadi* (the tenth day of every *décade* of days) to the two Committees. Each was overseen by a 'national agent' appointed by and accountable to the Committees also. All the unofficial bodies that had proliferated in the localities, such as local Revolutionary Armies, were abolished. The twenty-seventh of March 1794 saw the dissolution of the Paris Revolutionary Army—a move that heralded the demise of sansculotte dominance of the government—and on 1 April the Council of Ministers was formally abolished and each department was put into commission headed by a member of the governing committee. But far from bringing an end to the Terror these moves widened and deepened it. The 'left-wing opposition'—Hébert, Ronsin, and others—were arrested, convicted in a rigged trial, and guillotined. Shortly afterwards

---

[69] Ibid. 142–3, 153.

Danton, Desmoulins, and Fabre—close boyhood friends—were 'framed' and executed too: they were accused of being involved in a financial scandal but their real offence to people like Robespierre and St Just was that they wanted some respite in the Terror. Now, on 16 April, all conspiracy cases were transferred from the special *ad hoc* revolutionary courts in the provinces to the Revolutionary Tribunal in Paris, and on 10 June (22 *Prairial*) a law decreed that witnesses were virtually dispensed with, and the accused was denied defending counsel. The effect was immediate. Between March 1793 and August 1794 2,639 people were guillotined, and over half of these (1,515) died during June and July 1794.[70]

But by now the members of the twelve-man Committee of Public Safety were bitterly quarrelling with one another. Furthermore, it had infringed the jurisdiction of its twin committee, the Committee of General Security. But the decisive Battle of Fleurus, on 26 June 1794, proved the catalyst of change. By and large the 'Plain' in the Assembly and Parisian public opinion generally had become nauseated by the tumbrils and the perpetual fall of heads. Yet Robespierre and St Just saw no reason to stop and found enemies of 'Virtue' everywhere. St Just hinted darkly at further prosecutions—of unnamed persons. The deputies demanded a law giving them immunity from the law of 22 *Prairial.* Robespierre (whose appearances at the Convention had become sporadic) returned on 26 July 1794, denouncing few names but seemingly threatening everybody. Swiftly a plot was framed among those who felt most threatened and when Robespierre returned the next day he was shouted down with cries of *à bas le tyran* and arrested. His friends tried to raise the Commune against his accusers but failed. The Convention declared them outlaws and hunted them down. Robespierre and St Just were guillotined on 28 July 1794—the famous '9 *Thermidor*'.

The dismantling of the Committee and its apparatus of Terror throws additional light on the nature of the Committee of Public Safety. Henceforth a quarter of the members of each Committee had to retire every month and were ineligible for immediate re-election. On 1 August the Law of the 22 *Prairial* was repealed, on the 10th the Revolutionary Tribunal was purged, and its infamous president, Fouquier-Tinville, guillotined. The Terror was over: only forty more victims were guillotined by the end of the year. On 11 August the Committee of Public Safety was deprived of its superintending role in government and left to look after only war and foreign affairs.

How far, then, does the Committee of Public Safety conform to the ideal characteristics of a dictatorship expounded above? Certainly it was a crisis

[70] Doyle, *The Oxford History of the French Revolution*, 274–5.

committee, set up to deal with a dire emergency. Next, it was certainly armed with despotic authority to do whatever it thought fit to save the Republic, limited only by the complementary functions of the Committee of General Security. But the third test, surely, fails? This Committee *was* responsible to a higher authority—the Convention—which designated it, gave it its powers, and could (and ultimately did) terminate it. But if we accept this, we need not deny that the Committee was a dictatorship, merely that it resembled that of early Republican Rome. But *is* it necessary to accept this? The Committee established a dominance over the Convention by its control of the armed and militant Commune and the Jacobin chain of clubs, not by free exercise of the Convention's vote. So placed, it was able to pressure the Convention to give it a free hand. At least, then, from December 1793 to the guillotining of Robespierre in July 1794 the Committee can fairly be described as a 'dictatorship'.

It was the creation of a minority, the triumphant leaders of the Mountain, itself a party among republicans, who in their turn did not include all the people in France. As in the name of liberty France now possessed the most dictatorial government it had ever known, so, in the name of the people, it now had the political system which, of all systems in its history, probably the fewest people liked. The ruling group knew that in a free election it would not be supported.[71]

8.1.3. MILITARY INTERVENTION IN POLITICS

The experiences of Rome, of the medieval Italian city-states, the activities of such corps as the Mamluks, the Janissaries, and the Streltsi all attest the antiquity—and ubiquity—of military intervention in politics. But these troops lacked any political motivation; their motive was individual self-interest—the desire to put 'their' man into power so as to receive better pay and conditions.[72] Such military intervention differs essentially from military intervention as we know it today. Its seed-plot was the French Revolution and Empire, because hereby were engendered three elements which separately and conjointly form the necessary conditions of such a novel kind of military intervention.

The first is the professionalization of the officer corps. This opened a gap between the armed forces and the politicians for, under the *ancien régime,* policy-making and the task of fighting both lay in the same hands—those of the aristocracy. The second was the rise of nationalism and the nation-

[71] Palmer, *Twelve Who Ruled,* 128.

[72] The great exception is the English Revolution of 1642–60. But it was a unique antecedent and generated no forces of attraction in the world such as would stimulate further adventures on this pattern.

state. Nation replaced dynasty as the object of military loyalty. It provided the military with a civic religion and an overriding set of values. It provided them with an ideology. So, whereas in the *ancien régime* loyalty to state and ruler were synonymous, this was no longer so; it had to be demonstrated to the troops that the government they served was synonymous with and representative of the nation. The third element, closely associated with this both historically and logically, was the substitution of the dogma of popular sovereignty for the divine authority of kings. In the dynastic state the most that soldiers could do was to replace the monarch by another monarch, or rule through his person. Only the monarch conferred legitimacy. But once *vox populi* is *vox dei*, then any Tom, Dick, or Harry who can muster even a mere show of popular support can claim to be the legitimate government. This popular support was assumed to underlie the dictatorship of the Committee of Public Safety and the numerous *journées* when the Paris Commune or *sections* of it used armed force against the Convention. Not once in all these *journées* were the people of France consulted, but in not one of them was the action taken not carried out in their name. The infinite malleability of this new political formula was fully grasped by Napoleon. 'The appeal to the people', he wrote 'has the double advantage of legalizing the prolongation of my power and of purifying its origins. In any other way it must always have appeared equivocal.' And again: 'I did in no way usurp the crown; I picked it up from the gutter. The people set it upon my head.'[73]

However, 'military intervention' admits of several degrees. One might range these in a spectrum. At one pole the army is acting constitutionally, 'in aid of the civil power'. However, as government comes to depend on its support *the army* may use the government's dependency to blackmail it. This can develop into, effectively, military *indirect* rule, that is to say, directing the policies of the government from behind the scenes, including evicting the government for a more compliant one. Finally comes direct military rule by the military: this generally assumes the form of a take-over of government by a section of the armed forces which is, or purports to be, representative of the rank and file. It is here that one must be very careful. The army may play a dominating active role in government. Usually the ringleaders form a military junta which appoints a civil cabinet to execute its orders. But it may be that the military, having once overthrown the civil government and established its military leader(s) in its place, returns to the barracks and plays at most a supportive role (in case there is any opposition) and lets 'its' man get on with it. Direct active rule by a body of military men who represent the political views of the troops (or purport to) ought to be

[73] Quoted, Napoleon, *Vues politiques* (Paris, 1939), 65, 66–7.

distinguished from the usual term 'military regime' or 'military dictatorship' by a special term. It should be called a *statocracy*: the active rule of the army as such. It is the *nec plus ultra* of all the military regimes. But it cannot be emphasized too strongly that the intervention of the army does not necessarily lead to a military regime at all. Not all regimes brought about by a military intervention are necessarily 'military regimes'—they may be simply regimes of military provenance. The most famous contemporary illustration is, perhaps, the accession of General Charles de Gaulle under the threat of armed insurrection.[74]

The relevance of this analysis is to distinguish the role of the military under the Directory from what it was under Napoleon. Until 1795 the usurpation of power was carried out by the sansculottes of Paris in *journées* of a popular and insurrectionary character. But by 1795 the army had been reconstituted and became a political force once again, and from that year ever more obviously decisive. On 22 August the Convention voted a new constitution with the executive vested in five directors, working to two legislative Chambers. For the first election, however, two-thirds of the members of both Chambers were to be taken from the members of the Convention. A clamour immediately arose in the *sections* of Paris which had now fallen under Royalist influence. On 13 *Vendémiaire* (5 October) they marched on the Tuileries. Facing them, under Barras, were the regular forces, with Napoleon in charge of the cannon. Here he launched his 'whiff of grapeshot'.[75] The insurrectionaries fled; and by this it was established that the regular army was once again the ultimate bulwark of the civil power. Thus the Right had been defeated; on 18 *Fructidor* (4 September) 1797 it was the turn of the Left. Whereas in *Vendémaire* the army perpetuated the rule of the Thermidorians, in *Fructidor* it was called in by one faction of Thermidorians to suppress the other. Napoleon (in Italy) sent orders to General Augereau to suppress the 'Left inclining' members of the Directory—which he duly did. He ordered the arrest of the 'soft' directors, Carnot and Barthélemy, as well as of General Pichegru and fifty-three Deputies. When one of these asked Augereau by what right he did so, the general replied 'By the right of the sword'. The rump of the Council of the Five Hundred was then surrounded by troops and forced to pass the law by which the recent elections in no less than forty-nine *départements* were annulled and the victorious faction charged with filling the vacancies.

[74] For the above analysis I have relied on S. E. Finer, 'Morphology of Military Régimes', in R. Kolkowicz, and A. Korbonski (eds.), *Soldiers, Peasants and Bureaucrats: Civil Military Relations in Communist and Modernising Societies* (G. Allen & Unwin, London, 1982), 281–310; id., 'The Retreat to the Barracks', *Third World Quarterly*, 7:1 (1985), 16–30, and *Man on Horseback*.

[75] The famous phrase is Carlyle's.

Napoleon now took himself off to Egypt, a not very successful enterprise. During his absence the enemy re-opened its offensive and scored smashing victories on the Rhine and in Italy. Internally, too, matters had gone from bad to worse and the financial situation was disastrous. It was in these circumstances that Sieyès and Roger-Ducos decided that the Directory must be overthrown and a new constitution enacted. They were looking 'for a sword'. When their first choice, Joubert, was killed in action, they bethought themselves of Napoleon. On 8 October he arrived unannounced from Egypt.

Up to this point the army had intervened in support of the civil power. On 18 *Brumaire* (9 November) it intervened against it, thus heralding in the Consulate and the Empire.

8.1.4. CONSULATE AND EMPIRE: POPULIST AUTHORITARIANISM

Napoleon's Consulate and Empire was *not* a military regime. It was an authoritarian regime ruled, not by a dictator, but by an autocrat. The *coup d'état* of 18 *Brumaire* 1799 was not very military. It was in fact thoroughly bungled, and only the timely action of Lucien Bonaparte (Napoleon's brother) rescued it. The two Chambers were ringed by 300 guardsmen, and when the Chambers refused to establish a committee to enact a new constitution soldiers cleared the hall. A rump quorum was assembled which adjourned the legislature for six weeks while a committee prepared a new constitution. Meanwhile government was vested in a provisional government of three consuls—Ducos, Sieyès, and Napoleon. If this bungled affair was a 'military intervention' it certainly was one of the most nominal. Furthermore, once the Moor had done his work, the Moor could go: the military as such received no special consideration whatsoever and for its part never sought to meddle in the civil polity. For instance, in Napoleon's Council of State—a conclave of top advisers—only four members were generals.

The result of the coup was the constitution of the Year VIII: the Consulate. Executive power was vested in three consuls, but, as first consul, it was effectively in Napoleon's hands, the other two acting as advisers. Yet they had to work to a legislature. This complicated structure reflected Sieyès's dislike of the common people. It rested on a very complex form of indirect election. Each commune voted a list of persons, numbering one-tenth of its citizens, deemed worthy to conduct public business. This list then proceeded to elect one-tenth of its number and these made up the departmental list. This in its turn elected a tenth of its members—this was the national list. The choice of members was vested in a new body, the Senate. From this list first the Consulate appointed twenty-four members and these co-opted others to form a body of sixty. These sixty then drew up a list of 100 members for the Tribunate and 300 for the Legislature. The Tribunate could discuss or propose legislation but not vote on it whereas the Legislature could vote but not discuss it, and neither Chamber had a legislative initiative. That came from the executive, in brief, from Napoleon working with his Council of State. The power delivered to the executive was therefore immense, but it should not be supposed that the members of these bodies were nobodies. On the contrary, nearly all had been a member of one or other of previous legislatures. What is more, although their powers were shackled they could still make things difficult for the executive. Finally, the Senate could advise on the constitutionality of such laws as were passed.

This Constitution was then put to the people in a plebiscite. The official figures were 3,011,007 in favour and only 1,562 against. But these figures were rigged. Lucien Bonaparte, who conducted the plebiscite, had told his official to add between 8,000–14,000 'yes' votes per candidate. Sutherland reckons that the adjusted figures mean that about 1,500,000 voted 'yes' and 1,500 voted 'no'.[76]

From then on the regime became increasingly autocratic, especially after Napoleon had won the Battle of Marengo in 1801. That gave him undisputed authority. He had already embarked on the civil reforms that were to make him justly famous: the pacification of La Vendée, a successful fiscal reform, a superintending administrator (the prefect) in every one of the *départements* answerable only to him, the establishment of a nation-wide network of primary and secondary schools, and the codification of the laws and decrees of the Republic in a clearly written single document. His crowning difficulty lay in making his peace with the Church, and this he had negotiated with the Vatican by the Concordat of 1801. But to his mind the legislative Chambers were becoming obstructive—for instance, over the peace treaties he had signed, such as the Treaty of Lunéville (1801)—while they seemed to be dragging their feet interminably in drafting the Civil Code. By the spring of 1801, it is true, only six of Napoleon's bills had been rejected, but he feared the fate of the Concordat, a most contentious issue, when that came up in the Session of 1801–2. Most astutely he used the constitutional provision that stipulated that one-fifth of the membership of the two Chambers must be renewed in 1802: but it did not say how or exactly when. Napoleon therefore called on the docile Senate to name the members who should remain as deputies: and by this simple device sixty (opposition) names were dropped from the Legislative body and twenty from the Tribunate. This purge sufficed and Napoleon got his legislation.

[76] Sutherland, *France 1789–1815*, 339–400.

In that year Napoleon signed the peace treaty of Amiens with England. At last France was at peace. In these circumstances Napoleon moved a step further towards autocracy by getting the legislative bodies to propose him as life consul. Approved by them, it was to be put to a plebiscite. Meanwhile a new constitution was drafted. Napoleon was to name his own successor. The Senate's independence was further weakened by the first consul's right to nominate fourteen of its members and to add to the membership distinguished notables who had not been presented through the electoral colleges. The Legislative body lost its power to ratify treaties of peace or alliance which only the first consul might negotiate, and the Tribunate was reduced to only fifty members. Neither Chamber had to meet regularly. Furthermore, with the approval of the Senate by a *senatus consultum* he could himself amend the constitution, and he alone had the right to nominate the members of this body.

This constitution was drafted before the results of the plebiscite were known. The vote for the Life Consulate was 3,568,000 in favour to 8,374 against. Two years later Napoleon completed his journey to autocracy: on 3 May 1804 the now-domesticated Tribunate expressed the wish that 'Bonaparte be proclaimed hereditary Emperor of the French'. The Senate and the Legislative body drew up a bill which then became an organic *senatus consultum*. It was then submitted to the people for ratification: 3,572,000 voted 'yes' to 2,569 'nos'. The Legislative body disappeared and the Tribunate is not heard of after 1808. The emperor was sole ruler.

How was his rule maintained? Not by the show of military force, to be sure—nor even by its presence. It was partly based on the genuine popularity of Napoleon. Furthermore, the Concordat and the pacification of La Vendée had removed the main sources of discontent. When Napoleon returned victorious from Marengo he found that deserters from the draft had formed robber gangs called *chauffeurs* and that banditry was rife—he soon put paid to that. Moreover, Napoleon demanded far smaller drafts than had the revolutionary regimes—between Years VIII and XII he conscripted some 200,000 men, which is about half the number conscripted in the single levy of the Year VII. In contrast to 1801, well over 90 per cent of the conscripts levied up to 1808 fulfilled their obligation.[77]

But there was a darker side. The country was honeycombed with spies and informers and watched over by a vigilant and efficient police. 'The basis of this structure was the Code Napoléon; then came the judicial system, then the police and the prisons; then the Censorship and meaningly, along-

---

[77] Sutherland, *France 1789–1815*, 377.

side all this, military courts, special tribunals, arbitrary imprisonment and deportations.'[78] The various types of prison were filled not just via the courts, but by way of orders signed by a *grand juge* or the *ministre de police*. Did the citizen have any remedy? In theory, yes. The minister was supposed not to detain a prisoner without charge for more than ten days, but if he did there followed an extremely lengthy and tortuous procedure culminating— again in theory—in the Legislative body denouncing the minister to the High Court of Justice. In practice, over a span of ten years the system never declared that a single person had been arbitrarily arrested.[79]

Little by little the press was closed down. In 1800 the Paris press was cut from thirteen papers to nine, then cut further to a mere four in 1811. Prior censorship had been introduced in 1805 and after 1807 only one newspaper was allowed in each *département*. At the same time the official *Moniteur* carried or distorted or utterly suppressed news according to the emperor's will. Journals were not spared, either. In 1810 a set of imperial censors was set up and ninety-seven of the 157 presses in Paris were closed, while publishers had to take out a licence and swear an oath.

The emperor, it must be remembered, was not a kindly figure; he was imperious. As he had said when re-introducing indirect taxation in 1805: 'Do I not have my gendarmes, my Prefects, and my priests? If any one should revolt, I will have five or six rebels hanged and *everyone else will pay*.'[80]

Napoleon was not a 'dictator', for his rule was not to confront a crisis. Napoleon was an *autocrat*, and his regime was an authoritarian one—very authoritarian. We have already outlined the authoritarian implications of the 1802 constitution. But meanwhile, more and more appointments—of electors, chairmen, magistrates, senators, and public servants of all kinds— fell into Bonaparte's hands and transformed a nominally democratic govern- ment into an oligarchy of officials and experts appointed and dismissed by a single guiding will. This, 'at the beginning of the nineteenth century', says Thompson, 'was a new theory of government.'[81]

This illegitimate regime by a usurper who had made his own rules and justified them by an appeal to the people represented a new type of regime, comparable only to the Greek 'tyranny'. It was Palace rule justified by the sovereignty of the people. In this way it was a compound of Palace (which was the executive government) and Forum (the popular base). It was this kind of populist autocracy to which Sir Henry Maine drew attention. 'Since that time [i.e. since 'rulers became delegates of the community'] there has

---

[78] J. M. Thompson, *Napoleon Bonaparte: His Rise and Fall* (Blackwell, Oxford, 1951), 196.
[79] Ibid. 198.
[80] G. Lefebvre, *Napoleon from 18 Brumaire to Tilsit, 1799–1807*, trans. H. F. Stockhold (Routledge & Kegan Paul, London, 1969), 186–7. [81] Thompson, *Napoleon Bonaparte*, 190.

been no such insecurity of government since the century during which the Roman Emperors were at the mercy of the Praetorian soldiers.'[82] By various routes—it may be by the victory of an insurrectionary army (e.g. in Latin America since 1810 and in countries like Algeria today) or by some military coup which installs a military man or a group of them as supreme rulers and then 'validates' them by a popular vote, usually based on fear and fraud— the Palace/Forum regime has become a commonplace throughout Latin America, Africa, and South-East Asia, that is, in the succession states of the great European empires.

Why then do I claim the French Revolution as the most important single event in the history of government? In those few years it bequeathed to us the universalistic 'Rights of Man and the Citizen' which is the charter of all would-be nation-states, and a commonplace among the old-established European ones and their overseas extensions; the ideology, the new secular religion, of nationalism; citizen armies and the *levée en masse*; and military interventions and the Palace/Forum type of polity—the regime of populist autocracy. Moreover, and this is the significant point, all four of these are still alive, working like a leaven throughout the globe. In that sense the revolution is a Permanent Revolution. Nothing was ever like it before and nothing foreseeable will turn this Revolution back. The truth of this will become manifest in the chapters that follow.

---

[82] H. Maine, *Popular Government* (John Murray, London, 1885), 158.

4

The Constitutionalization of the Absolute
Monarchies of Europe, 1815–1871

1. THE TYPOLOGY REDEFINED

*T*he American, and more significantly, the French Revolutions worked a
change in the ordering of society and in consequence drastically altered
the typology of polities we have been following till now. For as a result of
the secularization and democratization of society after 1776, and particularly
after 1789, two hitherto great Orders, each capable (in principle) of ruling a
state on its own, namely the Clergy and the Nobility, ceased to be viable
ruling strata. Consequently the two pure types—Clergy polities and Nobility polities—totally disappeared. By the same token so did all their hybrids.
Of our previous ten types we are left with only three. These are the Pure
Palace, the Pure Forum, and the Palace/Forum. Given the degree of
democratization in the world, the Pure Palace type persists only in some
principalities of the Third World, such as Saudi Arabia. It is not worthwhile keeping it in the typology, which therefore reduces itself to two main
types only—the Forum and the Palace/Forum—which will be recognized
immediately as, in other words, some kind of democracy, and authoritarianism. This is somewhat like Machiavelli's reduction of polities into those
ruled by princes and those ruled collegiately. But these categories are so
wide that they conceal at least as many differences as they reveal. Something
more fine-meshed is required.

It can be provided by pursuing the status of the two Orders, the Clergy
and the Nobility (including in the latter *hacienderos, caciques,* in short, the
'historic oligarchies'[1]), after these have lost their potential to act as the
ruling élite. These great corps do not disappear—they simply decline, to the
status of *corps intermédiaires,* that is, pressure groups and the like. Furthermore, to anticipate, in Europe neither departed the scene without a great
struggle. They remained immensely powerful groups within the state
throughout the nineteenth century, their power only waning gradually;
they were not spent forces until, perhaps, 1918.

[1] As described in Finer, *Man on Horseback,* ch. 9, 'The Façade-Democracies'.

In this sense they still form part of the Palace/Forum and the Forum types but dichotomize both of these into two major classes: the Pluralistic (if they are present and active) and the Monistic (if they are absent or wholly inert). But post-1800 the Church and the Nobility were not the only forces in the state. Two new forces emerged, side by side with the still-active Church and Nobility, the fruits of the Industrial Revolution. These are respectively organized Labour and organized Capital. And these two groupings also form part of the class of plural societies, whether of the Forum or even the Palace/Forum type. Admittedly it is possible just to conceive of a wholly monistic Forum polity. It would be Robespierre's Jacobin *une volonté une*. Though this did not exist (subject to a later qualification), it is this concept and the intention to make it come true in practice that makes for the two possible classes of Palace/Forum polity: the pluralistic Palace/Forum type, which is authoritarianism (e.g. Franco's Spain) and very much like old absolute monarchy writ large; and the monistic Palace/Forum polity, which we used to call totalitarianism.

This can be put by way of a two-by-two matrix, thus:

	Pluralistic	*Monistic*
Palace/Forum	Authoritarianism	Totalitarianism
Forum	Liberal Democracy; Constitutionalism	Jacobinism

where 'pluralistic' stands for the active presence of (i) historic oligarchies of clergy and nobility, and (ii) new forces of organized labour and capital. The so-called 'totalitarian' model is a twentieth-century phenomenon, and consequently falls to be discussed later. But the matrix contains two terms which we have had occasion to use without giving them any precise definitions. These are 'liberal democracy' and 'constitutionalism'.

2. LIBERAL DEMOCRACY AND CONSTITUTIONALISM

A state can be liberal and not democratic; equally, a state may have a constitution without being constitutionalist. Hong Kong at the time this is written [i.e. before 1997] exemplifies the first; the constitution of imperial Ethiopia, which simply stated that all powers resided in the emperor, is an example of the second.

For present purposes a democracy can be defined as a state where political decisions are taken by and with the consent, or the active participation even, of the majority of the People. This definition deliberately begs the question of 'who are the People?', because answers to it explain why, when, and how the qualification 'liberal' applies. As a key ideology of the nineteenth century, liberalism demands a much wider discussion than is offered here. This must be deferred to a later page, for liberalism is a protean term that may connote an ideology, or a movement, or a package of measures and which, moreover, differed from country to country. In all these respects it resembles the Enlightenment, and indeed it is this movement's nineteenth-century manifestation. But, as in the Enlightenment, despite all the complications and aberrancies, a hard core of principle persists. This might be described as the precedence of the individual over the state: hence it demands that what it regards as the basic political freedoms of the individual be protected from the state. What these are is discerned by various routes—for example, natural-rights theory, such as Locke's 'life, liberty, and property' or the American Declaration of Independence's 'life, liberty and the pursuit of happiness'. These rights are held to be self-evident. They are also inalienable. For the moment it suffices to say that in the nineteenth century they consisted, roughly speaking, of a conflation of the rights conferred by the American Constitution and those listed in the French 'Declaration'. Perhaps the very minimum deemed acceptable to the liberal persuasion is to be found in the Constitutional Charter grudgingly conferred by the restored Bourbons on the French people in 1814. It promises equality before the law, equal access to all civil and military offices, freedom from being charged or arrested except for offences enumerated in pre-existing legislation, freedom to follow one's own religion and likewise to publish one's views, and the inviolability of one's property except for compulsory purchase for legally justified reasons.

Now this ring-fencing of certain liberties against intrusion by the state will apply whether the state is a democracy or not. It is all the same to the individual if he is dispossessed of his property by a despot or a popular majority. This is why, as we have stated, it is in principle possible for a state to be non-democratic and yet liberal. It was something of this kind at which the proponents of enlightened despotism were aiming. The difficulty arises from the uncertainty as to how long or under what interpretation these civil rights will be observed under different sets of rulers. It is precisely at this point that the ideal of a fixed constitution arises. But let us put this aside for the moment so as to consider the situation where the 'People' rule. For we are not considering liberalism *per se* but exploring the meaning of liberal *democracy*.

The 'People' are not a solid lump, nor are they necessarily congruent with the electorate. Who are they? If the People are to be less than the totality of adults in the society, then by what criterion is one to delimit this minority—the *pays réel* as against the *pays légal*, as the French put it? Is it to be by literacy or knowledge of the constitution or some other such educational accomplishment? Or by a property or an income qualification—a *démocratie censitaire*? If so how much education and/or property? What does a 'majority of the People' then signify? Given an electorate of a certain size, whether restricted or not, what proportion of this counts as a large enough majority to to be empowered to legislate? The question is relevant because a plurality or even a simple majority might not be thought sufficient if the state contains permanent minorities which can never become majorities and are consequently as much at the mercy of the state as they would be under a despotic monarchy. Sometimes this matter goes deeper still; there are some issues, of religion or nationality, for instance, which are too heartfelt to be negotiable. In such cases liberalism, though recognizing that in the last resort the 'legal majority' must prevail, tries to protect the minorities as it does the civil rights of the individual, and by much the same methods. All of them would have to be protected from 'pure' majoritarian rule. This calls for the slowing down of the decision-making process so as to give time for a minority to persuade the majority or even to become a majority in its own right. All manner of institutional devices have been designed to ensure that the contested decision is very hard to make: for instance, second chambers, the separation of powers and similar checks and balances, federalism, or complicated legislative and administrative procedures. As to those issues that are extremely intractable or even non-negotiable, they would require that the constitution itself must be changed: this is usually painfully difficult and slow.

Whatever exception be taken to the way the argument has been developed here, the drift must be perfectly clear. Liberal democracy is *qualified* democracy. The ultimate right of the majority to have its way is conceded, but that way is made as rough as possible.

This definition of liberal democracy overlaps with the second of the concepts we are dealing with—to wit, *constitutionalism*. In a sense, as we have said earlier, all states have constitutions if this term be thought of as the totality of its political arrangements: it would not be far-fetched to say that in the Third Reich Hitler's will, according to the *Führer-Prinzip*, was the constitution. But *constitutionalism* is a different matter. It consists in (1) restricting the powers of the government to conform to the ideals of liberalism, that is, the limitation of arbitrary rule and the guarantee of the immunities of the individuals and associations that make up the society; (2) defining these rules either through the mixture of written law, conventions, and common law principles, which is the British way (and very rare indeed) or, as is all but universal today, by codifying them in a written document; (3) treating this constitution as the supreme law of the land, all other acts of government having to comply with these rules; and (4) abiding by it. Short of these four principles the civil rights of individuals would be open to interpretation, change, or even suspension according to the will, even the whim, of the ruler. This applies, be it noted, whether the ruler is an elected legislative assembly or a monarch, and for the reasons we have already advanced. In brief, there would be no certainty. One of the most important reasons why the Americans produced a written constitution turned exactly on this point. They felt that the principles which they regarded as the time-honoured rules of the British constitution and their birthright had been perverted by the British Crown-in-Parliament. Having decided to reclaim these rights and, indeed, improve on them, they tried to impart fixity to them—and this by way of writing them down (which included manifold institutional devices to ensure that they stayed put). All the written constitutions that were to follow, beginning with the French and its preambular 'Declaration of the Rights of Man and the Citizen', were inspired by the same purpose.

Not all constitutions are restrictive of power. Some, like parts of the Brezhnev constitution, are enabling of power.[2] But the commonly acquired meaning of constitutionalism is that the constitution in question is to *guarantee* the rights of subjects. Sartori has defined the constitution as being, precisely, a fundamental law or set of principles and correlated institutional arrangements to restrict arbitrary power and ensure limited government, and, at another place, as 'a frame of political society *organized through and by the law* for the purpose of restraining arbitrary power'.[3] Examining the history of the term 'constitution', he maintains that its 'present-day conceptualization . . . really gained ground and acquired a definite connotation only in America during the years 1776–1787'.[4] By the nineteenth century, however, that connotation had spread all over Europe as well as in the United States.

In the nineteenth century, all over Europe as well as in the United States, a general agreement prevailed as to the basic meaning of the term 'constitution'. In 1830, and especially during the 1848 revolutions it was very clear on both sides of the Channel what people were asking for when they claimed a constitution. If, in England, 'constitution' meant the system of British liberties, *mutatis mutandis* the Europeans wanted exactly the same thing: a system of protected freedom for the individual which—according to the American usage of the English vocabulary—they called a 'constitutional system'. Having to start from naught, people on the Continent (as

---

[2] See my *Five Constitutions*, 28–9, on the Brezhnev Constitution of 1977.

[3] G. Sartori, 'Constitutionalism: A Preliminary Discussion', *American Political Science Review*, 56: 4 (Dec. 1962), 860.   [4] Ibid. 859.

was first achieved by the Americans) wanted a written document, a charter, which would firmly establish the overall supreme laws of the land.[5]

3. COMPETING IDEOLOGIES: THE NEW MAP OF EUROPE AND THE PRINCIPLE OF LEGITIMACY

For twenty-five years Europe had been in turmoil: it had experienced the Revolution, unending wars, the deposition of monarchs, the incessant alteration of frontiers. After Waterloo the overwhelming desire of the potentates assembled at the Congress of Vienna in 1815 was to get back to where things had been before. That was not always possible, especially in the areas Napoleon had conquered and occupied, but the Congress did what it could. It remodelled the map of Europe as little as possible, and where it could not it worked on the principle of the balance of power, realized through dynastic exchanges of bits of territory—the principle of 'compensation'. And it restored, wherever possible, the exiled kings and princes to the thrones from which they had been driven: the principle of 'legitimacy'.

France was returned to its 1790 borders. The Austrian Netherlands, later to be called Belgium, was ceded by Austria to combine with Holland. Prussia received an important stretch of territory on the middle Rhineland. A German Confederation of thirty-nine states—which included both Prussia and Austria—was established under the presidency of Austria, which received back Lombardy and Venetia as compensation for giving up the Netherlands. The pope went back to his Papal States. The Bourbons were restored in Naples. The little duchies of Parma, Modena, and Tuscany were placed under Austrian princes. Piedmont won back Savoy and received Genoa. The Bourbons were restored in Spain, the House of Braganza in Portugal. And in the Baltic, Norway was taken from Denmark and united with Sweden. Switzerland was declared permanently neutral.

Monarchy was the rule, then, but with very few exceptions it was absolute monarchy. This was to change; by the end of our period only Russia was not a 'constitutional' monarchy. This momentous transition was fought out in terms of competing ideologies. I shall not dally to attempt a full explication of the term 'ideology'. Great wars and civil wars of the sixteenth and seventeenth centuries had been fought between rival religions. There were some Enlightenment figures who held their convictions with religious fervour. But it was not until the French Revolution that we find self-consistent intellectual philosophies of a this-worldly nature being held

---

[5] Sartori, 'Constitutionalism: A Preliminary Discussion', 854.

with the millennial fervour that had marked the religious conflicts. These ideologies were in truth so many secular religions.

They may be reduced to four. They were liberalism; what may be described by the catch-all expressions of traditionalism or conservatism; nationalism, sometimes of the liberal persuasion and sometimes of the conservative disposition; and what passed for 'socialism' at this early stage, when continental Europe was hardly touched by the industrialism so precociously developed in Britain.

3.1. *The Spread of Nationalism*

Of nationalism we are already aware. And we showed how French nationalism provoked counter-nationalisms in such countries as Spain, Prussia, and Germany–Austria. This heady ideology spread until it covered virtually the entire Continent and Ireland. It spread quickly enough in the former 'sister-republics' of France, notably Italy, the Rhineland, and Poland. Then it moved to the Balkans, where first the Serbs and then the Greeks fought the ruling Ottoman power, until the former obtained autonomy in 1829 and Greece obtained full independence in 1830. Meanwhile it was spreading in the German Confederation, not only to its ethnic German components, but to the non-German parts of Austria, especially in Hungary and the northern and southern Slav territories. In all these countries nationalism went hand in hand with liberalism until at least 1848, after which it flirted with and then married Conservatism. At all events it would have been hard to find a country which was not by 1848 affected by the fever.

But for the most part this fever was a middle-class condition. Outside the national states of the west, the nationalist movement had no mass basis except in Ireland. The most traditional and backward or poor sectors of a country were the last to be involved in such movements. Instead, they were the province of that narrow stratum lying between the aristocracy, great landowners and the capitalist class (where this existed), and what went for 'the People'—effectively, the educated: teachers, priests, shopkeepers, artisans, and students (the last being very important as the catalysts of the 1848 revolutions).

However, as the educated middle classes perceived it, the nation-state had to be a self-sufficient, viable entity, large enough to look after itself. This was to copy the paradigm of the western 'historical' national states such as France, Britain, and Spain. But the further east one went, the less the paradigm applied. There, the nationalities were either small and/or scrambled up with others. The middle-class nationalists of the greater nations (Prussians, Austrians, Magyars) which ruled such lesser national identities were not prepared to grant them independent nationhood. Some argued that they were not 'real' nations, others that the course of events would reduce them to mere provincial idiosyncrasies, like Catalans in Spain, or the Occitans in France. Or, they could emasculate them via the schools system and the systematic enforcement of their own language—Magyarization, Germanization, Italianization.

3.2. *Liberalism*

We have already said that the essentials of liberalism were the limitation of arbitrary government by institutional controls (usually including a representative assembly) and guaranteed specified rights of the individual against encroachment by government irrespective of its complexion. But British, French, and German versions of liberalism were notably different.

Britain already had what the Continental countries were seeking. She had a representative Parliament that acted as a most powerful check on the executive—indeed, after 1834 one that could and did control the executive to make itself sovereign. Her peoples had long enjoyed the personal rights that the European liberals were demanding. The distinctive feature of British liberalism was its positivism. This is the very hallmark of the outlook of Jeremy Bentham and the jurist John Austin, and the school of Philosophical Radicals generally. There was no truck with any 'rights' that were not embodied in law, no reliance on historical precedent or prescription. Bentham mocked at 'Lady Matchless Constitution', he called natural rights 'nonsense on stilts', and dismissed the German Savigny's historical approach to jurisprudence as resembling a man who wants to cook a dinner but instead of receiving a cookery-book is given the past set of household accounts. Institutions were to be judged solely by whether they served a useful purpose. Every person was the judge of his own interests, and everyone was to count as one and nobody more than one. An elected parliament would thus provide a snapshot of the sum of interests; the majority would then, definitionally, register the greatest happiness of the greatest number. The difficulty lay in that individuals, though their choice must be respected, might not act in an enlightened way; hence the noxious interference of 'sinister interests'. The notion that the sum of free-willing interests produced the greatest good of the greatest number, when applied to economics by Ricardo and his school, yielded the argument for free trade and *laissez faire*, later vulgarized in the tenets of the Manchester school. Bentham's crude and uncompromising effort to reduce issues to a quantitative, 'cost–benefit' 'calculus of pleasures and pains' was later highly modified by John Stuart Mill's attempt to incorporate the 'quality' of pleasure into this calculus. It humanized the philosophy but at the cost of self-consistency.

John Mill and his fellow British liberals (unlike Bentham and James Mill) fought extremely shy of universal suffrage, and indeed this was a marked feature of earlier-nineteenth-century liberalism throughout Europe: it was a middle-class creed. Nowhere was this more marked than in France, where, with some justice in view of their recent experiences, they equated democracy with mob-rule. French liberalism delimited itself on the basis of wealth: the *pays légal* as against the *pays réel*. It advocated a moderate constitutionalism which, by the division of powers and parliamentary control, tended 'rather to limit than appropriate the action of the State and the government'.[6]

Benjamin Constant (1767–1830) is typical. He strongly opposed a wide suffrage: his obsession was to safeguard individual liberties. Popular sovereignty meant to him that no faction or person might arrogate itself a sovereignty not delegated to it by the People. But, he hastened to say: 'There is a part of human life which necessarily remains individual and independent, and has the right to stand outside all social control. Where the independent life of the individual begins, the jurisdiction of the sovereign ends.'[7] Many of the rights claimed by Constant and such liberals as Royer-Collard were to be found already in the Charter of 1814 conferred on France by the restored Bourbon, Louis XVII and outlined in Section 2 above. To these the liberals added, *inter alia*, security of person and family, freedom of industry, and jury trial. But, as Constant and his fellow-liberal Royer-Collard (1763–1845) insisted, these rights could only be made secure and certain by political guarantees. The first was a representative assembly consisting of two Chambers of different composition and with equal powers. The second was the separation of powers; but whereas Constant wanted ministers to be responsible to the Chamber as in Britain, where according to him the king (as against the Crown) played no active part in government but acted as a mediator when the three powers fell into disaccord, Royer-Collard wanted ministers to be responsible to the king. It was generally agreed that judges were not to be dismissed and that all cases concerning the statutory liberties of the citizen should be tried by jury. A free press was a further political guarantee in the sense that it acted as a conscience and interpreter between the government and the public. Fourth came the grant of independence to local authorities; but this proved chimerical, so deeply had Napoleon's centralization taken root. Finally came resistance to oppression—to be secured by the formation of a National

[6] G. de Ruggiero, *The History of European Liberalism* (OUP, Oxford, 1927), 75.   [7] Ibid. 161.

Guard recruited from the middle class and independent of the gendarmerie and the army.

German liberalism was bound to be intermixed with German—or shall we call it Pan-German?—nationalism. Germany's fragmentation into thirty-nine states posed such a challenge. But the demand for liberal constitutions and bills of rights came almost exclusively from the professional middle classes—lawyers and university professors dominating: they found little or no support among the population, which was still 90 per cent agricultural and, for the rest, lived in tiny towns.

There are no great names in German liberalism, like Constant or Royer-Collard at least, unless we accept the early works of Fichte and particularly Humboldt advocating the very minimum of state activity: the 'night-watch-man state'. For the greater part, the demands of liberals echoed those of their French counterparts. For an example one might well take the Frankfurt Parliament that arose from the revolutions triggered off by the French Revolution of 1848. The Frankfurt Parliament proceeded to draft a constitution. Its institutional arrangements fall to be discussed elsewhere, for at the moment we are interested in the freedoms that it contained. They deal with citizenship and emigration, equality before the law, the abolition of titles of nobility and its privileges, freedom of the person, expression, and learning, the rights to petition and assemble, the security of personal property, procedural rights in the law courts, and local autonomy. This list shows the close affinity between German liberal demands and those in France; and since, according to de Ruggiero, Italy played only a 'modest' part in developing liberal thinking and Belgian liberalism followed much the same path as France[8] (except that its political institutions were closely modelled on the British constitution), it can fairly be concluded that on the Continent liberalism, with only minor variations, presented the same package, made similar demands, and followed the same intellectual route.

3.3. *Traditionalism*

Not so its great opponent, traditionalism (or conservatism). This stood firmly by the principle of 'Throne and Altar'. Its exponents saw the French Revolution as the climax of Enlightenment, which they perceived as a false trail that had ended in bloodshed, anarchy, war, massacre, and the desecration of the Holy Church. At the Restoration rulers sought a new principle of authority in place of all this: the Church, particularly the Catholic Church, had undergone an extravagant revival and this provided one tradi-

---

[8] de Ruggiero, *The History of European Liberalism*, 158, n. 1, 275.

tionalist ingredient of such a principle. The Throne, that is, monarchy as against popular sovereignty, provided another. For the eastern powers—Prussia, Austria, and Russia—a simple recourse to divine right—'the Grace of God'—sufficed as it also did for the rulers of many of the petty states the Vienna Congress had restored. Stendhal's portrait of the duke of Parma seeing a Jacobin under every bed is not an idle caricature. Everywhere the authorities trembled at the word 'Jacobin'. They had been given a fright, but they had not learned the lesson.

In the eastern powers their dynastic appeal to Throne and Altar did not require any great philosophical underpinnings: religion and tradition sufficed. It was not so in Western Europe, particularly France and Germany. There a line of thinkers elaborated a comprehensive anti-liberal philosophy. They were the anti-Enlightenment. For them the state was no mechanical contrivance; it was an organic growth. Its nature was expressed in its own *telos*, and this could only be discovered from, and was cumulatively defined and redefined in the course of, the community's history. Thus man did not derive his personality from the 'natural order' and from this construct the state, as the liberals maintained; just the reverse: the state, or rather the society it embodied, anteceded and transcended the individual, and it was only in, by, and from this state that man acquired his personality. It follows that all traditionalists denied that authority was derived from the People or that Reason alone could build a new society or that there were natural rights anterior and superior to the total social organism; they affirmed that the free life of the individual was the creation of the state and not the other way round. They rejected written constitutions, for these seemed to them to embody all such false claims.

Such a creed ran in complete conformity with the post-1814 aggressive and Vatican-orientated Catholicism known as Ultramontanism. Each—traditionalism and Ultramontanism—drew strength from the other. So, before attempting the thought of the traditionalists it seems wise to start with some notion of Ultramontanism.

Because of its persecution of the Church, France was particularly receptive to the appeal of the Ultramontanes after the Restoration and this is precisely why it was so formative and creative in French traditionalism. This reinvigorated and aggressive Catholicism found fervid devotees in the French ruling circles. The Church expanded its influence further by fostering Catholic lay societies, among which the most important was *la Congrégation de la Vierge*, founded before 1815 by former pupils of the Jesuits. In this, clerics and laymen pledged themselves to use for the good of the Church any useful information or influence they could. The Society consisted of a central society and affiliated groups: the former numbered 1,400 members, the latter 48,000.[9] French ruling-class society was thus riddled with extreme Catholic doctrine by these 'Ultras', and it was their excesses as embodied in the actions of Charles X that led to the Revolution of 1830.

The connection between Ultramontanism and traditionalism is vividly illustrated by Pope Pius IX's 'Syllabus of Errors' of 1864. The 'Errors' are the exact mirror-image of the Liberal 'Truths'. They included:

That the Church ought to tolerate the errors of philosophy leaving to philosophy the care of their correction . . . That every man is free to embrace and profess the religion he shall believe true, guided by the light of reason . . . That the eternal salvation may (at least) be hoped for, of all those who are not in the true Church of Christ . . . That the Church has not the power of availing herself of force, or of any direct or indirect temporal power . . . That ecclesiatical jurisdiction for the temporal causes—whether civil or criminal—of the clergy, ought by all means to be abolished . . . That the civil government—even when exercised by an infidel sovereign—possesses an indirect and negative power over religious affairs . . . That the best theory of civil society requires that popular schools, open to the children of all classes, should be freed from all ecclesiastical authority . . . That the Church ought to be separated from the State and the State from the Church . . . That it is allowable to refuse obedience to legitimate princes; nay more, rise in insurrection against them . . . That in the present day, it is no longer necessary that the Catholic religion be held as the only religion of the State, to the exclusion of all other modes of worship . . . That the Roman Pontiff can, and ought to, reconcile himself to and agree with, progress, liberalism and modern civilization.[10]

With this as background let us pass on and review traditionalism through the eyes of some of its foremost exponents. In France the outstanding names are de Maistre, Bonald, and Lamennais. The first has been called 'the Praetorian of the Vatican'.[11] Rarely has the case for the state as an organism been so elegantly put—for instance, 'you count the grains of sand and think that the sum total is a house'.[12] A state is an organism, powered by forces from the distant past. It coheres through the soul of its people, one expression of which is patriotism, a term which assumes already the notion of a *patrie*. The embodiment of this *patrie* is the monarch: the *patrie* is patriotism incarnated in a man and loved in him. But, given the king, this fatherland incarnate, what does *his* authority depend on? De Maistre answers: it is God. But where to find this voice of God? De Maistre replies: in the Church. Where in the Church? The Church is itself a monarchy:

[9] F. B. Artz, *Reaction and Revolution, 1814–1832* (Harper and Row, New York, 1963), 15.
[10] Quoted, H. Bettenson (ed.), *Documents of the Christian Church* (OUP, Oxford, 1943), 379–81.
[11] E. Faguet, *Politiques et moralistes du dix-neuvième siècle*, 1st Ser. (Paris, 1899), 96.
[12] Ibid. 10.

which is as much as to say the Church is the pope. The Papacy is absolute and it is infallible.[13]

Bonald reaches the same conclusion by a wholly different route. When it comes to explaining the state, his view is patriarchial. Just as in the family the man acts as head of the household and the household thus owes him obedience, so, in the state, does the king act, and so, further, in the universe does God stand in relation to the king. The universe is monarchical.[14] 'I am a man of the pre-1789', said Bonald and he defended the *ancien régime* through rose-tinted spectacles as a system of liberties founded on the liberties of corporations, individuals, and property. He even says 'I am liberal'.[15] But when he comes to the present and the future he has nothing material to say. What he advocates—or so it seems—is pure despotism: no periodic parliaments, no independence of judges, no written charter in lieu of the ancient unwritten constitution of France, no freedom of conscience.[16] Divine (that is to say Catholic) revelation is absolute, so much so that free discussion and even toleration must be prohibited. The people obey the king, the king obeys God, and the way to God is, of course, through the Church and its head, the pope.

Lamennais, however, is far more original than either. He was brought up as a passionate Catholic in Brittany, the most Catholic area of France. To him, doubt was like lacking oxygen. Starting from so absolute a faith he had no difficulty in constructing a theory of intransigent theocracy. In this he resembles de Maistre and Bonald: 'horror of individualism, and instead, the need to gather up, to concentrate humankind—which would otherwise disperse and disseminate itself as dust—around an idea and in a unique morality.'[17] And here his thought ties up with the organic theory of the state in sentiments that echo Burke. It is quite wrong, he says, to think that we read and thereby derive information. Not at all! What is thought at the present moment—even universally—is only an individual opinion, a hallucination. The truth is that the human race is composed of men of the past, the present, and the yet to come and should be considered as one entity, one whole. And the judgement of those who have passed away and those living now and (we must infer) those yet to come, can only be Christianity.

Now his extreme opinions suffered a complete change at the 1830 Revolution. He became convinced that absolute monarchy was doomed in France. Therefore the Church had made a mistake—it had tied itself to a particular regime which hung upon it like an albatross. And so in an overnight conversion Lamennais did not merely advocate the separation

[13] Ibid. 47–50.   [14] Ibid. 80.   [15] Ibid. 114.   [16] Ibid. 115.
[17] Ibid. 92.

of Church and state, but espoused all the liberal demands that he had hitherto hated: freedom of conscience, of thought, of expression, of the press, of propaganda, of association, and of teaching. In this remarkable *volte-face* Lamennais became the founder of a movement that by the century's end was to prevail over Ultramontanism: he had invented 'Liberal Catholicism'. With a small group of friends he founded the journal *L'Avenir*. He seriously thought that the pope would follow his advice and went to Rome to try to convince him. He was dealt a stinging rebuff and ultimately left the Church altogether. But his friends, notably Lacordaire and Montalembert, continued his general line from inside the confines of Catholic orthodoxy. This current of Catholic opinion became so influential that the archbishop of Paris supported the 1848 Revolution, and the president of the Constituent Assembly was the Christian socialist, Buchez.

German political traditionalism was not so widely rooted in Ultramontane doctrines, though it is significant that Schlegel, Novalis, Adam Müller, Stolberg, and Haller went over to Rome. Hegel, if we are to count him as a traditionalist and not a liberal (in a way he was both) was quite certainly not Ultramontanist but a Protestant, whose thought neither derived from nor coincided with that of the Roman Catholic Church.

All these Germans were 'communitarian', opponents of the mechanical view of the state, promoters instead of its organic and evolutionary nature. Their views were admixed with other elements, of which nationalism was the most important. Another, quite compatibly, was romanticism which drove them to admire the Middle Ages. The link between romantic individualism and the organic view of the state was, precisely, the nation. For instance, the jurist Savigny rejected the idea of rights as innate principles and instead saw them as the spontaneous and evolutionary creation of the national spirit—the *Volksgeist*—in a similar way to language, customs, folklore, and so forth. He rejected written constitutions precisely because constitutions could not be constructed but must evolve in their own way. He pursued a revival of ancient Teutonic law. Frederick von Schlegel—a convert to Rome—believed that the nation, defined by linguistic unity, was the basic unit of history. The state exists to preserve the nation and that is why the true goal of history is best served by conservative principles. He regarded the Middle Ages as a paradigm, combining as they did political and religious authority but preserving the integrity of the individual nation. Adam Müller's line was in conformity with Roman doctrine, opposing individualism in the name of authority, tradition, and the organic community. The highest realization of the individual's personality lay in membership of a Christian state under strong leadership.

Hegel is unquestionably the most original and also the most influential of all the names we have cited. It is impossible to encapsulate Hegel's views in a few sentences. Society is one great organism, it is the nation; to capture its nature and essence, its *Geist*, one must have recourse to its history. The state encapsulates it and 'straightens out' its inherent contradictions. The individual is a personality only in so far as he is a member of this community. This represents a higher self than his day-to-day caprices and therefore the whole duty of man is to obey the state. That does not mean rule by caprice. On the contrary—the relationship between the state and the citizen must be expressed by law. In explicating this, Hegel stands out as no mere reactionary but as the protagonist of the *Rechtsstaat*, and in this peculiar sense a constitutionalist.

What it boils down to is this. First the primacy of state over individual:

The State is the Divine Idea as it exists on earth, we must therefore worship the State as the manifestation of the Divine on earth and consider that, if it is difficult to comprehend Nature, it is infinitely harder to grasp the essence of the State . . . The State is the march of God on earth . . . The State must be comprehended as an organism.[18]

And from this?

The really living totality, that which preserves and continually produces the State and its constitution is the *Government* . . . In the Government, regarded as an organic totality, the Sovereign Power or Principate . . . is the all-sustaining, all-decreeing Will of the State, its Highest Peak and all-pervasive Unity. In the perfect form of the State in which each and every element . . . has reached its free existence, this will is that of *one actual decreeing Individual* . . . it is *monarchy*. The monarchical constitution is therefore the constitution of developed reason and all other constitutions belong to the lower grades of the development and the self-realization of reason.[19]

All such propositions—expressed as they are in cloudy and labyrinthine trains of language—lead us to the ineluctable conclusion: the best and the highest form of constitution, of government, of the state, in the entire world is the monarchy of William III of Prussia.

We might next have mentioned the socialist thought of Saint-Simon and Fourier, but at this stage (i.e. over the first three-quarters of the nineteenth century) these Utopians played no significant role in the conflict of ideologies. In every one of the revolutionary capitals in 1848 the labouring poor came out in favour of 'the democratic and social republic'. All three terms are significant: 'democracy', because the prevailing liberal policy was a

---

[18] Quoted, K. R. Popper, *The Open Society and its Enemies*, vol. 2 (Routledge & Kegan Paul, London, 1962), 45.   [19] Quoted, ibid. 45–6.

restricted and/or indirect suffrage; 'republic', because the liberals were still wedded to a monarchical executive that would 'confer' a constitution, instead of this being the will of an elected constituant assembly; and 'social', because the liberals thought in purely political terms and recoiled from the slightest notion that property was not sacred. But what, in practice did this 'social' dimension amount to? It boiled down in practice to the 'right to work' advocated by Louis Blanc, and for this reason—in Paris and also in Vienna—the provisional governments set up the so-called 'national work-shops'. The idea was noble, but in practice the entire enterprise became a system of temporary outdoor relief. Not until the 1870s did European industrialization on a British scale arise. Until the 1860s there was no 'proletariat' in the Marxist sense: merely the ill-paid artisans, a few fac-tory-workers, wage-labourers, and the like. Socialism as a mass force did not develop until the 1860s at the earliest: and so it will be dealt with at a more appropriate point when we come to discuss industrialization.

I said that liberalism—and nationalism—were middle-class creeds; but in fact it is difficult if not impossible to make a perfect fit between these ideologies and social stratification. To simplify, we can nominate four categories: the landed aristocracy and the new aristocracy of money (the so-called *haute bourgeoisie*), the middle class, the labouring poor, and the peasants. Their political strength and their political attitudes could vary greatly from one country to another. Thus, France had developed a govern-ing crust consisting of former aristocrats, many of whom had turned back to landowning, which was rapidly coalescing with a *parvenu* wealthy entre-preneurial sector styled the *haute bourgeoisie* to distinguish it from the *petite bourgeoisie* which consisted of the artisans, traders and shopkeepers, and the like. But in the German states and Austria the aristocrats had survived the Revolution with their privileges intact and their political influence as strong as ever, while the 'middle class' consisted among others of the learned professions and officials. (This is why the revolutions of 1848 in those countries are sometimes called 'the revolution(s) of the intellectuals'.) In Hungary there was virtually no middle class at all: the country was stratified into the peasantry on the one hand and larger and smaller landowners on the other, and it was the latter who were the fiercely liberal nationalists who made the 1848 Revolution.

But one point must be stressed: these leading and moneyed classes dreaded the 'labouring poor'. In many states the rulers and court regarded them much as Afrikaners used to regard the Bantu—with anger, fear, and contempt: in short, they recoiled from any notion of democracy. They foresaw it as the mob rule of the French Revolution, and above all things they were terrified of losing their property. Their frenetic determination to hold on to it at whatever cost was what divided them from the labouring poor and their 'social' republic. It was this fear of being expropriated that Marx was talking about in 1848 when he said that Europe was 'haunted by the spectre of Communism': it was not 'communism' as we have known it today in the least, but the fear of losing one's property. In Paris, Berlin, Vienna this antagonism finally burst out in working-class insurrections which the richer sections of society, with the police and the army as their instruments, put down with the utmost ferocity. For instance: one of the most prominent liberal leaders in Vienna was Füster, chaplain to the students. The divide between liberals and the labouring men could not be more vividly illustrated than by his furious harangue to these workers: 'Do you think', he asked, ' that we have thrown out our lords and nobles to let ourselves to be ruled by you? Then you are much mistaken.'[20]

For the period we are now considering the great ideological battle was three-cornered, between the liberals and the traditionalists with nationalism admixed with both; and this was reflected in the pace and form of the constitutionalization of Europe.

4. CHRONOLOGY

This is not meant to be a full chronology of the major events in Europe, 1815–75, but simply a selection of the most important dates in constitutionalizing the absolutist states. The stages by which this proceeded are well-marked. After the 1815 settlement the Continent was puncuated by revolutionary surges followed by repression: thus, the revolutionary waves of 1820, then of 1830, then of 1848. Then, in the 1860s, the three most intractable areas of such revolutionary attempts—Germany, Italy, Austria—were finally constitutionalized, but not by revolutionary means. They were settled by the outcomes of war and statecraft.

CHRONOLOGY

1809	SWEDEN	New constitution
1812	SPAIN	Liberal constitution
1814		Napoleon abdicates. Louis XVIII king of France
		Grants Charter
		Congress of Vienna opens
	NORWAY	Its constitution accepted by Sweden
	SPAIN	Ferdinand abolishes constitution

[20] Quoted, P. Robertson, *The Revolutions of 1848: A Social History* (Harper Torchbook, New York, 1960), 227.

1815		Napoleon returns, Louis XVIII flees, Napoleon defeated at Waterloo, Napoleon abdicates, Allies enter Paris, Louis XVIII restored. Second Treaty of Paris. Congress of Vienna closes
1816	GERMANY	Carl August of Saxe-Weimar grants constitution
1817	GERMANY	Wartburg student liberal festival
1818	GERMANY	Constitutions in Bavaria and in Baden
1819	GERMANY	Constitutions in Württemburg and Hanover. Diet of the German Confederation passes the Carlsbad Decrees to put a check on revolutionary and liberal movements
1820	SPAIN	Revolution and restoration of 1812 constitution
	ITALY	Revolt in Naples
1821	ITALY	Austria suppresses Naples revolution
	GREECE	Revolt against Turks
1823	SPAIN	French restore Ferdinand of Spain. Constitution abolished
1824	FRANCE	Charles X (Ultramontanist) succeeds to throne
1826	PORTUGAL	Liberal constitution
1828	PORTUGAL	King Miguel revokes the constitution
1830	FRANCE	Charles X issues five anti-liberal ordonnances. The 'Trois Glorieuses', i.e. the July Revolution. Charles flees, Louis-Philippe of Orleans becomes king
	GREECE	Recognized as independent state
	GERMANY	Revolutions in Brunswick, Saxony, Hesse–Cassel
1831	ITALY	Revolutions in Parma, Modena, Papal States suppressed by Austria
	GERMANY	Constitutions in Saxony and Hesse–Cassel
	BELGIUM	Following rising in 1830, breaks with Holland and is recognized as sovereign state: a parliamentary constitution
1832	BRITAIN	First Reform Bill
1833	GERMANY	Zollverein established. Constitution granted in Hanover
	SPAIN	Civil war, ends 1840, with victory for constitutionalists
1837	GERMANY	Constitution of Hanover suppressed
1838	BRITAIN	The 'People's Charter'
1844	GREECE	Constitution
1845	SWITZERLAND	Catholic cantons form 'Sonderbund'
1846	GERMANY	Professors meet in Frankfurt
1847	SWITZERLAND	War of the Sonderbund; latter defeated and dissolved
	PRUSSIA	United Diet summoned

1848
January   Revolution in SICILY
February   Constitutions in NAPLES (10th),
                                 TUSCANY (17th)
                                 Revolution in FRANCE, abdication of Louis-Philippe,
                                 proclamation of republic (21st–24th)
March   Revolution in VIENNA, Metternich resigns (18th–
                                 19th), BERLIN (19th)
                                 Revolutions in VENICE (12th); PARMA (19th);
                                 MILAN (22nd); ROME (14th)
                                 PIEDMONT declares war on AUSTRIA (23rd)
April   GERMAN pre-parliament at Frankfurt (4th)
                                 AUSTRIAN constitution repealed (25th)
                                 FRANCE National Assembly meets (27th)
May   PRUSSIA invades DENMARK (2nd)
                                 Second revolution in VIENNA (15th)
                                 GERMAN National Assembly at Frankfurt (18th)
                                 PRUSSIAN National Assembly meets (22nd)
June   AUSTRIANS defeat PIEDMONT at Vicenza (10th)
                                 AUSTRIANS suppress CZECH revolt (17th)
                                 In PARIS, General Cavaignac suppresses rising of
                                 workmen (23rd–26th)
July   AUSTRIAN Reichstag meets (22nd)
                                 AUSTRIANS defeat PIEDMONT at Custozza
                                 Constitution in PIEDMONT (14th)
August   Truce between AUSTRIA and PIEDMONT (9th)
                                 Emperor Ferdinand returns to VIENNA (12th)
                                 Truce between PRUSSIA and DENMARK (26th)
September   Kossuth proclaimed king of HUNGARY (12th)
October   Third revolution in VIENNA (6th)
                                 Windischgraetz retakes VIENNA (31st)
November   Republican constitution in FRANCE (12th)
December   AUSTRIA: Emperor Ferdinand abdicates in favour of
                                 his nephew, Franz-Joseph (2nd)
                                 RUSSIAN National Assembly dissolved; constitution
                                 granted (5th)
                                 FRANCE: Louis Napoleon elected president of the
                                 Republic (10th)
                                 GERMAN National Assembly proclaims Fundamen-
                                 tal Rights (28th)

1849
January   PRUSSIA suggest German union without AUSTRIA
                                 (23rd)

February | Grand Duke of Tuscany flees (7th)
ROME proclaimed republic under Mazzini (9th)

March | AUSTRIA: constitution granted (4th)
Reichstag dissolved (7th)
PIEDMONT and AUSTRIA resume war (12th)
AUSTRIAN victory at Novara, Charles-Albert abdicates in favour of Victor-Emanuel II (23rd)
Frederick-William IV elected 'Emperor of the GERMANS' (28th)

April | Frederick William rejects imperial crown (3rd)
HUNGARY declares independence from AUSTRIA (14th)
FRANCE sends troops to papal states (25th)

May | Revolt at Dresden crushed by PRUSSIA (3rd–8th)
Military revolt in Baden (11th–13th)
Garibaldi enters ROME (11th)
FRANCE: National Assembly dissolved (26th)
PRUSSIA adopts three-class suffrage (30th)

June | DENMARK receives Liberal Constitution (5th)
Working-class demonstration in PARIS (13th)
GERMAN National Assembly dispersed by troops (18th)

July | French take ROME (3rd)
BADEN insurgents surrender to PRUSSIA (23rd)
AUSTRIA restores Grand Duke of TUSCANY (26th)

August | HUNGARIANS surrender to RUSSIAN troops (13th)
VENICE surrenders to AUSTRIA (22nd)
AUSTRIA rejects PRUSSIAN scheme of Union

1850 | PRUSSIANS withdraw from DENMARK
Insurrection in Hesse–Cassel, where AUSTRIAN candidate prevails over PRUSSIA, thanks to RUSSIA
PRUSSIA: constitution granted
GERMAN Union Parliament meets at Erfurt
Universal suffrage abolished in FRANCE. Freedom of press restricted in FRANCE
PIEDMONT: Cavour appointed minister

1851 | FRANCE | *Coup d'état* of Louis Napoleon. Favourable plebiscite for a new constitution

GERMANY | The Confederation Diet appoints a Reaction Committee and abolishes Fundamental Rights

AUSTRIA | The constitution abolished

1852 | TUSCANY | Constitution abolished

	FRANCE	Gives Louis Napoleon monarchical power. *Coup d'état*—Napoleon proclaimed emperor as Napoleon III
	PIEDMONT	Cavour becomes premier
1853	FRANCE	Plebiscite in favour of imperial constitution. RUSSIA and TURKEY at war
1854		BRITAIN and FRANCE at war with RUSSIA. The Crimea, battles of Alma, Balaclava, Inkerman; siege of Sevastopol
1855		PIEDMONT joins Crimean War versus RUSSIA. Sevastopol and Kars taken by Allies. Nicholas I of RUSSIA succeeded by Alexander II
	PIEDMONT	Monasteries and Orders abolished
	AUSTRIA	Concordat with Vatican gives state control of education, censorship, and matrimonial law
1856		Peace Congress of Paris ends CRIMEAN War
	AUSTRIA	Amnesties Hungarian insurgents
1858	FRANCE	Orsini tries to assassinate Napoleon. 'Treaty' of Plombières between FRANCE and PIEDMONT
	PRUSSIA	William, prince of Prussia, made regent for insane king
1859	ITALY	PIEDMONT refuses AUSTRIAN demand to disarm. Revolutions in TUSCANY, MODENA, PARMA. PIEDMONT and FRANCE at war with AUSTRIA, and are victorious at Magenta and Solferino. Villafranca Treaty cedes Lombardy and Parma to PIEDMONT. Cavour resigns
	FRANCE	Amnesty and extension of political rights
1860	ITALY	Plebiscites in TUSCANY, PARMA, MODENA, ROMAGNA in favour of union with PIEDMONT. Garibaldi takes Palermo, Naples. PIEDMONT invades PAPAL STATES. Plebiscites in NAPLES, SICILY, UMBRIA, and the LEGATIONS favour unification. Cavour recalled to office. First Italian Parliament meets in Turin
	AUSTRIA	Constitution (the October Diploma)
1861	ITALY	Francis II of NAPLES surrenders Gaeta. Victor Emanuel proclaimed king of Italy. Cavour dies
	PRUSSIA	William I succeeds to throne. German Progressive Party founded
	AUSTRIA	The Constitution centralized (the February Patent). Hungarian Diet dissolved, government by imperial commissioners

1862	ITALY	Garibaldi, trying to take Rome, defeated at Aspromonte
	PRUSSIA	Bismarck becomes premier. Governs without budget till 1866
1863		POLISH insurrection suppressed by PRUSSIA and RUSSIA
1864	ITALY	The Kingdom renounces claims on ROME. Florence made the capital
	PRUSSIA	Defeats DENMARK. Latter cedes Schleswig, Holstein, and Lauenburg
	RUSSIA	Establishment of Provincial Councils
1865	AUSTRIA	Constitution temporarily annulled. Transylvania incorporated in Hungary
1866		ITALY and PRUSSIA at war with AUSTRIA. PRUSSIA defeats AUSTRIA at Sadowa. Cedes Venetia to Napoleon III. Plebiscite in Venetia in favour of union with Italy. PRUSSIA declares German Confederation (the Bund) dissolved, invades and takes Saxony, Hanover, and Hesse, makes peace treaties with Württemberg, Baden, Bavaria. AUSTRIA withdraws from Germany. National Liberal Party founded
	SWEDEN	Legislature with only two Chambers *vice* four Estates
	DENMARK	Constitution altered to favour king and Upper House
1867	ITALY	Garibaldi's attempt on Rome defeated at Mentana
	GERMANY	North German Confederation formed with Prussia as head
	AUSTRIA	The Ausgleich of Austria-Hungary—Hungarian Constitution of 1848 restored, a dual monarchy with common foreign and military policies
1870		FRANCO-PRUSSIAN War. France defeated—revolution in Paris, proclamation of republic, siege of Paris. ITALY seizes Rome
1871	FRANCE	Capitulation of Paris. National Assembly meets at Bordeaux. Thiers elected French president. Communard rising in Paris. France cedes Alsace and Lorraine, makes peace
	GERMANY	William I proclaimed German emperor at Versailles

5. THE CONSTITUTIONS OF EUROPE, 1809–1875

Broadly speaking, the course of constitutionalization runs from absolutism to parliamentary government and from west to east, reaching Germany and Austria-Hungary only in the etiolated form we shall be calling constitutional monarchy (of a singularly authoritarian kind), and missing Russia altogether. Even by 1875 only the French Third Republic and the Confederation of Switzerland were democratic, for although the German Empire enjoyed universal suffrage from 1870, the Reichstag which it elected enjoyed very qualified powers and was far from being sovereign. All the rest were based on a franchise determined by the amount of taxes paid or property owned, and sometimes with other disabilities, such as indirect election, as well. As time went by, the movement to broaden the franchise strengthened and reached more and more states, but universal manhood suffrage was rare before the 1890s.

A large majority of the constitutions tended to be, initially at least, *octroyées*, like the French Charter of 1814 which was given to the French people as an act of grace by Louis XVIII who still claimed to be king by the Divine Right. But some constitutions, such as the Belgian (1831) or Hungarian (1848), sprang from revolution, and others from a representative constituent assembly convened by the monarch.

At the outset, the modal type was so-called 'constitutional monarchy', and at the end, for the most part, parliamentarism. Let us explain.

1. At the Restoration many monarchies were what they had always been—*absolute*.

2. In others, however, the absolute monarch or prince conceded a constitution as an act of grace: and what he had freely conceded could, it was understood, just as easily be withdrawn. These can be styled '*self-limited*' *absolutisms*. We might add that many of these, especially in Germany, persisted for a century, and in the course of that time became so firmly entrenched that it was inconceivable that the monarch should withdraw them. They had turned into one or other of the next two types.

3. The '*constitutional monarchy*'. I put this in inverted commas because I take the definition from a most influential work on systematic politics by the Swiss scholar Johann Bluntschli (1808–81). Bluntschli was a professor of law. His great work is the *Lehre vom modernen Staat*, in three books: *Staatslehre*, *Staatsrecht*, and *Politik* (1875–6). The first of these titles is translated into English as *The Theory of the State*.[21] Bluntschli had a very clear and distinct idea of 'constitutional monarchy'. By it he means a monarchy that is a freestanding and hereditary chief executive working with an elected legislature, and where the king takes all executive decisions through ministers responsible to himself alone, not to the elected body. He insists on this again and again, and to make sure, lists the 'false ideas' of constitutional monarchy.

[21] J. K. Bluntschli, *The Theory of the State*; authorized trans. from the 6th German edn. (1892; 2nd edn. published 1895).

These include: that the king has executive power only, that he is purely passive, 'that the royal power is exercised by the ministers', that the 'king reigns but does not govern', and that the king must obey the will of the majority.[22]

The distinguishing principle is the responsibility of ministers. It is this that differentiates between the constitutional monarchy as defined by Bluntschli, and what is best called parliamentarism or parliamentary government. In the former the ministers are appointed by and dismissed by the monarch and are responsible to him alone. In the latter, they are responsible to the legislature which can force them to retire, or, if the legislature is very strong, can actually impose them on the monarch. Hence type 4, *parliamentary government*. This brings us to the fifth and final type: the *parliamentary republic*, which is nothing but a *parliamentary regime* in which the hereditary monarch has been replaced by an elected president—as in the French Third Republic.

Absolute governments were to be found in Naples and the Italian states generally from 1815, and in Spain at intervals punctuated by the return of the 1812 constitution and subsequent liberal constitutions from 1815–20 and thereafter. Of the self-limited absolutisms we might first notice Holland— in 1814 King William I granted a Charter along the lines of the French *Charte*, but less accommodating: 'I can reign without ministers, it is I alone who governs and I alone am responsible', he said. This was in sharp contrast to the constitution of Norway, enacted by an elected constituent assembly in 1814, and maintained under the joint monarchy of Sweden when it was united with that country in 1815. The most numerous are those of the petty German states, whose rulers granted constitutions in 1818–20 and 1830–4. The *Bund*'s Diet represented the whole but possessed few powers. This *Bund* lay heavily under the influence of the Austrian chief minister, Metternich, the arch-reactionary who used repression, censorship, and an army of spies throughout the Habsburg dominions (which at that time included Lombardy and Venetia) and extended this not only to the German states but to the petty Italian ones also. Article 13 of the *Bund* said that the German princes and kings were to grant constitutions to their subjects. Between 1818 and 1820 the rulers of Bavaria, Baden, Nassau, Württemberg, Lippe, and Hesse-Darmstadt granted charter-type constitutions, in which the Diets tended to be weak and ministers were responsible to the ruler. Nevertheless, these rulers and their successors tended to act upon them and they underwent some evolution in the course of years. This burst of constitution-granting was ended by the Diet's Carlsbad Decrees of 1820, inspired by

---

[22] Bluntschli, *The Theory of the State*, 426–31.

Metternich, which discouraged any further advances. But these were resumed after the French July 1830 Revolution, in Brunswick, Hesse-Kassel, and Saxony, until this movement too was ended by the *Schlussprotokol*, carried at Metternich's insistence in 1834. Most of these constitutions were bicameral, the Upper House representing the landed nobility, the Lower Houses following the lines of the old Diets. In all cases the ruler was given ample powers and rights.

Finally we may mention the new kingdom of Greece, which moved from, effectively, an absolutism to a constitution (1843) where King Otho ruled with a very heavy hand until he was deposed and replaced by a new king in 1862, after which a parliamentary constitution was introduced.

The constitutional monarchies were more numerous and more important. Furthermore, many evolved into parliamentarism within a brief time. The earliest was the Swedish of 1809, which built upon the constitution already described, that had been enacted and negotiated with the Diet by Gustavus III in 1772. France, governed by the Charter of 1814 until the Revolution of July 1830, was similarly a constitutional monarchy. For the purposes of this classification we can also categorize as constitutional monarchies Denmark, and the Second Republic and the Second Empire of France of 1848–52 and 1852–70 respectively. Later in the century, between 1850 and 1870, three extremely important constitutional monarchies were created. They resulted from the Prussian constitution of 1850, the Austrian of 1867, and the German constitutions of 1867 and 1870.

A number of the constitutional monarchies evolved into parliamentary ones in the course of this period; the July Monarchy of France (1830–48) edging towards but never quite making this transition, and similarly with the authoritarian Second Empire, which became increasingly parliamentary between 1860 and the closing months of the regime in 1870, when everything was conceded to the legislature—except that the principle that ministers were responsible to it was still in doubt. Belgium was a parliamentary monarchy by virtue of a revolutionary assembly in 1831, and was similar to the British. The short-lived Frankfurt Constitution of Germany and the Hungarian one of 1848 were both parliamentary. In Holland the former constitutional monarchy became parliamentary in 1848, Denmark likewise in 1848–9. Piedmont adopted a parliamentary system in 1848, and Greece became parliamentary in 1862. The period closes with the débâcle of the Second Empire and the transitional phase of provisional government from 1870, until the Organic Laws of 1875 established the long-lived Third parliamentary Republic (1875–1940), a parliamentary monarchy but with an elected president and not a hereditary monarch in place.

There is a rough chronological order to the constitutionalization process.

The year 1814 ushered in France, Holland, Norway, numerous petty German states, Spain (for part of the time), and (ephemerally) Piedmont and Naples. The July Revolution in France gave it a new impulse, adding Belgium and another handful of petty German states. The next wave was sparked off by the overthrow of the July Monarchy in France in February 1848. Piedmont, Denmark, Switzerland, and (for a few brief months 'Germany', Austria, and Hungary) entered the class of constitutionalized states. By 1848, therefore, one could observe a bloc of constitutional or parliamentary monarchies which included all Scandinavia, Britain, France, Belgium, Holland, Piedmont, and some lesser German states, to which one must add the *sui generis* Switzerland by its seminal constitution of 1848. Spain and Portugal had also enjoyed spells of constitutionalization. In brief, the entire western half of Europe from Scandinavia to Spain and from the Atlantic to Piedmont and bits of Germany was now constitutionalized.

The year 1848, the 'Year of Revolutions', was followed by a period of reaction when any constitutional changes were in the direction of authoritarianism: in France, Prussia, the German states, Austria-Hungary, and the Italian states south of Piedmont. To the west lay the constitutionalized countries cited above, to the east the three absolutist monarchies of Prussia, Austria, and Russia. But between 1860 and 1870 the dam finally broke. In 1860–70 Piedmont, with its parliamentary constitution, was able to unite all Italy behind it and endow it with its own *Statuto*. In 1867–70 Prussia united all the smaller German states behind it and endowed them, in the new German Empire, with constitutional monarchy (albeit of a most authoritarian kind—and worse in practice than in theory). And in 1867 Austria, defeated by Prussia and Italy in the 1866 'Six Weeks War', finally gave way. In place of the unitary Austrian state, a dual monarchy consisting of Austria and Hungary was set up with common functions confined to little more than the armed forces and foreign affairs. Austria proper became a highly authoritarian constitutional monarchy in the strictest Bluntschli sense, while in contrast, Hungary reverted to its 1848 Constitution and became a parliamentary monarchy. Thus by 1870 all states in Europe had become, in one way or another, constitutionalized—with one exception. This was Russia. There the tsar still reigned absolute and by divine grace.

It would be too time-consuming and not particularly helpful to our exercise in this chapter to describe all these constitutions in any detail. There is a strong case, however, for looking at the constitutions of the Great Powers—Britain, France, Italy, Germany, and Austria—as they were at 1875.

5.1. *Great Britain*

We have hardly mentioned Great Britain in this survey. Its 'legitimist' condition, its own particular *ancien régime*, lasted until 1832. Up to that point the balance in the constitution of Crown-in-Parliament had remained unaltered. The legislature had remained subservient to the party in power—the Tories—through the use of the Crown's resources of patronage and the corruption exercised through its ministers on its behalf. But in the Napoleonic wars the ministers' stature *vis à vis* the monarchy grew, especially after the accession of George IV in 1820. This saw the 'waning of the influence of the Crown'.[23] In 1830 the Tory Cabinet split apart on the issue of the removal of the disabilities of Roman Catholics (Catholic Emancipation). The ensuing election was the first for over a century to defeat the government. Instead of the Tories, the Whigs came to power and introduced a bill to reform the electoral system. It suppressed a number of ancient constituencies which were now either totally uninhabited, such as Old Sarum, or in the control of a handful of voters under the influence of the great landowner of the district: hence 'pocket' or 'rotten' boroughs, by which the landowner class was able to return its nominees to the House of Commons. These suppressed parliamentary constituencies were replaced by new ones, mostly in the newly industrialized towns of the Midlands and the North (though the preponderant majority of members continued as before to come from the South). In addition the franchise was widened on a property basis: in the boroughs those householders who paid £10 per annum in rates and, in the counties, the various classes of leaseholders who paid £10 per annum and also tenants paying more than £3.50 per annum. The electorate, previously numbering 435,391, was expanded to 652,777, equal to 3.5 per cent of the population.

This reform was the precondition of full-blooded parliamentary sovereignty. The matter was tested in 1834. King William IV turned the Whigs out and installed his own (Tory) prime minister (the Duke of Wellington) instead: Parliament was dissolved and a new general election called. The Whigs rode back to power triumphantly, which proved beyond any dispute that the king could no longer pick his own prime minister but had to accept the man who could command a majority in the House of Commons; and, since this majority was the product of popular consultation, this was tantamount to saying that the electorate, via the Commons, chose the government it preferred whether the monarch liked it or no. The system which had been devised so that the king might control the Commons

[23] A. S. Foord, *His Majesty's Opposition, 1714–1830* (Clarendon Press, Oxford, 1964).

became the means by which the House of Commons, through its leaders, controlled the king; and thus all the power of the House of Commons and of the Crown became vested in the same men, who guided legislation and took charge of the administration at the same time. By the same token the power of the House of Lords was cut off, since disagreement with the House of Commons could be set aside by the Crown creating peers to swamp it, at the behest of the ministry. With the extrusion of the monarch and the now unimpaired responsibility of ministers to the House of Commons, British parliamentarism had become fully fledged. In 1867 the Second Reform Bill extended the franchise to include most of the 'artisan class', and the electorate, which had grown by natural increase to 1,056,659 in 1866, was nearly doubled in size to 1,995,085, or 7.7 per cent of the total population. From that point the political parties, which had existed ever since the 1660s in the form of 'connections' and were localized with no central headquarters, began to become solidary formations endowed with central organs, and the alternation of the two main parties became an entrenched two-party system.

5.2. France: The Third Republic

'Rien ne dure que le provisoire.' France had become used to codified constitutions, but the constitution of the Third Republic is, by contrast, simply three Organic Laws passed in 1875 in a mode that would have left the way open for the return of the king. That he did not return was due to the obstinacy of the legitimist pretender, the comte de Chambord. He declined to accept the tricolour.[24] As time slipped by, the republicans became the majority faction, and the royalist option was lost for ever.

As soon as Paris heard that the emperor had capitulated to the Prussians at Sedan (2 September 1870), the fall of the Empire and the establishment of the Republic was proclaimed. The Assembly fled to Bordeaux and elected Thiers chief executive of a provisional government. Paris fell and France capitulated by the Treaty of Frankfurt. New elections returned a royalist Assembly, the workers of Paris erupted against it and held power for a month as 'the Commune' until this was bloodily crushed by Thiers's forces. The monarchist majority in the Assembly, frustrated by the comte de Chambord's insistence on the white Bourbon flag, found itself electing Thiers as president of the Republic. He resigned in 1873 and was succeeded

[24] Mocked by Anatole France in *L'Île des Pingouins*: here the royalist colour is green (not the Bourbon white) and the pretender is given the name of Prince Crucho. Asked by a committee of royalists to assume the throne, he answers solemnly, 'I shall enter Alca [i.e. France] on a green horse' (Calmann-Lévy, Paris, 1908, Bk. v. 2).

by the royalist General MacMahon. Since Chambord still remained obdurate, in 1875 the Assembly set MacMahon's term at seven years, and passed three Organic Laws establishing a framework of government which left the way clear for Chambord to change his mind and return. That did not happen and these Organic Laws became the new constitution.

They were of the simplest character. The 'Declaration of Rights . . .', which had usually formed the Preamble, was dropped. Government was vested in a president and an Assembly that consisted of a Senate and a Chamber of Deputies. The president had all the usual attributes of a chief executive and head of state, of which two were critical: he appointed and dismissed all officers, and this included the Ministers, and, with the concurrence of the Senate, he could dissolve the Chamber and call fresh elections. The Chamber of Deputies numbered 597, including the members from the colonies (treated as part of metropolitan France), elected by universal male suffrage. The Senate consisted of 300 members selected by colleges composed of the municipal councils and certain *ex officio* personages. Under the 1875 Law the senators were life-appointments but under the extensive amendments of 1884 the Senate was elected for nine years with one-third of members retiring every third year. Both Senate and Chamber possessed the legislative initiative (as indeed did the president also), with the proviso that the budget and taxes must start in the Chamber.

Ministers did not have to be parliamentarians, but had the right to attend sessions and speak in them. In practice only parliamentarians were appointed—reflecting the parliamentary nature of the régime. The Organic Law says specifically that ministers are 'collectively responsible to the Houses for general policy and individually responsible for their personal acts—the British formula, in fact. It seems clear enough but in fact was ambiguous. Its meaning was given definitive form in the crisis of 1877, the so-called *Seize mai*. New elections had thrown up an overwhelmingly republican Chamber of Deputies. MacMahon forced the choice of the Chamber (Jules Simon) to resign as prime minister and appointed instead the royalist duc de Broglie. He then dissolved the Chamber and called fresh elections. In these every scrap of pressure the government could call on was brought to bear, for instance, the replacement of prefects was utilized to defeat the republicans and produce a royalist majority. The republicans, led by Gambetta, fought under the cry of *se soumettre ou se démettre*. In the event the republicans, though somewhat reduced, still had a clear majority. MacMahon had no alternative but to appoint the republican leader as prime minister. From then it was clear that the prime minister had to be the choice of the majority in the Chamber. Furthermore, presidents fought shy of ever dissolving the Chamber again. Henceforth it always ran its full legal four years. The powers of the president had been reduced to nullity. The Chamber was all, and the ministers in place were its servants. It could dismiss them *en bloc* or pick them off one by one.

The Republic was a parliamentary government without qualification. But it did not turn out like Britain's at all. There were three main reasons for this. In the first place a British Cabinet was kept in place by the discipline of one or the other of the two major parties. France never developed a two-party system but, on the contrary, threw up a large number of smallish factions which, undisciplined at the polls, were even more so in the Chamber. The result was a series of never-ending combinations and permutations of party majorities and hence of Cabinets. The Third Republic was notorious for its 'dance of the portfolios' and the debility of its executive. Secondly, this fragmentation could not be cured—as in Britain it could—by the dissolution of the Chamber and fresh elections. Consequently deputies never had to consider their policies or conduct as they would have had to were an election to take place at any moment. It became 'the House with sealed windows'. And finally, the house-rules of the Chamber gave inordinate powers to the deputies. Bills went to a committee before they reached the floor of the House, where what was debated was not the text of the bill but the committee's frequently hostile report. The weekly agenda was not set by the government but by a committee of all the competing groups in the Assembly. Any deputy could propose increases in public expenditure. Ministers were perpetually fighting off snap votes on an 'interpellation' from the floor. The Third Republic had abandoned a strong executive in favour of the two Chambers, which in turn had abandoned their powers in favour of the individual senator or deputy. It was parliamentarism carried to an extreme.

5.3. *Italy*

As we noticed, in 1848 King Charles-Albert of Piedmont conferred a constitution on his people. It is styled the *Statuto* and it was this Piedmontese document that, under the leadership of Piedmont, was adopted in each of the country's constituent political divisions and states and so became the constitution of united Italy. It is interesting that it did not have to be amended in order to expand in this way, and the reason is that there is no provision for amendment. As in Britain, constitutional change was brought about by simple Act of Parliament, no differently than Acts on the most mundane of topics. The *Statuto* is still important: the present Italian constitution is founded upon it.

The *Statuto* was a liberal document just as the year of its promulgation was the Liberal Year: and it was granted by Charles-Albert precisely because he wanted to win liberal support in his war to drive the Austrians out of Italy. Indeed, unlike the French or the German constitutions, it contains a bill of rights which is redolent of the pristine liberalism of that Liberal Year. Though the Catholic faith is pronounced 'the official state religion', all others are tolerated. The statute guarantees equality before the law, equal access to all civil and military appointments, forbids arbitrary arrest, protects the inviolability of the home, and grants freedom of the press and of assembly (except for outdoor meetings, which were controlled by the police) and affirms that 'without exception' all forms of property are inviolable. Any state acquisition must be done in due legal form.

It established a structure basically similar to the British or French—fully parliamentary, and where the sovereign power was vested in two legislative Houses and the king. The latter possessed the veto power but in practice never used it. Otherwise his powers were similar to those of any chief executive, and this of course included the appointment and dismissal of all officials. The ministers were his ministers just as those in a British Cabinet were the queen's. They exercised all the powers in the king's name and, though it was not explicit in the *Statuto*, these ministers were (by convention) responsible to the lower house of Parliament. The king attended all Cabinet meetings. In itself this gave him little influence in domestic affairs, but in practice he exercised considerable power, especially in war and foreign policy, because the fragmentation of the parties presented him with a wide choice of prime ministers. Finally, the king had the right to dissolve the Chamber of Deputies and, owing to the lability of parties, frequently did.

The two Houses had equal powers except that finance bills had to come to the Chamber of Deputies first. (In practice, however, the Senate would usually yield to the Chamber.) The senators were life-appointments. Some sat *ex officio*, others had to be paying at least 3,000 lire per annum. The legal term of the Chamber of Deputies was five years but it was frequently dismissed earlier for *elezione anticipate*. It consisted of 508 deputies elected on a narrow franchise which took in barely 2.5 per cent of the population. (In France the suffrage was universal and in Britain it was 7.5 per cent at this time.) What is more, this franchise was not decided solely on financial qualification, that is, a *censitaire* suffrage; in addition, there were a variety of educational tests.

Finally, unlike most others, this constitution set the quorum of each of the two Houses at the absolute majority of the members. There were marked contradictions between the liberal theory and the actual practice of government: for instance, although Italy was in the forefront of Europe in its criminal code, thousands of people were arrested on suspicion, and imprisoned for years, only to be released, eventually, for lack of sufficient evidence. Furthermore, for all its resemblance to the British model, the way this constitution worked was its polar opposite. It was much more like the French model than the British and suffered from similar defects of practice, only more so. Cavour, Piedmont's prime minister and the architect of Italian unity, died in 1861, and his supporters divided into a Right and Left, initially distinguished by disagreement over the speed and the means required to complete the unification. Until 1876 the Right was in control, carrying, successfully, the enormous burden of meeting the budget deficit and generally establishing the rule of the constitution through the newly unified country. Once it had completed its work, in 1876, a popular reaction set in against its autocratic methods and its high levels of taxation. That year saw the 'fall of the Right', a landmark in Italian constitutional history. There was little to choose between the programmes of the Right and the Left, and both had to impose the same high levels of taxation, and so forth. But there was an immense distinction in the tone of political life, a tone which, *mutatis mutandis*, is recognizable in Italy even at the present time.

For the Right and the Left were not solidary parties at all but, on the contrary, loose aggregations of coteries, each following its own parliamentary leader. The Left never had a specific programme and never acted as a united party after 1876—it was a confederation of chieftains and their hangers-on and was based on a patron–client relationship which reached down to local clienteles which they fostered and it nurtured. This clientelism started up in the backward south where for centuries the population, fearsome of authority (and with good cause), had formed self-defensive secret societies like the Camorra and the Mafia, and where individuals, sensing how weak they were *vis-à-vis* the authorities, 'commended' themselves to a local boss in return for protection. From the Mezzogiorno this nefarious system honeycombed the rest of Italy and politics came to be informed by the networks of extended family ties and patronage, admixed with administrative pressures, corruption, and abusive local administration. As a result, allegiances of groups in the Chamber swithered and altered all the time and one administration was barely distinguishable (if at all) from its predecessor: this was what was styled *trasformismo*.

Furthermore, as in France, parliamentary procedure helped to break up the party system still more. All bills had to be referred to a committee, and Cabinets were so sensible to the danger from these—particularly the budget committee—that it was not uncommon for them to make the composition of a committee a matter of confidence in the Chamber. Furthermore, the ministers were subject to the 'interpellation', though its excesses were perhaps curbed by the requirement that the vote be not taken immediately but the next day. This made Cabinets slightly more stable than in France: but not by much. In France the average life of a ministry at this time was some 8.5 months—in Italy it was 13.5.[25] In brief, the political system was based on local manipulation. It was riddled with corruption. It was acephelous. The portfolios danced but the tune was always the same.

5.4. 'Germany'

Prussia and Austria, the two great powers, were locked in intense rivalry for control of the *Bund*. In 1848 the wave of revolutions frightened the king of Prussia into granting a liberal-type constitution, which he soon withdrew. The Frankfurt Parliament spent 1848–9 drafting a federal constitution which would include all the German states except Austria. It was to be headed by the king of Prussia as emperor of the Germans. But the king of Prussia refused the invitation, and by 1849 Austria's armies had subdued the revolts in its provinces. The Frankfurt Constitution was dispersed and Prussia and Austria again vied for pre-eminence in the *Bund*. They were still Divine Right monarchies and from 1849 both entered on a phase of reaction, reversing the hopes of the Frankfurt liberals by increased centralization, and strengthening the bureaucratic-military apparatus of their autocracies. This did not still the German nationalism which had given rise to the Frankfurt Parliament, but with the two reactionary Great Powers watchfully frustrating one another in the effort to control the *Bund* it could find no outlet. In 1866, however, the Prussian chancellor, Bismarck, manoeuvred the Austrians into a war and, having defeated her, created a North German Confederation. In 1871, after she had defeated France, Prussia completed the unification of Germany, building on the constitution of the North German Confederation to bring the southern states into what now became the German Empire. In this federal empire Prussia was by far the wealthiest, most populous, and most powerful state, and the political system of the empire worked as it did because the empire's constitution was enmeshed with Prussia's: in short, the king of Prussia wore another hat as emperor of Germany, and any default in the powers of the one was made up by his powers under the other. This is why it is essential to describe the Prussian constitution before that of the empire.

[25] A. L. Lowell, *Government and Parties in Continental Europe* (London, 1896), i. 211, n. 2.

5.4.1. PRUSSIA

Frederick William IV of Prussia dissolved the representative assembly he had granted in the 'March Days' and promulgated his own constitution in December 1848. It was to have been revised by an elected assembly but this offended the king and he dissolved it in April 1849. He then abolished universal suffrage and substituted instead an extremely restrictive electoral system, which will be described in due course; and the new constituent assembly elected on this franchise revised the earlier constitution in a more conservative direction than ever. William promulgated this in 1850 and it remained in force until the defeat of Germany and downfall of the Hohenzollern dynasty in 1918.

The constitution included a bill of rights, but this was nugatory since there were no means for giving effect to them. For instance, it laid down 'freedom of instruction'—but there was no statute to give effect to this, so that the old school law remained operative—and therefore no school might open without the permission of the government. Similarly with the guarantee of freedom of indoor assembly: the police had to be notified of every meeting to discuss public affairs, and had the right to attend such meetings and the powers to break it up. The constitution was amendable by a simple majority vote in both the Chambers on two separate occasions with a twenty-one-day interval between them. The king, hereditary in the Hohenzollern line, was the head of state. All statutes required his consent. He appointed directly or indirectly to all state offices. He could confer titles of nobility. He enjoyed a civil list voted him in perpetuity. Ministers, appointed by the king, were responsible only to him. Though they might appear and speak in either of the two houses on request they did not resign on an adverse vote, for they did not form a Cabinet—each member was independent of his fellows, since each was responsible to the king and not to the legislature.

The legislature was the *Landtag*, and consisted of a *Herrenhaus* and a House of Representatives. The composition of the *Herrenhaus* was a matter for the king. In practice it consisted mostly of landed gentry. The House of Representatives had 433 members and sat for a five-year term, having been elected on the 'three-class system' combined with indirect election and open voting. The basic electoral division was a unit of 250 voters who elected an elector. These electors then met together in each district and elected the representative to the House by simple majority. But to vote in these primary elections, a roll of income-tax payers was compiled and the total sum they paid was divided into three: those who paid the first third of the taxes between them, another and less wealthy class who together paid the next third of the tax, and a third class which comprised the rest of the electorate. Separately and by majority vote each class chose by absolute majority one-third of the voters in each basic unit. The obvious result was to dilute the voting strength of the majority of electors while enhancing that of the wealthy. Dawson, writing in 1908, estimated the first class of primary voters at only 3–5 per cent of the electorate, the second class from 10 to 12 per cent, and the third class 85 per cent. The working class was so totally misrepresented that it was not till 1908 that the Social Democratic party returned its first representative to the House.[26]

The powers of the two Houses were identical and they had to consent to all laws, taxes, loans, and the annual budget. As a result of Bismarck's notorious constitutional coup of 1862 they lost their power to appropriate the taxes. Both Houses possessed legislative initiative but it was usually the government that put forward legislation. However, the *Landtag* could and sometimes did obstruct, so that ministers had to be wary.

5.4.2. THE GERMAN EMPIRE

The German Empire was a federal state in which the preponderant power was Prussia, the lesser states retaining privileges roughly in proportion to their size. Its chief organs were the emperor, the *Bundesrat*, and the popularly elected *Reichstag*.

The executive powers of the federation were vested in the emperor, and were not, at first view (but only at first view), very extensive. Even these were shared with the *Bundesrat*, so that the emperor had little power except in military and foreign policy. But he was also king of Prussia, which was grossly preponderant in the federation. Because he wore this hat as well as that of emperor he was able to exert considerable power. As emperor, he held supreme command of the army to which he appointed the highest officers; but as king of Prussia he appointed the lesser officers too. Again, it was as emperor that he told the chancellor to introduce a bill, but it was as king of Prussia that he told Prussia's representatives in the *Bundesrat* to support it. Furthermore, it was as king that he would tell the chancellor the amendments he would accept on behalf of the Prussian *Bundesrat* delegation, which was so large that it was likely to carry a majority. As to ministers, in law there was only one federal minister, namely the chancellor. He had subordinate ministers, but they were not colleagues. The chancellor was in no way obliged to resign on a hostile vote in the *Reichstag*. As chancellor he headed the entire body of federal officials, and presented bills to, and steered the *Reichstag*.

[26] W. H. Dawson, *The Evolution of Modern Germany* (T. Fischer Unwin, London, 1908), 435.

This *Reichstag*—which we would assume at first blush was the more important chamber—was elected for five years by direct universal suffrage! At one bound Bismarck made the empire appear as democratic as France and much more so than Britain. Its powers, too, gave this impression, for it had to consent to all laws. In fact its powers were highly circumscribed because the chief revenue laws were permanent and could not be changed without the assent of the *Bundesrat*. Furthermore, appropriations for the army were virtually determined by the law that fixed the number of troops needed, and which was voted not annually but for several years at a blow. In fact the *Reichstag's* chief activity was to criticize and amend government bills. This it did effectively, but the fact remains that it was reactive and not proactive.

Its powers were weakened still further by the emperor's power to dissolve it at any time, providing he had the support of the *Bundesrat*. In parliamentary governments the power to dissolve complements the power of ministers to see if they enjoy the confidence of the nation; but the German ministers were responsible solely to the emperor. This power to dissolve was used, in fact, simply to break down the *Reichstag's* resistance: as, for instance, when it refused to pass the anti-socialist law in 1878; again when it refused to fix the size of the army for the next seven years; and in 1893 when it refused to permit changes in the military system. In every case, after dissolution the electors returned a *Reichstag* that supported the government's plans.

In fact, the more one looks at the constitution, the more the *Bundesrat* appears the more important of the two Houses. It consisted of delegates— one might almost say ambassadors—sent by the kings and princes of the states and the senators of the free cities, and all members of a state delegation had to vote together. Its members numbered fifty-eight, of which Prussia had seventeen and (by virtue of an arrangement with Waldeck) another three, thus twenty in all. The state with the largest delegation after Prussia's was Bavaria, which sent six members. It will be seen, then, that Prussia had to win over only ten votes to wield an absolute majority.

The powers of this House were very great, though it hardly used its power of legislation, most bills originating in the *Reichstag*. But the *Bundesrat* was also part of the executive, for it could make ordinances for the completion of laws and regulation of the administration, had an extensive auditing authority, and could appoint to various offices. Furthermore, it disposed of a judicial power in that it was the body that decided disputes between the federal and the state governments on the interpretation of federal statutes, and decided controversies in public law that arose between the states themselves. It was privileged, too, for it could sit when the *Reichstag* was in recess, while the reverse was not the case. Hence it could sit in permanent session until its current work was finished. As a conclave of the (virtual) ambassadors of the various states, and a home of unending compromises, it met in secret, to prevent its dissensions becoming public knowledge.

Most importantly, it was the instrument through which Prussia ruled the nation. This was so because the central, federal government of the Reich received very extensive powers indeed *vis-à-vis* the individual states. Article 4 of the Constitution reels off its competences. They included customs duties and taxes, the army and navy, the consular service, and the protection of foreign commerce, and many domestic matters too. The latter included, for instance, posts and telegraphs, transportation on riverways passing through more than one state, extradition between states, railroads, canals, citizenship, travel, weights and measures—and so forth. Furthermore, it included all civil and criminal law. This great catalogue of powers did not entail a correspondingly large bureaucracy because, unlike in the United States, they tended to be executed by the several states themselves, with the federal government exercising supervision. Thus the federal government would enact a tariff, then make regulations, but the collection of the duties would be done by state officials.

The powers of the several states were by no means uniform, and Prussia, with three-fifths of the total population, was privileged over the rest. First, she had the perpetual right to have her king as the emperor of Germany. Next, amendments to the constitution required only an ordinary vote in the *Reichstag*, but would fail in the *Bundesrat* if fourteen votes were cast against them: and as Prussia had seventeen votes it follows that she could veto any proposed changes. It was even laid down that all bills relating to the army, navy, customs and excise, and the revision of regulations for collecting the revenue were also subject to her veto, since Prussia's vote in the *Bundesrat* was decisive if cast in favour of the *status quo*. Most of the states agreed by conventions between themselves and the state of Prussia, which effectively put their armies under the control of the emperor. Only Bavaria, Saxony, and Württemberg exercised their constitutional rights in respect to their armies: notably the power of appointing all officers below the rank of supreme commander.

Otherwise, the powers reserved to the states varied. Special rights were mostly enjoyed by the southern states. Thus Bavaria, Württemberg, and Baden were exempt from federal excises on beer and brandy, Bavaria and Baden retained their own postal service, Bavaria had complete control of its armed forces in peacetime, while Hamburg and Bremen retained their right to be free ports (a privilege later surrendered).

This government, quite dissimilar from those we have just been

examining, is an archetypal constitutional monarchy. Through the conflation of the emperorship and the Prussian monarchy, the ministers, acting in
the king's name and exclusively answerable to him, ruled the nation. The
Bundesrat was no check on any despotic tendencies of the monarch, because
Prussia controlled the *Bundesrat*. The *Reichstag*, elected on universal suffrage as
it was, might have been expected to impose the popular will on the
government; in fact it was an ingenious device by which Bismarck gave
the constitution the trappings of parliamentary democracy while robbing it
of the substance. The *Reichstag* contained enough parties (four main ones)
for the chancellor to manœuvre between them, so that the government was
usually able to carry its measures. Its legislative initiative, even if it resulted
in carrying a bill of its own making, was shipwrecked if opposed by the
chancellor. Its chief function turned out to be to act as a nuisance and a
gadfly to the government in matters it did not approve; for if the government wanted a measure, it had to have the *Reichstag*'s assent. Its obstructive
function therefore did give it some power to negotiate deals and compromises with the government of the day, but this power was mitigated by the
government's ability to concoct coalitions of support among the main
political parties. In fact, the *Reichstag* was rather like the US House of
Representatives *vis-à-vis* the president: to put it in Bagehot's famous phrase,
'a body hanging on the verge of government', reactive rather than proactive,
obstructive rather than creative.

5.5. *Austria*

In 1848 the wave of liberal revolution struck Vienna and the emperor hastily
granted a constitution, while in Hungary the Assembly of Deputies drew up
its own constitution on the basis of the liberals' 'Ten points'. By 1849 the
imperial generals had repressed the uprisings in all the Habsburg lands and
a bleak period of reaction followed which lasted until the Seven Weeks War
with Prussia in 1866. Defeated, the central government had to come to terms
with Hungary and its own insistent liberals. The result was the famous
Ausgleich of 1867 which transformed the formerly unitary empire into a dual
monarchy of Austria and Hungary. The two states each recognized the same
emperor, there were common ministries for foreign affairs, war, and finance
(the latter being only a common treasurer for assigned funds), and annual
'Delegations' where sixty members from each state convened to decide
matters of common interest, communicating with one another in writing,
and in Latin, so as to make clear that neither German nor Hungarian was
the superior tongue. A decennial treaty regulated such matters as tariffs,
currency, and the military system.

Hungary reverted to its 1848 parliamentary constitution which we have already described. Austria (composed of seventeen provinces of the former unitary state) adopted a constitution embodied in five statutes, which were described as 'fundamental law', one of which was a bill of rights. Their provisions could only be altered by a two-thirds vote of both Houses of Parliament.

The basic form was the common one of a monarch as chief executive, working with a bicameral legislature: emperor, *Herrenhaus*, and *Reichsrat*. The emperor's powers were what we have come to expect in heads of state. All his acts had to be countersigned by a minister nominally responsible to the legislature. Read literally this suggests parliamentary and not constitutional monarchy. But read in conjunction with clauses in the fifth bill, 'On The Executive Power', it appears not: for this bill, though providing for impeachment proceedings against a minister for unconstitutional conduct whilst in office, did *not* introduce the more important principle that the Cabinet as well as ministers needed the confidence of the legislature. This signified that the executive could only be dismissed in the event of unlawful conduct, but otherwise all it required was the emperor's confidence. Whether the form of parliamentary government was more closely observed at Vienna than at Berlin, the upshot was much the same: an executive independent of popular control. Furthermore, this independent power of the monarchy was reinforced by the extraordinary Article 14. This allowed the government to legislate in emergencies without the consent of the *Reichsrat* at all while it was not in session (a matter within the competence of the emperor), and in practice this power was used extensively to sail right over the head of the *Reichsrat* at the emperor's pleasure.

The *Herrenhaus* was composed of noblemen and imperial nominees. Its powers were identical with those of the Lower House, except that the latter was the first to be seized of the budget and the bill fixing the size of the army, so in consequence it could veto acts of the *Reichsrat*.

The *Reichsrat* was elected for six years, unless dissolved sooner. Originally its members were chosen by the provincial Diets but this was abandoned in 1873 and put fully in the hands of the electorate. On this basis each district elected one representative. But this electorate was constituted in a manner that was all but medieval. The representatives from each province elected through four *curiae* of voters (later five, when a 'general' *curia* was added)—the great landowners, the cities, the Chambers of Commerce, the rural communes—and provinces were divided into electoral districts for each *curia*. The catch, however, was that entry into any of these *curiae* required a property qualification: landed property or tax contributions (to the tune of at least 10 guilders per annum). The result of the two principles combined was that even in 1896, when the fifth general *curia* was added and the franchise correspondingly broadened, 5.5 million voters in this new *curia* elected only seventy-two deputies, as compared to eighty-five elected by some 5,000 great landowners in the first *curia*, twenty-one deputies by the limited number of electors in the Chambers of Commerce, while nearly 400,000 propertied voters elected 118 deputies in the towns, and 129 deputies were elected by the rural communes' 1,500,000 voters.

The *Reichsrat*'s competence was limited by the privileges of the provincial Diets, and these were specified in the constitution, so that Austria was less a unitary state than it appeared. The powers of these Diets were absolute in respect of local government, higher education, raising local taxes, and altering their mode of voting. They also exercised powers in subordination to any general laws made by the *Reichsrat* and these included legislation on churches, primary and secondary schools, and any matter in the power of the *Reichsrat* which it chose to delegate to them.

Here, then, was another constitutional but thoroughly authoritarian monarchy. The ministers were in practice the servants of the Crown and not of the *Reichsrat*. Since the latter could obstruct, however, ministries were always resigning. Whereas Germany had five chancellors between 1871 and 1917, Austria had twenty. This was in most part due to the *Reichsrat*'s composition, for it reflected every ethnic group in an extraordinarily poly-ethnic state, all of them quarrelling fiercely with one another, making governments difficult to sustain but easy for the emperor and court to manipulate. There were some forty political parties which formed them-selves into about twenty 'clubs' in the Chamber. They were formed chiefly on ethnic lines. At the same time as representing ethnic groups, the clubs might stand for clerical, liberal, agrarian, and (later) even socialist interests. To make matters more confusing, their names and affiliations were con-tinually changing.

The emperor, then, was far from being a figurehead, so much so that he actually used his veto against a Bill passed by both Houses and frequently used his power to issue emergency decrees. Thus any responsibility of ministers in the parliamentary sense is delusive: they were remote from popular control, and this gave extensive and intrusive powers to the enor-mous bureaucracy over which they presided. True, there was a bill of rights but it did not impose a legal restraint on legislation and some of its clauses were scanty generalities which required legislation to give them effect, while still others were limited or qualified or even contradicted by statutes passed regardless. The right to sue officials for injuries done in the course of their official duties was impossible because no procedure for doing so was enacted. The right of assembly was virtually turned into its opposite by the qualifying legislation. An association had to acquire an official certificate which could be refused if the authorities deemed it illegal or seditious, had to provide them with the by-laws and their reports to members, and had to report their proceedings. The police were entitled to sit in on these meetings and could dissolve the association if it went beyond the items stated in its by-laws. To forestall conspiracy, associations were forbidden to communicate with one another. As to public meetings held by persons not belonging to a regular association, the police could virtually forbid these at pleasure. Lowell commented: 'The Austrian police is . . . the most inquisitorial, the most minutely and severely vigilant in the world.'[27] Likewise with the freedom of the press. The constitution guaranteed this and further stated that there should be no censorship. In fact the business of printing could not be carried out without a licence, every number of a periodical had to be submitted to the police before it was published, and periodicals issued fortnightly or more often could not be started up until the government had received a deposit to ensure that fines would be duly paid. If this was not done they could be suppressed.

The only recourse of the private citizen was to the administrative court, the *Reichsgericht*. But this course suffered two disabilities. In the first place this court could exercise moral force only—there was no machinery for giving effect to its decisions. Secondly, it could not question the legal validity of a statute that had been passed in due form. It could question only the validity of bureaucratic actions pursuant to that act.

6. CONCLUSION

So, by the 1880s every state in Europe excepting Russia was a constitutional monarchy. But whereas three of the Great Powers, Britain, France, and Italy, were parliamentary monarchies, in Austria and Germany the legislature was an ancillary, a 'body hanging on the verge of government' which vested in the hereditary monarchy and the bureaucracy and military of which the monarch was the supreme head. The three western powers were liberal, the two eastern ones authoritarian. But the movement towards constitutionalizing monarchy had gathered a momentum that took it out of Europe, further and further east: past Russia, which had its foretaste in 1905, into Turkey, which had indeed endeavoured to reform itself in this sense since at least the 1870s, to Egypt at about the same time, on to Persia in 1905, and into India and China; while its British model was replicated in Canada, Australia, New Zealand, and South Africa.

[27] Lowell, *Government and Parties*, ii. 92

This momentum was made all the greater by the now overwhelming military and economic power wielded by the West. This was the fruit of the industrial revolution which, having made Britain the workshop of the world, by 1860 began to take rapid hold of much of Europe and particularly Germany, whose industrialization proceeded at a frantic pace after Unification, surpassing Britain's from about 1900.

Yet to confine industrialization to this context is to demean it, to render it parochial, of significance only to the propulsion of constitutional forms overseas from Europe and the United States. The fact is that industrialization was the most significant event in world history since agriculture succeeded food-gathering and hunting over 5,000 years before. The long agricultural age in which we have spent all our time so far had come to an end. Industrial society had arrived.

5

Industrialization

*T*he industrial and technological revolution which began around 1770 and is still in full flood today ushered in an entirely new phase of world history. It 'made a far more drastic break with the past than anything since the invention of the wheel'.[1] 'From then on, the world was no longer the same . . . no revolution has been as dramatically revolutionary as the industrial revolution—except perhaps the Neolithic revolution. Both of these changed the course of history, so to speak, each one bringing about a discontinuity in the historic process.'[2]

Three major principles characterize the revolution. The first was the substitution of machinery for hand-labour: regular, tireless, anonymous mechanical energy instead of human skill and effort. The second was the use of inanimate sources of power, especially the conversion of heat into work: hence an almost limitless supply of energy to operate the machines. The third was a new abundance of raw materials, as witnessed, for instance, by using mineral substances (e.g. coal) for animal or vegetable ones (e.g. wood, charcoal).

The political developments we have just been considering—the consti-tutionalizing of European absolutisms—owed nothing to this industrializa-tion process except in precocious Britain where the advance of the industrial middle class was universally recognized and, possibly, in Belgium. Elsewhere in Europe, we must agree with Barraclough's assertion that 'industrialization was a product of the last quarter rather than of the first two-thirds of the nineteenth century; it was a consequence rather than concomitant of the "railways age", which by 1870 had provided the continent with a new system of communications'.[3] The notion, often vaguely adumbrated, that consti-tutionalization rode on the back of industrialization and the 'rise of the working class' is quite wrong. The working class certainly provided the cannon-fodder of the liberal revolutions, but its influence once the battle was won was minimal. Louis Blanc's plan of social workshops may be

---

[1] *Cambridge Economic History of Europe* [hereafter referred to as *CEHE*], 8 vols. (CUP, Cambridge, 1953–78), i. 275.
[2] C. Cipolla (ed.), *The Fontana Economic History of Europe: The Industrial Revolution* (Collins/Fontana Books, Glasgow, 1972), 7.
[3] G. Barraclough, *An Introduction to Contemporary History* (Penguin, Harmondsworth, 1966), 43.

quoted to support a significant proletarian input, and so might the publication of the *Communist Manifesto*. These meagre exceptions prove the rule: one swallow does not make a summer. It was not till after 1870 that we begin to see powerful social democratic parties of working men, and finally the extension of the suffrage. Industrialization was not the progenitor of constitutionalization: that was a liberal achievement. When industrialization burst into its full flood after 1870, it was to bring not constitutionalization but democracy: a very different matter indeed.

So, industrialization was the world's hinge of fate, but to explore all the ramifications of this great fact would take us far beyond the limited purview of this *History*. Here I want to draw attention to three facets of the process which are of particular relevance to this book. I shall consider, first, the effects of the industrial revolution on the aims and techniques of government; next, its effects on warfare; and finally, its generation of two new classes, capitalist and 'proletarian', and, as a concomitant, the changing of the entire agenda of government.

1. INDUSTRIALIZATION'S EFFECTS ON GOVERNMENT

In this new Industrial Age, government took on two new characteristics, characteristics moreover that were to intensify as the years rolled by up to the present day and will continue to do so, without doubt, into the future. Government became unprecedentedly intrusive. And it was unremittting. There is a sense in which, as Jean Dunbabin argues,[4] 'nobody was governed before the later nineteenth century: it would certainly be foolish to maintain that either royal or princely government in the twelfth century operated according to fixed rules or over all the inhabitants of a defined area'. To be GOVERNED 'is,—what?' We must take the views of Proudhon with a large pinch of salt: Proudhon was a proto-anarchist, an arch-anti-centralizer, an advocate of workers' self-rule by *mutualité*. Furthermore, he was writing at the period of Louis Napoleon's authoritarian Presidency. For all that, his answer contains a subtext and it is this that is of value to us: government was an *intrusion*.

To be GOVERNED [he wrote in 1851] is to be watched, inspected, spied upon, directed, law-driven, numbered, regulated, enrolled, indoctrinated, preached at, controlled, checked, estimated, valued, censured, commended, by creatures who have neither the right nor the wisdom nor the virtue to do so. To be GOVERNED is to be at every operation, at every transaction noted, registered, counted, taxed, stamped, measured, numbered, assessed, licensed, authorized, admonished, pre-

---

[4] J. Dunbabin, *France in the Making, 843–1180* (OUP, Oxford, 1985), 277.

vented, forbidden, reformed, corrected, punished. It is under the pretext of public utility and in the name of the general interest, to be placed under contribution, drilled, fleeced, exploited, monopolized, extorted from, squeezed, hoaxed, robbed; then at the slightest resistance, the first word of complaint, to be repressed, fined, vilified, harassed, hunted down, abused, clubbed, disarmed, bound, choked, imprisoned, judged, condemned, shot, deported, sacrificed, sold, betrayed; and to crown all, mocked, ridiculed, derided, outraged, dishonoured. That is government; that is justice; that is its morality.[5]

2. THE CAPABILITIES OF GOVERNMENT

The new capabilities of government can be summed up in an acronym: PEP. 'P' stands for 'plenty' as measured by the vast expansion of national wealth, outstripping a huge population explosion. Europe had moved and was destined to move still further and further away from the subsistence level of the Agricultural Age. 'E' stands for 'energy'—access to almost unlimited sources of natural energy, and its harnessing to inanimate machines in lieu of human skills and labour. The final 'P' stands for 'penetration' and this term needs some explication.

By *penetration* I mean the ability of the government to act directly upon the population by its own agents, instead of through intermediate local bigwigs. Such penetration could be expressed, to use an earlier term, as the new-found 'intrusiveness' of government into the homes, occupations, and daily lives of the citizenry. As stated here, 'penetration' is meant as a summary variable which is composed of three elements. They are, to begin with, the surveillance of the population, and the control and direction of that population's activities. The first of these three implies acquiring information. The other two, together, imply government action.

This formulation can and indeed must be explicated in terms of its *parameters*. One parameter is the state of information technology. Another is movement, that is, the speed at which messages and freight can be carried. A third is energy technology. The fourth is bureaucracy, and the final parameter is wealth, defined as the sum total of extractable resources.

Some of these parameters have hitherto remained fairly constant over time whereas others have advanced.

[5] P. J. Proudhon, *General Idea of the Revolution in the Nineteenth Century*, trans. J. B. Robinson (Freedom Press, London, 1923; first published in France, 1851), 293–4, with some alterations from Benjamin Tucker's translation in *Instead of Books* (New York, 1893), 26 and quoted in R. Nozick, *Anarchy, State, and Utopia* (Basic Books, Blackwell, Oxford, 1974).

2.1. *The Constants*

One parameter that hardly changed up to the industrial revolution was *movement*. Messages could travel much faster than armed forces. Beacons, semaphores, smoke systems, even drums (as in Africa) could convey information within hours. But these were primitive messages: 'the enemy is coming', 'on foot', 'by land'; 'the Armada has been sighted and attack is imminent'. Sophisticated messages had to be carried by couriers and this depended on the speed of the horse and the distance between relay stations. The fastest information service before the coming of the railways was the Pony Express: this covered the route from Saint Joseph, Missouri, to Sacramento, a distance of 1,966 miles, in ten to eleven days. Relays were established every 10 miles, eighty riders were employed, half in one direction, half in the other. Each rider usually covered 50–60 miles (much longer distances in dire emergency). The average rate of travel, then, was between 179 and 196 miles a day.[6] Earlier, in the sixteenth century, a message sent by the fastest courier between Venice and Nuremberg—some 360 miles as the crow flies, but in fact traversing the tortured defiles of the Alps—took four days, an average of 90 miles per day. Between Madrid and Venice the average speed was 40 m.p.d., between Constantinople and Venice 41.5 m.p.d.[7]

The fact is that up to the industrial revolution the speed on land was determined by a completely constant technology: either you walked or you rode a horse. It takes a great jump of the imagination to realize that when a Roman legion was transferred from a place such as Gaul to a station in, say, Illyria, it *walked* that entire distance. So, for that matter, did Alexander's troops and so did Napoleon's. The speed of armies—and these, remember, were the sinews that held states and empires together—was altogether slower, therefore, than the carrying of messages. Alexander's daily rate of march varied from 19 to 7 m.p.d., averaging some $12\frac{1}{2}$ m.p.d. But this was only when the whole army was on the march. Cavalry or mounted infantry could move between 46 and 30 m.p.d.[8] Luttwak puts the marching-rate of Roman infantry as high as 25 m.p.d. In the third and fourth centuries this was too slow to adapt to the new strategy of mobile defence which

---

[6] I owe this interesting piece of information to my colleague, Professor Rodney Needham, who cites his reference as W. W. Beck and Y. D. Haase, *Historical Atlas of the American West* (University of Oklahoma Press, Oklahoma, 1989).

[7] F. Braudel, *Civilisation and Capitalism, Fifteenth to Eighteenth Centuries*, vol. 1, *The Structure of Everyday Life*, trans. S. Reynolds (Collins, London, 1981), 424; *The Mediterranean and the Mediterranean World in the Age of Philip II*, 2 vols., 2nd edn. (Collins, London, 1973), i. 364.

[8] D. W. Engels, *Alexander the Great and the Logistics of the Macedonian Army* (University of California Press, Los Angeles, 1978), app. 5, pp. 153–5.

depended on a central reserve of cavalry to move to any point of danger. The effect, he says, was to double the rate of march to 50 m.p.d.[9]

Cavalry *raids* were different. Akbar raided Gujarat, 600 miles away, with 3,000 horsemen, and it took them nine days in the saddle. Compare mass infantry armies with their baggage trains: the Abbasid armies took a whole year to move down from Khorasan to Mesopotamia. The usual speed of the pre-industrial army was 15 m.p.d. while the bullocks and baggage moved at some 4–5 m.p.d. Napoleon's usual rate of march was some 10 or 12 m.p.d., but when actively engaged he moved his troops at high speeds. In the 1805 campaign, for instance, Soult moved 275 miles in twenty-two days' sustained marching, but Davout led the Third Division 80 miles in forty-eight hours, of which thirty-six were spent on the road, and in the first Italian campaign, at Castiglione, Augereau marched his division 50 miles in thirty-six hours.[10]

A second parameter, access to energy, did show signs of some movement. In the Middle Ages greater and more sophisticated use was made of wind and water. Water-driven corn-mills came in in the sixth century, and in the eleventh century water-power was used for fulling cloth, driving sawmills, lifting water, turning lathes, and by the fourteenth century could in theory be used to drive any machine. Indeed, in France, which was well endowed with water-power, the water-mill competed successfully with steam-power until the 1860s. But after about 1350 the flow of invention slowed down.

Finally, the size of the bureaucracy relative to the population also moved—but not unidirectionally. It may well be that the civil servant–population ratio in Sumeria was greater than that of France in the eighteenth century. China, with a population of some 200 million at this time, was still administered by the 30,000 established civil servants who comprised the senior and the junior classes of the bureaucracy. Of course this figure does not take account of the innumerable 'runners' who infested the *yamens*, and this points up a general difficulty in comparing numbers of civil servants: what exactly are we to count as a civil servant? In France today both the schoolteachers and the police would be reckoned as civil servants, whereas in Britain they are not.

---

[9] E. N. Luttwak, *The Grand Strategy of the Roman Empire* (Johns Hopkins Press, Baltimore and London, 1976), 186.

[10] D. G. Chandler, *The Campaigns of Napoleon* (Weidenfeld & Nicolson, 1966), 148–9.

2.2. *The Advancing Parameters*

The parameter that made the greatest advance prior to the industrial revolution was that of information technology, and its advance can be summed up in two words: alphabetization and printing.

The art of writing is of course coeval with the inception of organized states—everything before that is definitionally prehistoric. The first systems of writing effectively confined it and the secrets it unlocked to the very few. Hieroglyphic script took a long time to master, and so did the Mesopotamian cuneiform. We have school primers of the time that show us how it was imparted. The parallel is Chinese, where as many as perhaps 30,000 separate characters, each denoting some thing or another, must be learned by heart. Modern schoolchildren do learn enough characters to become literate, but only at the cost of several years' relentless drilling. In all these cases literacy used to be the preserve of a very small coterie whose command of it gave them enormous social, political—and religious—power. The alphabet democratized literacy. Already in full use in the Levant by *c.*1100 BC, a version of the Phoenician-Jewish alphabet was taken over by the Greeks *c.*900 bc. This flexible facility, with a mere twenty to twenty-six letters to learn, could adapt itself to any language. When we say it 'democratized' literacy we do not mean that every Jew or Greek was able to read and write. We simply do not know. But apparently even uneducated Athenians in the fifth and fourth centuries BC were able to read: an Athenian could describe a complete ignoramus as 'He can't read, he can't swim'. Roman legionaries were not necessarily literate, but a country where election squibs and posters were stuck on notice-boards bears witness to a literate society. And the entire empire became covered by a network of schools.[11] Reading and writing created a new, broader political constituency.

So matters stayed for some two-and-a-half millennia until 1455, when literacy became far more widespread, almost, one might say, commonplace, by an ancillary invention: *printing.* Printing made written works accessible to the common man and the political public was immensely enlarged. The Bible, translated into the vernacular, became a revolutionary document. The Reformation, its offspring, gave rise to a multitude of competing sects: the tracts and pamphlets of the Great Rebellion in Britain alone fill several volumes. Nor were these pamphlets confined to religious matters: the Religious Wars in France made most important contributions to political theory, the Mazarinades were political polemic.

---

[11]   C. Cipolla, *Literacy and Development in the West* (Penguin, Harmondsworth, 1969), 38–9.

3. PRE-INDUSTRIAL AGE GOVERNMENT

3.1. *Poor Control of Territorial Perimeters*

Because armies were so slow and messages took so long to move between them and the capital, the central control of the peripheries was weak and empires tended to disintegrate by breaking away at the fringes. We have given several examples of this: for instance, the break-up of the Persian Empire at its Aegean borders and the progressive whittling-down of the Abbasid Empire from both west and east until it consisted only of its central portion, Iraq.

3.2. *Limited Public Policy*

Generally, the smaller the state the more the government could do, if it wanted: the limiting cases are some of the chartered or free cities of Europe, but also any garrison city in Asia. In such cities the authorities could and did enforce a multitude of by-laws, most of them relating to market regulation, others (particularly in Moslem cities) to religious conduct, some—but pretty rarely—to the provision of schools and hospitals. Even so, most services were provided by voluntary effort—by *liturgies*, as in the Greek and Roman cities. This is how churches and mosques and caravanserais, fountains and aqueducts, and the like were generally provided. But not so the central government. This confined itself to little more than to provide an army, law and order, and taxation to pay for these. Sometimes these might be accompanied by physiocratic measures such as the Chinese canal system, or the eighteenth-century French and Prussian state manufactories. But these were ancillary to the fiscal system, designed to expand the tax-base. The core functions were extremely limited.

3.3. *Dependence on Local Élites*

With slow communications and few administrators governments had to look to laymen for assistance and who else could these be but the most influential men of a district? The common experience was a governmental hierarchy that only reached down so far and then made an interface with local individuals, nominally under their orders but, in fact, powerful enough in their own right to drive bargains with them. *Buzones*, *seigneurs*, 'notables, 'gentry': we have met with and described these many times over in the pre-industrial states, so there is no need for repetition here. It is worth recalling, however, the elementary arrangements for maintaining order and control of the common people: by armies of spies and delators, and by co-responsibility units like frankpledge in England, or the *li-chia* and *pao-chia* in China.

3.4 *The Incompetence of the Bureaucracy*

It was not just the sparseness of administrators that made governmental penetration so shallow, but corruption and, more importantly, inadequate information retrieval.

Previous chapters have dwelt on the widespread, indeed one might almost call it endemic, corruption in the pre-industrial state. The ideal of selfless, devoted public service is largely a late eighteenth- and nineteenth-century European and American phenomenon. Till then it was taken for granted that one went into government service in order to make money out of it. The effect of the consequent widespread corruption was to distort or even frustrate the intentions of government. What government wanted and what it got were often very different things.

As to information retrieval: the larger empires such as the Abbasid, the Chinese, and the Mogul successfully divided their administrative functions between specialized departments; but in many cases—pre-Petrine Russia could serve as an example—the departments were either too many for the range of government business (hence, overlapping) or too few (so that each department was a rag-bag of different functions). Then again, even with a satisfactory division of functions, working convention could hamper efficiency: for instance, if an official could only communicate with his opposite number in another department via his departmental head who sent the file to the other departmental head who passed it down until it reached its appropriate level, decisions were enormously time-consuming.

Perhaps much more time-consuming and prone to error were the practices of retrieving stored information. Even today—and quite frequently—a misplaced file is enough to halt an entire operation. As far as I know, there is no study that brings together the methods adopted in the past. We know that clay tablets were sorted and stored in earthenware pitchers, that Roman imperial records were scrolled up and kept in boxes (the *scrinia*), but there is no book that follows the developments through time.

Even so, the point may be illustrated by cataloguing the working practice of the British Treasury over some 400 years. In 1677 the Treasury was put into commission and it was decided that its secretary was to keep minutes for future action. The inspirer of this enterprise, Sir George Downing, initiated a number of other books such as the Customs Book, the Letterbook, and so on. The latter, for instance, contained copies of all letters written by the secretary for the Board of Commissioners. In those days

Treasury papers were folded twice, and docketed and numbered on back and sides. As matters became more complicated and more and more information began to attach itself to a docket, odd bits of paper were written on and folded with the rest. Not till 1868 did the secretary order that each original paper be kept flat, filed to a tag, and put into a jacket: behold, the file!

Information about the provenance of the paper was written on the front of the jacket. This also contained references to relevant files elsewhere. Later the cover was marked off into one column for memoranda and one for minutes. In 1904 the contents of the file were rearranged so that they could be read forwards, as in a book. All these arrangements lasted until the First World War. The search for papers was often a slow business and frequently the clerk in charge had to visit the Paper Room to interview the clerks in charge there. The war radically altered the system. Hitherto, each file related to one letter and all relevant letters were tied together with it into a so-called 'bundle'. Now the concept became one of 'one subject, one jacket', so that all such letters and so forth were put together into one file, which of course became very fat. Meanwhile, modern methods of retrieval were slowly making their way in. The first proposals for installing a telephone were made in 1881—the system consisted of three telephones only! Not until 1889 were typewriters introduced—and not until 1892 was a third lady typist employed! Electric light came in at much the same time—1894–5; until then the office had used candles.

One final but very important word on information retrieval: even if local information was gathered efficiently and duly passed upwards to the central government, it by no means followed that the appropriate authority would have access to it. We have seen how kings and emperors were surrounded by courtiers and officials. These could act as a barrier to communication, so that the prime mover of the entire political system could issue orders that were based on faulty information. A story is told about the great Ch'ien-Lung Emperor of China. The Manchu emperors, as we have had occasion to show, had developed their own private system of gathering information from every part of the empire. Ch'ien-Lung was a considerate man, particularly in entertaining visiting sages. When news was brought him of the arrival of such a man he invited him to breakfast. The poor man did not dare to eat and said he had already breakfasted. 'Oh, and what did you eat?' asked the emperor, to which the sage replied, humbly, 'Two eggs, Sire'. 'Two eggs!' exploded the emperor 'But you must be rich. They are so expensive I cannot afford them. Why, they come at about 100 cash apiece.' 'Ah', replied the sage, catching on quickly, 'You see, those are Imperial eggs that you eat, especially chosen for the Imperial Majesty. As for me I have to buy the poorest and cheapest, in the markets, where they cost two cash apiece.'

If we had to sum up the nature of government in the pre-industrial era, government's role was architectonic, that is, its role was to provide the most basic of frameworks for an ocean of *sponte acta* and self-regarding activities.

4. THE INDUSTRIAL REVOLUTION—FROM *c.*1800 TO THE PRESENT DAY

4.1. *Energy and Wealth*

Unlimited natural resources have fuelled energy, and energy has produced plenty. This has lifted the industrialized economies out of their previous marginal subsistence economy. It has also produced large surpluses that can be turned to military and civilian use. But at the same time it has created new imperatives for public action—the prevention of industrial accidents, the regulation of hours of work, the improvement of environmental public health—and so one could go on.

There are, alas, no precise figures for national income in the eighteenth century. Hence we have no base from which to measure the vast expansion in the standard of living and amenity that have taken place since then. We have to content ourselves with indicators, not with a completed time-series. Perhaps the most striking indicator is that, since the industrial revolution, man has 'increased his productivity a hundred times over'.[12] If we compare consumption of coal with its hypothetical alimentary equivalent, '[then] by 1800 the UK was using perhaps 11 million tons of coal a year, by 1830 more than double that figure, by 1845 twice as much again, and by 1870, over 100 million tons'. The last amount cited is equivalent to 800 million calories of energy, enough to feed a population of 850 millions for one year—at a time when the population was only 31 million.

Another way to put this is that by 1870 the capacity of Britain's steam-engines was about 4 million horsepower, equivalent to the power that would be generated by 40 million men.[13] Or compare these figures: in 1860 Britain was burning 132 million tons of coal, equivalent to 1,057 million megawatt hours.[14] But in 1960 it was burning some thirteen times as much: 1,809 million tons of coal, generating 14,472 million megawatt hours. But coal was not the only natural source of energy: it was between 1860 and 1890 that oil extraction was begun and the internal combustion engine was perfected. By the 1900s electricity also became a source of energy and, in the mid-twentieth century, atomic power. Hence the expansion in megawatt hours went far beyond what the figures for British coal production suggested. In

[12] *CEHE*, i. 328.   [13] Ibid. ii. 326–9.   [14] Cipolla, *Industrial Revolution*, 11.

1860 the world production of energy from all inanimate sources was 1.1 billion megawatts—in 1960 it was 33.5 billion megawatts.[15] The resultant rise in living standards can be illustrated by two indicators. Life-expectancy in pre-industrial society was some thirty years; nowadays it is over sixty. A household in pre-industrial society spent from one-half to three-quarters of its income on food; today food would take up about one-quarter. In Europe, prone for all its pre-industrial history to an agricultural economy where some 80 per cent of the population worked the fields, life, as we have seen, was lived at bare subsistence level, where the frequent food scarcities, or heavier taxes, drove populations to revolt.[16] That Europe was no more. Instead of scarcity there was a surplus, instead of marginal subsistence there was amenity.

4.2. *The Great Innovations*

It would be out of place here and doubly otiose, since the story has been recounted a dozen times, to give a chronology of the advances that make up the industrial revolution. Our needs are served by attention only to what, after all, is the point of this chapter: the great changes wrought in the provision of energy, the access to information, and the carriage of goods and men. However, two general remarks need to be made. First, Britain was precocious. It was not till the 1860s that noticeable signs of industrialization appeared on the Continent, and not till 1870 onwards that the now-great power, Germany, became fully industrialized at a prodigious rate, catching up with Britain. The second point is the primacy of the railway in the industrialization process. Long habituation has exposed British schoolchildren to learning about flying shuttles and spinning jennies and the consequent rise of factory production using the power-loom; but, on reflection, one might well ask whether this was not simply a concomitant to the industrial revolution rather than a prime mover. The prime mover was, surely, the railway. It took a long time for the railways to develop from Newcomen's fixed steam-pump of 1712 and Watt's invention of the steam condenser in 1765 and his patent for converting the machine for rotary motion, and the coming of the first passenger railway line, the Stockton and Darlington, in 1829. But by the 1840s a railway mania had developed and the country was quickly criss-crossed by a network of lines. Continental Europe followed this example, though at some remove. By the 1860s, however, it too

---

[15] Ibid. 12.

[16] For a full discussion of this problem, see C. Tilly, 'Food Supply and Public Order in Modern Europe', in id. (ed) *The Formation of National States in Europe* (Princeton UP, Princeton, 1975), 380–455.

was furiously investing in railways. The railways burnt coal and used iron or steel, which also required coal; so the result was a self-generating process by which these three heavy industries developed, and located themselves in favoured places where coal and iron could be worked together; such places, for instance, as the Saargebiet and the Ruhrland in Germany.

By 1985 the world production of coal was 3,114 billion tons. The age up to about 1880 has been called the Age of Steam and Iron. It was succeeded by an age when two different forms of natural energy emerged to compete with it: electricity and oil. During this period, too, the world began to change over from iron to steel. This was due to the introduction—largely in Germany (Britain clinging to its old-fashioned methods)—of the Gilchrist–Thomas process, in which full-scale production began in 1879. By 1890 this method was responsible for 64 per cent of the steel in continental Europe, as against only 14 per cent in Britain. World output rose from about a half-a-million tons in 1870 to nearly 28 million in 1900. (Symbolically, the Eiffel Tower was completed in 1889.) In 1985 estimated world steel production was 690 million tons.

Electricity had been a gentleman's hobby in the eighteenth century and its origins, unlike those of the cotton-machine and steam-engine inventions, which were the work of self-taught artisans and the like, lay in scientific exploration. The basics had been discovered relatively early. Volta produced his 'pile', that is, his cell, in 1800, and by 1831 a number of inquirers, including Davy and Faraday, had laid open all the phenomena involved in the telegraph, light, and power. But although Faraday had shown how mechanical motion could generate electric current, an electrical industry did not take off till sixty years later. Then electricity began to be used for electroplating, then the electric light globe, then electric traction, and finally the delivery of power to industrial plants and to the home consumer. By 1985 the world generation of electricity had topped 9,675 billion kilowatt-hours. (kWh).

Meanwhile oil had begun its career in 1870 with a miserable 5.5 million barrels per annum. It did not really take off until it was 'cracked', that is, converted into petrol. As such it made a potential source of gas for an engine and that engine, the internal combustion (i/c) engine, was invented by Otto in 1876 and then, in 1886, was used for locomotion: in short, the motor car (automobile). The applications of this type of engine were manifold and caught on rapidly: the oil-fired ship, the submarine, and the aeroplane all evolved from the original Daimler two-stroke engine. By 1985 the production of crude oil had reached 2,669 million tonnes, that of petroleum products 2,770 million tonnes.

The social and political effect of the i/c engine was profound because it so enormously increased the tactile outreach of government. The number of passenger motor vehicles produced in 1985 was 30.4 million, that of commercial vehicles, 11.4 million. So, armies no longer (save in dire straits) footed it to the front but were moved at double or more their pre-industrial speeds. (Over longer distances, however, rail preserved a clear superiority.) More important by far in respect of this outreach was the increased use of the aeroplane for civil or military purposes. Military aircraft now speed faster than sound, a passenger flight from London to San Francisco, Tokyo, or Hong Kong will take between thirteen and sixteen hours only. Distance has shrunk. A letter mailed from England to Italy will travel airmail within a day-and-a-half—before spending that number of *weeks* (at least) in the maze of an archaic distribution system. (Much the same is true of letters to North America.) Some idea of the revolution in transportation is gleaned by the following indicators: in 1985 the passenger-kilometres covered by rail was 1,770 billion; that covered by air, 1,361 billion. Thus the internal and external distances among states had shrunk to what—in internal matters at least—was near instantaneity. The effect of this could only be to magnify the state's capacity for penetration.

Next we must turn to information technology. This was transformed by the invention, simultaneously by Morse and Wheatstone, of the means of sending messages over distance by electrical impulses passed through a wire. Its immediate customers were the developing railways. Next, a way was found to send two messages simultaneously in opposite directions. By 1850 the American Telegraph Company was sending 2,000 words an hour. The invention was so handy that even economically backward states in Europe such as Austria took it up, and in 1860 so did Turkey. In 1849 the telegraph poles stretched for 2,000 miles, in 1869, for 110,000. The messages sent along them similarly multiplied from less than a quarter-million in 1852 to nearly 19 million in 1869.[17] More significant was the development of submarine telegraphy. It was pioneered across the English Channel in the 1850s, and in 1865 a cable was laid across the Atlantic. There followed a burst of cable-laying between nations that criss-crossed the entire globe. By 1872 it was possible to telegraph from London to Tokyo and Adelaide. The most striking symbol of the telegraph's success was in 1871, when the result of the Derby was sped from England to Calcutta in five minutes.[18]

The telephone was another distance-cutting invention, made by Bell in 1876, but which, unlike the telegraph, was a domestic consumer good. By 1985 there were 123 telephones per 1,000 of the world's population. But the

[17] E. Hobsbawm, *The Age of Capital* (Weidenfeld & Nicolson, London, 1962 repr. 1975), 76.
[18] Ibid. 76.

next advance in telecommunication was breathtaking: the possibility of sending long-distance signals by the emission of radio waves, without the need for wires to carry them, had been demonstrated theoretically by Clerk-Maxwell in 1864, and had even been tested experimentally by Hertz in 1886. But the working system was not set in place until Marconi did so in 1895. Hence the expression 'wireless', appropriated by those who bought commercial receivers. This was an amenity, and spread like wildfire. Today, in the western industrialized states it would not be too bold to say that it had reached saturation point; in 1983 there were 1,450 million sets in operation throughout the world, an average of 310 for every 1,000 people. From now on communication by speech became virtually instantaneous: either by telephone, radio-telephone, or wireless telegraphy (using the Morse Code). By 1926, too, by an adept adaptation of telecommunications, Baird transmitted the first moving pictures on television and from then on the industry never looked back. Here again there are countries like the United States or Great Britain where the number of units has reached, virtually, saturation point. By 1983 there were 630 million television receivers throughout the world. Just so, governments can commmunicate face to face with entire populations, inside their very houses.

However, the greatest of all breakthroughs in telcommunications developed c.1946–7 with the invention of the transistor. The transistor has laid open the path to the microprocessor of today: an invention hailed by some as the greatest technological breakthrough of the century, and one which so divides today from yesterday as to be hailed as the initiator of a 'second industrial revolution'.

The first half of the century used the tube—commonly called 'valve'—to construct a machine for radio, long-distance telephony, and television. It was also used in the construction of 'computers', machines that would complete millions of arithmetical exercises in a fractional time, whereas its more complicated operations were beyond the range of the human brain altogether. Such computers reached extraordinary sizes: the famous ENEAC computer used 17,468 tubes, filling a large room. But in 1947 the transistor was invented—a component made of semiconductors, of which the cheapest and most suitable turned out to be silicon. It was first employed practically in 1960 when computers began using hundreds of thousands apiece, and by the 1970s had been refined into the familiar microcomputer of today. This is now the fastest-growing branch of industry in the United States, with Japan and Western Europe also manufacturing on a huge scale.

The computer, large mainframe, small mainframe, desk-top, lap-top, 'notebook', according to the work and speed which is required of it, has become ubiquitous. We can skip its application to everyday amenity—the microwave oven, the video-recorder, and the like. Its application to industry is more germane to the earlier part of our treatment, since it speeds up production, enables the manufacturer to produce articles of irregular shapes, such as aircraft wings, and even automates factories, where production is carried out by programmed machines, using a mere handful of men as supervisors. In this sense the microprocessor may be regarded as an enhancement of the conquest of energy we have already described.

Our interest here, however, is with its informational uses. It can store enormous quantities of data in a very small space—on a number of diskettes. It can—by using an appropriate 'programme' (provided ready-made nowadays by a software system)—systematize all this stored information. And it can retrieve, as desired, elements of this information at a single key-stroke. It is all but instantaneous and the higher-powered machines do their work in milliseconds. To give one or two very homely examples: libraries once used card-indexes (unless, like the Bodleian at Oxford, they still consist of huge leather folios in which the entries are handwritten). From card-indexes they proceeded to the micofiche—micro-copies of titles and authors on film, to be read through a reading-machine. Nowadays the modern library is one where at the touch of a key the appropriate book-title can be called up on screen. Or, to take another homely but less pleasant application and one that is far more intrusive: taxation. For certain types of earnings the tax is withheld by the government at source. To carry out this operation it must first know enough of your circumstances to issue you with a 'code', which will act as the guideline for the subsequent taxation, and this has to be processed by computer. Then the tax has to be calculated. And only then can it be deducted at source. In brief: information acquisition, retrieval, and communication have all been revolutionized.

This brings us to the last of the four components of the innovations introduced by the industrial-revolutionary process, that is, the growth of bureaucracy. I have already mentioned that comparisons between countries are difficult. But let us take Herman Finer's figures as a base, for all their inherent inaccuracies. In 1821 the number of bureaucrats in Great Britain was 27,000; in Prussia, 23,000; in the United States 8,000. (No figures from France were available.) In 1881, however, we find that Great Britain has 8,000, France 379,000, Germany (not Prussia) 452,000, and the United States 107,000.[19] But Richard Rose's tables, which cover Britain, Germany, and the United States (not France, unfortunately) in 1985, yield the follow-

[19] H. Finer, *Theory and Practice*, 1167.

ing (central government servants only): Britain 1,056,000; Germany 855,000; United States 3,797,000.[20] In brief: in Britain the number increased from 27,000 to 1,056,000. In Germany it increased from a figure of 23,000 (plus about a quarter of that number in the lesser states, hence some 30,000), to 855,000. And in the United States (largely due to its immense military programme) it rose from 8,000 to the huge total of 3,797,000.

We have looked at the literally stupendous leap in energy production, the immense new capability for collecting, storing, and retrieving information, and the great multiplication of the numbers of public officials. It should and indeed it does follow that penetration should have expanded in similar measure. And it has. The entire argument of this chapter has been elegantly summarized by Professor Anthony Giddens.

The expansion of surveillance in the modern political order, in combination with the policing of 'deviance', radically transforms the relation between state authority and the governed population, compared with traditional states. Administrative power now increasingly enters into the minutiae of daily life and the most intimate of personal actions and relationships. In an age increasingly invaded by electronic modes of the storage, collation, and dissemination of information, the possibilities of accumulating information relevant to the practice of government are almost endless. Control of information, within modern, pacified states with very rapid systems of communication, transportation, and sophisticated techniques of seques-tration, can be directly integrated with the supervision of conduct in such a way as to produce a high concentration of state power. Surveillance is a necessary condition of the administration of states, whatever end this power be turned to. It is not only connected with polyarchy but more specifically with the actualization of citizenship rights. The provision of welfare cannot be organized or funded unless there is a close and detailed monitoring of the lives of the population, regardless of whether they are actually welfare recipients or not . . .[21]

And so our wheel has come full circle. It began with that catalogue of the intrusions of the state into our daily lives as perceived by Proudhon: it has to be said that he was only some fifty or so years ahead of his time. His description would fit the world of today very well indeed. And we must not forget either Jean Dunbabin's perceptive comment: that there is a sense in which we were not 'governed' before the late nineteenth century. In terms of its 5,200 years duration, government began yesterday.

---

[20] R. Rose, *Understanding Big Government: The Programme Approach* (Sage, London, 1984), 130. The proportions of national employment employed in 1980 by government in one shape or another (e.g. public enterprises) was Great Britain 31.7%, Germany, 25.8%, and USA 18.8% (ibid. 132).

[21] A. Giddens, *The Nation-State and Violence* (CUP, Cambridge, 1985), 309.

5. INDUSTRIALIZATION'S EFFECTS ON WARFARE

An earlier chapter described the mass armies of the French Revolution and Empire and how, in abeyance until 1870 onwards, such mass armies increasingly engulfed the entire nation, and ended in the wars of 1914–18 and 1939–45 that, truly, embraced every able-bodied adult in the country. This military explosion was a fruit of industrialization.

Once continental Europe had industrialized, c.1870, it became wealthy. Between 1871 and 1914 population swelled by 70 per cent, from 293 to 400 million; the combined lignite and coal consumed by Britain, France, and Germany rose from 160 million tons per annum to 612 million, and these countries' production of pig-iron increased nearly fourfold, from 7.5 to 29 million tons per annum in 1913. In principle all this new wealth might have gone to improve living standards. But the claims of warfare were primary. Much of the increased wealth was spent on expanding military power, but the increase of any one country's capability was immediately matched by its rivals. Hence escalation: in 1709 the usual number of artillery pieces per 1,000 men was two or three, but in 1916 the French had 2,000 guns for every 10 kilometres of front line, and in 1942 the Russians at Stalingrad had 4,000 guns on every 4 kilometres of front. The size of the armies similarly increased: in the eighteenth century the average size of a large field army was 47,000 men, in the American Civil War the Federal troops alone numbered 622,000, but by the First World War the men mobilized totalled 63 million and by the Second World War this figure had risen to 107 million.[22] And naturally, expenditures kept pace with this increased military establishment. Germany, for instance, had spent 10.8 million marks on the military sector in 1870, 28.8 million marks in 1880, but 110.8 million marks in 1914. Austria-Hungary's expenditure rose from 8,200 million marks to 34,400 million marks between 1870 and 1914. In that last year the proportion of GNP spent on the military was 6.1 per cent in Germany, 6.1 per cent in Austria-Hungary, and 3.4 per cent in Britain.

Although most of the advances in military technology stemmed from industrialization, some were simply incremental improvements in existing weaponry. This is especially true of firearms. It is an extraordinary thought that there had been no significant advance in this field once the bayonet had turned the musketeer into a pikeman as well. The new inventions, small as each of them was, cumulatively revolutionized tactics. The first was rifling: firearms were smooth bore. Rifling had been used for a long time for

---

[22] Except where especially noted, the figures in this and the following are derived from the *Encyclopaedia Britannica* (1989).

hunting-pieces to enhance their accuracy, but they were too slow to load for general military use. The bullet had to be rammed in to fit the rifling, which took time and was not always successful. But in 1849 Minié discovered the simple principle that a lead slug could be slipped into the muzzle and the force of the charge would make it expand into the grooves of the rifling. At a stroke the range of the weapon was extended from some 200 yards to 1,000. This immediately upset the role of cavalry. It was suicidal for it to charge over open ground if it was receiving five times as many bullets as before. Likewise, the use of artillery had to be changed. Guns had been used to wheel in to some 200 yards of the enemy before firing grapeshot and canister. The Minié-type rifle kept them away at ranges where this ammunition was ineffective. Then in about 1865 breech-loaders replaced the older muzzle-loaders. In their 1866 campaign the Prussians used the needle-gun: the French responded with its superior *chassepot*, with the extended range of 1,200 yards.

Next came attempts to turn these single-shot weapons into repeaters. Many experimental types were thrown up, but the Belgian Mauser became the universal model after 1889. Smokeless powder, first used by the French in 1885, greatly increased the muzzle-velocity of the rifle; it was now lethal at some 3,000 yards and accurate up to 1,000. Efforts now turned on making a firearm that would fire several shots in a very brief period. The Gatling Gun was one of the first inventions in this field: it could hold 400 cartridges and give continuous fire for long periods, but it never saw military service except in the United States' invasion of Cuba in 1898. The French *mitrailleuse* was another early variant, but the French badly mishandled its tactical use in the Franco-Prussian War and for a time the entire concept of the multi-firing gun fell into abeyance. The first really successful machine-gun was the one invented by Hiram Maxim in 1884. It could fire single-shot or up to thirteen rounds per minute. It was ideal, too, for smokeless powder. These guns were first used by the British in a colonial war of 1895, but then were employed extensively in the Russo-Japanese War of 1905.

The advent of the rifle and the machine-gun should have brought about a profound change in infantry tactics. It took a long time for this to sink in among the American contestants in the Civil War, but finally it did. Men began to defend themselves from the deadly rain of small-arms fire by digging firepits and protecting them with earth and wood ramparts. These were impervious to all but the most suicidal frontal attack: one man in his firepit could hold off three attackers. The same lesson could have been learned from the Russo-Japanese War, where the tactic was practised against machine-guns. Cavalry charges were out, static defence had the better of the frontal attack. But the Europeans dismissed the American Civil War as an aberration, and took little notice of the Japanese. Instead, they actually hardened their dogma: to throw cavalry against breech-loaders with 1,000 yards accuracy. They sent their infantry forward in closed formation exposed to rifled 25 cm field-guns. They persisted in frontal attack when experience had shown this was futile. It was with these tactics that the opposing alliances opened their offensives in 1914. Once these were stopped, as they soon were, the armies found themselves forced back to the firepit and the barbed-wire entanglements of the American Civil War, until a line of trenches, studded with machine-guns, kept the one from the other and turned the war into one of attrition.

But for the rest, the tactics and strategy of warfare followed the pattern of industrialization: first steam and iron, which brought the railways, next the manifold uses of the i/c engine (motorcars, aeroplanes, and ships), and finally the age of the atomic bomb and rocket propulsion.

5.1. *Transportation*

Railroads could transport greater bodies of troops at greater speeds than ever before. For instance, in 1830 a regiment was transported between Manchester and Liverpool, 34 miles, in two hours instead of the usual three days' marching time; again, in Napoleon III's Italian 1859 campaign a French force of 120,000 men reached their destinations in eleven days, whereas by foot it would have taken two months.[23] In addition, railways could transport their supplies along with the troops, so that these had a longer staying-power in the field. Thirdly, the troops arrived in good shape for battle, and casualties could be evacuated to the field hospitals more rapidly. Finally, the railroads could transport any number of troops, the limits set being only those available for fighting—previously, simple logistics had contained the size of armies engaged.[24]

In fact not all these advantages could be realized. The earliest use of railways to move troops had been to quell insurgents. In the 1860s both France and Prussia–Germany saw some advantages in using them to deploy their troops straight on to the battlefield, but their initial efforts to do this ran into the severest obstacles. The Prussian railroad deployments against Austria in 1866 were so ineffectual that the battles were fought without their assistance, in the old way, with the troops requisitioning their supplies on the ground. The Franco-Prussian War did not see much of an improvement, except that the railways alone were what allowed the Germans to keep their siege of Paris going. The reason for the inadequacy was not due to railways

[23] M. Howard, *War in European History* (OUP, Oxford, 1976), 97.   [24] Ibid. 98–9.

as such but to a poverty of imagination, a failure to foresee the entailments of the railroad approach. For instance, provision trucks became jumbled up in disorder with the troop trucks, and it took so long to sort them out that the troops had to forage for their provisions. Again, even if the train duly arrived at its railhead, it took a great deal of time to detrain the supplies and get them to the troops. Then there was congestion—lines were often blocked for days. In addition, the railroad was a thin, inflexible high-way—how did one distribute the supplies among the many units that, inevitably, were deployed all along and around the railhead? It took much time before these problems were sorted out. But, for all that, the weight carried by the 1914 armies was many times that of the 1870 figures. The miles of track had all but doubled. Whereas in 1870 thirteen double-tracked lines deployed 350,000 Germans in fifteen days, in 1914 thirteen lines brought 1,500,000 men to the western front—more than four times as many per train as in 1870.[25] The World Wars of 1914–18 and 1939–45 could not posssibly have taken the shape they did, nor been pursued, without the use of the railway.

But steam-power did not confine itself to the armies. The introduction of explosive shells showed that the wooden navies of the Crimea were totally obsolete. They were replaced by ironclad steamers. The first great trial of strength between these new craft was the celebrated duel of the *Merrimac* and the *Monitor* in 1862, and the absoluteness of the steel steam-powered battle-ship was confirmed by the Japanese destruction of the Russians at Tsushima Straits in 1905. In 1906 the British, now engaged in their naval race with the Germans, introduced the new concept battleship, the *Dreadnought,* and it was with battleships of this size that the Battle of Jutland penned back the German fleet to its base for the duration of the war.

But by this time the era of steam and steel was drawing to its close. A new invention in transportation had been made. This was the petrol-powered i/c engine, initiating the age of oil-power. This type of engine was amazingly versatile, making possible the automobile, the airplane, and the submarine.[26] The motor car in no way supplanted horse-drawn trans-port but it made for greater versatility and speed. In the First World War it was used, apart from carrying staff, mostly in skirmishing all around the railroad, and in helping to distribute supplies from the railhead to the extended forward positions. All the same, its use at a decisive moment could be critical. At the Marne in 1914 the Germans decided not to extend their line westward to go round and behind the capital, but instead to contract their line and pull those forces to the east. This left their right flank open,

[25] M. van Creveld, *Supplying War* (CUP, Cambridge, 1977), 111–12.   [26] Ibid.

but the Allies could not get troops there in time to take advantage of this dramatic opportunity. An entire new division was available in Paris but it was impossible to rail them to the front in time, for the train could take only half the division—3,000 men. At this moment Galliéni, the governor of Paris, rounded up all the 600 taxis in Paris and, making them take five men apiece on two separate journeys, hurried the whole division into the battle-line. His intervention proved decisive. Reinforced on their right, the French Sixth army attacked the German flank and forced the German troops to retreat along their whole line. Paris was saved.

It was a short step to armour the automobiles, but these could not travel cross-country until, finally, their wheels were replaced by caterpillar tracks: the British had invented the 'tank'. First used in the 'surprise at Cambrai' in 1916, the tanks broke through the heavily mined and dug-in German lines, but without infantry to follow up the penetration was soon halted. In 1917 the Allies stepped up their production of tanks and these were to prove the decisive weapon in penetrating and then rolling up the German front.

Another application—to the warship—might have proved decisive too, this time from the German point of view. The i/c engine made the submarine possible. Until 1916 British sinkings from submarines were held at a tolerable level, but then the Germans decided on unrestricted submarine warfare. The riposte was the convoy system, highly successful but not sufficient to obviate a formidable tightening of rationing.

Finally, the i/c engine brought about the precocious development of aircraft. At first the planes were used only for artillery spotting and general reconnaissance. Bomb-carrying and aiming equipment was primitive and the chief instrument for this was the German Zeppelin. Their raids drew no distinction between military and civilian targets, and in all, between January 1915 and the end of the war, they had made fifty-one raids, dropping some 200 tons of bombs, killing 557 people, and injuring another 1,358. Their effect on British morale was considerable, hampering war production, and tying up twelve Royal Flying Corps squadrons and a huge force of anti-aircraft guns manned by 12,000 men. The carnage would have been far worse had it not been for the invention of the incendiary bullet in 1916 which, bursting inside the integument of the airship, sent it crashing in flames.

Thus the technological revolution had decisively altered the parameters of military strategy. This was now three-dimensional warfare; and it cannot have escaped attention that in the primitive use of the motor car we have the armoured column and the tank, in the skies the airplane, under the seas the submarine: in short, the three essential components of the German war plan of 1939—blitzkrieg, saturation bombing of non-military targets, and the submarine blockade.

5.2. *Information and Communication*

Signals communication is the nervous system of an army. Without it the best-equipped force in the world is simply a collection of tiny, individual, face-to-face units, none of which knows where its companions are or what they are doing.

Here again technology transformed the situation. Via the telegraph and the Morse Code, the High Command could communicate with commanders hundreds and indeed thousands of miles away. The British were the first to apply it in the field during the Crimea; it proved decisive in the suppression of the Indian Mutiny in 1858; and thereafter it became the standard means of communicating with the far-ranged armies in the American Civil War, operating over a whole half-continent. The telephone, on the other hand was neglected in the nineteenth century. However, at the close of the nineteenth century the radio-telephone had been developed and this became widespread; for, among other things, it eliminated the greatest drawback of the field telephone, namely the ease with which the lines could be cut, especially after artillery bombardment. By 1914 Marconi's development of wireless telegraphy found its military counterpart in the field radio. At first these were limited because non-portable and later, when they became portable, they were clumsy and extremely heavy to carry about. But these defects were overcome and the First World War saw the radio established everywhere as a system of intercommunication. So, not merely had an ubiquitous network of communication been established, but it was one where transmission was instantaneous.

Six entire armies were engaged on both the French and the German side; they could not be controlled or co-ordinated except by an efficient signals system. Tolstoy's description of the Coalition's armies at Austerlitz provides a vivid picture of the 'fog of war' in the days of the horse. An almost identical account of the muddle and disaster that befell the Russian armies in the days of the motor car is portrayed by Solzhenitsyn's *August, 1914*, his account of the early days on the eastern front. The disparity in the dates underlines the similarity between two armies who have lost touch with their component parts.

5.3. *The First World War, 1914–1918*

In the early weeks the armies on both sides were as mobile as they could contrive to be. Unbelievable as it seems now, cavalry were being used in frontal charges against machine-guns. But this mobility ended, pretty well, with the German defeat at the Marne and their subsequent retreat. From then onwards both sides tried to protect themselves in a way the generals had read all about and rejected—in firepits, protected by earth and barbed-wire and, very soon, machine-gun posts. The Germans were far quicker than the Allies to see the advantage of the latter: for instance, Lord Kitchener and his staff refused the offer of the War Office to increase the ratio from two guns per battalion, and General Haig declared it a 'much over-rated weapon'.[27] In fact it came to dominate the battlefield. The lines of trenches were developed into labyrinths that gave depth to the defence and enabled reinforcements to come forward rapidly, the barbed wire and machine-guns dominated the ground between them and the enemy. The High Command on both sides reached a similar conclusion. The name of the game was to destroy the enemy's emplacements and deny him reinforcements by artillery fire, and then, charge the enemy. This strategy depended on the development of heavy artillery, which we have not so far mentioned. Apart from the light artillery, both sides had developed very heavy guns—for instance, by May 1915 the British army was using eighty guns of 4.7-inch, fifty 5-inch howitzers, 130 4.5-inch howitzers, forty 6-inch howitzers, and twelve 9.2-inch howitzers. On the Somme, in 1916, the number of heavy guns on the eighteen-mile front of the British attack was one heavy gun every fifty-seven yards, at Messines it had risen to one every twenty yards. In addition the guns had been improved. The German 'Big Bertha' attained a range of 76 miles and all light artillery had a range of some 10,000 yards. Repeated attempts by both sides to break through brought only the most enormous casualties, and no break in the stalemate. Artillery fire and the barbed wire machine-gun post were the everyday stuff of campaigning. Hence Wilfred Owen's bitter poem:

> What passing-bells for those that die like cattle?
> Only the monstrous anger of the guns.
> Only the stuttering rifles' rapid rattle
> Can patter out their hasty orisons.[28]

This kind of warfare did not merely exact a monstrous sacrifice of human life. It called for vaster and vaster quantities of shells and other munitions to sustain the siege. And this insatiable demand for more shells, more artillery pieces, and the like brought about the transition from peacetime liberalism to all-encompassing impressment of the whole nation.

In no country was this more marked than in Germany which, it must be remembered, was blockaded by the Allies. Here Walter Rathenau was the

[27] B. H. Liddell-Hart, *A History of the First World War* (Pan Books, London, 1972), 142–3.
[28] Wilfred Owen, 'Anthem for Doomed Youth', in *The Poems of Wilfrid Owen*, ed. and introd. Jon Stallworthy (London, 1990).

great organizer. He set up special War Companies to run industry and replace competition with co-ordination, encouraged the scientists to make ersatz materials, controlled prices, and rationed food, imposing two meat-less days a week and a diet of turnips and potatoes mixed with flour. In 1916 a National Service law put every male aged between 17 and 60 at the disposal of the minister of war. In Britain the issue came to a head over the shortage of munitions—the trench war of attrition was using up undreamed of quantities of ammunition. In May Asquith appointed Lloyd George to a newly created Ministry of Munitions, with legal powers that gave him all but dictatorial control over industries. France too had its munitions crisis. Special boards of industrialists were set up to meet government orders and allocate scarce raw materials, while trade unions had to accept some direction of labour.

5.4. The Second World War, 1939–1945

The character of the Second World War was quite different from the First. It was a war of movement, strategy, and tactical surprise. Yet little of this was contributed by new technology. Indeed, on the whole technology remained constant; the only difference—a significant one certainly—being the refinement that was brought into the various types of *matériel*. The two great innovations were radar and rocket technology.

Radar greatly influenced the war at sea because it blunted the German submarine blockade. This continued to prove damaging, but without radar it could well have proved decisive. As for rocket technology, this was first used operationally by the Germans, but only towards the end of hostilities in late 1944 when the 'flying bombs' and then the V2 rockets began to rain on Britain. A third and quite revolutionary invention was the harnessing of atomic energy. In 1945 the Americans dropped two atomic bombs on two Japanese cities and abruptly brought about the surrender of Japan and the end of the war in the east. But this was merely embryonic: the use of atomic bombs and artillery was only just commencing its career that would usher in an entirely new approach to war.

Reverting now to the older technologies: in naval warfare it was a matter of smallish groups of highly trained servicemen utilizing very complicated weapons systems. But this was even more true for the second of the technologies, aerial warfare. The bomber and fighter had come a very long way since 1918. Fighters were now metal monoplanes, bombers larger, slower, but with complicated bomb-aiming equipment. All were armed with radar systems to warn of approaching enemy craft as well as identifying their own. So powerful were the possibilities of such planes that it was widely believed, in Britain at any rate, that the bomber would 'always get through', and its effects were conceived in apocalyptic terms. The vision of winning a war by the sole use of air-power enchanted some theorists, notably the Italian Douhet and the Englishman Trenchard, with his doctrine of 'carpet bombing' (of civilians, naturally). The use of aircraft went, of course, much farther than this. The Germans, for instance, started off by using them as tactical ground support and their Stukas proved deadly to enemy forces on the ground. It came to be perceived that armoured columns could do little if attacked from the air. Aircraft revolutionized the strategy and tactics of naval warfare too. When the *Prince of Wales* and the *Repulse* were bombed out of existence by the Japanese air-force, an epoch had passed. Capital ships yielded place to the aircraft-carrier.

At first sight the tactics of land warfare seem to have been revolutionized in the twenty-one years of peace. This is the impression long given by the German concept and use of *Blitzkrieg*. Here the i/c engine came into its own, with fast-moving tanks and motorized troops to keep up with them. In fact matters were not that simple. The chief reason the Germans broke through in Poland and then in the Low Countries and France was not a superiority in their number of tanks but the fact that so many of these were brought together in six armoured divisions. The plan was for these divisions to punch a hole in the enemy's line, move through it, and fan out inside the space created so as to demoralize the now-separated flanks of the enemy army, during which time the motorized infantry raced in to hold the ground. This was the tactic of *Schwerpunkt und Ausrollen*, and one reason it was so successful is that the French were still fighting the last war. To prevent another Schlieffen Plan they had fortified their north-eastern frontier with the Maginot Line, which was certainly unassailable by frontal assault. But the Germans columns simply outflanked and got behind it, making it useless. Meanwhile their own divisions raced towards Paris. With hindsight, one can easily see how the German assault could have been thwarted by tank counter-assaults, by the sowing of land-mines, by fast-moving infantry and tracked artillery.

On both sides the technical problems raised by the new, more advanced technologies of war demanded the services which were best provided by trained sections of the population—motor mechanics, drivers, radio operators, post-office engineers. Thus armies acquired enormous 'tails' to keep the fighting troops going.

The Germans suffered much less than the British in the opening years of the war; it was not until Barbarossa and the halting of their armies in Russia that their civilians began to feel the pinch. But the German economy had been on a half war-footing since the Nazi conquest of power. In 1939

Germany was a thoroughly regulated economy. Its main distinguishing characteristic was compulsory membership and subordination to the state of the previously existing, but free, industrial federations and economic associations. Wages were fixed, prices controlled, raw materials and labour were all rationed. For all that, the economy was not properly prepared for war. In the *Blitzkrieg* phase, 1939–42, this hardly mattered since the wars were all *Blumenkriegen*, achieved at small costs in men and *matériel*. By January 1942, in the first phases of Barbarossa, Speer, minister of armaments, quickly stepped up the munitions output. The third phase of the German war economy ran from mid-1944 to May 1945. Quality of armaments now counted much less than quantity and highly trained workers and professionals were called up along with everybody else, while reliance was put on conscripting the womenfolk and the use of 'slave labour'. The Allied air-raids became increasingly effective, especially on main rail communications. When most of its cities had been reduced to rubble, Germany capitulated in May 1945.

The British experience was different. Basically, great trouble had been taken to establish all the procedures and the shadow ministries for activation if war broke out. Indeed even before it did so, when the country had just agreed to guarantee Poland, the British government had stated its intention to set up a Ministry of Munitions and apply universal military service. One well perceives shadows of the problems of the last war. As soon as war did break out these shadow ministries were activated, complete with their staffs. Ration-books were already in print. But all this turned out to be on paper. Perhaps the 'phoney war' lulled the government. At any rate, once the real war started and the German blockade began, the country was ill prepared. The calculations for the quantities that could be imported turned out to be excessive and food-rationing was instituted. May 1940 saw one of the most drastic measures ever passed by Parliament: in one single day all the stages of the Emergency Powers Bill were completed, and the government received almost total authority over civilians and their property. By the middle of 1941 the administration had swung into full activity. The Board of Trade regulated the retail trade, civilian industry was concentrated, all vacant factories were put to some kind of use, consumers were catered for by 'utility' goods, clothes- and food-rationing were applied by a 'points' system. By the end of 1941 49 per cent of the population was being used on some kind of government work. Since even this would not be enough, the government introduced the allocation and direction of labour, and the conscription of women.

By this path the British war economy converged with the German. The entire economy was under state control, materials and goods were allocated and rationed, and above all, the entire adult population was part of the war effort. Add to this the wreckage of British cities by German bombers and the more-than-equivalent retribution handed out to such German cities as Dresden and Hamburg, and we have the lineaments of what was now total war.

The war had melded civilian and soldier into one community of service, it had transcended status, and reduced the wealthy to the same sparse rations as their servants. The equality of shared experiences, obligations, sacrifices, and the sense of being part of one great common enterprise created a new consciousness of society, and a new outlook on politics. In this sense it *democratized* politics: it gave a sense of self-importance to every citizen. This can only be appreciated in the light of the third of the great aspects of the industrial revolution: the rise of and subsequent struggle between the industrial capitalist class on the one side, and its creation, the industrial proletariat, on the other. So we must retrace our steps to 1870 yet again, and trace the rise of the working-class movements in the industrialized states.

6. INDUSTRIALIZATION'S EFFECTS ON SOCIETY

6.1. *Industrialization in Full Flood: From c.1900*

'The elements of a conflict are unmistakeable; in the growth of industry and the surprising discoveries of science; in the changed relations between masters and workmen; in the enormous fortunes of individuals and the poverty of the masses; in the increasing self-reliance and closer mutual combination of the working population; and, finally, in a general moral degeneration.' Thus the words of the Papal Encylical *Rerum Novarum*, in 1891. Though the last opinion is highly contestable, the remainder of the sentence is nothing but exact. It is an excellent and concise summary of the nature of that age.

The central event and key to the entire period is the emergence of an industrial proletariat. This expanded *pari passu* with the intensity of industrialization: greatest in the 'older' industrialized countries, Britain, Germany, and Belgium, with France lagging somewhat; establishing itself in industrial towns and conurbations in distinct new localities in Sweden, the Netherlands, northern Italy, Hungary, Russia, and Japan. One indicator of its advance is the growth of towns; for though great cities could and did arise simply as magnets for the desperately poor of the hinterland, this was not the case in Europe, whose cities were centres of industry, or ports, or providers of commercial services. In 1850, in Europe and the United States,

19 and 14 per cent respectively of the population lived in towns of 5,000+ inhabitants; by 1910 they had in aggregate risen to a total of 41 per cent. Some 80 per cent of the population (as against 66 per cent in 1850) were living in towns of over 2,000 inhabitants, and rather more than half in towns of over 10,000.[29]

Some historians apply the term 'proletariat' to the poor artisans and the like such as made up the revolutionary mobs of the French Revolution, but what we are observing here is a quite new phenomenon: the emergence of a new class. It is an *industrial* proletariat. It is the child of a second new class, the industrial entrepreneurs—the capitalists. These were a distinct element among the possessing classes. They did not derive their capital from the land or from professional qualifications or from commerce or even full-scale 'cottage' industry. On the contrary, the landed rich looked on them as vulgar *parvenus*, the educated despised their lowly, self-taught origins, and the wealthy commercial patriciate stood grandly aloof. It was a self-contained class. It consisted of self-taught folk of common origin who possessed an exceptional mechanical aptitude and an eye for turning it to profit.

It created the proletariat by the conditions of work which it imposed. It closed down cottage industry and 'putting out', alienating the worker from his tools and depriving him of his freedom to decide his own hours and conditions. It concentrated the workers in towns—that is, urbanized the countryside. And within each such concentration there were further concentrations—the factories. Factory production or its equivalents in the mines and the docks imposed on the working class conditions they had not met with before: they had to work with somebody else's tools, all under the same roof, disciplined by the sound of the bell, by fines for being late or other delinquencies, and by the threat of the sack. The concentration of workers in one workplace was soon translated into a feeling of joint concern, of common consensus, of collective action. It was the new version of that one place to which all repaired and where they felt as a community and where they heard the news and the Word being preached at them from the pulpit: the church or chapel. It was this that could give a simultaneous message to the great masses. The factory served as a mere part of a nation-wide network of surrogate chapels.

Such were the new *dramatis personae*. Their appearance registered three new developments: first, the ever-wider extension of the franchise (carried via mass parties), workers' protective associations against the capitalist, and socialism *vis-à-vis* individualism—the quest for a new social order. These have their corollaries in the formation of mass parties which competed

---

[29] E. J. Hobsbawm, *The Age of Empire, 1875–1914* (Cardinal, London, 1987), 49.

nation-wide for popular support (backed by promises of state intervention), and the resultant expansion and professionalization of the bureaucracy. The effects were the abandonment of free trade, the demise of *laissez-faire*, the vogue for 'new liberal' philosophies promoting the idea that the state has positive supportive duties towards its citizens, and the spawning of more and more 'collectivist' policies intruding into the free market-place.

No one of the three developments 'drove' the others. They were independent in origin but highly interactive in action. For instance, the extension of the franchise was by no means always due to the pressure of strikes: but the widespread strikes in Belgium in 1893 created the climate for the extension of the franchise in 1894 just as the 1902 strikes did in Sweden and the waves of strikes in Italy just before 1912. Similarly, it is unusual—to my knowledge, unknown—for the extension of the vote not to be supported by socialist parties wherever these might exist. Again: in some countries, of which Britain is the prime example, the trade unions formed the basis of a mass socialist party, whereas elsewhere, as in Germany, the trade unions, though mostly of Marxist orientation, were not organically linked with the Social Democratic Party. Nor was it trade-union pressure as such which compelled governments to concede a wider franchise. In short, the decision to extend the vote was by no means uniformly a response to pressures from below. It was just as likely to emerge from political rivalries at the top. It is significant that Disraeli and Bismarck, both conservatives, should have gone for a wider franchise in the same year, 1867. They did so because they believed that the new electorate would be conservative, not radical; the desire to call a new world of electors into being to redress the balance of the few old rich ones was prominent in Giolitti's universal franchise of 1912. In brief, we have to look at every individual country to fathom when and how the interrelationships of the three developments came about.

6.2. *The Extension of the Franchise*

A question that never seems to be asked is why the extension of the franchise was ever demanded at all. In fact de Tocqueville does address this question, and as the paradigm of his answer one can look at what happened in Britain. The 1832 Reform Act extended the vote to, *inter alia*, the so-called £10 freeholder. In 1837 Lord John Russell declared that this was where it would stop, so earning the contemptuous nickname of 'Finality Jack'. The Chartist movement was very much a demand for universal manhood suffrage, but it was easily contained by the authorities. Yet in 1867 a much wider franchise was freely conceded—for there was no logical answer to the simple question: 'If the £10 freeholder, why not the £9 freeholder and if . . .'—*und so weiter.* 'When a nation modifies the elective qualification', wrote de Tocqueville,

it may easily be foreseen that sooner or later that qualification will be entirely abolished. There is no more invariable rule in the history of society. The further electoral rights are extended, the greater the need for extending them; for after each concession the strength of the democracy increases, and its demands increase with its strength. The ambition of those who are below the appointed rate is irritated in exact proportion to the greater number of those who are above it. The exception at last becomes the rule, concession follows concession, and no stop can be made short of universal suffrage.[30]

The following is a brief chronology of the extension of suffrage in Europe:

Austria	1907	Univeral male suffrage
Belgium	1894	Universal male suffrage
France	1870	Universal male suffrage
Germany	1870	Universal male suffrage
Hungary		Remains at 5 % population
Italy	1882	Widened to 2 million=14% population
	1912	Universal male suffrage
Netherlands	1857	2% population, enlarged by Reform Acts to 14%
	1894	Universal male suffrage
Norway	1898	From 16.6% to 34% adult males
Spain	1900	Universal male suffrage
Sweden	1909	Universal male suffrage
Switzerland	1874	Universal male suffrage
United Kingdom	1830	Some 2% population
	1832	Reform Act extends to 3.5% population
	1867	Some 7.7% population
	1884	4.38 million=15% population
	1918	Universal male (over 21) suffrage and female (over 30)
	1928	Universal suffrage

---

[30] A. de Tocqueville, *Democracy in America* (Vintage Books edn., New York 1954 and 1990; orig. pub. Alfred Knopf, New York 1945), vol. i, ch. 4.

6.3. Trade Unionism

The 'labour movement' comprised several different organizations each serving its own purposes; such as co-operatives, for example, mutual benefit and burial clubs, educational associations, and the like. These organizations interacted in their own national ways. Of this broader labour movement the main component was the trade union as a defensive organization, fighting for better pay and conditions on the factory floor, and this is what we are concerned with. Trade unions were in existence even before the industrial revolution, finding their first niches in the small factories of artisans.

Britain is regarded as the original home of trade unionism, and indeed it did make an early start there, because the law was comparatively lenient in this respect. In Austria, for instance, 'associations' were not freely permitted until 1870, and in France not till 1884, when the 1791 *loi le Chapelier* was repealed. In Britain the Combination Acts, 1799 and 1800, declared them criminal conspiracies against the public, but these laws were repealed in 1824 and 1825; not that trade-unionists necessarily escaped harassment after that, as in the case of the six unfortunate Dorsetshire farm-labourers who were sentenced for administering unlawful oaths and deported to the colonies: the so-called Tolpuddle Martyrs. In 1871, however, legislation declared unions exempt from prosecution on grounds of 'restraint of trade'. The unions of that period were craft unions, and 'respectable', based on the model of the Amalgamated Society of Engineers which had been founded in 1851. The unions' immunity to prosecutions was, curiously, reversed by the judges in the Taff Vale case (1901), which declared them liable for losses to the employers caused by their strike action, but this situation was remedied by the Trade Union Disputes Act of 1906. Henceforth the unions enjoyed virtually complete legal immunity—not curtailed until the Thatcher reforms of the 1980s.

In 1868 the unions came together in the Trade Union Congress. This successfully resisted efforts to politicize it, as was happening everywhere on the Continent. In 1880 Hyndman founded a Marxist Social Democratic Federation, but it attracted few takers. In 1893 a largely Scotland-based Independent Labour Party was formed under the leadership of Keir Hardie. In 1900, however, the bulk of trade unions and socialist organizations combined in a new organization called the Labour Representation Committee, with the express purpose of getting working men elected to Parliament, and in 1906 this body changed its name to the Labour Party. In these ways did the British trade unions avoid entanglement with socialist and particularly with Marxist theories, while approved socialist organizations could rely on mass electoral support from the unions. The Labour Party, it has been constantly repeated, 'grew out of the bowels of the trade union movement'.

In Germany the relationship of trade unions to Marxist socialism was much closer. The first socialist trade unions, the *Gewerkschaften*, were founded by two socialists. In 1878 Bismarck, alarmed by the showing of socialism in the *Reichstag* elections, clamped down an anti-socialist law and under it many of the *Gewerkschaften* were dissolved. They were succeeded by local unions called *Fachvereine*, supposedly non-political but which often successfully evaded the law. The anti-socialist legislation was repealed in 1890, and in that year a *centrale* was established, the General Commission of Trade Unions, and German trade unionism began to expand rapidly. The membership in the *Gewerkschaften* unions (the great majority of them adhering to the General Commission) grew from 419,162 in 1897 to 743,296 in 1902, to 1,886,147 in 1907. However, unlike Britain, two other *centrales* were in existence. There was a group of non-political unions, founded on the British model, the *Gewerkvereine*, first formed in 1868 and regularly excluding Social Democrats. In 1907 their membership only numbered 109,889. Then there were the Christian Trade Unions, obviously non-socialist, whose *centrale* was founded in 1894 (the decade in which the Vatican had issued *Rerum Novarum* and taken a positive stand on substantive rights for workers). In 1907 they had 54,760 members. Altogether, then, the number of unionized workers in 1907 stood at some 2.5 million.

By and large, Austria, Switzerland, and Belgium followed the German example. In Austria's case the law permitting trade unions rested on the 1870 Organic Law which, *inter alia*, removed from the unions the restrictions on combinations for influencing labour conditions. But Austria's early promise was blighted by the Great Depression of the 1880s, and when the union movement was relaunched in 1888 most unions were formed on a Social Democratic basis. In 1907 501,094 unionists were affiliated to the Social Democratic *Gewerkschaften*, and these formed by far the largest proportion of unionized labour.

The status of the Belgian unions was laid down in the 1898 law under which they could be incorporated provided they were not political. In fact most of them were. Here the movement comprised a number of central organizations: the Socialist-Labour, the Catholic, and the Liberal parties each having their own affiliates. The grand total membership (1903) was 148,483.

French trade unions had been forbidden till 1884, after which they began to grow quite fast. In 1906 the number of workers in trade unions was 896,012. Contrary to the examples we have been citing, French trade unionism was very fragmentary and schismatic. To begin with, there was a clear and very sharp, almost antipodal, difference between the trade unions which believed in workshop negotiations and courted parliamentary support and those who had no trust in parliaments and elections whatsoever but believed in direct action. One influence on this trade-union movement was Marxism, represented by the faction of Jules Guesde. But France was still largely agricultural and her industries tended to be small-scale and widely dispersed. These conformed very closely to the thought of Proudhon, which was strongly anti-state and looked towards a national federation of co-operating units of production. These ideas were somewhat confusedly combined with the Marxist orthodoxy which believed that it was essential to gain control of the state apparatus. The Guesdists would have no truck at all with the 'bourgeois parties' although they sat in parliament. But there a second tendency manifested itself—the one embodied in the views of Jean Jaurès. A humanist, and a socialist only because of his radicalism, he committed himself entirely to the Dreyfusards. In view of the combined onslaught of the Catholics, the military, and conservative elements of society—the people who had 'framed' Dreyfus 'as it transpired in so gross and wicked a manner'—Jaurès brought his followers together with members of other, even 'bourgeois', parties in a 'rally to the republic', and he refused to follow the Guesdist line of allowing the new, republican Cabinet to sink because of Marxist self-seclusion. The breach between the two tendencies widened; yet in 1905, for the sake of international socialist unity, they consented to amalgamate in the SFIO, the *Section Française de l'Internationale Ouvrière*—but with an expressed aim of non-co-operation with the bourgeois.

But neither of these two factions satisfied the direct-action *tendance*, and this found its most profound expression in the theory of syndicalism (*syndicat* being the French for trade union). It believed in constant struggle with the employers in the workplace. Whatever was offered must be refused. Thus the two sides, proletariat and bourgeois, would be polarized and forced to a show-down. And this must be launched from the proletarian side by a general strike of all unions, disrupting the capitalist order and leaving the field exclusively to the triumphant trade unions, which would take over and organize themselves to run the new proletarian state. This model, laced with copious infusions of Bakunin's anarchism, found a ready reception in the Latin countries, especially marked in Andalusia and Catalonia in Spain and in the area of the Romagna down to the heel of Italy. Here the French pattern was, *mutatis mutandis*, followed.

This account has, necessarily, brought us to mention socialism, the new great ideology of the age, since it affected the shape and outlook of so many trade-union movements in the various European countries.

6.4. *Socialism*

Marx's *Das Kapital* was published in 1867. It is unreadable and, except to the few and the very concerned who made a habit of reading this kind of lore, unintelligible. Yet by 1880 it was virtually canonical. It was transmitted by working-class leaders to the masses to form a new ideology, a lay religion, and in so doing it welded together the disparate sectors of this working class—artisans, small shopkeepers, non-manual and white-collar workers, along with the industrial proletariat itself. All these could come together in a single political party on an agreed socialist programme and it is characteristic of Continental socialist parties that each did develop such a programme, usually consisting of a statement of basic philosophy followed by a list of immediate demands.

The basic theme of this socialism is that the state belongs and always has belonged to the stronger and wealthier class, who have exercised a virtual dictatorship over the rest of society; and the countless examples we have given of the chasm between the élites and the masses in the Chinese Empire, in Rome, in the European Middle Ages, and so on provides total confirmation of this assertion. Between these two classes, of the élites and the masses, there is a perpetual struggle. The élites have lived and lived well by exploiting the masses, notably by despoiling them of all their produce except what was necessary for their bare survival. Hitherto it has proved fruitless to try to eliminate the élites—they were the architects of their states and empires, which could not get on without them. The best that could be achieved was simply changing one élite for another. With industrialization, however, all this changed. The new or rising class of industrial entrepreneurs, the capitalists, and the industrial proletariat were doomed to slug it out over the issue of who got what from the product of the factory— the same as saying who had title to it, and why. Hence the struggles in the factory or mine over pay, conditions, and hours of work. But with industrialization the conflict of the ruling minority and the ruled masses became transformed. Marx claimed to have proved a basic law which showed that capitalism had inherent characteristics which inevitably drove the industrial capitalist class to grow both smaller and richer (by dint of successful takeovers and the creation of monopolies), while the working mass became larger and more and more impoverished. The intermediate classes of white-collar workers and the like would be sucked down into the proletarian mass and share its miserable destiny. So a huge gap between the few immensely wealthy concentrations of capital and the mass of working folk would continue to widen. The class struggle would intensify. But here again conditions would be different from the pre-industrial ones. There, the most that could happen was the replacement of one élite by another. This was no longer the case. The economy could not run without its workers, but capitalists were dispensable. What was required was a manifestation of worker power that would, literally, sweep them away and keep them away: the rule of the proletariat, exercised at first as a 'dictatorship' to make sure that no capitalist classes would remain. Society would become a one-class society, which was the same as a no-class society, and from this the fair division of the product of labour would flow: 'from each according to his ability, to each according to his needs.'

So: the doctrine preached the revolutionary overthrow of the capitalist classes, and the inevitability of proletarian victory. This followed ineluctably from the inherent laws of capitalist production, and this is why it was 'scientific' socialism, unlike its 'utopian' alternatives.

It was a heady doctrine for working people: their victory was assured. History was on their side.

> Du passé, faisons table rase
> Masses serviles debout, debout!
> Le monde va changer de base
> Nous ne sommes rien, soyons tout . . .
>
> *   *   *   *   *
>
> . . .
> Il n'est pas de sauveur suprême
> Ni Dieu, ni César, ni tribun:
> Producteurs, faisons nous nous-mêmes
> Decrétons le salut commun.
> C'est la lutte finale
> Groupons nous et demain
> L'Internationale
> Sera le genre humain.[31]

In what we may call mainstream socialism, promulgated in its Erfurt Programme (1891) by the German Social Democratic Party, there was an ambiguity in the word 'revolution'. The founders went all out for a mass membership and indeed, by 1912 they were the largest single party, with 110 *Reichstag* seats and 4,500,000 votes. 'The Social Democracy distinguishes itself from all other parties and stamps itself a revolutionary *party*': because efforts to remove the 'excrescences' of private owned capitalist enterprises are Utopian—'whoever wants to remove them must remove it [capitalism], their cause.' 'Against all parties standing there in common we Social

---

[31] From *L'Internationale* by Eugene Pottier (1888).

Democrats close our ranks. There are no compacts, no compromises ...',32

Elsewhere in this address to the Erfurt Congress (1891) Liebknecht states that '[we] cannot effect the passing of the means of production into the ownership of the community without acquiring political power . . ., that is, we fight for *power in the state*, for the "latch of legislation" which is now monopolized by our opponents in their class interest'.[33]

If anything specific can be retrieved from this maze, it seems (to me) that the Social Democratic leaders wanted to create a mass party in order to acquire legislative power by way of voting and parliamentary majority, not by violent revolution, and yet not by any compromise with any of the other political parties. It was clothed with the phraseology and general reasoning of Marx, and this made it sacrosanct. Yet all it boils down to is the quest for a parliamentary majority and no compromises with other parties.

So, was the party simply espousing the parliamentary route to socialism or was it advocating violent revolution? The woolliness of its official creed generated two major, diametrically opposed points of view. The right wing was the so-called 'revisionism' of Bernstein.

Bernstein first expressed his critique in a series of articles written in 1896 and followed up in 1898 by a ponderous tome translated, shortly, as *The Premisses of Socialism and the Tasks of Social Democracy*. His attack on Marxian orthodoxy is wide-ranging, but for present purposes one can concentrate on his demolition of the central predictions of Marxist theory. To begin with, Marx had affirmed in an unqualified way that the revolution (whatever that was) would and must occur because industrial capitalism had built up the infrastructure, processes, and real wealth of the community to the point when it became ripe for the proletariat simply to expropriate the proprietors as a going concern. In their time the industrial capitalists had taken over the state from its former, non-industrial bourgeoisie—this is the 'bourgeois revolution'. Society must experience this before the proletariat take-over from the industrial capitalists—the proletarian revolution. This was the 'ripening' theory: ineluctably the proletarian revolution must be preceded by a 'bourgeois' one. Bernstein disagreed entirely with this historicism and, in particular, with the way it committed the Social Democrat party to hold aloof from any dealings with the non-socialist parties in winning piecemeal reforms.

In particular, Bernstein demonstrated that Marx's predictions, as well as his analysis, were false. Marx had maintained that the crisis of capitalism

---

[32] R. C. K. Ensor (ed.), *Modern Socialism* (Harpers & Bros., London, 1907), 7, 8: the address by Liebknecht at the Erfurt Congress (1891).   [33] Ibid. 13

could demonstrably be shown to reside in its inherent tendency to polarize society into just two camps, and that the lot of the workers could never improve—on the contrary, they would suffer increasing 'immiseration'. Bernstein argued that this polarization was the reverse of what was actually occurring: the numbers and relative proportions of the middle classes were constantly increasing and the ratio of proletarians in society was actually falling. Next he pointed to the indisputable fact that, although the prole-tariat had not necessarily benefited as much as the proprietorial classes, they nevertheless had and were enjoying an ever-rising standard of living: so, no immiseration here. Marx had also said that the number of property-owners was decreasing as property was being concentrated into fewer and fewer hands by way of cartels and trusts and monopolies. Bernstein showed that this number had not decreased but increased as a result of private indivi-duals taking up shares in these companies via the new limited liability laws. If all these things were true, Bernstein had taken the very guts out of Marx's analysis. By contrast with the quest for the Holy Grail of revolution, Bernstein advocated alliances and compromises with the other parties and the governmental authorities to introduce reforms piecemeal and exert an influence, much as the Fabians were doing in Britain. (Bernstein had spent years of exile in that country.)

One can imagine the impact of this iconoclasm on the orthodox Marx-ism of the Social Democratic Party. A tumult of polemics followed. Bernstein's views were rejected. In practice, the Social Democrats had pursued limited objectives but wrapped them up in Marxist jargon and ideology. Bernstein had done no more—but also no less—than to make the performance of the party match its theory. In the post-war history of that party in Germany it was Bernsteinism that was to prevail.

But if reformism was one current of dissent in the socialist movement, there was also its diametrical opposite: no less than a belief that Marx's theory was correct and that this demanded neither moderation nor waiting for the ineluctable revolution to evolve through force of events, but that its goal must be violent revolutionary seizure of state power. This was the viewpoint of the tiny underground Russian Social Democratic Party—or at least, of that fraction of it that broke with the rest to become the 'majority' or Bolshevik faction; and its architect, theoretician, and prime mover was Lenin. The point was that, since Russia did not even have a parliament, any thought of progressing like the German Social Democrats, by capturing a majority in the legislature, was out of question. Lenin perceived that if socialism was to come in Russia it must be by a real, a violent, revolution. This called for a technique entirely different from the mass-party approach of the German party. Lenin did not go for a mass party at all. On the contrary, he conceived the idea of a band of dedicated professional revolutionaries, tightly disciplined and controlled by its leaders, that would stand in waiting until an opportunity came that would enable it to step in and take power in the midst of general crisis. The turmoil of military defeat was one of the more likely scenarios for such a crisis, and this was confirmed in 1905 when the country, shocked by Russia's defeat by the Japanese, erupted against the tsarist autocracy and demanded parliamentary government. This revolution was no mere flash in the pan: starting with the massacre of the workers led by Father Gapon on Bloody Sunday, January 1905, it led, through strikes and violent demonstrations, to an entire year of revolutionary activity. During the revolution many towns and cities had thrown up spontaneous assemblies or 'soviets' which took local control, and the two factions of the party battled to win them, Lenin's faction always in a minority. But despite the ultimate crushing of the revolution and the flight of the party-leaders abroad, Lenin kept tight grip on his faction and would brook no compromises outside nor rivals within it. Thus was the ground prepared for the great October Revolution of 1917.

Now all these varieties of Marxism agreed that the objective was the take-over of the state, because it was through the state apparatus that the dictatorship of the proletariat could be realized and the organization of socialist society secured. However, this was not the only possible socialist position: there was also anarchism. The orthodox Marxists held that after the revolution society entered into two phases: that of socialism, which continued the capitalist role of building up the wealth of the country, and then—and only then, when this wealth was sufficient—the 'withering away of the state', the stage of true communism. With this reasoning Bakunin completely disagreed.

Bakunin agreed with Marx on the importance of workers' associations and the need for violent revolution. Where he disagreed was in what the object of this revolutionary activity should be. It should not, as Marx maintained, be the control of the state apparatus, intact but at the service of the proletariat; rather, it should be the destruction of the state as such. The state was itself the father and mother of all human miseries, and the ideal position was one where no state apparatus existed, just spontaneously organized groups, freely co-operating. Between him and Marx there erupted a furious row. In 1864 a number of internationally minded socialists had formed an International: the First International. It consisted of delegations from the working people of a number of countries and was tightly centralized under its central committee. Marx was a leading light; but in 1868 Bakunin joined the International and challenged him. In 1872, when it looked as if the Bakuninites were likely to prevail, Marx contrived the expulsion of Bakunin and the International broke up. But this was by no means the end of anarchism as a powerful movement. Bakunin's doctrines found a welcome in certain areas where the conditions of industry and agriculture favoured it. It took a firm hold in Andalusia and Catalonia in Spain, and in parts of southern Italy. The newly founded Italian PSI expelled its anarchists in 1892. In Spain the movement took early hold— in 1873 it had 270 centres and 300,000 adherents. Its strength lay in the south, land of the *latifundios*, distressed lands exploited by absentee landords. What did its villages need the state for? They were virtually self-sufficient *pueblos*. Barcelona was different. It became a magnet for disaffected migrants from Murcia who brought their resentments and violence with them, and had a particular appeal to the secessionist feelings of the Catalans, alive to this day, in opposition to the centralization of Madrid.

One further point—being the loose, unstructured movement that it was and wanted to be, a variety of sub-anarchisms flourished, many of them small groups whose aims were almost nihilistic and devoted to terrorism and assassinations. They were responsible for the murder of President Sadi Carnot of France (1894), Empress Elizabeth of Austria (1898), King Umberto of Italy (1900), and President McKinley (1901).

Bakunin's anarchism was inspired by Proudhon (d. 1865). Proudhon had preached a version of federalism, according to which society ought to consist of small societies, co-operating with little or no central direction. Abolish property and also dismantle the state-apparatus and man would be liberated so that his better nature would at last have full scope. He envisaged a society of self-reliant workshops and peasant farmers. Now industrialization in France was not highly concentrated, consisting of a host of smallish towns employing small numbers of workmen dispersed through-out the country. For this reason Proudhonism corresponded to the objective facts of French economic life far more closely than did the notion of the centralized mass party that Marx and the German Social Democrats envisaged. Thus in the 1890s, as we have seen, three main *tendances* manifested themselves in French socialism. One was the Proudhonism we have just described. Another was precisely a Marxist mass party: this was the faction led by Jules Guesde. The third was a tendency which developed within the Socialist group of deputies in the Chamber. It arose out of the Dreyfus case. The Guesdists regarded this as a bourgeois matter and stood off from the battle. Jaurès saw it as a coalition of the darkest reactionary forces of Catholicism and militarism that threatened the very existence of the Repub-lic, and he was eager to join with other parties in a broad-based coalition of Republican defence. This raised in the French context a quarrel similar to the one Bernstein had in Germany. Nevertheless, as late as 1904, Jaurès had come in as arch-conciliator and the architect of a united socialist party in which all the tendencies were represented, the SFIO. But it was a very self-divided and fissionable party.

There was one final tendency in French socialism which has at least a historical importance. Proudhonism and anarchism had, as we have seen, a certain resonance in French working-class circles. They combined with militant trade unionism to form 'anarcho-syndicalism'. We have already outlined this viewpoint. The classic exponent of a further tendency was Georges Sorel, an activist, at that time in his Marxist phase. Sorel would not waste time, as the Webbs did in Britain, in arguing the point-by-point case against the feasability of the general strike or the desirability of trade-union control of their individual sectors ('The sewers to the sewer-men', they sneered). For him, it was the *belief* that the general strike would bring about the new order that was critically important. This was 'the myth'; the myth of the general strike. You cannot reason away a myth, argued Sorel: it is irrational; all it demands is faith. Consequently the anarcho-syndicalists would have no truck at all with parliamentarism in any shape. They stood for violent, direct action.

There remains the idosyncratic case of Britain. As we have shown, Britain differed from the Continent in two vital respects. First, it had developed a powerful trade-union movement. Secondly, it had two well-established parties, Liberal and Conservative, both of which, despite ideological differences on many issues, were committed in their own ways to increasing substantive benefits to working people. Old-age pensions (1908), the opening of labour exchanges (1909), and the social insurance schemes for health care and for unemployment (1911) were striking (Liberal) examples of this. But what the trade unions wanted in particular, for their part, was to be represented in Parliament by their fellow-workers and not vicariously by the Liberal Party's candidates. (Hence the foundation in 1900 of the Labour Representation Committee, which became the Labour Party in 1906.)

There remains one final and most important thing to say about all these socialist movements: they were internationalist. Marx's *Communist Manifesto* had declared: 'The workingman has no country', and demanded 'Workers of all countries unite; you have nothing to lose but your chains—you have a world to win.' It was this internationalism, the fear of a secret international conspiracy to subvert existing society that made governments so nervous. In 1889 the Second International was founded. It was a loose federation of national parties. It did not have a central executive until 1900. It stood for parliamentarism and in 1896 expelled its anarchist members. But it reaffirmed the primacy of the class struggle and the inevitability of revolution, although its main concern was to prevent war. This was not to be. In 1914, with only a handful of objectors, the parties of the International came to support each of their own countries. It was the end of the internationalist ideal of the unity of all the workers of the world. Blood proved thicker than water.

6.5. *Cross-Currents in Ideology*

From the 1890s three powerful currents of thought cut across one another. The first was the internationalism of the socialists, as against nationalism wherever this was to be found. Nationalism was not merely the ideology of the new capitalists and the landed traditionalists: it was rapidly becoming a mass ideology of national supremacy, expressed in such ways as 'Jingoism' in Britain, and the teachings of Treitschke and his ilk in Germany, together with the militaristic circles that surrounded Kaiser Wilhelm II, but here again, finding a spontaneous echo among the common people. In France the sore of Alsace and Lorraine still rankled. The only exceptions to this general rule were in the Austrian Empire where, after universal suffrage in 1907, the *Reichsrat* contained factions that were perfervidly socialist and yet, as nationalists, demanded their independence or at least their autonomy.

The second current was what we have for so long been discussing: the struggle of capital and labour.

The third was the ambiguous attitude of the powerful Roman Catholic Church. The Church, like the socialists, was internationalist. This divided it from the nationalistic elements in society. But it differed both from the nationalists and the socialists in its specific political and social doctrines. It made valiant efforts to mend its fences with existing regimes. In Germany, however, it came into collision with Bismarck over the state control of schools, though here it secured a qualified success: Bismarck found it expedient to break off the quarrel, and to come to terms with a new party founded on Catholic values, the *Zentrum*. In Italy the pope had forbidden Catholics to take any part at all—including voting—in the public life of the new monarchy. In France, the Vatican made an effort to promulgate the encyclical *Rerum Novarum* in 1891 and tried to reconcile its flock to rally to the Republic, the *ralliement* of 1894. All this ended in catastrophe owing to the attitude the French Catholic right took up in the Dreyfus case; instead of achieving a *ralliement*, the Church found itself deprived of the control of state schools and, in 1905, was separated entirely from the state.

There were, nevertheless, important positive gains for the working classes in this period which, suprisingly, were not out of tune with these basic philosophies. The Church in *Rerum Novarum* expressed a sympathy with working people and pleaded for a more equitable distribution of wealth.

The reactionary and conservative classes often showed a wise spirit of preventive modernization; Bismarck's social insurance in the 1880s is a prime case in point. The socialist contribution led to a profound shift in the agenda of politics. Hitherto it had been confined to war, dispensing justice, maintaining order, and above all levying taxes.

6.6. *The New Agenda of Politics*

Politics had now moved into a new mode. Political crises came and went: for example, the *Kulturkampf* in Germany, the international struggles to control pieces of African and Asian territory, the Boulanger and then the Dreyfus cases in France, women's emancipation and the Ulster issue in Britain. Whereas the chronic climate was one of struggles over suffrage, conditions of work, the length of the working day, and similar concerns, it was around the poles of capital versus labour that politics consistently revolved. Here labour was on the attack through what evolved into a new phenomenon, the 'mass party'. The non-socialist parties could afford their own different understandings of capitalism and so—except in the case of a Roman Catholic party—could not form into one single party. The socialists, on the other hand, could not afford *not* to do so; they were 'class' parties and their aim was to mobilize the class—so that this made them proselitize for a mammoth party on the road to capture a parliamentary majority. The mass party was a new political phenomenon. As Duverger has shown (in *Political Parties*), the initial parties, illustrated by the British eighteenth-century ones, were effectively the followings of aristocratic clans. The next phase, in the nineteenth century, was the age of the 'notables', that is to say, the candidates and their local leaderships were made of local notables who organized the local electoral support. These local coteries were what the French called the *comités*. Bit by bit, during the nineteenth century, these groups were drawn together by some form of central organization, which might be very weak as in France or, as in Britain, powerful caucuses backed up by central offices in the case of the two main parties, the Liberals and Conservatives. But it was not until near universal suffrage had emerged (see above, Section 6.3) that the notables lost their place in the parties where, by and large, the central bodies were now working to their own regional organizations of party members. As these parties grew very large, so they fell into the hands of professional party officials. This, said Roberto Michels, was the inevitable consequence of all large-scale organizations. The party might well claim and indeed think itself to be democratic, its members might well think that it was they who made policy. In fact it was nothing of the sort. The party had fallen prey, as all large-scale organizations must, to oligarchy. 'Who says organization, says oligarchy.' And the party was, in reality, a 'following' behind a small group of party professionals who evolved the party's policy and then set out to get the mass membership to endorse it.

The intellectual atmosphere, too, had changed radically from the days of 1848 liberalism. There was no more free market, no more free play of supply and demand. The consensus among social philosophers was now for state intervention in the interests of the working classes. The transition is particularly interesting in Britain, which was the original home of the individualized liberalism represented by J. S. Mill: the axiom of which was the distinction between other-regarding and self-regarding actions. Was the state really to stand aside and simply look on at individuals who were behaving in a self-regarding manner, certainly, but one that was manifestly harmful to themselves? Ought not the state prohibit such actions? And so, by this elision, early individualistic liberalism was overtaken by the views of T. H. Green and then, under the influence of German philosophy, through Bradley and Bosanquet, by an Anglicized version of Hegel which advanced the view that the State was but the macrocosm of the 'better' side of human nature made manifest. In practice this could only lead to the view that 'the gentleman in Whitehall knows best'.

Thus was ushered in the age of the mass party, of massive and ever-increasing bureaucracy, of the class struggle, and the resultant of all these: the politics of social welfare. The year 1914 did not mark the end of this stage, but on the contrary served merely as its threshold. These characteristics were all acccelerated, for the reasons we have explained, by the First World War, even more so by the Second World War, and after that they were to be the hallmarks also of the non-democratic communist and socialist systems of Eastern Europe. The trends were Europe-wide. In such a way was the constitutional state of the nineteenth century transformed.

Bibliography

ARCHER, J., *The Art of War in the Western World* (OUP, London, 1987).

ARTZ, F. B., *Reaction and Revolution, 1814–1832* (Harper & Row, New York, 1963).

BAGEHOT, W., *Literary Studies*, 4th edn. (Longman, London, 1891).

BARRACLOUGH, G., *An Introduction to Contemporary History* (Penguin, Harmondsworth, 1966).

BECK, W. W., and HAASE, Y. D., *Historical Atlas of the American West* (University of Oklahoma Press, Oklahoma, 1989).

BERLIN, I., *Against the Current: Essays in the History of Ideas* (Hogarth Press, London, 1979).

BETTENSON, H. (ed.), *Documents of the Christian Church* (OUP, Oxford, 1943).

BLUNTSCHLI, J. K., *The Theory of the State*, authorized trans. from the 6th German edn. (Clarendon Press, Oxford, 1885).

BOGDANOR, V. (ed.), *Constitutions in Democratic Politics* (Gower, Aldershot, 1988).

BOWLE, J., *Politics and Opinion in the Nineteenth Century* (Jonathan Cape, London, 1954).

BRAUDEL, F., *The Mediterranean and the Mediterranean World in the Age of Philip II*, 2 vols., 2nd edn. (Collins, London, 1973).

—— *Civilisation and Capitalism, Fifteenth to Eighteenth Centuries*, vol. 1, *The Structure of Everyday Life*, trans. S. Reynolds (Collins, London, 1981).

BRINTON, C., *A Decade of Revolution, 1789–1799* (Harpers & Bros., London and New York, 1934).

BRYCE, J., Viscount, *Constitutions* (OUP, New York and London, 1905).

BRYCE, J., *South America, Observations and Impressions* (London, Macmillan, 1912).

Cambridge Economic History of Europe, 8 vols. (CUP, Cambridge, 1941–89).

Cambridge Modern History, The New, 12 vols. (CUP, Cambridge, 1957–71).

CHANDLER, D. G., *The Campaigns of Napoleon* (Weidenfeld & Nicolson, London, 1966).

CIPOLLA, C., *Literacy and Development in the West* (Pelican Books, Penguin, Harmondsworth, 1969).

—— (ed.), *The Fontana Economic History of Europe: The Industrial Revolution* (Collins/Fontana Books, Glasgow, 1972).

COBBAN, A., *Historians and the Causes of the French Revolution*, Pamphlet, General Series, no. 2, The Historical Association (Routledge & Kegan Paul, London, 1946).

COMMAGER, H. S., *The Empire of Reason: How Europe Imagined and America Realized the Enlightenment* (Weidenfeld & Nicolson, London, 1978).

CONDORCET, MARIE-JEAN-ANTOINE-NICOLAS DE CARITAT, Marquis de, *Sketch for a Historical Picture of the Progress of the Human Mind*, ed. S. Hampshire (London, 1955).

CORWIN, E. S., *The Constitution and What it Means Today* (Princeton UP, Princeton, 1978).

CUNLIFFE, M., *American Presidents and the Presidency* (Eyre & Spottiswoode, London, 1969).

D'ARGENSON, R. L. V., *Journal et Mémoires*, édition Rathery, 9 vols. (Paris, 1859–67).

DAWSON, W. H., *The Evolution of Modern Germany* (T. Fischer Unwin, London, 1908).

DE RUGGIERO, G., *The History of European Liberalism* (OUP, Oxford, 1927).

DE TOCQUEVILLE, A., *Democracy in America*, vol. 1, H. Reeve text as revised by F. Bowen, further corrected and edited by P. Bradley, with a new introduction by D. J. Boorstin (Vintage Books edn., New York 1954 and 1990; orig. pub. Alfred Knopf, New York, 1945).

DOUGLASS, E., 'Sturm und Drang: German Intellectuals and the American Revolution', in Toth, *Liberté . . .*, 48–63.

DOYLE, W., *The Oxford History of the French Revolution* (Clarendon Press, Oxford, 1989).

DUNBABIN, J., *France in the Making, 843–1180* (OUP, Oxford, 1985).

ECHEVERRIA, D., 'Mirage in the West: French *Philosophes* Rediscover America', in Toth, *Liberté . . .*, 35–45.

Encyclopaedia Britannica (1911), (1989).

ENGELS, D. W., *Alexander the Great and the Logistics of the Macedonian Army* (University of California Press, Los Angeles, 1978).

ENSOR, R. C. K. (ed.), *Modern Socialism* (Harpers & Bros., London, 1907).

FAGUET, E., *Politiques et moralistes du dix-neuvième siècle*, 1st Ser. (Paris, 1899).

FARRAND, M. (ed.), *Records of the Federal Convention of 1787*, rev. edn. (United States, Yale Paperbound, New Haven &c., 1966).

FINER, H., *The Theory and Practice of Modern Government* (Methuen, London, 1932).

FINER, S. E., *Five Constitutions* (Penguin, Harmondsworth, 1979).

—— 'The Morphology of Military Régimes', in R. Kolkowicz and A. Korbonski, (eds.), *Soldiers, Peasants and Bureaucrats*.

—— *Comparative Government* (Penguin, Harmondsworth, 1984).

—— 'The Retreat to the Barracks', *Third World Quarterly*, 7:1 (1985), 16–30.

—— *Man on Horseback*, 2nd edn. (Westview Press, Boulder, Colorado, 1988).

—— 'Notes towards a History of Constitutions', in Bogdanor (ed.), *Constitutions in Democratic Politics*, 17–32.

—— 'State- and Nation-building in Europe: The Role of the Military', in C. Tilly (ed.) *The Formation of National States in Europe*, 84–163.

FOORD, A. S., *His Majesty's Opposition, 1714–1830* (Clarendon Press, Oxford, 1964).

FORSYTH, M., *Reason and Revolution: The Political Thought of the Abbé Sieyès* (Leicester UP, Leicester, 1987).

FRANCE, A., *L'Île des Pingouins* (Calmann-Lévy, Paris, 1908).

GIDDENS, A., *The Nation-State and Violence* (CUP, Cambridge, 1985).

GILBERT, F., 'Revolution', in P. P. Weiner (ed.), *Dictionary of the History of Ideas: Studies of Selected Pivotal Ideas*, iv. 152–67.

GODECHOT, J., *Les Révolutions (1770–1799)* (Presses Universitaires de France, Paris, 1970).

GREENE, J. P., *The Re-Interpretation of the American Revolution, 1763–1789* (Harpers & Row, New York, 1968).

HEINE, H., *Religion and Philosophy in Germany*, trans. J. Snodgrass (London, 1882).

HOBSBAWM, E. J., *The Age of Capital* (Weidenfeld & Nicolson, London, 1962 and 1975).

—— *The Age of Empire, 1875–1914* (Cardinal, London, 1987).

HORNWILL, H. W., *The Usages of the American Constitution* (Kennikat Press, Port Washington, 1925).

HOWARD, M., *War in European History* (OUP, Oxford, 1976).

HUFTON, O., *Europe: Privilege and Protest, 1730–1789*, Fontana History of Europe (Fontana Paperbacks, London, 1980).

JOURDEUIL, M., *Du Césarisme en France* (Librairie Muzard, Versailles, Paris, 1871).

KOLKOWICZ, R., and KORBONSKI, A. (eds.), *Soldiers, Peasants and Bureaucrats: Civil–Military Relations in Communist and Modernising Societies* (G. Allen & Unwin, London, 1982).

LEFEBVRE, G., *Napoleon from 18 Brumaire to Tilsit, 1799–1807*, trans. H. F. Stockhold (Routledge & Kegan Paul, London, 1969).

LIDDELL-HART, B. H., *A History of the First World War* (Pan Books, London, 1972).

LOWELL, A. L., *Government and Parties in Continental Europe* (London, 1896).

LUNDBERG, F., *Cracks in the Constitution* (Princeton UP, Princeton, 1980).

LUTTWAK, E. N., *The Grand Strategy of the Roman Empire* (Johns Hopkins Press, Baltimore and London, 1976).

MCDONALD, F., *The Formation of the American Republic 1776–1790* (Penguin, Harmondsworth, 1967).

MADISON, J., HAMILTON, A., and JAY, J., *The Federalist Papers* (Penguin, Harmondsworth, 1987).

MAINE, H., *Popular Government* (John Murray, London, 1885).

MAUDE, F. N., 'Conscription', *Encyclopaedia Britannica*, 11th edn. (1910–11), vi. 971–4.

MAYER, J. P., *Political Thought in France from Sieyès to Sorel* (Faber and Faber, London, 1943).

MAZZINI, J., *The Duties of Man (1844–1858)* (Everyman edn.; J. M. Dent, London, 1907).

MIDDLEKAUF, R., *The Glorious Cause: The American Revolution, 1763–1789* (OUP, Oxford, 1982).

MILL, J. S., *Representative Government* (Everyman edn.; Dent, London, 1910, repr. 1971).

MILLER, J. C., *Origins of the American Revolution* (Faber, London, 1945).

MONTESQUIEU, C. DE SECONDAT, *The Spirit of Laws*, trans. T. Nugent and revised by J. V. Pritchard (Encyclopaedia Britannica Inc., Chicago and London, 1990).

NAPOLEON I, *Vues Politiques*, Avant-propos de Adrian Dansette (Fayard, Paris, 1939).

NOZICK, R., *Anarchy, State, and Utopia* (Basic Books, Blackwell, Oxford, 1974).

NYE, B. B., and Morpurgo, J. E., (eds.) *The Birth of the U.S.A.* (Penguin, Harmondsworth, 1964).

PALMER, R. R., *Age of the Democratic Revolution*, 2 vols. (Princeton UP, Princeton, 1959), vol. 1.

—— *Twelve Who Ruled* (Princeton UP, Princeton, 1965).

POCOCK, J. G. A., *The Machiavellian Moment* (Princeton UP, Princeton, 1975).

POPPER, K. R., *The Open Society and its Enemies*, vol. 2 (Routledge & Kegan Paul, London, 1962).

PROUDHON, P. J., *General Idea of the Revolution in the Nineteenth Century*, trans. J. B. Robinson (Freedom Press, London, 1923; French edn. first published 1851).

REISS, H. S., *Political Thought of the German Romantics* (Blackwell, Oxford, 1955).

ROBERTSON, P. S., *The Revolutions of 1848: A Social History* (Harper Torchbooks, New York, 1960).

ROCHE, J. R., 'The Founding Fathers: A Reform Caucus in Action', in Greene, *The Re-Interpretation of the American Revolution*, 437–69.

ROSE, R., *Understanding Big Government: The Programme Approach* (Sage, London, 1984).

ROSSITER, C., *Constitutional Dictatorship: Crisis Government in the Modern Democracies* (Harcourt Brace & World, New York, 1963).

RUDÉ, G., *Interpretations of the French Revolution*, Pamphlet No. 47, The Historical Association (Routledge & Kegan Paul, London, 1964).

—— *Paris and London in the Eighteenth Century* (Fontana, London, 1970).

SARTORI, G., 'Constitutionalism: A Preliminary Discussion', *American Political Science Review*, 56:4 (Dec. 1962), 853–64.

SCHAMA, S., *Citizens* (Viking, London, 1989).

SCHAPIRO, L., *The Origins of the Communist Autocracy* (London School of Economics/Bell, London, 1955).

SIEYÈS, *What is the Third Estate?*, ed. S. E. Finer (Pall Mall Press, London, 1963).

SMITH, A. D., *Theories of Nationalism* (Duckworth, London, 1971).

SUTHERLAND, D. M. G., *France 1789–1815: Revolution and Counter-Revolution* (Fontana, London 1985).

TALMON, J., *The Origins of Totalitarian Democracy* (Mercury Book, London, 1961).

THOMPSON, J. M., *The French Revolution* (Blackwell, Oxford, 1944).

—— *Napoleon Bonaparte: His Rise and Fall* (Blackwell, Oxford, 1951).

TILLY, C., 'Food Supply and Public Order in Modern Europe', in (next entry), 380–455.

—— (ed.), *The Formation of National States in Europe* (Princeton UP, Princeton, 1975).

TOTH, C. W. (ed.), *Liberté, Égalité, Fraternité: The American Revolution and the European Response* (Whitston, New York, 1989).

TUCKER, B., *Instead of a Book By a Man Too Busy to Write One: A Fragmentary Exposition of Philosophic Anarchism from the Writings of B. R. Tucker* (Facsimile, New York, 1893).

VAN CREVELD, M., *Supplying War* (CUP, Cambridge, 1977).

VILE, M. J. C., *Constitutionalism and the Separation of Powers* (Clarendon Press, Oxford, 1967).

WEINER, P. P. (ed.), *Dictionary of the History of Ideas*, vol. 4 (Scribner, New York, 1973–4).

WOOD, G. S., *The Creation of the American Republic, 1776–1787* (University of North Carolina Press, Chapel Hill, 1969).

POSTSCRIPT

Editors' Note: This was the last chapter S. E. Finer survived to write. He had planned a further two substantive chapters, on the export of the 'paradigmatic' western state model and on the varieties and the vicissitudes of totalitarianism, respectively. Had he lived he would also, without doubt, have contrived to write a fitting endpiece to this his *History of Government*.

By way of an alternative we end here with Finer's conclusions to a lecture delivered in 1982 (the text is in *Government and Opposition*, xviii, no. 1 (1983), pp. 3–22), wherein he explained his vision of the 'History of Government' he was about to undertake. It is a tribute to Finer's singleness of purpose as well as to the quality of his analysis, that *The History of Government from the Earliest Times* is the work he had envisaged and hoped it would be.

I have advanced no overarching theory, propounded no all embracing formula, invented no key which by itself alone, will unlock all the *arcana imperii*. Simply and, I fear, cursorily, I have tried to run over some of the problems that arise from this project and outline some of the possible solutions to them. But I am wryly reminded of what I said earlier about writing one's first chapter, last. It seems to be now that one should never write a prolegomenon until one has written the book!

I have been talking about *how* to write such a book; but how to *write* it is quite a different matter. It is all the difference between considering 'the state as a work of art', and creating a 'work of art on the state'. Suppose, after all, one did indeed conceive it, as I suggested, as the entry of one polity and then another onto the stage of history — as first one theme and then another, in a great fugal movement; then, at the same time, transpose each theme in three ways, by way of structure, by way of actors, and by way of belief systems; and, in doing so, blend all these elements into one whole! Here, one can but try, but do one's best. At least, let the ambition be there; indeed, also, the prayer like the one that Abt Vogler utters, as he improvises at the organ: — and says — and hopes —

> . . . such gift be allowed to man,
> That out of three sounds he frame, not a fourth sound, but a star.

INDEX

34

C

VALENTINES PARK

Valentines

Cricket Ground

Band Stand

The Lake

Football Ground

Sch.

Hosp!

NEWBURY PARK STA.

HERTFORD RD

NEWBURY AV

CHURCH RD

BRANCASTER RD

DEVONSHIRE RD

St Johns Ch.

ST. JOHNS ROAD

Sch

Cha

Little Newbury

U.D.C. Depot

Fire Sta.

Tram Depot

Electric Power Stal.

MAGYSMITH AV

KIMBERLEY AV

GLENGARY RD

D

St Clements Ch

PARK AVENUE

Sams Green

SEVEN KINGS STA.

Ch.

Ch.

Ilford La

Goods Yard

OAKLANDS PARK AV

FRANCIS AV

Sch.

St Mary's Ch.

Ilford Cemet

ST MARYS ROAD

NORTH RD

MIDDLE RD

SOUTH RD

SALISBURY RD

LYNFORD

E

ILFORD STA.

STATION RD

HAVELOCK RD

Ch

Town Hall

Sch.

R.C.Cha.

Sch.

SOUTH PARK CRES.

South Park

ILFORD

Ilford Br

Swim Baths

Recreat. Ground

Cha

BEDFORD ROAD

WINDSOR ROAD

KINGSTON ROAD

HAMPTON ROAD

HENLEY ROAD

MONTRAVE ROAD

WINCHESTER RD

SOUTH PARK TER.

F

Little Ilford Level

School

Sch.

Uphall

Loxford Hall

Sewage Works

Fair Cross

G